Soviet Baby Boomers

Soviet Baby Boomers

An Oral History of Russia's
Cold War Generation

Donald J. Raleigh

OXFORD
UNIVERSITY PRESS

OXFORD
UNIVERSITY PRESS

Oxford University Press, Inc., publishes works that further
Oxford University's objective of excellence
in research, scholarship, and education.

Oxford   New York
Auckland   Cape Town   Dar es Salaam   Hong Kong   Karachi
Kuala Lumpur   Madrid   Melbourne   Mexico City   Nairobi
New Delhi   Shanghai   Taipei   Toronto

With offices in
Argentina   Austria   Brazil   Chile   Czech Republic   France   Greece
Guatemala   Hungary   Italy   Japan   Poland   Portugal   Singapore
South Korea   Switzerland   Thailand   Turkey   Ukraine   Vietnam

Published by Oxford University Press, Inc.
198 Madison Avenue, New York, New York 10016

www.oup.com

Oxford is a registered trademark of Oxford University Press

Library of Congress Cataloging-in-Publication Data
Raleigh, Donald J.
Soviet baby boomers : an oral history of Russia's Cold War generation / Donald J. Raleigh.
    p. cm.—(Oxford oral history series)
Includes bibliographical references and index.
ISBN 978-0-19-974434-3 (hardcover : alk. paper)
1. Baby boom generation—Soviet Union—History.   2. Families—Soviet Union—History.
3. Youth—Soviet Union—History.   4. Soviet Union—Social conditions—1945–1991.
5. Cold War—Social aspects—Soviet Union.   6. Social change—Soviet Union—History.
7. Moscow (Russia)—Biography.   8. Saratov (Russia)—Biography.   9. Oral history—Soviet Union.
10. Interviews—Russia (Federation)   I. Title.
HN523.5.R357 2011
305.2440947'09045—dc22   2011007313

3 5 7 9 8 6 4 2

Printed in the United States of America
on acid-free paper

In loving memory of my son, Adam Sanders Raleigh, 1986–2008

Contents

Acknowledgments

Until recently, my office on the fourth floor of Hamilton Hall at the University of North Carolina (UNC), Chapel Hill, was the only one along the corridor not occupied by someone affiliated with Carolina's distinguished Southern Oral History Program (SOHP). I must have walked past promotional posters and announcements about SOHP activities thousands of times over the preceding decade during which I researched and wrote a book on the Russian Civil War in Saratov province, a project for which I spent each summer sifting through voluminous archival collections in the Volga city. By the time I had finished the difficult-to-research monograph, I was itching to tackle something altogether new for me but also felt an intense attachment to Saratov. One day the inspiration came: why don't I write an oral history? Back then, I could count on one hand the number of books in Russian history based on this methodology. But I had never read a work of oral history. Besides, what would I write about? I answered my own question while attending the graduation from Knox College—my alma mater—of magna cum laude graduate Anna Obraztsova, whose parents and Moscow family I have known since 1976. Over the years Anna's mother, my dear friend Lyuba, shared stories of attending Moscow's prestigious magnet School No. 20, which offered intensive instruction in English, and of her friends, now scattered throughout the world. After picking up Lyuba in Chicago, we drove to Galesburg, Illinois, for Anna's 2001 graduation. At some point that weekend I baffled Lyuba, "Lyub, why don't I write my next book about *your* graduating class?" When I realized that a comparable school had existed in Saratov, I knew I had a topic, and one that appealed to me at that. There's a story behind the making of each book, and this is mine.

Although I shoulder sole responsibility for this study's shortcomings, it, more than most books, represents a team effort. I therefore am pleased to acknowledge the many people and institutions that, in so many ways, have supported, financed, or otherwise facilitated the researching and writing of this book since its inception. Above all, I wish to express my profound gratitude to the sixty individuals who took time to share their life stories with me. They also extended to me respect, hospitality, and sometimes their homes, family photos, and even friendship. I owe a special thanks to several 1967 graduates of School No. 20: to Lyubov Obraztsova (Raitman), Tatyana Koukharskaia (Arzhanova), Yelena

Kolosova, Yelena Proskuryakova (Zharovova), Yevgeniya Kreizerova (Ruditskaya), Vyacheslav Starik, Andrei Rogatnev, and Leonard (Leonid) Terlitsky. In Saratov, Nikolai Kirsanov helped me establish contact with many of his classmates, some of whom also went beyond the call of duty to assist me, especially Arkady Darchenko, Natalya P., and Aleksandr Virich. A class in his own in this regard, Aleksandr Konstantinov has served as an invaluable resource from the start. The project benefited as well by my interviewing two former teachers at each school: the late Nina Ivanovna Timonina and Roman Arkadyevich Kaplan, who taught at School No. 20, and Klara Eduardovna Starshova and Igor Andreyevich Molchanov, who taught at School No. 42. Principal at the time I began the project, Igor Andreyevich helped me locate members of the class of 1967 and several teachers.

I am also indebted to Russian colleagues and friends in both Moscow and Saratov. In Moscow, Oleg Kling and his wife Katya Orlova and children Dasha, Masha, and Vanya have made me family, as has Lyuba Obraztsova, her mother Liliya Aleksandrovna, and ex-husband Petya Obraztsov. I am also thankful for the support and hospitality I have received from Larisa Zakharova, and Feliks Burdzhalov and his wife Rita Orlova. In Saratov, Nina Devyataikina not only helped me jumpstart the project but also cheerfully aided me in innumerable ways. I likewise thank other colleagues in the History Department at Saratov University, in particular Velikhan Mirzekhanov, Anatoly Avrus, Mikhail Kovalyov, and Denis Belousov. Yelena Yarskaya-Smirnova and Pavel Romanov at Saratov Technical University contributed to this project as well by sharing their experience practicing oral history. Josif Gorfinkel and his wife Lyudmila Aleksandrovna served as my local arrangements, recreational, and emergency committees, kindly helping me at every step of the way. Viktor Semyonov extended friendship and his knowledge of old Saratov.

This book was made possible by the generous support of UNC's University Research Council, the Spray-Randleigh Fellowship program, a Chapman Fellowship from the Institute for the Arts and Humanities during the spring 2004 semester, and funds available to me as holder of the Jay Richard Judson Professorship. These monies funded research trips and transcription of the tapes by two conscientious and efficient assistants to whom I owe a great debt, Katya Karelina, who set the bar high, and then by Olga Kotik, who, in transcribing the bulk of the interviews, maintained Katya's standards. A John Simon Guggenheim Fellowship during the 2005–6 academic year allowed me to work through the 3,500+ pages of transcribed interviews and to draft the first three chapters of the book.

My study has benefited immeasurably from the insights and rigorous reading that my peerless colleague and friend, Louise McReynolds gave it. Emily Baran also pored over the manuscript—twice—with razor sharp eyes. Kim Gaetz and George Gerolimatos good naturedly read the manuscript at various stages, reporting on it to my graduate reading colloquia on Soviet history. Gary

Guadagnolo reviewed the penultimate draft, catching some glitches and inc013sistencies in usage. Marko Dumančić commented intelligently on early chapters of the book. I have also gained from discussing the study with Chad Bryant, Jacqueline Hall, James Leloudis, Beth Millwood, William R. Ferris, Robert Jenkins, Yasmin Saikia, Jehanne Gheith, Alexander Rabinowitch, Ronald G. Suny, Diane Koenker, Rósa Magnúsdóttir, Sharon Kowalsky, and the outstanding graduate students at UNC with whom I have had been privileged to work.

Moreover, I am happy to express appreciation for the intellectual companionship and supportive environment of the Department of History and the Slavic Studies community at Carolina and Duke University. It is difficult for me to imagine a better place to work. Or to make home: My colleagues', graduate students', and departmental staff members' expressions of support, friendship, concern, and affection during the darkest chapter of my life when I lost my son sustained me in more ways than they will ever know.

I eagerly acknowledge, too, the suggestions of the two anonymous readers for Oxford University Press and the enthusiasm and strategic insights of my editor, Nancy Toff. Thanks as well to her efficient assistant Sonia Tycko, to Lynn Childress, who copy edited the manuscript, and to team leader Jaimee Biggins, who saw the manuscript through production. Emily Baran prepared the index as if the book were her own.

Finally, it would have been challenging—and much less fun—to finish this volume without the loving friendship of Doug Ludy, Louise McReynolds, Stan Chojnacki, Barbara Harris, Alex and Janet Rabinowitch, Beth Holmgren, Mark Sidell, the late Fern Mignon, Jerry Bolas, David E. Williams, Chad Bryant, Joe Glatthaar, Rob Dewoskin, Al Calarco, my Al Anon family, and the new friends I made at the Bodhi Manda Zen Center in New Mexico.

I dedicate this book to my son, Adam Sanders Raleigh, 1986–2008, who text messaged me the night before he died that he wouldn't trade me for any dad in the world. I felt, and feel, the same way about him.

Donald J. Raleigh
Chapel Hill, N.C.

Soviet Baby Boomers

INTRODUCTION

In 1961, at the height of the Cold War, the leader of the USSR, Nikita Sergeyevich Khrushchev, promised the Soviet people that the Soviet Union would surpass the United States in per capita production by 1970 and attain communism by 1980. A vast improvement over socialism, which the state proclaimed had been achieved already in the 1930s, communism represented that stage in historical development when the inherently superior Soviet system would race past the capitalist order. Khrushchev's blueprint for communism included sky-high incomes; free vacations, trips to resorts, medical service, and education; a six-hour workday; free lunches in schools and workplaces; free day care and unprecedented maternity benefits; and the gradual reduction of fees for other service industries.[1] "But people didn't think it was possible," remembered Irina Vizgalova, born in 1950 in the provincial city of Saratov. "Even children. How could we? Because suddenly we didn't have bread here in Saratov. There was no milk. What kind of communism could there be when they passed out bread in school?" Her classmate Olga Kolishchyuk drolly recalled when, in conjunction with Khrushchev's campaign, the authorities hung a banner with his slogan "Catch up with and overtake America" across Lenin Street, Saratov's major thoroughfare. Shortly afterward, the state automobile inspection put up a poster suspiciously nearby, "when in doubt, don't pass [overtake] anyone."

Yet several other people their age taken in by Khrushchev's promises—who, as adults, ironically emigrated from Russia—dredged up different memories. Irina and Olga's classmate, Aleksandr Trubnikov, who today lives in Israel, trusted Khrushchev: "I even remember arguing with my friend whether we'd each have a personal helicopter in 1980, by which time we'd have built communism. I remember very well how normal this seemed back then." Trubnikov added, "I now see that our childhood minds were so tainted that we believed that we'd have a bright future. It's great that at least now I understand that they duped a huge part of the population." Similarly, Moscow's Bakhyt Kenzheyev, now a Canadian citizen, stressed how smugly satisfied Khrushchev's promise of overtaking America had made him when he was eleven years old and in awe of Soviet triumphs in the space race with the United States. "But then the year 1970 began and I was already twenty years old. I looked at Khrushchev's *Party Program* and realized that nothing had been done," observed Kenzheyev. "More than anything else," concluded Saratov's Viktor D., "reality shaped my worldview. And to a large degree, comparing reality with what was on the posters and with information from the press."

On the other side of the globe, on Chicago's working-class South Side, the frosty Cold War rivalry between Russia and the United States also shaped my own worldview, but my concerns—although I grew up poor—were more political than economic. Once designated the worst public school system in any American city with a population over a half-million, the Chicago public schools nonetheless deserved top marks at the time for subjecting the young and impressionable to frequent "duck and cover" air raid drills launched by a piercing siren blast, owing to the "Soviet threat," which I, for one, took seriously. Our humorless physical education teacher at Mark Twain Elementary, Mrs. Dickman, supplemented the drills with mandated and improvised fitness regimens and nagging reminders that we should "eat bread, not candy," so that we might be as strong as the Russians. On top of this, raised Roman Catholic, I clocked in hundreds of hours on my knees, praying for the conversion of the atheist Communists. During the Cuban Missile Crisis in October 1962, I remember being glued to the television set, fearing an imminent nuclear attack. In short, born in 1949, I grew up in "Dr. Strangelove's America."* The perceived Soviet menace helped fashion my generation the way the threat of terrorism defines today's.

Characterized by a state of tension, competition, conflict, and even threat of nuclear annihilation, the Cold War, the confrontation between the United States and the Soviet Union from the end of World War II to roughly 1990, represented a clash of two universalist ideologies, two ways of understanding the world. The dispute produced a stratified, bipolar global power structure in which the two superpowers towered over all the rest. Although there is general agreement that the Cold War dominated world affairs for almost half a century and continues to influence humankind, it has left a varied legacy for different generations living in different countries. What it meant and means to Russians my age is the subject of this book.

Through the life stories of the country's Cold War generation, *Soviet Baby Boomers* traces the transformative developments of the second half of the twentieth century that brought down the Soviet empire. Born shortly after World War II, the individuals I interviewed for this project graduated in 1967 from School No. 20 in Moscow or from School No. 42 in the provincial city of Saratov, both newly opened "magnet" secondary schools that offered intensive instruction in English. Most members of this cohort still live in Moscow, Saratov, or elsewhere in Russia; however, others have immigrated to the United States, Canada, Israel, and Western Europe. A number of them are dead. Members of the generation

---

* For those too young, or too old, to recall, Stanley Kubrick's 1964 jet-black cinematographic satire told the story of an accidental preemptive nuclear attack, and what might happen if the wrong person pushed the wrong button.

that began school the year the USSR lifted the first artificial satellite, Sputnik, into space in 1957, they grew up during the Cold War, but in a Soviet Union that increasingly distanced itself from the most awful features of the long reign of Josef Stalin (1924–53). Unlike earlier generations, whose success in transforming the country into the other superpower was tempered by ever-present shortages, deprivations, famine, terror, and the horrors of World War II, the Baby Boomers benefited in untold ways from decades of peaceful, organic, evolutionary development. They proved every bit as revolutionary, if not more so, than the preceding decades that established the Soviet system and that predated—and perhaps even determined—Mikhail Sergeyevich Gorbachev's coming to power in 1985 and his commitment to reinvent the Soviet system. During this genera-tion's childhood and young adulthood, the country's leadership dismantled the Gulag, ruled without terror, promoted consumerism, and opened the country in teaspoon-size doses to an outside world that feared Soviet-style Communism. Reaching their prime during the Gorbachev era, these Baby Boomers today con-stitute elements of Russia's and other countries' professional urban class.

In telling the story of this cross-section of the country's Cold War generation in its own words, I throw light on a critical generation of people who had remained largely faceless and ignored up until now. Focusing on how a group of individuals born in 1949/50 remembered their lives, I explore the margins among the political, the personal, and the professional. I seek, among other things, to answer five wide-ranging questions in order to grasp what it meant to "live Soviet"[2] during the Cold War. Who and what shaped the Cold War generation's worldviews while they were growing up? What do their life stories tell us about what constituted the "Soviet dream," and ultimately about the relationship bet-ween the growing emphasis on private life after 1945, the undermining of Marxist ideology, and the fate of the Soviet Union? How have they negotiated the chal-lenging transition to a post–Soviet Russia following the collapse of communism in 1991? How have their lived experiences both reproduced and transformed Russian society during the Cold War and afterward? In other words, how do their personal stories help us comprehend cultural transmission across generations? Finally, how do the memories of those who grew up in Moscow differ from those raised in a provincial city "closed" to foreigners and therefore to many direct foreign influences?

Equally important, this book is one of the first on post-1945 Soviet history to draw on the methodology of oral history. This approach appealed to me because, in the Soviet Union, where the boundaries between public and private life remained porous and the state sought to peer into every corner, it had been dan-gerous to remember facts that gave the lie to, or questioned, government-gener-ated fictions. Ideology was meant to replace memory.[3] During and after the dissolution of the USSR, Russian citizens began openly talking about their past, trying to make sense of it, and I saw obvious benefits in listening in. As Russian historian Darya Khubova put it, "It is sometimes said, and is almost true, that 'for us the documents are subjective, and the only things which might be objective are the memories.'"[4]

Indeed, the domestic climates in the two superpowers the year this Soviet generation—and mine—was born differed dramatically. In the United States, signs of postwar prosperity found expression in robust consumption. That year the U.S. automobile industry churned out bigger cars and more people bought them—some 6.2 million. The number of television sets in American homes had shot up from roughly 5,000 at war's end to 10 million in 1949. In January the first television soap opera, *These Are My Children*, began broadcasting. Months later *Hopalong Cassidy* became the first network western and *The Lone Ranger* premiered. The first Emmy Awards for television were presented in 1949, signaling the new medium's promise. It was a year of other "firsts" too. The New York Giants signed on their first African American players, the U.S. Army swore in its first enlisted woman, and Harvard Law School admitted its first female applicant. In the realms of technology and consumption, the first Polaroid camera went on sale, the first transcontinental dial telephone calls linked California with New York, and the Sara Lee Company in Chicago released the first frozen Sara Lee Cheesecake.

The emerging Cold War, however, cast a dark cloud on U.S. postwar prosperity, for 1949 also saw publication of George Orwell's *1984*, a dystopian classic about the horror of Soviet-style totalitarianism controlled by Big Brother and The Party. That April twelve nations formed the North Atlantic Treaty Organization (NATO), a collective defense bulwark against Soviet attack. In May the Federal Republic of Germany officially came into existence as the Soviet Union lifted the Berlin blockade, one of the first international crises of the Cold War. Afterward, the first allotment of Marshall Plan funds aimed at rebuilding war-torn Europe and minimizing the appeal of communism poured into West Germany. On September 21, Mao Zedong proclaimed the founding of the communist People's Republic of China. Two days later, the U.S. government announced that the Soviet Union had detonated its first nuclear device. The Cold War intensified at the start of 1950, when Ho Chi Minh launched an offensive against the French in Indochina and President Harry S. Truman ordered full-speed development of the hydrogen bomb. In June forces from communist North Korea invaded the south, transforming the Korean conflict into a full-scale war. After China entered the hostilities, Truman threatened to use the atomic bomb to achieve peace, instituting a state of national emergency. Alarm over communist activities in the United States mounted when a jury found former State Department official Alger Hiss guilty of participating in a communist spy ring. Overriding President Truman's veto, Congress passed the Internal Security Act requiring registration of American Communists.

Postwar prosperity was yet to come to the Soviet Union by the end of the 1940s, owing to the devastation of World War II, known in Russia as the Great Patriotic War, which destroyed one-third of the USSR's national wealth. The war left 27 million dead, including 17 million civilians; cities, villages, transportation, and communication systems ruined; and countless people homeless, injured, or otherwise victimized. (By comparison, U.S. war casualties amounted to 407,000 deaths; moreover, with the exception of the Japanese bombing of Pearl Harbor, the war did not rage on American territory.) A postwar famine in 1946–47 added to the Soviet tragedy, claiming an additional one to two million lives. The Fourth Five-Year Plan, implemented in 1946, aimed at reaching prewar levels of industrial production and at rebuilding the country's infrastructure by 1950. Restricting the manufacturing and consumption of consumer goods enabled the government to achieve the first goal, but not the more elusive second one. Just as it had before the Great Patriotic War, the country's Stalinist economic model privileged heavy industry in addition to making new allocations for atomic energy, radar, rocketry, and jet propulsion, leaving no funds for televisions or frozen cheesecake. Yet in 1948 Soviet propaganda declared that efforts to "reconstruct" the war-ravaged country had been completed, after which the birthrate began to climb.[5] We can thus speak metaphorically of a Soviet baby boom roughly akin to our own. By 1949 the Kremlin had demobilized the swollen ranks of the Red Army, ended the worst of rationing, and lowered the price of bread. This was prosperity, Soviet style.

During the Great Patriotic War, Stalin had loosened the Party's reins over society to facilitate the Soviet Union's wartime alliance with Great Britain and the United States. But now, suspicious of his former allies and of his own people who harbored expectations for a further relaxation of controls, Stalin clamped down. As early as 1946, the Communist Party Central Committee began to discipline the country's intelligentsia by attacking two major literary journals for their "servility" toward everything foreign, as Soviet propaganda stressed the superiority of all things Soviet or Russian. Plays by Western writers were purged from theatrical repertoires and leading artists, composers, writers, and film directors came under fire. This call for vigilance, an "anti-cosmopolitan" campaign to root out what ideologues deemed as Western influence, soon raged through the humanities, social sciences, and natural sciences with damaging consequences for linguistics, genetics, cybernetics, and other disciplines. These ominous developments increasingly took on a distinct anti-Semitic tone. Moreover, the year the Baby Boomers were born almost a million more inmates populated the Gulag than in 1941. The government carried out punitive deportations in Soviet Moldavia and forced collectivization of agriculture in the Baltic states, territories the Soviet Union had seized during the war. On December 31, a massive parade marked Stalin's seventieth birthday as his countenance was projected into the sky over the Kremlin, a reminder of how exaggerated the cult of Stalin had become.

With the benefit of hindsight, it appears that America's dread of the Soviet Union was also inflated. My own childhood fear of Russia, however, eventually evolved into an insatiable curiosity about, and affinity toward, my Russian counterparts that ultimately resulted in this book. Because Moscow enjoyed a privileged economic and cultural position within the USSR (and within the historiography of Russian history), I saw great benefits in making my project comparative by including a similar cohort of Baby Boomers from a large provincial city. It made sense to choose Saratov, a city I had studied since the 1970s, since Saratov—like much of the country but unlike Moscow—was physically off limits, that is, "closed," to foreigners until 1991. Lying on the western bank of the Volga River, Russia's Mississippi, some 535 miles southeast of Moscow, Saratov by the start of the twentieth century had become the flour production capital of the empire, a vibrant river port and rail center through which all of the political and social conflicts of late Imperial Russia swirled. The plight of the rural masses in particular, brought about by acute land shortage and overpopulation, had exalted the peasant in the eyes of the local intelligentsia, many of whom pined for pastoral utopias. As a result, Saratov province emerged as a center of Russian revolutionary populism, acquiring a reputation as one of the most radical Volga provinces well before the Revolution of 1917. Afterward, Saratov remained a major food-producing region, but Soviet power enhanced the city's significance as an industrial and manufacturing hub, resulting in hearty population growth into the 1970s. By the time members of the Cold War generation were born, the city's population had reached 473,000, and it swelled to 816,000 in 1975, when they were in their mid-twenties.[6] In 1951 the city began to mass-produce "Saratov" refrigerators, prized throughout the Soviet bloc. The city's factories and plants manufactured YAK-40 airplanes, machine tools, gear-cutting machines, industrial glass, ball bearings, synthetic fibers, trolley buses, chemicals, gas, electronics, and space communications equipment. Because many of these enterprises had ties with the Soviet military-industrial complex, the government closed the city to visitors from "capitalist" and even other countries.

Within Russia and the USSR, Saratov was also recognized as a leading cultural and educational center, renowned in the nineteenth century for its music conservatory, the third to open in Russia, and for the Radishchev Art Museum, the first to welcome the public free of charge. Founded in 1909, Saratov University had approximately 9,500 students when the Baby Boomers attended it. At the time, the Saratov Polytechnic Institute enrolled about 15,000 students and the Saratov Medical Institute another 5,500. In the early 1950s, Yury A. Gagarin, the first person to orbit the earth, attended a Saratov technical school, later renamed in his honor. In April 1961 Cosmonaut Gagarin brought his historical space flight to a triumphant, if unglamorous, conclusion by parachuting into a field outside Saratov, further firing the imaginations of members of the Cold War generation, then entering their teenage years.[7]

Stalin's death in 1953, which gave momentum to forces in Soviet society pressing for change, had a defining impact on the Baby Boomers. In the new climate, magnet schools in mathematics, science, and foreign languages targeting academically gifted children opened across the USSR, symbolizing the country's

School No. 42's B class on graduation night, June 22, 1967, sporting hairdos and skirt lengths that otherwise would not have been tolerated. Female students in particular griped about principal Vera Fillipovna's rigid interpretation of school dress codes.
Courtesy of Aleksandr Konstantinov

cautious embrace of the outside world amid the changing battlefields of the Cold War and a domestic climate of heady optimism that set apart the post-Stalin 1950s from the previous decade. One of these elite new schools, Saratov's School No. 42, started up in 1954. The graduating class of 1967 comprised fifty-six pupils divided into two groups of roughly equal size, Groups A and B, two-thirds of whom were female (thirty-eight of the fifty-six graduates). Six of the graduates have since died and several others have suffered strokes or other debilitating illnesses, sometimes due to alcohol abuse. Six live abroad (one in Germany, one in the Netherlands, three in the United States, and one in Israel), and five in Moscow. It proved impossible for me to ascertain the whereabouts of two others who left Saratov. Government and Communist Party officials and members of the cultural and technical intelligentsia sent their children to School No. 42; only a negligible percentage of the cohort came from working-class families.

I had more difficulty determining the class of 1967's ethnic or national composition, because, when enrolling children, administrators recorded the nationality indicated on a child's birth certificate, which was not always an accurate marker of one's ethnicity. (Soviet citizens were issued passports, which indicated nationality, only when they turned sixteen. At that time they could select the nationality of either parent.) According to school records, all of the students were Russian by nationality, except for five Jews, one Ukrainian, and one Moldavian. Yet my conversations with members of the class suggest that as much as 18 percent of it has some Jewish lineage, which popular anti-Semitism taught them to conceal. Two have Tatar surnames (the Tatars are a Muslim minority who speak a Turkic language). One parent of several others belonged to Saratov's Volga German minority that inhabited the Volga region since the eighteenth century (Stalin ordered their mass deportation to Kazakhstan and Siberia in September 1941). The loose generalization that can be made from the data is that the ethnic composition of the school roughly corresponded with that of Saratov, except that Jews were overrepresented and the city's Tatar population underrepresented. This profile is less the result of conscious policies than of the overall educational levels achieved by these two communities: Jews constituted, by far, the most highly educated national group in the Russian Federation, the largest of the fifteen republics constituting the Soviet Union.

Undoubtedly related to Khrushchev's blueprint for building communism made public in 1961, a government decree of May 27 called for the establishment of 700 new magnet schools throughout the country over the next four years and for improving language instruction in ordinary schools. In 1961, neighborhood School No. 115 in Moscow was converted into special School No. 20 with intensive instruction in English. Soon to become one of the preeminent schools in the city, School No. 20, like its Saratov counterpart, enrolled children of the cultural and technical intelligentsia, Communist Party officials, military officers, and only a handful from working-class families. A large number—the graduates themselves estimated that perhaps as many as half the class—were at least part Jewish. As in Saratov, the class of 1967 comprised two groups, A and B, until the ninth grade, when a third class, C (actually V in Russian) was formed, comprising students from A and B and newly admitted pupils. Whereas school officials in Saratov facilitated my project by allowing me to examine school records and by putting me in touch with several members of the class of 1967, school administrators in Moscow, stressing issues of confidentiality, refused to assist me. As a result, I had to enlist the support of my friend and 1967 graduate of School No. 20, Lyubov Obraztsova (née Raitman), who shared contact information and class photos with me. In time, I identified eighty-three 1967 graduates and confirmed that six others had died, but given Moscow's size and the far-reaching dispersal of this cohort owing to emigration, I failed to locate thirty-five members of Moscow's Cold War generation from School No. 20.

The Russian intelligentsia has understood the benefits of using generation as a conceptual frame to help measure social change within a historical context at least since the publication of Ivan Turgenev's *Fathers and Children* in 1862. The novel features a rising generation's intellectual challenge to the status quo in the wake of Russia's humiliating showing in the Crimean War and on the eve of the emancipation of the empire's serfs and introduction of other initiatives known as the Great Reforms. Some of the children soon populated the burgeoning revolutionary movement, giving way to successive generations also defined by a distinct bond created by destabilizing forces that made each age cohort conscious of its historical purpose. For the Soviet period, for instance, the events defining generations include the Revolution of 1917, the dark Stalinist 1930s, and World War II. But no destabilizing forces made the Soviet Union's Cold War or Baby Boom generation conscious of its historical mission; it grew up and experienced late socialism in a strikingly tranquil age, despite the Cold War. Importantly, the positive developments that shaped the Russian Baby Boomers have remarkable similarities to those that molded their Western counterparts, including me: the rise of a youth culture, the appeal of Western popular culture, more leisure time, a carefree attitude, economic growth, rising living standards and a consumerist culture, and the expansion of education.

There is virtually unanimous agreement that this generation has played a vital, even defining, role in transforming the climate of the contemporary world. For this reason, it is time to tell the Soviet Baby Boomers' story. By no means a homogeneous group, the individuals I interviewed undoubtedly had different expectations and life experiences than less educated, less well-connected, and rural elements of Soviet society. But they are a highly significant, critical component of the country's urban professional class, inseparable from the entire Soviet mass intelligentsia whose size grew exponentially in the decades following Stalin's death. Between 1965 and 1982, 12 million Soviet citizens graduated from college—including virtually all of those whom I interviewed. In that regard, the 1967 graduates' collective story tells the larger story of the upper strata of the entire Cold War generation that lived through the USSR's twilight years.

My understanding of the broader historical context in which the Baby Boomers' life stories are set is informed by the limited historical and sociological, and substantial political science literature on postwar Soviet history as well as by the personal observations I made during thirty-six trips I took to the country beginning in 1971. I likewise utilized quantitative and qualitative research on the period conducted by Western and Soviet social scientists, and the books, movies, and other publications identified by those I interviewed as having played influential roles in their lives. However, I privileged the oral testimony. I located and interviewed sixty Baby Boomers between 2001 and 2008. Working without assistants, I interviewed my subjects at their homes and dachas, at work, in apartments I rented, hotel rooms, parks, cafes, and even in a parked car. I taped them in Moscow, Saratov, New York, Montreal, Portland (Oregon), Ames (Iowa), and, over the phone, in Israel and on Cyprus. Approximately ten graduates from each school declined to meet me. In all, I interviewed thirty-one members of the Saratov cohort (more than 50 percent) and twenty-nine members of the Moscow cohort (about 35 percent). Conducted in Russian, the interviews range in length from one to three hours. Although I employed open-ended interview techniques to uncover my informants' remembered experiences, I formulated questions aimed at illuminating the themes noted above. I turned the conversations into dialogues by asking my informants what they believed I needed to know about them in order to shed light on the issues that interested me most. I use their real names in the pages that follow (except in eight cases when they asked to remain anonymous) not only because this convention distinguishes oral history from ethnography but also because—symbolically—most of the Baby Boomers are not afraid to reveal their identities.

Because individuals' values and beliefs evolve as a result of personal experience and changes within a larger sociohistorical context, people tell their stories in different ways throughout their lives. My book, then, is not only about specific historical events, but more so about what they mean to the Cold War generation today. Above all, I sought to comprehend how the interviewees made sense of the world, and the structure and patterns of Russian society as exhibited by representative individuals. Constrained and enabled by the range of stories available in a given culture at a given time, which people make their own, "life stories reveal the canonical rules of a society at a certain time, its mores, behavioral expectations, and taboos."[8] That said, the highly intelligent and well-educated people I interviewed structured their responses with a high degree of integrative complexity.[9] They felt comfortable in their own stories, which they already had available within in draft form before I pried them open with questions and we collaboratively coauthored the sources upon which this study is based. True, I confirmed or suspected in my informants' responses errors, conscious silences, exaggerations, inventions, and the co-opting of others' stories. Memory, however, is an interpretation of life events rather than a chronicle of the past. "Wrong" statements are nonetheless *psychologically* true,[10] especially because people often act on the basis of how they understand life events rather than on the events themselves.[11] Moreover, my project is not dependent on the accurate memory of any one of my interviewees: I searched for similarities, differences, and contradictions among many people's narratives to discern patterns across a number of lives and therefore to get more than one side of the story.[12] I used the oral evidence to uncover feelings, understandings, and judgments to reveal what events meant to people.

In sum, I created a composite narrative out of the Baby Boomers' individual stories that no one person could tell. I embedded it in larger historical narratives of Cold War; de-Stalinization of Soviet society after 1953; Khrushchev's "overtaking" America and opening up to the outside world; economic stagnation and dissent during the Leonid Brezhnev years (1964–82); the transition to a market economy during and following the collapse of the Soviet Union; emigration; the transformation of class, ethnic, and gender relations across this broad swath of time; and globalization. People are invisible to themselves in the enormous social transformations taking place around them. As a result, I looked for the connection between biography and history. My goal is to provide insight into how these historical developments were experienced by those living through them and to suggest, through their life stories, how Cold War Russian society functioned at a quotidian level.

Selecting the Baby Boomers' words to express my own viewpoint, I see my work as a collection of voices in my own "choral arrangement," to borrow a phrase from historian Kenneth Kann.[13] This arrangement underscores the revolutionary impact of decades of peaceful, evolutionary, organic development in transforming the Soviet Union out of existence, in changing it from a state that mobilized society to accomplish ambitious goals into a modern, highly literate, urban society that lost its coherence as the Stalinist economic model exhausted its potential—and the Soviet dream. An economy of scarcity under Stalin had made the new Soviet man, *Homo Sovieticus*, a peculiar kind of consumer; the rise of modern consumerism after World War II made him over into a consumer with expectations. While the Cold War generation grew up, systemic problems and a measured opening up to the world promoted private over collective values and this, in turn, exacerbated the troubles that increasingly made reform the order of the day. Deficits in what might be called the Soviet myth economy aggravated economic shortages: the Soviet Cold War generation grew up believing it lived in the best country in the world, but this perception came under assault when it reached adulthood and sought to find its own niche within it. The USSR figuratively expired in 1980, the year by which Khrushchev had promised the Baby Boomers that communism would arrive. Like food items that expire, the Soviet Union had not exhausted its shelf life, but the risk of it going bad shot up with each passing day.

My arrangement of voices also highlights the Baby Boomers' agency in participating in and constructing a new society and their own lives. Despite American Cold War black-and-white thinking that depicted Soviet citizens as either intransigent Communists or disgruntled dissidents, members of the Cold War generation were neither. Shaped fundamentally by their families,[14] they lived remarkably "normal" lives in a society quickly losing its uniqueness. Their lives aligned fully with the social rules and norms of Soviet society that ironically, as we will see in the following chapters, included forces that eventually subverted the system. That said, most Baby Boomers—like the CIA and Western academics—did not expect the disintegration of the USSR but, as anthropologist Alexei Yurchak argued, they were ready for the collapse when it came, finding it logical and inevitable.[15] Although the Baby Boomers routinely violated and reinterpreted the norms of expected behavior, many of them supported the values and ideals of Soviet socialism until they publicly came under fire. But others sensed the system was doomed and wanted out. What concrete experiences compelled one in six of the Baby Boomers I interviewed to emigrate to the United States, Canada, Western Europe, or Israel? (At least thirteen others did, too, among those who declined to be interviewed, died, or whom I could not locate. Many others contemplated leaving their homeland.) Most left Russia after the fall of the USSR made this option less difficult; however, they had entertained the possibility of doing so for years.

With the benefit of hindsight, the most important and transformative historical events—the end of the Cold War and demise of the Soviet Union—seem inevitable. But there is often little agreement over what caused these events or what they mean. The private memories—the personal recollections of the Cold War generation—are framed by broader collective memories, by widely shared accounts of events. As psychologist James Wertsch maintains, collective memory is a form of mediated action between people and the cultural tools, in particular narrative texts or stories, available to them; it belongs to a specific time, place, and history; it reflects a social position and perspective; and it undergoes change.[16] These observations are crucial to the story presented in the following chapters because, owing to the new information that became available to the Baby Boomers when Gorbachev in the late 1980s unleashed his revolutionary program to reform or to restructure the socialist system known as perestroika, the differences between how living in Moscow or Saratov shaped people's memories lost much of their significance. Gorbachev's most successful reform—glasnost, or openness, which ironically doomed the others—leveled the playing field: everyone in the country who wished now had access to the same flood of revelatory and even dubious information. Perestroika and glasnost contributed to a breakdown of the ideals of the socialist experiment, and to an uncritical interest in Western models and outmoded Imperial Russian forms. The result is considerable homogeneity in the Baby Boomers' assessment of the Soviet experiment, which reveals a social position and perspective—that of the well-educated urban professional class. Despite the wrenching economic difficulties many Baby Boomers endured in the 1990s during the bumpy transition to a market economy, the vast majority of those I interviewed remembered many, but not all, features of the Soviet system negatively and the post-Soviet period positively, in spite of real concerns over specific policies and developments. This is important because their collective memory today forms the continuity that connects and distinguishes generations. It allows individuals to locate their own lives in historical time, as these answers to my question, "How can your life story help me understand the fate of the Soviet Union?" suggest.

"I can't speak for everyone, of course, but I'd basically say that we went almost literally from Stalin[ism] to normal, developing capitalism. We still have far to go. It was hard enough, but we lived through this with the understanding that this was the deck of cards dealt us," replied Arkady Darchenko. "Many of us, including me, are happy that we lived to see this other life. Unfortunately, we will not live to see the complete transformation of our society. But it's great that we've gone through what we have. It was hard, full of all sorts of difficulties, yet it gave life meaning. I wouldn't want to continue living as we had in the 1970s," he concluded. Yevgeny Podolsky responded that he saw significance in "moving beyond the ideals they instilled in me during childhood to get to where I am today. Some got there sooner and some got there later, but this speaks to the fact that history does not deceive us. It has definite laws of development, and no artificial theories or teachings can change people," who, he emphasized, were now living a normal life: "Back then I was a true believer. I accepted what they told me as true, as how things really were, but got to the point where it all turned out to be a lie. Of course, you'll come across some who cling to their old views, but the upshot is that people understood that our former life, our history since 1917, was a terrible experiment."

Yet Leonid Volodarsky and Natalya Pronina cautioned against emphasizing only one side of the story. "We lived peacefully under Soviet power. I have to say that lots of negative things have been said about Soviet power, and they're true, but there was also lots that was good. There's no denying that," contended Volodarsky. Observing that the Baby Boomers "had it really tough," because they "lived through a revolution," he applauded stability, "which is very important for the overwhelming majority of people." Extolling the benefits of free education and health care, privileges that are part of her generation's collective memory, too, Pronina detailed, "I, someone from a family of very modest means, turned out to be someone after all. My parents, if they were engineers today, couldn't afford to send me to college. They couldn't afford to let me join any study or hobby group. They couldn't afford to hire someone to give me music lessons or foreign language lessons." Pronounced clinically dead, she also believed that she would not be alive today if it were not for the readily available and free Soviet health care system. "Back then a doctor saved me and it was free. She saved me because that doctor had taken the Hippocratic Oath, and she considered it her responsibility to save people. That's no longer the case. Today she wouldn't even know who Hippocrates was," insisted Pronina. Reminding us that shattered ideals nonetheless often remain attractive, she ended elegiacally, "That's what the Soviet period was. It has its positive qualities. There was a lot wrong with it, but there was a lot that was right. It's like today—there are some good things, and some bad."

1

THE REAL NUCLEAR THREAT

Soviet Families in Transition

"She remembered the Revolution and the postrevolutionary period. I therefore had not only a textbook understanding of history but also one from a live eyewitness, and this is very important," observed Saratov Baby Boomer Aleksandr Babushkin in telling me about the grandmother who helped raise him. Because attitudes toward authority are shaped mostly by the family, even in, or perhaps especially in, authoritarian societies such as the Soviet Union,[1] I began each interview by asking the Baby Boomers to tell me about their parents and grandparents. What they had to say on the subject confirmed the essential role families played in the USSR as repositories of information that might confirm or challenge official histories. The family backgrounds of two other Baby Boomers likewise highlight some of the ways in which the Russian Revolution, turbulent, Stalinist 1930s, and Great Patriotic War placed society under assault, generating memories that may have clashed with official ones created by the state.

Modest and unpretentious, Anna Lyovina, a 1967 graduate of Moscow's School No. 20, captivated me with the first words she uttered. Anna recounted that her maternal grandmother came from Moscow, "but not always, because she was born in America." Her father, a distinguished engineer, worked in Philadelphia at the time of the U.S. centennial in 1876. After returning to Moscow, this man, Anna's great-grandfather, founded an engineering firm that developed extensive international contacts. The Russian Revolution of 1917 turned this world upside down, however, disenfranchising the tsarist elite, now depicted as Soviet power's class enemies. Concealing their pasts, they had to invent new identities. By law, Anna's grandmother remained an American citizen until she married a Russian professor of physiology, M. O. Samoilov, the first person to introduce the electrocardiogram in Russia. Offered a position at Kazan University, one of Russia's oldest and best, Samoilov and his bride left Moscow for this vibrant Volga city, where Anna's mother was born in 1915, the youngest of four children. So as not to be drafted into the Red Army during the Civil War

(1918–22), her twin brothers, born in 1902, escaped to Siberia and from there to America, where they worked their way through Harvard.

Remarkably enough, in 1925 Anna's grandmother traveled to the United States as part of a delegation of educators sent by the Soviet Ministry of Education to familiarize themselves with American schools. She took her ten-year-old daughter, Anna's mother, with her. During the year they lived in America, Anna's mother attended school, learned English, and fell in love with the United States, while Anna's grandmother, who had not seen her sons for seven years, experienced a deep personal conflict. "Grandmother understood, of course, that they would not be able to adapt themselves to Soviet life," explained Anna. And her grandmother really could not stay in the States, because her husband, older daughter, and sister and their families were back in Russia.

Despite offers to work in Europe, Anna's grandfather decided not to emigrate. But tired of the weekly trek between his joint appointments in Moscow and Kazan, he remained in Moscow in 1930, where he died of a heart attack that same year. Afterward, his widow took a position teaching French and German at the university, but Anna's mother, as a professor's daughter, could not enroll there because of an affirmative action program for workers introduced by Josef Stalin. Undaunted, she cleaned animal cages at the Moscow zoo so as to qualify as a proletarian. "This corrected her application, and only then was she able to enroll at the university," Anna explained. Her mother's problems did not end with this stroke of luck. She graduated in 1937, the year of the Great Terror, and thus found it difficult to land a job owing to her "bourgeois" family background.

Trained in Zurich, Anna Lyovina's great-grandfather Aleksandr Venyaminovich Bari worked on the Russian pavilion at the world's fair held in conjunction with the U.S. centennial in Philadelphia. Anna's "American" connection became both a source of pride and of anxiety for her family, which shared this chapter of its history only with trusted individuals until after the demise of the USSR made it safe to speak openly about the past. *Courtesy of Anna Maslova (Lyovina)*

Rejected everywhere she turned, she accepted a position as a civilian worker in a labor camp until a well-connected neighbor found her a position in the capital at a research institute devoted to the study of frozen soil conditions. In Soviet Russia, who one knew mattered.

If it had not been for the Russian Revolution, it is doubtful that Anna's father, Fyodor Lyovin, the youngest of the five children resulting from the union of a peasant tailor and an illiterate Cossack seamstress, would have married into an academic family such as that of Anna's mother. The Revolution had not only benefited him but also his siblings: "All of the children received an education, all of them became scientists, and all of them made their way from Krasnodar to Moscow," boasted Anna. A graduate of Moscow University, her father specialized in ichthyology. But a dark cloud descended over him after he published his research abroad and turned down an invitation to teach at the ideologically pure Institute of Red Professors in the 1930s. Drafted as a rank-and-file soldier into a cavalry unit run by crude, semiliterate peasants, "he almost went nuts." When World War II broke out, they dispatched him to the front. After he suffered a broken leg in combat, his retreating unit left him with vodka and a hunk of bread. He lost consciousness, was taken prisoner, and ended up in a Nazi prisoner of war camp. Somehow managing to escape, he fell into the hands of a secret police unit that ferreted out "deserters" and either packed them off to the Gulag or shot them as a warning of what happened to those who "betrayed" the Motherland. Lyovin could have met this fate, but those who escaped before him told Soviet authorities of the selfless role he had played in planning their getaway. Incarceration by the Nazis deprived him of the benefits otherwise bestowed upon Soviet veterans; however, it did not prevent him from completing his graduate studies at Moscow University.

Meanwhile, Anna's grandmother had resumed teaching at Moscow University after the war. Her future son-in-law—Lyovin—was one of her students. He married his instructor's daughter and accepted a position at the university, but soon fell victim to Stalin's postwar anti-Semitic campaign even though he was not Jewish. (His surname Lyovin, in this case pronounced LYOvin, is usually Jewish [LEVin]). Yet no one cared, and he lost his post for "ideological" reasons. "He even wrote to Malenkov, but to no avail," injected Anna (Georgy Maximilyanovich Malenkov was viewed by many as Stalin's likely successor). Exiled to a remote biological station outside Moscow, Lyovin had to reinvent himself as a soil scientist.

The story of Irina Barysheva's parents, both from Saratov province, also reflects the impact of the Revolution on individual destinies. The last of thirteen children in a poverty-stricken family, her father was born in 1909. The destabilization brought about by World War I, revolution, and civil war guaranteed real hardship for him—begging, hunger, factory work at an early age—but, insofar as he was a proletarian, also opportunity. After signing up for the Communist

Youth League, the Komsomol, he soon joined the Communist Party [CPSU]. "And then things really took off. That is, his biography was exactly what was needed during the Soviet period. Ever the more so because he was 100 percent Russian. He quickly made a career in the Party," related Irina. "He was accepted everywhere without taking exams, at the university, and then at graduate school." Upon completing Saratov University with a degree in law, he obtained a second degree in Moscow as a Party functionary. Irina heard plenty about his commitment to various Soviet "campaigns": first to wipe out illiteracy, then to improve failing collective farms. During her toddler years, he participated in Khrushchev's crusade to plow up virgin land in remote parts of the country. "He was a Bolshevik by nature, not a Communist," Irina explained. He lived and breathed the spirit of the Revolution, not of the Soviet bureaucracy.

In contrast, Irina's mother's roots lay in Imperial Russia's gentry class. Unlike the poorer, more ethnically homogeneous, lower elements, her mother's family represented a mélange of Polish, Jewish, Gypsy, and Belorussian blood. Irina's mother was born in 1913, the last of eight children. Her mother, Irina's grandmother, died shortly thereafter. Her father, who had studied at an art academy in Kraków, served as a high-ranking tsarist official until the Bolsheviks seized power—and his property. Now a widower with a large family to feed, he was forced to take up work as an artist and to marry his former cook. The family lived in poverty. For this reason, Irina's mother appreciated her years in a Pioneer* brigade as the best of her childhood, "because they fed them there, and thanks to this she survived." Barysheva's parents met at school, where they became classmates, despite the fact that her father was four years older than her mother. Irina's father fell madly in love with her mother because she was fun and upbeat, while he was somber and serious; "such a difficult childhood left its trace," Barysheva observed. An excellent student, her mother nonetheless encountered difficulty pursuing an education because of her gentry roots. Irina's father's had a "correct" proletarian background, however, making it possible for him to help her enroll at the Saratov Economics Institute. She had to conceal not only her gentry origins but also the fact that one of her uncles had fled to America during the Revolution, and another to Germany. When the American relatives sent food parcels to Saratov during World War II, Irina's mother refused to accept them and thereby acknowledge that she had relatives abroad. "Otherwise they would have shot her, and they would have shot her child, too," believed Barysheva. Years later, Irina's brother corresponded with them—they live outside Chicago—until the American relatives offended their Soviet relations, whose overtures they misunderstood as an attempt to finagle an invitation to America.

---

* At age ten, children joined the Pioneers, a children's organizations formed to replace the prerevolutionary scouting movement.

The stories of Anna Lyovina's and Irina Barysheva's families suggest some of the myriad ways in which the Revolution transformed people's lives. They also illustrate how family lore, transmitted orally, offered missing pages not only to sanitized accounts individuals told publicly to negotiate the rules and practices of Soviet society but also to official histories. The latter often reduced complex historical forces to Manichean struggles between the dark forces of capitalism and the heroic and inevitable triumph of communism. A case in point, the *History of the All-Union Communist Party (Bolshevik)* or *Short Course*, published in 1938, became the self-serving catechism of Stalinism with which the Baby Boomers' parents grew up: Between 1938 and 1953, the *Short Course* was published 301 times in 67 languages with a press run of almost 43 million. After Stalin's death in 1953, the account fell under fire. The replacement textbook acknowledged the *Short Course's* shortcomings, but the 1969 edition dropped criticism of its negative influence. That is the textbook the Baby Boomers used in college.[2]

As an antidote of sorts, family histories archived facts, truths, partial truths, rumors, and even legends that families kept secret to hide suspect class backgrounds in view of an ever-changing Party line. Everyone's family story offered alternative or more complicated histories. This is significant because, upon coming to power in October 1917, the Bolsheviks sought to revolutionize the family as part of their far-reaching plan to fashion a new Soviet man and woman. In some respects they succeeded. Yet ironically, the new Soviet family helped to transform, and ultimately bring down, the system that sought to rethink it.

REVOLUTIONIZING THE SOVIET FAMILY

Between the Revolution of 1917 and the end of World War II in 1945, ideologically fueled policies and the shifting economic and political priorities of the state placed traditional family patterns under siege. Based on a vision of free sexual union, women's emancipation through wage labor, liberating women from the responsibility of housework, and an eventual withering away of the family, the Bolshevik Family Code of 1918 ended centuries of patriarchy, making women equal before the law. It made marriage a civil ceremony and divorce easily obtainable. It abolished the legal concept of illegitimacy, outlawed adoption (assuming the state would have the resources to raise homeless children), and, in 1920, legalized abortion. The most radical family code of its time proved to be a bad fit for a country impoverished and brutalized by the sustained crisis of World War I, revolution, and civil war, and a population that remained largely rural, peasant, and newly literate.

For these complex socioeconomic and political reasons, the state reversed its position by 1936. It now tightened up divorce laws, banned abortion, and attacked libertarian views of the family promoted during the Revolution. But one critical element of the original vision of how to rethink the family remained intact: the Stalinist state never claimed that women's place was in the home, because it needed their labor to industrialize the country. Although this ideological retreat from the revolutionary family code of 1918 and renewed commitment to strengthening time-honored family values took place when most European states promoted pronatal policies, there was something distinctly "Soviet" about the changes of the mid-1930s. They reflected the economic reality of millions of peasants and women joining the industrial workforce as part of a single-minded program of industrialization at breakneck speed and of ruthless collectivization of agriculture. This resulted in a double burden for women, who were expected to work outside the home and to do most of the chores within it. The changes likewise gave rise to a new Soviet elite comprised of cadres from humble social backgrounds sent to school and technical colleges by the state (Irina's father, for example), and to a program of targeted and arbitrary terror, the "purges," the bleakest chapter in Soviet history. Before the state largely shut down the Gulag following Stalin's death in 1953, an estimated 18 to 20 million Soviet citizens passed through it and another 6 million people were forcibly exiled to remote regions of the country.[3] We still do not know exactly how many perished as a result of state repression.

Obscuring the boundary between military and civilian involvement, World War II also battered the Soviet family. Destroying as much as one-third of the USSR's national wealth, the war caused an enormous imbalance in the country's male–female ratio. Census data reveal that in 1959 there were 20.7 million more women than men in the USSR, and 8.5 million more women than men under age forty-two. As late as 1975, the country's population of 253.3 million included 18.3 million more women than men, although by then the number of men and women under age forty-eight was roughly equal.[4]

The Great Patriotic War became a central moment in the evolution—and legitimization—of the Soviet system. Victory, the propaganda organs screamed, validated all sacrifices made before and during the conflict. But what about afterward? The torment and misery of war had given rise to hopes that life would get better in peacetime. Yet, in defeating the Nazis, the Soviet Union transformed its geopolitical situation by towering over Eastern Europe, thereby contributing to emergent strains in the wartime alliance with England and the United States. Withholding the true extent of the country's ruin from the population, the Soviet government vowed to rebuild the Soviet economy to even higher levels than before the war and gave top priority to "reconstruction." Offering only oblique reference to a famine that took one to two million lives in 1946–47, Soviet propaganda justified the renewed appeal for delayed gratification by emphasizing the fear of a new war. The call to sacrifice began to lose its grip in 1947 and 1948, however, as public consciousness turned increasingly to peacetime thereby constituting a change in the previous outlook.[5] By then the authorities had demobilized the Red Army, restored some prewar levels of industrial output, abolished rationing, and lifted the most stringent features of martial law.

This return to "normality" in 1948 gave rise to a Soviet-style baby boom beginning in 1949 and 1950. Those born at this time represented the first Soviet generation to come of age during a period of evolutionary transformation that lacked the wrenching adjustments and raw ideological fervor of earlier Soviet power. It was the Baby Boomers for whom Soviet power had to put up or shut up. It was crucially important that defeat of the Nazis not only determined how the Soviet people and leaders viewed the world and lived in it but also guaranteed that the rest of the world, particularly the West, would fear the Soviet Union as the other superpower. This was ever more the case as the USSR, before the end of the decade, consolidated control over Eastern Europe and manufactured an atomic bomb, while Chinese Communists fought their way to power in the world's most populous nation. Whether the Soviet Union deserved to be considered the other superpower is beside the point: The outside world feared it as such; Soviet leaders acted accordingly; and those growing up in the USSR after the war believed they lived somewhere special.

"MOTHER WAS LUCKY THAT SHE FOUND HERSELF A HUSBAND"

All but a few of the parents of the Baby Boomers whom I interviewed came from the upper strata of Soviet society. The family of one of them, Vladimir Mikoyan, belonged to the top Soviet elite. His paternal grandfather, Anastas Mikoyan, served in Stalin's Politburo for more than forty years. His maternal grandfather, Aleksei Kuznetsov, held the post of Party secretary of Leningrad during the war. Several others from Moscow and Saratov also came from the Soviet *nomenklatura*, an elite subset of Party members from which top-level government positions were drawn. Other parents fell into the next rung on the social ladder, comprising upper-tier Party and government officials, state economic managers, high-ranking military officers, distinguished scientists, and cultural figures. The majority of the parents belonged to the next category, the ranks of the mass intelligentsia—professionals (doctors, research scientists, professors, engineers, architects, artists, teachers, librarians, etc.), government or Party officials, or mid-level functionaries. A few could be classified as career military officers. Only a handful belonged to the working class. In most instances, at least one parent had ties to the Moscow or Saratov regions; however, Stalinist society was remarkably mobile. Most of the parents without local roots had moved to Moscow or Saratov on the eve of war to study, or else found themselves there during the conflict, when the government evacuated tens of millions of Soviet citizens. Owing to the massive casualties of World War II, some Baby Boomers never knew, or barely knew, their fathers.

World War II made the parents the "war generation," shaping their attitudes toward the Soviet system—by further legitimizing it—and its place in the world.

The war created new identities, often becoming the starting point of stories people told about themselves and their families. It generated expectations of how they ought to live after victory had been secured. Tempered by self-sacrifice, the war generation had already experienced deprivation and sometimes repression firsthand before the Nazi invasion. But even this could not prepare them for the hardships and misfortunes of the Great Patriotic War. In considering the cohort's parents, we need to keep in mind that we are dealing with the lucky ones—the *survivors*.

Although some parents proved reluctant to recount war stories to their children, the majority spoke openly about their experiences. Moscow's Leonid Terlitsky recalled that his father was sent to an officers' school and that months before graduation the whole class was dispatched to the trenches. "Out of close to three hundred people, five survived. So, my childhood was very much spent listening to his war stories. He shared his experiences with me in great detail to the point where I sometimes would think that all this happened to me rather than to him." The physical reminders of the struggle shored up an evolving collective memory that the government co-opted and mythologized to serve contemporaneous purposes (for example, "if it weren't for the war, we would be living better now"). The government's efforts met with success. Even today, after public discussion of the Soviet past discredited many core beliefs about the Communist system, the war remains a sacred topic for many: the Soviet *people* won the war at tremendous personal and collective sacrifice, regardless of the system.

The Baby Boomers tapped archived memories—ones they have shared before—in telling me about how the war impacted their parents. For a lucky few, the war provided the occasion for couples to fall in love. Lyudmila Gorokhova's Moscow-born father met her Kharbin-born mother at a dance in Saratov during the conflict that both survived unscathed. Evacuated from Moscow to Samara after the Nazi invasion, Sergei Zemskov's mother met her future husband there. His father disappeared in battle without a trace. Boris Shtein's father grew up "abroad"—in then-independent Estonia. The Soviet occupation on the eve of World War II brought him to Moscow, where he met his future bride when both were students. Yelena Kolosova's parents became acquainted in Moscow during the war, which interrupted her mother's education. She described to Yelena how, as Nazi forces advanced on the city, the government torched documents, and how black ash filled the air and bombs rained down on homes on the Arbat neighborhood, where many of her classmates lived. She joined a brigade that repaired frozen water mains and later met her future husband, evacuated from Sverdlovsk, at the Institute of Light Chemical Technology. Both of her parents had blemishes on their records: "One was the daughter of someone five minutes short of becoming an enemy of the people; the other the son of someone missing without a trace." But this gave them more in common. "They really were suited for each other and were madly in love with each other," maintained Kolosova.

For others, the war meant painful separation, sometimes with tragic consequences. Vyacheslav Starik's father came to Moscow from Ukraine before the war to study. Anticipating hostilities, his mother in 1941 wrote him not to return home. Starik recalled, "He didn't go, and the Fascists destroyed the entire family there in 1942." Tatyana Luchnikova's mother left Leningrad for Moscow to find work with her uncle. Her family members who stayed behind perished during the blockade of Leningrad. A spark flew between Tatyana Arzhanova's future parents when they met on a tram during evacuation at the start of the war. They fell in love, but her father-to-be was shipped off to serve in Mongolia and, after demobilization, completed his studies in Irkutsk. Her mother waited seven years for him to return to Moscow before they married in 1948. Vladimir Glebkin's father, a mathematician, served in the Moscow home guard during the war until Soviet forces discovered a strange contraption, which his father correctly identified as an autopilot device for planes. This not only got him out of the guard (which had a sky-high casualty rate), but provided him with a professional interest he would pursue the rest of his life. When Tatyana Artyomova's father was drafted, her mother and brother were evacuated to the Urals, where her mother toiled in a factory. Having survived the war, her parents decided to start a "second" family. Tatyana was the result. The outbreak of war found Irina Vizgalova's mother constructing an aerodrome near Kiev. After rushing back to Saratov she was evacuated to Bashkiria, where she sat out the rest of the war with her mother. Drafted into the Red Army, Vizgalova's father "returned safely from war, although he spent the entire war laying mines. God spared him. He wasn't even wounded," said a grateful Irina.

But for most, the hardships of war overshadowed all of its other aspects. Aleksandr Babushkin recounted that his father miraculously survived even though he was shell-shocked three times, and "three times my grandmother went to bury him." Natalya Yanichkina's teenage mother was evacuated to Central Asia after the Nazis invaded. She found work there with a geological expedition before malaria devastated her. Aleksandr Konstantinov's mother's first husband perished in the war; her second husband, his father, fell into enemy hands, an experience that almost cost him a stint in the Gulag. Fifteen years old when the hostilities broke out, Irina Garzanova's father enrolled in an artillery school evacuated from Leningrad. Sent to the war zone ahead of schedule, he arrived at the Belorussian front in late 1943, where he fell under machine gun fire. Medics amputated his left leg above the knee but saved his wounded right leg, which he afterward was able to use in a limited way. Declared an invalid, "he could have stayed home and bemoaned his fate," observed Garzanova. Instead, he graduated from Saratov University, accepted a position at the Polytechnic Institute, and "retired at age sixty-five in 1992, even though he could have, as a war invalid, retired at age fifty-five."

The enormous shortage of men after the war allowed them to have their pick of women. Valentin Ulyakhin's father was seventeen years older than his mother.

Natalya Yolshina was also the offspring of such a union. Her father, a physics teacher, left for war as a widower. He met his second wife at the store where she sold school supplies. Natalya P., whose parents, both from Saratov, married in 1948, was also a "late child." Twelve years older than her mother, her father, a "Communist by conviction," was thirty-nine years old when she was born and "ready to start a family." Natalya Yanichkina "practically didn't know" her father, who was fourteen years older than her mother. "Imagine the postwar generation. They had shot all the men."

Bakhyt Kenzheyev shared his mother's chilling account of what became of the young men who had gone to school with her. "Of the twenty boys in her class, only three returned from the war, and one of them was a complete invalid," explained Bakhyt. "Mother was lucky that she found herself a husband." But this meant that she defied tradition to marry a Kazakh Red Army soldier raised in an orphanage. His father's (mis)alliance did not go unnoticed by the military authorities. Ordered to return to his first wife, he refused, only to find himself discharged from the army and "left on the streets with his pregnant Lena."

Given Soviet postwar realities—missing fathers—all children were seen as legitimate. Tatyana Arzhanova knew her father mostly "through letters to Mama and me." Tatyana grew up with her mother and grandmother, who "didn't want

Yevgeniya Ruditskaya with her parents, between whom there was a "huge difference" in age: "When I was born my father was forty-nine years old and my mother was twenty-eight. This was my father's second marriage," she explained. *Courtesy of Yevgeniya Kreizerova (Ruditskaya)*

me to know him" and who told her terrible stories about his alcoholism. She later had an "unofficial" stepfather who lived with them for several years. Georgy Godzhello was raised by his mother and her parents and goes by his mother's surname because his parents never married. Godzhello said next to nothing about his father, who had a "second" family, but he enthused that his mother "is simply unique."

Some of the parents had married and started families before 1941; the older siblings resulting from this tended to have a deep influence on the Baby Boomers. Leonid Terlitsky's older brother, a jazz musician, not only convinced him to become an architect but also saw to it that he developed an appreciation for jazz, a leading source of American "soft" power. Recalled Terlitsky: "He was one of the first people in Moscow playing jazz bass. He took me to every jazz festival through my childhood." His influence did not end here: Terlitsky immigrated to the United States in the 1970s and credited this to his brother's influence. Viktor Alekseyev expressed gratitude to his brother, fifteen years older, for "enthusiastically supporting" his wish to enroll in the special English-language school. More important, Viktor's older brother helped him decide upon a profession. "It was he who told me that a new department was being opened at the university. He encouraged me, and I'm very grateful to him for that."

Whatever their family backgrounds, the war strongly affected the Baby Boomers' parents, becoming the defining feature of that generation. Given the hardships they endured, it is not surprising that they would place top priority on lavishing their own children with whatever benefits the postwar Soviet system could offer.

"THIS PROBABLY COULD HAPPEN . . . ONLY IN THE SOVIET UNION"

After 1917, "formers," the privileged elements of tsarist society disenfranchised by Soviet power, drew on their cultural capital—the knowledge they possessed, their behavior, moral qualities, aesthetic sense, good manners, and the like—to adapt creatively to the new conditions of Soviet life. Many of them thus recovered their social position and facilitated the upward mobility of their offspring by educating them.[6] Aleksandr Konstantinov's parents, whose paths crossed at Moscow University, fit the bill. Konstantinov was born in Moscow, but his parents had to relocate to Saratov when he was a preschooler because his father had been taken prisoner by the Nazis. As Konstantinov explained, "My father underwent some sort of verification as a result of which he managed to avoid being sent to the labor camps. However, he wasn't allowed to remain in Moscow. He told me he was given a choice: move to Baku, Saratov, or some other town—and he chose Saratov." In time his father became a professor at the Saratov Medical Institute and his mother a scientist at the Anti-Cholera Institute in Saratov.

Those disenfranchised by Soviet power also survived by marrying people from less suspect social origins. Owing to class politics that discriminated against "formers," affirmative action programs that privileged workers, and tremendous opportunities for upward mobility, some Baby Boomers were born into families of "mixed" social standing. Irina Barysheva is one of them. Another is Aleksandr Virich, whose mother was the daughter of Aleksandr Kovalevsky, a distinguished Saratov statistician, and whose father was the son of Ukrainian peasants who immigrated to the Far East during a routine famine. Virich's parents fell in love during their student years in Saratov. Later his father became Saratov's chief architect. The war also offered some an opportunity to refashion their biographies. For example, Aleksandr Kutin's grandfather, a bookkeeper for the Riazan-Urals railroad hub in Saratov, had experienced discrimination before the fighting. Awarded the Order of Lenin during the ordeal, his new identity as war hero replaced his suspect past as a tsarist official.

Rags to riches tales demonstrate the prospects for upward mobility in Stalin's USSR. Tatyana Artyomova's parents grew up in an orphanage in Ukraine. "Therefore, they achieved everything on their own." Both of her parents graduated from college, becoming, in her words, "typical members of the Moscow intelligentsia." Vladimir Glebkin's father from a peasant family became a distinguished mathematician. Lyubov Kovalyova's father was born in a poor village near Kursk in 1905. He later attended special courses for workers and rose quickly, serving as the main engineer of a large textile plant at the time of her birth. Vladimir Nemchenko's father was born into a Ukrainian peasant family. A war invalid, he met his future wife, a medical student, in Saratov, where he trained at the Higher Party School, which prepared Soviet functionaries. Olga Gorelik's mother came from a family of four that had been abandoned by their father. She became a

Born in 1919, Aleksandr Konstantinov's mother, Natalya Sergeyevna, graduated from Moscow University. Her first husband disappeared without a trace during the war, after which she married his friend and classmate Aleksandr Stepanovich Konstantinov. *Courtesy of Aleksandr Konstantinov*

professor of medicine and her sister a doctor. "This probably could happen to someone only in the Soviet Union because we're Jews and before the Revolution, for the most part, they were unable to get an education," Gorelik opined.

Some family genealogies reflect important trends and opportunities for those who served the Soviet state. For example, Andrei Rogatnev's maternal grandfather, who came from a poor peasant family, became a Civil War commissar at an early age. Andrei's grandmother was born to a Siberian gentry family with nine daughters. His grandfather met her when he asked to be quartered in a home with as "many girls as possible" in the family. She fled with him as the Red Army pursued their enemies, the Whites, teaching soldiers basic literacy. Rogatnev's paternal grandfather worked as a freight train brakeman and his grandmother as a laundress. Their off-spring, Andrei's father, joined the secret police. Rogatnev explained that, as a young Komsomol activist during the dangerous 1930s, his father found himself between a hammer and a sickle and had no choice but to accept an invitation to join the secu-rity forces. "He was probably lucky, too, that he immediately got involved in foreign intelligence work and didn't take part in the repressions and doesn't have any blood on his hands," reasoned Rogatnev. Andrei credited glasnost with helping him learn more about his father, who, he claimed, "became the NKVD's resident in Mussolini's Rome, and from there warned about the impending attack on the Soviet Union." Olga Gorelik's father worked as a journalist and war correspondent. His job took him to Stalingrad, to Budapest, and then to Kishinev in Soviet Moldavia (now Moldova). He met his bride to be, "an exceptionally pretty woman," in Saratov while on leave during the war, where she, a young doctor, worked in a hospital. They married before the end of the week, but had to commute until he returned to Saratov in 1949, after which he was appointed assistant editor of the local Communist Party newspaper, *Kommunist*. Larisa Petrova's father also served as a high-ranking official in the city Party committee and her mother as a school principal. They met in Saratov doing Komsomol work after the war. Irina Chemodurova's father made a career as a Party historian. A native of Dnepropetrovsk, he escaped to the Volga when the Germans seized the city, completing his education at Saratov University, after which he "was sent to take courses at the Central Committee." He became a specialist in the history of the CPSU, teaching this mostly unpopular subject at Saratov University and then in Ufa.

Only a handful of the Saratov Baby Boomers belonged to the working class. Natalya Pronina claimed to be one of them. So did Irina Kulikova, whose mother moved from the countryside to Saratov during the war. Too young to fight dur-ing the conflict, her father completed technical school and labored as a skilled metalworker at a local factory. Aleksandr Ivanov was born into a working-class family that lived next door to Kulikova.

A number of Moscow and Saratov interviewees were born to military fam-ilies, underscoring the prominence of military service in the USSR at that time. A career officer, Olga Martynkina's father faced regular transfers. As a result, her maternal grandmother raised her in Saratov. Olga Kolishchyuk's father was a colonel in the Red Army stationed in the Far East. Born in the Belorussian town of Vitebsk, her mother had fled with her family from the Belorussian front to Saratov during the war and met her husband when she went to Siberia as part of a youth brigade. Olga was born there. Afterward she spent two and a half years in China with her parents, where her father was posted. When her parents relocated to Saratov in 1955 they initially lived with her grandparents. After his family perished during the war, Sergei Zemskov's father studied in a military school in Leningrad and later in a military academy. Born in 1911 into Moscow working-class families, both of Viktor Alekseyev's parents grew up in harsh material circumstances. His father made a career in the military, returning to Moscow when Viktor was a young child. A military engineer, Sofiya Vinogradova's father achieved the rank of lieutenant colonel and could have climbed even higher had his family been willing to leave Moscow. Tatyana Luchnikova's father served in the Soviet rocket forces. She spent part of her toddler years in Khabarovsk before the family settled in Kazan. Tatyana moved to Moscow in the ninth grade. Georgy Godzhello's father was a career military man, as was his maternal grandfather who helped raise him. Aleksandr Trubnikov's father had an army career before settling down as an engineer at a Saratov factory.

More likely than their Moscow counterparts, some parents of the Saratov cohort had been sent to the Soviet periphery, where their skills were needed as a payback to the state for their free higher education. As a result, a number of Saratovites were born on the fringes of the USSR. Irina Tsurkan's half-German mother met her future husband from Moldavia on the Pacific island of Sakhalin, which fell into Soviet hands as a result of the war. After completing his studies in Kishinev, Irina's father worked in Sakhalin as an engineer. Her mother had arrived there from Saratov as a young physician. Irina was born on the island. Aleksandr Virich's parents served a stint in Vladivostok upon completing their degrees. Born there, Aleksandr returned to Saratov with his parents in 1951. Larisa Petrova was born in Tashkent, Uzbekistan, and lived there until she was seven years old. After the war the Soviet government fortified its hold on the Baltic states reincorporated into the Soviet Union during the conflict, by exiling large numbers of the countries' inhabitants to Siberia, settling Russians in the area, and posting military units in the region. Yevgeny Podolsky's parents worked in Kaunas, Lithuania, between 1946 and 1952, when they relocated to Saratov where his grandparents lived. Yevgeny said that he came from a military family but failed to mention that his father worked for the secret police in Lithuania.

Members of the Saratov cohort who spent their toddler years in Siberia waxed nostalgic about the natural wonders of the place. Galina Poldyaeva lived with her parents on the Kamchatka peninsula between the ages of three and six. Fading photographs evoked memories of the train ride between Moscow and Vladivostok, the boat trip from there to Petropavlovsk-Kamchatsky, and killer whales at play. Then there was Kamchatka itself. "I remember," said Poldyaeva, "how snow covered everything because the settlement was made up of single-story wooden homes. When there was a blizzard or heavy snowstorm there was snow up to the chimneys, and in the morning soldiers would dig us out." Natalya Pronina grew

Yelena Zharovova's father, Vadim
Nikolayevich, an engineer from
Izhevsk, married Anna Vasilyevna, a
history teacher from Moscow, in 1947.
Yelena's father was drafted into the
Red Army in 1953, after she was born.
*Courtesy of Yelena Proskuryakova
(Zharovova)*

up in Siberia outside the Gulag capital, Magadan. Her mother, from Saratov, and
her father, from Michurinsk, met there in the transportation industry. Pronina
insisted that "no one in Saratov had such a childhood, and that's because the tiny
little settlement where I lived was surrounded by Mother Nature." As she put it,
"You could play wherever you liked, run about freely, associate with others freely.
It was like a wild life preserve." Her parents did not move back to Saratov until
1960, when she became the "seventh" Natasha, the diminutive form of Natalya, at
school. The contrast between the physical beauty of the deep hinterland and the
grim built environment of Soviet power jarred her: "My impression was that
Saratov was a hot, dusty, dirty city." Arkady Darchenko's parents accepted assignments in Siberia after his father graduated from the Saratov Polytechnic Institute
in 1949. His father served as chief clerk at a mine along the upper Yenisei River
where Arkady was born in the town of Abakan. "These were the very places where
Lenin was once in exile," he recalled. Unlike Pronina, Darchenko spoke openly
about the Gulag: "The chief clerks and foremen had been sent there as a mandatory
way of paying back the state. But the workforce, for the most part, was made up of
prisoners mostly from Western Ukraine. Each day," he added, "they drove the
inmates dressed in black pea jackets to work and back. They escorted them with
German Shepherds. I can still see it. It was sometime in '53 or '54, when I was four
years old, and it got carved into my childhood memory." Darchenko remembered
the impression Saratov made on him in 1956: "There was no embankment, and no
bridge. There were natural beaches right on the riverbank. There were huge barges

with watermelons, which they unloaded by tossing them. Some of them fell into the river. We kids retrieved them and ate them."

During their schooldays, only two of the Baby Boomers, both from Saratov, experienced the death of a parent. Aleksandr Virich lost his mother when he was fourteen, but had little to say about how her loss affected him. His father remarried a "well-paid doctor," so the outward manifestations of Virich's family life did not change radically. This was not true of Galina Poldyaeva, whose father died when she was thirteen. Recalled Galina: "I didn't have any worries until my father was no longer with us, and my mother hid her feelings from me. Of course, all of our relatives helped us." They received other support as well: "Our school had a very active local committee that provided assistance. They helped all the time."

Because it remained hard to obtain a divorce in the Soviet Union owing to a 1944 decree and to a severe housing shortage, the Baby Boomers were spared the complications arising from being from a broken home (but not the problem of parental conflict due to the inability to get a divorce or to secure separate housing). The Soviet system eased up on the draconian 1944 legislation after Stalin's death, but did not implement real changes until 1963. More important, the government introduced a form of no-fault divorce in 1968, after which divorce rates shot up. Taking advantage of the new laws, the parents of some Baby Boomers divorced about the time their children entered college. In contrast, divorce would become part of the Cold War generation's personal stories and something that distinguished them from their parents' generation.

Arkady Darchenko had vivid memories of his toddler years in Siberia: "The most amazing thing was the tall grass that you could get lost in. And the enormous mushrooms my size!"
Courtesy of Arkady Darchenko

"I ALWAYS REMEMBERED HOW HURTFUL 'LITTLE JEW' SOUNDED"

Nationality remained a problematic category of self-identity throughout Soviet history, complicated by state affirmative action programs for minorities, targeted discrimination (as in the case of the Volga Germans and other nationalities exiled during the war), popular prejudices, religious bigotry, and corruption. The country represented a true melting pot of peoples, but this only made ethnic intolerance more apparent when it occurred. As children, the Baby Boomers paid little attention to their classmates' family backgrounds or nationality. Part of this had to do with the success of Soviet propaganda (depicting the Soviet Union as one big happy family), part with the socioeconomic status and attitudes of their parents, part with the innocence of childhood, and part with how people remember. Aleksandr Konstantinov claimed, "I made it to the university before I realized that there was such a thing as anti-Semitism." Yet he admitted that "on the street kids called sparrows [a bird often seen as a nuisance] 'Yids,' but I didn't know what the word 'Yid' meant." His not being Jewish made it possible for him to conclude that "nationality problems didn't concern people at all."

Some of the cohort's grandparents and parents of Jewish descent, however, experienced official discrimination or everyday anti-Semitism, which has a long and violent history in Russia. This is particularly the case because of the last wave of state anti-Semitism in Stalin's final years, when many Jews lost their jobs as a result of the campaign to root out "cosmopolitanism." In currency since the late 1940s, the term marked someone accused of rejecting Soviet values in favor of "reactionary" bourgeois ones. The so-called Doctors' Plot,* made public shortly before Stalin died, gave rise to fears that a new purge was about to be launched targeting Jews. Boris Shtein remembered that his maternal grandfather lost his teaching post for including "too many citations from American sources in his doctoral dissertation. He was fired at the very start of the 1950s for cosmopolitanism." Although Leonid Volodarsky's father had joined the CPSU at the front, "he was afraid of everything." His son explained: "I understand why. There was the front, war, and after the war things were rough, too. The campaign against cosmopolitanism was underway when he graduated from the institute. And, of course, no one gave work to a Jew. He got by taking on some difficult

---

* Marking the culmination of postwar state-sponsored anti-Semitism, the Doctors' Plot refers to a government announcement in January 1953 that nine Kremlin doctors, six of whom had typically Jewish surnames, had killed several prominent Party leaders and planned to murder others. Alarmingly, the government condemned Soviet Jews as Zionists and agents of Western imperialism. After Stalin's death, however, the new Soviet leaders acknowledged that the plot had been a fabrication.

odd jobs." Sofiya Vinogradova remarked that her mother "was born at the wrong time." After graduating from Moscow University in 1949, she could not find work until 1953. The situation improved after Stalin's death, but too slowly for some. Lyubov Raitman's mother, for instance, had trouble landing a job, despite her credentials. "It's what they call the Fifth Point," clarified Raitman, referring to a quota system for Jews identified according to the fifth item on their Soviet passports indicating nationality. Eventually, Raitman's uncle found her mother a job as an editor.

There is some inconsistency or ambivalence in the interviews regarding the sensitive subject of whether members of the Cold War generation themselves experienced anti-Semitism during their childhood. When presented with passports at age sixteen, Soviet youth could opt for the nationality of either parent. Because of popular anti-Semitism and official discrimination against Jews, those with one Jewish parent often chose the nationality of the non-Jewish parent. Several Saratovites never mentioned that they are part Jewish. Their silence probably represents a way of coping with Saratov's more overt anti-Semitism. Yevgeny Meyer claimed not to have encountered any anti-Semitism growing up, yet he took his mother's (Slavic) surname, Podolsky, prior to completing school and competing for college admission. Aleksandr Trubnikov, the only one of the cohort to have immigrated to Israel, acknowledged that the problem of anti-Semitism is "sufficiently complicated." Trubnikov's mother is a Jew, but he was considered a Russian because his father was Russian and he had a Russian surname. His mother's family suffered at the hands of the Nazi invaders, but afterward he did not believe she endured any discrimination—at least as a Jew. "Besides, she was a woman. She did not have to hold any high positions. She did not have to join the Party. It was men who experienced discrimination," he stressed.

It is hard to untangle the knotted strands of ambiguity concerning one Saratovite who asked not to be identified. Her family knew anti-Semitism first-hand: her maternal grandfather, who had taught at Saratov University, "was asked to leave in 1952." That same year her mother "was asked to leave the Economics Institute." (She later defended her candidate's degree, a rough equivalent to our Ph.D. at the USSR Academy of Sciences.) Two of the interviewees' classmates told me that, when they met her on the street several years ago, she poured her heart out about the anti-Semitism she had suffered growing up. Yet her former classmates saw things differently: in almost identical language they volunteered that she was "strange" and had a "difficult personality." Several of her colleagues intimated the same to me. I therefore had certain expectations when I interviewed her, which she met: she seemed suspicious, even embittered. She never married. Although she is a successful professional, she cast herself as a victim. My encounter with her reminded me that there always are multiple truths. In this case, her personal qualities might have constrained her professional and private life as much as discrimination had, yet the latter might also have determined her attitudes and outlook on things.

According to Moscow's Mikhail Markovich, "half of our class were Jews or else had one Jewish parent." Many of their parents came from territories belonging to the former Jewish-populated Pale of Settlement in Ukraine. Born in Kirovograd, Igor Litvin's Jewish itinerant parents eventually settled in Moscow. His father arrived at age fourteen, finished some economics courses, and found a position with a Soviet trade organization in Riga, Latvia, on the eve of the Nazi invasion. His mother's family perished in the war, leaving her an orphan at age sixteen. Lyubov Raitman's father, from Vinnitsa, Ukraine, studied architecture in Odessa before coming to Moscow for graduate work. He met his future bride, daughter of a Moscow lawyer, in the capital and married her in 1943. Leonid Volodarsky cast his Jewish parents' marriage as something of a "misalliance" because his mother came from a Moscow family belonging to the intelligentsia, and his father from a poor family in Ukraine. His father's experience demonstrates two contradictory policies after the war: an affirmative action program for veterans and anti-Semitism. Volodarsky's father was admitted to the Foreign Language Institute without the need to pass entrance exams because he had been a front-line soldier during the war. In due course, he found a position teaching English there. Yet Volodarsky believed his father would have had even more professional success had not "nationality hindered him."

Unlike their Saratov counterparts, the Muscovites of Jewish heritage felt their "otherness" already in childhood. Although Mikhail Markovich maintained that "there were utterly no problems ever connected with" his being half Jewish, that is not how his classmates remembered things. Lyubov Raitman's first encounter with her "otherness" came when she was about five years old and her village nanny took her for a walk. An attractive child with dark hair and inquisitive eyes, Lyubov caught the attention of another nanny, also from the village. When the other nanny asked Raitman "what's your nationality?" she replied that she is Russian. "What kind of Russian are you? You're a little Jew!" Raitman did not know that her parents were Jewish, "but I understood that this is bad and I always remembered how hurtful 'little Jew' sounded to me." Yevgeniya Ruditskaya explained that being Jewish did not pose any difficulties for her at school, "but outside of school I felt anti-Semitism." So did Leonid Terlitsky: "Of course there was street anti-Semitism but I was a tough kid growing up in Moscow, and I didn't take shit from anyone so I was in a few fist fights in my childhood when you try to prove your point of view through brute force." His experience ran in the family: "So was my brother who broke someone's nose for that very reason, and so was my father who was called a kike on a tram right after the war. He was wearing a civilian overcoat over his military uniform. Someone called him a dirty kike and accused him of spending the war in Uzbekistan. So he threw that son of a bitch off the tram."

Saratov's German minority also endured state-sponsored discrimination— both during World War I by the tsarist government and again, during World War II. Since the eighteenth century, Saratov and neighboring Samara province had been home to the Volga Germans. Stalin ordered the mass deportation of these, and other Soviet Germans, some 750,000 people, to Kazakhstan and Siberia in September 1941. Yet some escaped this fate because they were married to a Russian or other Slav. Vladimir Kirsanov's Volga German mother stayed in Saratov "only because my father was Russian. They didn't touch such women." Be that as it may, "it was very rare" that a German was able to remain in Saratov. "Basically 99.99 percent were deported to Kazakhstan and Siberia. My grandparents went there and practically all of my relatives," he volunteered. Irina Tsurkan's maternal German grandmother escaped deportation because she was married to a Ukrainian. Gennady Ivanov's Volga German mother avoided deportation, but he insisted it was owing to the arbitrariness of Soviet officialdom. "They summoned her and the committee members said, 'Why do this to a young girl of twenty? Why ruin her life? What kind of threat does she pose to us?' And they let her stay." Ivanov probably did not tell the full story; later in life his mother moved to Aktobe, now in Kazakhstan, where she died. She undoubtedly had relatives there who had been deported in 1941.

"CHILDREN WITH GRANDPARENTS HAD A BETTER CHILDHOOD"

Owing to the serious imbalance in male/female ratios after the war, 85 percent of Soviet women between the ages of twenty and fifty-five (the official retirement age for women) worked, and by the 1960s more Soviet women than men had high school diplomas and college degrees. As a result, the USSR set world records for the number and percentage of working women with secondary and higher technical educations, distinguishing themselves on the world stage in terms of the diversity of the positions they filled. But the outpouring of women into the labor force complicated child rearing, regardless of Western observers' admiration for Soviet achievements in providing maternity leave and affordable day care. The Cold War generation's mothers received fifty-six days off after giving birth and the right to stay home for a year without pay before returning to their jobs. A survey conducted by Soviet sociologists in 1962, however, revealed the material difficulties families faced in raising children: a shortage of children's facilities, lack of time on the part of parents (especially mothers), unsatisfactory living conditions, and low pay. Survey respondents recommended expanding the network of day care and other children's facilities; lightening woman's load at the workplace; and involving husbands more in caring for children and in sharing responsibility for housework.[7] In 1960 only 13 percent of preschool-age children in the USSR attended state nurseries, and Saratov failed altogether in meeting its targeted plan for their expansion.[8]

Around 1950 the Soviet family remained a multigenerational one, owing to tradition, housing shortages, and economic necessity. Grandmothers—*babushki*—in particular, often kept families afloat by taking on the tasks of childrearing, shopping, cooking, and running the household. Sofiya Vinogradova, for instance, called her grandmother "the head of the household." True, some Baby Boomers had an altogether different experience. One of them, Yevgeniya Ruditskaya, recounted, "Unfortunately, I didn't know my grandparents. My maternal grandmother was shot during the war and my grandfather perished at the front. And on Papa's side no one survived either." Viktor Alekseyev's grandfathers had died before Viktor was born. He had memories only of his paternal grandmother who lived with the family until she passed away when he was four years old. Lyubov Kovalyova's paternal grandparents died when she was a toddler, and her mother's parents lived in a village in Ukraine. "They came to live with us for a year or so only at the very end, when they were helpless," divulged Kovalyova. All of Igor Litvin's grandparents died before 1950. "Children who grew up with grandmothers and grandfathers had an altogether different childhood," he believed.

Those with grandparents agreed. During their preschool years, a good number of Baby Boomers lived with their grandparents because of their parents' work schedules or unsatisfactory living arrangements. Galina Poldyaeva's maternal grandparents, who lived in Voronezh, took care of her when she was a toddler while her parents were stationed in far-off Kamchatka. In fact, she called her grandmother "Mama"—to the chagrin of her real mother. After Poldyaeva's parents returned to Saratov, she vacationed each summer in Voronezh, and her parents even discussed sending her to live with her grandparents again because they had a large apartment in the center of town. Aleksandr Babushkin lived with his maternal grandmother since his parents did not receive a separate apartment until 1957, and then only a one-room flat. Because Olga Martynkina's father served in the military and moved frequently, her maternal grandmother brought her up in Saratov so that she did not have to change schools. Martynkina never mentioned her mother, and this makes her grandmother loom even larger.

Vladimir Glebkin lived with his paternal grandmother outside Moscow until the end of first grade. His father worked so much that Vladimir by and large interacted with him only in the summer when the family vacationed. Because Sergei Zemskov's father served in Murmansk, where his mother became a school principal, Zemskov mostly lived with his grandparents at their dacha outside Moscow. Yelena Kolosova resided with her paternal grandparents in the provincial town of Kursk until she was four years old, because her maternal grandmother in Moscow suffered from tuberculosis. Yelena warmly recalled that Kursk "was its own special sort of world that enriched me with its customs, outlook, and hospitality." A grimy, inconvenient train that "literally, as they say, stopped at each goat" linked her world in Kursk with Moscow. After Yelena moved to Moscow her "beloved" maternal grandmother who lived with her family spoiled her. Although she received a miserly pension, she "spent it on me," emphasized Yelena. "Mother thought she was a bad influence on me. I would have to agree."

As Sofiya Vinogradova quipped, "Children with grandparents had a better childhood than those without." "A grandmother and grandfather, that's true

Olga Martynkina and her parents in 1953. Owing to her father's military career, her parents settled in Moscow, not their native Saratov, after he was demobilized, by which time she was a student at the Saratov Conservatory and did not consider moving. *Courtesy of Olga Zaiko (Martynkina)*

love, of course," gushed Galina Poldyaeva. Irina Garzanova attended day care for only four months after coming down with one infection after another. "They took me from there and I was raised by my grandparents" who resided with her family. In addition, her maternal grandmother's sister Baba Lyulya, who never married, moved to Ulyanovsk oblast where Garzanova worked as a physician, to look after her infant son. Vladimir Nemchenko was reared mostly by his maternal grandmother and harbored some resentment toward his father, who "had no time" for him, especially when he offers unsolicited advice now. Likewise, Irina Vizgalova's maternal grandmother brought her up. "My grandmother was exceptional," Vizgalova told me. "I was lucky." Born in Siberia, her grandmother began to lose her hearing during the Civil War. Completely deaf by age thirty, she taught in a school for the deaf but came to Saratov to tend to her grandchildren. She read lips well and they learned sign language. Gennady Ivanov's maternal grandmother, a gynecologist, retired to look after him so that his mother, also a doctor, could devote attention to her research.

Some Baby Boomers recalled with fondness summer visits to grandparents who did not live in Moscow or Saratov. The most evocative example comes from Vyacheslav Starik, who spent three months each summer in his grandmother's village located in the backwaters of Orel province. His great-grandmother, who was still alive when he was young, had given birth to thirteen children, nine of whom survived, including his grandmother, who was "barely literate" and who "could write but only with difficulty." (He did not get to know his grandfather, killed by a garbage truck, a misfortune Starik blamed on the long shifts people worked under Stalin and the safety violations that accompanied such policies.) It was not easy to reach the village. Starik described taking the train from Moscow to Orel, and from there another train to a station at Verkhovie, site of a factory that produced evaporated milk. "If I see in a store evaporated milk made in Verkhovie, I buy it," stated Starik. His parents would inform their village relatives by telegram that they were arriving, and they would meet their Moscow relations at the station with a cart and pair of horses, which trudged another seventeen kilometers to the village. Starik's family brought sausage, candy, and other presents to the kolkhoz, which remained "hungry enough" so that farm women stole grain from the threshing floor to feed their poultry flocks. The village store sold next to nothing, just sugar and gingerbread with an inedible filling that was, according to Starik, "a hundred years old." Visiting the countryside most summers, Starik saw before his very eyes "how living standards in the village improved." Electricity replaced kerosene lamps. The chairman of the kolkhoz got a telephone. Battery-operated radio receivers appeared. Then televisions. True, there was still no road leading to the district center, "but on the other hand it was ecologically clean." Boasted Starik, "Unlike many city children, I knew the difference between a horse and a cow."

No one among the cohort had more famous grandfathers than Vladimir Mikoyan, grandson of Anastas Mikoyan, a longtime member of Stalin's Politburo, and of Aleksei Kuznetsov, hero of the defense of Leningrad during the 900-day blockade of World War II. His grandfather on the Mikoyan side expected that the families of his four surviving sons (one had perished during the war) spend part of the weekend at his dacha, because a family "had to behave like a family." Vladimir felt lucky in that he later worked for ten years in the United States as a Soviet diplomat. But this had a downside to it. "I didn't communicate with my grandfather, who back then still had a sharp mind. And there was a lot that I could have asked him and learned from him," regretted Vladimir. That said, he volunteered that his grandfather "told me himself" that he kept a loaded pistol handy, prepared to take his own life if the security police ever came to arrest him. He feared shaming himself if tortured and wanted to soften the blow to the family. Fear of arrest was a legitimate concern for Mikoyan, because of the fate of Vladimir's other grandfather, Aleksei Kuznetsov, whom Stalin had shot in 1950.

The heavy male casualties during the world wars and lower male life expectancy made grandfathers an endangered species. Viktor D. lost both of his grandfathers already during World War I. One of Leonid Volodarsky's grandfathers died in 1941; the other, who worked in a store in Omsk, was killed by bandits during a robbery. Some interviewees knew their grandfathers only vicariously.

In recounting the revolutionary pedigree of her maternal grandparents, Tatyana Arzhanova told me that her grandmother, born into a Siberian peasant family with thirteen offspring, was taken in by her godmother to work as a nanny. In 1918 she joined the Communist Party and sometime during the Civil War married a Polish socialist. When she was eighteen years old, she gave birth to Tatyana's mother and soon thereafter was sent to Moscow to study. Although he was forty-three when the war broke out, her grandfather was drafted. The family believed he died in September 1941. Ambiguous language in his war letters led family members to suspect that his own men might have killed him because he refused to surrender. Widowed without knowing it, her grandmother waited years for him to return.

Those blessed with grandfathers underscored the influence they had on them as they grew up. Galina Poldyaeva spent a lot of time with her grandfather who, in her words, "taught me how to walk correctly." He paced back and forth like Stalin in an army jacket and boots, a style that Galina imitated while sporting a Panama hat. He also instilled in her his passion for hunting and the chase. Grandfathers served as role models especially for male Baby Boomers, whose fathers were busy earning degrees and advancing careers. Georgy Godzhello's grandfather played a crucial role in his life, because Godzhello did not see his father. Andrei Rogatnev also held his grandfather, a dedicated Communist, in the highest regard. "I now understand," he told me, "that if all Communists had been like my grandfather and others that I knew, then, perhaps communism wouldn't have been discredited."

"SHE HAD AN ENORMOUS INFLUENCE ON ME"

The Baby Boomers' parents availed themselves of state-run day care facilities only as a last resort. One of the few to attend a state nursery, Saratov's Aleksandr Trubnikov generalized from his own personal experience: "Back then women didn't stay home with their kids. People believed that the most important thing was work, and that children needed to grow up as part of the collective. I went to a nursery school. I had grandmothers, but since we lived far away from them they didn't look after us." Trubnikov added, "Back then they had round-the-clock nurseries where parents could leave their kids during the week, but I didn't spend the nights there, because my parents didn't work shifts." Lyudmila Gorokhova attended a facility where her mother worked as a day care provider. But owing to its distance from their home, Gorokhova remembered that "they didn't drag me back and forth because we had what was called an extended day facility. I spent the night there. I virtually lived there." Moscow's Tatyana Artyomova also attended day care and took part in an extended day program at school, because her grandparents were dead. Later her mother hired a babysitter and then quit work to become a stay-at-home mom when Artyomova was in second or third grade.

Some families hired nannies in cases in which grandmothers still worked, lived elsewhere, were sick, or no longer alive. Usually young peasant women, the nannies influenced the Cold War generation by exposing their charges to a distinctive frame of reference: that of the countryside. The nannies had different values, they spoke village Russian, and they tended to observe religious practices and holidays. Given the bleak situation on the postwar collective farms, peasant youth looked for ways to escape to the cities; working as a nanny seemed like a one-way ticket out.

Aleksandr Konstantinov's nanny, a village girl from Ryazan province, was roughly eighteen years old when she came to work for his parents. Konstantinov's mother's family had belonged to the Ryazan gentry, and it is instructive that the "formers" continued to turn to local peasants to provide this service. Konstantinov's nanny was the daughter of Auntie Fenya, who had been hired by her former Ryazan masters after the Revolution. Konstantinov acknowledged his nanny's

Aleksandr Konstantinov visited his childhood nanny in Ryazan oblast around 2007. She spent many years in Moscow, then in Saratov, before she returned to the Ryazan countryside. *Courtesy of Aleksandr Konstantinov*

influence on him: "The things she told me greatly differed from what my parents had to say. Moreover, she was critical of my parents." He recounted: "I saw some things in them from her point of view, for instance, the oppression of one person by another. I saw this in how my parents treated her. It was not nice, and I always defended her." According to Konstantinov, she "wasn't really religious," but she went to church and "had Easter cakes blessed. It was more of a superstition." Konstantinov observed that "it wasn't accepted" in Saratov to have a nanny, who was usually called a housekeeper. "It was more common in Moscow."

His classmate Olga Kamayurova was raised by her paternal grandmother and nanny, whom Olga remembered as "an absolutely humble and charming woman, as unselfish as they come." She not only brought up Kamayurova and her brother but also Olga's own daughter and began to raise her daughter's son. Olga Gorelik was less than a year old when her nanny, Galya, began looking after her. "Back then many arrived from the village when they were young and got hired," explained Gorelik. "We were like girlfriends." Galya, who was "not very literate," took care of Olga until she turned five, when her parents decided to send her to kindergarten for a year before starting school.

As Konstantinov observed, it was more common for professional families in Moscow to hire nannies. Yelena Kolosova's mother was unable to take even a few months maternity leave: "I always had nannies, and then I had a grandmother who no longer worked," detailed Yelena. Even when Kolosova lived with her grandparents in Kursk, Nanny Dusya helped raise her. Kolosova's grandparents took in Dusya when she returned to Kursk after her husband had been killed during the war. She lived the rest of her life with them. "For me, Dusya was like having yet another grandmother," added Kolosova. Dusya celebrated religious holidays and taught Yelena how to bake the traditional Easter cake, *kulich*, and to make the accompanying sweetened cottage cheese, *paskha*. Tatyana Arzhanova's nanny, Vassa Efimovna, or Vasyena, who also came from the village, liked to take Tatyana to the movies, "and when there were some scary moments she'd cover my eyes with her skirt," remembered Arzhanova. Anna Lyovina idealized her nanny, an illiterate peasant from Tambov province with a "natural sense of beauty and harmony" and "a real Christian worldview" who never judged others. "I now understand," reminisced Lyovina, "that she had an enormous influence on me." She took Lyovina to church (her parents allowed this providing her nanny made no attempt to have her baptized). Lyovina marveled over how her nanny went to bookstores to admire the illustrations in art books she could not read. When Lyovina gave birth to her first son, her nanny brought her an art book, *Reproductions from the Metropolitan Museum*.

"BACK THEN WE WERE ALL ATHEISTS"

Anna Lyovina's nanny may have exposed her to a "real Christian worldview," but the Baby Boomers grew up in an emphatically secular public environment. The

Communist Party launched an antireligious campaign at the end of the 1920s that destroyed or closed most churches and monasteries, making it difficult, and dangerous, for the Cold War generation's parents to remain openly religious. World War II brought changes in state policy, when the government struck a deal with the Orthodox Church. In exchange for the church's support of the war effort, the government allowed many churches to reopen. After the war, the Kremlin maintained its softer stance toward religion, realizing the foreign policy benefits that came with it as the Cold War escalated. But the status quo changed once again in 1958, when Khrushchev started to shut down churches, monasteries, and theological seminaries, and intensified antireligious propaganda.[9]

While many citizens saw the antireligious campaign as a form of repression, these controversial actions did not necessarily contradict the spirit of the time. In their autobiographical account, Moscow intellectuals the same age as the Baby Boomers, Pyotr Vail and Aleksandr Genis, argue that "the intelligentsia had no room for God." This remnant of the past seemed incompatible with science, progress, and communism. It was not that belief in God was harmful or dangerous, but "embarrassing." Indeed, a manual issued by the government at the time, *The Atheist's Companion*, stated categorically that "religion serves as a break to social progress." By 1960 the question "Is there a God?" seemed comical in comparison with "Is there life on Mars?"[10] Irina Vizgalova spoke for many: "Back then we were all atheists. They raised us that way. I grew up like that." Influenced by her atheist parents and by the media hype over the Soviet Union's launching of Sputnik, Irina Garzanova teased her very religious maternal great-grandmother: "How can there be a god up there?" Undaunted, the old woman took Irina to church. Vyacheslav Starik grew up "a complete atheist." Visiting his grandmother's village each summer did not change things because, as he put it, "There wasn't a church there. It had been destroyed." Religious holidays were loosely observed, he noted, "but there was no religion."

Outwardly complying with the state's official position, some families remained tolerant of religion. It played no role in Yelena Kolosova's young life, but an icon of St. Nicholas hung above her nanny's bed. Andrei Rogatnev explained that it was not that he grew up with a hostile attitude toward religion, but "without an opinion of any kind." Having attended a church school in his youth, Lyubov Kovalyova's father became an atheist as a member of the Komsomol and later of the Party. Be that as it may, she recalled, "We had a tolerant attitude toward religion, there was no harsh denunciation of it." Yelena Zharovova remembered that "at home we didn't poke fun at religion. I knew that there's a God. I sometimes went to church, although I didn't know any rituals or prayers." Viktor D.'s father in Saratov did not know if there was a God, but he taught Viktor that there is a higher power summoning people to adopt a moral point of view. "In effect," reflected Viktor, "it's the essence of all the best that humankind has lived through, the suggestions for living worked out over the centuries found in any religion."

Despite ruthless state policies toward religion, the Baby Boomers' grandparents, especially grandmothers born before the Revolution, kept religion alive. Many of them did not hide their religiosity—a "privilege" that came with age in the Soviet Union. Galina Poldyaeva's grandmother was a believer, but her mother, a committed atheist, refused to have Galina baptized. Vladimir Kirsanov's family had no believers, except for his Volga German mother who had attended the local Protestant church before the Soviet regime blew it up. Aleksandr Kutin told me, "My maternal grandmother was very religious. And all of my maternal grandfather's relatives were also religious. Many people their age were." Aleksandr Ivanov insisted there was nothing religious about his family, but then confided that "an icon hung in the apartment," that his parents had him baptized, that his "grandmother sometimes went to church," and that he had "a Godfather." Tatyana Kuznetsova's maternal grandmother did not go to church, but believed in God. Recalled Tatyana: "Everyone baked Easter bread and colored eggs." Natalya P.'s maternal grandmother taught her a prayer when she was little. However, her father, a Communist "really chewed out Grandma. It wasn't that he was afraid that someone would find out, but he really strongly believed in what he did." A self-described "atheist by nature," Natalya Pronina acknowledged that religion nonetheless played a role in her life: "The other kids in my class didn't know that my maternal grandmother was an Old Believer. Insofar as this was forbidden back then, she carefully kept this hidden."* Moscow's Vladimir Glebkin remembered that religion played no role during his childhood, yet admitted that his grandmother was religious: "However, she wasn't a fanatic. My father and mother, they, too, didn't forget, well, customs, especially on Easter."

Some grandmothers took things further and arranged to have their grandchildren baptized, even though this involved some risk because priests had to report baptisms to state authorities. Not uncommon was the experience of Arkady Darchenko, who confided, "My parents aren't religious, but my grandmother was. My great-grandmother, who looked after me when we first arrived in Saratov, was very religious. When I was five she took me to church and had me baptized." Similarly, Olga Kamayurova told me, "You know, as Communists, my parents were atheists. My grandmother had me baptized in church secretly, probably when I was about three years old. But afterward, until I reached adulthood, I wasn't at all interested in religion." Neither was Irina Tsurkan, who also knew she had been baptized: "They did so on the sly, entrusting this to some granny who lived in our building. She took me there, baptized me, and brought me back. And everyone acted as if no one knew a thing about what had happened." Mikhail Markovich mentioned that the women in his mother's family

---

* The Russian Orthodox Church underwent a schism in the mid-seventeenth century, after which those rejecting reforms introduced by Patriarch Nikon continued to practice old rituals. The Old Believers comprised numerous subdivisions, which were persecuted by both the tsarist and Soviet states.

harbored a deep respect for religion and that his grandmother became a church elder in her fifties. "And believers had me baptized."

One Muscovite, Valentin Ulyakhin, became an Orthodox priest after the collapse of the USSR, thereby fulfilling his father's own dream. Born in Krasnodar in the Kuban region in 1907, his father had attended a church primary school and would have become a priest if the Russian Revolution had not made this impractical. He kept his spiritual thoughts to himself during the Stalinist 1930s, but not during the war. Repeating a popular saying, Father Valentin quipped, "There are no atheists in the trenches." Although he did not become a conscious believer until the death of his father in the mid-1970s, Valentin had been introduced to the church: "I remember how Grandma and I prayed in the Church of the Redemption, how she lit candles, how we took Communion, because I was still very young back then and could take Communion without confession." Ulyakhin admitted that his classmates "were non-believers. Perhaps they believed, but if they did they kept it secret."

Most of the Jewish Baby Boomers also observed that religion played no or little role in their childhood, and this is not surprising given the high levels of education among this group. Moscow's Leonid Terlitsky maintained that his "father was well educated in Jewish law and tradition but the family was secular." Moreover, many parents belonged to the Party. Yet even in such cases, religion, or religion as custom, had not completely disappeared from everyday practices. As Yevgeny Podolsky reminded me, "Religion back then was forbidden, and the authorities carefully monitored this, especially among families of Party members." That said, he confided that "sometimes grandmothers might say something about it." Olga Gorelik's Jewish family belonged to Saratov's Party elite and kept an atheist veneer, but her maternal grandmother was a believer. "I remember perfectly well that Grandmother went to the synagogue. She knew Yiddish. I also understood some. However, no one ever taught me, and in general my parents had no desire to do so. On the contrary, they believed that everything they had had been given to them by Soviet power. And, in fact, that's the way it was." Viktor Alekseyev linked religion with cultural tradition, noting that his grandmother knew Yiddish, and "somehow kept up these traditions." Yet they didn't impact his father, a Party member: "In general religion left no trace on his worldview. I never noticed any."

The generational split within families between the Baby Boomers' grandparents and parents regarding religion bequeathed a mixed legacy. The Soviet state may have taught the Cold War generation that religion was an embarrassing remnant of the past; however, the need to learn how to "act Soviet" in dealing with it transformed religion into a political issue. Said Terlitsky: "So many chose to sort of follow the rules and keep quiet just to stay alive." Be that as it may, most families observed cultural practices with religious overtones, especially at Christmas and Easter or during Hanukkah. Doing so further separated public from private life while providing elements of continuity with Russia's pre-Communist past. There is also the question of one's innate spirituality. Saratov's Larisa Petrova captured this point best: "We were all atheists. Religion didn't interest us. We didn't go to church, but at heart there was something." She elaborated, "We always believed in some sort of higher power. You'd be anxious about an exam and say 'God help me.' You know, we always said the word 'God,' 'God help me.' We didn't even think about it." There is also such a thing as a spirit of the time. Cited earlier, Vail and Genis emphasized that the highly secular Soviet age of science that had seemingly made religion obsolete in the early 1960s, in time created a spiritual vacuum that needed to be filled in some people.[11]

"THIS SEEMED ALTOGETHER NORMAL TO US"

Upon coming to power, the Bolshevik government confiscated all private housing and established a monopoly over it, thereby obscuring from the start the lines between public and private life. In contrast to Western Europe and the United States, the housing strategies of individuals and families were not based on independent choices, but on state policies determined by ideological preferences. Making control over living space a political rather than an economic issue became such an effective strategy that it amounted to a form of symbolic yet discreet violence.[12] This is especially the case because Stalin's government gave low priority to housing, despite the enormous population influx into the cities as a result of rapid industrialization and collectivization of agriculture, and later from the devastation of war. Horrendous overcrowding became the norm for virtually all but the most privileged. Most Soviet citizens lived in communal apartments (*kommunalki*), an unofficial symbol of Soviet power at the everyday level. Each room or cluster of rooms in apartments and homes intended to house single families now accommodated several different families, often multigenerational ones, who shared not only bathroom and kitchen facilities but also the full range of human emotions and dysfunction that come with overcrowding.[13]

After World War II, class considerations, the whims of local authorities, Party membership, an individual's value to the state, and corruption, as before, governed housing policies. The vast majority of the population continued to live in communal apartments, managed by a person responsible for making sure inhabitants shared bathroom and kitchen facilities and cleaning responsibilities. The housing manager could also monitor the inhabitants' comings and goings. If communal housing policies represented optimal conditions for molding the new Soviet man and woman of the Stalin era, then a mass exodus into individual apartments provided ideal conditions for molding the post-Stalin *Homo Sovieticus*. Making the expansion of housing a top priority, Khrushchev mass produced prefabricated modular apartment complexes known colloquially and not unaffectionately as *khrushcheby*, "Khrushchev's slums," whose appearance transformed the Soviet urban landscape. Urban housing stock doubled between 1950 and 1965. One hundred eight million people moved into new apartments between 1956 and 1965.[14] The exodus out of the *kommunalki* proceeded rapidly. It began with the political and Party elite, spread to highly educated professionals and skilled workers, and finally to lower and unskilled elements. The trend intensified under Leonid Brezhnev when, between 1965 and 1978, 10.5 million people a year moved into their own quarters.

Despite the rapid expansion of housing, the state failed to meet its citizens' rising expectations, in part owing to the astounding rate of urbanization in the postwar Soviet Union. In 1959 the urban population made up 52 percent of the total. This grew to 62 percent by 1970, to 70 percent by 1980, and to 74 percent by 1990.[15] In 1970, 23.7 percent of married couples lived with at least one parent. In 1979, by which time most of the Cold War cohort had married and had become parents, this figure remained substantial at 19.7 percent. (In comparison, the corresponding figure for the United States was approximately 1.5 percent.[16]) The inadequacy of the urban housing stock proved to be another source of dissatisfaction. As late as 1959, only 34 percent of urban residents enjoyed running water, and only 2.2 percent had hot water. Indoor plumbing was available to 31.4 percent of city dwellers, central heating to 22.4 percent, and bathing facilities to 8.9 percent.[17] It is therefore not surprising that Soviet citizens continued to see inadequate housing as a primary concern.[18]

At the time, four types of housing existed in the Soviet Union: individual (often wooden) homes (usually found in rural areas and in provincial cities); government apartments distributed through the workplace; government flats at the disposal of municipal authorities; and cooperative flats that individuals purchased. The construction of cooperative apartment buildings reflected not only the government's commitment to improving living standards but also economic realities: people had money to spend, yet little to spend it on, and the housing shortage remained acute. By 1977 more than two million Soviet families dwelled in cooperative apartments, and an estimated one million families were "in line" to purchase one.[19]

The most graphic memories of living conditions shared by the Cold War cohort have to do with life in communal apartments. "Can you imagine what a communal apartment was like?" asked Saratov's Irina Tsurkan, who lived with her parents in a one-room communal apartment. She described a long hallway with six rooms off of it, each inhabited by a separate family. "Whenever there was a holiday, there was company in each room. There was singing, all sorts of noise, a real uproar." When Olga Kolishchyuk's family returned to Saratov in 1955, they moved in with her grandparents who occupied a single room "six meters long," she claimed. Irina Kulikova's family "lived in a communal flat without indoor facilities."

In Moscow, Viktor Alekseyev, his parents, older brother, and grandmother occupied a communal flat until his father received a two-room apartment through work when Viktor was ten years old. Anna Lyovina's family rented a room in a "hut" before occupying a shabby apartment in a barracks outside Moscow. "Excuse me, but the toilet, God knows where, was on the street," she recalled. Under Khrushchev the family moved back to the city into a communal apartment. Igor Litvin's family dwelled in an apartment located in an old wooden building on the outskirts of Moscow known locally as the "Jewish house," because "no one but Jews rented rooms and apartments" in it. Recalled Litvin: "In 1956 or 1957 when Eisenhower was supposed to visit Moscow, it was decided to raze all of those small houses." After they demolished the building, his father obtained a two-room communal flat in central Moscow, where they remained until his parents bought into a co-op when Litvin was in college. Bakhyt Kenzheyev remembered "eighteen people lived in my grandmother's three-room apartment." Then he, his parents, and sister moved into a separate communal flat. "It was in the basement. It was a room of sixteen square meters for the four of us." He added that, from today's perspective, "the poverty we lived in back in the 1950s is simply unimaginable. But we were nevertheless happy because we didn't know any better." Tatyana Arzhanova lived with her mother, grandmother, stepfather (temporarily), and nanny in a two-room third-floor communal apartment adjoining a cinema whose sounds penetrated the apartment's walls. "I don't know anyone in the West who could imagine such a family life." She described the unventilated kitchen without hot water situated in the corridor. Because the bathroom in the apartment had an occupant, Auntie Katya, Arzhanova and her family had to bathe in the public facility across the street. "But this seemed altogether normal to us," explained Tatyana. Her mother always met her downstairs when she returned home "because it really was awful to go upstairs." The entranceway served as a haven for local drunks who relieved themselves there because there were no toilets nearby. "It was disgusting," objected Arzhanova. So much so that she scrubbed down the stairs before her friends came to visit on her birthday and other occasions. Her mother also waited for her at their entranceway for safety reasons: Arzhanova's mother often found documents or purses abandoned by thieves. Once her mother came across an otherwise empty bag with a real treasure in it, a recording of Tchaikovsky's First Piano Concerto. Since her family had recently acquired its first Victrola, they "listen[ed] to it with great pleasure." Leonid Terlitsky's family lived in communal apartments until he was fourteen years old. Terlitsky's reality seemed altogether normal, too: "The family was large. We lived in a single room. There was always food on the table. There was always clothing on our backs. I went on summer vacations with my parents."

Moving into a new government flat or co-op amounted to a new way of life. Yevgeniya Ruditskaya resided with her parents in a one-room flat in an apartment with ten other families. They managed to exchange this room for a larger one in another building and eventually to buy a cooperative apartment. "I remember how Mama walked into the apartment and said 'I can't believe it. Is this really mine?'" reminisced Ruditskaya. Arkady Darchenko recalled that most people in Saratov lived in communal flats: "But then, before our very eyes, they began to move us out of communal flats into our own. People could see that a lot of new living space became available and people began to live on their own. More things began to show up in the stores." Olga Kamayurova's family lived in a communal flat in which they shared a kitchen with two other families until 1963, when they purchased a co-op. "The apartment was considered luxurious. It had three rooms and was located in a brick building with all amenities. My mother's salary allowed her to hire a housekeeper."

Saratov's "housing market" offered another variant: individual wooden homes, usually without indoor facilities, similar to ones in villages, found especially in the Glebuchev Ravine neighborhood, which was packed with them. They too sometimes housed more than one family. Galina Poldyaeva lived in such a home until her father, a worker, was given an apartment in 1961. Olga Martynkina resided with her grandmother: "She had her own house with a garden. Then they tore them down and built apartments. Grandma had a cooperative apartment—a one-room apartment with a large kitchen, a good apartment." Aleksandr Ivanov's family also lived in a small house at first. Then "they built the *khrushcheby*, which in principle was state housing," he explained. "Some were given these apartments, but not us. My parents had to buy a co-op apartment with their own money."

Those who did not experience communal living were the children of the Party or government elite, of prominent professionals or cultural figures, or of some high- to mid-level professionals or Party workers. Vladimir Mikoyan, grandson of a member of Stalin's Politburo, grew up in a well-appointed private home. But this had its downside. "To be honest," he recalled, "I never liked living in a private house because I couldn't invite friends over, owing to the contrast." When the family moved into an apartment when Mikoyan attended School No. 20, he could finally ask classmates to his place. Son of a KGB official, Andrei Rogatnev lived in an apartment located in a building the Ministry of the Interior constructed for its employees. Olga Gorelik's father was deputy editor of Saratov's Party newspaper and later assistant to the head of the local Party organization. "We lived in a building next to the State Bank. Basically, it was a state within a state," remembered Gorelik. Several of her classmates, also the children of Party officials, grew up in the same or neighboring downtown building. On a more modest scale, Georgy Godzhello lived with his mother and grandparents in a "very small" two-room apartment. His grandparents occupied one room of eight square meters, and he and his mother the larger one of eighteen square meters. "But we always had a shelf of books," he recalled. Tatyana Artyomova's family of four also inhabited a small two-room flat. "I really loved this apartment and thought it was really a good one because it had high ceilings and large windows. The small room was very tiny and had only a bed and a desk. Nothing else would fit. That was my brother's room. The rest of us lived in the bigger room."

All but a handful of families improved their living arrangements during the 1950s and 1960s. Conditions for Irina Barysheva's family, who inhabited two small rooms on Saratov's main thoroughfare, did not get better because, even though her father distributed apartments, they could not buy one since they "lived on only one salary." Similarly, Natalya Yanichkina replied that "we didn't live in a communal apartment, but didn't move into a new flat." Irina Kulikova's father worked at a factory that built its own apartment houses for its employees. "People live even worse than us. We'll wait our turn," he told her. But her father died before receiving an apartment, so the family lost out. "Things improved, but only through our own efforts. We didn't get a thing from the government," regretted Kulikova.

No matter how intrusive the state, one's personal space, substandard as it might be, could serve as an arena of what historian Moshe Lewin calls hidden resistance.[20] It was here that people often spoke their minds (although the street was better), told jokes (frequently at the system's expense), listened to foreign radio broadcasts (or chose not to), read and discussed literature (official and otherwise), entertained guests (usually trusted friends), celebrated holidays (including religious ones), nourished each other, bickered, and made love. It was here that one could personalize otherwise look-alike furniture and belongings. It was here that children learned to read between the lines, when to "speak Soviet," and when to bite their tongues. Moving into individual flats strengthened the nuclear family. And what went on in families reproduced Soviet everyday realities, but also, in time, transformed them.

"THE LESS YOU KNOW, THE BETTER YOU'LL SLEEP"

Because remembering could be dangerous in Stalin's Russia, the parents of the Cold War generation practiced caution in talking about certain aspects of their lives. Despite the heady optimism of the Soviet 1950s, the legacy of mass repression and the subculture of violence it created cast a shadow over the Baby Boomers' childhood. During Stalin's terror, fear of others had even spread to family members, as some people sought to distance themselves from their arrested relatives by fleeing to other locales, by falsifying family histories, or by relying on personal connections to stay afloat in the sea of uncertainty. Yet repression could also strengthen family ties and identities because the whole family of someone designated an "enemy of the people" became vulnerable to persecution.

After Stalin's death, the post-Stalin leadership shut down most labor camps and "rehabilitated" many of those who had passed through or died in them by acknowledging the victims' innocence and restoring the property and rights to those still alive. Memorial, a nongovernmental organization set up during perestroika, estimates that the authorities rehabilitated 612,000 people between 1953 and 1957. But in declaring camp inmates innocent, the Party leadership did not name the guilty or publicize rehabilitation procedures, since the new policy represented more of a political than a legal move. The state failed to institutionalize the process of reintegrating Gulag survivors into the system. It did little to mitigate survivors' anxiety, depression, trauma, and fear of rearrest as they dealt with arbitrary officials and ambivalence at all levels—even from family members—in their attempts to have their property restored, to find jobs, and to obtain housing. Historians of the Gulag point to how the pathology of the camp system and its subculture affected everyone in Soviet society. This made it possible for the state to offer rehabilitation at the price of silence in this Khrushchevian "deal" with society.[21]

Saratovites and Muscovites shared similar stories about their families' first-hand experience with repression, the great equalizer in Soviet society. Olga Kamayurova's maternal grandfather in Saratov was repressed in 1937, when her mother was thirteen. He died locked up. Irina Kulikova's maternal great-grand-mother, a peasant, was arrested (and later rehabilitated), "simply because she let her tongue wag." Olga Martynkina's family also "suffered from the personality cult," a euphemism for Stalinism. Her uncle's father-in-law perished in prison, making her aunt an "enemy of the people." Martynkina's husband's uncle also spent time in Stalin's labor camps. The family lived in Tomsk at the moment of his arrest after which "they left Siberia immediately for Saratov, so as to escape." Aleksandr Kutin's uncle had been sent to camp because he had had been taken prisoner of war. Calling the Stalinist policy of incarcerating liberated Soviet POWs "vile," Kutin underscored that rehabilitation proved to be bittersweet. "Life simply didn't work out for him," he maintained. "They didn't give him suitable work."

Moscow's Boris Shtein related that his grandfather's brother "was destroyed and the rest of his family exiled to Baku." The return of the repressed to Moscow when the Gulag shut down left an indelible memory on Shtein: "My grandfather helped them a lot. These were close acquaintances and relatives and he tried hard to help them materially. People lived with us before returning to their homes." He likewise recounted that his mother told him how she and his grand-mother "sat at the window each night until a certain hour when they came after people. And only then they went to bed. According to my mother's stories, at least half the people in the building were arrested," he said.

Yelena Kolosova's paternal grandfather ended up in Stalin's Gulag. His crime: he had survived a Nazi concentration camp and lived to tell about it. Her maternal grandfather also became a victim. He "was supposed to have been repressed," shared Yelena, "but he committed suicide so that his family would not fall into the category of the family of an enemy of the people." Mikhail Markovich's great-grandfather perished in the Gulag and his wife and older chil-dren passed through the camps. The children later acquired a higher education, but "none became a Party member," observed Markovich. Yet this deep-rooted detachment from the regime was not true of numerous other families, illus-trating that the social pressures to comply, complicated by the dynamics of gen-erational change, could produce Communist believers, too. For instance, Vladimir Sidelnikov's maternal grandparents, both peasants, were repressed after someone denounced them. His grandmother spent fifteen years in the Gulag near Magadan. Raised in an orphanage, Sidelnikov's mother nonetheless became a hard-edged Communist who did not blame the system for her own mother's misfortune, dismissing it as a "terrible mistake."

Although arbitrary, the terror targeted Old Bolsheviks, consuming those who made the Revolution, as Moscow's Sergei Zemskov's account confirms. Zemskov comes from a family of revolutionaries, many of whom were repressed in 1937. Some of them survived the ordeal, especially the women, one of whom was his grandfather's sister, who languished for almost twenty years in the camps. His own grandmother "sat" for five years. Zemskov vividly recalled how, when he was about seven years old, he encountered at the family dacha former Gulag inmates who had been rehabilitated. Zemskov especially remembered that, "despite all, they preserved the romantic notions they had toward the Revolution. Not a single one of them became embittered or talked about how much he or she had suffered." Some voiced hostility toward Stalin or Beria, head of the security police, but their ideological and moral commitment to the system never wavered. "They made a huge impression on me," maintained Zemskov.

Repression struck closest to home for Saratov Baby Boomers Viktor D. and Natalya Yanichkina. Viktor's father "sat" it out in Siberia before being allowed to return to Saratov in the mid-1950s. Natalya's mother and grandmother were charged with "cosmopolitanism" in 1952 and repressed. According to Yanichkina, her mother and grandmother (she barely knew her father) "had lots of furniture and things that had been brought from [East] Germany after the war. When my mother began wearing clothing not seen elsewhere, someone denounced them. This turned out to be a kind of show trial, and that's why they imprisoned both mother and daughter." Yanichkina's mother threw a hunger strike during her interrogation until they brought her child, ill with pneumonia, to see her. Afterward, the police packed her mother off to far-off Vorkuta. Yanichkina's care fell into the hands of her "very old" great-grandmother and step-grandfather, who raised her until her mother was amnestied and then rehabilitated after Stalin's death. Although cut short, the prison sentence took its toll. Her grandmother suffered a heart attack in the camps; she and her husband divorced after her release. And her mother decided against starting a second family. "She's not a nun, but she was afraid."

Some families managed to avoid the terror, yet in recounting *how* they did so, the Cold War generation emphasized that things could have been otherwise and that, in this way, their families could just as easily have been swept up into the whirlwind. Aleksandr Virich's grandfather was a distinguished prerevolutionary statistician. "He was lucky, for he died in time, in 1934. He would have been repressed in 1937," averred Virich. Vladimir Kirsanov's father's peasant family left for the city before collectivization. "I don't know what would have happened to them had they stayed," he wondered.

Moscow's Andrei Rogatnev shared how his grandfather, an Old Bolshevik and Civil War commissar, left the Red Army to take up a diplomatic post. This saved him. "Our entire family understands this simply as a coincidence, as good fortune." Tatyana Arzhanova's grandfather turned in his Party card to protest the arrest of innocent friends. He died in the war, which "probably helped from falling himself into the meat grinder." A kick in the temple by his favorite horse killed Bakhyt Kenzheyev's Kazakh grandfather in 1923. After his grandmother died a year later, Bakhyt's father and his siblings were placed in an orphanage. If Kenzheyev's grandfather had lived five years longer, "he would have been shot, in which case the children would have ended up in a children's home in Siberia as enemies of the people," claimed Kenzheyev. Anna Lyovina's grandfather, it will be recalled, died in 1930. "I know this sounds blasphemous, but the fact that he died in 1930 saved him," she reasoned. Moreover, her aunts were expelled from the university for attending church. Others voiced relief that no one in their families had been purged, that no one, as Galina Poldyaeva put it, "fell into the meat grinder."

Repression remained a taboo topic in some families. Olga Martynkina remarked that her grandmother "kept everything secret." Irina Tsurkan's grandmother told her "the less you know, the better you'll sleep, and never told us a thing." Natalya P. maintained that her parents "didn't discuss such things." But she—and others—still found out what was going on, and that is the point. "I can recall that we had a neighbor who venerated Khrushchev, because he freed him [from the Gulag]. He was very intelligent and soft spoken." Similarly, Irina Garzanova remembered meeting the son of her mother's friends arrested in the 1930s for drawing a picture of Hitler. He languished away in the camps until 1956. No one "spoke about this as long as he was in camp," related Irina. "But when he returned, of course, the matter was discussed. He'd drop in to visit with us often." As a young adult Natalya Yanichkina would want to know more about her mother's ordeal in Vorkuta, but "when I was young we didn't discuss it," she stated. "I knew that Mother had been repressed, but back then we didn't use the term, which appeared much later. I knew that my mother had been imprisoned, and I was ashamed of this. I didn't want to know a thing." Andrei Rogatnev lived in a large building housing agents of the secret police. During the repression of the 1930s waves of arrests rolled through the building. "We children grew up together and we continue to get together, but no one ever said that someone else was the son of an enemy of the people, the son of someone who had been repressed. They protected our childhood."

It is hard not to agree with Anatoly Shapiro that "there were repressed individuals in practically every family." "And when that was the case," agreed Viktor D., "the whole family suffered, not just the repressed." Moreover, as Shapiro maintained, "Fear was instilled in my parents, and it exists even today. I also was afraid. It was passed on genetically." Vladimir Glebkin corroborated that his parents "to the very end did not believe that the harsh Stalinist system had come to naught; this fear remained with them always." As a result, parents inspired in their offspring awareness of the need to be cautious—a survival skill that arguably came at the system's expense, for it ineluctably raised the question of why this was the case. Anatoly Shapiro's parents feared talking about politics because, as he put it, "the children might say the wrong thing to someone on the street and there would be repercussions." When his grandparents wished to keep something from the children, they spoke in Yiddish. Vladimir Sidelnikov's parents did not tell him that his maternal grandmother had endured a fifteen-year Gulag sentence. "You couldn't back then, because I might have let the secret out," elaborated Sidelnikov. Andrei Rogatnev remembered telling jokes about Khrushchev. Andrei's father, a KGB agent, warned him, "Andriusha, please don't tell anyone this at school."

Neither of Pyotor Krasilnikov's parents in Saratov, both Communists, mentioned politics in his presence. He explained: "They lived through 1937, and things remained strict enough for some time after Stalin's death. Therefore, there were practically no such conversations." Similarly, because Vladimir Kirsanov's mother's Volga German family had been deported during the war, "fear of repression lingered. Generally, they spoke little about politics at home," he recalled. Olga Kolishchyuk admitted that "during my childhood they told me that I had to bite my tongue, because the cult of personality was a dangerous thing. You might blurt out something as a joke and then there'd be a knock on the door at night and they'd take your parents and you'd remain an orphan. And they told me over and over again not to say anything out of stupidity."

"IF I DIE, CONSIDER ME A COMMUNIST"

The first postwar attempt to study the Soviet family, the Harvard Project, based on interviews of émigrés conducted in 1950–51, reveals what constituted the Soviet dream for the Baby Boomers' parents, most of whom were born in the decade following the Revolution of 1917. On the eve of World War II, this generation voiced the greatest enthusiasm for the Soviet experiment. The Harvard Project concluded that prewar *Homo Sovieticus* believed in success and approved of specific features of the Soviet welfare state such as government ownership of the means of production, free education and medical care, and social mobility. Yet the new Soviet man and woman also expressed widespread hostility toward the collective farm system, resented the terror, and felt an enormous gap between themselves and their top leaders. Further, they either totally believed what the state told them or totally rejected it.[22]

World War II hardened these attitudes toward state propaganda but also transformed this generation's expectations. Delayed gratification—an inherent feature of the Soviet system from the start—began to lose its appeal just as the state called for further self-sacrifice to ward off the new threat of conflict as the unfolding Cold War exacerbated the paranoid social and cultural climate that characterized postwar Stalinism. After Stalin's death in 1953, however, the impetuous Khrushchev (1953–64) ended rule by terror, improved the bleak living conditions, sought to reduce tensions with the non-Communist world, eased the misery in the countryside, slammed Stalin at the Twentieth Party Congress in 1956, fashioned a new social contract based on his populist leadership style, and promoted the Thaw in Soviet cultural life—a period rich in promise characterized by an episodic relaxation in censorship restrictions and openness that had a tonic effect on the intelligentsia. Rejecting terror, the Party sought compliance by different means, including a dispersal of authority and calls for exemplary personal conduct. Its success in all of these areas underscored dazzling accomplishments in the Soviet space program and scientific-technical revolution. In the short run, Khrushchev's denunciation of Stalin and the Party's acknowledge of former "falsifications" may have increased the public's confidence in the system and its trust in the media. It was at this time that an independent public opinion emerged in the Soviet Union.[23]

This is important because a far larger percentage of the Baby Boomers' parents belonged to the Communist Party than the population at large: *at least one of the parents of 80 percent of the interviewees joined the CPSU.* They thus constituted the system; the values and attitudes they instilled in their children helped to determine the fate of the USSR. In 1956 (when the population was approximately 200 million) the CPSU had 7,174,000 members and candidate members. Only 11.2 percent of them had attained a university-level education, and only 25.8 percent had completed a secondary education. As a cohort, therefore, the parents of the Cold War generation belonged to the most educated strata of the Communist Party. Enrolling their children in the elite magnet schools can be seen as a perk of Party membership, but it also had much to do with the parents' own educational levels.

Roughly 75 percent of Party members at the time were male. During the 1950s and afterward, the Party stepped up efforts to attract women into the organization but, as Vyacheslav Starik stated, "For the most part, it's traditional in Russia that the woman is more family oriented. The man is the go-getter." Besides, many of the interviewees' fathers became Communist Party members during the war, when the high death rate of Communists at the front and efforts to expand the size of the Party transformed it: There were 3.4 million Party members and candidates for membership in 1940 and 5.76 million at war's end. Igor Litvin, for instance, explained that his father joined the Party in 1941, "when there was such a high level of patriotism." Many became Party members at the front. Leonid Terlitsky recalled that his father used to joke about this: "During the war a commander comes to his troops and says, 'Who wants to join the Party,' and one of the soldiers answers, 'If I die consider me a Communist. If I survive, please don't."

Terlitsky's anecdote touches upon a vital element of Soviet public life: Party membership remained a key to success and was even necessary in some professions. A high percentage of the interviewees explained that their parents became Party members because they had to do so. Lyubov Raitman described her father as a conscientious Party member who attended meetings and paid dues, but as someone who "never was a committed Communist." An accomplished architect, "he had to be a Party member in order to head up a studio," she added. Yevgeny Podolsky defended why his mother joined the Party circa 1965: "She had already become the chief doctor at a sanitary inspection station in Saratov. And it was expected back then that someone in a position of authority belong to the Party."

Aleksandr Virich maintained that his stepmother enrolled in the Party's ranks because "in Russia at the time it was impossible to defend your dissertation if you hadn't joined the Party." An engineer recruited to extract war reparations in occupied Germany, Valentin Ulyakhin's father "had to" join the Party in 1946. "Back then when someone ended up abroad," explained Valentin, "they demanded that he be a Party member." Drafted into the army in 1953, Yelena Zharovova's father joined the Party when he got stationed in Leningrad. "The Party organization requested that he be transferred back to Moscow to his family," she explained, adding that her father "quit the Party as soon as that became possible when he was already an old man." Yelena Kolosova's father felt compelled to accept an invitation to become a Communist after being elected a member of the Academy of Sciences. She recalled that her family treated politics "with a peculiar sense of humor and sometimes a biting one." Irina Garzanova had a similar explanation for her father's becoming a Communist: "We could say that they made him join the Party after heading up his department for a year. However, as soon as he could quit, he did."

But there were committed Communists among them, too, especially within the Saratov cohort. Olga Gorelik cast her father as a true believer, who did not see Party membership as a ticket to success: "We lived very modestly. We didn't have any luxuries—no car, no magnificent apartment. Nothing." Aleksandr Trubnikov's father lectured him that "under capitalism I never would have achieved what I did." Born in 1914 to a cook and an alcoholic who got crushed to death by a train, he obtained a higher education and became an army engineer. "Socialism and Soviet power," he reminded his son, "elevated us." Natalya Yolshina described her parents as rank-and-file Communists who inculcated in her universal values such as honesty and responsibility. "Ours was a 'correct' family, and I was a 'correct' child," affirmed Yolshina. Both of Vladimir Sidelnikov's parents belonged to the Party, but he stressed that his mother in particular, an instructor at a Moscow neighborhood Party committee, "was an ardent Communist." So were some parents who did not become CPSU members, such as Natalya Pronina's; she regretted, "I can honestly say that this was not by choice."

Some parents refused to join the CPSU because of the compromises they felt they would have to make as Party members. Georgy Godzhello recalled that, when his mother declined an invitation to become a Communist, she expressed her support for communism, but explained that she might have a problem "subordinating herself to Party discipline." Some parents paid a price for staying outside the Party's ranks. Irina Vizgalova's father was invited to join the Party so that he could become a full professor, "But he felt he could get by without being a professor, and therefore he didn't join," she related. Vladimir Glebkin believed that not joining the Party posed "a serious problem" for his father: "Everyone said that, had he joined the Party, he would have become an academician a long time ago." Be that as it may, Glebkin stressed that his father achieved much without taking this step.

"EVERYONE UNDERSTOOD THIS AS A GREAT LOSS"

Family history, personal experience, and an array of other considerations determined the Baby Boomers' parents' attitudes toward the Soviet system, regardless of whether they belonged to the Party or not. These positions changed as more—critical—information became available after Stalin's death. When Soviet radio announced on March 6, 1953, that Josef Stalin had died, many found it impossible to fathom him gone, because all of the accomplishments of Soviet power, including victory in World War II, had been credited to him. Many shed tears of grief and tears for the uncertainty awaiting them. Marking a turning point in public consciousness, Stalin's passing even made an impression on the young Cold War generation. "Believe it or not," Leonid Terlitsky told me, "but one of my first memories is of the day when Stalin died. It's very vague because I was only three years old. But I do remember sort of the inner feeling of that day. It was unlike any other day." Saratov's Aleksandr Babushkin had vivid memories of 1953, "even though I was four years old. I remember there was a black loudspeaker. Our neighbors listened attentively to it and cried." Irina Garzanova recounted "that there were lots of people, some kind of demonstration on Lenin Street. There were portraits of Stalin." Yevgeny Podolsky recalled, "I was in my bedroom, in bed, when my mother came in. She was crying, tears were pouring down. I naturally also began to cry and asked, 'What's wrong?' And my mother said, 'Stalin died.'" Podolsky continued, "People cried, because everyone understood this as a great loss," including Irina Kulikova's maternal grandmother who had been repressed. Repeating the oft-told tale that Stalin simply was not in the know about the repressions, Irina's mother told her that "Grandmother cried when he died and even I did, despite the fact that she and I had suffered."

Some of the interviewees remembered their parents' disparaging remarks about Stalin after he died, a reaction that became more pronounced as a result of Khrushchev's denunciation of Stalin at the Twentieth Party Congress in 1956. The attack emboldened writers, movie makers, and even some historians, an otherwise ideologically safe group, to press the limits of the permissible. It likewise encouraged families, particularly those that knew repression firsthand, to talk about the injustice done them, for doing so now represented the Party line. "The entire country breathed a sigh of relief," according to Viktor D., whose father had been repressed after the war. "After the Twentieth Congress the police in Saratov stopped checking to see if my father was at home. In 1957 my father was fully rehabilitated. It was now possible for me to enroll in the English-language school and later in medical school. Before [the Twentieth Party Congress] that would have been unlikely or would not have happened at all." Olga Martynkina did not forget her grandmother saying, "'Well, thank God, finally!'" Tatyana Artyomova recalled, "Both Papa and Mama admired Khrushchev for finding the courage to

The Baby Boomers remembered the ubiquitous portraits of Stalin in public places—even after he died. At the end of 1953, Natalya Pronina and her kindergarten class celebrated the New Year in Magadan with the assistance of Uncle Frost (the Soviet Santa Claus). *Courtesy of Natalya Altukhova (Pronina)*

do so, since he was one of them." Her classmate Tatyana Arzhanova believed her mother and grandmother's discussions about Khrushchev's dethroning of Stalin affected her at a subconscious level. When being put down for a nap, she imagined seeing the faces of Lenin and Stalin in the elaborate patterns of the Oriental rug hanging above her bed. There was no doubt in her mind: Lenin was good, while Stalin was bad. "This is connected with the repressions and with what happened to my grandfather's, grandmother's, and mother's friends," she clarified. Aleksandr Konstantinov shared that he "remembered the Twentieth Party Congress well. It was clear that Stalin was a monster, and it was wonderful what Khrushchev did." Olga Kolishchyuk reminded me "that there were Party meetings everywhere. Everyone was in shock, because before Stalin had been considered a god." Leonid Terlitsky echoed this point: "all of a sudden we heard that Stalin was not what we thought, not what we were told he was, but something very different." Still, he remembered that his parents "were careful to tell me not to talk to anyone about it. It was sort of a taboo [topic]—any criticism of the government, don't talk about it outside the house. That was the rule."

Yet Natalya Pronina claimed the congress made no visible impression on her parents: "None at all. I can say that for certain." Arkady Darchenko's experience may help us grasp why. His parents did not share with him their reactions to Khrushchev's denunciation of Stalin, he explained, because "they were afraid to comment, especially since they had worked in the Gulag [as did Pronina's]. They didn't discuss politics at home. My father never joined the Party and my parents were afraid. They still are, by the way. As they say, 'Who knows what might happen?'" And there were others such as Olga Gorelik's father who, while not approving of the repressions, saw Stalin "as a remarkable and talented leader."

There were also households in which parents did not see eye to eye on the Stalin question. Irina Barysheva remembered that her Party-member father from working-class origins "believed in his communisms and socialisms so much." From Russia's gentry class, her mother "was raised differently and was more critical of the authorities." Barysheva overheard conversations at home as her mother and her friends exchanged whispered secrets. Her mother had a particularly close friend whose husband, the editor of the local paper, had been shot without a trial or investigation. But his wife did not know his fate. For years, corrupt officials extracted bribes from her, offering in exchange bland assurances that her husband was alive and that she would soon be able to correspond with him. Then the Twentieth Party Congress took place and she found out the bitter truth. "She wrote such a letter to the Supreme Soviet that Mama was afraid that they'd arrest her and shoot her." Concluded Irina: "That's probably when I first heard about the personality cult." Soon thereafter the government rehabilitated the executed Communist, offering his widow a small monetary compensation. "It was the money that offended her most," noted Barysheva. As a sign that things had changed, no one reacted to the hostile letter she had penned to the government. She later went insane, spending her last days in a mental asylum, while her aggrieved children joined relatives in America when emigration became possible in the 1970s.

"WE BEGAN TO GET MORE INFORMATION"

Khrushchev began opening up the Soviet Union to the outside world as part of the thawing of public life, not only because the more internationally minded and pro-reform elements of society supported this policy but also because of Khrushchev's own fascination with the West. Confident in the Soviet system's ability to pass the tests associated with invidious comparison with the West, particularly America, he believed that by definition everything Soviet was better, and if it just so happened that this was not obviously so at the moment, then it was destined to become the case in the not-too-distant future. This act of faith resulted in a much welcomed expansion of foreign contacts that trickled down throughout Soviet society. It involved allowing Western tourists to resume travel to the USSR in 1955, displaying Pablo Picasso's cubist art in Moscow in 1956, translating certain Western writers, and promoting cultural exchanges. Two particularly consequential examples of the latter are the Moscow Youth Festival in 1957 and the opening of the first U.S. exhibit in Moscow in 1959. Made possible by a bilateral agreement recently signed by the two superpowers, the latter put on show cars, kitchens, and everyday products associated with the American way of life.

For two weeks beginning on July 28, 1957, an estimated 30,000 foreign youth in their twenties and thirties attended the Moscow Youth Festival, exposing Soviet youth—including the Cold War generation's parents—to Western music, ideas, fashion, and behaviors. Calling themselves "shtatniki" (Stateniks) or "bit-niki" (Beatniks), Soviet youth sang "Love Potion Number 9" and adopted the expression "See ya later, alligator."[24] For a short spell, Picasso's doves of peace replaced the otherwise ubiquitous hammer and sickle.[25] Jazz musician Aleksei Kozlov called the festival "'the beginning of the collapse of the Soviet system,'" while film critic Maya Turovskaya stressed that Russians could "touch and smell the outside world for the first time in three decades."[26] The result, as Vladimir Sidelnikov crudely put it, was that "after the festival our Russian wenches began to give birth to Negroes."

Natalya Yanichkina described how the Moscow Youth Festival reverberated in Saratov: "We didn't have a television, but back then people would visit their neighbors to watch [the festival on] TV. I recall there was some special event here, too, and the city was spruced up." Yanichkina summoned up memories of sewing new dresses for the occasion and of how her mother looked like Lolita Torres, an Argentinean movie star popular among Soviet cinemagoers in the 1950s and 1960s, a fact that reminds us that the "West" was not the only source of outside influence on Soviet life. Yanichkina understood the festival as "an event of national significance" for her country. "There was dancing, fireworks; it was almost like a carnival. There's a park of culture and leisure in Saratov. Mama went there with her girlfriend, but didn't take me along because I had come down with the mumps." It was more than a fleeting moment in Soviet cultural life. As she put it, "We began to get more information, not the kind you speak about in the kitchen in private, but public, open, information."

Saratov's Natalya Pronina attended the Moscow festival with her parents. "You have to see documentary films from the time," she insisted. "People danced in the streets. People of all nationalities. You'd be walking along, and there'd be one nationality and you're of another. Then we'd join hands and dance. It was spontaneous. People wanted to do it, their hearts were in it. The interaction was completely free." Equally vivid is the impression made on Pronina of befriending a Chinese girl in the hotel where her family stayed. "Although we didn't understand each other's languages, we got along really well. We drew, cut out some dolls, and I had a very positive impression of the Chinese. Both my parents and hers were pleased that we got along."

Bringing Soviet citizens into contact with U.S. technology and consumer goods, the American exhibit also had a profound impact on the popular imagination. The Stalinist system had avoided making comparisons with capitalism so as to justify economic autarky and isolation. Promoting the slogan "catch up with and surpass America," Khrushchev believed that the Soviet system would overtake the United States in all measures. In this sense, those who visited the U.S. exhibit in Moscow in 1959 "were viewing their own future."[27] The American exhibition opened in the summer of 1959 in Sokolniki Park. In the American exhibit's dome, a huge screen flashed alluring slides of American highways, supermarkets, cities, and college campuses. The exhibit comprised eight themes ranging from work and agriculture to medicine and basic scientific research. Sipping free Pepsi Cola, Soviet visitors saw an IBM computer in use, a Disney produced "Trip across the U.S.," and examples of American consumer goods. One of the structures featured a model home, new cars, boats, camping gear, and a Jungle Gym set. The exhibit conveyed a real sense of technological superiority, thereby undermining Soviet propaganda, and undoubtedly the authorities' confidence in the Soviet system's ability to withstand the competition. The Soviet media counterattack depicted the exhibit as a "tacky display of excess and bourgeois trivia." It controlled admission, banned the Americans' distribution of free cosmetics, and promoted rival cultural events. Yet, according to official statistics, 2.7 million Soviet citizens visited the exhibit. The real figure might be as much as 20 percent higher.[28]

In justifying the expenditure, the United States Information Agency (USIA), the propaganda wing of the State Department, saw the exhibition as "the largest and probably the most productive single psychological effort ever launched by the U.S. in a communist country."[29] At this exhibit, Vice President Richard M. Nixon and Khrushchev angrily debated the virtues of their respective countries—and ideologies. This episode is often called the "kitchen debate" because it took place against the backdrop of an American dream kitchen in a model ranch house. Consumption had become as much of a front of the Cold War as had outer space.[30] The setting allowed Soviet critics to trivialize the preponderance of consumer goods, making the commentary gender specific by claiming that the exhibit was intended more for women's eyes. But some visitors knew better.

As a nine-year-old, Moscow's Leonid Terlitsky had no chance of getting into the exhibit, but his mother did. "She brought back a lot of catalogs and a lot of brochures of American cars, and American kitchens, and American homes, and other stuff." The exhibit made a "huge impression" on Aleksandr Konstantinov's mother: "She had a lot to say about it. The organization of scholarly research amazed her. She told us about the system of grants, about American kitchens, American cars, and the general style—light-hearted, cheerful, and open." Some others, especially in Saratov, experienced the exhibit vicariously, as Aleksandr Trubnikov's account reveals. "I, of course, didn't see it; but acquaintances of my parents did and they told us about the altogether amazing displays that were there. This struck me as being strange. However, they explained to me that the capitalists had squeezed the last drop of blood from the poor workers, and that soon they'd stop putting up with this."

Afterward, a bilateral agreement between the superpowers resulted in regular USIA exhibits opening in the few Soviet cities not closed to foreigners. The parents of Viktor D. from Saratov visited the American exhibit in neighboring Volgograd in the mid-1960s, after which Viktor traveled the 400 kilometers on a motorcycle to see it for himself. "I liked it. The cars, the technology, the motorcycles, and all the informational handouts. It was back then that I saw my first real American," reminisced Viktor. "I received a great deal of pleasure, seeing everything and remembering what I saw. We saved the interesting catalogs and the other things they gave us." Viktor emphasized that he would not have made the trip if America hadn't fascinated him. "Hardly. You wouldn't find me traveling to the zoo in Rostov. Or to the one in Saratov for that matter."

"THE WORLD BEGAN TO OPEN UP JUST A LITTLE"

Khrushchev's measured opening up of Soviet society and easing of restrictions on cultural life also made it possible for some parents to travel abroad. Saratov's Natalya Yanichkina remembered that the father of her classmate Galya Kiselyova, a member of the local Party elite, traveled to Africa. "It might have been for outward appearances, but nevertheless the door was open for some," remarked Yanichkina. The disparity between Moscow and Saratov in this regard, however, was enormous: none of the parents of the Saratovites I interviewed went abroad at that time. As "the world began to open up just a little," Tatyana Arzhanova's unofficial stepfather went to Rome for the Olympic Games in 1960. Leonid Terlitsky's parents, a musician and administrator in the Red Army Symphony Orchestra, began traveling abroad while Leonid was in school—to Yugoslavia, Hungary, then to England, and even the United States. Terlitsky recalled the impression made on him of the books, records, catalogs, and brochures for cars, kitchens, and houses that his mother brought back to Moscow. "Plus I had relatives in the United States, and there was contact with them." Indeed, two of Terlitsky's father's sisters had left for New York before the Revolution. His mother arranged for a clandestine meeting with them during a visit to the United States. Then there was the time friends of the family's American relatives visited Moscow in 1961. "We were still in our old room, and all of a sudden these two nice Americans in clean clothes walk into our grimy neighborhood where we lived. It was quite an experience." When Yevgeniya Ruditskaya was in eighth grade, her mother journeyed to Italy. "She returned absolutely sick. She was in shock," after observing the standard of living there. "For several days she couldn't even talk about it," reported Ruditskaya. Vladimir Glebkin's mathematician father began attending conferences and symposiums abroad in 1956 or 1957. Anatoly Shapiro's parents worked in Austria after the war. In 1965 his father, a lawyer specializing in international trade, frequently began traveling abroad and recounted his impressions and adventures. Work assignments also took Lyubov Kovalyova's father to Eastern Europe and to the United States in the 1950s. "I remember that when he traveled to America he brought back a film shot on a video recorder," she recalled. Seeing video shots of San Francisco, New York, and Washington fascinated her.

Both of Lyubov Raitman's parents went abroad while Lyubov attended School No. 20. Her mother went first, in 1960 or 1961. A French-speaking editor for a scholarly journal in the natural sciences, she was included in a group of scientists who left for France on a program of "academic tourism," that is, tourism with a didactic, professional purpose. "They liked her, despite the fact that she was a Jew and did not belong to the Party," shared Raitman. "They included her in the group because she could serve as a translator. This was probably the most important event in her life." As Lyubov explained, "It was simply impossible to

Leonid Terlitsky (bottom left) in 1954 with his parents, older brother, and a neighbor girl in the communal flat they lived in during his early years, where they hosted American relatives who visited in 1961. Terlitsky's brother had a profound influence on his taste in music and on his decision to emigrate. *Courtesy of Leonid Terlitsky*

hope during those years that there was a chance this dream would come true. It was a miracle." Of course, Soviet tourists had to be on their best behavior, for "in each group of this sort there was supposed to be, and always was, an agent of the KGB." But to the group's pleasant surprise the one chaperoning them "didn't really hide his role and behaved with dignity. And he got along with my mother very well." The exhilarating sensory overload transformed her, and affected those with whom she shared her observations back home in Moscow. Evaluating her mother's experience, Raitman said, "They were people just like us, but they were free. She sensed a different life. And then there was Paris. It all made a strong, strong impression on her."

And on Lyubov, too. Allowed to exchange little money, Soviet tourists nonetheless found ways to scrimp and save in order to bring back gifts to their loved ones. "I remember that she brought me an absolutely fabulous little skirt. Neither my girlfriends or I ever had anything like it again," gushed Raitman, who added that earlier her uncle had brought her a pair of gloves from Paris, "such beautiful crimson gloves," which replaced the tatty mittens she normally wore. "I'll remember them my entire life. Gloves, like grown ups had!" Raitman's father, a distinguished architect, visited Ghana yearly between 1962 and 1964. "He brought back a Philips transistor tape recorder, which created an incredible furor among my friends. When we had a party at school I'd take the tape recorder and we'd record each other singing and then listen. It was a wonderful toy."

Because those who traveled abroad had to be cautious in sharing their impressions outside the family and circle of trusted friends, they often "told us what they were ordered to say, and not how things really were," maintained Vladimir Sidelnikov. Consequently, the deep impact the "material encounters" with the outside world made should not be underestimated. For instance, Marina Bakutina's Party-member mother, who taught English at the Institute of Foreign Languages, went abroad as a translator at international conferences and exhibits. "She was in New York in 1958 or 1959 and brought back a View Master. It was truly a window on the West. I don't know how to say 'Wow!' in Russian. There was nothing else like it. No journals, no films, no television broadcasts, especially during those years, were comparable to the 3-D View Master," enthused Marina, who "can still see New York, the Rockefeller Center, as if it were yesterday. She also brought back the album from *My Fair Lady,* my favorite musical." Marina, who lives in Portland, Oregon, today, linked the subversive impact of seeing the world vicariously through the View Master as part of the prehistory of her decision to emigrate. Concluded Tatyana Arzhanova: "As kids, the greatest impression made by these trips turned out to be the things people brought back."

A handful of Baby Boomers themselves spent time abroad during their early years, but mostly were too young to appreciate the experience. Anatoly Shapiro was born in Austria. Saratov's Olga Kolishchyuk had only vague recollections of the time she spent in China when her father served in the Soviet Red Army.

Living abroad left an indelible mark on seven-year-old Andrei Rogatnev, however, who was in Hungary during the Soviet invasion of 1956, because his father served in the KGB. Andrei exonerated Soviet actions by ignoring them, focusing instead on the transgressions of the Hungarian "freedom fighters." He recalled the "Russian troikas," when Hungarian freedom fighters tied three people bound together at the leg to the back of a Soviet "Pobeda" automobile, dragged them through the streets of Budapest alive, doused them with gasoline, and torched them. "I saw all of this with my own eyes," he underscored. "This strengthened my belief even more that our cause was right."

"THE FAMILY WAS YOUR SOCIAL NET, YOUR SAFETY NETWORK"

Acknowledging the existence of independent public opinion, Stalin's successors remained determined to shape it: The postwar Soviet Union had one of the largest and most complex public communication systems in the world, aimed at inculcating values that the state deemed desirable. And even when it failed to do so, it mostly succeeded in shutting out ideas that might weaken the Party's grip on society.[31] As Leonid Terlitsky put it, "There were, of course, millions upon millions who believed it, who honestly believed it. This is the nature of any propaganda, especially Soviet propaganda. If someone tells you over and over again that your hair is green, you finally start to believe it. Or to have doubts about it at the very least."

As a closed society, the USSR made it difficult for outside observers—and perhaps even for its own leaders—to understand how attitudes toward authority and other core values, molded primarily by the family, shored up, or offered an alternative voice to those promoted by the state. Ultimately, an individual's lived experience finds expression in the values one espouses and in the identities one takes on, and all of this begins in the family. While true that political authorities make decisions that shape orientations and the choices available to people, the family imparts its own values that determine how individuals respond to circumstances. Within any historical situation, people pick their fates and live their lives both as passive objects and as active agents.

Families have histories—memories—often passed on orally, but also with the help of photographs, official and private documents, possessions, and other symbolic reminders of the past. Soviet state policies made memory dangerous, yet they could not prevent family memories and personal encounters with Soviet power from challenging sanitized official histories. The Baby Boomers' grandparents, after all, were born before the Revolution, and many of them, especially the women, observed religious practices on the sly. Moreover, most families knew state repression and violence firsthand. They also experienced the state's efforts to refashion the Soviet family, followed by a return to traditional pronatal family values. Then came total war, and expectations of what peacetime might bring, followed by Stalin's death and Khrushchev's Thaw. Rule without terror, the loosening up of censorship, attempts to improve living standards, growing foreign contacts, and a foreign policy of peaceful coexistence must be seen as the Party's recognition of what the Soviet people wanted. In responding to—and shaping—"public opinion," however, the state became far less successful at keeping out unorthodox ideas. As a result, the Soviet family, an amalgam of traditional as well as egalitarian features, underwent sweeping changes while the Cold War generation grew up and attended school. Authority in the family shifted from patriarchal to more open forms as three-generation families, which had persisted in the cities, gave way to the nuclear family—and eventually to a falling birthrate. As a result of state policies of modernization, the Soviet family more closely came to resemble those in other industrialized nations. According to the 1959 census, the average family in urban Russia had 3.5 members. The postwar birthrate fell in the 1960s owing to expanding educational and job opportunities for women, social mobility, and improved living standards. In addition, the number of people who took advantage of no-fault divorce, introduced in 1968, made clear that many people had stayed locked in unhappy marriages because they had to do so.

The shift to the nuclear family, facilitated by the beginning of a mass exodus from communal to private flats, created opportunities for deepening attitudes associated with the Thaw and for forming an independent public opinion. Ironically, this is ever more the case owing to other peculiar features of Soviet reality. Social life remained centered in the family. As Leonid Terlitsky reminded me, while he was growing up he went to an occasional movie, but there were few restaurants or clubs to go to: "There were no activities outside the family, and the family was your social net, your safety network," he stated. He also claimed that "no one in my family believed the government. No one would have a relationship with the government unless he had to." At the other end of the spectrum, some parents remained ardent Communists. But Vladimir Prudkin's parents represent what appears to have been the most typical archetype among the Baby Boomers. Prudkin observed that his parents, like those of his classmates, were liberal thinkers but not hostile toward the system that defined and rewarded their success. "In this regard they were conformist enough in their external behavior and at work, but their thinking placed them on the side of what we might call the free movement."

2

OVERTAKING AMERICA IN SCHOOL

Educating the Builders of Communism

On October 4, 1957, a Soviet R-7 intercontinental ballistic missile lifted off from the Baikonur Cosmodrome in Kazakhstan with a 184-pound polished silver sphere called Sputnik ("Traveling Companion"). The size of a beach ball, the world's first artificial satellite contained two beeping radio transmitters that allowed observers to track its orbit. A decade earlier, the RAND Corporation had foreseen that the launching of the first artificial satellite to orbit the earth "would inflame the imagination of mankind, and would probably produce repercussions in the world comparable to the explosion of the atom bomb." RAND was right. A dazzling public relations victory, Sputnik's appearance demonstrated, according to the *New Republic*, that the USSR had "'gained a commanding lead in certain vital sectors of the race for world scientific and technological supremacy.'" Future Sputniks, informed *Newsweek*, "'would be able to sight and even photograph just about every point on earth.'"[1] Worse yet, cautioned the *Chicago Daily News*, "'the day is not far distant when they could deliver a death-dealing warhead onto a predetermined target almost anywhere on the earth's surface.'"[2] As one historian wrote, Sputnik was "the shock of the century."[3]

Other Soviet successes and "firsts" in space followed hard on the heels of Sputnik, fanning fears that "the Russians" were beating the Americans at what we believed we did best. Technology, after all, had become a deciding factor in the Cold War superpower competition since 1949 when the Soviet Union had ended the U.S. nuclear monopoly. Less than a month after the alarm caused by Sputnik, the USSR put into space the much heavier Sputnik II, which carried on board scientific instruments and a dog named Laika.[4] In 1959 three Soviet space missions, Luna 1 to 3, had sent back to Earth images of the far side of the moon. On April 12, 1961, Soviet science propelled the first man into space, Yury Gagarin. The Soviet space program also launched the first space flight with more than one cosmonaut aboard. It accomplished the first space walk. And it boasted the first woman in space, Valentina Tereshkova, too.

The launching of Sputnik inspired fear in the West, but confidence in Soviet citizens, for the triumph complemented the Thaw in cultural life, denunciation of Stalin's crimes, robust economic growth, and rising living standards that characterized the country in the decade following Stalin's death in 1953. Not surprisingly, given the Cold War competition between the superpowers for the hearts and minds of the Third World, Soviet propaganda capitalized on the world's shocked reaction to Sputnik's launching, depicting the achievement as but one of many spectacular technological advances underway in the USSR. Moreover, in 1957 Khrushchev dreamed up the slogan "Catch up with and overtake America," which became the underpinning for his new *Party Program* approved by the Twenty-second Party Congress in 1961. The program assured citizens that the USSR would surpass the United States in per capita production by 1970 and build a Communist society by 1980.

The Party authorized Khrushchev's blueprint for building communism hard on the heels of Gagarin's historical space flight, which left a lifelong impression on the Baby Boomers. "We were most proud of his achievement," affirmed Saratov's Natalya Yanichkina. Moscow's Leonid Terlitsky remembered the excitement—classes were cancelled—when Gagarin's mission succeeded: "Everyone poured into the street in an absolutely unprecedented expression of joy. It was absolutely spontaneous. It was like the Yankees won the pennant." That same year, the government issued the "Moral Code for the Builders of Communism," which the Cold War generation committed to memory. Beginning with "devotion to the cause of Communism, love of the socialist Motherland and of the socialist countries," the code articulated collectivist values and patriotic commitment that youth were expected to manifest. "There was nothing wrong with this," claimed Natalya Yanichkina. "It's almost the same as the Ten Commandments." Natalya Yolshina concurred that "the basic postulates of Christianity did not fundamentally differ" from the code.

How successful were Soviet schools at bringing up "the worthy builders of Communism," as a popular 1965 housekeeping manual called this generation?[5]

KHRUSHCHEV'S EDUCATION REFORMS

There were no alternatives to highly centralized government-run schools in the USSR, which gave top priority to educating the builders of communism. State ministries controlled the curriculum, viewing teachers as instruments of state power. The year the Baby Boomers were born, the USSR introduced compulsory seven-year schooling, later extended to ten years, and then, in 1958, to eleven. Emblematic of Khrushchev's never-ending turnarounds, the government in 1964 returned to a compulsory ten-year education usually comprising four years of primary and six years of secondary education, to take effect in 1966. The class of 1967 was the first to complete the new ten-year curriculum.

The Baby Boomers' school year ran from September 1 to June 1 (until late June for the upper classes), Monday through Saturday, from 8:30 until 2:00 or 2:30 P.M., with twenty-four to thirty-two class periods of forty-five minutes a week. Pupils enjoyed a five-day fall break to celebrate the anniversary of the Russian Revolution, a twelve-day winter break (December 30–January 10) to celebrate the New Year, and an eight-day spring break (March 24–31). They were graded on a five-point scale, with "5" representing the equivalent of an American "A." The state banned corporal punishment in schools. When the interviewees attended school, the number of contact hours devoted to the sciences increased while the number of hours devoted to Russian language and literature, geography, and mechanical drawing decreased (as did foreign language instruction, except at the magnet schools). The time devoted to military training, physical education, shop and home economics, and practical excursions peaked in 1959, but then declined.

Moreover, Khrushchev's denunciation of Stalin forced a rewriting of history texts and, in 1962, to counteract pressures from below for even greater cultural liberalization, the introduction of a new subject, social studies, which focused on study of Marxist-Leninist texts, Party documents, and the pronouncements of Soviet leaders.[6] Two years later, Soviet schools further strengthened political indoctrination, promoting an atheistic, materialist view of the world. As Tatyana Luchnikova put it,

Tatyana Arzhanova's mother accompanied her across Moscow's Pushkin Square to her first day of school, on September 1, 1957, weeks before the launching of Sputnik. Soviet school children wore uniforms to school and customarily brought flowers to their teachers at the start of the school year. *Courtesy of Tatyana Koukharskaya (Arzhanova)*

"You had to be stupid not to understand. At school they told us there was no God." Luchnikova remembered reading in school textbooks that "you could traverse the entire globe and not find evidence of God." She elaborated, "We'd open the textbook and read what was written there because we had to answer questions to receive a grade. We'd repeat what was in the textbook. It never occurred to us to analyze anything. Like zombies, we simply followed along what was written."

Khrushchev's reforms affected teachers and how they taught. In 1957 the government set up a national teachers' union and reconsidered pedagogical practices, paying more attention to how children learn. Ironically, whereas the United States introduced sweeping reforms to make schools more competitive in science and math following the launching of Sputnik, the Soviet Union instituted reforms in the second half of the 1960s in response to American educational models, deemphasizing rote learning and creating a more relaxed atmosphere in elementary school, measures that came too late to affect the Baby Boomers. In other words, elements on both sides of the Iron Curtain feared that the other side had the edge when it came to educating its young people. Despite the alarmist mood in the United States, some educators who visited the USSR noticed plenty to criticize, especially teacher-dominated classrooms with little discussion, lots of factual learning, and virtually no individual research.[7] Journalist Susan Jacoby, for one, saw few examples of "high quality" teaching, underscoring, instead, the more "formally drawn" line between students and teachers that reminded her of the Catholic schools she had attended.[8] The debate over which superpower had better schools intensified in 1970, when a Russian-born American educator Urie Bronfenbrenner extolled the virtues of the Soviet school system for placing as much emphasis on *vospitanie*, or correct behavior, as it did on developing children intellectually. As much a critique of what he believed were disturbing trends in America, Bronfenbrenner's work argued that the centralized Soviet system did a superior job of socializing its young people, producing the type of society it desired thanks to "generous emotional support coupled with a firm insistence on propriety and collective conformity. In short, the individual was still very much at the service of the collective."[9]

But this was often in theory only. Doggedly determined to raise industrial production levels, convinced that Soviet schools were "divorced from life," and troubled by youth's desire to attend college rather than to join the ranks of the proletariat, Khrushchev pushed through a reform in 1958 calling for pupils to spend part of their school week acquiring practical work experience in industrial and other enterprises. He also proposed that all children work after eight years of schooling and before completing high school. These measures proved impractical to implement, immensely unpopular, and easy to circumvent, despite government efforts to propagandize this "polytechnic" approach. For instance, the Pioneer manual glorified the life of a worker named P. A. Samsonov, emphasizing the positive features of combining work and learning: "The more I read, the more I love the profession of being a worker and take pride in it,"[10] the hero contended. Not surprisingly, the post-Khrushchev leadership dropped these calls for mandatory polytechnic training, which virtually none of the interviewees recalled. Moscow's Anna Lyovina did only because they interrupted her future husband's studies. Assigned to a chemical enterprise, he injured his arm there, "thanks to an alcoholic," she claimed.

"SCHOOL NO. 42 TALKS WITH GOD HIMSELF"

Saratov's School No. 42 opened on September 1, 1954, at No. 18 Radishchev Street. When the class of '67 was in fifth grade—also in the historic year 1961—the school settled into a new, well-equipped building on the Twentieth Anniversary of the Komsomol Street. The school's class of 1967 comprised two groups, A, formed in 1958 when the pupils were in second grade, and B, formed the following year, each with twenty-eight students. Later in the Soviet period, the more capable students could be found in A and the less accomplished ones in B, but this was not the case back then, at least in the special schools. True, Aleksandr Babushkin (a member of the A class or *ASHnik/ashniki* [pl.]) boasted "that the level of the A class was intellectually higher" than that of the B class; however, it was actually the status and privileges of their parents that distinguished the two groups back then.

Most *ashniki* agreed with Vladimir Nemchenko that "there was, to all intents and purposes, no difference" between the groups, the parents of whom, according to Natalya Yolshina, "belonged to the intelligentsia: doctors, teachers, engineers." But "a small percentage of parents of the A class worked in the oblast committee of the Party," she added. In a status-conscious society such as the Soviet Union that distinction was paramount. Interviewees from both classes readily rattled off the names of the children of the local Communist Party *nomenklatura* who attended school with them. Despite the widespread sense that the parents of the *ashniki* belonged to the Communist Party elite, Olga Gorelik—herself the daughter of the deputy editor of the local Party newspaper—pointed out that "there were children of Party officials, but not many. There were four of them." Some of these individuals found excuses not to meet with me, thereby giving credence to the gossip their classmates told about the difficulties the children of the former Party officials endured after the collapse of the Soviet system. An exception, Tatyana Kuznetsova, never mentioned her father's privileged position: "For us," she stated, "there didn't exist such a thing as important parents and unimportant ones."

The majority of members of the B class (*BESHnik/beshniki*), however, called attention to the distinction between the two groups. As Irina Tsurkan quipped, "It's probably the children of the Party officials who claim there was no difference." Her classmate Aleksandr Virich echoed her sentiments: "Their parents' status was higher. We were not as privileged, but represented the second tier of the intelligentsia." Olga Kamayurova agreed that "some sort of difference was noticeable. Those in the A group seemed more elite. It seems to me, both now and back then, that they were a bit stuck up." It is not that children in the B class did not have influential parents. But, as Irina Tsurkan pointed out, "There were fewer of them, and they were probably a rank below." Concluded Aleksandr Konstantinov: "The A group was made up not so much of people with connections as of people of privilege, among who were several children of Party officials. They formed a nucleus around which an elite group was fashioned. The group also included the children of trade officials. We, too, came from the privileged stratum, but we were not of their ilk." Irina Barysheva reminded me that the "cultural intelligentsia did not envy" those who belonged to the commercial establishment, for, as her class-mate Larisa Petrova put it, "they lacked culture." Revealingly, no one recalled any significant conflicts between the A and B classes, although, "for the most part, we associated with those from our own class," remembered Aleksandr Kutin. Aleksandr Virich agreed, "Although we had some contacts, there were no particular friendships."

Despite the minor advantages children of the A class might have enjoyed in regard to their parents' privileges, members of the B class emphasized they had—and have—the edge when it comes to personal qualities. Actually, both classes see the B class as unique in that many of its members remain friends today and still get together regularly. Maintained Larisa Petrova: "We simply had a wonderful class," while the A class was "more stand-offish." Arkady Darchenko elaborated, "We were closer and the friendship that's lasted among us for forty years is worth mentioning." Irina Kulikova believed the reason for the cohesive-ness of class B boils down to the human factor: "We were much simpler in our relations, in our behavior, and in everything else. It didn't matter what kind of family a child came from, from a worker's or a professor's." Galina Poldyaeva claimed that it was only in the upper classes that she and her classmates became aware of what each other's parents did. "We never felt it mattered what family you came from. It never entered our heads."

Members of the class of 1967 had attended at least a dozen different primary schools before transferring to School No. 42. They concur that it "was much nicer, and cleaner" than, as Aleksandr Trubnikov put it, "my neighborhood school." "It was the top school, which was opened for the children of high-ranking officials," exclaimed Irina Barysheva. "Back then it wasn't acceptable to use this term, but it existed nonetheless." Natalya Yolshina stressed that "it wasn't just anybody who went there." Lyudmila Gorokhova's experience was typical. She had been the "star of the class" at her elementary school, but when she enrolled in School No. 42 "it turned out that I wasn't a star but ordinary." "For Saratov, the English school is somewhat legendary," remarked Aleksandr Virich. "Ninety-nine point nine percent of our class went to college." Those who attended the school knew "that they would become relatively well-known leaders of science and technology in Saratov and perhaps in Russia." "Of course it was an elite school," boasted Irina Chemodurova. "This was reflected even in our conversations back then. We'd say, 'School No. 13 talks with School No. 19, School No. 19 with School No. 42, and School No. 42 with God himself.'"

The school's composition made it special in another regard, too. Natalya Yanichkina explained, "Our school didn't have any of the serious disciplinary problems encountered in ordinary schools. There was no hooliganism, which in an ordinary school would be an everyday occurrence." Aleksandr Trubnikov concurred. "Selectivity is selectivity. Let's just say that we didn't have anyone who became a criminal." Irina Garzanova opined that "the main thing was the atmosphere of the school. It's wonderful when there's a friendly, creative atmosphere in any collective, and at school all the more so." Similarly, Olga Kolishchyuk recalled, "The school offered a fine education and demanded good behavior and decency. It was head and shoulders above the others." There was tremendous peer pressure to succeed, and the students who did not perform well "went to other schools and were practically straight-A students there."

Although the Saratovites sounded off about the elite nature of the school, virtually all of them commented that, as children, they paid no attention to issues of social distinction. But "often it was the parents who competed. And those from the working class who got in did so only because they needed to have a certain percentage of workers and peasants," explained Aleksandr Virich.

Aleksandr Konstantinov (back row, third from left) recalled that, on the first day of school in Saratov on September 1, pupils were taught how to sit correctly at their desks. They were instructed to place their hands flat on the desk with the right hand on top of the left so that they could readily raise it to answer questions. *Courtesy of Aleksandr Konstantinov*

"It was the same everywhere back then, beginning with the Supreme Soviet and ending with a school or kindergarten." Natalya P. volunteered that two of her classmates in the B class from working-class families were admitted "to improve the school's profile. They couldn't take children of only the intelligentsia." The fathers of the two pupils in class B may not have been "ordinary" workers. One of them, a chauffeur, "drove around someone from the *nomenklatura*," recalled Irina Barysheva, while the other was a skilled fitter who "traveled all over the world" to show customers how to use Soviet engineering tools. Neither of their children confirmed Barysheva's observation that their fathers were special in any way. In fact, one of them, Aleksandr Ivanov, remarked that "we were all from average families," thereby demonstrating the power of Soviet propaganda—and the role that a family's cultural capital can play in constraining and enabling decisions that young people make. Ivanov found that School No. 42 simply was not a good fit. He enjoyed physical education, shop, and physics lab, not English, and especially not Russian, for which he received Ds. He left School No. 42 after the eighth grade to study at Saratov's Aviation School.

Things turned out similarly in the A class, which at one point enrolled a pupil from a large working-class family, Yura Gusev. According to Natalya Yanichkina, one or both of Gusev's Russian-born parents had been taken to Germany during World War II. All too aware of the fate of Soviet POWs who returned home, they fled to Australia, where their children were born, but returned to the USSR in the 1960s when the post-Stalin leadership welcomed back expatriates. With poor knowledge of Russian, the oldest child, Yura, and then the rest of his many siblings, enrolled in School No. 42. Gusev's father labored in a local factory, while his mother stayed home to take care of their large brood of children. Yanichkina remembered that "the school helped this family out a great deal. We held school concerts, for instance, and collected money for the 'curriculum fund,' which went to the family for clothing and other things." But Yura did not graduate from the school: "When he showed some musical talent, he left to study at a military school specializing in music and graduated from there," recalled Yanichkina.

It bears repeating that the Saratovites claimed that, as children, they took no notice of nationality, with the exception of one interviewee of Jewish descent. As Vladimir Kirsanov observed, "These questions don't interest children. I can't remember any conflicts in school on these grounds." "Regarding nationality," confirmed Arkady Darchenko, "it's worth noting that we simply didn't think about such things back then. Even now I can't say with any assurance who belongs to what nationality." Irina Vizgalova remarked that "as an adult I understand that there were other nationalities apart from Russians, but back then we were all the same. Nationality didn't concern us at all." Olga Kolishchyuk also maintained that "we didn't pay any attention to this whatsoever. Only now, I'm able to say that there were Russians, Jews, Ukrainians, Belorussians, Tatars, and an Armenian."

"CHILDREN OF SORT OF THE CREAM OF SOVIET SOCIETY"

In 1961, neighborhood School No. 115 in Moscow was converted into special School No. 20 with intensive instruction in English. "We, in fact, were the first graduating class when kids went through the full program of a special school," explained Leonid Terlitsky. When the switch took place, the parents of roughly half of the fifth-grade class of School No. 115 opted to keep their children in the new magnet school. Igor Litvin was one of them. "They had to accept us," he made clear. But during the next two years the administration rid the school of weak students and of pupils from families not likely to intervene should their children flounder. Mikhail Markovich recalled that school administrators carried out this weeding out process "very tactfully." According to Vyacheslav Starik, "they gathered together the parents of the previous students and warned them that the load would be substantially greater than in a regular school, and therefore some of the parents transferred their children." As a result, Sergei Zemskov observed that his classmates' parents came from the "intelligentsia" and "rather high-ranking Soviet officials," but there was "practically no one from the working class in this school." Mikhail Markovich believed that the school's principal welcomed the children of top Party officials, thereby creating a certain social—or perhaps psychological—inequality. Elaborated Markovich: "It was a question of clothing, of tape recorders. There were no tape recorders back then. Yet several had them."

The new magnet school drew pupils from an ever-expanding pool of potential students from nearby and surrounding neighborhoods. The technical and scientific intelligentsia populated the neighborhood, which became more elite as apartment complexes of various ministries and even the Politburo were built on nearby Aleksei Tolstoy Street. Owing to the school's location and its almost instant reputation for excellence, it is not surprising that "a lot of kids in the school were children of sort of the cream of Soviet society, high-level Party officials," as Leonid Terlitsky observed. "We had one of [Politburo member] Anastas Mikoyan's grandchildren in our class. We had the daughter of the TASS* general director in our class. We had children of several high-level diplomats in our class. We had children of several high-level KGB officers in our class. We had children of famous scientists and artists in our class."

Like their Saratov counterparts, many Muscovites responded that they did not interest themselves in what their classmates' parents did. Calling herself "average" with a "Soviet understanding" of things, Lyubov Kovalyova looked upon everyone at the time as equals—as she had been taught. "Only much,

---

* The Soviet Union's official news agency.

Moscow's School No. 20 opened in a former neighborhood school weeks before the Twenty-second Party Congress endorsed Khrushchev's new *Party Program.* It promised the builders of communism that their generation would achieve communism by 1980. *Courtesy of Yevgeniya Kreizerova (Ruditskaya)*

much later, I can tell you in all honesty, I understood that we were children of very different parents. And our possibilities were probably very different, even though we were grouped together in the same class." Yet others sensed back then when someone came from a famous family. For instance, Anatoly Shapiro had a crush on Nadya Goryunova, daughter of the general director of TASS who, according to Shapiro, was one of "the five most important ideological leaders in the country." Another pupil from an elite family was Sasha Rukavishnikov, the son of well-known sculptors and grandson of one of Moscow's main architects.* Aleksei Yefros's grandfather "discovered" painter Marc Chagall and founded the journal *Foreign Literature.*** The B class included Vladimir Prudkin, son of an acclaimed actor at the Moscow Art Theater, and Yelena Kolosova, whose father became a member of the Academy of Sciences.

---

* Rukavishnikov left School No. 20 to attend a special art school, after which he became a well-known sculptor.
** Yefros died several years before I began this project.

The A and B classes in Moscow saw each other as competitors, but not to the same degree as their Saratov counterparts. Tatyana Arzhanova believed the A class "was more academically minded, more diligent, more hard-working, and more aspiring." It also seemed to her that students in the A class showed keener interest in studying science, while the B class was more inclined toward the humanities. This "split" reflects a popular, but by then waning, public discussion between "physics and poets" regarding who offered the most to society, fueled not only by the well-acclaimed technological advances of the period but also by the popular film *Nine Days of One Year*.* With the establishment of a third, C, class in the ninth grade, however, the rivalry between the groups eased. One of those transferred to the new class from within, Sergei Zemskov, recalled that "it was a real tragedy" for those involved at the "emotional" level. Mikhail Markovich, among others, hinted that pupils who misbehaved were placed in the C class, the "rowdy class." According to Vyacheslav Starik, the C class comprised pupils "from various social strata, with various degrees of preparation, with diverse cultural habits." He gave as an example Vladimir Mikoyan, grandson of a Politburo member, and Mark Milgotin, who, after the collapse of the Soviet Union, purportedly emerged as a leading figure in the Russian mafia. Even Mikoyan admitted that "they gathered all of the hooligans and under-achievers there." Not only: the C class included the daughter of the ambassador of Afghanistan, and Boika Dionisyeva, the daughter of Bulgarian diplomats. Tatyana Luchnikova joined the C class when her family moved from Kazan when she was in the ninth grade. Her father, a military engineer, served in the rocket forces.

As in Saratov, many Muscovites claimed to have paid little attention back then to ethnicity; however, they could not ignore the fact that a large percentage of the class was Jewish. Sergei Zemskov estimated that "about half his class" was. Lyubov Raitman explained that many Jews such as herself lived in the center of Moscow, where the school was located. Moreover, "traditionally, in Jewish families parents wanted their children to receive a good education and made this a priority." Leonid Terlitsky was of the same mind: "Jews have this knack for giving their kids the best education available, putting themselves into debt in order to do so, and evidently a lot of the parents of my classmates in School No. 20 were of that set of mind because the class was full of Jewish kids." Terlitsky underscored that "we weren't any different from other kids. We were all secular Jews. It was an ethnic rather than a religious category. Many of the teachers were Jewish, too."

---

* Directed by Mikhail Romm in 1962, the film depicts the conflict between old and new. It features a scientist who thinks independently, as well as sinister omens reminding viewers they lived in a dangerous, nuclear age. Indeed, in an ironic twist the scientist succumbs to radiation.

СПЕЦШКОЛА N 20
ФРУНЗЕНСКОГО РАЙОНА Г. МОСКВЫ
ВЫПУСК 1967 Г.

10 КЛАСС „Б"

When School No. 20's B Class posed for graduation pictures in 1967, the West remained an imaginary place. Today ten members of the B Class live abroad. *Courtesy of Lyubov Obraztsova (Raitman)*

"I'M VERY GRATEFUL TO MY PARENTS"

The Saratovites believed their parents sent them to School No. 42 because, as members of the intelligentsia, they appreciated the value of knowing a foreign language, particularly English, which, in this Cold War environment, was becoming the most widely taught foreign language in the USSR. "My mother looked to the future," explained Tatyana Kuznetsova. "She realized that a child would need to know another language." Likewise, Larisa Petrova noted that "the most important attraction was that the school taught English, and, secondly, had a reputation in Saratov for its discipline and outlook on teaching, and, to be blunt, it had a higher cultural level than in other schools." "Apparently my parents already understood back then that a child needs to know a foreign language," remarked Olga Gorelik from an elite Party family. One of her classmates was Natalya Yanichkina, whose mother had been imprisoned in the Gulag. Commented Yanichkina: "I think Mama wanted to make the point that I was as good as they were." Something else motivated Yanichkina's mother: "School No. 42 was very prestigious back then, and Mama, as if to make up for the lack of maternal love I experienced when she was away, wanted to give me everything she couldn't give me earlier." Some ended up at School No. 42 when it raided top teachers from other schools. For example, when Aleksandr Trubnikov finished first grade, his teacher received an offer to join the staff at School No. 42. "They allowed her to pick two students from her class to take with her, and she chose a girl and me." At first his parents were not keen on the idea, because the school was far away from where they lived. "There also was the problem of work shifts. But my mother insisted that I be given a chance. That's how I ended up there."

The Saratovites remembered having to "compete" for a slot by passing an exam and interview with school officials before being admitted. When Aleksandr Konstantinov's parents heard that a second class was being formed at School No. 42, they sought to enroll him there. He explained, "insofar as I was an 'A' student I had a good chance of getting admitted. I went for some sort of interview and everything went well, except for the fact that I mispronounced the letter 'Sh.' They told me that they might let me in if I was able to correct this. I went to a speech therapist and repeated 'sh-shilly-shally and sh-shiney shoes.' They admitted me that fall." Irina Barysheva related that "Papa once again went off somewhere on some campaign and we didn't make it back [to Saratov] in time for the exams." Although her mother lobbied to get her admitted, Irina acknowledged that her father's position as manager of the factory that sponsored School No. 42 "probably played a role" in her getting in.

A handful of pupils enrolled after the initial selection as slots opened when students moved, opted for other schools, or were encouraged to leave. Turned down the year before when she had trouble pronouncing her r's, Irina Chemodurova joined the A class in third grade. "I studied with a language teacher for a year," she recalled, before replacing someone who had left the class. Moving to Saratov in 1960, Natalya Pronina joined the A class in fifth grade. Private tutors likewise prepared her for admission. She remembered, "I passed the exams, very tough ones. I had to demonstrate that I had mastered the material." Similarly, Yevgeny Podolsky did not enroll in School No. 42 until the fifth grade. "I had to work hard at the language, because I had to make up four years, and the principal admitted me under the condition that if I didn't catch up with my classmates during the year, I'd have to leave the school." "It turned out," he sheepishly explained, "that they built the school next to my father's factory, and he became the school's sponsor." The eighth Natasha in the group, Natalya Yolshina joined the A class in seventh grade. Before then she had attended a special music school where a classmate who had enrolled in School No. 42 infected Yolshina with the desire to go there. "She elatedly told me about School 42, about how everyone wears the same uniform, about the boys in jackets with high collars, about how they carry satchels, and about how they speak English during recess." Yolshina's parents hired a teacher from the school to tutor her so that she could learn as much English as those already enrolled.

"A NEW SCHOOL FOR THE CHILDREN OF GIFTED PARENTS"

Vladimir Prudkin, "Kuzya," clarified what motivated his parents to get him admitted to Moscow's School No. 20. "Stalin left the scene and shortly thereafter the so-called Thaw began. It's as if the realization of the need for contacts with the outside world arose, and most likely my parents understood that even a minimal knowledge of a foreign language was necessary." By this time magnet schools offering English, French, and Spanish had opened, but his parents "felt that English would soon become the international language." He observed that the selection of pupils was carried out privately, but probably "according to a quite widespread phenomenon called *blat,* or connections." This all but assured that it became "an elite school." Indeed, according to Bakhyt Kenzheyev, "the majority of children came from the *nomenklatura.*" He saw himself as an "odd duck," since his parents were not of that caste. Yet his father, a Kazakh, took advantage of his own form of *blat*: he enlisted the support of the Kazakh union republic's representative in Moscow to get Bakhyt admitted. Other Muscovites confirmed that parents pulled strings to win a coveted slot for their children in the school; however, they also remember an admissions interview. Vyacheslav Starik enrolled in School No. 20 in 1961, "the year Gagarin made his flight." His parents hired an elderly woman to teach him English once it became clear they were wasting their rubles on violin lessons. He performed well during the interview. Tatyana Artyomova likewise took private English lessons to prepare for her admissions interview, which she sailed through, "because I had straight A's at the school I had attended and because I acquitted myself well on the exams," she explained. Lyubov Kovalyova also mentioned "some sort of interview at School No. 20 that I passed." Lyubov Raitman stressed how unusual this was: "We had an admissions interview, a small exam for eleven year olds which, as a matter of principle, was altogether atypical for schools. This was something new. That is, you could get turned down." Only later did she realize that her mother's workplace petitioned in order to help Raitman get admitted.

Some parents who knew English encouraged their offspring to study the language. This is true of Vladimir Glebkin, whose father "very keenly felt the importance of studying a foreign language. He learned English on his own, and not badly, but he also told me that it was essential to master English." Owing to a speech impediment, Glebkin was admitted on probation, during which he saw a speech therapist to improve his pronunciation of the "L" sound. Similarly, Lyubov Kovalyova's father began studying English on his own as an adult and persuaded her to try out for School No. 20. Tatyana Arzhanova recalled that an old woman working in the nearby bath house informed her mother and grandmother that her granddaughter went to School No. 115, which was being transformed into an English-language school. A teacher of English, her mother taught Tatyana enough of the language to pass her interview.

A somewhat different path led Yelena Kolosova, now of Houston, Texas, to School No. 20. On the advice of her grandmother's friend, a well-known translator, Yelena began studying English at age five with "an absolutely wonderful English-woman." Since "Russian did not come easy to her at all," they spoke only in English. Kolosova thus had a strong command of the language before enrolling at School No. 20. Her parents decided to send her there after reading a satirical article in the paper about "a [new] school for the children of gifted parents." Yelena was admitted, after which she "didn't have to do anything for a long time."

As in Saratov, the parents of those in Moscow who joined the class after its initial formation hired tutors to prepare their offspring for admission—often teachers from the school whose moonlighting increased the odds that those they tutored would get in—but also enlisted the help of valuable personal connections whenever possible. Viktor Alekseyev joined the class in the sixth grade. In order to compete, he "crammed day and night," studying with his older brother, a student at the Institute of Foreign Languages, and with a private tutor. During the "admissions interview," Alekseyev fumbled, but the teachers took a liking to him. Admitted conditionally, he had to pull himself up to the same level of his classmates during the first quarter. "I truly had to work day and night on the language." Sergei Zemskov emphasized that his mother—herself a teacher of English—had attended School No. 115 and had many fond memories of, and personal ties to, the neighborhood. "Besides, it turned out that the head of curriculum at School No. 20 had been in my mother's class in school. Despite the fact that the school by this time had already become something of an elite one and that there were some diffi-culties in sending me there, they nonetheless transferred me to the school." Leonid Terlitsky enrolled at School No. 20 in the middle of seventh grade, when his parents took him out of the neighborhood school, because he "was turning into a young gangster." He and another person "spent about six months in private lessons" with a teacher from the school. Joining the B class in the eighth grade, Yelena Zharovova studied English with a private tutor to ready herself for entrance exams in English and mathematics. The transition proved difficult. Reminisced Zharovova: "I had to get used to new kids, to new teachers, to new relationships. The atmosphere was different; teachers treated us differently. If in my school they used the familiar form of 'you' when speaking to you, here they used the formal form of 'you.'"

"SHE WAS A REAL COMMUNIST"

A Soviet school's success had a great deal to do with the personal qualities of its principal and vice principals (one for curriculum and another for the physical facilities). The Saratovites appreciated the special climate that reigned at No.

42, even if they complained about it at the time. Most of them, especially the women, spoke about the "very strict," and even "iron" discipline at No. 42, personified by the school's "authoritarian" principal, Vera Filippovna Echberger. A product of the Stalinist system, Echberger has a personal story that remains hard to pin down. Tatyana Kuznetsova commented that "she was, as far as I know, German. And that probably showed." Then why had she not been deported at the start of World War II like other Saratov Germans? The only answer I have comes from Irina Barysheva, whose father knew Echberger from their Komsomol days, when they campaigned together to wipe out illiteracy. At the start of the war Echberger's husband, a true believer, left for the front on a so-called "Communist train," filled with Party loyalists willing to sacrifice themselves for the war cause in order to whip up patriotism. Because of him, intimated Barysheva, Vera Filippovna, a German, was allowed to remain in Saratov. Her personal circumstances deepened her loyalty to the system. Teacher Klara Eduardovna confided in me that Vera Filippovna held on to her portrait of Stalin.

Irina Barysheva complained that it was hard to escape Echberger's watchful gaze, for Vera Filippovna would "stand at the door and check the length of our skirts. She always had a ruler in her hand. And we weren't allowed to wear bangs." Natalya P. remembered that "when our principal, Vera Filippovna, visited our class we had to show our hands and, if she noticed that anyone was doing their nails, she'd punish them. We weren't allowed to wear adult hair-dos. We didn't dare think about wearing makeup!" If the girls tried to get away with wearing makeup, Echberger sent them home to wash up—or hauled them into the bathroom to do it herself. Natalya Yanichkina recounted that "the school nurtured an asceticism in us, not allowing us to 'let our hair down.' They'd loosen up a bit if there were a dance. That was different." There was no "conspicuous consumption" back then, as Natalya P. put it, and "we were all dressed modestly." For instance, the girl's uniform comprised a brown dress with a white collar covered by a black apron. "But on special occasions the apron was replaced with a white one," remembered Yanichkina. Girls also had to wear socks, even in the heat. Yanichkina described how, as Soviet consumer industries expanded, the girls wanted to wear hose and pantyhose: "The first one-size hose appeared, for example. And the income level of the pupils' parents allowed them to buy or 'obtain' nylon stockings. But Vera Filippovna forbade this and we had to wear what everyone else wore, so that no one stood out." Concluded Yanichkina: "On the whole, she was probably right in this regard. But as children, we thought this was unfair."

As teenagers, the young women tested Echberger's regulations, especially her insistence that the girls wear braids and not cut their hair. When one of them saw in the newspaper *Pioneer Pravda* illustrations of recommended hairstyles for girls, which included deviations from Echberger's sense of decorum, they launched a revolt. Citing the newspaper article to justify their making a fashion statement, the girls, one by one, cut their hair—to Echberger's dismay. "It was a real revolution," boasted Irina Barysheva.

Photographs of Vera Filippovna say it all. A strong, formidable-looking woman with a military bearing, a stern, even harsh, expression, and an aura of self-confidence, Echberger had no trouble taking other people's inventories and setting the "correct" tone at school. Aleksandr Ivanov called her "a woman with a man's personality." She enhanced her authority by knowing all that she could about her charges. "She was an amazing woman, who knew each pupil by name, and the names of their parents," Aleksandr Babushkin remembered. "She knew what made each student tick." As the remarks about Vera Filippovna's cultural war against the girls' growing consciousness of fashion suggest, Echberger recognized what trouble to expect from her pupils. In the seventh and eighth grades some of the boys sneaked into the bathroom during recess to drag on cigarettes. Aleksandr Ivanov related what happened when word of this reached Echberger. "Things went so far that during recess she, a *woman*, went into the men's room. She was standing there [when we came in]."

Irina Garzanova grossly exaggerated that Vera Filippovna "was already approaching seventy back then" to drive home the point that Echberger stood on the other side of a great divide separating the generations. From a child's perspective, it must have been hard to imagine that Vera Filippovna had once had a childhood. That said,

Although it might not seem obvious to viewers of this photo, several female Baby Boomers remarked that Vera Filippovna (right) softened her look for graduation night in 1967 when she presented diplomas to Olga Kolishchyuk and others. Echberger's "iron discipline" extended even to teachers. Irina Vizgalova remembered that teacher Klara Eduardovna "once had been sent home to change because she came to school in a colorful blouse rather than in a white one." *Courtesy of Aleksandr Virich*

it coincided with the Bolshevik Revolution of 1917. In fact, Echberger's penchant for iron discipline may have had something to do with her Bolshevism. She "was a principled woman," insisted Larisa Petrova. "She was a real Communist in the positive sense of the term. She was honest, and she loved order and discipline. She mixed up each class by placing children of well-off parents next to children from ordinary families." Although committed to broadening the social profile of the school's student body, "she didn't pick children from families of alcoholics or from other antisocial elements." Patent privilege violated her Soviet egalitarianism. Irina Garzanova received a reprimand from Echberger for being driven to school at the start of the school year. "That was not allowed," explained Garzanova. "Like good Soviet children, we were expected to use public transportation." Viktor D. voiced respect for Echberger's success in creating a built environment conducive to learning, but criticized her for "being afraid of childhood pranks and for exaggerating their importance." He clarified that "she'd panic a bit and not always investigate things fully." He believed he "suffered from her" as a result. Tatyana Kuznetsova saw a softer side to her. "We feared her, but she actually was a very pleasant, kind-hearted woman. When we'd see her on the street after we graduated she'd greet us warmly. She could be really charming, but in school she was strict."

"HE WAS A BORN ADMINISTRATOR"

The photos suggest he looked like Khrushchev or like *kolobok*, the small personified round loaf of bread coveted by animals of prey in Russian fairytales: short, bald, thick-set, and seemingly obtuse—except for the piercing eyes. Georgy Godzhello, himself an educator, gave Anton Petrovich Potekhin top marks for creating "extraordinary" conditions. "As someone who turned out almost with the same kind of job, I perhaps understand him better than others. He was able to create optimal conditions and pick a teaching staff." Moreover, he had a gift for admitting talented children. Sofiya Vinogradova called him "a very good manager, who got along very well with children and teachers. Back then I didn't understand this," she added, "but now I can appreciate it." Once the children of the Party elite began attending the school, he managed to expand it by building a second edifice and a swimming pool. He had the students put in a wonderful garden and attend to it. He kept bees. He planted apple trees. "And we didn't suffer because of this," concluded Starik. Mikhail Markovich explained why: "He arranged to sell the produce and used the money to buy tape recorders, movie cameras, and the like."

Most of the Muscovites fondly summoned up memories of Anton Petrovich's peculiarities, his light touch on many disciplinary issues, and his constructive way of dealing with problems and of meting out punishments. "We had a wonderful principal, Anton Petrovich, with very charming eccentricities," recalled Andrei Rogatnev. One of them was pretending to be deaf whenever his charges asked him for something. Another concerned Latin America. Vyacheslav Starik warmheartedly brought up that Anton Petrovich opened each school year on September 1—a

Some Baby Boomers expressed positive feelings about principal Anton Petrovich (center, surrounded by teachers and members of the C class). Vyacheslav Starik called him "a born administrator," forged in the fire of the Russian Civil War when one-person management became the order of the day. *Courtesy of Vyacheslav Starik*

real ritual in Soviet schools—with a speech. No matter what burning issues of the day needed mentioning, he ended each oration by sharing his views on the situation in Latin America. "Why did he have such a thing for Latin America?" No one knew, but they could count on Anton Petrovich ending his annual homily in this manner. Boris Shtein found Anton Petrovich interesting "in that he sometimes could recite whole paragraphs or give entire lectures in verse. He was blessed with natural gifts. He became one of the first in the country to be given the rank of 'people's teacher.'" He also had a thing about protecting the parquet floors, making students change their shoes at school. Andrei Rogatnev reminisced how Anton Petrovich taught the students to polish the school's parquet floors until they shone like his bald head. Once, when he slipped off his jacket and draped it over a chair, one of the students dropped a large-toothed comb into the breast pocket so that it protruded. Mikhail Markovich told me Anton Petrovich began the social studies lesson by taking out the comb and asking to whom it belonged.

Sergei Zemskov was enthusiastic about Anton Petrovich, who also taught social studies. "He was simply the most marvelous person. He had wonderful classes. It's hard to say what the content was, but they were good-natured human interactions." Anton Petrovich's approach to diffusing a mutually hostile relationship between sixteen-year-old Zemskov and his Russian literature teacher, Galina Aleksandrovna, won over Sergei for good. Zemskov had no idea how Anton Petrovich knew about the strained relationship, but one day he invited Zemskov into his office, where he told Sergei that Galina Aleksandrovna's infant had taken ill. He asked Zemskov to take her medicine for the infant. "You can well imagine the look on her face when I rang her bell." But Anton Petrovich's strategy solved the problem.

Mikhail Markovich recalled that Anton Petrovich, born in 1899, had worked as principal of a military school and also had served in some sort of "penal" forces before taking charge of School No. 20. "Yet he was utterly blessed from birth with a sense of the magnificent and of good," and with an appreciation for hard work. Markovich added that Anton Petrovich "was strict with the boys, but was altogether lenient with the girls," especially the pretty ones. His ability to get things done and his disciplinary practices made an abiding impression on Markovich, who recounted how Potekhin enlisted a nearby sound recording establishment to sponsor the school. As a result, "we had our first radio station." "I remember Anton Petrovich when the first Beatles group formed [at school]," continued Markovich. "We set up something like a discotheque. I looked up; he was standing, leaning against a shovel, taking it all in altogether benignly. He understood."

Then there were the punishments. When in the tenth grade Markovich and another student were sent out of the classroom for a misdeed, Anton Petrovich had them paint the school fence, "like Tom Sawyer." When Lesha Yefros broke a teacher's chair, Anton Petrovich exiled him to the cabinetmaker's workshop for two days to repair broken furniture. Vyacheslav Starik recalled a craze the boys went through. "We disassembled practically all of the school furniture. It was a period when we were fascinated with jousting like knights." This came to an end when a teacher sat down and the chair collapsed under her. "And when they noticed how much furniture we had taken apart, there was a huge scandal. They dragged us off to the wood shop—we had a home mechanics class—and we reassembled all of the furniture there that we had taken apart," said Starik.

"All of the teachers had enormous respect for him," maintained Markovich. He let a teacher, Roman Lvovich, smoke in class, "which was altogether incomprehensible in Soviet times." He also turned something of a blind eye to the students' smoking. When the boys gathered in the attic to light up, he'd chase them away. "But he'd bang against things when he came, as if he were announcing that Anton Petrovich was coming. We'd scurry out of there in time, and he never caught anyone. But he'd punish people for hooliganism" and for coming late to school. Vyacheslav Starik likewise remembered that Anton Petrovich categorically forbid marking the end of eighth grade with alcohol, throwing a real scene when he came across several males from the class carrying open bottles on the street.

None of the females complained about Anton Petrovich the way their Saratov counterparts did about Vera Filippovna when it came to fashion, but they disliked the school uniforms. Lyubov Raitman hated it and the Pioneer kerchiefs, "which were supposed to be ironed, accurately tied, and which we 'forgot' whenever we could." That was "especially true of the girls in the upper classes. It simply didn't look good. It looked much prettier without the kerchief. So we used any opportunity." In winter when it was cold in school, they would don a cardigan to cover the kerchief. "But, by and large, to the very end of our studies there was the so-called Pioneer outfit." The Moscow variant included a navy blue skirt, a white shirt, the mandatory kerchief, "but, still, not that awful brown dress with the black apron" (worn in Saratov). In sum, owing to Moscow's more liberal and open environment, the school authorities and many of the teachers allowed their charges an element of personal autonomy when it came to the dress code.

Some of the Muscovites had mixed feelings about Anton Petrovich—and about his teaching. Vladimir Glebkin conceded that Potekhin's administrative capabilities benefited the school materially, but did not understand how Potekhin ended up in the field of education. He seemed "far removed from learning," claimed Glebkin. "It seems to me that if he had been a foreman at a construction site, he would have been in his own element." Lyubov Raitman cast him as "a terrible Communist, an insufferable historian who taught history and social studies." Vladimir Mikoyan criticized his teaching of social studies: "It could have been interesting, but it wasn't the way he taught it. Anyhow, perhaps Anton Petrovich had to stay within certain limits." Some were institutional, but others may have been self-imposed. "But you have to give him his due," opined Anatoly Shapiro. "He set up this school, and he was a very good administrator, yet he likewise was a man of his time, and that was Stalin's time."

"NOT ALL SCHOOLS IN SARATOV GIVE SUCH A FOUNDATION"

Olga Kolishchyuk stressed that No. 42 "was a fabulous school." Pyotor Krasilnikov elaborated "They put into place the nuts and bolts there, and did so at a very high level. Later, we simply developed them more narrowly in college." "Not all schools in Saratov gave such a foundation," opined Tatyana Kuznetsova. Official records confirm the success of its pupils: fifty-four of the class of 1967's fifty-six graduates enrolled in college, a figure that vastly surpassed the national average attained by elite specialized schools (approximately two-thirds).[11]

Foreign language instruction amounted to 30 to 40 percent of the teaching time in the ninth and tenth grades, compared with 6 to 8 percent in regular schools.[12] As Aleksandr Trubnikov put it, "They not only taught English there very well, but they taught those who wanted to learn. The teaching methods were good, the teachers were good, and they demanded a great deal from us." However, "all of the other subjects were, in my view, the same as in any neighborhood school." Natalya P., herself an educator, appreciated the standard school curriculum: "The school provided us with a good, broad education, not a narrow one. We even studied art. They taught us how to sew." Of course, the school sought to inculcate values. They "were very similar to how I was brought up at home," said Natalya Yolshina. "You had to be smart, and you had to be educated. You had to work hard and honestly, correctly. You had to apply yourself." Olga Kolishchyuk underscored "respect for others, intelligence, love for literature, no matter what we became, and friendship."

Most of its graduates agree that the school deserves top marks for teaching English as best it could—given the circumstances. Recalled Natalya Pronina: "We had English every day and English literature three times a week. We studied history, modern history, in English. We even studied some physics in English, and geography." Natalya Yanichkina noted the drawbacks of introducing special subjects taught in English. "They did this with history and they began to do the same with physics by translating an ordinary textbook into English. But this was all done as an experiment, since for the most part our understanding of the language at that time was not deep enough to allow us to study physics. The result was neither English nor physics."

Attending school in a closed city in a closed society certainly made itself felt. As Yevgeny Podolsky added, "We had practice only among ourselves and with our teachers, because back then there were no foreigners in Saratov." According to Natalya Pronina, "they taught us English well, but those who taught us English hadn't been abroad, and naturally they had an accent." Besides, "one had to use literary English as in our textbook published in 1949. It was as old as we were." Natalya P. remembered reading *Lorna Doone*, which she called "an absolutely awful book. But apparently they simply had enough copies to go around. There was a real problem with textbooks." And with audio equipment: unlike School No. 20, the Saratov school lacked a modern language lab. "But there were several record players, a handful of records, and one or two tape recorders," Aleksandr Konstantinov informed me. "And all of this was the initiative of the teachers."

All school systems inculcate values and what societies believe constitutes good citizenship. Olga Kamayurova astutely observed that because their "entire life was politicized it would be hard to say that this somehow stood out at school." Arkady Darchenko made the point that "it seemed to us that that's simply how things were. That's why it didn't seem political. Even the Pioneer movement. We took it to be like your Scout movement. We were just hanging out." Aleksandr Konstantinov believed that, "in comparison with other schools, it was far less politicized. It all depended upon the teacher." Yet Yevgeny Podolsky called attention to the fact that "in history and the social sciences things were heavily politicized and the textbooks were written in such a manner that when you look at them today they seem funny." Besides, "each day we had a political information session and the children had to be aware of current events," recalled Tatyana Kuznetsova. They had to subscribe to newspapers and discuss articles from them. As a result, Podolsky and others "for the most part believed, because we didn't know anything else. There was no other information until the later grades when we began to listen to foreign radio broadcasts."

Regardless, the graduates concurred that the school prepared them well for college. "After graduation, or already in the ninth or tenth grade we could converse rather freely in English," marveled Aleksandr Kutin. Pyotor Krasilnikov agreed that the school did a fine job of teaching conversational English. Natalya P. may have hated *Lorna Doone*, but she enjoyed reading *Jane Eyre*, and, in tenth grade, Oscar Wilde's *The Portrait of Dorian Gray*. When Olga Martynkina later enrolled in the Saratov Conservatory, she got by in language classes owing to what she had learned at School No. 42. "I didn't have to study, I didn't attend classes." Back then the only undergraduate program in English was offered by the Saratov Pedagogical Institute, where a full third of the class of '67 enrolled upon graduation. Those who went to the Pedagogical Institute excelled. "We already knew everything," boasted Olga Kolishchyuk. "We only had to clean up a few things and do some polishing." Others maintained that this proved to be the case even with the weaker students.

Galina Poldyaeva's sharing perhaps sums things up best: "Of course, we had to learn by heart a lot of what they taught us. We, of course, understand today that there were lots of shortcomings and that things could have been done differently. But we were only children back then, and we didn't think about such things."

"THE SCHOOL HAD VERY TOUGH REQUIREMENTS"

The atmosphere at Soviet schools often sharply deviated from the climate at home. As someone who had not attended day care, Anna Lyovina formed a negative view of school from her older sister who "always came home in tears and who saw school as a torture chamber." She detailed: "Therefore when I went to an ordinary school, I, too, cried each day. It devastated me that we had to sit with our hands folded, that we weren't supposed to move, that we had to write only in a certain way, holding our pen not in a way that was comfortable, but as one *should*." To ease her anxiety, her parents transferred her to another school, but things were not much better for her there. Her "liberation" came when she "ended up at School No. 20." Lyubov Kovalyova volunteered that "it was always friendly there and I enjoyed myself." Andrei Rogatnev made the same point: "You left the warmth of home for the warmth of school." Given the quality of the pupils, "there were always interesting conversations, interesting associations," noted Kovalyova. Mikhail Markovich elaborated, "Each of us had some distinguishing feature. And if someone took a stab at something, he tried to do it well."

Tatyana Arzhanova remembered that she and her classmates spent as much time with each other as possible, linking up on public transportation, since there was no system of school buses in the USSR. "We couldn't simply go to school; we had to go together," no matter how complicated this became. What did they do when they arrived? "We were supposed to do calisthenics before the first period," recalled Yelena Zharovova. "The school was equipped with a loud-speaker system used to broadcast the exercises. But we exercised only on special days when someone from the administration remembered. Otherwise we simply chatted during the music, showed up late for the calisthenics, or got ready for our first class."

School No. 20 matched the success of its Saratov counterpart, with virtually everyone eventually enrolling in college. Tatyana Artyomova believed that her B class had five gold medalists (students with perfect records) and ten or eleven silver medalists (students with near-perfect records), a number constituting half the class. "We studied an awful lot. They gave us a lot of work," recalled Artyomova. "I never worked at any point in my life as hard as I did in school. There wasn't a single free moment. The school had very tough requirements." Another medalist, Yelena Zharovova, concurred: "I studied an awful lot, and sometimes didn't go to bed until two or three in the morning. And I wasn't the only one like that." Zharovova elaborated that the school system inculcated in her "responsibility for what you say or do. And perhaps shame if you didn't work to the max." Marina Bakutina was of the same mind; the school instilled in her "a very serious attitude toward learning and toward obtaining knowledge." Vladimir Bystrov emphasized the quality of language instruction. "It turned out that for twenty-one years I didn't have the opportunity to practice my English. But when I first visited America in 1988, after a week I began to speak English." Vladimir Prudkin knew "the map of London better than the map of Moscow. Many, many years later," he remembered, "when I first arrived in London, I got my bearings, as if I already knew things by heart." Vladimir Glebkin also praised the language instruction and the well-equipped language lab. "We each had our own tape recorder. We could record how we pronounced things and compare it with a master recording and hear our shortcomings. However, what was interesting was not listening to individual tapes, but acting out short skits during class." He gave the example of staging scenes from Dickens's *Pickwick Papers*. By the seventh grade, he recalled, "We already had excellent knowledge of the language." Comparing the school program with that of ordinary schools, Lyubov Raitman commented that "we had more English-language lessons each week, and then, in the upper classes, several subjects taught in English, English and American literature, a subject called regional geography, and a little bit of history." The other subjects paralleled what one would find in ordinary schools.

Otherwise critical of Soviet education, the American reporter Susan Jacoby acknowledged the positive role of native speakers and language labs in the specialized schools in Moscow.[13] Indeed, Yelena Kolosova applauded the "endless assignments in the language lab, and also contact with native speakers." Kolosova welcomed the lessons "where we compared native speakers of the language from South Africa with those from India." Anna Lyovina shared Kolosova's enthusiasm. "It was wonderful! Besides, there were lots of visitors. Any delegation that came to Moscow would drop in to socialize with us. That is, we heard real language, which was very rare for the time." Lyovina later encountered professors at the Institute of Foreign Languages "who never saw foreigners and didn't know how to correctly pronounce some things." She believed the "system

School assemblies were held to observe political, cultural, and social events and to welcome foreign visitors. Students at School No. 20 enjoyed a much looser dress code than their Saratov counterparts. *Courtesy of Yevgeniya Kreizerova (Ruditskaya)*

of teaching English [at School No. 20] was very open and free for those times. I can't imagine how our principal was able to achieve such freedom. Our teachers experimented." She recalled the day John F. Kennedy was assassinated. "All of the scheduled activities were cancelled. They told us today we're going to have a press conference. Pretend you're journalists from different newspapers. Formulate some questions."

Anatoly Shapiro pointed out that, from today's perspective, much about the school program seems politicized, but that was not the case back then. "It couldn't have been otherwise." Marina Bakutina professed "not to remember anything that was politicized. On the contrary, the teachers of English were sometimes dissidents." Nor did Vyacheslav Starik remember any politicization: "Yes, we were Pioneers, and they enrolled us in the Komsomol. The external attributes existed. But I can't say that they forced us." Yelena Kolosova understood politicization as a personal matter, casting principal Anton Petrovich and history teacher Nadezhda Petrovna, with her stiff appearance, as the bearers of politicization. Kolosova shared, "It depended upon the instructors' cultural level and upon their method. I think that we were happy enough that politics was watered down there. There was humor. They knew who they were dealing with. There were funny things such as civil defense and the like. They were, of course, a product of the time," she explained. Yet even Anton Petrovich could have a light touch. Georgy Godzhello related that many of the boys "forgot" or left at home the Komsomol badges that Anton Petrovich liked students to wear.

Eventually they conspired to drop them down the toilet, which they did without serious consequences. He also recalled a class discussion of Mikhail Sholokhov's novel about collectivization of agriculture, *Virgin Soil Upturned*, when one of his classmates queried: "What sort of Communist is it who says that, for the sake of the Revolution, he's ready to mow down women and children with his machine gun?" Nothing came of this question. "No one brainwashed us," underscored Leonid Volodarsky.

"ALL OF THE TEACHERS WERE EXCELLENT"

At Saratov's School No. 42 a single homeroom teacher taught the children until the fifth grade, when they began to switch teachers for some subjects. Students in the B group loved their homeroom teacher Aleksandra Sergeyevna Fadeyeva. "She was like a mother. We adored her," said Olga Martynkina. Many shared Irina Tsurkan's view that the teachers "had very colorful personalities" and played an enormous role in shaping their charges' worldviews. "As I now understand," opined Irina Chemodurova, "the contingent of teachers was very strong. They taught us how to think, not only to learn things by heart." Exclaimed Aleksandr Konstantinov: "Actually, all of the teachers were excellent! Except for a few individuals, they were all interesting." Arkady Darchenko echoed these sentiments: "Basically, the teaching staff was very strong. There were simply wonderful teachers of English." Not all of their classmates would agree, but most Saratovites remained grateful to those who prepared them so well for college.

Natalya P., today a teacher of English, acknowledged that "from today's perspective, some of them used strict methods that were tied to the [Stalinist] regime. The older ones were brought up and worked both before and during the war. They weren't at all able to shed this, but the young ones were marvelous." She also complained that there was considerable turnover among English teachers in the B class, unlike in the parallel A group. Her classmate Aleksandr Kutin shared her objection: "We changed our English teachers like gloves." Some interviewees hypothesized that the A group had more stability in this regard because the school administration did not wish to invite criticisms from local Party leaders whose children attended the school. There was an exception: Klara Eduardovna Starshova, whom members of the B class cited most frequently as a favorite teacher. The daughter of a devout Communist who taught at Saratov University, Klara Eduardovna was a child of the Twentieth Party Congress and of Khrushchev's denunciation of Stalin. This—and her youth—gave her more in common with the class of 1967 than with her parents' generation. Klara Eduardovna began teaching at School No. 42 as a newly minted graduate of the Saratov Pedagogical Institute where, she told me, she had had "little practice with the language." As a result, she and three girlfriends spoke English among themselves. Her efforts were not in vain, for she made a favorable impression on future gold medalist Aleksandr Konstantinov. Like him, Irina Tsurkan remarked that Starshova "was like an older sister." Irina Vizgalova praised her too. "She's a charming person and the most amazing thing is that, although so many years have passed, she remembers who is where, what they do for a living, how many children they have, and their problems."

Tatyana Ivanovna Zorina, who taught Russian language and literature, also made a deep and abiding, if not always favorable, impression on her pupils. An older woman, Zorina had survived the blockade of Leningrad and therefore commanded, and demanded, respect. She taught the class of '67 from the fifth grade, becoming class B's homeroom teacher in the ninth and tenth (final year) grades. Viktor D. found her "very peculiar" and suspected that she was becoming senile. "She was a very strange woman," concurred Irina Barysheva, "who was not afraid to express what, for that time, were seditious ideas," tolerating unconventional readings of Soviet classics from her pupils. Barysheva recalled that, whenever she took an independent position, Tatyana Ivanovna still gave her an A for the day and never "forced" her to adopt an official point of view. "Another would have slammed me with Ds. All of the other kids valued this and really liked Zorina," volunteered Barysheva. Olga Kamayurova knew her classmates liked Zorina, but Olga had reservations: "Perhaps she treated us correctly, but she was crude and without ceremony. I never found that to be pleasant. I'm very thankful to her that I write without making errors," confided Aleksandr Kutin, who admitted she was "original, strict, and had a sharp tongue." Zorina was Olga Kolishchyuk's favorite teacher. "She was strict, but fair. And she could really interest us in the subject. She had absolutely brilliant Russian, fabulous Russian, classical Russian, without any slang." Irina Garzanova recalled how Zorina would tell them, "Don't be offended. I'm responsible to your parents. I'm preparing you for college. All of you will get in."

The Saratovites who became scientists or went to medical school after graduation often had positive things to say about their science and math teachers at School No. 42. Vladimir Nemchenko and others praised Roza Vasiliyevna Galaguz, who taught chemistry so well that although Irina Chemodurova saw herself as "a typical student of the humanities," she enrolled in the Chemistry Department at the university because of Galaguz's influence. Even more sang the praises of their bearded physics teacher, war veteran Mikhail Dmitryevich Benevolensky. Yevgeny Podolsky remembered, "His classes were a real pleasure. He had a great sense of humor." Viktor D. called him a "man with an exceptional heart and with outstanding knowledge" who demonstrated "a love for teaching and for children." According to rumors, he even raised several orphans. Irina Vizgalova recounted that, "like many girls in our class, I didn't understand a thing about physics, even though we had an absolutely charming teacher. We really liked him. He was too kind, and didn't give Ds." He also inspired Aleksandr Trubnikov: "He was loud-mouthed, very lively, and taught physics well. It probably was because of him that I studied physics in college."

Because history was the most patently politicized discipline, a personal problem involving one otherwise exemplary teacher turned into a scandal of sorts. Before the ninth grade Albina Ivanovna Baklanova taught history. "She was famous in the city," recalled Irina Barysheva. "They wrote about her in the papers; they came to film us for television; we were a vanguard class" that participated in and won various citywide academic "socialist competitions." Viktor D. appreciated her because "she worried about each pupil and put her entire heart into her teaching." For this reason, Irina Barysheva and her classmates complained when they learned that Baklanova would no longer be teaching them. Everywhere they turned, the students were blandly told that she had opted to resign. But Baklanova refused to meet with them when they went to her home. Altogether by chance, Barysheva claimed to have found out what happened from her father because the factory he directed sponsored the school. It turned out that one of his skilled workers who helped out in the school's workshop became romantically involved with Baklanova. "During the Soviet era this was unacceptable, ever the more so because he was willing to leave his family for her. This was incompatible with the calling of a Soviet teacher. To make a long story short, they suggested that she quit 'of her own accord,'" explained Barysheva. This indignity occurred before the Soviet government relaxed divorce laws, when concepts of what constituted suitable behavior on the part of teachers—and good Communists—made such liaisons problematic. "When a new teacher of history showed up in the ninth grade," lamented Aleksandr Konstantinov, "she proved to be Communist to the core. She wasn't mean, but it was awful, and the contrast was so obvious." "Honestly speaking," volunteered Irina Chemodurova, "she almost killed my desire to study it."

Some Saratovites griped about how some teachers made them feel, but most of the disgruntled ones complained about grades they believed they did not deserve. Natalya Yanichkina, for example, groused about her Russian literature teacher, Valentina Nikolaevna: "She was from the old Stalinist cadres. She would all but disrupt an entire class simply because it seemed to her that a girl's hairdo was not right or because her hair was braided, say, on one side." Fortunately, continued Yanichkina, "Lidiya Vasiliyevna Yermolova replaced her. She was more democratic. She'd express views that were not part of the school program, or tell us her opinion of an author, or of some situation. She was my favorite teacher." Irina Garzanova praised her teachers except Aleksandra Ignatyevna Dolgova: "the only one I don't recall with gratitude, because we didn't get along. My only two B's were in mathematics." Yevgeny Podolsky's bête noire was biology teacher Galina Lyudvigovna, whose B prevented him from graduating with a silver medal. Irina Barysheva got good grades from chemistry teacher Roza Vasiliyevna Galaguz until the ninth grade, when Irina fell in love with a university student who would become her future husband. "I simply wasn't into chemistry," she owned up. But that did not prevent her from demonizing Galaguz, who gave Barysheva a D for the fourth quarter, which would have resulted in expulsion from the school. She and her mother appeared before the school council, at which all of her teachers spoke on her behalf except for Galaguz. "And, as a result, under pressure from my homeroom teacher, the principal, and, here, once again, I think it was important who my father was," she was allowed to retake the exam in August, when she received a B for the course, "and thereby remained in school." Aleksandr Virich clashed with his geography teacher and Russian language teacher, Zorina. The first disagreement "ended in mutual love between me and the geography teacher." But Virich's charm did not work on Zorina. She gave him Cs in language and literature, "but didn't prevent me from getting Bs on my graduation exams," he remembered.

"WE SIMPLY DIDN'T HAVE ANY WEAK TEACHERS"

Mikhail Markovich had nothing but admiration for the teachers at School No. 20 and for how they related to their students. "For the most part the teachers were brilliant." According to Andrei Rogatnev, with rare exception "the teachers were tremendous, simply tremendous." Anatoly Shapiro claimed they not only "were excellent" teachers but also "honest and decent" people, especially those who taught English. "They were really capable and devoted," observed Viktor Alekseyev. Vladimir Bystrov praised his first teacher of English, Irina Yakovlevna Yurina, who "left a long time ago for America during the first wave of immigration." Leonid Terlitsky recounted how "she taught us the English terminology of jurisprudence. She set up a trial." Mikhail Markovich remembered that the mock "English court" involved swearing on a Bible, and this during a state campaign to close churches. She also organized an English-language choir. Lyubov Raitman applauded Yurina too as an "absolutely extraordinary teacher, who, before coming to the school, worked as a translator for the Soviet tourist agency, Intourist. She shared many personal reminiscences and experiences, and she had very good English. She had a great voice and knew many American songs." Anatoly Shapiro likewise expressed gratitude for Yurina, who, as head of the curriculum, recruited "a group of very talented young, gifted teachers of English," including his first English teacher, Maya Naumova Turovskaya, who also left for America. Georgy Godzhello called Turovskaya "the most outstanding, most brilliant teacher," adding, "we simply didn't have any weak teachers."

Something else about the school's English teachers stands out. Soviet teachers were among the strongest believers in socialist values.[14] But things were more complex than that at School No. 20 during the 1960s. As Igor Litvin understood, "They were not only teachers but some kind of dissidents, who, if they hadn't been fired from their former jobs, were at least told that it was time for them to leave." Litvin elaborated, "Since the new possibility emerged of working in the special schools—there was no fixed curriculum—the neighborhood department of education took them on. And there they could be creative." Although they differed from one another in every possible regard they had one thing in common:

"They did not belong to the mainstream of Russian education." Litvin later studied English at the Moscow Pedagogical Institute, where we "waited for interesting classes like the ones at school. It was only during my fourth year there," he recalled, that he "understood that there simply weren't such teachers there." Vladimir Prudkin drew similar conclusions about the teachers at School No. 20: "When I got older I began to understand that it was our good fortune that there were not only such good pupils, but also teachers, because they also selected the teachers in an elitist way." Pointing out that most of the teachers came from the same age cohort as the Soviet "sixties" generation (the *shestidesyatniki*), which in Russia refers to those who attended college during the Thaw* and came of age at the start of the 1960s, he maintained, "It's clear that the teachers sympathized with this group." Moreover, "the more liberal" among them "eagerly took in liberal ideas, and all kinds of contact with Europe and the West." In this regard, stressed Prudkin, "It was altogether obvious that the teaching staff was in full agreement with the ideas of Khrushchev's Thaw." He added, "Perhaps 90 percent of them were people who somehow almost felt that they were free." There is no reason to doubt Prudkin's observations, for Soviet authorities took notice of the tolerant climate in the special schools, repeatedly expressing dissatisfaction with Moscow's Special Math School No. 2, which they shut down, seeing it as a breeding ground of potentially dangerous activities on the part of both pupils and teachers.[15] Vladimir Shlapentokh confirmed that the post-Khrushchev leadership adopted a negative stance toward the special schools for this very reason.[16]

One teacher who fired the Baby Boomers' imaginations is Roman Kaplan, "Romashka," who improved the Muscovites' language skills in the ninth and tenth grades. Leonid Terlitsky, who remains close to Kaplan today, appreciated that "he was friends with everyone and still is, with [Nobel Prize poet Joseph] Brodsky, with Baryshnikov, with every meaningful cultural figure of the time." As teenagers, they commended his unorthodox approach to teaching, his theatrical readings, and his manner. "I'll never forget the time he came into the classroom and read Kipling's poem 'If.' My, how he read it! He's very dramatic, and absolutely cast a spell over us," gushed Lyubov Raitman. Kaplan made a lasting impact on Mikhail Markovich for traveling each week to Leningrad to see his wife, something the students found terribly romantic. He also smoked Marlboros. "Back then that was a rare thing, and *he smoked in class*," marveled Markovich. Like many other girls in the class, Tatyana Luchnikova "was in love with Roman Kaplan."** In addition to Kaplan, Vyacheslav Starik extolled the

---

* As mentioned on p. 53, Khrushchev's inconsistent liberalization of cultural policy is loosely known as the Thaw; however, the term also refers more specifically to the period before and immediately after the Twentieth Party Congress of 1956, where he denounced Stalin.

** In 1996 Luchnikova published a collection of her poems, *Cross of Love*, which she presented to her former teacher at his restaurant. According to Luchnikova, Kaplan told her, "Tanya, come to the Russian Samovar and sell as many of your books as you would like." The book is *Krest liubvi* (New York: Context Publishing House, 1996).

virtues of Gennady Petrovich Nikiforov, who taught English, not only at School No. 20 but also on TV. "Later I even saw a film in which he played Churchill. He grew plump for the part." Then there was a Jesus-look-alike from Moscow University who had translated Stalin's writings. Out of personal interest he visited the school several times a week to offer a few classes.

Most of those in the B class spoke passionately about their Russian language and literature teacher, Nina Ivanovna Timonina, "an altogether marvelous teacher," in Vladimir Bystrov's estimation. Andrei Rogatnev believed that, thanks to her, "I can say without boasting that I write grammatically." Marina Bakutina spoke for many others in describing Nina Ivanovna's daily rapid-fire dictation requiring mastery of "the most insidious spelling rules." Marina despaired over the D's she received on the exercises. "I begged my parents to take me out of the school. I remember how much I practiced at home, and gradually I began to get Cs, then Bs, and finally As." Yelena Kolosova agreed that Nina Ivanovna was "her favorite teacher of all time," because of Nina Ivanovna's "extraordinary respect for her pupils." Sofiya Vinogradova expressed envy that the B group was so lucky. "When she sometimes taught us we felt very fortunate. Such artistry. I can't describe it. You'd have to hear it and see it." Mikhail Markovich praised the A class's Russian literature teacher, Olga Aleksandrovna Lanskaya. "It's to her credit that I followed this path and do what I now do." "She was of course confined by the school curriculum, but sometime in the 1960s this began to loosen up, and we quickly raced through that which was required." She, and Nina Ivanovna, had their classes read and write summaries of Alexander Solzhenitsyn's *One Day in the Life of Ivan Denisovich*—the shocking novella published in 1962, which reminded readers of the dark chapters in the Soviet past and the shortcomings of the Soviet present—and other controversial works. Markovich credited these efforts with "opening them up."

Now co-owner with ballet superstar Mikhail Baryshnikov of the Russian Samovar restaurant in Manhattan, English instructor Roman Kaplan keeps in touch with some of his former students. This photograph was taken at an informal reunion of the B Class at Andrei Rogatnev's Moscow apartment in 2005. *Courtesy of Donald J. Raleigh*

Some teachers made lasting impressions on their young charges for the strangest of reasons. Yelena Kolosova mentioned Yury Borisovich Seminovker: "I think they jailed him for black marketeering. There were such rumors." Vladimir Glebkin enjoyed his enigmatic physics teacher, not because of the subject, but because of how he taught. He "opened his heart" to those fascinated by physics and "tried not to get into things too deeply" with those who did not understand the subject. Anna Lyovina remains grateful to her homeroom teacher, Galina Aleksandrovna, who helped Lyovina detach from a clinging classmate from a troubled home whom "no one wanted to be friends with." Marina Bakutina reminisced about how her classmates poked fun at a teacher of English literature her classmates for some reason called Marzipan. He pronounced the word "realism" as "brealism," totally unaware of the additional "b" when he said the word, but able to discern it when he had his charges repeat the word as he pronounced it. Boys in the C class could not resist the opportunity to tweak the name of a tenth-grade English teacher, Semyon Anisimovich Sheiman, whom they called Semen Onanisimovich [Masturbation] Shame-on-You.

Those that got into trouble for causing disciplinary problems had critical things to say about some of their teachers, while others reacted negatively to teachers who appeared as spokespersons for the regime's official value system. Leonid Volodarsky observed that "there were teachers who loved their subjects and who loved children, and there were teachers who perhaps loved their subjects, but who did not like children." Sergei Zemskov pointed out that the teachers at School No. 20 "felt that the school had to be better than average, and that their professionalism also had to be greater." He believed they "denied themselves creativity" and that a "rigid pragmatism" held sway. "That is, you had to be well prepared, and you had to move on to prestigious colleges. All of this was factored down to the last 't.'" Some of the interviewees reviled history teacher Valery Mikhailovich, who condescendingly told his students that "at your age Zoya Kosmodemyanskaya [a Komsomol partisan heroine during World War II tortured by the Nazis] was hanging from a rope."

Lyubov Raitman found objectionable her math and homeroom teacher in the middle school years, Rada Fyodorovna Kostenko. "She was terribly Soviet and had a very Soviet disposition." Raitman detailed the time the KGB in 1962 arrested a colonel in the Soviet military intelligence, Oleg Penkovsky, staging a show trial broadcast on television. Convicted of spying for the Americans and British, Penkovsky was executed. Kostenko launched into a tirade against him during a math class, which prompted her pupils to misbehave. This set her into a rage. According to Raitman, Rada Fyodorovna bellowed, "Well, it's people like you who grow up to become Penkovskys." "We were terribly proud of this," boasted Raitman. "That's the awful fool she was." Admitting that most of her classmates shared Raitman's assessment, Yelena Kolosova confessed she "absolutely loved Rada Fyodorovna Kostenko. I don't have a problem with such people. At heart they're more reliable and predictable, because they're not hiding behind pleasant veneers." Recognizing Rada Fyodorovna's "Soviet qualities," Boris Shtein also came to her defense. "She was a very lively person, not unfeeling, with real heart."

"GREETINGS TO SARATOV FROM BRISTOL"

Some of the Saratov English teachers had spent time abroad in countries where English was spoken as a second language, such as India or Burma, and one of them, according to Olga Martynkina, had been a translator for the UN. But those attending Moscow's School No. 20 were taught by teachers with stronger English and had far greater opportunity to encounter native speakers of English than their Saratov counterparts living in a "closed" city. By opening the country up in the 1950s, Khrushchev made it possible for a trickle of foreigners to visit Saratov while the Cold War generation attended School No. 42, but by the late 1960s, Saratov, home to numerous defense-related industries, became totally off limits to foreigners from the capitalist world. Like many of her classmates, Irina Chemodurova remembered that before then Saratov had a sister-city relationship with Bristol, England, and that the head of the school's curriculum department, Nina Alekseyevna Bobrovnikova, traveled to England. A document in the school album for the 1966/67 academic year indicates that, after the first official visitors from Bristol came to Saratov in 1956, several delegations from Saratov toured England. During the time the Cold War generation attended School No. 42, Saratov sent an exhibition of children's art to Bristol and also a photo exhibit of scenes from performances in Saratov theaters of plays written by English playwrights.*

Most of the Saratovites have some vague recollection of the visitors from Bristol and of some of their teachers traveling to England. Arkady Darchenko stated that "we were in the fourth grade at the time, and I remember that it was mainly teachers, probably of the Russian language." Aleksandr Babushkin recalled tiny blue flowers planted along the riverfront: "They told us that they brought these flowers from Bristol and planted them." According to Aleksandr Kutin, the head of the school's curriculum and one or two other teachers had traveled to Bristol as tourists. Natalya Yanichkina corroborated this: "Delegations of teachers visited Saratov, but there were no children. I remember that our teacher had a pen on which was written 'Greetings to Saratov from Bristol.'" Yanichkina also mentioned a delegation that visited Saratov shortly before they graduated—perhaps the last. "Some sort of Englishman, I believe, visited and socialized with us. I think he gave some lectures at the university. I can even recall what he looked like."

---

* Shakespeare's *Hamlet, Anthony and Cleopatra,* and *The Two Gentlemen of Verona*; Jerome Kitty's play about George Bernard Shaw, *Dear Liar*; and Oscar Wilde's tale, "The Star-Child."

A young teacher at School No. 42 at the time, Klara Eduardovna Starshova met with a delegation of three English women who visited Saratov in 1958. When the authorities chose her father, a devout Communist, to host them at home for tea, her family anguished over what to serve the visitors, given the limited possibilities. Klara Eduardovna told me her most vivid and unexpected memory of the encounter involved the response to her remark about the virtues of the English-language Communist newspaper issued in England, *The Daily Worker*, one of the few available in the USSR. Her guest Barbara astonished her by lambasting the paper for its lack of objectivity.

Shortly thereafter, Saratov closed, not to reopen to the West until the Gorbachev era. In the meantime, the authorities replaced Bristol with Bratislava, then in Czechoslovakia. Summed up Arkady Darchenko: "We corresponded mostly with people from 'brotherly' countries, with Czechs, Slovaks, Poles. But to travel abroad, no, there was nothing like that."

"BACK THEN THEY ONLY CAME TO US"

In contrast to their Saratov counterparts, the Muscovites had regular contact with foreign visitors, who not only provided opportunities for them to speak English but also a chance "for the foreigners to be shown something," as Vladimir Glebkin so aptly put it. Because of his technical skills, Glebkin welcomed foreign delegations to the school's radio center: "I remember that, already from the seventh grade, I told these foreign delegations about everything." Lyubov Kovalyova remembered that "many delegations visited the school, and we always performed for them. We had a choir. We sang, with enthusiasm, 'Do Russians Want War?' and 'Jingle Bells.' I think all of them liked it." Andrei Rogatnev recalled British guests, "But there was no exchange yet. Back then they only came to us." Vyacheslav Starik summoned up memories of visitors from Canada, and once a delegation from either Australia or New Zealand. When the Brits visited, "we told each other dirty jokes." (Afterward, some of the males "practiced" their newly acquired vocabulary at Mayakovsky Metro station, where Intourist often took tourists because of the station's exceptionally stunning mosaics.) For Leonid Terlitsky, "one of the memorable guests was writer James Aldridge, who visited the school with his Egyptian wife." Boris Shtein boasted that "somewhere I still have the book *For Whom the Bell Tolls* with Mary Hemingway's autograph." These encounters made Bakhyt Kenzheyev hunger for even more contact with foreigners. When he was sixteen years old, he paid a call on the House of Friendship, which hosted foreign delegations, expressing a desire to practice his English. The staff invited him to meet with English-speaking visitors. "I was very surprised and probably went there for about half a year and met with tourists," noted Kenzheyev. "I think they probably thought that I was a young KGB agent, but I was simply a kid who wanted to speak English."

The Muscovites also got to mingle with visiting foreign school children their age. In the eighth grade, children showed up from England. Marina Bakutina cringed telling me about her reply to a visiting English teen who asked about Moscow. "I began to recite by heart a passage from our English textbook about what a great metro Moscow had, about when it was built, about how much marble was used in constructing the subway. It was an altogether inappropriate reply. I remember very well the look of amazement on the girl's face." Americans whose parents worked in European embassies also visited the school. "We socialized with them quite freely," recalled Igor Litvin, "although I now think that there probably was someone in our group who [might have informed on us], but I don't know who." When Lyubov Raitman was in the tenth grade, a large group of American school children paid a visit. "We spent several days with them. We went places with them, to museums, to Red Square, and elsewhere. It was *terribly* interesting. They attended classes with us, sat next to us, boys and girls. We spoke with them, and later corresponded with them." Raitman and others exchanged letters with their American or British pen pals. Yevgeniya Ruditskaya became pen pals with a girl from England, "but then I had to end this because my mother had a top security clearance and they wouldn't let me," she regretted. The KGB often monitored these innocent childhood contacts.

"NO OTHER SCHOOL IN SARATOV HAS THIS"

Both schools offered unique summer opportunities for the Baby Boomers that they remember fondly, for the programs—in some regards extensions of the school year—contrasted sharply with the boilerplate, state-subsidized summer Pioneer camps that most Soviet youth attended. Some of the Baby Boomers attended Pioneer camps, too, but the camps were not popular among the intelligentsia, who sought other ways to care for and enrich their children. Viktor D. claimed that there were more than 350 Pioneer camps in the Saratov region back then, "but it seemed scandalous to send their children there, and not because conditions were bad." As a result, Aleksandr Trubnikov reported that "the majority from our class did not go to camp." Each year Olga Kamayurova's parents took her to the Black Sea. "Back then this was simple and easy. I never went to camp, neither to Pioneer Camp, nor to any sport camp. I simply wasn't drawn to that sort of thing," she explained. Aleksandr Babushkin expressed gratitude to his grandmother. "She showed me much of the then Soviet Union. There's practically not a place that we didn't visit." Although he vacationed at the Black Sea several times with his parents, Aleksandr Trubnikov observed that "few could afford [going to the sea]. It was expensive, even for some who went to our school." Instead of camp and trips to the sea, each summer during the 1950s Yevgeny Podolsky's grandmother took his sister and him to the village of Chadaevka in the Saratov region. "I'd remind you that this was not today's village. There was mud up to our knees, no roads, nothing. We lived in our landlady's cottage with dirt floors, but things were very clean. That was our vacation." A rare exception, Lyudmila Gorokhova loved Pioneer camp, perhaps because she lived at state day care facilities when she was a preschooler. "For the ten years I was in school I attended Pioneer camp twelve times. That is, some years I went for two sessions I liked it so much," she recalled.

The local Party elite sent their children to the USSR's most prestigious Pioneer camps, which were located on the sea. Tatyana Kuznetsova fondly recalled the time she and classmate Irina Kositsyna spent at Kabardinka, on the Black Sea, where kids from Cuba vacationed with them. Downplaying her family's privileged position, Kuznetsova claimed she did not go to local camps "because of the terrible Volga mosquitoes." Irina Chemodurova also spent time at an elite camp, Adler, where, at the age of seven, she saw Khrushchev. After graduation, Olga Gorelik with Larisa Petrova attended Artek, the most prestigious Pioneer camp in the Soviet Union. "We lived in the same building," noted Gorelik. "Her father also worked in the oblast (provincial) Party committee."

Despite the intelligentsia's reservations about Pioneer camps, most looked favorably upon sending their children to an alternative—to Camp Labor and Rest, an option that became available thanks to the initiative of School No. 42's teachers. The Saratovites raved about spending a month living in tents following the eighth and ninth grades. "Children today can only envy us," crowed Galina Poldyaeva. For her, camp began each year with vivid memories of the journey to an island in the Volga, Chardym, in a huge iron motorboat, powered by an automobile engine. "All of the kids attending the camp, and all of the tents, in pieces, were on the wooden deck. And Mikhail Nikolayevich [their physics teacher] would say, 'Sit still. If someone rocks the boat, we'll drown.'" "No other school in Saratov had this," boasted Aleksandr Trubnikov. "And it's not because we were the English-language school, but because we lucked out with our gym teacher, Igor Andreyevich," who organized the camp. Trubnikov described his memories of the Volga camp as "wonderful ones. It was really a great summer camp," he told me. "I think this is what I enjoyed most about my school days. This was real happiness, when you're young, when you don't yet work, and when you're on the Volga." Remembered Trubnikov: "I drank right out of the river. You'd swim, take a sip, and swim further. It was so clean! These memories are probably the happiest from my school years." This is where many of them cemented lifelong friendships. Arkady Darchenko clarified why: "In our class a large enough group went practically each year. We did just about everything ourselves. We purchased supplies and took turns cooking on open campfires. And group work is the sort of thing that bonds people. Likewise, there were conflicts and romances."

Like others, Irina Tsurkan found the experience transformative. Raised by strict parents who barely let her out of their sight, Irina remembered what the camp signified for her: "It meant tents. It meant taking turns keeping the

The Saratov Baby Boomers enumerated the many reasons why they enjoyed living in tents at Camp Labor and Rest on an island in the Volga. Aleksandr Konstantinov recalled what might have been one of the main ones: "It meant freedom for us, especially from our parents!" *Courtesy of Aleksandr Virich*

campfires burning. It meant doing some fun work on nearby kolkhozes. I remember that they sent us city kids to weed carrots. We good naturedly weeded and weeded. Not a single carrot was left. We pulled them all up!" Up until that point, Tsurkan suffered from all sorts of inferiority complexes, owing, in her view, to her exacting upbringing at home. She recalled, "It was at camp that I revealed my more interesting side. I returned home a different person, and people treated me differently. I came to feel that I was no worse than anyone else, and perhaps better at some things." Pyotor Krasilnikov saw the socialization experience as a rite of passage. "At first we listened to the songs of the older kids. Then we ourselves became upperclassmen and others listened to us and we taught them."

Not everyone attended Camp Labor and Rest, because some parents did not allow their children to do so, and because some Baby Boomers did not want to go. Natalya P.'s parents insisted she vacation with them on the Black Sea. "This totally distressed me," lamented Natalya. "I didn't need their trip down south to the sea; I wanted to go to camp with my classmates! But my parents were strict and didn't let me go." Irina Vizgalova did not participate because she spent each summer visiting her grandparents in Volgograd oblast. Others did not attend camp, "because not everyone liked living in a tent and roughing it," explained

Aleksandr Trubnikov. "To be honest," confirmed Larisa Petrova, "I always loved comfort, and never really cared for tents."

"ONLY ENGLISH IS SPOKEN HERE"

During the summer the young Muscovites spent time at the dacha, visited relatives, attended camp, or traveled with their families. Mikhail Markovich visited his grand-parents in Yasnaya Polyana, where he enjoyed "a village childhood during the summer." This meant that he was left to his own devices and "was absolutely free," he recalled. "We played all of the childhood games, including stealing apples from the neighbors' trees." "Although travel was confined to the country," Yelena Kolosova appreciated her parents because they "miraculously managed to find untouched nature reserves" to visit. Viktor Alekseyev remembered going to the Black Sea every other year. "It was mainly with my mother or with my aunt, my mother's sister." By the time he had completed school his father had salted away enough money to buy a small dacha outside Moscow, where they spent subsequent summers.

Some Muscovites attended Pioneer camps, but they and their parents harbored the same reservations about the experience that their Saratov counterparts articu-lated. Viktor Alekseyev volunteered, "I went to Pioneer camp several times, and wasn't, to put it mildly, in ecstasy." He had a list of grievances that others shared: "the discipline, the overcrowdedness, and the level of the teachers in comparison to ours." Yevgeniya Ruditskaya "couldn't stand the Pioneer camp." She explained that "it made an awful impression on me, because there were altogether different kids there who really differed from the children I went to school with." Ruditskaya experienced anti-Semitism in the Pioneer camps "and that's why I hated them." "It was never inter-esting there," quipped Tatyana Artyomova, "because the other kids were strangers."

But "everyone was one of us," Artyomova waxed lyrically, recalling the glo-rious month she spent at a special English-language camp organized by School No. 20 during the summer of 1964, after she finished seventh grade. The camp was the brainchild of the younger teachers and some of the parents. Leonid Terlitsky gave credit to Irina Yakovlevna Yurina: "She was the moving force behind organizing an English summer camp, a month in tents outside of Moscow on the territory of one of the military bases where we would use a can-teen to eat, and we spent the month speaking only English." Lyubov Raitman thanked "the influential parents of several of our classmates," who struck a deal with a military unit stationed near Moscow. The unit provided large soldiers' tents that accommodated up to six people. According to Marina Bakutina, each of the parents was given an assignment in preparing for the camp. "My parents were asked to make a poster, which my father did: 'Russian is forbidden. Only English is spoken here.'" Anna Lyovina emphasized how lucky she and her class-mates were that "all of the teachers did it out of sheer enthusiasm. After all, no one *made* them." She elaborated: "Do you understand what kind of enthusiasm and energy is needed to organize all of this, to arrange things, to figure out

Yevgeniya Ruditskaya (third from right) fondly remembered vacationing with both her parents at the Black Sea. This was unusual given Soviet workplace vacation policies, which often meant that married couples had to take their vacations at different times. *Courtesy of Yevgeniya Kreizerova (Ruditskaya)*

where we'd live and what to feed us? And to achieve all of this in our bureaucratic system? Can you imagine how many documents they needed? They pulled it off. I thank my lucky stars that it all turned out, and that I ended up at that school." Vladimir Prudkin called it "a gift of fate, especially in the USSR."

The experience made "a very powerful impression" on Tatyana Artyomova and others. They began each morning singing songs in English and learning new vocabulary. "It was lots of fun, it was really interesting, and it helped us grow closer," insisted Lyubov Raitman. Tatyana Arzhanova maintained that the camp experience resulted in bringing the A and B classes closer together as well. Lyubov Kovalyova believed that, apart from having a good time, they took part in some "socially useful" work, too, in nearby fields. Yet it was summer, and the emphasis was on enjoying themselves. Leonid Terlitsky fondly reminisced, "We would play soccer using English terminology and have various activities. Even our coach, who didn't speak a word of English. He learned. He had to learn corner kick, penalty kick, that sort of stuff." The girls basked in the sun, hiked, and hung out at a nearby stream. Although they were not supposed to wander off on their own, "like all kids, we were interested in going exactly where they forbade us to go," said Lyubov Kovalyova. She also recalled, "There was one more absolutely marvelous thing. We took turns at night duty. We guarded the campsite, and in the morning one of the teachers would come to check on us."

Passionate about soccer, the males at School No. 20 continued their team competition at camp. Five members of the B Class's team were interviewed for this book (Viktor Alekseyev [far left], Leonid Terlitsky, Sergei Zemskov, Vladimir Glebkin, [second, third, and fourth from left], and Vladimir Prudkin [third from right]). *Courtesy of Lyubov Obraztsova (Raitman)*

The school administration looked upon the opportunity as something to be earned: because of misconduct, Leonid Volodarsky and several others were not allowed to take part in the adventure. Several others earned the opportunity, but did not like it. Yelena Kolosova found it "a bit hard" to spend 24/7 with others, even her friends. She remembered, "There was no room for my inherent insularity. Although I'm someone who is very loquacious, I'm really a reserved person." Moreover, her first severe allergy attack darkened her memories of the camp. "I don't even recall what provoked it, but the memory's a vivid one. So is the memory of what my complexion looked like. I was covered with awful scabs and they sent me back to Moscow first chance they got."

Lyubov Raitman acknowledged that, when she and her friends were by themselves they spoke Russian, but "nevertheless, we tried [to speak English]" and the teachers did their best to uphold the English-only rule, "punishing" those who got caught violating it. For example, one night Andrei Rogatnev and Shurik Lapson, who now lives in Skokie, Illinois, whispered to each other in Russian in their tent about the next day's soccer plans. Recalled Rogatnev: "Suddenly the tent flap was flung open. It was pitch dark. A flash light shone in our eyes. 'Lapson, Rogatnev! Tomorrow while all the others go to the river for a swim, you can dig a ditch.' That's how they taught us English." Vladimir Sidelnikov confided that he and a few others, "got drunk behind the teachers' backs." But it was not only such things that bonded them and made the camp special. Lyubov Raitman believed that interaction with the teachers that summer contributed to the shaping of their outlooks: "They broadened our horizons, that is, our access to information." Sharing their knowledge and sometimes firsthand experience in England and America, the teachers presented these cultures in a positive light. "It was not exaltation, it was not servility toward America, but it was recognition of the positive in literature, in art, in history, in geography, in all aspects of life. We learned a great deal during that month."

"IT WAS ALL ABOUT LENIN, LENIN, LENIN"

The state exposed children and young adults to a pyramid of age-based youth organizations designed to provide fun, inculcate values, develop talents, and carry out political indoctrination. Soviet school children between the ages of six and nine belonged to the Young Octobrists, named after the October (Bolshevik) Revolution of 1917. At age ten, children joined the Pioneers formed to replace the prerevolutionary scouting movement. Celebrating its fortieth anniversary in 1962 when the interviewees were in sixth grade, the Pioneer organization sponsored a national campaign involving youth in all sorts of activities in which the Baby Boomers took part.

Pioneers were instructed to study hard, to be honest, and to learn how to get along with others. They took an oath upon joining the organization, "to dearly love my Soviet Motherland, to live, study, and struggle as the great Lenin bade us and the Communist Party teaches us." They wore a uniform, a red kerchief, and a badge with the motto "Always Prepared," the response to the Pioneer call, "Be prepared to fight for the cause of the Communist Party of the Soviet Union!" They had a salute, rules, and responsibilities. The Pioneer manual told them how to behave, how to dress and groom themselves, how to be polite, and how to look after themselves,[17] in short, how to be "an example for all."[18] Making no mention of Stalin, the manual had plenty to say about Khrushchev's initiatives. "Grow corn!" it directed.* "Unlike any other crop, corn is important for the national economy."[19] The handbook emphasized that the Seven-Year Plan adopted in 1959 set the goal of accelerating the creation of the material and technical basis of communism.[20]

As Saratov's Olga Gorelik maintained, "We were Octobrists, then Pioneers and we wanted to be. Even though it was a special school, there was no irony in any of this." For Moscow's Bakhyt Kenzheyev joining the Pioneers was "one of my most 'wonderful' childhood memories." Except for one thing. The school had invited a writer to the ceremony, requesting that he tie the red kerchief on

---

* Khrushchev sought to introduce and expand the cultivation of corn to increase livestock herds and consequently meat and dairy production and consumption.

Young Pioneer brigade from School No. 42's B Class on Pioneer Day, May 19, in the fifth or sixth grade, with their popular home room teacher, Albina Ivanovna Baklanova. Principal Vera Filippovna dismissed Baklanova, ostensibly for becoming romantically involved with another teacher. However, Vera Filippovna might have seen Baklanova as a rival who threatened her position. *Courtesy of Aleksandr Konstantinov*

one of the pupils. Kenzheyev reported, "I was short and puny and my status when I was ten years old was zero so I was standing there at the end of the line and I was eager for this old Soviet asshole to tie the kerchief on my neck, but he overlooked me. So it was a major disappointment."

All of the interviewees later joined the Komsomol organization, the Communist Youth League that catered to young people between the ages of fourteen and twenty-eight, but some did so only out of necessity. "When they accepted us into the Komsomol," explained Igor Litvin, "everyone really wanted to join. God forbid that you didn't get picked. There would have been a certain stigma. That is, you *had* to be a member." Membership in the Komsomol, a training ground for Party membership, was far from universal in the USSR, but those with aspirations to enroll at a university needed to join. "I really didn't want to join the Komsomol," volunteered Saratov's Pyotor Krasilnikov. "I didn't understand why I had to join. But the times were such that, if you would have said that you didn't want to join, they'd not have given you your diploma upon graduating, so I had no other choice."

Vladimir Ilich Lenin stood at the center of the Soviet belief system and thus of the Pioneer and Komsomol organizations. According to Moscow's Igor Litvin, "there was a mythologization of Lenin." Vladimir Bystrov acknowledged that he "revered Lenin. That was the line they filled our heads with." Georgy Godzhello observed that "we truly believed what we were taught. We had no doubts." Vladimir Sidelnikov confided, "I adored Lenin, ever the more so because my mother told me so much about him and even named me Vladimir in honor of him." Saratov's Olga Gorelik remembered that everything associated with Lenin "was sacred for us." Olga Kolishchyuk agreed, "We looked upon him as a member of the family, as a protector, as a teacher, and as a person to imitate." Olga Kamayurova recalled, "We sang a song that now seems like gibberish: 'Lenin is always alive, Lenin is always with you.'" As Tatyana Kuznetsova shared, "He was everything. Open any of our textbooks and his portrait's on the first page, be it *Our Native Language*, or the *ABCs*."

The Cold War generation back then held Lenin in high regard, but often not Stalin, owing to Khrushchev's anti-Stalin drive during their childhood and return to "Leninist principles." Bakhyt Kenzheyev admired Lenin but had "no illusions" about Stalin "because of 1956, and then there was another Party congress in 1961, a year full of all sorts of scandals. Then there was *One Day in the Life of Ivan Denisovich*. Besides that, I had a maternal uncle who had spent ten years in Siberia, and two paternal uncles who had been shot." As Aleksandr Konstantinov put it, "Many probably were under the impression that Lenin, unlike Stalin, was a good man, who wanted the best. Of course, people

Portraits of Lenin could be found in all public buildings, including Soviet schools. A portrait of Lenin observes Arkady Darchenko on June 22, 1967, addressing his classmates and their parents on graduation night. *Courtesy of Aleksandr Virich*

nevertheless looked upon him with some cynicism because he was forced on us." Back then Leonid Volodarsky believed "that if Lenin were only alive, then everything would be fine. I think that no matter who you ask," he stated, "they'd say that Lenin did everything correctly, and that Stalin perverted everything." Viktor Alekseyev certainly felt this way. "We didn't know the entire truth back then." He emphasized that his views on Lenin "began to evolve much later" than those of some of his classmates. He gave the example of his classmate and friend Igor Altshuller, "who far earlier was exposed to all of the damaging influence of *samizdat* [self-published forbidden works] and foreign radio broadcasts."

The abrupt changes in the Party line toward Stalin confused many, since before 1953 Soviet propaganda had attributed victory in the Great Patriotic War to him. "His influence was absolutely enormous in that regard," remembered Galina Poldyaeva. As a child, Irina Vizgalova also linked Stalin to victory in war. "Well, Stalin, Stalin, Stalin. Back then it was believed that it was all Stalin's doings that we won the war. But all of our misfortunes came from him." Tatyana Kuznetsova sensed a certain public anxiety over Stalin when Soviet newspapers wrote about repressions. "How could all of this have come about? How had things really been? After all, people left for war with his name on their lips, 'For the Motherland! For Stalin.'" As Aleksandr Trubnikov reasoned, "Stalin is a complicated matter. When I was really young, Nikita Sergeyevich [Khrushchev] denounced the Stalin cult. And when we finally began to understand things, this cult began to return once again. I remember that, already in 1963–64, no one had anything negative to say about Stalin anymore." Consequently, added Trubnikov, "Our poor history teachers simply didn't know what to tell us! It was as if Stalin had made mistakes and had some shortcomings, but, on the other hand, he won the war. That was the most important thing, the war. There's a saying, 'war justifies everything.'"

As they grew up, some of the interviewees had a change of heart about Lenin. In the lower grades, Yevgeniya Ruditskaya associated Vladimir Ilich with the ideals of the Russian Revolution and proletariat. "But then in the upper grades I began to understand what's what." But for most the realization came later. It did for Aleksandr Trubnikov who remembered, "The propaganda system was so comprehensive, so all-encompassing that it was hard to think something other than that Lenin was a genius who showed us the bright path. I didn't think otherwise until I attended the university." When Bakhyt Kenzheyev enrolled at the university, a friend poured scorn on communism. "I was shocked. After all, how could that be? Communism was such a good idea. I think that until I was twenty I thought that Lenin was good." Admitted Anatoly Shapiro: "I understood that Lenin was a bandit and a scoundrel only after graduating from college, when I was older." When he attended school, Yevgeny Podolsky "accepted what they said about him. Back then, no one said anything bad about him, and it never even crossed anyone's mind. Lenin remained some kind of ideal." As Olga

Martynkina summed up, "From childhood we read books about Lenin. It was all about Lenin, Lenin, Lenin. Lenin gave us everything. Yet later, when you begin to mature and grow wiser, when you begin to read other kinds of books, you understand."

"CATCH UP WITH AND OVERTAKE AMERICA"

Although Soviet statistical compendia commonly compared Soviet achievements with what had (not) been achieved under the tsars, the real unit of measurement was the United States,[21] especially after Khrushchev in 1957 launched his campaign to catch up with and overtake America. Saratov's Aleksandr Kutin found the slogan appropriate "because there had to be some kind of competitive incentive. And we could never have said 'let's catch up with and overtake Kenya.' That would have sounded stupid," he retorted. Kutin saw an unexpected benefit in the campaign: "In order to catch up with and overtake America, you had to at least know how America lived. They allowed us to know, but, of course, in small doses."

The slogan came to encapsulate Khrushchev's new *Party Program* that, from a Soviet child's perspective, promised the moon, not just traveling to it. Life was wonderful, because it soon was going to get even better. Their Pioneer manual made clear the Communist Party's goal: to build a Communist society. "*It will be the best, the most just and the happiest society on earth.*"[22] In this society everyone would work and create to the full extent of their talents and abilities; everyone would receive whatever they required to satisfy their needs; everyone would be able to live an interesting life, free to draw on the material and cultural abundance.

Growing Soviet consumerism, price reductions on basic necessities, and triumphs in the space race in and after 1957 gave just enough credence to the propaganda to make some Soviet citizens optimistic, and to make Western observers anxious. Tatyana Luchnikova remembered that "I was very happy because I was born in the very best country in the world." This brought to mind something she had memorized at school: "I know of no other country where man breathes so freely." Luchnikova wrote poems in this vein as a schoolgirl that appeared in newspapers targeting youth. Saratov's Natalya Pronina remembered Khrushchev saying, "'Today's generation of Soviet people will live under communism.' I'll never forget this remark. It was drilled into me since childhood. We once believed in this, because we saw with our very own eyes that we were living better and better." "You have to give credit to propaganda," mused Saratov's Aleksandr Trubnikov. "I, and many of my friends, too, believed in socialism, further still, in communism, which was even more special." Trubnikov elaborated, "When you know nothing other than this life it seems that that's how things ought to be, especially when they tell you so 24/7. We live better than anyone in the world and soon we'll start living fabulously. Perhaps there were those who felt otherwise."

There were. Khrushchev promised what he ultimately could not deliver, and this did not escape the attention of some Saratovites as they entered their teen-age years. A bemused Olga Gorelik replied that she "never tried to overtake anyone." Skeptical of Khrushchev's boasting, she "took it all in for what it was." According to Trubnikov, his classmate Arkady Korchmar "drew caricatures, batches of them, of Khrushchev's adventures in Africa and elsewhere. They were like comics, like what you see in cartoons. He understood things far better than I did at the time. He knew." "I was confident that we would truly achieve com-munism by 1980," remarked Arkady Darchenko. "People indeed believed that we were on the right path, and that soon we'd achieve it. But when we were a bit older, we realized that we weren't heading in that direction. We understood already during the Khrushchev years."

Yet some Baby Boomers realized this earlier than others because, in 1962, bread, the staple of the Soviet diet, briefly disappeared from shops in Saratov. "I won't even speak about meat and other things," said Yevgeny Podolsky, who remembered that "people began to blame Khrushchev for the economic diffi-culties—after all, he himself had invited criticism." We already heard from Irina Vizgalova, but her claim that even children did not think it was possible to build communism bears repeating: "How could we? We didn't have bread here. There was no milk. What kind of communism could there be when they passed out bread in school and there were long lines for bread?" Many interviewees dredged up memories of queuing up at night for bread before the shops opened in the morning. Aleksandr Trubnikov had a sardonic take on the matter: "We harbored no doubts that we lived in the greatest country in the world, that we had fine futures ahead of us, and that life was steadily improving. Then, all of a sudden, things got so good that we were without bread in 1962." Even though this epi-sode did not yet shake Trubnikov's faith in the system, he admitted that not all of his classmates shared his optimism. Moreover, the economic situation trig-gered full-scale riots in the city of Novocherkassk in southern Russia. Even though the regime brutally suppressed the disorder and news about it, rumors about the shootings, which left twenty-four dead and dozens wounded, circu-lated widely throughout the USSR.[23]

Some Saratovites had further reasons for doubting Khrushhev's promises or for questioning his policies or ability to rule. Irina Vizgalova laid into his unpop-ular currency reform in 1961, which many feared would devaluate their savings as had been the case under Stalin: "Everyone was extremely disappointed. This was hard to swallow, that money became worthless." Olga Kolishchyuk remem-bered that "we were in shock when he took off his shoe and pounded it [at the UN]. Some of his pronouncements also humored us, but we hoped that you Americans didn't have good translators. Not all of what he said was translat-able." Olga Martynkina had a list of complaints: pounding his shoe at the UN, giving the Crimea to Ukraine [this became an issue only after Ukraine became independent in 1991], and forcing corn on the country. "He was called the corn man," she snipped, for the Soviet economy began producing candy, beer, sausage, and other items from corn, which also became the subject of jokes and the symbol of his failed agricultural policies in general. A joke from the time has it that Khrushchev received a Nobel Prize for agriculture for managing to sow grain in Siberia and to harvest it in Canada, a reference to the Soviet need to begin purchasing grain abroad at the end of the Khrushchev era.

Although the Moscow Baby Boomers lived better, they were even more skeptical of Khrushchev's plans to build communism. As Yelena Zharovova remarked, "That future seemed to me at the time so unattainable that I didn't get all caught up in it." Most agreed with Leonid Terlitsky that "Khrushchev was maligned mostly because he had destroyed the economy. Since the war there hadn't been a time when people couldn't buy bread." Living near one of Moscow's train stations, he had vivid memories of people from the suburbs and small towns outside of Moscow showing up to buy bread. "They would buy it by the sack full, taking it back to the whole village or for the whole family." This distressed Muscovites. "There was no sausage, no meat, nothing or very little that people could buy with money, and that caused a real uproar. I think that was the primary reason behind the dislike of Khrushchev," he argued. Terlitsky also found the carrying out of the corn campaign especially ludicrous, "but if you try to explain anything about this country from a logical point of view you're bound to fail."

Yelena Kolosova cast Khrushchev as "a comic, yet somewhat romantic" figure, but one tainted by Stalinism. "Who was there to catch up with?" she queried. "We were very proud of our space program without a doubt and, later, of all that a totalitarian state could achieve by blood." Andrei Rogatnev chastised not only Khrushchev's closing, using bulldozers, of an avant-garde art exhibit in Moscow in 1962 but also his corn campaign, the belligerent shoe-thumping stunt at the UN, and the drive to overtake America. Evoking the Pioneer call, he snickered, "We were prepared, only we didn't know for what." He then shared a joke he heard "not out loud in Red Square, but in the kitchen at home": Khrushchev and Kennedy agreed to compete against one another in a race. The next day's issue of *Pravda* informed readers of an international competition involving Khrushchev and Kennedy to see who could run the fastest. Nikita Sergeyevich, *Pravda* reported, came in second, and Kennedy next to last. Rogatnev also recalled a remark that his classmate Vladimir Bystrov made in tenth grade English class. Formulating statements in English using subjunctive "if" clauses, Bystrov volunteered, "If my grandmother would have had two packages of margarine, she wouldn't have been grandmother, but a food store."

Although critical of his economic policies, many Moscow parents evaluated Khrushchev's *political* reforms positively. Lyubov Kovalyova's father, a Communist, believed he was a progressive leader, and, unlike earlier Kremlin figures, accessible to the public and "more democratic." Viktor Alekseyev's father looked upon Nikita Sergeyevich favorably, because "the Thaw was felt everywhere. It happened slowly, but people began to feel freer." Anna Lyovina remembered that, for her parents, his ouster was a "huge shock, because they deeply respected Khrushchev, despite the fact that they understood that he was uneducated and part of the Stalinist system." Still, as Lyovina reckoned, "If you place everything on the scales, my parents believed the good outweighed the bad, and I think they're right." Leonid Volodarsky's parents, "people of quite liberal views," thought that everything Khrushchev said about Stalin "was correct and necessary." Khrushchev's denunciation of abstract art and hostile encounter with leading members of the cultural intelligentsia in 1962, however, disappointed many who otherwise backed his de-Stalinization. "It seems to me that, on the whole, my parents evaluated him positively owing to the Twentieth Congress," weighed in Boris Shtein. "But I remember the conversations at home after his meeting with the intelligentsia [in 1962]. Much changed." Historian Vladislav Zubok concurs, arguing that the chance for a common cause between the impetuous Kremlin leader and the intelligentsia might have overcome Stalin's legacy and reformed the Soviet project.[24] It is not for nothing that the monument on his grave depicts a Janus-like figure, half black and half white.

In Saratov, Yevgeny Podolsky's Communist Party member parents felt relieved at Khrushchev's ouster, because "he was basically part of the same cohort as Stalin," yet had dealt a terrible blow to their belief system, so much so that they never trusted him. Later, under Leonid Brezhnev, when the regime softened its position on Stalin, emphasizing that his policies had won World War II, his parents told him: "See, it turns out that Khrushchev wasn't altogether right after all." Pyotor Krasilnikov explained that, to understand his parents' positive reaction to Khrushchev's ouster, it is necessary to consider what preceded it: bread shortages. His grandmother, moreover, resented him for levying a tax on trees. "She had no livestock and had to pay for her apple trees. So her husband chopped them down." Aleksandr Konstantinov's parents understood Khrushchev's removal "as some sort of reversion toward a tougher policy. We understood that Khrushchev was no saint. He was crude. But he accomplished much."

Many Baby Boomers had a hard time separating out their childhood memories from their adult attitudes toward Khrushchev, since hindsight gave them the ability to judge him in more textured ways that may have obscured what they had thought about him in the past. Irina Tsurkan realized when she became a doctor that "he ruined alternative medicine, all sorts of folk remedies, which he called 'voodoo.' He returned from America and said that everything was available in tablet form, that everything had already been invented. Many formulas were lost. We certainly can't thank him for this." Others, however, came to appreciate aspects of Khrushchev's nonstop reforms or, more commonly, the climate of optimism and renewal he nurtured in the post-Stalin years. Moscow's Vladimir Bystrov had a strong opinion about Khrushchev's efforts to break up the power of the centralized Moscow ministries. "He was absolutely right. Things have turned out that way now, but back then they didn't let him do it." Despite the threat of nuclear war during the Cuban Missile Crisis of 1962, Saratov's Olga Kolishchyuk remembered Khrushchev's promotion of peaceful coexistence and that he was depicted as "the messenger of peace." "We thought about America and hoped that everything would be good there, too, that people would be sane there, too, that there would not be war, and that our leaders would somehow reach agreement and there wouldn't be any tensions."

Others expressed appreciation for the Thaw. As Moscow's Viktor Alekseyev put it, "Some freedoms began to appear. Despite the fact that all of this was very gradual, nevertheless the Thaw at the end of the 1950s and beginning of the 1960s was felt everywhere." Praising Khrushchev's accomplishments in promoting the Soviet space industry and military, Pyotor Krasilnikov believed the bread shortages had been "artificially created in order to arouse the masses against him." His classmate Gennady Ivanov also saw them as a provocation. Crediting Khrushchev with promoting a climate conducive to creativity, Sergei Zemskov found that this had come to an end by the time he entered the workforce, when they began to pay far more attention to copying the West. "You'd come with an idea, let's say, and the first question that arose was 'And over there in the West? Do they have this? If they don't have it, then why do we need it?' Under Khrushchev this question never arose." But it did: Tsurkan, as well as those who harped on Khrushchev's corn campaign, underscore this blind copying of the West that Zemskov claimed to have experienced only later.

The slogan to catch up with and overtake America, which may have doomed the Soviet Union to failure, bombarded the Baby Boomers and penetrated their consciousness, sometimes in mysterious ways. Moscow's Vladimir Sidelnikov, for instance, put an unusual spin on the slogan: "I believed that we'd catch up with and overtake America. Khrushchev said that today's generation of Soviet people will live under communism. He wasn't that far off the mark. We now live as if under communism, if you put 'communism' in quotation marks."

THE FLIP SIDE OF NOSTALGIA

Some of the interviewees' memories of their schooldays open windows onto less nostalgic aspects of their childhood. For example, Aleksandr Konstantinov confided that one characteristic feature of his and other Saratov schools at the time was what he called their criminalization: "What I mean by this is that some of the boys were connected to city gangs, sort of like *West Side Story*. Your prestige at school—in the restrooms where the pupils smoked—was dependent on who your 'protectors' were." The detail he provided belies the otherwise sanitized image of the school. "I was protected since the 'king' of the riverbank neighborhood nicknamed the 'Italian' lived in our building and was friendly to me. This gang world was a fact of life for us boys." Konstantinov emphasized that "at school Matveev, who was two or three years older than me, was 'king.' Everyone feared him. They began to respect me in school after he told one of the older boys in the bathroom not to touch Konstantinov because 'the Italian's behind him.'" Gennady Ivanov recalled a mostly Tatar gang from the Glebuchev Ravine neighborhood, and another dubbed the Industrialists, but insisted "there were no hooligan groups in *our* school." Although these and other gangs occasionally caused trouble at School No. 42, it had an advantage: "We came from different neighborhoods of the city and, if they came to pester us, we could enlist the help of those from our neighborhoods, in which case no one could equal us," boasted Ivanov.

Some Saratovites' passionate recounting of one episode made as much of an impression on me as others' silence on the subject, or claims not to remember the incident at all. A handful of females brought up the event concerning the B class, which remains a conversation topic today among them. The case in point took place during the final weeks in school as stress mounted in regard to taking exit exams, especially the mandatory composition on a topic in Russian literature that students needed to pass in order to graduate. The fractured memories reflect complex issues involving childhood jealousies and rivalries, and also reveal a large measure of collusion between pupils and teachers. So much depended upon the results of this hour-long essay—one's standing within the class, what college one could get into, the school's and teachers' reputations—that pupils, their parents, and teachers worked the system to obtain favorable results by learning in advance the writing prompts from which graduating tenth graders had to choose. In other words, what would be seen as outright cheating in the United States was acceptable in the Soviet Union. Irina Barysheva came clean: "It's a secret to no one that we found out the topics in advance and prepared drafts the night before." This is the case "even now" in Russia's schools. But something went terribly wrong back in 1967. This time the authorities had managed to keep the real prompts secret, except from one girl, the "class favorite," who knew the new themes but did not tell a soul. "After that we ostracized her," justified Barysheva. Natalya P. saw her classmate's behavior as an act of betrayal. "It was her father who gave her away. He said, 'M—wrote all night. She needed to receive a medal.' No one spoke with her at graduation. She was all alone."

Having to write on a topic for which students had not prepared the night before distressed Barysheva. It was "something unreal," she claimed. Like others, she had picked one of the five themes the night before, written a crib, and memorized it. Her father checked her work before sending her to school, where, to her dismay, she realized her efforts had been in vain. When she learned the new prompts for which she had not prepared, Barysheva drafted an essay on Soviet writer Mikhail Sholokhov, avoiding one on the nineteenth-century poet Nikolai Nekrasov, whom she "didn't understand." But this upset her homeroom teacher Zorina, who told her "Ira, I'll even sneak you a crib sheet, but don't write on that topic. Write on Nekrasov." She then took her into the hallway. "Have you lost your mind? That theme is unfair. How can you critique the craftsmanship of

Sholokhov?" Zorina even tried to talk Barysheva's mother into convincing her to select the question on Nekrasov. Yet Ira stuck to her guns. Zorina gave her an A on the essay, but the outside commission assigned the essay a B, because her interpretations deviated from the Party line. Zorina, her "favorite teacher," appealed and Barysheva eventually got an A. Barysheva believed her father who managed the factory that sponsored School No. 42 had interfered on her behalf once again: "Sponsors, after all, are sponsors—and that means pipes, indoor plumbing, bricks, and other materials [the school needed]."

None of the Muscovites brought up gang activities at school or cheating on the final exam. But "children are children," as Vladimir Bystrov put it. "Between classes we ran and goofed off. We did all those things. Not in school, but near the school after classes." "Of course, conflicts arose, and fights, and everything else," clarified Sergei Zemskov, but "afterward it was hard to imagine what had caused them." Mikhail Markovich remembered: girls and also relations with those in authority. Some resented the Pioneer leader, Nikolai Alekseyevich,

Lyubov Vilenskaya and Natalya Khamidulina, members of the Saratov B Class, pore over a class assignment. Now a physician, Vilenskaya lives in the New York area, as does Khamidulina's daughter, who married an American. *Courtesy of Aleksandr Virich*

"a not very smart and hyperactive creature."[25] Leonid Terlitsky wryly remarked that Nikolai "wasted his irrepressible energy on attempts to organize the students at the school into future builders of communism." The male students resented Nikolai Alekseyevich, among other things, because he squealed on smokers. Pupils in the older class of '66 took their hostility out on him in a vindictive hazing incident that caused him to wet his pants.

Vladimir Mikoyan told how the C class challenged Anton Petrovich's authority. During a break between classes, Sergei Zemskov boasted to a group of classmates that he had stayed up all night reading nonconformist poet Yevgeny Yevtushenko's cycle of poems, "The Bratsk Hydroelectric Station," smitten by its honesty and boldness. "I remember how we crowded around him listening. Then Anton Petrovich appeared." When he ordered them to their seats for their social science lesson, Zemskov defiantly replied that he would not take his until he had finished reading the poem. According to Mikoyan, "we all left. We simply walked out. And out on the street we agreed not to return to school. We wanted to punish the principal." No one in the C class went to school for three days as telephones rang off the hook. "We graciously went back," bragged Mikoyan. One can only imagine the negotiations that went on behind the scenes to smooth things over so that everyone saved face.

Encounters at school with foreign visitors offered lessons for a society opening up to the outside world—and for the guests. One group of visitors used the school assembly called in their honor to disparage the Soviet system. To the dismay of teacher Olga Konstantinovna, none of her charges rose to the defense of the maligned motherland. Recalled Vyacheslav Starik: "When all of this was over and we were alone with her, she began to rip into us, 'Why didn't we, conscious and active Komsomolites, put an end to the flood of slander and spiteful criticism?' And we had to honestly confess that we didn't understand what the slanderers had actually said. This was a big relief for her, for it turned out that we weren't secretly anti-Soviet after all, but ordinary C students." Tatyana Luchnikova brought up an episode that caused the school administration profound embarrassment. It took place during the visit of a group from England, when a British guest "left her boots in the cloakroom. She took off tall black boots, and someone stole them. So," concluded Tatyana, "even in magnet English School No. 20 there was theft." Luchnikova did not know whether the boots were found and returned to their owner, but she expressed surprise that no one else had told me about the incident.

"IT WILL BE THE BEST . . . SOCIETY ON EARTH"

Saratov's School No. 42 and Moscow's School No. 20 attracted children of the *nomenklatura*, of Party and state officials, of career military officers, and of the technical and cultural intelligentsia. Their student bodies were diversified by a few token children of working-class families, but this Soviet style affirmative action program met with limited success. In both cities these *were* schools for the "children of gifted parents." Except in a few instances, parents used their influence, connections, and pull—*blat* in Russian—to get their offspring enrolled in these schools and, since at least one parent of roughly 80 percent of the Baby Boomers belonged to the Communist Party, they tended to be well connected. When necessary, they hired private tutors to prepare their children to enroll in the school or to get through academic subjects that gave them difficulty. As the most educated group in the Soviet Union, Jews were overrepresented in both institutions, especially in Moscow, where a high concentration of Jews inhabited the surrounding neighborhood.

Devoted Communists set the tone at both schools, whose built environment represented the best the Soviet Union had to offer. Principals Vera Filippovna and Anton Petrovich selected seasoned teachers but, given the special need for instructors of English, they often had to take on newly minted teachers or, as was especially true of Moscow, those with nonconformist views. In both cities some of the younger teachers imbibed the spirit of the Thaw, thereby making enduring impressions on their young charges who mostly raved about those who instructed them at the special schools. These teachers were also flexible in dealing with their young pupils, and often generous in organizing enrichment experiences such as special summer camps outside the parameters of the Pioneer movement. Such activities, and the relationships that grew from them, mitigated the otherwise strict regulation typical of Soviet schools.

Two mutually reinforcing indices highlight the elite nature of both schools: their near-perfect college placement record, which places them within the top tier of elite schools in the Soviet Union, and universal Komsomol membership. Joining the Komsomol simply was something one did to facilitate getting admitted into an institution of higher education, even if one had doubts about the official youth movement. Both markers also strengthen the case for studying this cohort of individuals, since they represent a highly articulate and influential element in society, whose views contributed to the sustainability—and erosion—of the system.

Given that, how successful were Soviet schools in bringing up the builders of communism? Designed to educate, as well as to inculcate values and to indoctrinate their pupils with belief in the advantages of communism, School No. 42 and No. 20 deserve top marks for preparing their charges to compete academically, and for teaching them English, given the restrictions and limitations of the Cold War. They instilled in their charges basic human values that would be appreciated in most societies. And they did so in a climate of heady optimism fueled by Soviet technological achievements, by elevated consumer expectations bolstered by palpable improvements in living standards, by an opening up to the outside world, and by Khrushchev's campaign to overtake America and his new *Party Program*. The latter revealed that delayed gratification—the promise of a radiant future—no longer was a viable option. That is why Khrushchev risked naming the year when the Soviet system would achieve true communism, and why Soviet propaganda told the Baby Boomers that theirs "will be the best, the most just, and the happiest society on earth." Despite the optimism of the era, these promises had a hollow ring to them. As the Russian writers the same age as the Baby Boomers Vail' and Genis put it, "Anyone could look out the window and see for themselves that so far everything was still the same: the broken bridge, queues for potatoes, drunks in the bars. Even the orthodox Communist understood that this landscape would not change radically in twenty years."[26]

As schoolchildren, some of the interviewees may not have doubted this, but they now had a unit of measurement they would use to gauge how well the Soviet system functioned. For some, misgivings appeared early, after the disappearance of bread and other essential items, especially in Saratov, which made a mockery of the ubiquitous propaganda extolling the virtues of communism whose achievement, Soviet citizens were told, was right around the corner. Economic difficulties, combined with Khrushchev's endless campaignism, growing personality cult, foreign-policy failures, and attacks on Party organs, turned public opinion against the First Secretary—but not the Soviet system— by the time his comrades ousted him in 1964. Many in Soviet society continued to appreciate Khrushchev's dismantling of the Stalin cult; however, others found his attack on Stalin disconcerting.[27] De-Stalinization affected the Baby Boomers directly in that history texts were revised before their very eyes. To counter any potentially negative fallout from this, the Communist Party increased the contact hours devoted to political indoctrination while they attended school. Slavic studies scholar Catriona Kelly concluded that, during these lessons, pupils heard about self sacrifice for the common good, but learned even more about how to bend the rules and that they could think whatever they wanted as long as they maintained outward decorum.[28] In retrospect, it seems clear that the government stepped up such measures because the message it wished to convey to the builders of communism had competition, some of which was nurtured by what they did in their free time.

3

"UNCONSCIOUS AGENTS OF CHANGE"
Soviet Childhood Creates the Cynical Generation

"For the most part, our family was an average Russian family of moderate means," explained Saratov's Aleksandr Virich. "We always had decent food; we went to the theater, to the movies, to the circus, and to whatever else that was of interest. We didn't differ from other average people of our time. We had a quiet, peaceful, happy childhood." Similarly, Moscow's Igor Litvin believed his childhood "was quite happy, and I see it today through rose-colored glasses." His classmate Lyubov Kovalyova called her childhood "a very good one, as I understand today. But I didn't doubt that even back then." True, according to state propaganda, a Soviet youngster *had* to have a happy childhood. Propaganda aside, the Baby Boomers' childhood did differ in qualitative ways from that of their parents, who were brought up during the cataclysmic Stalin years. By the 1960s, the emergence of the good life resulting from postwar recovery and peaceful, organic change placed a new accent on leisure activities and consumption in the Soviet Union. The Cold War generation's parents benefited from this development. So did their offspring, all of whom emphasized that they had a "normal," "happy," "exceptionally happy," even "wonderful" childhood.

Most of the Baby Boomers' families were well off by Soviet standards and some of them very much so. Vladimir Glebkin reminisced, "Back then the state supported science and my father was a talented and successful scholar. Therefore we didn't have any problems with our standard of living. For that reason my childhood was very happy, materially speaking." Yet others from both cities recalled that they had happy, but not necessarily materially abundant, childhoods. As Olga Gorelik recognized, "Our family had a full life, but that did not refer to furniture or material things. My father made sure there were always a lot of books at home; however, for the most part, everything else was difficult to get hold of." Yevgeny Podolsky reflected that "with the passing of time, we probably remember the good things and forget the bad. Hence, when you look at your childhood from the perspective of a fifty-year-old, you recall the good, although, in evaluating that life today, you see that it was very difficult. I see how my parents worked, how we lived. It was hard, because wages were low, and they worked a lot and worried about supporting our large family." Anatoly Shapiro shared that he had "some very sweet childhood memories, but we felt the lack of material things and money."

Despite the Baby Boomers' stable and comfortable childhood, many of them as adults realized that this formative period in their lives also bred cynicism that would develop more fully in the 1970s. This paradox involved not only material issues but also beliefs and attitudes nurtured by the Cold War generation's identification with a larger global youth culture.

"WE LIVED FOR RECESS AND FOR LIFE AFTER SCHOOL"

Childhood is the ultimate age of discovery. "Like all of the other kids," stated Moscow's Georgy Godzhello, "I had an enormous range of interests." "It's easier to tell you what I wasn't interested in," quipped Tatyana Artyomova. Saratov's Tatyana Kuznetsova pointed out that "sometimes these interests turned into professions." They did for Arkady Darchenko, whose childhood love of physics reflected the spirit of the time. "Right after I started to go to school, physics became my thing. Back then there was a cult of physics. I knew exactly what I wanted to become, and where I'd go to college already as a child," he recalled.

Yevgeny Podolsky observed how the ethos of the era defined how many youngsters spent their free time. "During my childhood years we were interested in space, space, and space. That's how it was." He took pride in the fact that Yury Gagarin, the first person to orbit the earth, had studied in Saratov and had completed his 1961 space flight by parachuting into a nearby field. Leonid Terlitsky remembered, "We had chess tournaments until we turned blue." And not surprisingly, since chess was also in the news: in 1960 Soviet citizen Mikhail Tal became the youngest international chess champion at age twenty. Other Soviet victors followed, including Boris Spassky, Viktor Korchnoi, and, later, Anatoly Karpov. "Many of us collected things," recounted Viktor Alekseyev and others. Larisa Petrova collected stamps, a hobby that became a "special passion" for Natalya Pronina. "At an early age," Mikhail Markovich began to play Preference, "a rather complicated card game." Akin to Bridge, the game became popular among the Cold War generation in both cities.

Most of the males mentioned being fascinated by electronics, model building, and photography. Interested in radios and electronics, Saratov's Aleksandr Kutin bragged that he "can fix a television even now." He also "became enamored with building model boats." Pyotor Krasilnikov became a radio buff, "probably owing to the influence of our physics teacher. It was back then that the first pocket transistor radios appeared, and my parents were pleased that I was at home and not running around somewhere on the streets," he remembered. Moscow's Vladimir Glebkin also developed a real passion for electronics and radios, which eventually fed into his professional interest in physics. His father bought him do-it-yourself kits. Even though Glebkin's first efforts to construct a receiver fell short, he successfully built a transistor radio and a tape recorder so that he could record the Beatles. Aleksandr Virich was partial to photography. "It was interesting and prestigious because, when you engaged in photography, you'd curry favor with the girls." Virich remembered the unofficial school newspaper the Saratov boys put out on March 8, International Women's Day, entitled *Our Girls Are Better than All the Others.* "It was huge, with tons of photographs." Because only a few families had automobiles at this time, the interviewees had nothing to say about cars except for Sergei Zemskov, whose Opal-owning grandfather taught Sergei how to rev up the engine.

Many female Baby Boomers loved theater, ballet, dancing, reading, hanging out with friends, and other pastimes, some of which, as in the case of the males, were gender specific. Larisa Petrova reasoned that her interests "were probably the same as most children. I loved to play with other kids." Olga Gorelik liked to read, draw, go to the movies, and spend time with her girlfriends. Natalya Yanichkina enthused, "Like all the girls, I wanted to become an actress and joined the school club." Irina Tsurkan remembered, "I wrote to all of our famous actresses. Some replied, others didn't. I became close friends with Natalya P. and we bought *Hamlet* and other plays and played theater at home." Olga Kamayurova enjoyed music and "played with kids my age on our street. Then there was the beach and trips to the country." Natalya Pronina's mother "insisted" that she learn how to embroider. "I finished my first piece of embroidery under threat of punishment. But I completed my second piece on my own free will, and because I wanted to," she claimed.

The Baby Boomers loved sports, in part owing to far-reaching media coverage of the USSR's victory in the 1956 Olympic Games in Melbourne, the second games in which the Soviet Union took part. Saratov's Pyotor Krasilnikov attended a sports club and remembered, "I especially liked volleyball, and then I boxed for a while with Gena Ivanov." Viktor D. recalled "constant participation in neighborhood, city, and oblast-wide competitions. I took first place in my neighborhood for skiing." When he broke his leg in the eighth grade and had to spend two months lying in a hospital bed in traction, his classmates and teachers tutored him "so that I didn't fall behind." Moscow male Baby Boomers "were fanatics about soccer. We played soccer after school practically every day. It was our main love," claimed Vyacheslav Starik. According to Saratov's Natalya Yanichkina, "the whole class loved basketball and organized tournaments." Olga Kolishchyuk and some of her classmates took up gymnastics. Then, she related, "We took up folk dancing. All of us loved to dance and, to uphold the school's honor, we performed in various competitions. We performed on a television show 'Dance with Us,' and our group won." Olga Kamayurova enjoyed different diversions in winter and summer: "In winter there was the skating rink, which we went to each day. It was like a narcotic. I couldn't get by without a fix.

In summer it was the beach and swimming." After the large outdoor pool opened in Luzhniki in Moscow, Yelena Kolosova frequented it. Marina Bakutina described her father as "a big adherent of a healthy life style regarding physical activity." As a result, after school Maria skied, skated, and swam competitively. "I remember that I was the only girl at school called a sportsman." This had a downside: "I spent a lot of time in the swimming pool at the expense of socializing with my fellow classmates," she regretted.

Tatyana Arzhanova voiced a common sentiment: "We lived for recess, and for life after school." Except in one regard: having grown up during hard times, the war generation lavished private lessons of all sorts on their children, even when they lacked interest or talent. Marina Bakutina spoke for many when she shared that "my parents gave me access to everything that you could possibly familiarize a child with." Olga Gorelik's parents made her take music lessons even though she "lacked any special interest" in it. Natalya Yanichkina had a similar experience "even though I had a tin ear. But, once again, you had to give a girl back then a good humanities education," she justified. Irina Vizgalova told me her parents sent her to a music school, "but it didn't work out." Olga Kamayurova took piano lessons, "but these ten years didn't elicit anything in me other than aversion," she admitted. "After I left home I never once sat down at the piano

By age ten Olga Martynkina already demonstrated real talent and interest in the piano, and eventually she left School No. 42 to enroll in a special music school. A graduate of the Saratov Conservatory, she is a pianist at the Saratov Theater of Ballet and Opera. *Courtesy of Olga Zaiko (Martynkina)*

bench." Natalya Pronina felt the same: "Papa believed that a child needed to know how to play an instrument. I wasn't very enamored with the idea. It requires a lot of diligence that's difficult to maintain." Apart from music lessons, Olga Martynkina's parents also sent her to ballet school. "Then they proposed that I go to a choreography school, because I showed some talent in this area."

The males complained, too, about music lessons, which had become a new rage in part owing to the extraordinary popularity of American pianist Van Cliburn, who won the Tchaikovsky International Piano Competition in Moscow in 1958, becoming the first foreign star on Soviet TV.[1] Gennady Ivanov groused, "I wasn't all that interested in music, but I took piano lessons when I was a kid. I can't say that it ever became a goal of mine or a lifetime hobby." Vladimir Nemchenko admitted that "I never fell in love with music, probably because I attended music school for four years. My parents made me." Because Kolya Khabarov attended music school, he could not walk home from school with his friends. Irina Kulikova reported, "I saw him coming, clutching a folder of music. I said to myself, 'Poor Kolka is going to music school.' But then we look and see that he's coming from the school, waving the folder. I said, 'Kol, what's wrong? What happened?' 'They kicked me out,' he said, with a grin on his face."

Natalya P. and others spotlighted the down side of their parents' good intentions. "For instance," she said, "I studied music since I was six years old. I studied ballet, music at the music school, and something else. And then I got sick. It had something to do with my heart. I was nine or ten." The doctor who examined her identified the problem: "'So, we have ballet, music, the English school. Figure skating has become popular, too. Maybe you'll enroll the girl there, too?' She added, 'She's simply tired.' So they dropped me from ballet [instead of music], which grieved me greatly, because I couldn't stand music." Moscow's Tatyana Arzhanova explained how her mother "transferred all of her unfulfilled desires, her striving to study music, to me." Despite the fact that Tatyana did poorly on the test to assess her musicality, her mother convinced the school to take her into the preparatory class. "Strange as it sounds," Arzhanova remembered, "in time I developed, or it manifested itself, perfect pitch." But, "it was a burden for me that I didn't think I needed." Besides, "all of my friends remember the music school because, owing to scheduling conflicts, they didn't let me attend birthday parties," she complained. Forced to take piano lessons, Yevgeniya Ruditskaya recalled "for the most part the piano drowned in my tears. For two years they tormented me, and then I quit."

The schools instilled and nurtured many of the Baby Boomers' interests by sponsoring clubs devoted to academic subjects—history, math, physics, English literature, and so on—as well as to sports and music and other enrichment activities such as photography and electronics. Many of them also joined clubs or took part in activities organized at Pioneer palaces. Lyudmila Gorokhova recounted that "somewhere around five or six o'clock I, without fail, went to some kind of club." She completed ballroom dancing classes and classes in gymnastics and acting. After school, Natalya Pronina took part in the literature club and in one for math. "Back in our time everyone could join as many as they'd like," she stated. Viktor D., for instance, joined volleyball, basketball, ping-pong, and handball clubs. As Pioneer leaders, Olga Kolishchyuk and others volunteered to work for the same teacher who had taught them in elementary school. "We'd come to her class, help her correct homework, and organize various things. And each year we put on performances such as Cinderella," related Olga. The Saratovites also had positive memories of the woodwind ensemble for boys and string orchestra for girls, directed by Stepan Ivanovich Lendyuk, a former military musician who, according to Viktor D., "loved to teach." Viktor enjoyed the band: "It gave me a great deal, because my family is not musical at all." The band took part in parades and other public functions. Aleksandr Ivanov mentioned that, apart from the band, there also was a folk instrument ensemble, in which he played the alto sax. Ivanov took part in the May Day celebrations and other events.

The Muscovites took advantage of their access to the country's best theaters. Mikhail Markovich remembered, "We went to the Taganka Theater. After the theater opened when we were in eighth grade [in 1964] we didn't miss a single premiere." Igor Litvin confirmed the craze over theater. "For example, there was the Theater of Satire, and my parents knew one of the actors. I saw practically all of the performances." Sofiya Vinogradova recalled that she "went to the Bolshoi Theater, and to all the others. To get tickets, we queued up at night and took numbers." In the upper grades she "went to see particular actors." It was not just the classics that drew her, but the plays "that they put on with difficulty." Marina Bakutina waxed nostalgic: "There was a period in my life when the Moscow Art Theater dominated. I remember I even collected programs." An impression was made on Anatoly Shapiro and others when Vladimir Prudkin's father, actor Mark Aleksandrovich, visited their school along with other well-known stage performers.

Apart from clubs and cultural activities, the Baby Boomers spent considerable leisure time, and in some regards came of age, in the courtyard (*dvor*) of the apartment building where they lived. Enthused Saratov's Irina Vizgalova: "We had a wonderful courtyard, and courtyard friends. Back then we all played together, not like today. The courtyard was closed in, and children of various ages came there to play together." Olga Gorelik remembered she "hung out there from morning until night," not only because her parents worked long hours but also because "the desire to hang out was enormous." Until she was five years old, Natalya Yolshina lived in an old home with a yard and "courtyard friends, boys and girls." When they moved into an apartment near the Volga, "there was also a courtyard, and kids from our courtyard and from the neighboring one played together," she reported. The names of the games they enjoyed are unfamiliar to us, but not how they were played. For instance, Aleksandr Virich volunteered "like all young lads, we ran around, hung out, played *Shtander* [Spud] and Cossacks and Robbers. And we fought." When they were younger, they played war, not Russians against Germans, but "ours vs. yours," according to Aleksandr Ivanov, "with sabers and water pistols."

Moscow's Igor Litvin explained that the building in which his family lived on Malaya Nikitskaya was "a special one, about which you could write a separate book," because a number of those from the *nomenklatura* lived there, including the son of writer Maxim Gorky. "When we got older and began to flirt, we came to the courtyard to do so." Litvin also commented how, each May, parents and their offspring cleaned the yard and planted flowerbeds. They set up a ping-pong table. In the winter they flooded the yard to make a skating rink. Children of all age groups hung out there. Today Litvin appreciated the practical side of things: "I understand that such an arrangement helped out parents who worked. They didn't have to look out after the children because there was a certain amount of self-organization. No one ever strayed from the courtyard. It was its own secluded world."

Many interviewees idealized the yard, but as Saratov's Aleksandr Trubnikov pointed out, "Where else could we play?" "The street had its own rules," he elaborated. "The building was packed with people. Several families inhabited each apartment, and all of them had lots of children, therefore the courtyard was packed with kids. The children grouped together by age. We played with each other, and fought with each other, all according to rules of the street." The mixed neighborhood in which he lived included young criminals who, according to Trubnikov, "smoked what today's called marijuana. But back then we called it *anash*, or hash. Marijuana grows everywhere. It's very widespread. They used to sell it for kopecks, and this meant that anyone could try it." Trubnikov was about eight years old when he first smoked pot. In Moscow Anatoly Shapiro remembered, "We smoked cigarettes [in the courtyard]. I began to smoke at age fourteen. We'd all gather there and smoke. We socialized. We didn't hit the bottle, well, we practically didn't drink." But Vladimir Sidelnikov, a recovering alcoholic, remembers it differently: "It all began, of course, in the courtyard."

"THE MAIN THING IS RELATIONSHIPS"

Friendship lacks a definition that works for all times, places, and peoples, because the phenomenon is a cultural and historical one that changes over time: the type of society determines the nature of friendships.[2] What was "Soviet" about the Cold War generation's friendships, as Russian émigré sociologist Vladimir Shlapentokh notes, was that friends served as critical sources of information, as substitutes for the mass media. They also played an economic role. They borrowed money from each other and devised ways to beat the system, to find a job, to place their children at work, survival strategies often intertwined with the second economy. They helped to determine how leisure time was spent.

In this regard a friendship could threaten a family's hold over someone by exposing that person to outside influences. Given the Stalinist legacy, friendship's most important virtue was trust: people regarded as friends only those whom they knew for a long time.[3]

Saratov's Aleksandr Konstantinov, who has lived in Moscow since his student days, expressed a common sentiment in saying that the friends he made at School No. 42 "are perhaps even closer than those I made at the university." His classmate Aleksandr Virich reminded me that, owing to the gender imbalance at school, he "considered all the boys who went to school with him" to be his friends. According to Pyotor Krasilnikov, "as we were growing up there were three or four groups. Our group began to smoke together, and then began to hit the bottle together." Vladimir Nemchenko, Aleksandr Trubnikov, and Valentin Bobrov became "an inseparable threesome" because they lived nearby and attended the same school. Later Trubnikov befriended Yevgeny Podolsky, who had nothing but positive things to say about Trubnikov, "who really looked out for me and who had a huge influence on me." Bonding at camp on the Volga, they studied together, often stayed at each other's homes, and prepared for college entrance exams together. They remain close today, despite Trubnikov's emigration to Israel. Olga Kamayurova befriended Nelya Yegorova, who now lives in Germany. Olga reported that she and Nelya "skipped school. We hid our briefcases in her attic among the potatoes and then rode to the outskirts of Saratov, where we hung out. Later I lied and said that I had been sick. I simply couldn't endure attending school for six days in a row each week."

Moscow's Tatyana Arzhanova hung out with a group of three or four other friends, with whom she remains close even today, despite the strains of separation caused by emigration. She recalled that they corresponded with each other when they attended different childhood summer camps. Igor Litvin credited his friends with shaping his worldview "because my entire childhood passed namely among my friends from school," who remain "special." Illustrating his point, he mentioned classmate Yakov Gluz, who immigrated to America in 1977. They have corresponded ever since, even though Litvin's father feared the consequences of Igor's writing to a Russian émigré in America. "But that was my condition for remaining in Russia," explained Litvin. "I said, 'I must correspond with him, because I can't believe I live in a prison.'" Viktor Alekseyev developed a lasting friendship with Igor Altshuller, who later emigrated to Holland. Far more critical of the Soviet system than Alekseyev, Altshuller's decision to emigrate after becoming disappointed in Gorbachev's reforms influenced Alekseyev's own decision to leave Russia. Altshuller later came to America after being diagnosed with cancer and when he died was living with Alekseyev.

But not everyone felt so fortunate when it came to making lifelong friends at school. Years after they graduated, Moscow's Tatyana Arzhanova encountered an

Vyacheslav Starik, Yury Seliverstov (deceased before I launched this oral history project), and Mark Milgotin became buddies as members of School No. 20's C Class. In the 1990s the Russian newspaper *Kommersant* alleged that Milgotin was one of the country's top ten mafia gangsters; today he is a successful businessman. *Courtesy of Vyacheslav Starik*

embittered classmate. Recalled Tatyana: "She got all upset remembering those who had offended her, although I never noticed it." Her classmate Vyacheslav Starik believed this had something to do with gender: "I can say with assurance that the boys' company was far more democratic, with far fewer class differences." Remarks made by some female Saratovites support Starik's point. Tatyana Kuznetsova observed that "there were a few of our classmates who kept a bit to themselves." Natalya Pronina, who enrolled in School No. 42 in the fifth grade, told me that "several of my classmates still consider me an outsider."

The Saratov B class in particular prides itself in remaining close even today, but not everyone felt or always felt so attached to the group. Olga Kamayurova and Irina Tsurkan began attending reunions and parties only recently. Until then they felt no need to do so. Admitted Kamayurova, "They sang songs they all knew, they reminisced, they recalled old teachers. Even now I don't have any nostalgia for my school years. I can't say, as they do, that our 'school years were wonderful.'" She related that, at a recent reunion, "one of our former classmates leaned over to me and said: 'I remember it all as a nightmare.' And I agreed with him." Irina Tsurkan felt similarly: "I was surprised when we finished school that our classmates wanted to get together. They did so regularly; however, I wasn't interested in how they lived or how things turned out for them. I was so satisfied with my own life. Then I found fulfillment professionally."

"WE READ AN AWFUL LOT"

The Soviet Union prided itself in being *the* "most reading" nation, especially this generation. Irina Chemodurova called reading "her single and main passion." "I learned how to read when I was five and still love to read," claimed Aleksandr Trubnikov. The male Saratovites cited as favorite authors Mark Twain, Alexander Dumas père, Jack London, Guy de Maupassant, Bret Hart, and Soviet writer Aleksei Tolstoy. These Western authors were available in the Soviet Union not only because they told a good story but also because they described racial prejudice or some other negative features of life abroad or, as in the case of Jack London, advocated socialism and workers' rights. Back then certain magazines became the rage. Vladimir Nemchenko remembered the anticipation he felt when either his father or grandfather subscribed to one of the Soviet Union's oldest weekly illustrated magazines, *Ogonyok* (Little Flame), because it introduced Soviet readers to foreign authors. Yevgeny Podolsky underscored the excitement of getting hold of popular literary journals such as *New World* and *Foreign Literature*, which his family subscribed to with difficulty. "There was a waiting list," he recalled, "and they gave out subscriptions with a catch, that is, if you wanted to receive a decent magazine you had to subscribe to four Party newspapers or magazines such as *Party Life*, which no one bought and no one read." *Foreign Literature* first published Walter Scott and other "children's things. But there were practically no contemporary [foreign] works published." Owing to the difficulty they had obtaining good books, "we traded books a lot and borrowed all the time from each other," shared Tatyana Kuznetsova. They also visited the library.

Reading conferred status. Moscow's Igor Litvin recalled that "during the winter, we'd congregate at the radiator in the stairway and tell each other about what we read. There was a science fiction series with Belyaev* and other writers, such as the Brit, H. G. Wells. We read few American authors at the time. Ray Bradbury and others came later. You'd be ashamed not to know something. If you didn't, you'd keep silent, run home and open a reference book so that the next day you'd be able to show that you knew." Mikhail Markovich concurred that "we read everything, read a lot, and shared our impressions." Tatyana Arzhanova pointed out that "back then it was very popular to buy the collected works of authors. Everyone had subscriptions. I especially remember the summer I spent in the country at an acquaintance's of my grandmother and mother. She had a huge library with collected works. I read all of Balzac that summer, and all of Jack London." Yelena Kolosova

---

* Widely read throughout the entire Soviet period, Aleksandr Belyaev was an immensely popular science-fiction writer known for his technological innovations and novels about biology.

remembered, "when I came home from school, I'd sit on the floor in front of the bookshelf in my parents' room, from which would fall out either Irving Shaw's *Young Lions** or something else, and I'd simply lose myself in it. That's how all of Hemingway got read." Vladimir Bystrov liked Jack London, science fiction, "and Hemingway, O'Henry, and Sidney Porter." Dostoyevsky had a profound effect on Georgy Godzhello. He also liked Jules Verne, Sir Arthur Conon Doyle, Jack London, and Hemingway. Two volumes of the latter's writings were translated into Russian in 1959, in part because of his support for the Cuban Revolution.[4]

At school the Baby Boomers were raised on the same Stalinist literary canon as their parents; however, it began to broaden as the Soviet Union opened up. They did not take the advice of their Pioneer handbook, which urged them to read books on Lenin, Soviet power, Khrushchev's Seven-Year Plan, and Pioneer heroes.[5] As Irina Vizgalova remarked, "I read a great, great deal, and of course not about the subjects they recommended at school, but others." The Muscovites had an easier time getting hold of rare, foreign, and even illegal items. Explained Leonid Terlitsky: "You couldn't go to the library and pick up a book printed in a foreign language unless the book had been approved. I started reading English early on because one of the kids in school whose father was also a musician began to travel even before my parents' orchestra because he played in the Bolshoi Orchestra." He put together a fairly decent library of books in English. "It wasn't much, but there were a couple of shelves of books of various kinds, from James Bond to whatever, and they were loaned out," remembered Terlitsky.

Vladimir Prudkin remembered—correctly—that there was a short period in the 1960s when the authorities began to issue "books that before then could not have been published in Russia. They began to publish Bulgakov. Kafka suddenly appeared and books by Kierkegaard. Then this ended." A Soviet writer who fell out of favor with the Stalinist regime before he died in 1940, Mikhail Bulgakov, became something of a cult figure among elements of the intelligentsia when his internationally acclaimed novel, *Master and Margarita*, was first published in the USSR in sanitized form at this time. Woven around the premise of the Devil's visit to the atheist Soviet Union, the novel deals with Pontius Pilate's sealing of Christ's fate. The Moscow Baby Boomers found *Master and Margarita* a milestone in their young lives, but no one in Saratov mentioned it, ostensibly because it was harder to come by in the provinces and not something local teachers felt comfortable teaching. Recounted Viktor Alekseyev: "It was really popular at school, as reading outside of class. We discussed it among ourselves and quoted from *Master and Margarita*, pages of which we knew by heart. I remembered entire passages." Tatyana Arzhanova read Bulgakov in the tenth grade. *Master and Margarita* "was a real event, a real shock." She explained why: "We never

---

* Born Irwin Gilbert Shamforoff in New York to Jewish immigrants from Russia, Irving Shaw became an accomplished playwright, screenwriter, and author of international bestsellers, most notably *The Young Lions* (1948), one of the most popular World War II novels.

knew anything about the Bible. We read the myths and legends of ancient Greece and Rome. Maybe in families more intellectual than mine they read the Bible as a source of culture and art, but that came later for me. The first revelation in that regard was *Master and Margarita*."

The publication in 1962 of Solzhenitsyn's literary bombshell, *One Day in the Life of Ivan Denisovich*, also created a euphoria among Soviet readers, because the story destroyed the illusion anyone might have harbored that some prisoners had languished in Stalin's labor camps for a valid reason, "We read it," remembered Muscovite Viktor Alekseyev, "and what's more, our teacher Nina Ivanovna included it in the school program. We even wrote a composition about it in the upper classes." Lyubov Kovalyova "liked it a lot." But not all three classes read it in school, and not everyone liked it. Sergei Zemskov related, "Back then I didn't read it. My mother read it, and everyone else read it." When Zemskov later read the novella, he reacted negatively to it: "Time and again, I caught some tampering of facts, some lies. Then you don't believe the rest of it."

The Saratovites read Solzhenitsyn's novella, but not as part of the school curriculum. Natalya Pronina read it back at the settlement in Siberia, where her family lived before moving to Saratov, and disliked it: "It's not worth talking about, but he has a lot wrong in the novella. He editorializes a great deal, and subjectively, in each of his works." Yet reading the work transformed others. Irina Chemodurova boasted that "I still have the first edition of *One Day*. I had to read it." Aleksandr Babushkin remembered that "it made a shocking impression. It opened our eyes," but "when it was at its peak in Moscow, it was greatly limited here." Yevgeny Podolsky and others devoured it in college. "I read it during a lecture my freshman year. I was shaken, of course."

"I SOMEHOW UNDERSTOOD THIS ALL BY MYSELF"

The circulation and reading of "self-published" forbidden works (*samizdat*), usually typed with multiple carbon copies, or of these works published abroad and smuggled into the Soviet Union (*tamizdat*), became widespread among the Soviet intelligentsia about the time the Baby Boomers enrolled in college. Yet some were already exposed to samizdat during the upper grades at school. The phenomenon was far less pervasive in Saratov than in Moscow. Only one Saratovite, Yevgeny Podolsky, averred that "lots of *samizdat* circulated" and that he read it "already in the upper grades at school." Moscow's Vladimir Glebkin recalled that Bakhyt Kenzheyev and Vladimir Prudkin were the main sources of information about *samizdat*. Prudkin confirmed this. Whether or not the Baby Boomers read *samizdat* at that time had much to do with their parents. Lyubov Raitman's parents got their hands on rare volumes of poetry by Russian masters Boris Pasternak, Osip Mandelshtam, Marina Tsetayeva, and Anna Akhmatova, all unavailable for sale. She read them with great interest in her mid-teens, eager to share her impressions with her closest girlfriend: "I wondered whether I should or not. I nonetheless told her. I wanted to give her the books, but didn't know if I should or not. I eventually gave them to her." She likewise recalled when her parents' friends brought over Solzhenitsyn's works. "There were evenings when people sat at our round table with thin sheets of cigarette paper on which typists reprinted Solzhenitsyn's novels. They circulated them. And some people read faster than others, who held up the flow of these pages. I remember that we read *Cancer Ward*. I really wanted to tell my closest girlfriends about this, but I knew not to. I somehow understood this all by myself." She added, "I knew, and can't recall just how or explain whether they said to me not to tell my friends at school things I heard at home when my parents' friends discussed politics. I didn't do that, and it was as if it were normal."

Raitman's intuitive sense of caution was something instilled in the Baby Boomers at home already during their early years. Saratov's Aleksandr Konstantinov explained that "there were things about which it was better not to speak. This was clear to us already in school." Leonid Terlitsky recalled that "it was sort of a taboo—any criticism of the government, don't talk about it outside the house. That was the rule, although there were pretty vivid discussions about it around the family table." According to Vladimir Mikoyan, "the spirit of caution was inherent practically in everyone. It was the general atmosphere. People knew where and how best to express their opinions. It was impossible to completely stifle the expression of one's own opinion." Yelena Zharovova described how "at home it was customary for us neither to believe in the printed word nor, for that matter, what we heard over the radio." How did she learn how to read between the lines? "It was in the air. I can't even tell you, people simply doubted everything they read. And once you got the general picture, whenever they sharply criticized something, you'd look closely at it to see how things really are," she said. "If there was outside information, you could judge things for yourself, but if there wasn't, then we'd more likely think that things were the opposite of what was written."

This built-in caution made an act of school-age defiance even more remarkable. Some of the Muscovites emulated the *samizdat* phenomenon by secretly cobbling together an issue of their own class *samizdat* magazine, comprised of their poems and drawings about life at school. Vladimir Glebkin remembered "that there was a great deal of commotion. Somehow it reached school officials and they searched almost everyone, but didn't find the magazine. It existed—I held it in my hands—but it somehow vanished in thin air." Leonid Terlitsky designed the magazine cover. Emphasizing that it was "funny stuff" with "nothing really political about it," he nonetheless ascribed importance to the endeavor: "The fact that we engaged in this outside of official channels was in itself an act of dissidence of sorts, because those were the days when a good typewriter would be put under lock and key, let alone a Xerox machine, and it was that technology that really finished off the Soviet Union. It started with the tape recorder, then it went through the VCR phase, and it ended up with the Xerox machine and with the Internet."

"EACH FILM WAS AN EVENT"

Apart from family, school, the general ideological climate, and books, Saratov's Gennady Ivanov saw film as a key factor that shaped his worldview. Although the number of television sets grew significantly at the time, programming remained limited. Cinema remained far more influential than television,[6] which became the primary venue for high culture. New films got noticed. For instance, Viktor D. recalled *Amphibian Man* in 1962, which "was released all at once in practically all of the movie theaters in town. Back then there were about fifty of them. And all of them were packed." The film sold 65.5 million tickets in 1962, becoming the most popular Soviet movie of the year.[7] "For the most part movie going meant a great deal in our lives. Television appeared only later, when I was in fifth grade," remembered Saratov's Olga Gorelik. "All of our films, Soviet films, were in fact good, even the comedies and musicals. We liked all of our films and would go to see each three or four times." Gorelik thought the entire class went to see the Czechoslovak film, *Lemonade Joe* (1964), and that all of her classmates liked *Quiet Flows the Don*, which she called "a classic." Aleksandr Ivanov loved patriotic movies about war and Soviet agents because "our soldiers were always victorious." Arkady Darchenko credited his interest in physics with seeing *Nine Days of One Year*, about physicists and scientists. Released in 1962, the film was the number one choice of respondents to a survey carried out in the early 1960s of favorite films.[8] The girls in his class, he added, "loved *War and Peace*. But the Soviet film *Hamlet* made the same impression on everyone. Here's a film that probably everyone in the class loved, even though we were only in eighth or ninth grade." Like all "normal kids," Aleksandr Virich and his classmates frequented the cinema. And, like all normal kids, they sometimes cut school to do so, because when they attended a matinee, they paid only ten kopecks, instead of the usual thirty to fifty kopecks, depending upon the location of the seats.

Western films proved far more popular than Soviet movies.[9] Although the government controlled which films reached Soviet audiences, mostly selecting foreign movies that presented the capitalist world negatively, this approach backfired, for viewers saw what they wanted to see. Even experimental films coming out of Eastern Europe, especially from Poland, Czechoslovakia, and Hungary, could present the authorities with a dilemma. Take the example of the 1964 Czechoslovak film *Lemonade Joe* by Oldrich Lipsky. Part of a Czech New Wave series, the film was a parody of an American western that featured a Kolaloka [Coca-Cola]-drinking hero. The film's lighthearted anticapitalist message did not sit well with Moscow censors, who decided that Soviet viewers missed the parody. The censors shut it down after two weeks. Saratov's Tatyana Kuznetsova remembered that "the entire class wanted to see it really badly so we cut our classes."

Soviet viewers eagerly fell into line to see American films, even when some were shown without subtitles. *Gentlemen Prefer Blondes* (1953), starring Marilyn Monroe as the stereotypical gold-digging dumb blonde, proved to be a huge hit in the Soviet Union. Lyudmila Gorokhova gushed, "The film simply stunned me, and it remains my favorite film ever since." *Gentlemen Prefer Blondes* ranked high on Viktor D.'s list of favorite films, too. Gorokhova also detailed her interest in *McKenna's Gold* (1969), starring Gregory Peck, Omar Sharif, and Julie Newmar. The film features how the lure of gold corrupts all sorts of people and is alive with violence, chase scenes, conniving criminals, and Apache Indians bent on keeping the gold out of the hands of their enemies. Gorokhova loved the movie "because of its unusual ending," which involves Apache spirits bringing down the walls of the canyon on top of the gold to prevent the fortune from falling into the hands of greedy outsiders. Gorokhova's assessment of these films suggests how misguided the government's efforts proved to be: "They bought a lot of American films. But they bought those that were cheery, witty, and gave you something to think about."

The Muscovites also became animated when I asked about favorite films. Teacher Roman Kaplan made an abiding impression on Marina Bakutina when he regaled the class with descriptions of the foreign films he had enjoyed at closed showings. She especially remembered his passion for the 1966 French film *Man and Woman* directed by Claude Lelouch. "It was like forbidden fruit, which later was released for mass consumption." Igor Litvin rattled off the names of the movie theaters he attended regularly: Flame, Art, and Barricade. "We went there all the time, and we saw all of the new films that were released." Litvin added that "in our childhood we saw all of the Chapaev movies [about a Soviet Civil War hero] and *Striped Trip*," the most popular film of 1961, which Litvin "went to see a hundred times. And *Paris Secret* [1964] with Jean Mare. I was amazed that when American children visited they didn't know Jean Mare." Later, Litvin went to the House of Architects, House of Films, House of Literary Men, and House of Culture opened by the All Union Theatrical Society, which became "hotbeds of culture" because they showed otherwise prohibited films not available for mass consumption. There were "showings of the first films of Tarkovsky*, showings of the first American films," especially westerns. Vladimir Bystrov singled out *The Magnificent Seven* (1960), starring Yul Brynner, Steve McQueen, and Charles Bronson, which took the country by storm. "It was a shock, simply a shock back then, because it was so different. The genre of the western was, of course, quite interesting for us boys. I saw it seven times."

The Muscovites appreciated Soviet classics from the 1950s and 1960s as well. Anatoly Shapiro recalled that "back then there were many wonderful movies such as *The Cranes Are Flying* (1957)," a Thaw-era production documenting the cruelty and psychological damage wrought by World War II. Yelena Kolosova

---

* Andrei Arsenyevich Tarkovsky won international acclaim for his early films *Ivan's Childhood* and *Andrei Rublev*, and was highly regarded among the Soviet intelligentsia. Although he produced less than a dozen films, each turned out to be a major cultural event.

told me, "We were a bit too young when they released Kalatozov's *The Cranes Are Flying*, but old enough for *Ballad of a Soldier* [1959, another international Soviet hit, this one about love during war]. I recall that entire episode with [Marlen] Khutsiev's movie *I'm Twenty Years Old* [1964]." Kolosova had in mind the corrections and cuts censors forced the director to make to the original film, shot in 1961. The significance of state interference was not lost on her: "That is, it was part of the growth of our public awareness as a member of society, because each time, as always in Russia, it's some sort of political event." She mentioned the films of the most cerebral of Soviet directors at the time, Tarkovsky, whose *Andrei Rublev* brought him international acclaim. "The volume of film releases in the Soviet Union cannot be compared with that of Hollywood but, on the other hand, each film was an event. And like very many things in Russia such as publications in *New World*, it was always something that you simply had to see. Everyone had to, not only so that you could take part in conversations but also because they really were worth seeing."

"IT WAS DIFFICULT TO GET HOLD OF THINGS"

During the Baby Boomers' childhood the appearance of stylish clothing—and the desire to acquire it—represented but one element of the emergence of Soviet mass culture at the time. The Soviet government fueled interest in fashion but sought to control tastes. It produced more shoes and new synthetic fabrics. It allowed French and Italian film festivals that familiarized viewers with foreign styles.[10] It introduced the permanent wave. Soviet newspapers and magazines began to write about fashion, hairstyles, cosmetics, perfume, and other topics of interest to women, encouraging them to pay more attention to physical attractiveness. For example, the issue of *Ogonyok* published on International Women's Day in 1960 spotlighted perfumes, now made accessible thanks to the expanding Soviet chemical industry that no longer needed precious oils.[11] Disputes over fashion at the time reflected an emerging public opinion mediated by literature and journalism.[12] As the Soviet Union opened, ideas of fashion circulated, often clashing with older notions and creating demands for hard-to-come-by items of clothing. *Clothes for Young People*, a booklet published by the government in 1959, decried the "imitation of the worst traditions in foreign fashion" and "making a show of originality." The *stilyagi*, who wore tights suits and short skirts, became a target of official ridicule from the late 1940s into the 1960s, because the government saw their fascination with American jazz and "glaring costumes" as behavior unbecoming the ideal Soviet youth. "Young people, in short, should be dressed as miniature adults."[13] An advice book opined that "the intelligent, cultured person doesn't wish to look like a *stilyag*" and instead wears cleans shoes, is tactful, and doesn't talk with his hands or "spit over his shoulder while talking."[14]

Saratov's Arkady Darchenko remembered that "back then, toward the end of our school years, tight pants were the rage, and jackets with padded shoulders, but we weren't allowed to [wear them]. Our school principal was a mini-Stalin who dictated what we could wear." But she had less control over what her charges wore once they left school. Aleksandr Virich recalled that in ninth grade Aleksandr Konstantinov was the first to wear a dark jacket with shoulder pads. "As soon as he turned the corner, he changed into a handsome dark suit with a white shirt and tie." Darchenko concurred that "of course, people wanted to be fashionable, but it was difficult to get hold of such things. It was impossible to buy them, and we needed to 'get hold of' them. The meaning of the verb 'get hold of' is probably uniquely Russian," he explained, because it means acquiring something with great difficulty. "Various fads passed through. Jeans, for example, but they came later. Probably at the university; we also had to 'get hold of' jeans." As Pyotor Krasilnikov explained, his family's limited financial resources made it hard for him to "get hold of" things. "I was satisfied with whatever my parents were able to buy me from time to time. I knew that I'd not be able to buy name-brand jeans."

The Saratovites fought an uphill battle in trying to dress stylishly, owing to the school uniform and to Vera Filippovna's culture war. Irina Chemodurova grumbled that the girls could not paint their fingernails or wear makeup or nylon stockings until graduation night. "And until ninth grade we weren't

The Baby Boomers' families went to great efforts to assure that they would be dressed stylishly on graduation night, June 22, 1967. Because the event was popularly viewed as the end of childhood, the graduates could now bend the rules and sport adult clothing and hairdos as this photo of Saratov's B class suggests. *Courtesy of Aleksandr Virich*

allowed to wear wristwatches." "And no perfume," added Irina Kulikova. Natalya Pronina griped that the girls had to wear their hair "combed back, with two small braids, or into a ponytail with large bows." Instead, the girls liked to "wear their hair teased back. It looked terrible." Galina Poldyaeva concurred that "those who had long hair had beehives. It was awful." Irina Kulikova reiterated that she and others had run-ins with Vera Filippovna when they tried to wear such hairdos to school. Poldyaeva related that, when those receiving graduation medals for their academic performance went to be photographed, Vera Filippovna rescheduled the session, making the girls return in braids.

The sewing skills girls learned at school expanded their clothing choices. "Practically any girl in our class could make herself a dress," claimed Olga Gorelik. "We even had something of a competition." They took each other's measurements, bought inexpensive material, and sewed outfits that they modeled at home fashion shows, "just like on television." They did this, noted Gorelik, because the Soviet consumer industry gave stylish clothing a low priority. "Therefore the girls, especially in the upper grades, sewed for themselves to have something to wear at parties." Olga Kolishchyuk remarked that "all of us loved clothes and tried to dress according to the fashions available to us. If it was the fashion to let our hems out, we let them out. If the fashion was to wear something else, we wore something else." Kolishchyuk acknowledged her mother's influence. "By Saratov standards, she was always a very fashionable woman and always dressed with good taste." Olga Gorelik also credited television with broadening her fashion consciousness. "Slowly a certain taste was formed. And, later, when we were at the university, all the girls wanted to dress in a contemporary way." It was then that mini-skirts appeared.

The Muscovites had more options available to them: the local dress code was more lax, some of their parents traveled abroad or knew people who did, and Moscow attracted foreign visitors who dressed differently. Leonid Volodarsky believed he "was the first to have a pair of jeans in school, and that was in 1967. One of my father's friends brought them from abroad." Igor Litvin became aware of foreign-made products when he went ice skating and saw that someone had "imported skates from Canada or somewhere. I understood already in the ninth grade that there was a distinction. Jeans appeared. The first Beatles tapes appeared. Someone had the first tape recorder." Yet even these comparatively privileged youth had limited choices. Moreover, not everyone cared about clothes: Mikhail Markovich claimed "we didn't pay any attention whatsoever to clothing, and that carried over to college." When they attended camp or lived at the dacha, "we'd wear sweat suits and Keds." Graduation appears to have been a rite of passage: "I remember that they bought me my first real English-style suit for graduation night. My father gave me a watch when I enrolled in college."

"THESE WERE FAR LESS SERIOUS SINS"

The Soviet Union deserved high marks not only for how much its citizens read but also for how much they drank. Drinking was so embedded in everyday life that popular attitudes on teenage drinking and related vices remained lenient. "Of course, we drank and smoked," confessed Saratov's Aleksandr Trubnikov. "These were far less serious sins than listening to Western music. They were simply incomparable. Drinking was always considered normal in Russia." At home, Aleksandr Virich's parents allowed him to have a glass of wine and, by the time he was in tenth grade, vodka. Vladimir Nemchenko owned up that, when he got together with his friends, Vovka (Vladimir) Kirsanov, Sasha (Aleksandr) Trubnikov, and Valka (Valentin) Koloskov, they often downed a few bottles of wine. Nemchenko opined that "alcohol is a pernicious thing because it imperceptibly takes over." (It did in Koloskov's case. After losing his license to practice medicine, he worked at a construction site. "They found him beaten to a pulp, with a broken skull," lamented Nemchenko.) Moscow's Leonid Terlitsky recounted that "we would skip classes, go out, and drink a beer. In later years we would drink into oblivion, anything with an alcoholic content." By the time he was in eighth grade, Vladimir Sidelnikov and Mark Milgotin drank heavily. Acknowledged Sidelnikov: "We drank like Russians. That's what I did in my free time. I also studied, but in all honesty I'm amazed that my brain endured it." Although drinking remained primarily a male pastime, Saratov's Tatyana Kuznetsova recalled that "there were two or three girls in the class who gave themselves permission in the tenth grade to try it."

Just about the entire group tried smoking. Some became addicted, but most never let smoking become a habit or else managed to quit after becoming aware of health risks as adults. Still puffing away today, despite having suffered a stroke, Aleksandr Virich came clean that he "began to smoke in the tenth grade on New Year's. Before then," he "just smoked a little." Growing up in a family of smokers, Moscow's Yelena Kolosova first lit up when she was fourteen, but did not like how it made her feel. She tried it on and off when she was in her early twenties, but "it never grew into a habit."

The Saratovites detailed the coed parties some of their classmates threw at home, which may have been more common there, because the city lacked the amenities of Moscow. According to Irina Kulikova, "we got together for the first time in ninth grade at Lenka Kovalkova's, whose parents left. My grandmother called: 'I'll come to chaperone.' She was the only one with us. It was wonderful. There was no getting drunk, no smoking, nothing. There was soda pop, food, and dancing. From nine at night until morning." Although no one admitted to excessive drinking, Irina Garzanova remembered that "from the eighth grade the boys already hit the bottle. They began with wine, then switched to something harder." Natalya Pronina got together with her classmates from the A class at Vera Miachinskaya's place on holidays. Natalya admitted that the girls drank alcohol, too: "It was a large group. Six girls and six boys. Just as it was supposed to be at that age. We played records. There was a Victrola and a piano. Sometimes we played popular songs, simple things with banal lyrics. We ate, drank alcohol, and danced and danced and danced. And there were some teenage romances, too." In describing how they celebrated birthdays and New Year's, Larisa Petrova perhaps summed things up best: "There were no excesses. I recall this today and am amazed. Some of the boys liked to get a little tipsy, but there were no drunks lying under the table, no fights, no crude sex."

Drinking and smoking may have been more culturally acceptable than listening and dancing to Western music, but the Baby Boomers felt the appeal of international youth culture. Tatyana Arzhanova explained how young people learned about dances that were the rage in the West. Tatyana Soboleva joined their class in the sixth grade after she and her parents returned from Paris. "She brought a dance with her, either the Twist or the Shake and she showed us how to do it." Mikhail Markovich mentioned that "there were dances when we were in the upper grades," and that some of his classmates formed musical ensembles. The Beatles served as a special inspiration. Galina Poldyaeva told me that, in Saratov, "we got interested first in the Twist, and then the Charleston. Sasha Konstantinov taught us how to dance the Charleston, and he and I danced together." "The boogie-woogie and Twist were banned," Aleksandr Virich reminded me. "How did we get out of this situation?" At Aleksandr Konstantinov's suggestion, they studied ballroom dancing at the local Pioneer Palace. "All of us danced the waltz, tango, 'a gentlemen's selection.' We learned several especially well in order to open school dances." Virich recounted how pleased the teachers were at first: "Konstantinov, Darchenko, and I danced with all of the girls and teachers." Playing the same waltz music over and over soon bored the teachers, who left the pupils to their own devices. "We plugged in a tape recorder brought from home, turned off the waltz, and put on the boogie-woogie. Forty minutes passed. After that, when word spread, the teachers returned upstairs." But they had someone standing guard, who sounded the alarm. "We turned the waltz back on, the boogie-woogie off, and returned to dancing the waltz. That's how we got out of the situation," remembered Virich.

"I STILL HAVE THE BEATLES' GREATEST HITS"

On graduation night, the B class at Saratov's School 42 sang, in English, "Sixteen Tons," the battle cry of the (exploited) American miner, made popular by Tennessee Ernie Ford. But if it had been up to them, they would have performed a Beatles song. One thing that all of them—in both cities—agreed on is their love of the Beatles, whose music, in part, became accessible with the state's mass production of tape recorders. As Saratov's Aleksandr Virich recalled, "Our family bought a tape recorder and I wanted to tape everything," especially the Beatles. "It's impossible not to love the Beatles. Not only because they were banned here in Russia. I think the whole world loved them." Larisa Petrova remembered that the "Beatles reached us in 1966. We could understand them, ever the more so because we attended an English school." Beatlemania overwhelmed Yevgeny Podolsky: "I worship them even today, my entire generation does. They banned them, but forbidden fruit is always sweet. Then the dissemination of tapes began. It turned out that there, in the West, they don't live so badly after all and they sing well. This was a very significant moment."

Shortages stimulated unusual forms of resourcefulness in the Soviet Union. To meet the profound demand for Beatles music made popular by foreign radio broadcasts, black marketers and other enterprising sorts made their own primitive 78-rpm recordings on used chest X-ray films. Although the Soviet government declared the X-ray phenomenon illegal and the Komsomol formed music patrols to curtail their production, millions of "records" continued to be made and distributed this way. According to Viktor D., "you'd listen to them three times, and naturally the emulsion would rub off and erase the recording. Nonetheless, the Beatles made a huge impression on everyone." "It was 1965, I think, when they brought me the Beatles on the sly," recalled Natalya Pronina. "I first heard them on recordings made from used chest X-rays that showed people's ribs." Years later, when they were no longer banned she heard them on television. "I was sometimes amazed at how clear they sounded. Even the words were comprehensible."

The problem of "getting hold" of tapes and crude recordings of the Beatles made listening to them difficult. "They didn't jam them, but for all intents and purposes what we listened to was the tenth copy on a tape recorder," noted Aleksandr Trubnikov. Official attitudes toward the Beatles, as well as the predispositions of many parents, likewise complicated listening to Western groups. Trubnikov volunteered that "all of this was for all intents and purposes banned. If they had caught us with a copy of a tape, say, of the Beatles at a school party, we would have gotten in deep trouble." Vladimir Kirsanov remembered how much the Beatles upset the father of one of his classmates: "'How can this be? It's disgraceful! What in the hell is this?'" His own father "was amazed that you could listen to classical music and then, all of a sudden, have some Western tapes with some scoundrels' songs, recorded somewhere in underground studios on X-rays." Yet Natalya Yolshina clarified that listening to illicit recordings "didn't have any hostile or political undertone. Rather, it was simply a bit of youthful rebellion." She emphasized that "there were no political discussions on the subject, nothing at all like that." The fact that "forbidden" music had to be obtained on the sly just made it another hard-to-get commodity. "This was the Cold War, and I thought this was normal."

Some tried to emulate the Beatles. According to Galina Poldyaeva, Pyotor Krasilnikov "played the guitar very well and had a great voice." As a result, "we knew the Beatles and the Rolling Stones and all of the hits from those times." But the Beatles reigned supreme. Concluded Arkady Darchenko: "I don't know anyone from our generation who doesn't love the Beatles. Even now, I still have the Beatles greatest hits."

The Beatles and other Western music and trends were easier to come by in Moscow. As Leonid Terlitsky explained, "My first exposure to the Beatles—and the Beatles were gods for us—happened because one of my classmates brought in, I think it was 'A Hard Day's Night,' or even before that, 'Meet the Beatles.' Not only that, his parents went to the West and brought back the records and a couple of John Lennon buttons and Paul McCartney pins." Terlitsky added that "we'd all get together and play the record on a good Phillips player in someone's house while we were playing a Russian version of Bridge."

Mikhail Markovich believed that School No. 20 had the first Beatles group in Moscow, thanks to Tanya Marchenko, whose father worked in the Soviet embassy in London. "She returned to school with the first 45-minute cassette of the Beatles, which they played during breaks between classes. A Beatles group appeared at school, comprising kids who had been playing for some time. Volodya [Vladimir] Glebkin played the bass guitar." Lyubov Raitman stressed that studying English made the Beatles especially appealing. "We listened to songs and deciphered and learned the words." Andrei Rogatnev became a Beatles fan in 1962, when he and Glebkin formed a beat-group. Rogatnev emphasized the importance of foreign radio broadcasts. "We caught the BBC wave through

As young teens in Moscow, Andrei Rogatnev and Vladimir Glebkin performed Beatles music at school. This would have been impossible in Saratov, a fact demonstrating yet another difference between "open" Moscow and "closed" Saratov. *Courtesy of Vyacheslav Starik*

the interference. We caught it and tried to copy it onto a tape recorder through the crackling and din of the jamming. We jotted down the words as we understood them. After all, it was very hard to understand." Rogatnev's examples drive home the point: "Was it 'yesterday' or 'yes today'? Take 'Michelle,' for instance. Michelle was perhaps 'me shall.' After all, if we say 'I will,' then perhaps we could say 'me shall'? Why not? These were the discussions we had." Rogatnev remembered performing the Beatles in the ninth grade to a group of visiting school-age kids from Britain, something that never would have been allowed in Saratov. His parents placed no restrictions on him. "And it wasn't only my parents who were so good. I think it was the same with all the kids." Indeed, at school, Rogatnev and Vladimir Glebkin spent a lot of time broadcasting in the school's well-equipped radio center. "And at the same time we made copies of the Beatles and Rolling Stones," boasted Rogatnev. Today, Glebkin believes that his love for the Beatles was a natural reaction to the government's attempt to impose its own tastes on young people. As a result, "the Beatles and all of Western culture penetrated very deeply among young people."

"WE GREW UP LISTENING TO THESE SONGS"

The Khrushchev era saw a resurgence not only of what has been called Soviet "mass song," with its optimistic gloss, but also of the elusive genre of pop. According to Irina Chemodurova, "the majority of us were keen on variety show music when tape recorders first appeared in 1961 or 1962. They were enormous, with huge knobs. Naturally, some of the kids had them, those who had more access." But soon the so-called poet bards took the country by storm. In the 1960s Aleksandr Galich, Bulat Okudzhava, Vladimir Vysotsky, and others began crooning their songs to their own solo accompaniment on the seven-stringed guitar. Circulating on privately recorded tapes, guitar poetry represented the most widespread form of unofficial popular and perhaps even antigovernment culture at the time. Viktor D. recalled that "sometime around the sixth grade the entire class fell for Okudzhava at the suggestion of Seryozha Arkhangelsky. I think he was the first to bring tapes of Okudzhava to school." Okudzhava visited Saratov when the Baby Boomers were in the tenth grade, giving two concerts but not the scheduled third one. "Something happened," remembered Larisa Petrova. "He smoked on stage and threw his cigarette butts. I later heard that it was seen as a scornful attitude toward those in the audience. And a cigarette hit someone in the front row. That was enough for the authorities." Arkady Darchenko and others learned the songs at summer camp, on the Volga. "Several guys in the group played the guitar really well. They sang Okudzhava. Vysotsky was just making his debut. When we first heard his songs we didn't know whose they were, but we liked them enormously and all of us sang them. Each night," he continued, "when it began to grow dark, we gathered around the campfires on the riverbank and sang until two in the morning. We grew up listening to these songs, to these poet bards."

Moscow's Mikhail Markovich confirmed that "everyone sang all of those songs at campfires in the 1960s, Vysotsky, Galich. And it was fun." Viktor Alekseyev never became a fanatic about them, but he admitted, "I liked them. It seemed to me that they expressed nontypical feelings that were in opposition to official poetry and literature. The bards were very, very appealing people."

Vysotsky, especially, became something of a Soviet cult figure. His tough-guy songs represented an attractive alternative to official sanitized culture, because his lyrics dealt with life in the raw, with topics such as prison life, crime, the unheroic aspects of war, sex, drinking, cramped living quarters, and food lines. Vysotsky was also an acclaimed actor at Moscow's trendy Taganka Theater and appeared in Charles Bronson-like roles in movies. Sustained gossip about his counterculture life style added immensely to the officially decried Vysotsky cult. Vysotsky touched something vital in Viktor D.: "At that time he was one of the few who understood the human soul, who could express in a satirical, poetic form repressed feelings, the aspirations of the majority." Natalya Pronina agreed that Vysotsky's songs struck a respon-sive chord and explained why they sometimes offended the authorities: "The song 'And All Is Quiet in the Cemetery' has lyrics such as everything was as quiet as could be and as proper as could be. And although there's nothing at all in the song that makes an analogy to the country at large, that's exactly how we understood it. That it's like a cemetery, see? We young people under-stood this as a political song."

"WE REACHED THE AGE, AND ROMANCES BEGAN"

Under Stalin, sexuality was so brutally repressed in the USSR that Russia's leading sexologist, Igor S. Kon, called government policy "sexophobia in action." The Khrushchev Thaw permitted some research on sexuality and the term "sex" even entered public discourse; however, the Soviet press preferred the more euphemistic "intimate relations."[15] Although the system remained prudish and hypocritical when the Baby Boomers came of age, Kon concluded that, by the 1960s, it was "clear that both the value orientations and the sexual conduct of Soviet youth were moving in the same direction as those of their counterparts in the West," and "the overall trends in sexual behavior within Soviet society were, in the main, the same as the West."[16] Changes in social structure and culture resulted in earlier sexual maturation and onset of sexual activity. Premarital sex became more socially acceptable, as did homosexuality (although none of the interviewees admitted being gay or talked about the subject). As in the West, these changes created a gap between the Baby Boomers and their parents in terms of sexual values and behavior.[17]

Few of the Baby Boomers had anything to say about the troubled terrain of individuality, privacy, and sexual practices. This is not surprising. Soviet schools—like American schools at the time—offered no sex education. A few learned about sex at home or from movies and hearsay, but most learned about sex from each other. The moralizing official advice on sex for this generation, which a Finnish sociologist calls "learned ignorance," emphasized the dangers of masturbation and the risks of venereal disease.[18] The few gynecological handbooks available for girls extolled the benefits of getting married as a virgin. Although family planning using contraceptives appeared in the 1960s, they remained hard to obtain. The Soviet medical profession rejected the birth control pill, instead praising the virtues of condoms (known colloquially as "galoshes"), IUDs, and diaphragms. Because of the difficulty getting hold of reliable birth control, abortion, legalized in 1955, remained the most widespread form of birth control for the Cold War generation until the 1990s. In 1985, the abortion rate per 1,000 women of reproductive age was six to ten times the analogous rates in Western Europe.[19]

The Baby Boomers spoke readily about teenage flirtations and romances. "I don't think our school differed from any of the others," stated Aleksandr Trubnikov. "We reached the age, and romances began. Even Soviet power couldn't do anything about this. Basic instinct was at work." Gennady Ivanov piped in "that practically everyone had their first love at school," but emphasized how rare it was "that someone remained with someone from school all their life." But were the Baby Boomers sexually active at this age? Like others, Aleksandr Konstantinov remembered that "as far as I know, up until the tenth grade, relations between boys and girls in our group were quite innocent, with perhaps one exception. But if we are to go by what people said back then, a select group of 'golden youth' in the A group beginning in the seventh or eighth grade began to throw parties with alcohol and perhaps even sex." None from that group admitted this. Aleksandr Trubnikov believed that sexual activity "depended on the neighborhood you lived in. My neighborhood bordered on Glebuchev Ravine, where there were always loose morals. Many of my neighborhood friends were older and more experienced than me. They taught us everything and introduced us to the right people. But at school, as far as I remember, there was no particular activity observed."

Therefore, the majority described relations between the sexes at school as pure and innocent. Irina Tsurkan felt "that's to the credit of this particular school and its particular atmosphere." More to the point, "there weren't any incidents whatsoever of vulgarity." But this had its downside, too. "That is, we probably were naïve compared to other children," she suggested. According to Moscow's Tatyana Artyomova, there were "many school romances. But I want to say that these were very mature spiritual relationships." In other words, "since the people were on a very high level, their relations were of the highest level." Yelena Kolosova found love at any age humbling, and "all of my being in love unrequited." Because love as a theme was plastered on the pages of Russian literature, she found it "simply impossible not to be in love." She also "wouldn't have known what would have happened if her feelings had been reciprocated." After all, she found that older men—her father's graduate students and even one of her teachers—were attracted to her. "They always had enough sense not to go too far, because they were dealing with a girl of fifteen or sixteen." Moreover, the boys her age, Mikhail Markovich claimed, "related to the girls in a respectful way. We didn't touch them. We went out with them and went to the theater with them." Markovich, however, conceded that "because of girls" the boys sometimes "settled things with their fists until they drew blood."

Quite a few recalled the crushes they had while in school. Saratov's Galina Poldyaeva divulged that girls in the B class "were in love with Petya (Pyotor) Krasilnikov, a handsome and gifted boy." Krasilnikov remembered the time as "an awkward age. We were becoming adults. We were interested in going out with girls and in nature outings. We sang songs, built campfires. I taught myself how to play the guitar, and I'd take my guitar with me on all of our nature outings or get-togethers on birthdays or on holidays." Because the B class comprised twenty girls and eight boys, Aleksandr Virich opined that "we had so many girls that it didn't make sense to argue over them. We'd get acquainted, argue, go out, then go out again, then argue again, then find new girlfriends." Natalya Pronina told me that "all of us girls in the A class were in love with Sasha [Aleksandr] Trubnikov. He was very smart and well read, but mainly it was his inner charm. He played the guitar and sang Vysotsky." Many of the Moscow males considered Tatyana

The Baby Boomers needed a ready supply of 2-kopeck coins to use public phones. This photo of Leonid Terlitsky and a friend, taken near School No. 20 in 1966, hints at the diverse uses of telephone booths at the time. *Courtesy of Leonid Terlitsky*

Arzhanova the beauty of the B class. Georgy Godzhello, the tallest boy in class, was her first boyfriend. "If Godzhello liked a girl, she must be worth something," Arzhanova believed. More to the point, "the feeling that others like you, that you have a friend, a girlfriend, a group of friends, people you like to be with and who are well-disposed toward you" impacted her life. "If I hadn't had that stage in my life, I would probably have turned out to be a different person."

Viktor Alekseyev described the transformation he remembered taking place at school. First the boys avoided the girls, then friendships emerged, and next some attachments that the boys talked a lot about. "Or there was some petty jealousy or rivalry among the boys over a very popular girl. The same was true for the girls." Regarding sex, Alekseyev emphasized how hard it is to generalize about an entire generation. That said, he knew "some who began very young, while at school, and others who did so rather late, at the end of their college days. I was somewhere in the middle," he admitted. "But I have the impression, perhaps an erroneous one, that we became sexually active later and that it was a much bigger deal than it is for young people in Russia today." Indeed, his classmate Leonid Terlitsky did not believe that people at school were sexually active: "Not really. There were some kinds of sexual experience but nothing major, only a small minority I would say had had sexual experiences at the time. No, we got into some serious drinking at that tender age of sixteen, and that's about it."

"EVERYONE LISTENED TO WESTERN RADIO BROADCASTS"

The Baby Boomers listened to foreign radio broadcasts, especially by the time they reached the upper grades. Many of them did so because their parents tuned in, or because they wanted to enjoy Western music or practice their English. Those who denied listening to Voice of America and other stations came from families closely connected to the political system. Quite a few observed that they paid more attention to political events, and consequently took note of the broadcasts more seriously, after they had enrolled in college, and especially after the Soviet invasion of Czechoslovakia in 1968. Despite jamming and Soviet counterpropaganda condemning foreign broadcasts, people found ways to listen if they wanted to. Ironically, the government jammed Western broadcasts, but at the same time produced a receiver in Latvia—the Spidola (later known as the VEF)—that could pick them up. Vladimir Prudkin observed that for a time under Khrushchev the Soviet government stopped jamming the broadcasts altogether, but stepped up the jamming once again in 1968. Concluded Prudkin: "It made an impression, when here in the USSR there were many things you couldn't talk about that they talked about over there."

The BBC began beaming signals to the Soviet Union in 1946, Voice of America (VOA) in 1947, and CIA-funded and Munich-based Radio Liberty (RL) in 1953. Germany's Deutsche Welle (German Wave) rounded out the list of most important foreign broadcasts, but eventually thirty nations got involved in the activity.[20] After the Soviet Union started jamming foreign broadcasts in the winter of 1948, VOA engineers concocted ways to circumvent the interference, and Soviet listeners found ways to adapt their receivers. Targeting the Soviet intelligentsia, the early hard-hitting broadcasts focused on issues with which Soviet listeners could identify: the impossibility of traveling abroad, the Gulag, the horrors of collectivization, the depressed living standards, privileges of Communist Party members, government hostility toward religion, restrictions on the intelligentsia, and grievances of ethnic minorities. Characterizing VOA as a "servant of Wall Street," Soviet counterpropaganda depicted the Russian-speaking broadcasters as "clearly the dregs of the earth, outcasts from all humanity, which they themselves realize."

The VOA toned down the broadcasts following Stalin's death in 1953, offering more news and entertainment such as "Music USA," launched in 1955, while Munich-based and CIA-funded Radio Liberty continued its uncompromising propaganda. In 1958, the United States Information Agency (USIA) made English-language broadcasts available around the clock. After the two superpowers signed a cultural agreement that year governing a vast array of reciprocal exchanges of radio and television programs, films, artists, students, faculty, scientists, agricultural specialists, athletes, youth, and even civic groups, the United States replaced its aggressive psychological warfare with a more evolutionary one that promoted the soft power of the symbols of American mass culture such as blue jeans, chewing gum, jazz, rock music, stylish clothing, and cultural stars.[21] By the mid-1960s, however, the VOA, BBC, Radio Liberty, Deutsche Welle, and other stations began broadcasting political trials back in the Soviet Union. Civil rights activist Liudmila Alekseeva believed that the number who listened to VOA and Radio Liberty eventually reached 34 million daily and 82 million weekly listeners,[22] concluding that "it would be difficult to exaggerate the impact on Soviet society of foreign radio broadcasts beamed to the USSR," and that their influence was "felt by all of Soviet society, from its highest to its lowest strata."[23]

Saratov's Arkady Darchenko remembered he began listening "as soon as I was able to figure out electronics myself. We had a VEF. I fixed the wave band so that they couldn't jam us. I listened all the time. Yes, this was around tenth grade and afterward." Vladimir Nemchenko boasted that "already from age seven I knew what Voice of America and German Wave were. I had a receiver in the shed. I sat up at night and listened." Aleksandr Virich claimed that "all of Russia listened." Fine-tuning his remark, he added, "Everyone who was even somewhat of a member of the intelligentsia did. The lower classes didn't listen, but the majority of workers, of skilled workers, they all listened." He, too, explained how easy it was to outsmart the state's jamming process. "Our jammers worked at all frequencies our radios received. But no one realized that you could insert a special band in an empty slot in an ordinary VEF, which was adjusted so that it picked up the VHF wavebands. Everything came through perfectly!" Viktor D. recalled, "We believed some things, but not others." Viktor, who listened with his father, considered it a "violation" of his rights that the Soviet government considered listening an anti-Soviet act.

Listening ran in families. In Moscow, Anna Lyovina recalled that her mother "listened all the time." Igor Litvin's father had a Spidola. "He, of course, listened, but didn't make any commentary on what he heard," observed Igor, who listened, too, but to the Rolling Stones and Beatles. A jazz fan, Leonid Terlitsky preferred the "Jazz Hour" on Voice of America. Leonid Volodarsky remembered, "I liked the Beatles, and the Rolling Stones. I followed them closely. I'd listen to BBC World Service's Top Twenty. If I could, I'd listen to Radio Luxembourg, but it was hard to catch it." Volodarsky's parents "strictly told" him "not to tell anyone about this, but we nonetheless discussed this among ourselves at school." Lyubov Kovalyova listened, because, she maintained, "It was really interesting to compare the understanding of an event here with the view of the event from there." Lyubov Raitman recalled she tuned in "from age ten or so. I remember the crackling sound, and the voices that broke off. It was very interesting!" Fluent in French, her mother could not pick up French-language broadcasts in Moscow but could when they vacationed on the Crimea. Coincidentally, her family encountered the Volodarskys while vacationing there, where they got to be friends. Lyubov recalled that Volodarsky's father, who taught English, listened to BBC and Voice of America on the beach and translated what he heard for them. Bakhyt Kenzheyev's father never spoke about politics but listened each night after the kids went to bed: "The first thing we bought when we saved up a little money was a radio," recounted Bakhyt. "He listened to BBC and to Voice of America." Tatyana Artyomova had no trouble picking up stations, characterizing the pastime as "absolutely normal." Underscoring the intellectual atmosphere at school, she noted that "if you found out something new, you'd discuss it with the others."

Saratov's Arkady Darchenko agreed, "We no longer were afraid. We were from a different generation. We often discussed what we heard at school, since we listened to the same things." Aleksandr Babushkin confided that "we talked about the broadcasts and considered this normal. I don't believe that in our circle it was seen as something extraordinary."

Aleksandr Konstantinov began listening "when the radio receivers appeared," that is, when he became a student at Moscow University. Some Muscovites also date their serious listening to their college days. "That information became important, probably from the time our troops invaded Czechoslovakia," responded Mikhail Markovich. "We began to understand that we lacked information." Leonid Terlitsky concurred: "At that time we would all listen to Voice of America, to Voice of Israel, to various enemy voices. We were avid listeners." Tatyana Luchnikova claimed her mother "really loved to listen to VOA. She couldn't live without it." Luchnikova joined in only after finishing school. "It was really interesting because they said a lot about dissidents."

In contrast, the Baby Boomers' parents with the most to risk—almost always Party members—claimed to have tuned in less, if at all, to foreign broadcasts. Anatoly Shapiro remembered, "My father tried to listen late at night. He feared all his life because he traveled abroad and worked for the Ministry of Foreign Trade. I understand all of this now, but thought it was strange back then." Marina Bakutina suspected her parents did not listen because "they were Party members and my father was in the army and my mother was eligible to travel abroad. It really was dangerous, because they could put an end to foreign travel." Olga Gorelik claimed her father, assistant editor of the Saratov Communist newspaper, listened "only once out of professional interest, but I think he had already retired." Irina Tsurkan believed her parents did not listen "because of me. I was the only child. Their fear was probably exaggerated." Nor did Aleksandr Trubnikov's parents tune in. As for him, he said, "It was simply impossible. You had to make colossal efforts, and why did I need that?" But he began to listen in college: "And by then I began to really get interested in such things." That said, Trubnikov emphasized that "you had to listen to them secretively. You had to be careful." Some of these feelings still lingered when I asked Natalya Pronina whether her family listened to foreign radio broadcasts. She barked, "I don't have to answer that question. It was forbidden to listen."

Despite the need to be cautious when listening to foreign radio broadcasts, some Baby Boomers reminded me that, from their perspective, there was nothing explicitly political about their doing so. Saratov's Aleksandr Kutin listened to VOA's English news broadcasts because they were accessible and comprehensible, and because, as he put it, "It helped me with the political information classes. I'd record the news on my tape recorder and report on it in English at school the next day, and everyone would applaud me. The best pupils did the political information reports, but it was also something of a joke." Natalya Yanichkina acknowledged that "back then I didn't pay much attention to what was said, but was more interested in saying that I listened to Voice of America. Ever the more so because it was jammed, and everything that's secretive and off limits always sparks one's interest. But what they had to say didn't interest me at all." Several others claimed that they realized that neither superpower had a monopoly on the truth and that, as Aleksandr Kutin opined, "You had to chose somewhere in the middle." Yevgeny Podolsky remarked that "it was of course very interesting to me back then, but I believed it was propaganda. But later I began to see all of this differently. By then we had lost faith." Recalled Pyotor Krasilnikov: "Back then I simply wanted to pick up some other information. I'm not saying that it was objective or not." "When they broadcast things that deviated from our radio broadcasts, I didn't believe it," asserted Olga Kamayurova. "It seemed to me that they were slandering us, that's what they pounded into our heads. I was quite naïve."

Moscow's Yelena Kolosova groused about the quality of Voice of America, "which irritated me with its unintelligent propaganda," comparing it with BBC, which her family loved for its "balanced approach and objectivity." Despite her critical remarks, Kolosova appreciated VOA and other stations because "it was information. It was impossible to get by without it, because you had to try to find out about certain events. Especially the Sinyavsky-Daniel trial [in 1965]."* Her mother listened to music on German Wave, because she knew the language. They also listened to Radio Israel, especially during the Six Day War in 1967. They listened during the invasion of Czechoslovakia. They listened to everything tied to Solzhenitsyn. Several of her classmates also found fault with the broadcasts, but it is hard to say whether this is due to the effectiveness of Soviet counterpropaganda or to the programming's real shortcomings. Vyacheslav Starik explained that "it's a question of mentality. It's simply that foreign powers don't want what's good for us. We couldn't expect anything good from them. They had their lives, we had ours." Vladimir Glebkin lost faith in the broadcasts shortly after graduating from school, when he heard a BBC report about an incident for which he claimed to have had firsthand knowledge. "I began to notice that, from time to time, they indeed had a purpose in conveying information," he detailed. "The fact that our side said that all of those foreign voices lie, that they're the mouthpiece of American propaganda, well there's something in that."

"EVERYTHING SOUNDS ROMANTIC WITH A SPANISH ACCENT"

Among the most accomplished spin doctors of the twentieth century, Soviet propagandists pounded into the Baby Boomers' heads that "the number of socialist countries would soon surpass the number of capitalist ones, and that the transition to socialism was possible in a peaceful manner, without revolution," recounted Aleksandr Trubnikov. In the aftermath of World War II, and especially during their school days, the final blow was dealt to colonialism, especially in Africa, which the Soviet government depicted as evidence of the march of progress and further decline of the capitalist world order. "At that time," remembered Trubnikov, "they taught us that Africa had awoken. It had cast off the yoke of colonialism, and all the countries on the dark continent in a wink became socialist. I really didn't understand who Patrice Lumumba was in the Congo. I read the papers and thought that colonialism was a very bad thing and that Africa became free and that everything instantly was now good there."

But then the Cuban Revolution brought Fidel Castro to power, eventually resulting in a superpower crisis that brought the world to the brink of nuclear war. Africa remained remote and other. Not so Cuba, and once the love affair with Cuba began, Latin America became more accessible, too, at least the voice

---

* In 1965, the new Brezhnev leadership arrested writers Andrei Sinyavsky and Yuli Daniel, for slandering the Soviet system in works they published abroad under pseudonyms. Both were sentenced to labor camps at a show trial held in early 1966. By raising fear of a return to Stalinism, the trial helped to galvanize the dissident movement.

of actress Lolita Torres and the soccer prowess of Pele, Didi, and Vava. The Cuban Revolution allowed Soviet citizens to vicariously relive their own revolution. Reminisced Saratov's Viktor D.: "There was the affable Comrade Fidel who invited us to help him. We helped him, and the country prospered." "Cuba, my love, island of crimson dawns," crooned Olga Kolishchyuk. "What an unusual love we had for Cuba. They were all heroes there and everything was wonderful." "Cuba! Oh, we loved Cuba!" enthused Natalya Yolshina, "because Fidel was a national hero; he was handsome, with a beard, and quite the orator." Yolshina remembered a special school assembly when "a teacher got up on the stage and said 'Children! A wonderful thing has occurred in Cuba.' The insurgents, the revolutionaries, have won! We gave a standing ovation, we were so happy. Although, we understood very little. We always loved Cuba." Aleksandr Trubnikov concurred that "we loved Castro. He was simply a national hero who, on a tiny little island, defied terrible bourgeois America. He became our friend and began to build communism." Castro's success created expectations: "We were even fonder of Che Guevara. He was, as they now say in Russia, even cooler than Castro," commented Trubnikov.

Yet certain issues confused the Baby Boomers. "Somehow I couldn't understand why they live so poorly over there," volunteered Aleksandr Trubnikov. Hindsight enabled Viktor D. to distinguish between Big Politics and his own: "The fact that Cuba was a direct threat to America, well none of us really understood this, at least among those my age." Although positively disposed toward helping Africa and Cuba, he quipped, "We expressed amusement that we exchanged grain for sugar cane. Did we really need it?" According to Aleksandr Konstantinov, "we knew that Cuba existed, that there was a charming man there, Fidel Castro, with a beard, who was able to speak for six hours without a break. Initially people felt that the Cubans were a heroic people, yet not for long." Once again, things look clearer with the benefit of hindsight: "It was pure ideology," concluded Aleksandr Virich. Yet the relationship left a legacy of sorts. Arkady Darchenko visited Cuba in 1993, after the USSR no longer existed and its aid to Cuba had dried up. Despite the parting of ways, he "felt that these people were very open and friendly. When you walked along the street someone would run up to you and say 'Hey, Americano, give me a dollar.' I'd say in Russian, 'I'm not an Americano, I'm Russian.' 'Ah, Russo. Do you want a drink?' In general, they related differently. They were taught, 'Americano' is bad, and 'Russo' is good."

Castro cut a romantic figure for many of the Moscow females. Lyubov Kovalyova remembered, "Cuba, Fidel Castro, with the handsome beard. We learned all about it, and made a montage at school. We read poems, taking turns with 'Cuba-si, Cuba-si, Cuba-si, Yankee-no.' We did this with great enthusiasm. Cuba was our ally, we were friends." Lyubov Raitman also recalled singing "'Cuba, my love, island of crimson dawns.' We didn't know what was going on there. Revolution. Romanticism. Fidel, who was so attractive. I can't say what I understood at the time about America's position." Tatyana Artyomova maintained, "People liked Cuba thanks to Fidel, because he was so handsome. All of the other leaders were bent over with age." Yelena Kolosova explained why Cuba held appeal for her generation: "Hemingway [then so popular in the USSR] was on the side of the [Cuban] Revolution." As a result, "we were one with Cuba. And this made things similar to the situation during the Spanish Civil War." In fact, "it seems to me that Cuba was one of the myths of Soviet power. Besides, everything sounds romantic with a Spanish accent."

The Saratov interviewees had remarkably little to say about Cold War fears, even during the Cuban Missile Crisis, lending credence to the aphorism that "what you don't know won't hurt you." "I was in school during the Cuban Missile Crisis. I didn't know about it, but on my way home from school the newspaper *Izvestiya* was posted somewhere on a fence. And it contained an article 'How *The Times* Got into a Fix,'" recalled Aleksandr Konstantinov. "There was a fake photograph in *The Times*, which allegedly depicted Soviet soldiers and bases in Cuba. That very same paper the next day wrote about the 'wise' decision to remove our missiles from Cuba. Everyone got a kick out of this. We didn't realize that we had been on the verge of war." Olga Kamayurova also stated that "with the benefit of hindsight we now know how terrible the Caribbean crisis really was, after all, we were on the brink of nuclear war. But we didn't know the whole truth back then." Irina Garzanova was not afraid, for Cuba seemed so remote. "Of course, if it had happened on Kamchatka or Sakhalin, it would have been another matter," she conceded. Irina Vizgalova's uncle, "an old Party military man," was in Cuba at the time, but his memories privileged the ordinary: "He told us that Cubans eat green tomatoes and feed red ones to the pigs. And they eat squid. He got tanned there and wrote letters. If you believe him, he mostly rested there," she recalled.

Igor Litvin and other Muscovites, however, knew of the "strong confrontation with America. There literally was the feeling that war could begin tomorrow. And we feared it." "Poor Cuba," he felt. "Everyone was afraid of the crisis, I think, because of all the people here who lived through war." During the emergency, Anatoly Shapiro's father told him that "nuclear war was possible and that the world could end." This made an impression on the twelve-year-old, although "I couldn't understand who was right and who was at fault." Tatyana Artyomova's parents routinely vacationed in the fall. "They left on vacation. I was at home with my nanny. They returned home within a week because they were afraid that something might happen and they needed to be at home. I remember that very well." Andrei Rogatnev's father, who worked for the KGB, was mobilized during the crisis. "All of us expected war," recalled Andrei.

"THE CHINESE BECAME ENEMY NUMBER ONE"

Following Mao Zedong's establishment of the People's Republic of China in 1949, the new Communist kid on the bloc signed a thirty-year Treaty of Friendship,

Alliance, and Mutual Assistance with Stalin's Soviet Union, feeding Western fears of a Red menace. But Chinese suspicion, the Soviet leadership's overbearing and insensitive behavior toward Beijing, and growing differences over international political strategies resulted in a rift between the two Communist giants in the late 1950s and early 1960s. As the differences evolved into an open split in 1962, China challenged the USSR's dominance of the world Communist movement, claimed chunks of Soviet territory in the Far East, and slammed the Soviet Union as a "social imperialist" state. The Kremlin expressed disapproval of Chinese domestic policies, especially the decade-long Cultural Revolution launched in 1966, a violent and radical mass movement promoted by Mao to root out "bourgeois" elements in the Communist Party and society at large, resulting in chaos and economic instability. The tension between the two Communist giants escalated into the Ussuri River crisis of 1969 over Damansky (Chenpao) Island, a violent border clash in which the Chinese were determined to show the Soviet leadership that they would not back away from military conflict.

Natalya Yolshina remembered that, when she attended school in Saratov, "there was friendship between our nations, and we danced Chinese dances, always in Chinese outfits. China, our brother. Brothers for a century!" Both cohorts recalled the ever-present Chinese-made consumer goods on the Soviet market. "All of us had wonderful blue Chinese outfits made out of wool," related Olga Martynkina. "We had fur coats and Chinese toys." Galina Poldyaeva could visualize the Chinese towels, enamel dishes, and the Keds, of which she had several pairs. Moscow's Vladimir Glebkin told me that he and his family had "blue trousers made in China. They were of a very awkward cut, but very durable. Therefore, when you had to do some dirty work, you'd put on these trousers and know they'd live up to the job." Tatyana Luchnikova claimed that, at the time, "all of our clothing was made in China."

Following the public acknowledgment of the Sino-Soviet split, the Soviet media ridiculed the Chinese Cultural Revolution. Lyubov Raitman related that she found the social experiment "terrifying. The throngs of identically dressed people, marching, gazing at Mao. It made a disturbing impression." Especially since the climate in Khrushchev's Russia differed so much. Viktor Alekseyev agreed that the Cultural Revolution made a strange impression "against the background of the Thaw taking place here at home." As a result, China soon became enemy number one, "the new Mongol hordes, with atomic bombs in their quivers,"[24] posing both a revisionist ideological and a political threat. However, many interviewees linked the Sino-Soviet split to the crisis of 1969 over Damansky Island. Arkady Darchenko recalled, "We were taught that China was 'brother number one.' But then the events of 1969 took place: 'What enemies they all are, what vermin!'" Aleksandr Ivanov's cousin who served in the army told his family that "the army was almost on full military alert to fight with the Chinese." The confrontation dumbfounded Olga Kolishchyuk, who had spent several years in China as an infant, where her parents were stationed. "How could this be? When we were there things were fine and we were like brothers. And then suddenly this." The episode made an especially deep impression on Yevgeny Podolsky, who, as a college student, took part in a labor brigade in Siberia. When his group changed trains near Irkutsk, they heard an announcement over the loud speaker that the Moscow-Beijing train was passing through en route to China. Prepared to assault the Chinese, "we rushed to the platform, but they cordoned us off. We were surrounded by police, by troops from internal affairs. We threw a scene." Etched in Podolsky's memory is "the passing red train, well illuminated, packed with Chinese standing at the windows reading Mao Zedong." But there's more. During the two months he labored at the construction site, the Chinese broadcast in Russian, urging "Russian girls to wait for their hot Chinese lovers," who would soon reach Irkutsk. "We were outraged."

When the friendship soured, Saratov's Natalya Yolshina recalled being told that "they changed their views, but we continued to stand up for ours, the correct ones, so we stopped being friends." Natalya Pronina, who had met a Chinese girl during the Moscow Youth Festival of 1957, made a distinction: "These hostile relations stemmed from how the two countries' leaderships got along, not from the attitudes of ordinary people. We didn't understand." Pyotor Krasilnikov certainly did not. Later serving in the Red Army some sixty kilometers from China, he harbored no animosity toward the Chinese either. "It was a shame about our lads who perished on Damansky. But I think that politicians started this. The blood of our lads is on their conscience."

The 1969 shelling of Damansky Island also struck anger and fear in the hearts of Muscovites. Vladimir Bystrov remembered, "I was very glad when we bombarded Damansky Island. I took patriotic pride in this." Vladimir Glebkin recalled the change in relations between the two countries "came like a bolt from the blue, especially since his father's textbook had been translated into Chinese. No one understood the essence of the conflict and how it could have arisen." The events gave Anatoly Shapiro cause to fear China, "knowing that it was a large country with an enormous number of people who could pour in here." Leonid Volodarsky also heard Chinese radio broadcasts in Russian: "They were so aggressive, naïve, and uninteresting that they irritated me."

A significant number of Baby Boomers called the popular mood toward China in the Soviet Union one of condescension: "You know, the 'great friendship' was like a stock phrase. Then there were the incidents over Damansky Island and the others. Yet this was so far away that the attitude of most, up until now, is slightly, well, not exactly racist, but people think the Chinese are strange," explained Saratov's Aleksandr Konstantinov. Yevgeny Podolsky confirmed this: "We thought that the Cultural Revolution was funny and that they weren't normal." Natalya Yanichkina concurred: "The Cultural Revolution was presented to us as vandalism. Take the killing of sparrows. They shot them so that they wouldn't eat grain." Olga Kamayurova admitted, "We used to make fun of them. That's how official propaganda represented China to us, and that's how we regarded the place." Moscow's Vladimir Prudkin voiced a similar sentiment. "They reprinted articles about how the Great Helmsman [Mao] swam across the Yangtze River. There, of course, was the feeling that this was half-Kafkaesque, and half-Gogolian." Tatyana Artyomova and her friends "didn't consider China an interesting or serious country." She clarified, "And that's understandable, because Chinese culture doesn't at all resemble Russian culture."

Naturally, not everyone bought into the great friendship garble nor into the new Party line after the Sino-Soviet split. The influence of family and other close contacts seems paramount here. Saratov's Aleksandr Trubnikov admitted that "to be honest, I never, even as a child, because of something my father said, considered the Chinese to be our friends." Nor did China interest everyone. China had no appeal for Aleksandr Babushkin, who acknowledged that his point of view might have been shaped by the negative things one of his teachers of English, who had grown up in Kharbin, a center of Russian émigré life following the Revolution, had to say about the Chinese. Lyubov Kovalyova found the country interesting perhaps because her father had traveled there before the Sino-Soviet split. Georgy Godzhello "always had colossal respect for China and for its ancient culture and civilization."

As adults, the Baby Boomers continued to harbor ambivalent, if not negative, impressions of China. Moscow's Vladimir Bystrov opined that he "doesn't like China," which he has visited four times on business since perestroika. After the dissolution of the USSR, Arkady Darchenko also spent a lot of time there. "I now have enormous respect for them precisely because of their goals," he told me. "It's the oldest of civilizations and one feels it in them. It's a very powerful nation and our neighbor to boot. And Siberia is underpopulated. Let's say, therefore, that my attitude is one of respect and fear." Ironically referring to the attempt by Czechoslovakian reformers to create a more humane "socialism with a human face," Aleksandr Trubnikov credited China with shaping his worldview in that "on the whole it was a distorted mirror of the Soviet Union. All of the features of Soviet power became more pronounced there when taken to their logical extreme and everyone was dressed in the same Mao jackets and ate the same hundred grams of rice a day. That was real socialism with a human face."

"'ABROAD' IS A MYTH ABOUT LIFE AFTER DEATH"

The Saratovites held more tentative attitudes toward the West than those of their Moscow counterparts, because Saratov was a closed city. This made Soviet propaganda more effective, especially because their parents had fewer firsthand experiences with the capitalist world that might serve as an antidote to combat the official Party line. To be sure, official propaganda emphasized the potential goodness of people everywhere; not they, but their capitalist socioeconomic and political systems were the enemy. Although the depiction of two Wests—of good people and bad socioeconomic systems—held sway, popular opinion in the 1950s and 1960s remained hostile toward Germany, owing to the torment Nazi Germany inflicted upon the Soviet Union during the Great Patriotic War. Moreover, Soviet propaganda back then also excoriated the German people. "Of course, there was hatred toward fascist Germany," responded Galina Poldyaeva. Arkady Darchenko elaborated, "When I was a kid I wasn't fond of Germany. Like any Russian, I had lost several relatives during the war. And this affects your view, of course. But now I think that's stupid. It would be like hating the French because of the war with Napoleon."

America held a special place in the Soviet popular imagination because its technological advances had already by the 1920s made it the modernist nation par excellence; however, the image was tempered by depictions of racism and exploitation of workers, and government criticism of jazz and Hollywood movies. The wartime alliance created in the USSR what historian Alan Ball called an "orgy of good feeling" toward America, yet it vanished once the Cold War intensified. Soviet propaganda resumed the attack, adding to the above list of America's shortcomings unemployment, crime, and the gap between rich and poor that affected access to education and medical care. It decried vulgar materialism, violence, cynical individualism, social stratification, narcotics, and pornography.[25] Soviet images of America softened under Khrushchev, who promoted peaceful coexistence and opening up to the outside world. Further, the attitudes of professional—and far more sympathetic—foreign-policy practitioners neutralized ideological prejudices of the Soviet leadership. As before the war, Soviet class-war rhetoric depicted the American people as victims of an unfair system controlled by capitalist warmongers, right-wingers, the Pentagon, Wall Street, and Texas oil magnates. But America became less intimidating, as a result of which most young people in the Soviet Union harbored more ambivalent views of their Cold War enemy.[26]

Khrushchev's September 1959 visit to the United States colored the impressions of the Baby Boomers' parents, and of the interviewees, too, because Soviet propaganda gave the journey top billing, for Nikita Sergeyevich was the first Soviet leader to see the stronghold of capitalism. A hefty propaganda volume on the "triumphant" trip issued in a press run of 1 million copies declared that Khrushchev had "throughout the universe revealed and glorified the genius of our heroic nation." The book acknowledges the fabulous cars and fine roads in America, and "American service, which is well known in the entire world," but only if green paper dollars are rustling in your pocket. It depicts Americans as talented and hard working, but also as victims of the "contradictions of capitalism," making them so preoccupied with money. The book observes that Americans like baseball more than books, and a well-appointed kitchen and bathroom over the theater or music. Such remarks reflected the success of the 1957 American exhibit and propaganda war. The Soviet government could not deny what its people had seen, so it cast them as the consequence of America's location, far from the theaters of war.[27] Importantly, the book underscores that peaceful coexistence was the "only possible form of existence."[28] This rhetoric struck a responsive chord among the Soviet people, who needed peace to enjoy the fruits of communism that was just around the corner. According to a public opinion poll of Soviet citizens carried out by Soviet sociologists in 1960, 96.8 percent of the respondents expressed confidence that war could be averted.[29]

Saratov's Natalya Yolshina acknowledged the impact of the Soviet information system in shaping her views toward the West. "General human values prevailed, and the fact that people everywhere were the same was perhaps the main thing." Reminding me that Saratov was a closed city, she said she "never had any contacts with foreigners" but never felt any "animosity or ill will" toward the West. She assumed that "things were much better here. No one is oppressing anyone else. We have no unemployment. And it's marvelous that we have free education and free medical care. It's wonderful to live in the Soviet Union!" In contrast, "everything is more complicated there. There's endless competition, the survival of the fittest." Maintained Galina Poldyaeva: "We always felt sorry for the unemployed. They had nowhere to live, nothing to eat, and no place to sleep, whereas here everything was so good." They also learned that "the Negroes were repressed in the United States. We read *Uncle Tom's Cabin*. Of course, everything was one-sided and seems amusing today." Irina Garzanova reminded me that "propaganda is propaganda. I, for example, related to America negatively, in the sense that it threatened us. But I understood that it was military circles there that were responsible. It was advantageous for them to threaten us. However, the people were like us." As Aleksandr Konstantinov claimed, "We formed our ideas of the West mostly from caricatures in newspapers. The American was always depicted as Uncle Sam, with a striped flag and with striped pants." Konstantinov harbored prejudice toward the West back then: "I probably believed that there were people there who weren't interested in our country's well-being. On the other hand, I was interested and curious."

Some Saratovites emphasized that, although Soviet propaganda worked at the most general level, it also gave rise to reservations that evolved into genuine doubt. Explained Aleksandr Virich: "What kind of attitude could a school-age child have toward the West, when they drove home the point all his life that capitalism was rotting? But some ten to fifteen years later I understood that it was going to rot for a lot longer, and that for some reason its decay smelled like roses! We were young back then," he added. "We loved our country, we believed that in 1980 we'd have communism, although, for the most part, the adults already knew there'd be no communism." Aleksandr Trubnikov also felt this ambivalence. On the one hand, he affirmed the influence of everything he read and heard at school and over the radio and on television. On the other hand, it seemed strange to him that if Americans were all such terrible capitalists, "then why do they have such a high level of science and technology, and such a high standard of living? It was impossible for them to hide this from us," despite the Iron Curtain. "Even Soviet propaganda was incapable of doing so. This didn't make sense. There's such a terrible class war going on in the West with strikes and the like and, as they taught us, the working class would soon seize power because it's brutally exploited. After all, how much could it take?"

Studying English mitigated the worst effects of Soviet anti-Western propaganda. Viktor D. recognized this. "It brought me closer. I could imagine Hyde Park, I could imagine the Statue of Liberty. I can say that neither I nor anyone in my family ever considered Americans as enemies." Vladimir Kirsanov attributed his attitude toward the West to his school experience, "which without question shaped our worldview. We studied English literature, history, and so on. We became more broadly acquainted with world culture. Therefore, my attitude was normal." Irina Chemodurova prided herself in being "raised on Western culture. They brought me up according to the principle: English poetry, French prose, German music, and Italian art." Pyotor Krasilnikov recalled that back then he saw the USSR and United States as military and technological equals. "But I wanted more freedom. What kind, I can't remember, but perhaps to see more cowboy films, perhaps to chew chewing gum. From today's perspective, that's all trifling stuff. I wanted to travel abroad, but during the Soviet period that was very problematic."

Negative publicity about the West did not dampen the Baby Boomers' interest in the capitalist other, and often had the opposite effect. In 1966 Soviet citizens harbored "unequivocal disinterest in the 'Third World,'"[30] whereas 91 percent of those surveyed were interested in America and admired its technological progress and living standards. Abraham Lincoln and John F. Kennedy were enormously popular, and many people believed Americans were much like Russians.[31] Saratov's Aleksandr Babushkin agreed that he "was interested in how people lived there." Natalya Pronina admitted she was "really curious." Irina Vizgalova "wanted to communicate with people over there and to know more." Irina Tsurkan "envied their standards of living. There was the sense that everything there was very good. We were under the impression that to live well over there you had to work hard, and we saw that here you could work very hard and not get anything for your efforts."

Although the Saratovites appear to have had a more positive image of the United States than Americans had of the Soviet Union, they were not immune to Cold War fears. Said Viktor D.: "Here there also was a certain degree of hysteria. They charged this atmosphere, because, as with the situation between Cuba and the United States, there were American bases surrounding the Russian Federation. And there was Hiroshima and Nagasaki." Tatyana Kuznetsova also mentioned the trepidation she felt. "I would think, 'Oh, my, and if war breaks out? What if they suddenly attack us?' That was terrible. We knew for certain that we would never launch an attack against them." Olga Kolishchyuk insisted, "We were afraid of nuclear war. We thought that at any moment they could drop bombs on us and we'd no longer be alive. And we hoped that normal people lived there, too, who didn't want this." Yet Olga Martynkina claimed she and her friends "never thought about the Cold War. We knew that all of that exists, but it didn't concern us."

The Muscovites spoke more emphatically about the limitations of Soviet anti-Western propaganda, which, ironically, contributed toward an idealization of Western lifestyles and abundance. According to Tatyana Luchnikova, "it seemed to all of us that the West was inaccessible, dazzling, almost a place of shining asphalt and of crystal-clear clouds." Tatyana Artyomova concurred: "I think that, in general, Soviet-era propaganda was very unsuccessful. It was very unprofessional, because no one in our class believed that America was a bad country." Boris Shtein had relatives in Switzerland who had left Russia before the Revolution. "I remember that, in the 1960s, our families corresponded. We sent each other souvenirs. The West was always an open world to me." Shtein "never feared the West" and found mandatory Soviet civil defense classes "very silly and annoying. We put on gas masks. But I don't think anyone took this seriously." Leonid Volodarsky unabashedly admitted that "I idealized the West. I wanted to see Western cinema. I wanted to dress like them." Vladimir Prudkin agreed that his views back then were skewed "as if everything there was ideal." Igor Litvin saw America as "if it was some kind of promised land. As a child, I had the impression that it was a first-class country where people really did live freely, there were no obstacles, and the American dream could be realized. I always wanted to travel there."

Andrei Rogatnev spoke good-humoredly about the double standard inherent in Soviet propaganda, which depicted America and the West as "our enemy, but all the same with good music and decent films." From a privileged KGB family, he and his sister spent a lot of time at the family dacha in Zhukovka, a closed community built for the country's leaders, with a clubhouse that showed films each week. Before each foreign film, a specialist spelled out the shortcomings of "rotting Hollywood cinematography." For instance, the night Rogatnev saw *The Born Losers*, he recalled the lecturer's remarks: "And, he says, as an example of that vileness, we'll watch this disgusting film. And we, drooling, watched it with great pleasure."

Several agreed with Vladimir Glebkin that "at that time we were open to the West. We saw the shortcomings we had here, we felt them. The narrow-mindedness, not in school, but, let's say, on radio, on television, the limited nature of information and the form of that information, its crudeness, we saw all of this." It seemed to Glebkin that a country that could produce the Beatles was not all that bad and "was of an altogether different quality and more attractive" than Soviet propaganda would have it. Sergei Zemskov noted the limitations of propaganda—not only about the West but also about the heroic construction of communism in the USSR: "I'd say that the quality of life was apparent to everyone. Perhaps it was through our parents. It got through to us that there was a different standard of living, and, in general, a different atmosphere there that contrasted with official propaganda for the most part."

The critical-minded Russian, according to Bakhyt Kenzheyev, "believed that the Soviet Union was the worst place in the world, that the problems of the American poor didn't exist. All of this was expressed in the views 'if we only had your problems,' or 'if we only had your concerns.'" Kenzheyev remarked that no one understood the meaning of Watergate and other American domestic scandals: the Western political system interested the Cold War generation less than the Western standard of living and popular culture.

The latter especially fascinated them. Vladimir Bystrov "had dreams of going there." For Yelena Kolosova, "the West was above all literature, translations of all my favorite writers. And a way of life." Western culture and life appealed to Lyubov Raitman, who remembered, "My sources of information about that life were girl things." She recalled the French fashion magazines her mother brought back from Paris. "And I saw, for example, that women and children could look different than those surrounding me." Raitman likewise credited her teachers with providing them with positive information about America, because "we had incredibly limited possibilities for finding out." To illustrate this point, she told me about *Mosaic,* a journal published in English in Poland for those studying the language. "You couldn't possibly imagine how much we found out from this very thin publication." Difficult to get hold of, *Mosaic* printed the words to contemporary songs and stories about American and British schools. "In our youth, at a time when we thought we knew it all, there was a saying that we liked to repeat, half in jest, half seriously: 'There is no abroad. It's a myth about life after death.' But we nevertheless tried to find out about the abroad. We really wanted to know what it was like there." Vladimir Prudkin also credited his positive perspective to "the teachers who taught the subjects linked to language. They really loved their subject and naturally native speakers of that language." As a result, "they created the impression that there exists a world in which there are no problems, in which life is harmonious, even ideal, akin to heaven on earth."

The Baby Boomers' parents also profoundly shaped their children's attitudes toward the outside world. Born in remote villages in Saratov province, Viktor D.'s parents would have starved to death as children during the famine of 1921–22 if the American Relief Administration had not fed them. "Both my mother and father remember this well. They lived in a desolate village and received food from Americans who fed them twice a day and sometimes handed out clothing." Not surprisingly, "they often spoke about this. For that reason, I never had any negative feelings," detailed Viktor. He also pointed out that "back then they propagandized the meeting on the Elbe" between American and Soviet soldiers at the end of World War II. At home he likewise heard a lot "about the first wave of Russian migration to America and Canada [during the Revolution]. Many even corresponded with them, despite all."

Some interviewees recalled the impressions made on them when their parents returned from trips abroad, often with things as well as impressions. Marina Bakutina remembered "the artifacts that Mother brought back. They were a type of window to the West, to a world that we could glance at thanks to such things." Sergei Zemskov also concluded that "to a significant extent," the idealization of the West "might have had to do with the fact that many parents traveled abroad and this affected them." As a teacher of English, Tatyana Arzhanova's mother came into contact with foreigners and even dressed in an "English manner." "She adored England, and America was also not completely closed for her" because she worked from a very early age with a woman of Lithuanian descent who grew up in America. Similarly, Valentin Ulyakhin's father worked with Americans in the 1930s and cherished the wartime alliance. "He always spoke positively of America," divulged Ulyakhin. His father especially appreciated American Lend Lease, "and canned Spam." Tatyana Artyomova also recalled the atmosphere at home: "Perhaps we at that time didn't fully appreciate what was bad in the West. We saw more of the good." Yet Vyacheslav Starik's parents, both trained as economists, a highly ideological profession, had no interest in the West. Nor did Vyacheslav. "We were such a self-sufficient state that we didn't need anyone else. We have natural resources, human resources, knowledge. What else did we need? Ever the more so when you were propagating some sort of freedoms that were incomprehensible to us."

"WHEN THEY SHOT KENNEDY, IT WAS A TRAGEDY FOR US ALL"

Despite the tough stance President John F. Kennedy took toward Khrushchev and the USSR, the Soviet people, like the rest of the world, tended to find him irresistible—especially after Lee Harvey Oswald shot him dead in November 1963. Viktor Alekseyev observed that "such a handsome figure as the American president and the contrast with the Russian leaders for the most part evoked strong sympathy, simply on what I would call a purely emotional level." He also called attention to Kennedy's well-educated demeanor and the appeal of his glamorous wife Jackie. "All of this created a very attractive image and, accordingly, stimulated interest." Yelena Kolosova concurred: "It was all so romantic. Everyone talked about the fact that she had been a reporter and he a young congressman, and all of this took place in the country of the native speakers of the language we were studying. All of this took on emotional intensity for us, and almost became something personal."

In sum, the Soviet Union rediscovered America during the Khrushchev years, and Kennedy benefited from the deep public interest in the West. Viktor Alekseyev reminded me that, despite the strained official relationship between the two superpowers, "at the ordinary level people sympathized with, or in any case there was a great deal of interest in, America." For this reason, Kennedy's assassination struck hard. Natalya Pronina related that "when he was assassinated the entire country mourned as if he were one of our own. Evidently it was his appearance. You can see for yourself that he looks Russian." Leonid Terlitsky remembered when his father woke him up to tell him that Kennedy had been assassinated. Terlitsky wanted to roll over and go back to sleep, "for which my father gave me hell." "I remember the horror of the news report that November. I was sick at home. And the repetitive shots shown on TV of him hunched over, and then of Oswald and Ruby," detailed Yelena Kolosova. Now living in America, she moved from Ames, Iowa, to Houston, Texas. "Since the assassination, I've had a fierce hatred of Texas. The first time I flew into Dallas, I couldn't overcome that ominous feeling that the tragedy had taken place there."

Saratov's Aleksandr Kutin saw Kennedy's assassination as a calamity. "I can say that. Everyone was afraid. How could that have happened? Who would they replace him with? What might come of the agreement that already had been reached between the governments following the Cuban crisis?" I was struck to hear from Natalya Pronina the same rumors that reached me growing up in Chicago, where I attended "the first" John. F. Kennedy High School: "I even believed that one year they'd reveal the secrets behind his death. They told us that we'd find out in twenty-five years. How I wanted to fast forward to that moment, how I wanted to know who and why." Natalya P. fell under the influence of conspiracy theory. "It never entered the heads of the majority of the population that the mass media could name as the assassin not the person who killed him but, for political reasons, Oswald or someone else. Not because they couldn't find him, but because they had to substitute someone else because of politics." She was unaware that Marina Oswald grew up in Minsk, a fact that raised Western suspicions of KGB involvement in Kennedy's assassination. Moscow's Yelena Kolosova knew this. "Of course, that carried with it some fear because, if the whole thing had been fabricated, then per-haps there'd be some sort of revenge. It was all so strange and even then seemed far-fetched."

Natalya P. had a compelling explanation for the mystique of JFK. "For you, the president is an ordinary person, with all sorts of family problems, someone you can feel sorry for, someone you can relate to. He's one of, and comprehen-sible to, the people. People now understand, but not back then. The leader was an idol to whom everyone prayed." When Kennedy was assassinated "there was a great deal of sympathy, of course, and indignation on account of this."

"WE WERE THE CYNICAL GENERATION"

The distinctive features of postwar Soviet history define the Baby Boomers' gen-eration, as do worldwide trends such as the birth of a youth culture, the global-ization of Western popular culture, more leisure time, rising living standards, expansion of education, and a growing consumer culture.[32] Although formative experiences create age cleavages between all generations, the turbulence of Soviet history before 1953, followed by decades of peaceful, evolutionary change afterward, left a distinctive mark. Growing up under Stalin, the Baby Boomers' parents longed for improved living standards and stability. After 1953, the Soviet system delivered, but not enough to satisfy the Cold War generation as adults, who believed less and were promised more.[33] In judging Stalin, Khrushchev, and Brezhnev, both generations agree that the Khrushchev era was the best, but the parents believe the Stalin era was the worst, while their children save that distinction for the Brezhnev years—when they came of age.[34]

The Baby Boomers expressed agreement in regard to how they differ from their parents. Most of them emphasized combinations of five points. Their parents' generation: knew the fear of Stalinism; endured the hardships and trials of World War II; had values worth emulating caused by suffering; was less free; and was far less optimistic than their offspring. As Tatyana Arzhanova put it, "We didn't have to prove ourselves in some terrible ordeals, when you had to make a moral choice. We were lucky. My mother was afraid of practically everything." Yet these difficulties, according to Vladimir Mikoyan, made his parents' generation "more purposeful than ours." And, as Tatyana Kuznetsova suggested, "more pure, more good hearted, more open." As a result, avowed Irina Garzanova, her parents "put the good of the collective above their own personal interests."

Saratov's Vladimir Kirsanov emphasized, "My parents' generation was Stalin's generation. They were so suppressed by this regime that they withdrew from public life in all of its forms to live in their internal world." In contrast, "my generation was more interested in the outside world, and this evoked a negative reaction from our parents." "Our views," he opined, "were probably freer." Aleksandr Konstantinov concurred that "we had less built-in fear. As compared to 1937 [the height of Stalin's Great Terror], which for them was drenched in blood. We didn't know real repression. And generally there also was great openness." Yevgeny Podolsky linked his parents' "very secretive" nature to Stalinism. His generation "perceived things very differently. We were more open. We weren't afraid because we personally didn't experience the repressions. We didn't look over our shoulders." Moscow's Vladimir Prudkin stressed that, unlike his parents' generation, his "didn't have to endure such obvious repression and fear. In this regard our generation is luckier. Although it lived in very restricted conditions, there wasn't any heavy-duty intimidation." Khrushchev's denunciation of Stalin also profoundly affected the parents' generation, as Marina Bakutina underscored. "I know that for many people of my parents' generation this played an enormous role in that they began to see things clearly and this forced them to reexamine their values."

The Great Patriotic War also molded the Baby Boomers' parents. Saratov's Aleksandr Kutin recognized his parents' generation "had a hard life," because it won the war and then rebuilt the country, which was "half destroyed. Thank God that we didn't have to endure it." Olga Kolishchyuk felt similarly: "They lived through that horrible war. Our parents suffered more hardships than we did, more difficult times." Olga Martynkina believed her parents' generation was "more ideological" because of the war. "My father was a Communist, a commissar, who went through the war 'For the Motherland! For Stalin!' They were brought up differently." Moscow's Leonid Volodarsky pointed out that Soviet history provided few positive examples that could be used to bring up future generations, but the Great Fatherland War was one of them. "People didn't fight for Stalin or for the motherland, but for themselves. Everyone understood that Hitler wanted to destroy the entire country. It was a holy war."

Many interviewees saw the privations of war as but one more hardship on top of all the others their parents suffered from the start of Russia's revolutionary upheavals. For instance, Vladimir Bystrov's father, born in 1914, "was forced to leave home and become independent already at age fourteen." Then there were the harsh conditions of the Stalin revolution and forced industrialization and collectivization. Tatyana Luchnikova depicted her parents' generation as "that of the planned economy" that created all sorts of unplanned shortages. Acknowledging that the difference with her generation was "colossal," she opined: "They were used to living according to the rules." Saratov's Irina Vizgalova confirmed that the hard times her parents and grandparents lived through left an indelible mark. Distrustful, "they stocked supplies of salt, matches, and other essentials, just in case."

Baby Boomers from both cities depict themselves as luckier than their parents. "First of all, we didn't live through the horrible, horrible war. And, of course, we're more materially secure," explained Moscow's Anatoly Shapiro. "Those were very poor times and, for the most part, the great mass of people lived in poverty. Back then it was awful." Saratov's Aleksandr Trubnikov maintained that his generation is luckier because "we got to experience real life. Many of my friends' and acquaintances' parents died before they understood or saw anything." He clarified what he meant: "I now understand in what kind of world I live, and it's wonderful to experience freedom. Of course, there's the Chinese curse: 'May you live in interesting times.' It's quite appropriate, because we lived through precisely this kind of period." Trubnikov acknowledged that perestroika created awful hardships for his classmates, some of whom "lost confidence in tomorrow. But, as a matter of fact, even they understood that we're now living in the real world. This is probably the biggest difference between the generations. My father never understood what happened. He was old. He believed that the democrats sold Russia, that Soviet power was better."

Moscow's Igor Litvin and many others stressed that "our generation is more freedom loving. Second, we're far more pragmatic." Yelena Zharovova affirmed that their generation was "more pragmatic, less naïve, perhaps in an everyday sense in terms of belief in propaganda." Lyubov Kovalyova saw her generation as "better educated, freer, with broader views," and "less inhibited." Saratov's Aleksandr Babushkin insisted his generation "was, of course, emancipated." That said, he conceded that "nonetheless, our roots were planted by our parents." What struck Irina Tsurkan most was her parents' extreme caution. "Don't blab about that which you shouldn't blab about, don't say anything that can be misconstrued." "Our generation was freer," said Galina Poldyaeva. "And we had far more possibilities."

Saratov's Arkady Darchenko spoke for others in saying, "Most likely, our generation didn't differ all that much from that of our parents. But after us came a new generation that is completely different." For Olga Gorelik, it was also a matter of degrees: "Perhaps we were just a little bit freer, but you can't say that this was a huge thing. I believe that, to a certain degree, I'm a repeat of my parents." Natalya Yanichkina told me that "we're probably less inhibited or something, but at the same time we're products of our parents' upbringing. They had so many restrictions and for many years we were brought up on them too and have a certain internal self-restraint. Nevertheless, we're freer, but less so than our children." Natalya P. felt certain that her parents' generation passed on their ideals to the Baby Boomers: "I therefore think that there aren't any fundamental differences, although we're more democratic, we're freer, we're less inhibited. We grew up in different circumstances. Nonetheless, ideology was something that we had to deal with when we were in school?" "As a matter of fact," opined Moscow's Vyacheslav Starik, "our generation differed little. It's really hard for me, for example, to learn how to work for money." Vladimir Glebkin also believed that fear "is in me, because the Party system in the Soviet Union, although it began to get weaker and weaker, nonetheless continued to function."

Still, the Khrushchevian Thaw left a more permanent mark on the Baby Boomers than on their parents. "We nevertheless were shaped by the Thaw. We were more curious. We were more interested in that which was brand new," explained Saratov's Irina Chemodurova. Natalya Pronina concurred that "the Thaw exerted a powerful influence." Moscow's Yelena Kolosova represented her generation as "more self-assured, more open to interaction with each other and with other people." This was not accidental, owing to the Thaw and the greater flow of information. In short, "there were considerable ties with the West and we somehow felt ourselves part of the world. It's very important that we grew up feeling ourselves part of the world. We grew up with the sense that the culture of each nation is valuable."

Americans the same age of the 1967 graduates belong to the "1960s generation," but, as Lyubov Raitman explained, the Soviet 1960s generation was "the generation of our older siblings. It's the generation associated with the popular debate between physicists and poets. It's the generation" of the poet bards. "We caught the tail end of it." Leonid Terlitsky remarked that "we did not have a term attached to us. I think we were the first young generation growing up after the Soviet system showed the first signs of instability. In my mind, the real crash of the Soviet system happened largely because information began to come in. And with the introduction of the tape recorder to this country people had the technology to distribute information outside of official channels." They adapted it to create their own hybrid cultural forms that were both new, and all too familiar. What was distinctive about them defined the Cold War generation. Terlitsky came up with a label for it: the cynical one. "We were the cynical generation because we knew. We had the opportunity to learn that, what were being sold as universal truths, were nothing like it." Valentin Ulyakhin reminded me that the Soviet leadership saw his generation as a vanguard one that would build communism. Ironically, he concluded, "The tragedy of our generation is that we spent perhaps the best years of our youth going along that awful path to nowhere."

"OUR GENERATION TURNED OUT TO BE MORE OPEN"

The Baby Boomers remembered having happy childhoods not only because Soviet propaganda had it this way but also because their parents constructed a childhood for them reflecting the stability that came to the USSR in the aftermath of Stalin's death. This generation experienced no revolution, no terror, no World War II, no major social cataclysms, but evolutionary social change that proved to be revolutionary in its own way. Further, the state prepared them to be the first Soviet generation that would live under communism. Catching up with and overtaking America was not just about aggregate production statistics, since the Soviet Union, the propaganda organs screamed, had already forged ahead of the capitalist world in what really mattered: the system itself.

The circumstances in Russia and beyond when I interviewed the Baby Boomers early in the new millennium also shaped memories of their childhood. Except for truly traumatic moments, we remember positive things more readily than negative ones. When we factor in the weight of youthful confidence, and growing up in what may well have been the most optimistic period of Soviet history, it is easy to understand why the Baby Boomers today harbor positive memories about their carefree childhood years. Many of them recalled their childhood with nostalgia—although they do not think of it as such, but, rather, as the truth—in part because I interviewed them when nostalgia had seized hold of their country in the aftermath of a decade and more of political turmoil and economic uncertainty following the broken promises of the transition from communism to capitalism. As émigré Slavic studies scholar Svetlana Boym observed, this nostalgia does not represent a yearning for a return to a Soviet past, but for "the unrealized dreams of the past and visions of the future that became obsolete." We need to keep in mind that Soviet propaganda promised the interviewees that theirs will be the best, the most just, and the happiest society on earth. The dashed hopes and frustrations of the transition period following the collapse of the Soviet system made people long for an imagined past characterized by stability and normalcy, for the time of their untroubled school days.[35] A shattered and maligned ideal does not necessarily lose its appeal for proving to be wrong.[36]

On another level, the Baby Boomers' childhood *was* qualitatively different. The Thaw promoted a Soviet mass culture characterized by the poet bards and guitar poetry, stylish clothing, Sputnik, Soviet Olympic victories, world chess championships, and revolution in Cuba, to say nothing of the recurrent crises in the West and in its relations with the former colonial world. Their childhood was likewise characterized by the arrival of chewing gum, ballpoint pens, Fellini flicks, Hemingway and Salinger novels, Beatles music, the Twist, Marilyn Monroe, and *The Magnificent Seven*. This incipient globalization of youth culture took the edge off Cold War anxieties, too. So did the Soviet campaign for peaceful coexistence that made peace essential in order to achieve—and to enjoy—communism.

Saratov's Natalya P. maintained that "they managed to bring us up, the majority of us, with a strange sense of duty and sense of responsibility. I feel this even now." Soviet schools might also have met with some success in instilling values of collective upbringing, but the government found no foolproof way of fostering political orthodoxy while accommodating youth culture. The growth of education, access to foreign radio broadcasts, improved living standards, and focus on individualism all led to an erosion of ideology,[37] creating what Leonid Terlitsky called the cynical generation. Boris Shtein believed that, as a result, his generation not only lacked their parents' fear "but were far more critical. Thereby, it seems to me, our generation turned out to be more open to democratic changes." Shtein placed great importance on this: "I think that our generation was prepared for and destined for that which began in Gorbachev's time." For this reason, it is hard not agree with Moscow's Sergei Zemskov, who sees his generation as "unconscious agents of change."

4

THE BABY BOOMERS
COME OF AGE

The Baby Boomers came of age at the zenith of Soviet socialism, only to see the system crumble some three decades later. Ironically, much of this had to do with the Soviet system's very success at effecting social change, whose byproducts included rapid urbanization and a rise in the number of educated professionals.[1] On the eve of World War II, the younger generation in the USSR had voiced the greatest enthusiasm for their country. But by 1980, when the Baby Boomers were thirty years old, things were the other way around. The higher the educational level achieved by the younger generation, moreover, the weaker their backing was for the regime, with the exception that support for the system increased with income level.[2] Indeed, in the decades following Stalin's death people turned their attention away from state priorities to private concerns such as family and friends. The pursuit of new aspirations created a Soviet mass culture shaped by education, the media, and increasing contact with the outside world, which in time bred apathy and cynicism. As a result, not long after the confidence inspired by Sputnik, the Soviet government began to lose its grip over all segments of the population. The shifting attitudes did not necessarily result in a questioning of the core values of the Soviet model,[3] yet some Western observers noticed a certain malaise at the time. Sociologist Alex Inkeles, for instance, claimed that by the time it celebrated its fiftieth anniversary in 1967, the Soviet state had lost its vitality and imagination.[4]

But how did those coming of age during the Soviet 1970s, a crucial decade in the prehistory of M. S. Gorbachev's later efforts to revitalize Soviet socialism, remember this period? A survey conducted by Soviet sociologists in 1966 showed that Soviet youth wanted to land a satisfying job, earn a university degree, travel abroad, live well, obtain decent housing, improve their job qualifications, enjoy close friends, raise their children to be decent people, find true love, have a family, and buy a car.[5] How attainable was this Soviet dream?

"PERHAPS WHATEVER GOD DOES IS FOR THE BEST"

Mirroring a global trend, in the twenty-five years following Stalin's death in 1953 the number of students enrolled in Soviet institutions of higher education soared from 1.5 million to more than 5 million.[6] Soviet propaganda plugged the remarkable progress the USSR had made in educating its people since 1917—especially its women. When the Baby Boomers applied to college, women represented 44.4 percent of university students in the USSR, compared with 39.1 percent in the United States.[7] The Soviet Union also ranked first in the world in the percentage of women studying technological subjects (30.8 percent).[8] When the Baby Boomers graduated from school in 1967, only about 25 percent of those finishing nationwide continued their education, but virtually everyone from School No. 20 and School No. 42 did. Despite expanding opportunities, competition to get into the top colleges remained keen, but varied by discipline.[9] Soviet students applied to be admitted to specific departments, as a result of which they underwent enormous pressure to decide what professions they wanted to enter and to prepare for them already at school. The enthusiasm for math and physics began to subside as competition in the humanities at the top universities took on new intensity.[10]

The USSR lacked institutions comparable to American liberal arts colleges or community colleges, but supported a system of universities, polytechnic schools, and institutions with specialized profiles roughly matching what one would expect to find in professional schools at American universities—law, medicine, education, economics (business), and so forth. Thus those who attended medical school or law school in the Soviet Union did so as undergraduates. Those completing an institution of higher education received a diploma after five years of study.* Getting admitted to universities in the Soviet Union also differed from the American experience in that applicants applied to only one university during the summer following their graduation from high school. Their acceptance was based on how well they performed in school, on character recommendations (this is where belonging to the Komsomol took on meaning), and on the results of three entrance exams.

All applicants took a written and oral exam in Russian, and two other exams depending upon the subject area they wished to study. Gold and silver medalists received exemptions from some of the exams, depending upon their field of study. As in all other areas of Soviet life, *blat* (connections) could prove decisive in admissions. So could unofficial quotas for Jews and other minorities. The intelligentsia routinely hired tutors to prepare their offspring for the college

---

* Diplomas offered by pedagogical institutes required four years of study, but this was later increased to five years, too.

entrance exams.[11] This form of private economic activity increased one's chances of getting admitted, especially when those providing the service sat on the admissions committee. If the applicant failed to receive a high enough score on the admissions exam, he or she could attempt to get into another institution that held exams later in the summer or try out for the night school of his or her institution of choice. (Excelling in the evening division while holding down a job could serve as a springboard for getting admitted to the day division the next year.) Students could reapply to their chosen institution the following year or to a different one.

Soviet students attended institutions of higher education locally, except for a small percentage of super achievers or minority applicants from the provinces admitted to elite universities in Moscow, Leningrad, and a handful of other cities. To illustrate, all of the graduates of School No. 20 went to college in Moscow. All of the graduates of School No. 42 enrolled in Saratov colleges, except for gold medalist Aleksandr Konstantinov, who attended Moscow University. Although they viewed their graduation from school in 1967 as the end of their childhood, they continued living at home and they commuted to college, as dormitories housed only out-of-town students.

The Baby Boomers' stunning rate of college admission had much to do with the elite nature of the schools they attended, as well as with the value their parents placed on education. A great deal was at stake, particularly for males, because "you either went to college or into the military," as Leonid Terlitsky put it. According to Saratov's Irina Barysheva, "parents played a much more important role in their children's lives than now." Igor Litvin's father expected him to study economics and become a store manager—a lucrative position in the bribery-ridden, goods-short Soviet economy. "When I suddenly decided that I wanted to enroll at a language institute, he was simply stunned," said Litvin.

The graduates of Moscow's School No. 20 enrolled in the city's top institutions: Moscow University, the Moscow Institute of International Relations (MGIMO)—"certainly a good third of the class," according to Leonid Terlitsky—the Institute of Foreign Languages (IFL), the Pedagogical Institute, the Aviation Institute, the Energy Institute, the Institute of Economics, the Medical Institute, and others. The pressure at elite schools to get into top universities was felt not only by pupils and parents, but by teachers and principals, too, since how well a school's graduates fared in the admissions process determined the school's prestige.

Some teachers took proactive roles in helping their students. Anna Lyovina's homeroom teacher, for instance, dropped in on Lyovina's parents one day to tell them: "'Anna gets very nervous and is facing burn out. She should not be allowed to take admissions exams. If she does, she won't get into a single college.'" Heeding the advice, Anna's parents managed to obtain a certificate at the local health clinic exempting her from admissions exams. "My homeroom teacher saved me. I really would not have gotten in anywhere otherwise. She felt that," admitted Lyovina, who enrolled at the Institute of Foreign Languages. Boris Shtein remembered, "Somehow I got on bad terms with my homeroom teacher and, as a result, received a very poor character reference from her with which it would have been impossible to get admitted to college." Others were in the same boat as Shtein. "Anton Petrovich [the principal] and Nina Ivanovna sent the teacher abroad and, after this, we received normal character references," related a grateful Shtein.

Determined to study at the Physics Institute, Vladimir Glebkin encountered difficulties of a different sort. The year he completed school, he and Sergei Zemskov traveled with Glebkin's father to a ski resort in the Caucasus. Descending a mountain in poor visibility, Vladimir collided with a boulder dusted in snow, and this sent him sailing into a precipice. He would have perished if Sergei had not been with him, since Vladimir lost consciousness when his ski pole hit him in the eye. Realizing that Vladimir would not be able to make it through tough exams, his father convinced him to apply to the Patrice Lumumba People's Friendship University, where many Third World students studied. (Vladimir got admitted and teaches there today.)

The Baby Boomers spoke of the anxiety they felt preparing for college admissions. For gold medalist Yelena Kolosova this had much to do with the need to select a major beforehand. Yelena wanted to study art history at Moscow University, but her parents persuaded her that she would have to toe the Party line if she did. She also considered her other passion, biology, but a last-minute change in the admissions exam made her lose confidence in her ability to prepare for it, so she enrolled in the Chemistry Department instead. Valentin Ulyakhin became anxious for another reason. Although he performed well on his admissions exams at MGIMO, which trained diplomats, he recalled, "They didn't want to admit me, because I was very fat. I weighed 246 pounds." He got in, however, and graduated with honors in 1972.

Official records show that fifty-four of the fifty-six 1967 graduates of School No. 42 enrolled in college: eighteen at the Saratov Pedagogical Institute; thirteen at Saratov University; ten at the Medical Institute; nine at the Polytechnic Institute; one at Moscow University; and one each at Saratov's Institute of the Mechanization of Agriculture, Law Institute, and Economics Institute. The near universal college acceptance rate of the graduates of Saratov's School No. 42 belies an important consideration. As Natalya Yanichkina explained, "Some got in through patronage, some without, some because they knew a lot, some because they had money." Silver medalist Arkady Darchenko knew a lot, winning a slot in nuclear physics at Saratov University, as did Vladimir Nemchenko, who acknowledged a certain pecking order among colleges. "I'm not sure how to explain it, but those who went to the university would probably have a lot more in common with you than those who finished the Polytechnic Institute." The majority of females enrolled at the Saratov Pedagogical Institute to study English, the only institution in Saratov at the time that had such a program. Viktor D. got accepted at the Medical Institute "without bribes, without money, without anything," he maintained. "I submitted my documents, studied, passed the exams, and graduated."

It was difficult, but not impossible, to switch colleges. Galina Poldyaeva's aunt insisted she enroll at the Medical Institute. Yet her heart was not in it. Galina did well her first semester, "but by summer she began to perform abominably and gave up everything," lamented her friend Irina Kulikova. Poldyaeva then got into the language program at the Pedagogical Institute—but abandoned that to return to the Medical Institute to be with her fiancé: "My husband completed the med institute's army physician program, got his orders, and we left with a group of soldiers to East Germany." After five years there, the government stationed them in the Zabaikal region, "and as a result I remained without a higher education," which she much regretted.

Those who did not get admitted to their top choice college resorted to a variety of strategies to enroll elsewhere. Until her last year at school, Moscow's Tatyana Arzhanova planned to enroll at the Institute of Foreign Languages (IFL), but she became interested in medicine and prepared with a tutor to take exams in chemistry and physics. After receiving Bs, she decided to enroll at the IFL the next year. However, when a neighbor reminded her how expensive it was for her single mother to pay for tutors, Arzhanova tried out for, and got admitted to, the Food Institute, "a small and not very prestigious institute," where she became a straight-A student. With a transcript peppered with Bs and Cs, Tatyana Luchnikova was turned down by the IFL. She then considered MGIMO, but the admissions committee told her, "'don't waste your time.'" After getting rejected at the Institute of Cinematography (IC), she worked as a secretary, enrolled in correspondence courses at IC, and eventually transferred in as a regular student. Sofiya Vinogradova dreamed of becoming a doctor but feared that she would not get admitted to medical school, so she enrolled at the Institute of Chemical Technology. "Today I never would have gone into chemical technology," she insisted. She spent six "bad" years there, but landed a job upon graduation as a lab assistant for a "marvelously progressive comrade." While working there, she enrolled as a sophomore at the Medical Institute's night school and after a year switched to the day division, graduating in 1982.

Saratov's Natalya Yanichkina found a job as a draftsman's apprentice at the design institute where her mother worked after getting turned down by the Polytechnic Institute. She got admitted to the evening division the next year. One point short of getting admitted to the Polytechnic Institute, Pyotor Krasilnikov attended its evening division, too. This was hard on Krasilnikov: "All of my friends at school got admitted somewhere. I thought I knew everything, but I was punished for my conceit." Reflecting upon the matter, he concluded, "Perhaps whatever God does is for the best. I found work that I liked."

"I DIDN'T GET IN BECAUSE I'M A JEW"

A number of Muscovites believed anti-Semitism prevented them from getting admitted to their college of choice. Yevgeniya Ruditskaya bluntly told me "they didn't like to take Jews at the institutes." She spared me the details of her own experience of getting admitted to the Pedagogical Institute, but Igor Litvin did not. He dreamed of going to the Institute of Foreign Languages (IFL); however, "for the first time in my life I really felt that I wasn't welcome everywhere," he shared, owing to the "fifth point," that is, the fifth question on applications, regarding nationality. It began at school, where he had trouble getting a character reference. Several days after turning in his documents at the IFL, he received an anonymous call. "The person told me that all of the applications were divided into two piles. In one were those who would be admitted or who would be admitted on the basis of their knowledge, and in the second one those who would definitely not be admitted. You're in the second pile, so come fetch your documents. This is your friend speaking." A terribly discouraged Litvin suspected that classmate Leonid Volodarsky's Jewish father, who taught at IFL, had tipped Litvin off, but Volodarsky denied it. Desperate, Litvin turned to one of his English teachers, Gennady Petrovich, who said that "if I were in your shoes, I'd retrieve my application and try elsewhere." Another sympathetic teacher urged Igor to apply to the Moscow Pedagogical Institute. Despite receiving top grades on all four exams, Litvin later learned that some members of the admissions committee did not want to admit him because he was Jewish.

Vladimir Sidelnikov, a Russian who got admitted to MGIMO, which had become an institute where the Party elite sent their offspring, confirmed that anti-Semitism entered into the college admissions equation: "They didn't admit Jews. I attended school with many Jews, but it was the rare exception among them that got in," he stated. Anatoly Shapiro affirmed, "I didn't get in because I'm a Jew," reminding me that this took place shortly after Israel's stunning success in the Six Day War. What especially irked him was that, during the exams, he was waiting with his classmate Vladimir Mikoyan when the institute's rector passed by. Patting Vladimir on the head, the rector asked about his grandfather's health and assured him that "you'll get excellent marks" on the exams. "This took place right in front of me. But that's how things were back then," grumbled Shapiro. A month later he was accepted at the Moscow Finance Institute, "a very ordinary place. I studied there for five years and can't say anything good or bad about the place, only that those five years flew by," he related.

Vyacheslav Starik first suffered anti-Semitism when he tried to enroll in the Physics Department at Moscow University. During the physics exam he was asked a question that fell outside the parameters of the school program. "I had a surname that he didn't like," explained Starik, who had enough time to seek admission elsewhere. Trying the Moscow Aviation Institute where his parents taught, he got in without a problem owing to an antidote for anti-Semitism: "Well, perhaps my father's name played a role to a certain degree because he taught economics there."

Lyubov Raitman also encountered difficulties, but some were of her own making. She acknowledged, "I would have studied harder and more seriously." She tried out for the program in applied linguistics at Moscow University. "It was always hard for Jews to get in there," she explained. But officially she got rejected because of the D she received on the exam in mathematics. Lyubov still had time to apply to MGIMO. "I got a C on the history exam and had the feeling that my surname, my appearance, and my nationality were far more the cause than my insufficient knowledge of history. You feel this the way a teacher looks at you and asks you a question that falls outside the confines of the school program, and then bombards you with such questions." For a male this would have been a tragedy, because the prospect of serving in the army hung over them. "But for me it was simply a huge blow to my ego," admitted Raitman. "Everyone else enrolled somewhere except me." She then decided to apply to the IFL, not only because she was well prepared but also because the father of one of her classmates taught there. A friend of her parents, he promised to help her during the exams "because it was hard for Jews to enroll there as well. They got in with great difficulty thanks to their abilities and connections. Back then it wasn't a matter of direct bribes, although there was perhaps some of that, too." She fine-tuned her remark: "It was money that parents spent on private lessons with the very teachers who would then help out during the admissions exams. They helped by giving you the necessary grade." She also experienced a form of gender discrimination at the IFL: "For some reason that's unclear to me even today, they didn't accept young women into the translation department," griped Raitman. "I enrolled in the teacher training department and studied for five years with a group of nine women."

Since the age of fourteen, Leonid Terlitsky had prepared to enroll in the Moscow Institute of Architecture by working with tutors and attending evening classes at the institute for prospective students, but first he had to sit things out for a year. "I was flunked intentionally, because in 1967 there was the Six Day War, as a result of which the Soviet Union broke off diplomatic relations with Israel. Nineteen sixty-seven saw a wave of official anti-Semitism, and I think that was the only reason why I was not accepted." Terlitsky acquitted himself well on all of the exams except for drafting. He faced military service, "but the Almighty was watching over me. He got me into a car accident that I survived and, as a result of it, I pretty much faked being sick and not fit for service, and I got a second chance at school." He elaborated, "On the second try, my parents didn't take any chances. They bribed one of the school officials, and I was enrolled in the Moscow Institute of Architecture."

Because everyday anti-Semitism was more pronounced in Saratov, local Baby Boomers of Jewish descent were discrete about acknowledging their nationality when a surname or patronymic did not make it obvious. Ironically, none of them mentioned running up against discrimination in seeking college admission, unlike their counterparts in otherwise more liberal Moscow. Yet silver medalist Nikolai Kirsanov felt that attitudes toward nationality constrained his choice of college. Half Volga German, his surname is Russian, and Russian was the nationality stamped on his passport. When Kirsanov decided to try out for Moscow's Institute of International Relations, he remembered, "My relatives said to me, 'You don't need to do that, because you won't get in for certain reasons.'" Heeding their advice, Kirsanov enrolled at the Saratov Medical Institute. Kirsanov cannot claim that he was denied admission to MGIMO owing to the fact that he was Volga German, but this ambiguity was what made discrimination so effective.

"THEY TRIED TO BRAINWASH US AT THE UNIVERSITY"

The magnet schools prepared the Baby Boomers so well academically that those in both institutions who majored in English found that the preparation they had received at the special schools placed them far ahead of other students. Those who enrolled at Saratov's Pedagogical Institute—all female—became "A" students. Similarly, Igor Litvin recounted that, up until his junior year at the Moscow Pedagogical Institute, "I didn't have to do a thing." Frustrated, he turned to his instructors, but they discouraged him from trying. "They cranked out teachers, and heaven forbid you'd want to become a translator. They didn't want to teach us. They had their goal: to turn out ordinary teachers for secondary schools."

But the elite schools did not prepare the interviewees for the oppressive politicization of college-level instruction that Anna Lyovina called "awful." Going against the current, she switched from the daytime to the evening division of Moscow's IFL. "I did so after my freshman year. I thought I'd go out of my mind, because of the History of the CPSU [Communist Party of the Soviet Union], History of the CPSU, and History of the CPSU. It was torture. I couldn't stand it. Then there was Military Science. There was far less of it in the evening division," she said. Yet even there, "they constantly tried to indoctrinate us, 'You are translators on the ideological front. You will interact with foreigners and you have to be careful, you have to be grounded.'" An old Bolshevik who taught Party history regaled her charges about how she carried out collectivization. As a child, however, Lyovina had been exposed to a counternarrative: "My dear nanny would tell me that all of her relatives from Tambov province, hard-working peasants who fed Russia, were exiled to Siberia. I couldn't happily reply, Hoorah! Collectivization!" rationalized Anna.

Lyovina did not exaggerate the extent of the politicization, since the Central Committee had determined that the risk groups most receptive to alien ideologies were the artistic intelligentsia and students.[12] As a result, the Soviet government increased the number of required courses university students took on political indoctrination. For the Baby Boomers this meant mind-numbing classes in political economy, dialectical and historical materialism, the History of the CPSU, and the fundamentals of scientific communism.[13] Even Vladimir Sidelnikov, a true believer at the time, felt the heavy-handed politicization of the academy. "Why did I need these subjects?" he remembered asking himself. Ideology particularly constrained study of the humanities and social sciences. Tatyana Luchnikova, who attended Moscow's Institute of Cinematography, wrote her senior thesis on social confrontation in American cinematography, "because we could write only about confrontation. We couldn't write about the real American Hollywood." Saratov's Aleksandr Trubnikov came to realize that "they tried to brainwash us at the university, even more so than at school, but by then our contacts were different, and I already began to understand what a 'wonderful' country we lived in."

Complementing the growing politicization of university instruction, the Soviet government stepped up its repression of dissident activities following the 1966 show trial of literary critic Andrei Sinyavsky and short story writer Yuli Daniel. By raising fear of a return to Stalinism, the trial helped to galvanize the dissident movement. "We knew that the KGB existed," remarked Saratov's Aleksandr Konstantinov. "This didn't concern us at all at school. However,

This picture of Vladimir Sidelnikov (left?), taken when he studied at MGIMO and worked as a translator at the country's premier Pioneer Camp, Artek, suggests the influence of a larger youth culture on Soviet young people. It is unclear why the young man wrote in English "Tuva"—a desolate region in southern Siberia annexed by the USSR after World War II—on his jeans, but it was a daring thing to do at the time.
Courtesy of Lyudmila Sidelnikova

during the Sinyavsky-Daniel trial, we were older then, their existence began to interest me." Moscow's Lyubov Raitman remembered discussing the trial at school, because a short article on the court case appeared in *Daily Worker*, one of the two Communist English-language newspapers they read, and in *Moscow News*. According to Raitman, "we knew that this was unfair. We understood that this was a forbidden topic. They arrested *writers*." Leonid Terlitsky concurred that they talked about such topics at school, "but not in the way you might think. I mean, we were not actively seeking to join the dissident movement. For a variety of reasons all of us thought at the time that we all had to build a life *here*. We perceived ourselves in a cage. I certainly did." He added, "No one could imagine anything else. Maybe you'd get a job. Maybe you'd get an education with a job that would allow you to travel abroad, and that was certainly a goal of many in the magnet school because so many from our class enrolled at the Moscow Institute of International Affairs."

The KGB closely monitored university life, in 1971 arresting a group of students in the History Department at Saratov University and sentencing them to years at hard labor for setting up an independent Marxist reading group. Named after the group's leader, Aleksandr Romanov, the "Romanov affair" became a cause célèbre in the history of the university. Aleksandr Kutin, who read *samizdat* literature, acknowledged that, after the arrest of Romanov and his comrades, "we realized that they could punish us, too." Yevgeny Podolsky remembered the trial held in Saratov: "Even one student from our year suffered as a result of this. Although he didn't have anything to do with that group, one of his friends did, and he, for some reason, showed up at his friend's apartment where they had all gathered, after which the KGB naturally began to trail him too. Then they arrested him." They eventually released the student, but "they ruined his career. He was a straight-A student, but he had a really hard time finding work," reported Podolsky. The authorities imprisoned the others. As Podolsky concluded, "This disturbed the entire student body. When the trial took place everyone was really upset because we knew these people." University students reacted variously, to be sure, but he remembered that "they respected them for their courage, because we didn't believe they had committed any crime." Vladimir Nemchenko commented that "we all exchanged whispered secrets" about the Romanov affair. He also shared that a student in his own department got involved in some sort of "anti-Soviet" activity. "After they worked him over, he became reserved and unassuming." The Romanov affair reverberated throughout Saratov. Olga Martynkina, who studied at the conservatory, recalled: "Their fates were broken, and it's unclear why. They simply read some primary sources." Gennady Ivanov mentioned, "There was a dissident group at the [Law] Institute among the older students and they were locked up for two years. They raised questions that were unacceptable, although common sense would dictate that they had the right to ask them. Back then this was considered an anti-Soviet group." Thus, the Saratovites sympathized with the students victimized by the KGB, yet outwardly toed the Party line, suggesting how self-censorship instinctively became part of the Soviet socialization process.

Soviet leaders pinned the blame for the student disaffection on the qualifications of those who taught the required courses on Marxism, not on the subject matter itself. On July 24, 1974, *Pravda* published a Central Committee resolution "on raising the ideological-theoretical level of the teaching of the social sciences" at the Bauman Technical School in Moscow and Saratov State University. Knocking the rigid and irrelevant nature of the courses, the resolution observed that "more than half of the teachers in the departments of political economy and philosophy of Saratov University do not have a basic higher education in these specialties."[14] As everyone knew, these fields did not attract top students, but Party careerists instead.

"WE WERE BEWILDERED"

Stalin's death in 1953 and Khrushchev's denunciation of him in 1956 represented landmark events for the Baby Boomers' parents; 1968 became a landmark event for their offspring. On August 21, Soviet and Warsaw-pact tanks rolled into Czechoslovakia to crush the Prague Spring associated with Alexander Dubček. He and his associates had tried to do what members of the Soviet 1960s generation and intellectual community had expected from Khrushchev and still advocated. They wanted the government to open society further, to modernize its ideology, to decentralize the economy, and to offer more material incentives.[15] The Kremlin lied to its people that the Party and leaders of the Czechoslovak Socialist Republic had appealed to the USSR and its allies to provide urgent help. Justifying the invasion, the Brezhnev Doctrine declared that the USSR had the right to intervene in any bloc country threatened by imperialist forces, but the graffiti and placards Soviet forces encountered in Prague told a different story: "The Russian circus is in town. Don't feed the animals." "Proletariat of the world unite—or else we'll kill you." "The more tanks you have, the fewer the brains."

The invasion of Czechoslovakia may have united the intelligentsia in Prague, but it divided them in Moscow and Saratov.[16] With few alternative sources of information available other than the official media, most Soviet citizens supported the Kremlin's decision to overrun Prague. "Only later, when I was in Moscow, I learned about the demonstration on Red Square.* Back then we didn't know a thing," quipped Irina Chemodurova. Aleksandr Kutin concurred that the invasion "was little discussed, because we got practically no information from there." Arkady Darchenko remembered that "opinions differed sharply. There was one false report released by the mass media that, if we didn't invade

---

*   On August 25, 1968, seven demonstrators protested the Soviet invasion, five of whom were later sentenced to labor camps or to internal exile.

Czechoslovakia, the German hordes would once again be at our border. Many believed this." But the other half "said that this was nothing but a lie, another attempt at forcing them to accept socialism." Darchenko's uncle, who belonged to the invading forces, got burned in his tank when it was torched. "He always maintained that the invasion was necessary, but a soldier is a soldier. He couldn't see things otherwise, yet I told him that he had no business being there." Because of the invasion, however, "we began to understand that we lacked information," maintained Mikhail Markovich. This is why most interviewees date their serious listening to foreign radio broadcasts to 1968.

As Saratov's Vladimir Kirsanov emphasized, back then "we understood all of this differently." Aleksandr Virich underscored that the invasion took place in the summer. Like many, he had joined a student work brigade and had other things on his mind. "To be honest, we backed the invasion." Aleksandr Trubnikov believed that "what we did was right. I was convinced that you had to nip it all in the bud." Olga Kamayurova regretted that "I heard only official information and saw the invasion as the correct course of action for our country. There were no conversations at home on such topics in my presence. My parents were Communists who truly believed." Moscow's Vladimir Bystrov confessed, "We took pride in our army and in our country. I have upbraided myself ever since, but my views back then were inevitable, because we grew up this way." Andrei Rogatnev voted to expel from the Aviation Institute a classmate who had taken part in an "anti-Soviet" demonstration. Bakhyt Kenzheyev—who soon came to sympathize with Soviet dissidents—admitted that "back then I still believed in communism, and I justified the invasion to myself. If it weren't for the invasion, the Germans would have come." His case suggests how subversive an eventual loss of faith in the system could be.

There were enclaves of liberal thinking, however, among Moscow's student population. Yevgeniya Ruditskaya claimed she "understood what had happened in Czechoslovakia." Boris Shtein replied, "In our milieu it was severely condemned." Those who studied at Moscow University tended to oppose the invasion. According to Tatyana Artyomova, "no one supported it. They said, what a disgrace, what an idiot Brezhnev is." Viktor Alekseyev confirmed that "I don't recall anyone who was pleased with it or who even sympathized with it." In fact, all of Alekseyev's school friends "were very critically disposed." Aleksandr Konstantinov affirmed, "All of my friends were outraged" by the news.

Those in both cities troubled by the crude show of force acknowledged that their critical reaction remained passive, owing to indifference or fear. Involved in his first romances, Moscow's Viktor Alekseyev observed that they and his professional interests remained far more important to him. Recalling that he had been on vacation when the invasion was launched, Vladimir Prudkin confided that "I was more wrapped up in my personal life, and I wasn't politicized." Georgy Godzhello commented that "there were no major protests, but everyone understood that it wasn't a good thing." Natalya Yolshina remembered that there were conversations on the topic at Saratov University and that "they did not support the invasion," but "there were no strikes with placards, and we didn't march anywhere." Leonid Volodarsky maintained that "at the Institute [of Foreign Languages] I reacted like everyone else did, of course, but at home I was against the invasion." Aleksandr Konstantinov explained why young people felt the need to be restrained. "My cousin Sergei attended a meeting at his institute at which a resolution was carried to the effect that they supported the invasion of Czechoslovakia. 'Does everyone agree? Okay, I see everyone agrees.' But Sergei raised his hand and said, 'I'm sorry, but I disagree.' They didn't expel him, but for a long time afterward he held manual jobs."

Others recalled their parents' troubled reactions to suppressing the Prague Spring. Lyubov Kovalyova and her family returned to Moscow from the Black Sea when they got word of the march on Prague. "I remember that my father's mood soured and that he said that this was very dangerous, that it could be the beginning of war." Lyubov Raitman's parents' response remains etched in her memory. "We found out about this when we were in the Crimea. We found out by radio and in their group of close friends this was an awful shock. All illusions were lost." They eventually were: the Soviet invasion heightened the Cold War generation's awareness that official news reports were sanitized. It bred doubt. As Aleksandr Babushkin summed up, "We were bewildered, but then we began to see things differently." "All that left its mark, affecting us for the better," concluded Arkady Darchenko. "We began to understand things about our country that were not all that good."

"PEOPLE GOT HOLD OF WHATEVER THEY WERE INTERESTED IN"

Most of the Baby Boomers date the beginning of their serious reading of *samizdat* to the events of 1968, by which time more illicit literature was available. Saratov's Yevgeny Podolsky did not keep his reading of *samizdat* secret from his parents, both of whom belonged to the Party. "When I was at the university, we read a lot of *samizdat*," he confided. "We moved around little, traveled little, and, for the most part lived in a closed world. Then, all of a sudden, such things showed up. They greatly disturbed us." According to Olga Martynkina, "everyone read it" at the Saratov Conservatory. "We read Solzhenitsyn and other stuff. There were cases of repression." Arkady Darchenko spent the last years of his university days at a closed science city near Moscow, Dubna, where he got his hands on *samizdat*: "It was freer there, the institute is international, and all the available *samizdat* could be found there. Most of it was books published abroad in Russian and smuggled into the country. I read all of Solzhenitsyn in Dubna." Pyotor Krasilnikov believed that students at the polytech where he studied were less politicized than those at the university or conservatory. His classmate, Irina Vizgalova, however, remembered otherwise, thereby revealing how problematic it can be at times to generalize from one's personal experience. The unpublished works of Solzhenitsyn, she recalled, "were passed from hand to hand." Not settling for what others said about the works, she had "to read them myself."

The Saratovites active in the Komsomol or otherwise closely affiliated with the Party through their parents or work steered clear of *samizdat*. Vladimir Kirsanov observed that "my attitude toward dissident literature was fully in accord with my political views. Insofar as I was a staunch enough 'builder of the bright future,' I was indignant when I read in our paper a long article about *samizdat*. It included the names of many well-known Saratov university professors. How could our people take part in such unworthy activities?" An uneasiness still overwhelms Kirsanov when he sees one of these individuals today. "As Chekhov put it, 'Either they stole from him, or he stole from them, I no longer remember, but the feeling remains.'" Before perestroika, rationalized Olga Gorelik, "*samizdat* didn't make its way to me, probably because of the family I came from." Natalya P. explained, "You have to understand that it was all young women who studied at the Department of Foreign Languages. We were not at all interested in politics. We were interested in boys, in romance, in studying. Therefore, *samizdat* didn't circulate among us." Aleksandr Trubnikov "would have read it with pleasure," but, as he put it, "you had to search out this *samizdat*, and I didn't know anyone who offered me any. It was simply very hard to get hold of in Saratov." Aleksandr Babushkin felt similarly: "I had an enormous amount of information on hand, and I didn't need to read still more, and to have to search for it."

Moscow's Igor Litvin began reading *samizdat* when he was a student at the Pedagogical Institute, some of which he obtained on the black market. Aware of the dangers of keeping such literature at home, he nonetheless became bolder with age and "had an entire library." Anatoly Shapiro devoured Solzhenitsyn's *Gulag Archipelago* and the satirical writings of Vladimir Voinovich and Aleksandr Zinoviyev.* Summed up Lyubov Kovalyova: "If something came our way, we, of course, read it. I would say that people probably read everything that they wanted to read." Yelena Kolosova recalled in particular Boris Pasternak's *Doctor Zhivago*, because the print was so small. Although Kolosova appreciated the *samizdat* she examined, she made an astute observation: "It was enough simply to carefully read all of Russian literature and translated foreign literature to see that stupidity is stupidity and that terror is terror."

Owing to the danger of reading and keeping *samizdat*, families played central roles in its dissemination, thereby strengthening private life. Leonid Volodarsky's

---

* Vladimir Voinovich, the author of satirical fiction and poetry, is perhaps best known for his *The Life and Extraordinary Adventures of Private Ivan Chonkin*. Aleksandr Zinoviyev was a satirist and philosopher, especially known for his biting satire about daily absurdities during the Brezhnev years, *Yawning Heights*, published abroad in 1976.

parents showed him *samizdat* when he attended school. His father was a Party member, "but he was a man of very liberal views. There were few idealists," clarified Volodarsky. Lyubov Raitman recounted the time a French acquaintance of her mother's with diplomatic immunity showed up at their apartment in the late 1970s with a suitcase jam-packed with *samizdat* literature. "There was absolutely everything. I remember how we distributed this literature among our acquaintances, read it ourselves, and gave it to others to read. It was rather terrifying." The treasure chest included works by Vasily Aksyonov* and Aleksandr Zinoviyev. Her classmate Bakhyt Kenzheyev affirmed that "Lyuba Raitman's family helped me a great deal. It was in that home that I first saw *samizdat* books. It was a small window onto another world, but an extraordinarily important one." Another was at Moscow University, where Kenzheyev joined a literary group led by a poet Igor Leonidovich Volgin. "This young Volgin read us Mandelshtam, Akhmatova, Tsvetaeva, and Pasternak, told us their biographies, and without any politics. He risked a great deal. It was always possible to find some scoundrel willing to inform. Even now I can't understand why this didn't happen. The club functioned as a separate education that was objective and, of course, anti-Soviet," detailed Kenzheyev. Families also constrained some from searching out *samizdat*. Son of a KGB operative, Andrei Rogatnev volunteered, "We read some erotic stories allegedly written by Aleksei Tolstoy, but I didn't come across any dissident literature." Neither did Vladimir Sidelnikov, whose parents belonged to the Party and who studied at MGIMO. "At our institution there wasn't any *samizdat*," he contended.

"GOD SPARED ME"

The systemic shortcomings of the collective farm system, the difficulty recruiting workers for physically demanding jobs in remote places, and an official attitude that extolled the virtues of physical labor for the urban intelligentsia drove the Soviet government to enlist city dwellers for "volunteer" fieldwork at harvest time (usually without pay) or for participation in construction brigades (for money). Virtually all university students had to contribute their labor and many continued to do so as working adults. Student work brigades celebrated their fifteenth anniversary in 1973 with a major campaign involving more than 550,000 people. "We emphasize that this is a patriotic, volunteer movement of young men and women," one propaganda study reads. "The brigades become a school for breeding courage, stamina, and physical endurance, and for testing citizenship and comradeship."[17]

Yet some Baby Boomers failed the test, carping that participation in the brigades interfered with their educations, and that they found the work unpleasant, even if

---

* Vasily Aksyonov began publishing in the USSR in the 1960s. Appealing to Soviet youth, his works became instant classics. He later published works abroad, including *The Burn* in 1975.

they enjoyed the camaraderie. Saratov's Arkady Darchenko remarked, "You know, there's a great saying in Russian: 'the harshness of Russian laws is mitigated by the fact that their fulfillment is optional.' If we wanted to continue our studies, we had no choice. But we were always able to 'get out of it' somehow, yet we didn't." When he was not taking part in a construction brigade, Darchenko attended sports camps: "I was on the fencing team. Each summer I had the construction brigade and training. We were all like that." Indeed, Yevgeny Podolsky took part in a construction brigade only once, because after he became a member of the university's reserve basketball team, he spent summers training at the sports camp. Aleksandr Virich also belonged to a construction brigade only once, after which he wormed his way out of repeating his efforts. "I didn't go because I had already started writing my thesis."

Natalya P., who dug up potatoes on local state farms, remarked, "It was, as we say, voluntary-compulsory. It was possible to get out of it if you wanted, but it actually was fun. We didn't overdo it." Although others echoed this sentiment, the enjoyment represented the dark cloud's silver lining. Pyotor Krasilnikov recalled the "pleasure" of digging potatoes, cutting hay, and learning how to operate a combine. "We were young, we were with girls, there were dances, and we celebrated birthdays and organized picnics." The fond memories, however, came only after opposition to the idea of going. "It was the policy of the carrot and the stick. They suggested that we go, we refused, and then they told us that, if we didn't, we'd get our vacations in winter. I'd reconsider and say, 'Okay, I'll

The Saratovites did field work even before graduating from School No. 42. The partying that routinely took place afterward made these experiences memorable. *Courtesy of Aleksandr Virich*

go to the collective farm, but I need my vacation in August.' In this way compromises were reached. Plus there were financial incentives." Said a grateful Irina Chemodurova: "God spared me. I went to pull carrots only once."

The experience proved life changing for Vladimir Kirsanov. He concluded that "it wasn't so noticeable in town, but in the countryside the illogicality of the economy was quite obvious. All the shocking things I saw disturbed me." When Kirsanov shared his views with a member of his Party cell at work he was told, "You're mistaken, things can't be that way." Kirsanov, however, knew better. "But I needed a lot more time to process things and to change my mind. Until I reached thirty, I was a true builder of communism." Accompanying his own students on such adventures, his doubts began to grow. "It was especially awful for me to see unharvested fields. It was absolutely incomprehensible. I couldn't stand seeing it," he lamented, referring to red-stained fields of rotting tomatoes. Irina Vizgalova had a similar reaction to the Soviet countryside. "It was a revelation, the dirt, the mud, the attitude that no one needs to work. They'd ask, why should you do that when we don't have to do it? When we'd complete a task quickly, they'd say 'You're done? We thought you'd spend the entire week on it.'" The conclusion she drew from the experience: "It was a waste of time." The "stealing" and "plundering" were "awful." Vizgalova remembered a slogan the collective farmers chose to understand in their own way: "Everything here belongs to the kolkhoz, everything here belongs to me."

In contrast, the Muscovites recalled their involvement in work brigades with nostalgia, probably because the countryside seemed more exotic than it did to those living in provincial Saratov. Vyacheslav Starik saw benefits in joining expeditions to dig potatoes or in moving cabbage rotting in warehouses, both as a student and later as an associate at an aviation research institute. "It united our collective, because no one went there without vodka and tons of food. After lunch we'd fulfill our norm, spread the table, and everybody would mark the end of one more workday at the vegetable storehouse." Lyubov Kovalyova emphatically agreed: "It meant friends, it meant memories, it meant songs. And after we returned home the memories bonded us for years." Taking part in these activities also gave the Muscovites an opportunity to mingle with villagers. Kovalyova related that sometimes conflicts arose as village lads made advances at city girls. "But then we'd begin to mingle and even become friends." When she sprained her leg, the villagers took pity on her. "These were people who, at first glance, seemed like terrible thugs and who made an awful impression, but then we began to mix." Yelena Zharovova was enthusiastic about her experience, which the Physics Department at Moscow University made mandatory for freshmen. "I liked it a great deal because it really did bond us. I made a lot of friends in the building brigade." Apart from imparting confidence in one's ability to master something new, Yelena "learned to be independent because before this I probably was mother's little girl."

Saratov's Gennady Ivanov saw his involvement in the brigades as "a positive experience, and as an opportunity to earn some money." Moscow's Vladimir Bystrov participated in construction brigades as a young graduate student when he found it hard to make ends meet, so he had to do some moonlighting in a labor brigade. At the time, the Soviet government poured enormous resources into its last great construction project, the building of the Baikal-Amur Magistral* (railroad), or BAM, but Bystrov did not go. "When I began to take part in them the Ural region was being developed and the money was there, and not in BAM," he clarified. Vladimir Glebkin also underscored his taking part in summer building brigades "in order to accumulate some capital." It turns out that Glebkin did little building. "I have nothing but the best of memories of this. We traveled to Siberia with a student music ensemble and we not only worked, but performed."

"THE PARTY AND GOVERNMENT HAVE DECIDED . . ."

Upon graduating from college, the Baby Boomers were assigned to jobs (with a salary) by the Soviet government, usually for two years, as a way of repaying society for their educations and of assuring that no region would go without whatever specialists might be needed. The top students could count on the most desirable assignments, but the prominence of one's parents, connections (*blat*), whether or not a graduate was married (and to whom), bribes, and luck, among other factors, determined how things turned out. Parroting Soviet-era propaganda, Anna Lyovina mocked, "They instilled in us that we were the happiest, the most democratic society, that everything was wonderful. We have free medicine, free education! But everyone's forgotten that you had to work off this 'free' education for two years in some out-of-the-way place." Indignant, Lyovina exclaimed, "How many broken fates. How many life tragedies!" Yet whatever difficulties recent graduates may have encountered, all of the Muscovites received work assignments in the capital.

There is a story behind each, revealing the many ways the experience could affect their lives. After graduating from the Finance Institute, Anatoly Shapiro was placed in a Moscow bank, a job he abandoned as soon as his mandatory term expired. Assigned to a Moscow school to teach, Yevgeniya Ruditskaya recalled that "everything was wonderful, except that the school was far away." She dropped in at a neighborhood school, "where they had no math teachers whatsoever, so when I went there to inquire, they snatched me up." Upon graduating from the Moscow Aviation Institute, Mikhail Markovich was assigned to the Foreign Trade Publishing House's editorial office for publications on

---

* In 1974 the Brezhnev government launched the construction of the Baikal-Amur Magistral to link the European and Asian sectors of the USSR.

aviation. "This changed my life. I began to understand already as an upper-classman at the institute that aviation wasn't my calling. Instead, I found a profession that I could enjoy 24/7." Bakhyt Kenzheyev took a post in the Chemistry Department at Moscow University with the understanding that he eventually would enroll as a graduate student. But, Bakhyt recalled, "I had a crisis and slipped into a funk, because I had to decide whether I'm a chemist or a writer." By that time he had already published in Russia, and abroad, and the latter was a crime. Kenzheyev shared his doubts with his professors, "bitter enemies of Soviet power." One of them told him, "Bakhyt, if you leave us, Soviet power will destroy you. Stay here. You can do some translations for a couple of days a week. We'll pay you 100 rubles a month and you can write your poetry." Kenzheyev accepted the offer, remaining the department's unofficial "writer in residence" for five more years.

Although it was rare, some Moscow graduates received "free diplomas," which relieved the state of the obligation to place them. Lyubov Raitman explained that this was "sometimes the only way out for Jewish graduates who did not want to be assigned unwanted jobs in faraway places." Others felt pressured into taking free diplomas because the organization to which they had been assigned did not want them. Some young mothers also found the option attractive, even though it meant that they had to find employment on their own.

A noteworthy difference between Moscow and Saratov is that not all of the Saratovites received assignments in the city. For instance, Gennady Ivanov and his wife were assigned jobs in Saransk, in Mordovia, but there were complications: she was pregnant and he faced serving in the army. Ivanov returned to Saratov to work for the police, while his pregnant wife, released from her obligation, went to live with her parents in Tambov to give birth. The state sent Irina Garzanova to neighboring Ulyanovsk oblast upon graduation from the Medical Institute. She complained that "the majority remained in Saratov. Larisa Petrova was one of them, because her father worked in the Communist Party Oblast Committee. Even she admits this." She does admit this: "Of course, my parents used their connections to bring this about. Otherwise, I would have been sent to work as an ordinary village doctor." Olga Kamayurova worked for two years in a regional hospital in the town of Marx. "I wasn't assigned to Marx, but my husband was," she explained. "Our living conditions there were simply extraordinary. We lived on the fourth floor of a large building without water, heat, or indoor plumbing. How can people live like that at the end of the twentieth century?" Aleksandr Babushkin and his first wife, also a doctor, spent three years in Krasnoarmeisk in Saratov oblast. "It was very difficult," recalled Babushkin. "Books saved me, because I transported my entire library there. Besides, each Friday I fled for Saratov."

State policies at times worked at cross purposes, revealing how stressful job placement was for the Baby Boomers. For example, Arkady Darchenko spent his upperclassman years at the nuclear physics facility in Dubna. He recalled that "if I hadn't gotten married when I did, they could have sent my future wife wherever they liked. Therefore, we got married so we'd get sent to the same place." He had an invitation to work in Dubna, but when he graduated he received an assignment in Saratov, because the Party had implemented a new policy that required the best students to teach physics in local schools. Nobel prizewinner Ilya Mikhailovich Frank summoned Darchenko back to Dubna. "However, they wouldn't let us go for a long time. We were nervous wrecks," volunteered Arkady. Even the secretary of the Dubna Party organization intervened on Darchenko's behalf. As a result, Darchenko and his spouse returned there, but then the government made it more difficult to obtain a living permit for Moscow and Dubna. Despite pulling all the strings he could, Darchenko was told "'the law is the law. You must leave.'"

Yevgeny Podolsky was assigned to an aviation research institute in Saratov, but not without experiencing considerable angst when "the Party decided that all university graduates majoring in physics and mathematics would be assigned to teach in schools." Not enamored with the idea, Podolsky planned to serve in the army for two years after graduation, but the government once again threw him a curve ball. Determining that the country lacked specialists in automated control systems, the Party made physics majors spend an additional semester training to become specialists in this area. Those who refused had to teach in local schools. After an additional semester at the university, Podolsky chose what he called "the most desirable option, to end up at a closed [secretive] research institute, because the work would be interesting and the pay quite good."

The many women who majored in English at the Saratov Pedagogical Institute became teachers in local schools, instructors in Saratov colleges, or technical translators at one of the city's military-related factories and research institutes. Married when she graduated from the institute, Tatyana Kuznetsova remained in Saratov because her husband already worked in the city, accepting an assignment at the Polytechnic Institute. Also married, Lyudmila Gorokhova became a technical translator in an electronics firm, but Natalya P., who desperately wanted a teaching appointment, had to fight her way into one. It was "mostly the daughters of Party officials and generals who went to teach" at the Polytechnic Institute or Pedagogical Institute. Like Gorokhova, she started her employment history as a technical translator.

"IT WAS ALMOST LIKE PRISON"

A stint in the Red Army—notorious for its hazing practices and grim conditions—hung like the sword of Damocles above Soviet males not admitted to college. A university degree or a medical exemption released most young men from military service, apart from a summer's basic training and some activities organized by military departments at each institution of higher education, which also coordinated first-aid courses for women. For example, at the Moscow Pedagogical Institute, Igor Litvin and his classmates—mostly women—were designated "military translators." This spared them from the otherwise mandatory overnight maneuvers that involved shooting automatic rifles.

The two Muscovites who spent time in the army griped about the experience. Anatoly Shapiro saw military service as one of life's challenges that most shaped his worldview, "but in a negative sense. It was terribly negative," he recalled. Shapiro served as an officer in an antiaircraft unit located near Kuibyshev (Samara today) after completing college and a year's assignment as a young specialist. Escaping as often as he could on furlough to Moscow, Shapiro found his unit "dreadful, and the mental and intellectual level of the rank-and-file soldiers abysmal. Most were from the backwaters of the USSR, mainly from Uzbekistan." He spent some of his stay in Kuibyshev itself, where the cultural level was higher. "But even there the conversation would turn only to getting drunk—everyone drank an awful lot—or to women or fishing. These three topics," complained Shapiro. His service coincided with the Yom Kippur War of October 1973, "which was also unpleasant. I'm a Jew, do you understand?" As an officer, Shapiro did not endure hazing, but he

Leonid Terlitsky provided this 1973 photo of what he called a Soviet "ROTC" camp outside Moscow. As a student at the Moscow Institute of Architecture, Terlitsky (third from right) was required to attend the camp. *Courtesy of Leonid Terlitsky*

observed it, and this "was really unpleasant." After graduating from Patrice Lumumba University, Vladimir Glebkin spent a year in the army in the Far East on the Sino-Soviet border at Lake Khanka, where the situation was "very tense." His unit built concrete fortifications to fend off the Chinese. "While standing guard one could see our launch and a Chinese one testing each other's nerves." According to Glebkin, hazing "really does take place, and you have to stand up for yourself. I somehow managed to do so." Why had Glebkin enlisted? He explained, "My father believed that it was necessary," but "it was almost like prison."

Saratov's Vladimir Nemchenko, who joined the army for two years after gradua-tion, felt similarly. "I hated the army. All of the jokes about the dumb sergeants and generals are right on target. We mocked that bunch of uncultured blockheads." Several others also served, but they found the experience palatable. Having under-gone officer training in college, Aleksandr Virich shared that "service was not all that onerous. I might have remained in the army if it had been more interesting, but this was at a time when the army was beginning to decay." Pyotor Krasilnikov had a year-long stint in the army in faraway Zabaikal, despite the fact that he had gotten mar-ried, because he completed only the evening division of the Saratov Polytechnic Institute. Krasilnikov considered himself lucky on several counts. "Fifteen people from Saratov arrived and we were older, twenty-four and twenty-five years old, when the lieutenants in charge of us were twenty-two or twenty-three. Therefore, perhaps in part out of respect for our age, there was no particular hazing from the younger soldiers. It was simply work, but very far away from home." Viktor D. in 1975 had been assigned to an emergency orthopedic unit in Saratov, where he remained for two years. He recalled, "They drafted me into the Soviet army as a physician. I didn't go there on my own free will. It wasn't something I asked for, but it was an alternative to mandatory service as a rank-and-file soldier."

One Saratovite for whom School No. 42 was not a good match, Aleksandr Ivanov, left the magnet school to complete an aviation technical school. Drafted in 1969, he spent two years in Orenburg oblast, after which he "really wanted to join the army." Following six months of training, Ivanov became a second lieutenant. "There was hazing. I think that's existed since tsarist times, but not in the way they describe it today. I'm not against hazing. The older soldiers should help the young ones and teach them," he reasoned. Demobilized in 1971, Ivanov married the next year and went to work at the Saratov airport. "And in 1975 I left for Engels to serve in the army again. In all honesty, I went into the army to get an apartment. Thanks to the army I have all this [I interviewed him at home]." Ivanov added, "The second reason I did so, as I've already said, is because I like the army. I like military discipline."

"'A FOREIGN LANGUAGE IS A WEAPON IN LIFE'S STRUGGLE'"

As graduates of elite secondary schools and mostly top colleges, and as offspring of professionals, the Baby Boomers' collective career trajectory sheds light on a key element of the Soviet dream: guaranteed employment. The Soviet Union had a five-day, forty-one-hour work week when the Baby Boomers completed college. Disposable income was on the rise, and housing and services were improving.[18] At the time, women made up more than half of the country's labor force and a majority of its college graduates; the USSR had the highest rate of female employment in the world. In 1970, 86 percent of working-age women were employed (the figure was 42 percent in the United States): 71 percent of the country's teachers were women, 70 percent of its physicians (and 23 percent of Communist Party members). Employed women earned less than men everywhere, including the Soviet Union; however, Soviet female white-collar workers made progress toward equality.[19] Despite the double burden they faced, 85 percent of women favored working outside the home. They tended to be satisfied with their jobs, especially the skilled. But they wanted to work closer to home, better shifts, higher pay, a shortened workday, and more household appliances.[20]

Knowledge of English affected the Baby Boomers' careers in several ways. A good number of them majored in English in college and afterward became teachers of English in schools and colleges. A second pattern concerns scientists whose knowledge of English enabled them to read foreign academic literature in their disciplines. They also drew on their knowledge of English when foreigners visited the workplace or when they traveled abroad. Those trained to become Soviet diplomats and who were stationed abroad—all from Moscow—represent a third pattern. A fourth group of interviewees, mostly those who went into certain technical fields or into family medicine, had no practical need of English, and many of them forgot much of what they had learned; however, some of them drew on their childhood command of the language when they visited other countries, particularly during the Gorbachev era. A fifth group comprised those who immigrated to English-speaking countries.

Those who majored in English in college accepted teaching appointments at the college level, attended graduate school, or went to work as teachers in local schools. Saratov's Olga Kolishchyuk spoke for most of them: "English became my destiny." Assigned to teach at the Saratov Polytechnic Institute, she remained there her entire career. So did Tatyana Kuznetsova. "But I never associated with native speakers, so it's very hard for me to speak the language," she acknowledged. Natalya P. had no desire to remain a technical translator at the research institute to which she had been assigned. "I really disliked this job, despite the fact that it was considered a great place to work, so I quit and went to work part time at the Pedagogical Institute." To her dismay, Natalya worked part time for more than ten years, "until I defended my dissertation." Ignoring her father's wishes, she took a graduate degree in English, but not in Saratov, and this entailed lots of traveling and other difficulties. "Thus, I had to battle for my English, and therefore I madly love my profession." Hired as a technical translator, Lyudmila Gorokhova originally worked on Hewlett Packard computer manuals. She was employed at the institute for twenty years, "but not as a translator," which she saw as dull work. Instead, she found herself attracted to secretarial tasks, to typing, meeting guests, serving them tea—and to her boss, whom she eventually married.

After receiving her diploma from the IFL, Lyubov Raitman taught English at the Bauman Institute of Ferrous Metallurgy before assuming an appointment at Moscow University. She taught there until perestroika made it financially impossible for her to survive on her teacher's salary. After graduating from the IFL, Anna Lyovina settled into a job teaching English, but only after her oldest son began school. Even then, she taught in the evening division. "My husband came home from work and sat with the boys while I ran off to class. I never lasted anywhere for long because there was always something with my parents. How could I not help them? I'd quit work and take on something a bit lighter." Leonid Volodarsky graduated from the IFL, worked for a year in the Institute of Africa, and then enrolled in graduate school. "But it wasn't interesting. It was politics and you had to write what was necessary. I quit," he stated. Volodarksy found his "safety-valve" translating Western films. "There was a system of closed viewings here and I did some titles for them. I saw practically everything that came out in the West. I translated them and they paid me for watching movies." A graduate of the Pedagogical Institute, Igor Litvin taught English before switching to a job in a factory supply department that paid better and gave him more free time. While making a business call, he learned that another factory that had concluded an agreement with the British firm Wilkinson to produce razor blades urgently needed an English translator. Litvin talked his way into the job, which involved working with British visitors. After six years, however, Litvin quit to teach English in the evenings to adults. "I understood that you can't earn enough money to live on at your main job. I needed to work less for the government so that I could moonlight giving private lessons and working on translations. Taking on extra work is how you earned money."

The Baby Boomers who became scientists also believed that knowledge of English facilitated their careers. Aleksandr Konstantinov emphasized, "I was able to work independently as a scientist because I know the language fluently. It made it simpler for me to communicate with colleagues and to write articles in English for international journals, and this took me to an altogether different level." Yevgeny Podolsky, who went to work in a research institute in Saratov recounted, "I had to read a lot of foreign literature. I was riding high at the institute, because those people who completed ordinary schools had a hard time and often came to me for help." As an undergraduate physics major, Olga Gorelik read academic articles in English and continued to do so as a researcher. "There was a full-time translator, but I didn't need to use her services. Moreover, I was able to earn a little extra money writing summaries for those who didn't know the language. I felt superior to others because I knew the language." Arkady Darchenko, who changed his profession three times in his life, piped in

Lyubov Raitman (far left) translates for delegates to a 1974 conference on labor safety and hygiene in the mining industry, when she taught at the Bauman Institute. She later took a coveted position teaching English at Moscow University, which she held until perestroika forced her to quit teaching in order to accept better paying jobs to make ends meet. *Courtesy of Lyubov Obraztsova (Raitman)*

that he used his English "practically all the time." Darchenko spotlighted his need of English at the international nuclear institute he studied at in Dubna, where people communicated in Russian and English. "Then there were a ton of articles I needed to read in scholarly journals. Finally, I earned some pocket money translating articles when the professional translators had a backlog." He also needed English when he became an electrical engineer. "Once again, there was an enormous number of articles to read," he related. "Then they began to use computers, and all of the instructions were in English. I traveled a lot with exhibits, and I gave my commentary in English, even in China." Concluded Darchenko: "I changed my profession again in 1995, becoming a professional computer programmer, and English, well, I don't think any explanation of its importance is necessary. That is, I basically had need of the language all my life."

Knowing English aided Moscow economist Tatyana Artyomova in graduate school and beyond "in the sense that I wrote a dissertation on American corporations and could read any literature." Boris Shtein volunteered that "many of us who knew languages looked upon this as a second source of income. There was always the possibility of doing translations." Lyubov Kovalyova took advantage of such opportunities to earn extra money. Moreover, in 1985 she worked in Hungary:

Vladimir Kirsanov remained to teach at the Saratov Medical Institute in the 1970s after earning his candidate's degree there, a rough equivalent of the Ph.D. "Knowledge of English helped me a great deal," recalled Kirsanov, "in writing my dissertation and in reading scholarly literature." *Courtesy of Vladimir Kirsanov*

"While I was there I communicated with people entirely in English." As Vladimir Glebkin claimed, "Studying languages—whatever your field—is necessary, for it broadens your horizon. Knowledge of languages is power." He took his graduate degree at Patrice Lumumba and remained there as a researcher in radio-physics.

The cohort of Muscovites that graduated from the elite diplomatic training school, MGIMO, found their English skills essential. One of them, Vladimir Mikoyan, spent nine years in the United States as a spokesperson for the Soviet embassy. Although he articulated his irritation over America's "arrogance of power," he recalled, "I really liked this work. I traveled across the country, made numerous presentations, and mingled with people, and this gave me a great deal." After his tour with the embassy, Mikoyan worked in the Ministry of Foreign Affairs, but eventually lost his sense of purpose, admitting "perhaps it would have been important to find something that really captivated me." His fellow student at MGIMO Valentin Ulyakhin did. Ulyakhin studied Bhutai and lived abroad in Bhutan. He later went to work for the Ministry of Foreign Trade, but found bureaucratic discipline objectionable and quit. Enrolling in graduate school at Moscow's Institute of Oriental Studies, he defended his dissertation and accepted a research position there. Knowledge of English, he confirmed, "helped me in my scholarship." He maintains his appointment but also serves as a parish priest.

Then there are those for whom English played no determining role in their lives. Engineer Aleksandr Virich spoke for many when he observed: "For me, English played no role, unfortunately. I didn't use it." Irina Tsurkan "had no need for the language." True, after medical school, she said, "I read article abstracts of interesting and new things in English that seemed fitting and useful, but I saw that no one but me needed what I read." Natalya Yanichkina admitted, "I did not continue my language instruction, and we forget things if we don't use them. Besides, I really didn't have any passion for the language."

Yet some of those who did not use their English as young adults found it useful later in life. Anatoly Shapiro had little need of it until recently, when he came into contact with foreigners working in Russia. Georgy Godzhello likewise had "almost no" need of English, but it came in handy when he traveled abroad with sports delegations to France, Italy, and Finland. "It's deeply embedded in my memory," he maintained. "From the point of view of its practical application, language for me was not necessary," explained Vladimir Prudkin. Nevertheless, studying the language broadened his horizons: "I didn't feel like I was the inhabitant of a single country, but a citizen of the world." When Prudkin spent several months in America in the early 1990s, "the language returned. By the end, I spoke rather freely. I now understand everything spoken or written, but I speak with difficulty," he said. Leonid Terlitsky told me, "I didn't speak any English for ten years after school. When the time came when I needed it, I pulled it right out of memory. I got my first job only because I spoke English." Saratovite Gennady Ivanov retained some facility on "an everyday level. I understand most of what's said on television." He used the language when he served in Afghanistan, and later, when he went on business trips to the Netherlands or vacationed in Turkey. Saratov opera accompanist Olga Martynkina rehabilitated her English, too. "We had a piece in the theater in English, and I taught my charges a symphony by the American composer Philip Glass. Our soloists sang, and I worked with them, taught them. I have no problem with the language."

Some Baby Boomers made careers using their English, even though they did not train to do so at the university. Consider the fate of Tatyana Arzhanova and Bakhyt Kenzheyev, both of whom immigrated to Canada. Released from the need to accept a government-assigned position, Tatyana Arzhanova landed a job as an administrative assistant in the medical field thanks to her mother's contacts. Meanwhile, Tatyana's husband, who worked in the state Sports Committee, introduced Tatyana to his colleagues who invited her to accompany three groups of athletes to America as a translator. She traveled to the United States for the first time in 1974. "After this my life took a slightly different turn," she pointed out. Arzhanova planned to enroll in graduate school, but in 1975 received a job offer from the Department Servicing the Diplomatic Corps (DSDC). "When they told me how much I'd earn at the American firm, and how many D coupons

I'd receive for clothing,* I had no choice. I went to work where they paid well and where it was very interesting." She stayed there for three years before joining her husband for four years in Indonesia. Upon her return to Moscow she ran into difficulty finding a position, but in time the DSDC took her back.

Bakhyt Kenzheyev's arrangement at Moscow University allowed him to write poetry—and to work as a guide with Intourist, the Soviet agency that hosted foreign visitors. Intourist took him on for five seasons before firing him when he broke the rule against guides giving their home addresses to tourists. "Of course, I'd give them my address. I still have a few close friends dating from that period." Intourist taught Kenzheyev the right things to say to tourists from England and America. "At first, like a conscientious Soviet young man, I tried to lecture them. There was a brochure, *One Hundred Questions, One Hundred Answers*, and there were instructions on how to answer 'provocative' questions," he remembered. "If a tourist asked provocative questions you had to write a report afterward. Each day you were supposed to write a report for the KGB." Kenzheyev believed that Intourist fired him because he "had too many suspect friends, who had caught the attention of the police." Besides, he had published poems abroad in an émigré publication. He admitted that one of his foreign friends who accompanied tour groups to the Soviet Union brought Bakhyt "all sorts of literature, including anti-Soviet literature." Kenzheyev later published *Younger Brother*, a novel with autobiographical overtones about an Intourist guide.[21]

Aleksandr Trubnikov, who made use of his English both as a physicist and as an émigré to Israel, voiced the sentiment of others when he explained that his knowledge of English "played a role in everything. Karl Marx coined a wonderful phrase, 'a foreign language is a weapon in life's struggle.' Ever since I heard it, I've noticed that it's actually true. For me it was English. Of course, I've kept up with it my entire life. I've lived in Israel now for four and a half years. I don't know Hebrew. English is really important for me."

"I NEVER HAD THE OPPORTUNITY TO FORGET IT"

Soviet Jews experienced official and everyday forms of anti-Semitism. Ordinary Russians regarded Jews as smart, rich, clever, and hard-working people who stuck to themselves, in short, as "other." The non-Jewish intelligentsia perceived Jews as erudite, witty, sober, and more liberal than they were. There was an art to being Jewish in the Soviet Union. Finding themselves in an ambivalent situation, Soviet Jews at times tried hard to hide their nationality, while at other times they defended their right to be a Jew. In short, they sought to determine the circumstances in which they embraced their Jewishness. Statistics reveal the ambivalent position of

---

* A network of closed stores existed serving diplomats, foreigners in residence, tourists, and Soviet officials. Soviet citizens working with foreigners were often issued D (Diplomat) coupons, enabling them to buy items otherwise difficult to obtain.

Jews in Soviet society: they played disproportionately important roles in regard to their educational achievements, the number of Jews designated heroes of the Soviet Union, and the quantity of research scholars, but also in regard to the number of people punished for economic crimes. Although the Suez War of 1956 went unnoticed by Soviet Jews, not so the victorious Six Day War of 1967.[22] Igor Litvin, for instance, remembered that "when I studied at the institute we began to take great pride in Israel's war against the Arabs that Israel won."

Capturing the ambivalence of identifying as Jews, Yelena Kolosova, who is half Jewish, commented that "I was always somehow on the fence." "Christian by nature," Yelena admitted that "there were things you couldn't talk about and things best left unsaid. Like everyone, we learned that we somehow had to cover it up. It was impossible to hide it, but this meant you had to overcome it. It was a constant struggle." Her husband Em, for example, "had to demonstrate that he was much better than others." Also half Jewish, Moscow's Vyacheslav Starik claimed anti-Semitism "affected me a couple of times." The first took place when he tried to enroll at Moscow University; the second when he graduated from the Moscow Aviation Institute. Starik would have gone to work there, "but they didn't keep me, because of the fifth point." Starik turned his disappointment into an opportunity by enrolling at the Central Institute of Airplane Motor Construction, "where the level was higher." Invited to remain there afterward, he ran into an openly anti-Semitic Party member. "He couldn't do anything to me in an obvious way," stated Starik, "but behind my back he kept me from going abroad on business trips three times. That was the worst he could do to me. I didn't feel any anti-Semitism," he concluded, oddly.

But others did. Snapped Lyubov Raitman: "I never had the opportunity to forget it." Anatoly Shapiro insisted that, "while studying at the institute, and afterward when serving in the army, nationality meant a great, great deal." Although Sofiya Vinogradova never experienced discrimination working as a doctor, she complained that "the tourist business was completely closed to that nationality. Contacts with foreigners, too. We lost a great deal because of this." Vinogradova later revisited her remark about not experiencing discrimination. "The exception was when I wanted to go to med school." Yevgeniya Ruditskaya shared an incident that occurred when she vacationed in the Carpathians after her first year of college: "A young man began to court me, and when he found that I was a Jew he was in complete shock. He said he hated Jews and he couldn't imagine how such a nice and attractive girl like me could be a Jew." The second incident occurred in 2004. "When my mother died, someone wrote 'death to Jews' on the door of the building in which she lived," related Ruditskaya.

The situation of Saratov Jews appears to have been even more ambivalent. During my many visits to Saratov since 1990, I observed far more overt anti-Semitism than I ever did in Moscow, even among the intelligentsia. I suspect that is why fewer Saratov Jews spoke about it: they tried harder to assimilate. Olga Gorelik, for instance, insisted that "there was no anti-Semitism whatsoever," but when I pressed her, she reconsidered: "Of course, naturally there was.

They didn't hire people at work." At first claiming not to have experienced any anti-Semitism as a child, Yevgeny Podolsky thought again: "When I was a child the older kids often called us Yids, but without malice." Podolsky also related how, in the early 1960s when the government rekindled interest in an autonomous Jewish republic, Birobidzhan,* "our neighbor dropped in, the father of my close friend, and said: 'Well, aren't you going? Are you packing your stuff?' I remember that very well. It was very unpleasant, and we felt this all the time back then." Half Jewish but taken for a Russian because of his Slavic surname, Aleksandr Trubnikov acknowledged, "I didn't experience what many others experienced who had Jewish surnames." Ironically, Trubnikov is the only interviewee who now lives in Israel, an apt illustration of the art of being a Soviet Jew.

"IT WAS A CONDITION FOR ADVANCING MY CAREER"

Between 1967, the time the Baby Boomers completed school, and 1981, after most of them had spent a decade working or pursuing graduate degrees, the Communist Party admitted 8.7 million people to candidate membership and 8.4 million to full membership. Almost two-thirds of those joining during this period had remained active in the Komsomol before becoming Party members.[23] One parent of at least 80 percent of the Cold War generation belonged to the Party. Roughly one out of three of the Baby Boomers joined, but when their spouses are factored in the rate approaches that of their parents. Moreover, Party membership was probably higher among those unwilling to be interviewed or among those I failed to locate. The overwhelming majority of those who joined are men, especially among the Moscow cohort, where only two females among those I interviewed belonged to the CPSU.

Between 1950 and 1977, the percentage of those holding a candidate's degree (roughly equivalent to an American Ph.D.) that belonged to the CPSU shot up from 32 to 51 percent, and among those with a doctorate (a second Ph.D.), from 25 to 65 percent,[24] indicating a strong correlation between academic success and Party membership. Party saturation rates were higher in ideological fields (the social sciences, education, history) and lower in the hard sciences. Research scientist Aleksandr Konstantinov recounted that "they asked me to join. But, as was considered proper back then, I said something to the effect that I wasn't 'worthy,' that it was too early for me to consider it. And when they asked me again I said that I don't like to subordinate myself to others. One might say that I respectfully declined." Did this affect his career? "They always considered me a bit unreliable in that regard, but they overlooked this because I was an accomplished professional. I found the right words to convey that I believed that this was simply not my thing," he said. "The Lord spared me," quipped physicist Aleksandr

---

* In 1934 Stalin's government established the Jewish Autonomous Region in Khabarovsk region in the Far East, known as Birobidzhan, which became a forgotten Soviet Zion.

Trubnikov. "There was a long line at the university, and you needed to find some acquaintances to back you or to suck up to someone." Claimed Trubnikov: "I really never had any desire to join the Party. They said it was necessary in order to move up the career ladder, but I was never a Party member."

Attitudes toward Party membership ran in families. Nikolai Kirsanov, who joined the Party during medical school, justified his decision: "I understood everything differently than others. I was absolutely convinced that I was doing very important work in the Komsomol." Therefore, "when I was invited to join the Party, it was a huge honor." Larisa Petrova, whose father belonged to the local Party elite, claimed that she "wanted to join, and even asked to, but it was difficult." Membership did not shower her with perks or facilitate her career. She insisted, "At best, you'd get some food rations on holidays." Yet she also acknowledged her participation in prestigious international youth camps and coveted places she received in tourist groups owing to her Party card. Unhappy with the low pay of a young researcher, Vladimir Nemchenko quit graduate school to become a plumber after a friend convinced him he would earn a salary others would envy. He became a Communist. "I worked in shit up to my ears. I didn't earn my money for nothing," he rationalized. Nemchenko had to travel this path in order to become a supervisor. "Therefore I took it, and later I quit to become the chief mechanic of a repair department."

Two women in the class who became university instructors and who taught in fields with high rates of Party saturation aspired to join the CPSU, but were not invited to do so. Both of Irina Chemodurova's parents belonged to the Party. "At first I thought that I wasn't ready, but then I understood that I wasn't needed there. They always found someone better. I eventually realized that I would have to build my scholarly career by not belonging to the Party." Natalya Pronina lamented that she had no opportunity to join the CPSU. "Well, insofar as I was not known in Saratov for having eminent parents and, for the most part, made my own way, I didn't have the opportunity to join the Party, although I very much wanted to. I was utterly convinced that Party membership provided the opportunity to improve things in the country."

The evidence from the Moscow cohort also underscores the links between Party membership, career trajectories, and family attitudes. Like his parents, Vladimir Glebkin felt no burning desire to join the Party to advance his career: "I didn't have enough respect for those Party members with whom I had to deal," he commented. In contrast, Vladimir Bystrov explained, "Of course I joined, in 1978. I very clearly understood that without this I'd have no career. But it was hard to get in. They admitted only workers, then only graduate students, then only students, then only women." Had he encountered any true believers? "I personally never met any," he confessed. "By the time I became a Party member, everything was already obvious to normal people." It was to economist Tatyana Artyomova, who joined the CPSU in 1976, "because it was impossible to work as a college instructor if you weren't a Party member. It was like a license." Marina

Bakutina, both of whose parents were Communists, received an invitation to become one, too, during her senior year at the Institute of Foreign Languages. "They said that there was a unique opportunity available to particularly outstanding students and hinted that, if you wanted to receive a good work assignment, it was naturally in your best interests to join." Marina did and accepted an appointment at the IFL, where she taught until emigrating to the United States. Belonging to the Party also facilitated career changes. For example, Anatoly Shapiro in 1977 left a job he disliked at the Construction Bank of Russia to work at the Exposition Center "thanks only to knowing the right people there and to being a Party member," he owned up.

Those who did not belong to the Party saw their status as a matter of principle. Arkady Darchenko's father refused to become a Communist to advance his career. "This independent worldview greatly affected me. I also never joined the Party on principle because I never accepted its ideology," maintained Darchenko, even though the decision hurt him professionally. He never met any true believers, either: "As a rule, they were careerists in the most negative sense of the word. They'd lie to you and they knew that you understood that they were lying, and this encouraged them even more. That was the down side." When she lived in Balakovo, Irina Tsurkan encountered many itching to join the Party. "But you couldn't drag me into the Party." Neither Yevgeniya Ruditskaya nor her husband sought out Party membership. "People joined only for their careers, and what kind of career could I have teaching in a school?" She observed, "If I had wanted to become a school principal or a minister of education, I would have had to join the Party."

The female Saratovites whose husbands became Party members argued that they did so to promote their careers. "You need to understand that if you wanted to get ahead at work you needed to be a Party member," emphasized Natalya Yanichkina. She detailed the "absurdity" of how her husband got in: "He couldn't join the Party when he taught, because, at that time, the neighborhood committee needed to enroll eight workers and one member of the intelligentsia." Later "he tried to join the Party here in Saratov, already as the head of a construction site. It turned out that the time was ripe for him to join." She clarified: "An accident took place at work, and it was necessary to punish someone who was a Party member. But he wasn't a Party member, so they quickly enrolled him in the Party so that they could issue him a reprimand." Pathologist Olga Kamayurova declined invitations to join the Party. "I can't really explain it, but the very idea was unpleasant to me." However, her husband "joined the Party because he served in the army. He had to join. That was the situation back then."

Only one of the Saratovites who enrolled in the CPSU's ranks claimed to have done so for any ideological reason. Yevgeny Podolsky, whose parents belonged, became a Communist "because I had to," he said. "The situation was such back then that if you wanted to work and defend a dissertation, you had to become a member." Aleksandr Virich recalled, "I dragged out to the max my joining the Party, but further advancement at work was impossible without joining. I had to and became a member of the CPSU in 1987." Lest I miss his point, he hammered away, "First, I joined the Komsomol because I had to get admitted to college, then I joined the Party because I had reached my ceiling as a non-Party member." Making a career in the military, Aleksandr Ivanov "had to join." Irina Barysheva became a Communist because she made a promise to her dying father she would do so. "But once again, I didn't get by without connections. Probably everything's that way in Russia," Irina rationalized.

Nor did any of the Muscovites claim to have enrolled in the CPSU for any noble reasons, with the possible exception of Sergei Zemskov, who became a Communist in 1986 after Gorbachev promised real change. "Perestroika had already begun," he remarked. "That is, I didn't have any career reasons for doing so." His classmates, however, linked their membership to their careers. Said Anatoly Shapiro: "I joined the Party in 1974 when I was in the army, fully aware of what I was doing and consciously hating it all." Maintaining the step proved necessary because it "definitely helped me at work," Shapiro expressed "shame" for what he had done and confessed that his wife "constantly told me that she didn't respect me because I had joined. After all, many of my acquaintances didn't do so, and they achieved things without the Party." Mikhail Markovich enrolled in the Party in 1975, "understanding that I couldn't advance any further at work if I didn't become a Party member. I worked at a very good press that involved contact with foreign firms." Uninterested in politics, Georgy Godzhello claimed, "I joined the Party when they invited me. I don't know about the leadership, say, in the Politburo, but at the lower level everyone was normal."

Many of those who joined the CPSU stressed that Party meetings at the workplace lacked ideological charge. Vyacheslav Starik insisted that meetings at the Aviation Institute dealt exclusively with work-related and financial issues, and that "everyone understood that nothing gets decided at Party meetings." Tatyana Artyomova echoed this point: "You had to go to meetings, but at them questions about production were discussed. Nothing else, at least where I worked, but I assume it was the same elsewhere. How to build something, where to put a toilet, things like that." Party cells at the workplace also organized voluntary work Saturdays, *subbotniki*, to promote various causes; however, people mostly looked upon them as an occasion to socialize. Remembered Lyubov Kovalyova: "Afterward we'd set up a table for everyone, from the lowest assistant to the head of the laboratory, all fifty of us. There'd be potatoes, cabbage, herring and, of course, vodka. It was a lot of fun."

The Cold War generation did not know any committed Communists in their age cohort. Some Baby Boomers claimed to have been apolitical, but many decided on principle not to seek out Party membership. And those who joined did so to advance their careers. A political group like this probably had to implode.

"LIFE DROVE US APART"

The cohort born in the Soviet Union between 1946 and 1950 on average completed their education, took their first job, and gave birth to their first child between ages twenty-one and twenty-three. Virtually all—96 percent—married, and only 13 percent had no children.[25] Divorce had been simplified in 1965, and by 1970 the Soviet Union had the highest divorce rate in the world after the United States. Soviet women initiated divorce more often than men, citing their husbands' alcoholism and violence as the most frequent cause for the breakup of the marriage, followed by incompatibility and infidelity. By 1977 one in three Soviet marriages ended in divorce, but the rates were far higher in cities of European Russia, where most marriages terminated.[26] During the time the Baby Boomers attended college, 80 percent of freshmen believed it possible to find their one true love, and 92 percent of college students saw love as a factor in their own marriage. The high divorce rate thus might reflect unrealistic expectations spouses had.[27] Although love may have been highly regarded, both the state and many women supported pragmatic marriages that sacrificed romance for stability, seeing them as an antidote to rising divorce rates.

When the Baby Boomers came of age, the majority of Soviet marriages were homogeneous in social status and educational levels. Saratov data from the late 1970s, for instance, show that 63 percent of brides with a higher education married men with this level or one close to it. The Soviet majority looked favorably upon interethnic marriage, with the more negative attitudes coming from those far down on the social scale and, interestingly, the upper intelligentsia. But nationality endogamy remained the rule, except for Jews. Marriage rates among Slavic groups also were high.[28] Some of the interviewees married foreigners, but these were mostly second marriages registered during the difficult perestroika years.[29]

By the 1970s, Soviet women worked and benefited from social welfare programs, which made them less economically dependent on men. Although people did not see themselves as bargaining in selecting a mate, fictitious marriages and marriages of convenience to obtain living space or residency permits, to avoid undesirable government assignments, or to Jews or foreigners (in order to emigrate) were not out of the question. And some married when they got pregnant. The majority of cases of parental dissatisfaction came from the groom's parents because of the greater value of men in the postwar marriage market. Yet the position of women by 1970 had improved so much that, in the age cohort in which the Baby Boomers fell, there were 101.8 males per 100 females.[30] All but three of the sixty interviewees (one female and two male) married.

Many married the year they graduated from college, and children usually appeared early on. Olga Kamayurova rattled off her history: "We met when I was

Yelena Zharovova got married in 1975 at age twenty-five to a classmate, Ivan Proskuryakov, also a physicist and research associate at the Academy of Sciences. This photo of the young couple with Aloysha, their elder son, was taken in 1979. *Courtesy of Yelena Proskuryakova (Zharovova)*

nineteen and applied to get married when I was twenty. We got married the day after I turned twenty-one. My daughter was born when I was twenty-two." Vladimir Bystrov joked that he lived up to his surname (which means "fast one") and got married at the end of 1969. Aleksandr Babushkin "got married very young" to a classmate during his first year at medical school and a baby was born soon thereafter. To escape their grim living conditions, he went to work for the government and received "a fine four-room apartment." Yelena Kolosova met her future husband at Moscow University in 1967 and they married three years later. Pyotr Krasilnikov fell in love with someone he met at work. They "ended up in the same collective farm brigade" and married before he got drafted into the army. In 1971 Vladimir Glebkin married a woman who taught Russian to foreigners where he worked. Olga Kolishchyuk and her husband became acquainted at a New Year's Eve party and married that summer, in 1972. Andrei Rogatnev stressed that his wife comes from a similar family "and that's probably why we found each other."

Although it was uncommon, several females married out-of-towners. Moscow's Tatyana Artyomova fell in love with a student from Ukraine whom she met at Moscow University. Assigned to work in Ulyanovsk oblast after graduating from med school, Saratov's Irina Garzanova met her husband, also a physician. They settled in his home town of Lipetsk, where she lived for twelve years before returning to Saratov as a single mother. Olga Gorelik married someone from Odessa she met in Saratov who served in the army. Saratov's Natalya Yanichkina's future husband from Donetsk proposed to her the day after they became acquainted, while both were on vacation. "He had graduated from the Kiev Polytechnic Institute, was married, but was in the process of getting a divorce. He had a two-year-old child when we met. Within a month he visited Saratov and asked Mama for my hand," she related. His relatives who had worked in desolate Magadan, a capital of the Gulag, convinced the young couple to go to work there to earn double salaries that would enable them to establish themselves when they returned to Saratov. Related Yanichkina: "My mother was beside herself. We lived far away from his parents—he had a father who was quite authoritarian— and from my mother, who loved to take care of me. All of the problems of new-lyweds cropped up, since we had had little time to get to know each other." Moreover, "there were the extreme conditions of the Far North, with tempera-tures of 50 degrees below zero in the winter and freezing weather even in summer. Besides, it was a small town, where everyone knew each other. But we were young, and there was so much that was romantic in all this!" Summed up Yanichkina: "It was a good time for us. Life had its ups and downs, but we've been married for thirty-one years." Returning to Saratov when she was pregnant, they realized that they had not saved enough money to buy a flat, so they signed on for a second stint in Magadan, leaving their daughter with her mother. When they returned to Saratov in 1977, her husband had trouble finding work. "This was a period of pro-tectionism, when patronage opened doors for people. Our friend linked us up with others who had been up north. We befriended this group. They helped him and hired him for a well-paying job," she recounted.

Some bucked the trend by delaying marriage. Aleksandr Virich married "rather late," in 1975, "a year after I got out of the army," to a college English instructor. The oldest to wed, Olga Martynkina married a divorced physicist in 1983. In Moscow, Igor Litvin married a divorcee with a two-year-old daughter when he was in his late twenties. "We divorced. Then I got married again," he told me. The oldest Muscovite to marry, Leonid Terlitsky, who emigrated to the United States, met his first wife in Moscow before he left the country. "I came back eleven years later, married her, and took her out of here."

Most Baby Boomers maintained that the women influenced the men more than vice versa, probably because, as Saratov's Larisa Petrova put it, "I didn't join his family, but he, mine." Like many others, Arkady Darchenko held that his wife made him more cultured: "I was wild and she instilled in me better manners, besides everything else." Aleksandr Babushkin expressed appreciation for his first wife: "She even helped me study and channeled me into the right direction." Vladimir Prudkin treasured the fact that his wife, as he put it, "was very capable of self-development. There's been no one else with whom I've felt so intimate." Vladimir Mikoyan admired the fact that his wife "is good at understanding people," while "I, even now, cling to a certain naiveté."

Olga Martynkina and other Baby Boomers got married in Soviet "wedding palaces." The government promoted assembly-line weddings in these establishments to create new traditions as part of its ongoing campaign to limit the appeal of religion. The wedding attire reflects Soviet styles in the early 1980s. *Courtesy of Olga Zaiko (Martynkina)*

Not surprisingly, most of the women insisted their husbands influenced them little. Saratov's Olga Gorelik met her husband after graduating from college, when her worldview and values were already set. Her point: "Papa mostly shaped my worldview." Olga Kamayurova insisted her husband of twenty-five years "did not influence me at all." Galina Poldyaeva maintained her husband "didn't have any effect on me. I shaped him more."

Spouses or their families sometimes profoundly altered the Baby Boomers' political awareness. Saratov's Irina Tsurkan acknowledged her second husband got her to think. In short, "he affected me greatly and still does." He called Lenin a tyrant and opened Irina's eyes to things she had not considered or encountered before. Moscow's Viktor Alekseyev declared that his second wife's parents impacted him in all regards. A professor of physics and a surgeon of oncology, they never joined the Komsomol or the Party. "There isn't a single area in which they didn't open my eyes," Viktor said with gratitude, "beginning with politics and how to evaluate the Soviet past, because my wife's grandfathers perished in the camps. And this was always present in their family. Their outlook on politics, literature, and life in general also affected me, even more so than that of my own family." Anna Lyovina's parents were "in mourning" when she decided to marry, because her fiancé's parents had nothing in common with her own. She claimed her husband was "not at all ideological. He simply took in all that was going on around him with a smile. If it's hoorah, then hoorah. If there's a demonstration for the Motherland, for the Party, please. He didn't know any better." Their first disagreement came because her husband did not know about Soviet-era repression. "I opened his eyes," said Lyovina.

Reflecting national trends, roughly half of the Baby Boomers divorced, usually a few years after getting married or during perestroika, which placed new strains on relationships. Saratov's Natalya Pronina represents the first pattern: she graduated from the institute in 1972, married in 1973, gave birth in 1974, and got divorced in 1975. Explained Pronina: "He drank heavily. That's a national sickness. It's even part of our mentality." Now on his third marriage, Vladimir Nemchenko shouldered most of the blame for why he got divorced: "I'm ashamed to say there were other women. I chased after young women and fell in love." Tatyana Luchnikova married in 1973, but divorced in 1976 after her son was born. As we shall see, during perestroika she met a Norwegian businessman in Moscow and married him, only to find that her second marriage was not without problems either. Representing those who divorced during perestroika, Aleksandr Babushkin told me he and his wife "spent twenty-five years together, and got along well. But then I met another woman, fell in love, and had a baby. And we're very happy together and live in complete harmony." Pyotor Krasilnikov also divorced and remarried. "At first, everything's fifty-fifty, all of your worries, all of your concerns, but then the reproaches begin," he regretted.

Some interviewees admitted they had made a mistake by marrying into the wrong families or by marrying someone whose interests or lifestyle differed too much from their own. After falling in love with a dental technician, Saratov's Natalya P. got married when she and her boyfriend were twenty. Three days before the wedding, her parents tried to convince her that he was "from the wrong family." The head of her department at the Pedagogical Institute, who had married a dental technician, even admonished her: "'Natasha, don't get married. A dental technician is a special caste of people, not only a profession. It's a way of thinking, a personality type. Knowing you and what it means to be a dental technician—you don't have a clue—I know it won't work out,'" she warned. It did not, and Natalya took responsibility for her decision.

Viktor Alekseyev married an actress at the Moscow Art Theater in 1977. At first he found the bohemian theater crowd to his liking: "It was an extreme wing of the creative intelligentsia that had altogether different behaviors and interests from the one I consorted with, the scholarly intelligentsia." This gave Alekseyev much, but it also ended the relationship after five years. "She could not live otherwise, and I could not exist in that circle," he concluded.

Lyudmila Gorokhova remembered her first marriage as a nightmare. When her husband's pathological jealousy turned abusive, Lyudmila lived in fear and isolation: "I put up with it and decided to get pregnant so that it wouldn't be so terrifying and I wouldn't face being alone and childless, and then I'd leave him." She filed for divorce after the baby was born and moved in with her parents. Her love affair with her boss and future husband—who is twelve years older—began when they ended up on vacation together. (The Soviet practice of sending work cohorts on vacation together made it complicated for families to travel together, giving rise to vacation romances.) "We were together for twenty days in the south. We ate meals together, strolled together, lay on the beach together, well, that's it. He was mine," she explained. "The secret rendezvous began after we returned here. He joined me, when my infant was four, and we've been together twenty-five years."

Poet Bakhyt Kenzheyev married someone who found his address book in a phone booth and called him to return it. The relationship failed. Fearing that if he remained in the Soviet Union he would be arrested for parasitism, a code word used to frame anti-Soviet sorts who did not hold down full-time jobs, he became determined to marry a foreigner. When he proposed to a Canadian who worked for Progress Publishers, she offered to take part in a fictitious marriage in order to help him leave the country, but Kenzheyev refused; they married in 1979 and had a child. After their divorce, he married again, fathered two more children, and later married another Soviet émigré.

"SHE WASN'T THE DAY CARE TYPE"

The Baby Boomers sought to pass on to their offspring the same happy Soviet childhood they remembered. A good number of their children attended the same magnet schools or similar ones. There were three differences, however, between the Baby Boomers' and their parents' generations. First, the Baby Boomers had fewer children. At the end of the 1970s, 52 percent of Soviet families with children had only one child, a figure that rose to 61 percent in the cities (to compare, 37.7 percent of U.S. families had only one child).[31] Troubled by the dip in the birthrate at this time, the government accelerated its development of social services to ease women's lot. Second, grandmothers played a less prominent role in raising the Cold War generation's children than they had in bringing up prior generations, as a result of which the Baby Boomers had to rely more on liberal Soviet maternity leaves, state day care, nannies, and family support networks to juggle graduate school, careers, and marriage. Third, Soviet child-rearing practices shifted as the country opened. A Russian translation of Dr. Benjamin Spock's *Baby and Child Care* published in 1946 was issued in the USSR in 1970, just in time for the Baby Boomers to test it on their children. In justifying its publication, censors underscored that opposition in America to the Vietnam War came not only from Spock but also from young people raised on his principles. Moreover, Soviet pediatricians challenged Spock's ideas that went against deeply rooted traditions.[32] Recalled Natalya P: "I raised my son very democratically. I read Dr. Spock when he was born. He was completely free and I practically never punished him. Probably his upbringing was too democratic. But I'm pleased with my son."

Soviet women were expected to bear responsibility for child care; as in other industrialized nations this affected their professional life. "I finished school a year later than [my husband], because my daughter Maechka was born," related

Arkady Darchenko and his son in the early 1980s. "By this time I was already earning a decent living," recalled Darchenko, yet there was little for him to buy his child in Saratov stores. *Courtesy of Arkady Darchenko*

Yelena Kolosova. "I took an academic leave for a year, since there was no one to look after her. It was very hard to begin again after giving birth." Up until the time she had become a mother, Kolosova had competed academically with her husband, but then lost her ambition. "It was a very important moment that affected me the rest of my life. I never regretted what I might have become. I acquired so much being a mother." The birth of Lyubov Kovalyova's daughter delayed her dissertation and had a longer-term consequence: the time she spent in graduate school has been added to her pension eligibility age. Anna Lyovina had three children, but this, and the need to look after her parents, affected her career, because she had to settle for part-time work and for giving private lessons. Money was in short supply. "I tried hard so that our children would not feel our poverty," she remembered, by furnishing their apartment with second-hand furniture: "You could do anything you wanted at our place. It was fun. All of the other kids came to our flat." She sewed them outfits from whatever was available, including her own skirts, following patterns published in magazines.

State policies on maternity leaves improved in the 1970s, yet women still had difficulty juggling careers and families. Saratov's Tatyana Kuznetsova explained that the state allowed a woman to stay home from work for up to three years to raise their children. "I took off three years when my son was born, but when my daughter appeared, my mother helped out a little, and I stayed home for only two years." Irina Vizgalova stayed home after her two daughters were born, but returned to work when her oldest began kindergarten and the younger one went to day care.

Her mother, now retired, fetched them at the end of the day. Irina later gave birth to a son, and by this time her daughters were old enough to take him to kindergarten. Olga Kolishchyuk sat home with each of her two children for a year and a nanny took care of her daughter for another. "And then, at age two, we tried to send her to day care, but she wasn't the day care type." She got sick repeatedly, and "it seemed to us that she was afraid that we would leave her there, so once again, we hired a nanny," recounted Olga. Irina Garzanova gave birth to a son when she practiced medicine in Ulyanovsk. When her year-long maternity leave ended, they put him in day care, but he got sick without end. Her grandmother's sister came from Saratov, Irina recalled, "so that Andriusha could be at home with her and not in day care." Summed up pianist Olga Martynkina: "My grandmother warned me 'it's impossible to combine music with pots and pans,' but I somehow tried to do so."

"MY HEAVENS, THIS IS SO EXTRAORDINARY"

In accounting for the evolution of his worldview, one-time true believer Aleksandr Trubnikov underscored the significance of coming "into contact with lots of people. I began to travel to other cities, to Leningrad and Moscow. I began to interact with others. I began to listen to the radio, to 'Voice of America,' and to BBC." Many others also mentioned how visits to Estonia, Latvia, and Lithuania—the closest a Baby Boomer could get to traveling abroad without stepping foot outside the USSR—expanded their outlooks. Part of the Russian empire before 1917, the Baltic nations had become fiercely independent states in the interwar period, only to be forcibly taken over by Soviet troops at the start of World War II. Soviet "liberation" meant crushing local resistance groups and resettling Slavs into the area. The most "western" of the Soviet republics, the Baltic states had different historical and cultural traditions that opened Russian visitors' eyes to other possibilities, especially when Balts met Russian travelers with stony silence or other forms of passive resistance.

Saratov's Aleksandr Virich remembered that, when he traveled to the Baltic in the late 1960s, his group was not sold movie tickets when they asked for them in Russian. A decade later he returned with his wife. "She spoke German and they gave her everything and there were no problems. To be honest, they didn't like us there," recalled Virich. Irina Vizgalova had a similar experience in Lithuania. "I found it interesting that there was such order and that everything was so clean in Vilnius. The people, however, are very peculiar and would not answer our questions when we spoke in Russian. I found it offensive to a certain extent, but also odd." The living standard impressed her—as well as other, little, things. "Lithuania is especially famous for its whipped cream. Before this I had never seen whipped cream and all sorts of pastries. And all the bars!" Moscow's Boris Shtein knew Estonia intimately because his father was born there and often took Boris to Tallinn to visit relatives. "They treated Russians very poorly and that was understandable. I think I was aware of this already by age six," he confided. Besides, Shtein's father had explained to him "how Russia occupied

Estonia and how, after the war, many Estonian families were deported, among them many of our close acquaintances and even relatives."

Hearing about family members' trips abroad and encountering foreigners at home also broadened horizons. In 1956, 561,000 Soviet citizens visited sixty-one countries. Only a few Saratov parents journeyed outside the country and none hosted foreign visitors from the West, because the authorities had slammed the city shut. But Moscow was different. Moreover, if, in 1955, only 92,500 foreigners traveled to the Soviet Union, that figure shot up to 486,000 in 1956, and to 1,033,000 in 1964, and continued to rise.[33] Beginning in 1957 or 1958, people from America began to visit Anna's Lyovina's family. She recounted: "A cardiologist, Dr. White, who treated Eisenhower, considered himself my grandfather's pupil.[*] White came to visit us at home. It was a shock for me because he was altogether different, as if he were from another planet." Aleksandr Konstantinov met his first Westerners in the dormitory at Moscow University: "There was Mark Brayne, who taught me how to play the guitar. He later became a correspondent with Reuters."[**] Konstantinov also mentioned "a Frenchman, Bernard Kreise, who played in the Moscow University orchestra. He was a philologist who became a translator of Russian literature. But real professional contacts with foreigners started up after my first conference somewhere in Dresden, probably in 1976. It was there that I began to meet people whose articles I had read."

Like many students at the Institute of Foreign Languages, Marina Bakutina worked as a guide-interpreter for foreign tourists each summer. She recalled: "This is the first time I began to associate with Brits and Americans, and without an intermediary. I was alone with thirty of them, and this was very difficult because it was 1968 when I first began working with them and they tormented me with questions about what I thought of the invasion of Czechoslovakia. I could think whatever I liked, but not say it." She received daily briefings on how to answer provocative questions. Such interactions not only made the necessary political impression on nineteen-year-old Marina but also improved her English. She doubled up recalling the group of "well coiffed and neatly dressed" Australians, mostly elderly women, who showed up at the Intourist Hotel. "As we're greeting each other, one of them said 'We came here to die.' 'Oh my God, not on my watch,'" thought Bakutina. "In fact, they wanted to say 'today.'" Lyubov Raitman confided that her mother, a French editor at Progress Publishers, often brought French colleagues home to work, "but only in Papa's absence," for his job as an architect involved a security clearance. Yelena Zharovova cooked dinner for her scientist husband's American, German, and British colleagues. Andrei Rogatnev remembered when a professor at the Moscow Aviation Institute returned from a trip to America, stunning everyone with his account of the use of home computers. "Here a computer occupies half a room. How could someone bring one home?"

---

[*] Her grandfather, M. O. Samoilov, introduced the electrocardiogram in Russia.

[**] For over thirty years Mark Brayne served as foreign correspondent for Reuters and the BBC World Service. More recently Mr. Brayne runs Dart Europe, a global resource for journalists who cover violence and trauma.

Nineteen-year-old Lyudmila Gorokhova from Saratov met an American journalist in the Hermitage in Leningrad and "spent three hours talking with him
without a stop." Yet encounters of this sort occurred less often for the Saratovites
and mostly had an East European orientation. Olga Gorelik's journalist father
had friends in the bloc countries and welcomed many of them to Saratov, especially from Bratislava, Slovakia, Saratov's sister city. Tatyana Kuznetsova recalled
the time Gorelik's father invited a group of Czechoslovakian guests to the island
on the Volga where they camped. "We put up tents. We had a boat. Papa caught
fish, and Mama made fish soup. The visitors liked this a lot. They stayed with
us for several days and saw how we lived out in the wild." Larisa Petrova
corresponded with friends from Bulgaria, Poland, and Czechoslovakia she made
at international Pioneer camps, and even had occasion to meet a West German,
with whom she became pen pals. "I remember some concern on my father's part
when he saw an envelope from West Berlin," she divulged.

The Baby Boomers also continued to have vicarious encounters with foreign
cultures through movies and books. A film buff, Saratov's Olga Kamayurova
found ways to satisfy her love for cinema by joining a club. "I like the films they
used to show at film clubs, that is, complicated, sophisticated films not for ordinary viewers," she stated. "They showed us lots of such films, including, my
heavens, Fellini and Antonioni. It was like food for us movie lovers." Kamayurova
appreciated these opportunities: "Sometimes, when they picked some sensa-
tional film, I would think, my heavens, this is so extraordinary."

"WE SAW THAT THERE WAS SUCH A THING AS ABROAD"

Although Soviet citizens took the system for granted, the more the country
opened up to the outside world, the more they blamed the system, and not
specific leaders, for shortcomings. Foreign radio broadcasts, the growing number
of visitors to the USSR, cultural fads such as blue jeans, rock music, and chewing
gum all gave rise to invidious comparisons. So did the subversive influence of
Eastern Europe. Between 1960 and 1975, Soviet imports of better-made consumer
goods from the Eastern bloc tripled, as glossy popular magazines and lively journals from the bloc poured into the country. More important, between 1960 and
1976, 11 million Soviet tourists, in addition to official delegations and athletic
teams, traveled to Eastern Europe. Further, 2.5 million Soviet soldiers were stationed in the bloc countries, sometimes with their families. According to historian
John Bushnell, people's growing opportunity to draw comparisons with living
standards in Eastern Europe led to "mounting skepticism and cynicism about the
values and performance of the regime in other areas as well."[34] Contributing to
the erosion of patriotism and even Soviet self-legitimacy, foreign travel created an
unquenchable thirst for material goods and services, as well as envy and a sense
of humiliation over the Soviet Union's poverty and deficits.[35] While the mass

intelligentsia certainly had far more curiosity about London, Paris, and New York, than about Sofia, Prague, or Warsaw, the latter had become accessible. Indeed, all of the Muscovites and the overwhelming majority of Saratovites I interviewed traveled to Eastern Europe before perestroika in 1985, and most had done so already in the 1970s. The year they graduated from school, approximately 650,000 Soviet citizens visited the Eastern bloc; in 1972, when they left college, 936,000 did and, by 1976, the figure had shot up to 1,324,000.[36]

That so many of the Baby Boomers traveled abroad should not obscure the fact that travel involved voluminous paperwork, requests for character references, discussions with the authorities, indoctrination, and "nyets." Thus foreign travel could also be subversive in that it pointed to the Soviet authorities' suspicion of its own people. Moscow's Vyacheslav Starik went to East Germany on business in 1977, complaining that he spent half a year filling out forms: "Back then I belonged to the Komsomol. I had to show up at the travel commission of the neighborhood committee and prove that I was normal. I was married at the time, but didn't have any children yet. My daughter was born, by the way, when I was in Germany. In other words, imagine that, instead of carrying out the work that interests you, you had to sit and fill out forms, forms, and more forms." Anatoly Shapiro's trip to Bulgaria began with a visit to the neighborhood Komsomol headquarters for a conversation. "Everyone knew that you had to denounce the United States and the West, that they're bad and we're good. I remember that a young man asked me a question about Negroes in America, the Black Panthers, and about riots in Los Angeles."

Yelena Zharovova went to East Germany as a guest in 1983. "The family of a student from East Germany who wrote her undergraduate senior thesis under my husband's supervision invited us. They didn't let my husband go, but let me accept the invitation," she recalled. Zharovova did not understand why such trips proved to be so difficult. "I had to go for a discussion at the Party committee, where they could have asked me whatever they liked, including who the first secretary of the Communist Party of Indonesia was. That is, things that had absolutely nothing to do with my trip." She collected eleven signatures for the journey, "some of which I got routinely, but some of which I had to wait for," she griped. Natalya P. remembered being called in for an interview before leaving Saratov: "They asked questions about the history of the country we'd be visiting. They told us not to go out alone." Vladimir Mikoyan protested the onerous paperwork needed to visit Bulgaria. "I returned from a business trip to Switzerland, where I was part of a delegation on disarmament and decided to travel with my wife to Bulgaria a month after my return." Yet they told him at the Ministry of Foreign Affairs that he needed to attend a Party meeting and have everyone recommend him. "I said I'm going to Bulgaria to lie on the beach. I'm not going for political reasons, ever the more so because Bulgaria was an ally." The instructor from the neighborhood Party committee that led the tour tried to organize a meeting with Bulgarian anti-fascists during the stay, but

Mikoyan refused to take part, complaining, "I came to relax at my own expense." Tatyana Artyomova maintained that "the main problem for people like us was probably that we couldn't travel abroad freely."

Millions, however, thought the hassle involved in arranging foreign travel was worth it. Visiting Poland in 1976, Tatyana Luchnikova described the "wonderful, very polite people in Warsaw and the market. It's a fine country," she decided. That summer she went on a business trip to Bulgaria to write about the ballet competition in Varna for *Pulse*, a newspaper for youth. "I had a fantastic time. I liked Sophia so much, and the people are open and wonderful. I would have stayed there for the rest of my life, but that wasn't my fate." When Vyacheslav Starik visited Dresden, East Germany, the well-stocked shops overwhelmed him: "And I'm from Moscow. What if I were from the provinces?" Taking part in a student exchange in East Germany, Viktor Alekseyev noticed that "the standard of living was higher in East Germany than it was even in Moscow. And our German partners told us that, on the other side of the Wall, things are even better." Andrei Rogatnev traveled to Czechoslovakia in 1978. "I saw that the Czechs live better than we did. I was impressed when I went into a store and saw five different kinds of sausage and no line."

Something else irked Soviet tourists, as Natalya P. remembered: "We were allowed to exchange a ridiculously small amount of money—100 rubles. Or was it 30? I had wanted to buy some clothes, but decided not to buy anything." Instead, while in Poland "I sat in cafes, drank coffee, and simply observed what was going on. If I'm not mistaken, we even saw a film in English. We bought some exotic food items." Whenever Soviet tourists managed to exchange enough money, they did what Sofiya Vinogradova did in Bulgaria: "I brought back a suitcase full of children's things, because back then it was impossible to buy anything at home. It was possible only to 'acquire' things."

Those who traveled abroad later in the decade were less stunned by foreign living standards, because they had heard about them from friends and relatives who had their passports stamped earlier. Remarked Yevgeniya Ruditskaya regarding her visit to Prague in 1980: "You know, by that time, I already understood everything." Yelena Kolosova also visited Czechoslovakia in 1980. "There were no dramatic shocks for me, but I remember the Czechs' hatred, which was totally justified." Similarly, Saratov's Aleksandr Babushkin saw Yugoslavia in 1978. Prepared for the difference in living standards, Babushkin nonetheless noted "the smell in the stores was altogether different." Some such as Tatyana Artyomova understood the "cultured socialism" of the Eastern European economies as a function of the countries' small size. Saratov's Olga Kamayurova visited East Germany in 1976, where she was "astounded" by the standard of living. "But at the same time I understood that they deserved their standard of living. We deserved what we had, and they deserved what they had. When a country's smaller, people take better care of it."

Coming from a closed city, Saratovites found that foreign travel to Eastern Europe, especially to Czechoslovakia, opened their eyes in ways they had not expected. Arriving in the country on the tenth anniversary of the Soviet invasion, Vladimir Kirsanov met a young musician outside Prague who barked at him: "'We have a small, beautiful country. Why do you prevent us from living how we want?' Right then and there my view began to change a bit. You must understand that we saw the events of 1968 from the perspective of committed Communists." The experience left an indelible impression: "I remember the Czechs' dislike of Russians." Aleksandr Kutin traveled with the Komsomol to Czechoslovakia also on the tenth anniversary of the Soviet invasion. The group was warmly welcomed in Bratislava, the capital of Slovakia and sister city of Saratov, but things were different the closer they got to Prague. "We had to answer some tough questions and defend ourselves," he remarked. Natalya Pronina likewise visited Czechoslovakia on the tenth anniversary of the invasion. "They warned us not to go out and to draw our curtains if we were on the bus. They might throw rocks. Don't interact with anyone that day. But since I was much younger back in 1978, I, of course, went out." She encountered a local. "He said that in Czechoslovakia people live better than in the Soviet Union. Something to the effect that American buses are better than the Ikaris [Hungarian] buses we rode in. This really astonished me because I believed that it was simply impossible to be better than in the Soviet Union."

Soviet travelers came to appreciate the differences between East Central Europe—Poland, Czechoslovakia, East Germany, and Hungary—and the rest of the Warsaw Pact and Soviet zone. Sofiya Vinogradova laughed that, back then, "people used to say, 'A chicken is not a bird, and Bulgaria is not a foreign country.'" Anatoly Shapiro concurred, "We swam there, ran around, drank an awful lot. But we didn't feel that Bulgaria fundamentally differed from the Soviet Union or that it was a foreign country." East Germany, however, was another matter. Anatoly's father, a lawyer, spent nine years there; between 1976 and 1989 Anatoly often visited his parents who lived in East Berlin. Shapiro remembered "watching Western television broadcasts and movies." Saratov's Larisa Petrova visited Bulgaria in 1983 and 1984, and then Poland, Czechoslovakia, and Yugoslavia. She was enthusiastic about the private shops in Poland—and about the zucchini squashes. "We didn't yet have those cute little squashes." She found Poland irresistible: "But, then, I knew Poles for years from attending international youth camps, and my sister and I were always favorably disposed toward them."

The comparisons were not just economic. Aleksandr Konstantinov first went abroad after his sophomore year at Moscow University: "We got rewarded for our good schoolwork, for our successful presentations, with a month-long trip to the GDR.* Afterward I was in the GDR several more times. I also traveled to Poland," he recalled. East Germany was not without its minuses: "Everything was far more serious in the GDR than it was back home. We realized that people there were far more 'in the dark' than we were. It was just the opposite in Poland.

---

* GDR is the acronym for the German Democratic Republic, the official name of the East German state.

Poland was a free country. The people had a sense of humor and one that was uniquely Polish." Saratov's Natalya P. first went abroad in 1972, when she visited East Germany and Poland with a Soviet youth group. "I was full of impressions, but by the end I was eager to get home. I loved Poland. I remember the absolutely incredible impression the Catholic churches made on me, ever the more so, since here I didn't go to church. For the most part we didn't have any," she recounted.

Several Baby Boomers lived with their families in Eastern Europe for extended stays. Saratov's Galina Poldyaeva's husband, an army doctor, was stationed in East Germany between 1974 and 1979. "The standard of living was altogether different than ours," despite the level of destruction there during the war. She chalked this up to "a national character trait." "Things are so clean there. They scrub the streets with brushes. They wipe windows with special chamois. We hadn't seen such things before," she stated. "Why can't we create similar conditions? This question bugged me then and bugs me now." Galina drew a contrast. "Russians try to take good care of their apartments but, as soon as you step out into the hallway, it's terrible," she pointed out. Efforts were made to promote positive relations between Soviet troops and the locals, but Poldyaeva never attended these events. Living in Magdeburg on the border of West Germany, they were warned to watch their tongues on holidays when West Germans visited relatives in the East. No, she claimed, the Soviet rockets positioned nearby "didn't really weigh heavily on us. We thought everything was fine."

Saratov's Olga Kamayurova spent 1979 and 1980 in a small town in the Carpathian Mountains in Romania, where her husband served as the trade representative for Soviet gas equipment. The greater opportunities in Romania to listen to foreign radio broadcasts impressed Olga: "We listened to Voice of America there quite openly. There was no interference." She also commented on the standard of living: "It was a lot higher than ours, and that's why I decided to give birth there. I thought, why should I sit there for two years in vain? Everything was in abundance in the stores there. I don't think I'm revealing any secrets, but here the stores were empty." The locals treated them well, "but when we went to the capital it was different. When we went shopping we experienced an arrogant attitude toward us. When they understood who we were, we felt some contempt, a certain haughtiness," she remembered.

That such a striking percentage of the Baby Boomers visited Eastern Europe makes it easy to lose sight of the fact that some applications were rejected. Natalya Yanichkina's efforts to travel abroad "shattered" her ideals. "Well, maybe that's going too far," she reconsidered, "but I experienced great disappointment and great distress." A member of the Komsomol at the design institute where she worked while attending college in Saratov, she applied to go to East Germany as a tourist back in 1969 or 1970. "I filled out the necessary documents and application. There were several stages to this. The Komsomol committee had to approve the application, then a higher committee, then the Party committee, then it was sent to your workplace, and finally to the neighborhood Party committee," she detailed. But when she turned in the recommendation and documents to the Party organization at her institute, she ran into trouble. They said, "'They all seem to be active, conscious Komsomol members, but if they go there, they'll gape at everything, and come back screwed up.' There was the Iron Curtain, do you understand? Back then we really did feel it. My heavens, how I suffered! Precisely because I had put all my heart into Komsomol work, and then suddenly this distrust. And cynical distrust at that." Faced with such suspicion, "I thought, damn all this Komsomol work. It was as if they had slapped my hands. And when they spit in your face like this and when they say one thing and do another! How could this be? They say that the youth is our vanguard blah, blah, blah, but in fact, they treat you like this." Moscow's Tatyana Luchnikova was denied permission to return to Bulgaria. She remembered, "I was so upset and didn't understand. What did I do?" Luchnikova, who now lives abroad, concluded, "They simply deprive people of their Motherland. They put you in circumstances where you can't breathe. You can't live. You can't do anything. You have to stand at attention, as if you were in the army."

Despite individual disappointments, the country's opening meant some Muscovites even visited the capitalist other in the 1970s. During her fourth year at the Institute of Foreign Languages, Marina Bakutina won a coveted slot on a summer exchange program in Birmingham, England. "I remember flying into Heathrow and hopping a bus. We were glued to the windows. For all fifteen of us, it was our first trip abroad. Someone in our group said, 'They're rotting beautifully.' It was a spontaneous reaction" to Soviet propaganda that accentuated the rotting capitalist other. Bakutina related, "There were strict rules that we had to follow. To go out alone was fraught with very serious consequences." During the visit she lived in a dormitory with other Soviet students, except for a home stay in London. The trip proved subversive: "The teachers came to class wearing jeans, and they'd sit on the desk. For the first time we saw an altogether different style of teaching. And they sat us in a circle. It was so informal and natural. It liberated us," she emphasized. "For the first time I felt I could speak English without fearing I'd make a mistake."

When Tatyana Arzhanova accompanied sports delegations to America in 1974, the Soviet delegation—comprising all men except for Tatyana—was housed in a men's dormitory on Staten Island. She was compelled to join them "because [fearing defections] a Soviet delegation couldn't be split up. It was so unnatural." Otherwise the trip exceeded her expectations; local families took the Soviet visitors into their homes and organized the competitions. "They couldn't part with us. It was a time when Americans were discovering Russians. They wrote about us in all the newspapers." Writers from *Sports Illustrated* accompanied the Soviet guests. Arzhanova acknowledged that "I discovered a lot of interesting things for myself. It was like a fairytale. It was my first trip abroad and suddenly I was in America. There were a lot of memories, a lot that was striking, but the main thing I remember is that we turned out to be almost like family with the people around us."

Few members of the cohort managed to travel to the West at this time, but not for lack of trying. Lyubov Raitman got turned down when she put in a request to travel to France, but she was not surprised, because the application required the applicant to spell out why such a trip was essential. Sometimes politics got in the way of visiting the West, too. Saratov's Natalya P. expected to see England as part of an academic exchange in 1979, but the Soviet invasion of Afghanistan nipped these plans in the bud.

The Soviet government understood the risks involved in opening up. Didactic literature warned travelers about the psychological warfare carried out by the West, offering templates for how to behave abroad. Concerned over how citrus-deprived Soviet tourists might react to tables aching with food, travel etiquette books explained the correct way to negotiate a Smorgasbord. Whenever a Soviet tourist doubted how to behave, he or she was reminded that "V. I. Lenin illustrates for us an excellent example of behavior abroad."[37] Less they forget this, travelers to the West underwent special preparation and usually had to "prove" themselves on earlier trips to the Eastern bloc. Despite KGB briefings before each of his trips to Eastern Europe, Aleksandr Konstantinov emphasized that "the first real briefing of this sort that I remember occurred when I traveled to Italy in 1980. It was my first trip to a capitalist country. We all got called in by the Central Committee of the CPSU." Konstantinov was handed instructions to read: "I think there was the phrase that, if during a trip abroad we ended up in a train compartment with a person of the opposite sex, we immediately had to register a protest." He likewise recalled that "on the second day of the trip to Italy—there was a conference there—I really wanted to sleep and missed the opening and showed up late. One of the members of our group pressed, 'Why did you show up late? Why didn't you warn anyone about this?' I thus understood that he was put in our group to look after us." Konstantinov and his companions believed that "there had to be two of them, one obvious, the other clandestine, one dumb one, and one smart one. The obvious, dumb one collected information about everything, and the smart one only about what was important."

Those who violated the Soviet authorities' expectations for proper behavior abroad could suffer dire consequences, as Vladimir Sidelnikov found out. Enrolled at MGIMO, he prepared for a career as a Soviet trade representative in Finland, and in this capacity arrived in Helsinki in 1971 to work on his senior honors thesis. Sidelnikov, who had already begun drinking heavily at school, guzzled a half dozen Finnish beers one day, after which he left Helsinki with a Finnish female friend he had met when they served as translators at the prestigious Pioneer camp, Artek, the year before. Sidelnikov had failed to inform his Soviet colleagues that he would not return for the evening, and they undoubtedly assumed that he had defected. The decision he made under the influence of alcohol changed his life. "They sent me home for violating the norms of behavior of a Soviet citizen abroad," he stammered. The episode proved so wrenching that he suffered a nervous breakdown, resulting in an eight-month incarceration in a Soviet mental hospital, which he described as "a nightmare," and a two-year leave of absence from MGIMO. Thus began his adult struggle with alcohol and a debilitating neurological condition that made him an invalid by age forty.

Ultimately, firsthand experience abroad forced invidious comparison, as Mikhail Markovich, who took part in government delegations to England, soon realized. "Frankly speaking, these three or four trips a year allowed us to see what was going on here. I mean the stagnation." Comparison sometimes cut both ways. Some Soviet tourists concluded that things were not as good as they at first seemed in Eastern Europe—and even in the West. Natalya Pronina felt this way about Czechoslovakia: "It wasn't that life was better there but that there were more goods. These are quite different things. There can be lots of goods, but what if you can't afford to buy them? We were able to buy everything that was available in the Soviet Union, but they couldn't." In 1985 Moscow's Lyubov Kovalyova began an eighteen-month stay in Hungary. She believed that, had she arrived only as a tourist, the abundance in the stores would have shocked her. In the time she spent there, however, she realized that people had to watch how they spent their money: "I wasn't left with the impression that everyone lives better than we do. There they pinched each kopeck," she believed. Economist Tatyana Artyomova first came to America in 1980 to join her husband, who was teaching at Harvard. What she liked about America back then she still likes, and what she did not like, she still does not. Appalled at the cost of education, she asserted, "I had the impression that, in this regard, things were simply wrong. And in regard to health care, too." Vladimir Prudkin went to Italy in 1980; afterward, his theater work took him to "all of Western Europe and much of the world." As a result, he believed that his earlier admiration for Western individualism had been inflated and that, "owing to the totalitarian regime, the degree of spirituality was significantly higher here." The West had disappointed him. "I had a mistaken understanding that it was something of an earthly paradise, not only from the point of view of the development of civilization and its possibilities but also in regard to the development of the individual," he admitted.

THE IMPACT OF COMING TO AGE

One of the most consequential Soviet rites of passage, getting admitted to and attending college gave the Baby Boomers new insights into how the system worked and, more important, how to work the system. For the Jewish Baby Boomers, this also meant practicing "where, when, and with whom to be a Jew." The fifth point on applications—nationality—forced them to face realities they had rarely encountered at school as discrimination now constrained and enabled them in complex ways that were all too "Soviet."

Targeting university students as a risk group likely to fall under the seductive lure of alien ideologies, the CPSU stepped up its efforts to indoctrinate Soviet youth by forcing them to take five years of required, mostly resented, coursework. Developments in neighboring Czechoslovakia reinforced the Soviet leadership's belief in those measures. Many Baby Boomers accepted the government's version of 1968, but others had doubts that the KGB's subsequent crackdown on dissent at home did nothing to alleviate. The political climate in Moscow differed from that in Saratov. What young students might get away with in Moscow threatened local authorities far more in Saratov, who sent a clear message to the student population that there were limits to what was permissible. The lesson learned sharpened the growing distinctions between Soviet public and private life. Many Baby Boomers spoke of the discrepancy between their public behavior and the truths they shared in private only with trusted friends.

Governments reward loyalty, and the Baby Boomers—newly graduated, newly married, and newly hired—had other things on their minds than politics, particularly getting established in life, and this required acting Soviet and espousing the Party truth for everyone. The potential consequences of falling out of line, intensified political indoctrination, and sweet tastes of the good life yielded outward, but not necessarily inward, compliance. The state's measures, however, proved to be the wrong antidotes for the appeal of American and Western cultural symbols that spread more broadly throughout the 1970s. Necessity and conviction compelled the Soviet government to continue opening up to the outside world, yet the Kremlin's efforts to control this process proved to be one of the greatest delusions the leadership of the USSR made in the postwar era. The Soviet economy's mass production of tape recorders, for instance, made Western rock music and officially frowned upon Soviet bard poets more accessible. In addition to the Beatles, Rolling Stones, Elvis, and Bob Dylan, the Cold War generation added Stevie Wonder, Michael Jackson, Bruce Springsteen, Billy Joel, and Prince, among others, to their repertoire. Knowledge of English had made the world a smaller place.

The Baby Boomers came of age when alienated European and American youth took to the streets. Soviet youth, too, felt at odds with older generations and had some awareness of their foreign counterparts' activism, but their own anxieties were due to their age and not to any searching inventory of the system. Yet, growing up in the comparatively tranquil environment of the post-Stalin era, their formative experiences differed fundamentally from those of their parents. Visiting the Soviet Union at the time, journalist Georgie Anne Geyer noted that "it was a generation free of the fear that has permeated Russian life and it was a generation which...might just be able to give us a shadowy preview of what the future Russian man and world might be like."[38] Fast-forwarding to the Gorbachev era, Geyer's observations seem particularly prescient when viewed through the lens of an important survey of Soviet public opinion, which demonstrated that, ironically, the young and successful in the Soviet 1970s—the Baby

Boomers—were the most politically mobilized in that they had joined all of the correct political organizations (again, all of them had enrolled in the Komsomol). None of them belonged to nationalist or dissident movements or otherwise challenged the authorities. But they were also the most likely to listen to foreign radio broadcasts, read *samizdat,* and worm their way out of participating in Soviet voting and other public rituals.[39] When Gorbachev came to power, they were ready for sweeping change, even if they did not espouse it.

Historian David L. Ruffley takes issue with those who argue that the mass intelligentsia at this time came to reject the system that "had made them the most highly educated and materially affluent generation in all of Russian history." He maintains that the "children of victory" accepted the role of the Communist Party and worked within the system to solve the problems facing society.[40] There is a crucial distinction, however, between working within the system and believing in it. The Baby Boomers' attitudes toward the CPSU remained ambiguous, revealing a correlation between career trajectories and family attitudes in regard to those who became Party members. Virtually everyone who enrolled in the Party maintained that they had to do so in order to advance their careers. Although this is the same argument some made regarding their parents' generation, none of the interviewees professed to have been a conscious true believer—or to have known any, whereas a good number of them cast their parents as such. Voicing these opinions after the system's collapse, it is possible that their memories are revisionist on this point; nonetheless, this tells us how the cohort feels about Russia today. Anatoly Shapiro, for one, expressed shame that he had been a Party member. Belying the notion that those who joined the Party had to do so to advance their careers, Shapiro acknowledged having non-Communist friends who became accomplished specialists.

"It's better to see something once than to hear about it seven times," goes a Russian proverb. The desire to travel represented an important element of the Soviet dream that the government delivered on because, in forcing Eastern Europe to become "theirs," Soviet leaders had to make it accessible to its own citizens. Those who traveled—and the vast majority of the Cold War generation did—changed. Yevgeny Podolsky spoke for many: "They brought us up to believe that they were our 'little brothers.' But, as things turned out, it was the other way around. When I went to Eastern Europe and compared how they lived and we lived, it made an impression." Yelena Zharovova recalled that "the first impression of foreigners is, My God, they're just like us, but the second impression is they're so different." Those who never left the USSR changed, too. Aleksandr Virich mused, "I never had a desire to go abroad. Perhaps subconsciously, I understood that if I see that they live better there, I'd become a dissident, and who needs this?"

5

LIVING SOVIET DURING THE BREZHNEV-ERA STAGNATION

"Many jokes circulated back then that reflected how things really were," commented Natalya Yanichkina. "I remember one joke from the period when everyone is traveling by train and the tracks come to an end. 'Shake the train,' Brezhnev said, 'and let them think that we're still moving.' People told the jokes freely and weren't particularly afraid." One particularly biting one mocked his fondness for accolades he did not deserve, such as military decorations. "What would happen if a crocodile ate Brezhnev?" goes one of them. "It would be shitting medals for weeks." Irina Tsurkan touched upon another characteristic of the Brezhnev era (1964–82): "Back then," she related, "we drew up all sorts of foolish plans; everything was, in a subtly cunning way, broken, but living this way provided us insane pleasure. And we could find fault with Brezhnev on top of this. We could make fun of him and pick on him! We were unfair to him," she concluded. "We should thank him for creating the conditions that allowed us to live that way." How did the Baby Boomers remember life in the Brezhnev period? Why did the vast majority of them subscribe to the image of the Brezhnev years as a "period of stagnation"?

DEVELOPED SOCIALISM OR LATE SOCIALISM?

Leonid Ilich Brezhnev masterminded the coup that toppled Khrushchev in 1964. After presenting themselves to the Soviet public—and to the world—as a collective leadership, Kremlin leaders divided the spoils. But Brezhnev as First Secretary (later General Secretary) of the Communist Party and Alexei N. Kosygin as Chairman of the Council of Ministers (responsible for the economy) occupied the pinnacles of power. Brezhnev stressed the need to modernize Soviet agriculture and to build the world's most powerful military force. In contrast, Kosygin called for providing Soviet workers with incentives—longed-for consumer goods—that would result from giving enterprises more power to produce for a market, thereby weakening the stranglehold of centralized Moscow ministries. Similar reforms had already gotten off to a promising start in Eastern Europe. By the early 1970s, however, and especially after the Soviet invasion of Czechoslovakia in 1968, economic reform had become a dead issue as Brezhnev secured his position as the USSR's supreme leader. Brezhnev now pushed to improve the country's living standards and, in the aftermath of the negative fallout from the Soviet Union's crushing of the Prague Spring, to promote better relations with the United States by relaxing international tensions, an initiative known as détente. This policy and a sharp rise in world oil prices allowed the Soviet Union, an oil exporter, to spend on agriculture, consumerism, Siberian development, and defense, but not on industrial expansion.[1]

As a result, crisis conditions fell into place. The Soviet economy had become more complex, but in failing to implement Kosygin's decentralization reforms, planners found it increasingly difficult to manage the economy from centralized Moscow offices. The concomitant slowdown in industrial expansion in the 1970s began to erode the Soviet elite's confidence in the command-administrative system. There was also the problem of Khrushchev's unspoken legacy. In 1936, Stalin proclaimed that the Soviet Union had achieved socialism. In 1961, Khrushchev declared that the USSR would surpass the United States in per capita production by 1970 and attain true communism by 1980. Yet 1970 had come and gone. The Brezhnev leadership dealt with Khrushchev's promises as if he never had made them. Instead, Kremlin leaders rationalized that, under Brezhnev, the country had reached the historical stage of "developed" socialism, a term that implied an ongoing evolution toward communism.

Moreover, reacting to Khrushchev's endless assaults on the system and his attempt to divide the Party into agricultural and industrial constituencies, Brezhnev left authority relations untouched, promoting a policy known as "stability in cadres" that secured officials in their positions. This guiding principle of his rule enhanced his support within the Party, but it ultimately entrenched a gerontocracy, personified by the Politburo itself, which at the end of the Brezhnev era was populated by feeble old men. This turn of events proved demoralizing, because, since Stalin's time, upward career mobility had guaranteed the loyalty of Soviet officials and citizens and legitimated the system. It likewise encouraged corruption and the misuse of power throughout the system—and society. What later became known as Brezhnev-era stagnation found reflection in Soviet foreign policy, too. The Soviet invasion of Afghanistan in 1979 dealt a final blow to détente, as President Jimmy Carter put a stop to arms control negotiations and America withdrew from the 1980 Moscow Olympics. And that summer Polish miners launched the reform movement known as Solidarity, which represented a stinging critique of Soviet rule.[2]

Yet it took time for the Cold War generation to realize the real limits of the Soviet dream. During the Brezhnev era, Soviet propaganda organs, despite détente, continued to paint a picture of the United States—the preeminent symbol of the capitalist world—in somber hues as a place where the Almighty Dollar still ruled. American domestic and foreign policy gave Soviet propagandists plenty with which to work: the Kennedy assassination, Vietnam War, Watergate, race riots in urban America, economic crises, alarming rates of unemployment, and an angry youth movement, to name a few. Further, capitalism's own ideological critics from within debated what they saw as signs of decay in "late capitalism," a term suggesting that capitalism as an economic system, like others, is historically limited and destined to be replaced.[3] The fate of the USSR, however, suggests that the Baby Boomers were not only the generation of developed socialism but also of "late socialism": the system was approaching its limits and was fated to be supplanted, ironically, by (late) capitalism.

During Brezhnev's late socialism, the Baby Boomers earned acceptable salaries and lived in decent apartments. They owned basic household appliances and sometimes even automobiles. They felt deep appreciation for state ownership of industry, free education, subsidized day care, afterschool programs for children, socialized healthcare, generous paid vacations, subsidized housing, job security (and slack discipline), and an early retirement age (between fifty-five and sixty). In exchange for compliance, the system offered promotions, safety, stability, and privileges, including travel abroad.[4] Those who conformed also might have access to foreign goods, special stores, cash bonuses, dachas (country cottages), cars, and membership in elite professional associations.

But the further opening up of the Soviet Union encouraged the Cold War generation to make invidious comparisons. By the 1980s Soviet salaries averaged just over $200 a month, and $250 to $300 when factoring in other free privileges, whereas they fell into the $1,000–$2,000 range in the United States, Britain, and France.[5] The Soviet living standard placed the country between 20th and 30th in the world.[6] Although they knew that their counterparts in the West lived better materially, many Soviet citizens still believed in the advantages of the socialist system. In a national survey of the population in 1976, respondents evaluated the quality of their lives with a grade of "4" on a five-point scale, awarding the quality of life in socialist Czechoslovakia a "5," and life in the United States a "2" or a "3."[7] The Soviet intelligentsia in general, however, more so than the rest of the population, expressed dissatisfaction with the quality of goods available to them,[8] grousing about food deficits, long lines, and shoddy consumer goods, and the need for *blat*—connections—to obtain many coveted things. Owing to ubiquitous food shortages, many felt that agriculture should be privatized.[9] Furthermore, during Brezhnev's years in office, the Baby Boomers' evolving aspirations "magnified social envy," creating the desire to "keep up with the Joneses."[10]

It would be tempting, but naïve, to conclude that by the 1980s the majority of people had turned against state socialism; however, dissatisfaction with living conditions, and the growing feeling that the economic model itself needed tweaking, was one reason state socialism lost mass support when the time came.[11] To compete on the economic front, the Soviet system needed to supply more consumer goods despite the wayward work habits and low productivity of laborers, and the ideological subversion taking place as the country opened to the outside world. Under Stalin, the Cold War generation's parents wanted political peace and an improved living standard. Under Brezhnev, this was no longer enough: the growth of education had eroded support not only for the state's running of the economy but also for its record in human rights. To improve the country's image abroad, the Politburo engineered détente without softening its determination to squash dissent at home. It signed the Helsinki Accords in 1975, which not only recognized postwar borders but also the "universal significance of human rights and fundamental freedoms." One obtained the Soviet dream, however, by working the system, not by challenging it. None of the interviewees joined the human rights movement, although the vast majority sympathized with it, tested the limits of the permissible, and questioned aspects of the Marxist economic model. Later, a good number of them emigrated, especially during perestroika. Others considered the option and this speaks volumes to the health of the system.

"MUSCOVITES LIVE IN THEIR OWN SPECIAL WORLD"

The Moscow and Saratov Baby Boomers experienced the economic realities of late socialism differently. Saratov's status as a closed city placed it off limits to foreigners, except for those from Soviet bloc countries who had an official reason to travel there. The Cold War generation recalled visitors from Czechoslovakia in the 1970s, when Bratislava, the capital of Slovakia, and Saratov became sister cities. But the restrictions extended to just about everyone else, even Cubans. When Irina Chemodurova took her graduate degree in Moscow, she had a Cuban roommate. "She wanted to come here to visit, but as soon as she inquired at her embassy they told her 'don't even try,'" remembered Irina.

Most of the Baby Boomers did not give Saratov's closed status much thought until the Soviet Union opened and they became more aware of what they might have missed. That was because, as Aleksandr Trubnikov suggested, "When you're young, you're more interested in other things." Then, too, living in a closed city made it easier to believe in the system. "You have to bear in mind that I saw a foreigner for the first time when I was probably around thirty. Life was probably different in Moscow, but we stewed in our own juices." Aleksandr Konstantinov put the issue in larger context: "We knew that Saratov was closed, but that everything else was closed too." Then, too, according to Natalya Yanichkina, "we didn't feel that we lived in a closed city, because if someone's work or profession required a trip abroad, they went. For example, Galya Kiselyova attended school with me. Her father was the first secretary of the local trade union council. They were in Africa and someplace else." The city's closed status, however, troubled those who believed their professional lives would have been enriched had the restrictions been lifted. Tatyana Kuznetsova and others who teach English found Saratov's closed status "a pity," because it deprived them of contact with native speakers. Pianist Olga Martynkina averred that Saratov's closed status "was felt. We didn't have any actors or artists on tour, and they didn't let everyone from here go abroad."

The situation in Moscow differed so much that Soviet citizens inhabiting the provinces spoke about the capital with pride, admiration, and with sausage envy. Aleksandr Konstantinov recalled, "When I moved to Saratov as a kid, they called me 'Sasha the Muscovite.' People felt that Muscovites were privileged people. Muscovites, and those from Leningrad, too, were people from the two capitals, and people looked up to them." Konstantinov understood as a child that, after finishing school in Saratov, he would enroll at Moscow University or at the Moscow Conservatory. "Things probably would have turned out altogether differently had I remained in Saratov," he believed. "It's impossible to really carry out scientific research there. Despite this," he continued, "I consider Saratov my hometown and I remain an outsider in Moscow. The city remains 'other.'"

The economic difference between Moscow and Saratov made a far greater impression on the Cold War generation than the fact that Saratov remained closed to foreigners. Packed with military factories, Saratov offered competitive pay and perks for workers in the defense industry, but the economic situation, reflecting national trends, began to deteriorate in the late 1970s. The spasms of the Soviet economy affected Muscovites, too, but many of them could count on a special system of food orders at the workplace that provided them with otherwise hard-to-get items, and this, in an unintended way, benefited provincial consumers who coped with local shortages by traveling to Moscow for meat, other food items, and special purchases. "What's green, clatters, and smells like sausage?" queried Aleksandr Virich. "The train from Moscow that's approaching." He counted on two week-long business trips to Moscow each year in addition to short quarterly forays there to stock up on food. During the week-long stays he wrapped up his affairs early, freeing up at least two days for shopping. "Everything was planned out. I knew where all of the stores were, and what to look for."

Natalya Yanichkina described a typical trip: "I worked in a construction company and our trade union paid for half the cost of the trip. We'd hop on the train after work on Friday and arrive in Moscow the next morning. We'd spend all Saturday shopping and would leave Moscow on Saturday evening, returning to Saratov on Sunday morning." Because trade unions paid half the ticket price, people did not travel often. However, "people had to do it, for example, before a holiday or special occasion," acknowledged Yanichkina, "and they were thankful that an organization helped to make such a trip possible." Tatyana Kuznetsova certainly was. She expressed gratitude that she had the option to catch a train to

Moscow. "It was so easy and simple to get a ticket there for 14 rubles and a ticket back for 14 and to bring back everything you needed."

The vast majority of Saratovites indulged themselves in Moscow shopping sprees. One of the few who did not, Irina Chemodurova, insisted that shortages were in the eye, or stomach, of the beholder. "As strange as it may seem, our family was almost ascetic. If there is, there is; if there isn't, we'll do without. There were no privileges or no shortages." Olga Gorelik shared her resignation, but not Irina's coping strategies. "It was always hard to live in Saratov. If you had to go to Moscow, you had to go to Moscow," remarked Olga. "I didn't get bent out of shape over it." Nor did others. Olga Kolishchyuk's family lived off of her husband's salary, stashing hers away for annual summer shopping sprees in Moscow. "In Saratov you could get things only through *blat*. We'd go to Moscow for meat, sausages, delicacies, smoked fish, and for clothing, of course, and shoes, and everything," which, according to Irina Tsurkan, Saratovites called "imports." Aleksandr Kutin "never returned from a business trip to Moscow without meat and sausages. Moreover, it was more expensive here," he complained. "There you could buy it at state prices, and here only at the farmers' market." As a result, "I didn't like Moscow at the subconscious level." "All of Saratov was in Moscow," joked Galina Poldyaeva. Many of her husband's relatives lived there, "and they sent us parcels from there," she recalled. "But it was easier to make arrangements with a train conductor or go there yourself. People went there on business trips, to conduct research, to improve their professional qualifications."

Indeed, government officials from the provinces made a million trips a year to Moscow for seminars or conferences, and, in half the cases, without any legitimate reason to go.[12] The same was true of Leningrad and of the capitals of some Soviet republics. Irina Tsurkan related that once she spent two months in Leningrad on a research trip. "When we left there, a girlfriend's relative loaded us down with food. He worked at what we'd call a high-ranking sinecure or feeding trough, and he stocked us up with an inexpensive assortment of things out the back door." Irina brought home all sorts of tasty items unavailable in Saratov. "My husband was outraged," she related. "He'd eat the things with pleasure, but he wouldn't buy them himself."

Natalya Pronina spoke for many others when she pointed to a paradox in Soviet life: "The stores were empty, but people's refrigerators were full. Life was simply organized differently." Most of the interviewees agreed with Natalya Yanichkina, however, who saw the irony of traveling to Moscow "to buy sausage that was produced at a Saratov meatpacking plant. Some people thought that the meat was taken there because Moscow is the capital, and who, after all, comes to Saratov? No one. Everyone needs to see how wonderful things are in the capital." Although people saw this as a crude form of window dressing, Yanichkina added that "we were tolerant of it. People believed that's how it should be." Aleksandr Trubnikov understood that Moscow was a showcase:

"Foreigners had to see how good things were in the Soviet Union. They simply weren't allowed to visit Saratov, so no one was interested in how people lived there." For Olga Martynkina this "was the fate of provincial cities. Everything was sent to the capital. Traditionally, the standard of living had been higher there."

Arkady Darchenko and others, however, found this situation humiliating. "I simply didn't understand why we had to travel 800 kilometers for sausage. It seemed to me that something was wrong with our country. The people were the same here and there. So, why in regard to food were things so different?" As a student, Darchenko had spent time in the science city of Dubna outside Moscow, where "things were even better than in Moscow." Darchenko had in mind more than availability: "There were always lines in Moscow and crowds. But not in Dubna. I wondered why the entire country couldn't live that way. We understood that things weren't right, but this didn't turn us into active revolutionaries. We were busy doing our own thing." Natalya P. reacted "with indignation" over the difference in living standards. She often journeyed to Moscow for months when she worked on her graduate degree, leaving her child with her husband and parents: "I sent them endless packages of hotdogs and sausages through the train conductors." Blaming the situation on a lack of organization, Gennady Ivanov likewise found it "disgraceful." This former Communist turned his response, however, into yet another opportunity to criticize the West: "I realize that, with the Soviet system, you could hardly achieve the level of abundance you have in the West," Ivanov acknowledged. "But does it matter if there are two varieties of sausage or ten? Is that really the meaning of life?"

Perhaps not, but the inconvenience of obtaining such basics put the system on trial, as Yevgeny Podolsky suggested in placing the sausage-train phenomenon in broader perspective. In his youth, Podolsky believed Moscow was entitled to better provisioning because the most important people in the country lived there. "But the older I became," he explained, "the more discontented I grew over this. I remember the awful times in Saratov in 1962 and 1963 when there wasn't any bread, and they passed out a small roll in school each day." Like others, he mentioned the "terrible lines" for bread, and the so-called Zabaikal loaf "of rye, whose color was indeterminate. They baked bricks of it. It had a crust, but when you'd take it home and cut into it there was nothing but black dough. You could eat only the crust." There was no butter at times, either. In such cases his mother would buy sour cream and have him beat it. "They began to sell jars. When you cranked the handle it would turn the egg whisks and you could whip butter from sour cream."

Things got better until the mid-1970s. "Then the so-called sausage trains to Moscow appeared, when there was nothing in Saratov and people started to travel to Moscow. The trains were packed. This really irritated us and some discontent began to emerge." Others, too, observed that provisioning worsened in Saratov at the time. Irina Vizgalova reminisced about a time in the 1970s when "you could go to the store and buy only 200 grams of sausage, 200 grams of cheese, and that was it." She also recalled, "We didn't have any oranges, and there in Moscow they were piled up. Oranges, then bananas. You could find bananas only in Moscow."

Saratovites also hated how Muscovites treated provincial shoppers. "When you stood in line to buy something, they'd say to you, 'I need to buy just a little bit, but he's buying up so much that I have to wait in line for so long because of it.' I'd say, 'don't get upset, Granny, they'll bring you more, they'll bring it from us,'" recalled Aleksandr Kutin. Irina Vizgalova responded to hostile Muscovites similarly: "They thought that visitors bought up all of their things and there would be nothing left for them to eat, even though they received special food orders at work so that they wouldn't have to stand in line, and things were cheaper and more available." Aleksandr Virich added that Muscovites "who had relatives in the provinces and who understood our difficult life treated us well." Olga Gorelik's relatives did, but she admitted that other Muscovites "snubbed" her; after all, "Muscovites are Muscovites." Vladimir Sidelnikov agreed with the Saratovites that Muscovites resented provincial shoppers, but, like them, he saw a lesson in this: "I understood that if they come from Saratov for sausage, there's something wrong with the economy."

Saratovites likewise resented how some Muscovites made them feel inferior, as if a certain mindset marked someone from the provinces, and they felt a need to challenge this way of thinking. Irina Chemodurova admitted that she was "in awe of the big names" she encountered in Moscow, but she did not consider Saratov provincial because, as she explained, "there's a university here, and the same kind of people I saw in Moscow." Lyudmila Gorokhova recognized a difference in Saratov's favor: "Back in those years Moscow felt like a bazaar. We have more spirituality, more resourcefulness, or something." Whenever she visited the capital, Irina Vizgalova also squeezed in a visit to an exhibit or other cultural attractions. "We tried not only to make our rounds of the stores but also to have a cultural program—to go to the Lenin Mausoleum, to an exhibit, to an opening of something, or to do something else. We weren't all workers and peasants," she said derisively.

Many Muscovites might have railed against provincial shoppers and slighted them, but the Baby Boomer cohort claimed not to have done so. According to Vladimir Bystrov, "Saratovites don't vastly differ from Muscovites. I've been to Saratov. The people are the same." His classmate Georgy Godzhello believed "a well-bred person relates to others in a well-mannered way, a poorly bred person in an ill-mannered way," no matter where someone is from. Valentin Ulyakhin added that "the overwhelming majority of the population of Moscow comes from provincial towns. Therefore, Moscow, figuratively speaking, is a big village."

Still, "the difference between Moscow and Saratov was huge, and still is," observed Olga Gorelik. Natalya Pronina was of the same mind: "There's no difference between what was and what is. Muscovites live in their own special world. They don't live like the rest of the country does. Both then and now people in Moscow are better paid and receive the best goods." Aleksandr Babushkin confirmed that "Moscow's still better. It's a real beauty. It's reached a European level in terms of cleanliness and architecture." However, the rise of a market economy has benefited those living in Saratov. Olga Kolishchyuk's daughter now lives in Moscow. Explained Olga: "When we went to visit her recently she said, 'Mama, tell me what you'd like to buy here and I'll take you to stores to show you what's where.' 'Nothing,' I told her. 'We can now buy everything in Saratov.'" If before Olga and her husband would return home weighed down with things, they "now travel lightly. In this regard there's no comparison with before. Now the only problem is to have enough money. If you have money, you can buy anything you like."

"IT WAS IMPOSSIBLE TO GET BY WITHOUT *BLAT*"

Olga might also have said that, back then, the only problem was to have the right connections, or *blat*, because everyone resorted to acquiring goods and services *nalevo* (by outright illegal or at best questionably legal methods). "It was impossible to get by without *blat*. That's probably the way it is in Russia," lectured Saratov's Irina Barysheva. *Blat* represented the personal networks that Soviet citizens used, and the informal deals they made, often in the rhetoric of friendship, to obtain goods and services. The site where personal needs and relationships intersected, *blat* was made necessary by the Soviet economic structure that had created a socialism of deficits, and became an essential, even defining, feature of the economy. Everyone had it in some form or another depending upon one's social standing, and everyone resorted to it. Although Saratovites might have looked upon Muscovites with envy, they shared a set of common survival strategies to cope with systemic problems of the Soviet economy that everyone faced. *Blat* topped the list.

By this time the Soviet economy could not function without *blat*. In fact, economist James Millar called the Brezhnev government's accommodation of private trade and even the theft or personal illegal use of government property part of a tacit "little deal" struck between the government and its acquisitive citizenry.[13] It, too, should be considered, according to economist Alena Ledeneva, as yet another consequence of the highly centralized and controlled Soviet system of distribution. Yet the strategies ordinary people designed to make the system function for them also subverted it.[14] Ledeneva's ethnography of *blat* also points to a fascinating paradox: people she interviewed claimed *blat* permeated the system, but they did not admit their own role in it, recognizing *blat* when others resorted to it, yet describing the phenomenon in terms of friendship and mutual help.[15] The Baby Boomers, however, fully acknowledged their role in the economy of favors, perhaps because I interviewed them in the new millennium, after the Russian economy had stabilized and *blat* had lost some of its Soviet-era urgency.

But in the 1970s, across the USSR, the need to resort to *blat* made who one knew all the more important. "Everyone resorted to *blat*," affirmed Olga Gorelik. "What's there to say?" For instance, Olga Kolishchyuk remembered how her mother took charge of obtaining what the family needed: "She had acquaintances among pilots. She was a doctor [it was customary to pay Soviet doctors in kind], and they'd ask her, 'I'm flying to Moscow. What can I bring you?'" "There was nothing you could do about it. To recall this now is both funny and unpleasant," opined Vladimir Bystrov. "We couldn't buy a thing in the stores," remembered Yevgeniya Ruditskaya, "beginning with food and ending with everything else. Everything had to be gotten hold of through *blat*. That's how we lived." Viktor Alekseyev echoed these sentiments, noting that *blat* was needed not only to obtain food and clothing, "but also tickets to interesting events, or slots in tourist groups to popular places. All of this was mostly done through unofficial ties. Without them, there's little you'd be able to do." Anatoly Shapiro confirmed this: "There was inequality associated with *blat*, *blat*, and more *blat*, the need to acquire things through *blat*, to get in somewhere, to go somewhere, to eat somewhere. It was repugnant." Leonid Volodarsky agreed: "You felt the difference between yourself and others whenever you'd visit someone at home who was able to get hold of things. You could either protest or adapt yourself to the system." The inequality of it all also grated on Natalya P.: "I was offended that the daughters of Party officials could get hold of some wonderful boots, and I couldn't, because back then it was necessary to 'obtain' everything. It was a shame, yet we accepted this as a fact of life."

Saratov's Galina Poldyaeva and Irina Barysheva offered examples of how their families resorted to *blat* so that they could be well dressed on graduation night at School No. 42. "My mother had an acquaintance who married someone in the military," shared Poldyaeva. "They were stationed in East Germany. She sent me a parcel from there before graduation that had material for a dress and a pair of shoes—pointed high heels that were the fashion back then." Thus, despite the shortages, "we were well dressed because someone knew the head of a warehouse or a person knew someone somewhere who could get something." Irina Barysheva's family had a different form of *blat*: access to closed stores for Party functionaries, diplomats, and foreign visitors known as Berezki, where goods were exchanged for special coupons or purchased in foreign currency. "My father was sometimes given coupons for the Berezki. When I graduated from school, I needed a dress and shoes. My father and I went to Moscow, and he bought me shoes."

People also resorted to *blat* to save time. Natalya Yanichkina explained that, owing to *blat*, she did not stand in lines. "I had an acquaintance who worked in the sausage shop across the street. I'd go to her through the back door and ask, without humiliating myself too much, if she'd sell me a piece of sausage. It would all depend upon her mood. Sometimes she'd say no. I felt humiliated doing this." Aleksandr Virich related how *blat* worked during his work-financed shopping sprees in Moscow. "Let's say I had to make a call at the ministry. The parents of one of the officials lived in Saratov. Each time I'd cart an extra suitcase full of stuff for them. His job was to pack it; my job was to drag it back and deliver it. Thank God they lived only four blocks from me." Why did he do this? "When I'd show up and say to him, 'hey, listen, I need something,' he'd reply, 'Arkady Grigoryevich, we'll fix things for you right now. We'll go right now and settle things.'"

Irina Barysheva's testimonial suggests the complicated ways *blat* permeated the system, causing conflicts of interest and, ironically, even playing a role in determining Party membership. An acclaimed teacher, she taught English at a top school in Saratov. "The children of our local Party elite go there. And therefore my family had more possibilities than many others. I could get food items at distribution centers, because the parents of my pupils worked there." As she concluded, "My work gave me certain contacts, and there were others left over from my father. My husband was not badly connected either." When Barysheva promised her dying father that she would join the Party, she encountered difficulties after a teacher at the Party cell at the school where Irina taught, a respected old Bolshevik, voted against her, insisting Irina was an "aggressive schemer." Distraught, Barysheva tried to plead her case before the neighborhood Party committee. "But the solution proved to be quite simple," clarified Barysheva. "The first secretary of the neighborhood Party committee that admitted me into the Party was the parent of a girl in my class. He somehow covered up the matter, and they admitted me."

In sum, *blat* stood at the center of the systemic corruption permeating everyday life, from enterprises falsifying accounts to on-the-job stealing, private and illicit economic activity conducted during work hours, and freelance work, which the state frowned upon. The precariousness of people's living conditions, their personal qualities, the routine system of bribing and gift giving connected with *blat*, and the lack of fear of punishment fueled corruption, which, in an odd way, represented yet another form of private activity not controlled by the state and a lack of respect for collective property.[16] Ledeneva may have gone too far in arguing that *blat* subverted the Soviet system, but it certainly helped to undermine it. *Blat* also served to constrain and enable economic developments in the immediate post-Soviet Russia. As goods and services become more available, however, the need for *blat* began to recede.

"THE SHELVES BECAME EMPTY"

Apart from boarding the sausage trains to Moscow and resorting to *blat*, Saratovites shopped at farmers' markets or at a network of cooperative stores that did not exist in Moscow. As Galina Poldyaeva recalled, "My mother tried to buy everything at the farmers' market so that it was of good quality." According to Pyotor Krasilnikov, "in regular stores the potatoes were small and dirty. The quality was better in the co-ops, but they were more expensive." Irina Kulikova gave me an example: "If state shops were out of liver sausage, which sold for 3 rubles 80 kopecks a kilo, you could find it at the cooperative stores for 5 rubles 40 kopecks."

Saratovites also turned to legal second-hand goods or flea markets or to the illegal black market to satisfy their needs. Natalya Yolshina bought jeans and blouses at a flea market, claiming that "everyone went there." However, her family's modest means constrained her from turning to the black market. "Imported goods were always expensive on the black market, and for this reason it was practically off limits for us." Since shoes were forever in short supply, Galina Poldyaeva felt she had no other choice than to shop on the black market: "We'd have to go to some basements to get them, because it was impossible to buy normal shoes in the stores, or else we traveled to Moscow and stood in lines to get them." Irina Barysheva also admitted to shopping on the black market: "We knew who we could buy what from. And I bought good things from them. I'd economize on something and buy the jeans I really wanted, and they were brand names," she recounted. Barysheva saw looking nice as an act of self-affirmation, explaining why she and others went through such efforts to obtain desirable things. "Why did we have to wear only things made at the Red Army or Paris Commune clothing factories? We even had a word for this, to 'discard on sale'. You'd be walking along the street and every other person you came upon was wearing the same hat or coat. I never was able to be one of the pack. I probably got this from my mother."

Others helped make ends meet by using ration cards issued to family members who were World War II veterans. A doctor, Larisa Petrova praised the Soviet government's treatment of its veterans, especially those, like her parents, afflicted with diabetes. "We never left the sick unattended," she maintained. "They received privileged ration cards, and we used them. They gave them things you couldn't find anywhere. I recently used my father's cards." Irina Kulikova likewise recalled that "they supplied participants in the war, invalids, and pensioners with goods." Her grandmother had a friend, for instance, a war invalid, who received ration cards. "She received a lot and she shared this with Grandma. Grandma didn't eat everything and brought it to us."

The Baby Boomers fell into line for housing, too, often waiting for years, even decades, to move up to become next in line for a municipal or factory-built flat, or to buy into a cooperative. Acquiring their own flat became an obsession for many, because in the late 1970s, only 46 percent of families lived in apartments that had all or almost all of the main amenities.[17] Pyotor Krasilnikov regretted that "with my first wife, I was unable to solve the problem." It turned out that, before he married, he was ineligible for getting on the list for state housing and that, after he wed, he could not queue up because his apartment was 1.5 square meters larger than government standard. "The fact that the apartment didn't have any indoor facilities did not interest anyone. Back then it was also very hard to buy into a cooperative. You needed money and acquaintances." He and his second wife purchased their own flat only at the end of the 1990s. Olga Kamayurova and her husband bought into a co-op, but felt financially squeezed: "For fifteen years half of my salary went to pay off the apartment. We never had a chance in hell to receive one from the state." Irina Garzanova worked in Lipetsk, where her family waited for their own apartment for twenty years. "The line barely moved," she griped. "They built them rather quickly for those who worked in factories, but not for those on the general list."

How did the Saratovites comprehend the state of affairs in the economy? "Of course, it was a shame that we lived worse than in Eastern Europe," complained Pyotor Krasilnikov. "We worked as much, but got less, because on those very fields that we worked on in the summer, we saw that half of what's grown never makes its way to the consumer. I understood this all negatively, but I didn't know what we could do about it." Although people may not have been pleased with the state of affairs, they saw it as normal. "We were brought up that way. If that's the way it is, then that's the way it is," stated Irina Kulikova. Galina Poldyaeva, however, remembered being at a loss: "Why are the storefronts empty, but the store basements full? They never explained to us why this was the case when we studied political economy." Otherwise positive about her life in the Brezhnev era, Lyudmila Gorokhova did not understand why things produced locally were not available for purchase in Saratov, or why some items could be purchased in Moscow but not back home. "Lemons and oranges were considered delicacies that we'd bring back from there. But why weren't they on sale here?" Studying the political economy of capitalism, followed by a course on socialism, made Vladimir Kirsanov wonder. "Everything was turned upside down, and I had my first doubts back then, when I was a second-year med student. I anticipated perestroika."

If, as it has been said, expectations are premeditated resentments, the Soviet government must assume responsibility for the Baby Boomers' growing dissatisfaction with the economy. "It was drilled into us since childhood that today's generation of Soviet people would live under communism," emphasized Natalya Pronina. "We believed in this because we saw that we were living better and better." Yet at some point this changed, or people's perceptions did. When did the economic situation worsen? Aleksandr Kutin and others observed that, in the late 1970s, "the shelves became empty in Saratov." According to Olga Kamayurova, "it was all gradual. I can't recall exactly when it all began. I remember when there was nothing in the stores, but everything was available at the farmers' markets." Aleksandr Virich maintained, "There was nothing in Saratov. There was still sugar and tea, but the tea was bad. To get hold of good tea was a real high." "People had money," inserted Aleksandr Babushkin, "but there was nothing to buy." Natalya Pronina detailed that, when they attended school, "it was possible to buy everything locally. In 1967, for instance, there were 167 different types of lunchmeat in the store on Kirov Prospect." She, too, linked the shortages to the 1970s.

Even at its worst, "it wasn't that things were *always* in short supply," recalled Irina Vizgalova. They came and went, yet the overall situation continued to deteriorate. The government explained away the problems as "temporary difficulties, associated with growth," elucidated Aleksandr Trubnikov. "Things are getting better each year." However, the deterioration in the economy was "the case throughout the country. By the late 1970s socialism had actually began to decline. At the very start of the 1970s things weren't all that bad. But then it was real agony. Life began to get worse even in Moscow. Very much so when the oil money ended."* The vast majority of Saratovites seemed to agree with this sentiment; not so Party member Gennady Ivanov: "I think things improved a great deal here just before the start of the Gorbachev period. Auxiliary farms began operating in the Engels region.** As a result, we had fresh vegetables year round. Enormous poultry farms started up and chicken was available year round." He praised the local Party secretary, Gusev, for these "real" improvements. In Ivanov's scenario, perestroika ironically doomed this progress.

A few Saratovites voiced wistful appreciation for some aspects of the Soviet economy. Lyudmila Gorokhova remembered, "On your way home from work you'd buy what you needed. True, there were lines, but you could buy things at such low prices." Pyotor Krasilnikov waxed nostalgic that "on a salary of 180–200 rubles" in the Brezhnev era "we could squirrel away money for a rather expensive item or travel to the sea on vacation, which I can't do on my salary today." He claimed to barely make ends meet today, yet purchased a new apartment at the end of the 1990s—and a car. This aside, Krasilnikov hit upon something: the most oft-cited positive reminiscences of the Brezhnev-era economy concerned its capacity for providing affordable vacations, a real quality of life issue. Irina Barysheva related that she and her family "traversed practically all of Russia and the Baltic. Back then slots in tourist groups were very affordable." Olga Kamayurova agreed: "Since 1986 vacations have become off limits for me. Everything's now possible, but only if you have money. My income doesn't allow me anything." Aleksandr Babushkin mentioned that, economically speaking, his childhood knew shortages, "but we could permit ourselves a vacation each year at the Black Sea." Although otherwise critical of how the Soviet

---

* As a major oil-exporting country, the Soviet Union benefited enormously—but temporarily— when oil prices rose precipitously following the world oil crisis of 1973. Oil profits helped to keep the Soviet economy afloat and masked its declining performance.

** The Engels region is located directly across the Volga from Saratov.

economy worked, Aleksandr Virich saw a silver lining in the role Soviet trade unions played. "The unions were powerful and had impressive resources. We all received slots in tourist groups." He gave as an example the 100 rubles or so he paid for his family to vacation in Sochi. "And the trade union picked up the tab for all the rest."

"THERE WERE LINES EVERYWHERE"

Ironically, the better-off Muscovites voiced more critical assessments of the Soviet economy than the Saratovites, complementing the findings of a study of Soviet émigrés that revealed that Muscovites and Leningraders expressed less satisfaction with the state of the economy than others.[18] Yelena Kolosova reminisced that "all of my nightmares at the age of twenty-five had to do with how I would feed my family in May, when the reserves were used up." She remarked that her twenties and thirties were "spent providing for daily needs," while her parents and husband moonlighted to earn enough rubles to make ends meet. Things changed with the privileges and perks that her father received when he became a member of the elite Soviet Academy of Sciences: "Access opened up to a system of distributed goods. There were special food orders, opportunities to travel to resorts, tickets to things." What the food orders contained depended upon one's status, but most Muscovites received them. Vyacheslav Starik maintained that food orders "were democratically doled out at work," and that his institute's Party organization's main function was to assist employees in this regard.

Describing the strategies her family employed to cope with shortages, Lyubov Raitman, too, spotlighted "the system of food orders placed at work and passed out on holidays." Also "we had the habit, which died out only recently, of stocking up." In fact, Soviet women routinely carried string bags in their purses "just in case," to be used if they came upon something for sale. "I'll never forget those canned goods that I hauled home," injected Raitman. "When these Hungarian vegetables—green beans and peas—suddenly appeared they were sometimes available only for several days and then there wouldn't be any all winter. Therefore, we unfortunate women stood in line to buy our ten cans and try to stretch them out to last the winter." But it was a fact, she said, that "in Moscow, even during years of the greatest shortages, our refrigerators were not empty." She continued, "There were years when there was, say, no cheese, but we somehow managed to get it. We didn't have any underground sources, but we'd go to the far ends of Moscow when we knew it was available." Vyacheslav Starik retrieved a telling example, too: "When our child was young and lived at the dacha I spent three days a week searching for food. I had made a note of the stores and knew that on Wednesday I buy this at that one, and on Thursday something else. On Friday, laden with bags, we'd go to the dacha and feed our child. We brought food for the week ahead." "In order to feed my family,

I remember that I had to search for things in short supply all the time," related Yelena Zharovova. "There were lines everywhere. How much time I wasted standing in lines and going on shopping campaigns!" She volunteered that "things were nonetheless easier in Moscow." Yevgeniya Ruditskaya, whose in-laws lived in Odessa, confirmed this: "We routinely sent them packages of meat, groats, and cooking oil, because life there was even harder."

Sofiya Vinogradova never got upset over this aspect of life, but admitted, "Sometimes I'd wonder why things were this way. There was definitely resentment and disappointment." The more Vinogradova spoke, the more negative things she recalled. "I remember when my daughter asked for a school uniform. It was very expensive, and it wasn't available for sale. You had to 'acquire' it somewhere." She also dredged up memories of the time "when we stood in line for five hours to buy some sandals. It was better to go without them. I couldn't stand in line because I had to be at work. I could do so only on a day off. I now think this was wrong."

Who or what was to blame for the economic difficulties? According to Tatyana Luchnikova, "the system didn't work. I always thought that. It was an inner feeling I had that something was wrong." Yelena Zharovova was certain she knew what it was: "It was the incorrect policy of the Party and government regarding agriculture and the manufacture of consumer goods. That is, when heavy industry developed, light industry didn't. Also, the Soviet Union made itself obsolete because we lived thanks to revenues from the sale of oil." Tellingly, two Muscovites trained as economists also indicted the system. The government's efforts to explain away the shortages did not impress Anatoly Shapiro: "For years they said it was because of the war, that the war was to blame, then something else interfered. Yet we couldn't make things better." Shapiro understood already back then "that the socialist system was bad, that it was impossible to develop normally under it." Tatyana Artyomova did not know a single economist who defended the system: "It was clear to me back then that the economic structure was completely wrong. But it wasn't so simple to change it. You had to do it sensibly." Then, too, Artyomova observed that "there was the powerful feeling that everything would be okay. Wait just a bit and everything will get better."

Some of the Muscovites also blamed the "human factor," as M. S. Gorbachev would later put it. Assessing the Soviet economy, Lyubov Raitman concluded, "I believed people worked poorly, that they didn't know how to work and didn't want to." Tatyana Artyomova made a similar point: "It always seemed to me that, unfortunately, in the former Soviet Union things were hard for those who wanted to do their part, because no one supported them." She recalled the time when she proposed at work that the graduate program be overhauled and was told by a colleague, "'Tatyana Nikolayevna, wouldn't it be better for you to direct your energy at rearranging furniture at home?' They didn't want to make things better. Things were good enough for them." Vyacheslav Starik also maintained that the economic difficulties had more to do with how people worked. As a lesson for today, he pointed out that human "psychology changes more slowly than economic structures."

Or countries, for that matter. Historically, the Russian intelligentsia, largely professional rather than commercial, looked suspiciously at those involved in private economic activity. These feelings solidified under Soviet rule, which decried private economic activity, the dark side of daily life, but which made illegal private economic activity crucial to survive. Like others, Anatoly Shapiro considered black marketers "thieves." Tatyana Arzhanova remarked that "all my life I looked upon people involved in business as people belonging to another world, with whom I couldn't interact. It's the same for me here in Canada now [she emigrated] when we meet people from that world."

Viktor Alekseyev's reflections shed light on the extent to which deficiencies in the Soviet economy became more pronounced during the Brezhnev era. Viktor did not realize that the economic situation could be better until he got older, at which time he looked upon it as "a terribly unpleasant aspect of life you had to deal with. It was an inevitable part of the system, which could be changed very little. At an everyday level this began to irritate me more and more." He admitted the possibility that some aspects of the country's living standards continued to improve and that "perhaps, as we got older, we reacted more strongly to the shortages." That proved to be the case, for material conditions got better during the Brezhnev era in terms of the availability of housing, purchase of durable goods, more recreational opportunities, and a growth in the number of private plots. Yet these positive indices—and discrepancies in food availability felt especially in Saratov—failed to match growing expectations and the awareness that things were better across the border.

"IT WAS PREDICTABLE, IT WAS STABLE, AND THERE WAS NO FEAR"

Coming to power after masterminding a conspiracy to overthrow Khrushchev in 1964, Leonid Brezhnev promoted a policy of stability within Party cadres and beyond. Often seen in the popular consciousness as "confidence in tomorrow," this policy, by the late 1970s, had degenerated into what became known under Gorbachev as Brezhnev-era stagnation. This term referred to more than economic malaise: by the 1970s, widespread apathy and cynicism had become palpable. People spent less time and effort at work and got less emotionally involved in the public sphere. The role of family and friends grew, as did the sentiment that everyone exploited "their position for their own personal interests against the interests of the state and official policy."[19] As Vladimir Sidelnikov reminded me, people looted everything they could from work: "We ourselves stole everything, and that's why things got to be the way they were. Who's to blame? Ourselves? There's no one to blame."

The term "stagnation" became popular only after Brezhnev died and there-fore belongs to a specific historical context. Whether one accepts the term reflects an individual's social position and perspective. Some Saratovites—mostly former Party members—balked at using the term. With lives uprooted by the cataclysms caused by the move to a capitalist system after 1991, they looked back upon the Brezhnev era as one of stability. Vladimir Kirsanov is one of those who objected: "Insofar as we really didn't know any other life, it seemed altogether normal to us." He recalled a conversation he had with a law professor when Kirsanov was the deputy secretary of his institute's Party committee. "He said to me, 'You're a young man. You will remember these times as the best in your life.' That's what people thought then." Aleksandr Babushkin was of the same mind: "We had a stable, normal life. Everyone did his own thing. There were no illu-sions, no changes. We lived, we worked, we rested, we read, we went to the movies. Our life didn't change, but it was predictable, it was stable, and there was no fear." Pyotor Krasilnikov insisted, "There absolutely was no stagnation. You can't say that anyone starved. We worked day and night. We were confident that, if we set aside money, we'd be able to use it. Unfortunately, that's no longer the case today." Alexander Ivanov remarked, "As the common people say, he lived and let others live. I wouldn't say that we had it bad." Aleksandr Trubnikov concluded that, "as people like to say today, there was stability. Under Brezhnev things weren't so bad in regard to 'confidence in tomorrow.'"*

Viktor D. was one who felt that way. "True," he told me, "there was a disparity between what was said and done," but he ticked off many positive things. "The country picked up momentum, industry developed, factories and plants opened. There was no unemployment. There were no poor, no shootings. We traveled in space, we built BAM, we opened new mines, developed new industries. We have more stagnation today than back then." He admitted that "somewhere far away, in Moscow, they imprisoned dissidents," and that he knew of "two or three instances here in Saratov, involving people who expressed anti-Communist thoughts. But they did so more out of stupidity than out of any rational rejection of the system." A doctor, he observed that "health care was free and unequivo-cally on a higher level than now. Education was free, including higher education and graduate school." He went on: "People received apartments, they had confidence in tomorrow. Maybe everything was on a lower level than in America, but there was stability." On his salary, augmented by bribes and gifts, he could buy a cooperative apartment and build a dacha. "I could save up for a car and other things," he emphasized. "Back then the problem was that there wasn't much to buy and you had to 'acquire' things." Viktor admitted to ridi-culing Brezhnev at the end, but emphasized, "People in my circle had stable,

* During the economic turmoil associated with the transition to a market economy in the 1990s, President Boris Yeltsin's detractors employed the trope "confidence in tomorrow" in reference to the "good old" Soviet days.

normal, balanced lives." To Vladimir Nemchenko, Brezhnev also looks better in retrospect: "I didn't like him at all back then, but now I understand him." Reflecting on his own, difficult, experience during perestroika, he concluded, "Society itself is to blame for everything. It's true that the leaders are to blame for some things, but first you need to take your own inventory."

Other Baby Boomers from both cities emphasized the positive developments in their professional careers under Brezhnev. Moscow's Viktor Alekseyev, for instance, believed his work in psychology—a discipline suppressed under Stalin and now rehabilitated—spared him some of the downside of the Brezhnev years, because the discipline had some catching up to do and came into its own at that time. As a result, he claimed, "I never felt any stagnation at work." Others took issue with the term because they disliked aspects of their post-Soviet realities at the time I interviewed them. Saratov's Larisa Petrova recalled that the Brezhnev era "was a period of personal growth for me. I managed to improve my credentials, study in Moscow, and defend my dissertation. Now we cry over the fact that we can't get a lot done these days because everything depends on money." She also took issue with many Baby Boomers' view of the economy back then. "Under Brezhnev the food situation in Saratov improved. It was much better than in our childhood. It became possible for us to dress better. You can even see this in photographs. The gray mass that was characteristic of the 1960s gave way to far brighter colors in the 1970s." Moscow's Yelena Zharovova voiced similar sentiments, but with a twist: "I don't like the term stagnation because we developed, the country developed, everything developed, science developed, space developed, industry developed, but perhaps not in the right direction."

Arkady Darchenko and most other Saratovites, however, found stagnation "the most apt epithet for the Brezhnev period. There was so much despair. Everything surrounding us seemed irreparable. Take television," he offered, "which was unbearable. Our 'leading newspaper' *Pravda* elicited the same reaction, and the cinema was completely censored. Then there was the unpleasant political and economic side of things." Darchenko recalled trying to find chocolate or something else to buy for his son. "I searched the entire city and wasn't able to buy anything. So, I came home and stashed away this play money. Not in a bank. The bills were nothing but tokens. They were never worth the amount of money indicated on them. For these reasons, the stagnation was real. It was awful." According to Olga Martynkina, "everyone felt the stagnation when we were older. It was disgusting to see what was going on. But, on the other hand, there was a semblance of order." Aleksandr Virich remarked, "Perhaps it wasn't necessary to call the period one of stagnation," but the country "was developing in an incomprehensible direction. I realized that something was not right. Naturally, everyone cursed old-man Brezhnev, despite the fact that they swiped everything they could from work. He stole, and he let everyone else steal, too."

Most of the Muscovites found the term "stagnation" an appropriate one. That was not surprising, because they griped more about the economy even though—and perhaps because—they lived better than those in the provinces. According to Tatyana Luchnikova, "stagnation was visible because, if things had been normal, there would have been food in the stores but there were perpetual shortages." Anatoly Shapiro saw "absolutely nothing good about the economy." He argued that *blat* created a cohort of committed believers, especially among the military, yet not many among his Party acquaintances. "They lived better because they had privileges, a horrible word for me. Perhaps it was only a piece of bacon fat, but it belonged to them and not you. I understood them, but they disgusted me."

Several Baby Boomers found stagnation in other aspects of their lives. Viktor Alekseyev acknowledged that, in time, he fell under the influence of friends and of what he read. "I developed a more critical attitude and the sense that there was stagnation mounted. This was tied to the Czechoslovakian events and then, of course, to the events in Afghanistan." Valentin Ulyakhin dated stagnation to his parents' deaths in 1975 and 1976, and found it manifested in something no one else mentioned: "By this time they stopped persecuting you for going to church." Foreign travel also fed popular sentiments that the situation back home needed fixing. Mikhail Markovich highlighted the many aspects of Soviet reality that he considered funny. The comedian "Zhvanetsky* was famous at that time," explained Markovich, "and he described it all. How you go about getting a telephone and everything else." Accepting the humor in it all allowed Markovich to "keep morally healthy."

What irked Sergei Zemskov most was "running up against all sorts of far-fetched bureaucratic obstacles" that choked initiative: "When I began working, it would take three to four years for the simplest job. The bureaucracy managed to turn a routine procedure into a complicated one." Zemskov expressed utter amazement that the USSR managed to launch Sputnik in 1957 and send Yury Gagarin into space. "This is a mystery to me. I think it was aliens!" Yet Zemskov had an explanation: things had been better under Khrushchev. By the time Zemskov went to work, "things had gone to hell." He especially criticized the penchant for looking to the West before embarking on something new. "That is, you'd come with a plan for something and the first question they'd ask is 'And over there? Do they do this?' They didn't ask this question under Khrushchev." Yelena Kolosova also singled out the stifling Soviet bureaucracy for censure: "I wasn't aware at what moment stagnation occurred, perhaps because I fell in love with Em." They courted, married, and had a baby. Five years passed. "Then I woke up: there was Allende in Chile. And here? Reprints of *Gulag Archipelago*. I looked around. My God, it didn't seem like the same country in which I completed school. Such changes occurred between 1967 and 1973!"

---

* Born in 1934, Mikhail Zhvanetsky became a writer of satire and enormously popular stand-up comedian, appreciated for his monologues aimed at the shortcomings of Soviet and post-Soviet daily life.

exclaimed Kolosova. "Things were a bit easier and more serious, but at the same time more ridiculous." Kolosova mentioned all of the foolishness surrounding Brezhnev. "This bureaucratism became corrupt and arrogant, perhaps less frightful, like a Teddy bear, but the machine behind it was oppressive."

Vladimir Mikoyan reminded me that "there, of course, was stagnation. That's irrefutable, but it wasn't *felt*. We lived well for us. We knew that you couldn't find some things in the stores, but we got used to this." He elaborated, "Everyone knew that there were limits and norms. But it was hard to say what they really were, because they decide, and in each case they might do so differently. We lived with this, however, and I can honestly say that we weren't pessimistic." On the contrary: "This was the way the country was," he stated, "and we were born and raised within these boundaries. Of course, shortages irritated people, yet that wasn't that bad." As Marina Bakutina summed up, "The awareness of stagnation came only when they began to call the period that."

"IT WAS CONVENIENT . . . TO KEEP HIM IN POWER"

Stagnation also found reflection in people's shifting attitudes toward Brezhnev. Most Baby Boomers at first harbored hopes for bushy-browed Brezhnev and the new Soviet leadership, but had a change of heart by the mid- to late 1970s after he had survived several strokes, had been named Marshal of the Soviet Union, and been awarded the Lenin Prize for his ghost-authored books. As Natalya Pronina put it, "During the early years he was a real leader and people thought rather highly of him. That's not in dispute. However, this changed." Arkady Darchenko echoed these sentiments, adding: "Sometime in the mid-1970s, the idiocy turned into a real avalanche once they began awarding him all sorts of medals and titles and he could no longer speak clearly. By then it had become an awful spectacle." "What kind of leaders do we have when all of the members of the Politburo were his age and had to be led by the arm?" queried Yevgeny Podolsky. "There was disgust and mockery," averred Boris Shtein. An irked Vladimir Sidelnikov hated the hypocrisy: "Brezhnev preached one morality, but lived according to another." "There was the feeling that someone had applied the brakes," recalled Viktor Alekseyev. Concluded Natalya P.: "It was obvious that something had to give."

Several Baby Boomers had acquaintances who had met Brezhnev and who had positive things to say about him in his youth, thereby spotlighting the contrast between his early years and those of his decline. Lyubov Kovalyova shared that "I met people who worked with him. They spoke very highly of his energy and problem-solving abilities." Yet she, too, underscored the change after he became old and frail. "Even back then it seemed to me that he should have retired from politics." Vladimir Bystrov's grandfather, who had worked with Brezhnev in Dnepropetrovsk, "had a very high opinion of his organizational skills." That said, Bystrov asserted that "one shouldn't occupy the same position for so long. There should have been rotations."

Some Muscovites claimed to have disliked Brezhnev from the start. Igor Litvin believed that early on in Brezhnev's reign "people considered him an idiot." Lyubov Raitman remembered, "I always found it excruciating to listen to how he spoke. It was ungrammatical, silly, and meaningless. Not long ago they showed some documentaries from when he was young, but this is something I didn't remember. He always seemed awful to me." Agreed Viktor Alekseyev: "I saw Brezhnev from the beginning as something of a comic figure in all regards, his appearance, his behavior, and what he did." According to Leonid Volodarsky, "now many recall this period as the good times. Besides, leaders people laughed at didn't seem dangerous."

Saratov's Larisa Petrova believed that Brezhnev held onto the reins of power for so long because "it was clear to everyone that others manipulated him and that he wasn't in charge. Everyone saw this and worried." Moscow's Yelena Zharovova remembered, "I felt sorry for him when he was old. And later, when I read that he had twice asked the Politburo to let him retire and was turned down twice, I felt even sorrier for him. It was advantageous for some to keep him in power." She saw this as a tragedy: "They let an old man become the laughing stock of the whole world, and you must take this into account in evaluating him." Why did they allow this? "Because when a new leader comes to power a large stratum of the most powerful are replaced, too." "It's a shame," began Georgy Godzhello, "If our leaders had somehow rejuvenated themselves in time things would have been a lot easier, a lot better, and the country today would be altogether different." He elaborated, "There's the Chinese example, which is simply astonishing. There are the two Koreas, and the two Germanys. There's no going against the truth. History has shown that all large empires in time decline. And it's really hard on your nerves when it's your own country."

"PEOPLE TOLD THESE JOKES ABOUT HIM AND NO ONE WAS IMPRISONED"

Yet before empires collapse and revolutions topple old authorities, the latter need to become fully discredited in the eyes of the public. This type of desacralization of the old regime took place in France before the French Revolution of 1789, in Russia before the Revolution of 1917, and in the Soviet Union during the late Brezhnev era before the Gorbachev Revolution, when the Baby Boomers openly began to heap scorn on Brezhnev. As Olga Gorelik put it, "Everyone began to mock him on account of how he looked and his health." Galina Poldyaeva recalled that "it was unpleasant to watch," especially since, when he made an appearance, "everyone gave him a standing ovation. It gave me the creeps." Tatyana Arzhanova observed that "Brezhnev was considered a talking puppet and it was clear that someone in that state could not understand what was going on in the country."

Worse yet, fading apparatchiks packed the Politburo. "It was an embarrassment for our country," insisted Irina Kulikova. Natalya Yolshina stated that "in his later years Brezhnev at best evoked laughter, and at worst sarcastic laughter." She believed that eventually everyone shared the negative assessment of him, "because it had become so apparent, and it went on and on and on." Remarked Leonid Terlitsky: "He and his cronies were these gray faceless men without character or with a dull character and of low intelligence who were trying to run our lives." As a result, Terlitsky continued, "You had to somehow take control of your own life, and that was what our plans for the future were based upon, that we will be able to live a full, creative life in that system. It turned out be a total fallacy at least for me, and that was one of the reasons why I left this country." Viktor Alekseyev declared that "the older they got, the entire Politburo evoked a negative and humorous response. Not only in regard to good jokes. There was also a certain repulsion because of all those icon-like portraits."

People told countless jokes—a quintessential form of Soviet public opinion—about Brezhnev. Some feared doing so, but told them anyway, while most simply no longer were afraid. This is a key moment in the history of Soviet political culture. Andrei Rogatnev recalled that "you could tell the jokes out loud and there were no longer any punitive sanctions. Nothing of the sort." Aleksandr Trubnikov remembered that, by the time he established himself at work, "attitudes toward Brezhnev were expressed in jokes that circulated about him. He wasn't taken seriously; there was nothing but jokes at his expense." More to the point, "*no one was afraid of him.* At work you could quietly tell jokes about Leonid Ilich and no one would inform on you, even though in every organization there were people who reported on who said what."

"HE WAS EVEN WORSE THAN BREZHNEV"

Because the Soviet Union lacked an open, public procedure for selecting its top leaders, Brezhnev's death in 1982 caused alarm. "I recall how apprehensive everyone became when Brezhnev died," remembered Saratov's Olga Gorelik, who was at home at the time with her infant daughter and a pediatrician who had made a house call. They felt something was wrong. "That's because during such moments they typically played symphonic music on television. Knowing that he was ill, we thought it was the end. They finally informed us." Irina Vizgalova related that her grandmother "was terribly upset when Brezhnev died. She would say, 'What's going to happen now? The entire Soviet Union will collapse.' It was terrible when he died, but things didn't fall apart."

The Politburo's selection of Yury Andropov, former head of the KGB, as Brezhnev's successor alarmed many, as he had presided over the crackdown on dissent. "When Andropov came to power I became frightened, because my husband knew no restraint in telling jokes and there had been a time when they'd imprison you for this. I thought life wouldn't be as stable as it had been under Brezhnev," volunteered Moscow's Yelena Zharovova. Others believed that Andropov's tenure in the KGB allowed him a unique vantage point from which to assess the country's problems, and they hoped he would reinvigorate the Party and its policies. The mass media presented him as a progressive thinker, especially when he replaced ministers and regional leaders with younger Party members. Andropov survived only fifteen months in office, however, before succumbing to renal failure. Ill much of this time, Andropov nonetheless launched efforts to enforce worker discipline and raise productivity. "But with unsuccessful measures," explained Vladimir Bystrov. Vladimir Kirsanov regretted that Andropov died so soon: "I think that the majority of people were in favor of his attempt to bring order to the country. Unfortunately, he didn't have time and therefore it's hard to judge him."

When he died, the Politburo replaced him with Konstantin Ustinovich Chernenko, who many saw as Brezhnev's alter-ego and under whom the Soviet Union slipped into suspended animation. "After Brezhnev," quipped Natalya Yanichkina, "we had what we called the 'five-year-plan of lavish funerals,' as the septuagenarians populating the Politburo died one after another." Moscow's Lyubov Raitman decried the situation after Brezhnev expired: "Those years after his death were terrible, when everyone was replaced, Chernenko, Ustinov,* and the others." To illustrate the point, she told me about a conversation with the mother of one of her college girlfriends who was an "awful Communist, and who, in our youth, worked for the KGB and was fanatical." Reminisced Raitman: "It was after one of Chernenko's speeches, when I was at their place. She was absolutely crushed and shocked. She said, 'What a disgrace. How can it be that he's the head of our country? How could they let this happen?' Even committed Communists were appalled by what was going on." Yelena Kolosova recalled asking, "Who's Chernenko? He was even worse than Brezhnev, absolutely nothing more than a joke." According to Saratov's Larisa Petrova, "we were really afraid after the death of, what's his name, Chernenko. We feared that there would be another sick, old, decrepit leader no one wanted. How much could we take?"

"IF YOU INFORM ONCE, YOU'LL HAVE TO INFORM YOUR ENTIRE LIFE"

People also feared—but likewise cracked jokes about—the much-maligned KGB, who represented another essential feature of late socialism. One joke goes like this: "Two KGB agents pass each other in the corridor. One asks the other,

---

* Dmitry Fedorovich Ustinov became Soviet minister of defense and a member of the Politburo in 1976. During his tenure, the Soviet leadership invaded Afghanistan.

'what are you laughing about?' 'Someone just told me such a funny joke that I'm still laughing.' 'Really, tell me!' 'No, I can't, I just gave him ten years for telling it.'" How much did the political police meddle in the Baby Boomers' daily lives as they found their niche in the system? Although a good number of them emigrated, none who remained in the Soviet Union turned to open dissent. Moreover, none admitted to informing for the KGB—not that they would. Their experiences reveal that the Western imagination dividing Soviet citizens into diehard (or disingenuous) Communists and dissidents conceals a far more complicated yet commonsensical reality: most simply lived in search of the Soviet dream—or in search of the next sliver of sausage, staying clear of the KGB as best they could.

Of all the interviewees, only Moscow's Andrei Rogatnev made a career in the KGB, lasting until perestroika drove him into private business. Growing up in a KGB family, Rogatnev admired his father's "sense of duty and integrity" and "didn't see any alternative" other than to follow in his father's footsteps. Rogatnev's family was in Budapest during the Soviet invasion of 1956, an experience that left vivid, perhaps even traumatic, memories and made confident his belief that "our cause was right." His upbringing told: as a Komsomol activist and self-proclaimed patriot, he did not read *samizdat*, and he voted to expel from the Aviation Institute a classmate who demonstrated against the USSR's invasion of Czechoslovakia. He also married someone "from a similar family."

Rogatnev neither regretted the career choice he made nor justified himself. Instead, he seemed to personify the conflicting influences his generation faced. He may not have read *samizdat*, but he worshipped the Beatles and soaked up the Hollywood films shown to select audiences. He also loved a good joke, especially when it was at the expense of Soviet leaders. Traveling abroad affected him in the same way as it did his classmates. Visiting Czechoslovakia in 1978, he confirmed that its inhabitants lived better than he did. Prague's well-stocked shops, absence of snaking lines, and abundance of world-renowned beer delighted him. None of these experiences undermined his commitment to serving in the security police until the Soviet Union expired, but they helped to prepare him for life in post-Soviet Russia. So did the lifelong friendships and connections he made at School No. 20. Although his classmates spoke disparagingly about the KGB, many looked upon Rogatnev as one of their own. Adding a personal dimension to the otherwise faceless security organs softened them for those who had not had any run-ins with the KGB. Then, too, Rogatnev's work involved foreign, not domestic, surveillance.

But at home, the KGB suppressed dissidents and monitored the intelligentsia, while propaganda organs countered Western accusations of human rights abuses. Aleksandr Trubnikov explained how, at an everyday level, the Party explained away Western charges that people in the Soviet Union lacked basic rights, freedom of movement, for example. "They'd say, we have no unemployment and our medical system is free. We have confidence in tomorrow. We have equality. But there's a price that has to be paid for this. And we pay it. We have our laws, and they're better than yours. Who needs this freedom of movement if everyone in the West is poor and exploited?"

Such justifications did not sit right with many. Remarked Saratov's Arkady Darchenko on the topic of human rights: "I knew, of course, that we simply didn't have any. But I never took part in demonstrations on this account. I was busy doing my own thing." That said, continued Darchenko, "I supported Solzhenitsyn from the start, and Sakharov* even more, because he was someone who consciously did what he had to do, even though it cost him everything. In sum," wrapped up Darchenko, "I respected those people who struggled for human rights, but, in all honesty, I didn't myself. It was a special category of political people who were like that." Aleksandr Konstantinov volunteered that "we understood that things here were bad in regard to human rights. But the way the Western radio stations discussed the matter always seemed a bit artificial to us, because they harped over and over again on the same thing." Irina Chemodurova "strongly believed that everything was as it should be" in regard to the Party's crackdown on dissent, but changed her mind when she completed her graduate work in Moscow and witnessed the so-called Volobuev affair** unfold "before my very eyes" at the Institute of History. It was then that she "for the first time felt that things were not so simple." These three Saratovites studied in Moscow. Many of their classmates who remained in Saratov saw things differently. Olga Kamayurova, for instance, admitted "all of this passed me by. We took the word 'dissident' as some sort of swear word. How I regret that I was far removed back then from people who understood everything. There *were* people who understood things already back then. It's a shame that I wasn't one of them."

Most Muscovites agreed with Leonid Volodarsky's analysis of the Soviet human rights movement: "There was a lot of commotion. Only a very small number of people got involved. I believe they're heroes. They challenged the system. My acquaintances and I supported them, but we ourselves did not take part in demonstrations." Applauding the deep convictions of writers Sinyavsky, Daniel, poet Joseph Brodsky, physicist Andrei Sakharov, and other dissidents, Boris Shtein concurred that human rights was "an important subject for us." This was the case for him especially when his ex-wife applied to emigrate and encountered enormous problems. Igor Litvin kept informed of dissident activ-

---

* Andrei Dmitriyevich Sakharov was a Soviet physicist and political dissident who received the Nobel Peace Prize in 1975. Exiled to the city of Gorky (today Nizhny Novgorod), he was allowed to return to Moscow during the Gorbachev era and was soon elected a member of the Council of People's Deputies.

** P. V. Volobuev became director of the USSR Academy of Sciences Institute of History in 1970 until his dismissal in 1974. During this period, revisionist historians collided with the Brezhnev leadership, which imposed bureaucratic controls over the nonconformist historians by the time of Volobuev's ouster in 1974.

ities, particularly the Sakharov affair, by listening to foreign radio broadcasts. "I honestly don't know if I would have gone to take part in a demonstration of some sort had they asked me to. I found all of this really interesting, but in our milieu there wasn't any of that among my closest friends." Beginning in 1977, Litvin vacationed in the Crimea at a resort known as New World that attracted "dissidents, refuseniks*, the first devotees of karate, Osho,** and yoga. There were many people of this sort there. There were open conversations there. But here in Moscow I didn't socialize with such people."

Anatoly Shapiro did. He met the dissident author Vladimir Voinovich at a friend's dacha before the KGB forced Voinovich into exile. Shapiro also fell under the influence of Alik Polishchyuk, the executive editor of the journal *Asia and Africa Today*. Shapiro recounted that the KGB arrested Polishchyuk, who "lived in the neighboring apartment building, when they arrested Natan Shcharansky.*** Polishchyuk had ties with him. They followed Alik," remembered Shapiro. "He visited us at home, but I wasn't all that afraid." Polishchyuk emigrated when the KGB gave him the choice: arrest or emigration.****

In Saratov the KGB cracked down on dissident activities when the Baby Boomers were in college, targeting student groups at Saratov University, the Saratov Conservatory, and the Law Institute. This might have been a critical lesson, for unlike the situation in Moscow, none of the Saratovites admitted to having had any direct encounters with the KGB. Typical was the response of Pyotor Krasilnikov: "I knew there was such an organization, but it didn't touch anyone in my milieu. Therefore they didn't concern me much. There were even jokes back then about the organization." Aleksandr Virich acknowledged that people realized there was an informant in every group, "but in our time this wasn't that bad. It was okay for five or six people to gather in the kitchen and discuss things over a bottle of vodka. It was only if you'd begin to print and pass out leaflets that things got bad." Arkady Darchenko concurred, "You know, here there wasn't any uproar over political events as there was in Piter [the colloquial name for St. Petersburg] and Moscow, and within our circle we always felt free to speak our mind. We talked openly. Our conversations were the same. There

---

* Soviet citizens denied permission to emigrate abroad, mostly Jews, were known as refuseniks, derived from the refusal they received from Soviet authorities.

** Osho or Bhagwan Shree Rajneesh was born Rajneesh Chandra Mohan in central India. In 1981, Osho moved his ashram community to Antelope, Oregon, where the ashram's controversial lifestyle and reports of all sorts of abuses sparked enormous controversy that resulted in Osho's arrest and deportation on charges of immigration fraud.

*** Anatoly (Natan) Shcharansky is one of the original members of the Helsinki Group, the oldest human rights organization in the Soviet Union, which emerged in 1976. As a prominent Jewish dissident, Shcharansky applied to emigrate and was arrested and sentenced to fourteen years in prison in March 1977. Released in February 1986, he emigrated to Israel, where he founded the Yisrael B'Aliyah Party. He has also held several ministerial positions in the government.

**** After emigrating he became an official representative of Soviet Pentacostalists abroad.

basically wasn't anything special that set us apart." These testimonials suggest how the realm of the private gained depth and intimacy within a wider system of constraints.

In contrast to their Saratov counterparts, some Muscovites had intimidating run-ins with the KGB. One Baby Boomer, "Nina," who asked me not to use her real name, began to study Hebrew, associating with Soviet Jews preparing to emigrate. Many of them sought to remain anonymous by using pseudonyms. "Of course, the KGB followed them," she remembered. Later the KGB summoned her at work. "I was terrified and couldn't tell my parents a thing," but she confided in a classmate's mother who told her "Understand one thing. If you inform once, you'll have to inform your entire life." Taking the advice, Nina refused to cooperate with the police, who called her in three more times. At each encounter she denied she was a "Zionist." The last time she saw them she told the KGB that her fiancé forbid her to study Hebrew any longer. Upon parting, they gave Nina a telephone number to call in the event she "had a change of heart" about informing on those with whom she studied Hebrew.

The KGB tried to recruit Moscow's Bakhyt Kenzheyev: "There was one sympathetic investigator, and another mean one," recalled Kenzheyev, who wanted him to "prove" that he was a loyal Soviet citizen by meeting with them regularly to report on anti-Soviet activities, "in order to help your friends, since they might otherwise lose their way." When Kenzheyev refused, the KGB threatened to prevent him from publishing in the USSR and to get him dismissed from his university post. Fearing that his lifestyle would get him into deeper trouble, Kenzheyev knew he needed to find a way to leave the country. In the meantime, he had an opportunity to see how poorly the police functioned. After marrying a Canadian who worked in Moscow as a translator, Kenzheyev traveled with her and others from the publishing house that employed her to visit the historic towns, Vladimir and Suzdal. A year later his frightened mother phoned: "'Bakhytik, the police came and asked me and Papa why, a year ago, you spent the night in a hotel in Vladimir with a foreigner.' The police worked very, very poorly."

Not always. The KGB sent Vladimir Sidelnikov home from Finland in disgrace during his senior year at the Moscow Institute of International Relations. Before then, he had not feared them, because both his parents, owing to their positions, had "direct ties" with the KGB. "And if I hadn't gotten sick," Sidelnikov claimed, "I might have attended the KGB training school to become a professional intelligence officer." Sidelnikov shared that the KGB tapped his phone after throwing him out of Finland. Later he was locked up in a mental hospital after he had a nervous breakdown. "And that's a stigma for your entire life," he lamented. "You're like a prisoner. My parents couldn't interfere." There was more to his story than that: "I was in the nuthouse with dissidents. There was a guy from the Bolshoi Theater, a totally healthy person, who they put there simply because he applied to leave the country. That's how things were."

Tatyana Luchnikova expressed indignation that the KGB ran a "thorough check" on everyone who applied to go abroad and put a stop to her visits to Bulgaria. "They told me that I had to turn down some work that the Bulgarians offered me. I had earned a lot of money there." From the KGB's perspective, Bulgaria was not, as the popular imagination had it, just another Soviet republic. "They told me to say that I was sick and didn't want to go back." She fired off complaint letters, but to no avail. This was not Luchnikova's first run-in with the KGB. When she studied at the Moscow Institute of Cinematography, a French student invited her to a film preview at the French embassy. Afterward, she received a routine summons from her department chair, only to find that the call had been a KGB ruse. "They told me that if I were to continue seeing foreigners they'd expel me from the institute, and not to tell a soul about our meeting."

Lyubov Raitman's mother had an encounter with the KGB that cast a somewhat softer light on the organization. Despite the fact that she was not a Party member and was a Jew, she was included in a group that traveled to France in 1961. "In each group there had to be, and always was, a member of the KGB, observing and guarding, maintaining control and surveillance. There was one in their group, too, but he was one of those rare members of the KGB," noted Raitman. He looked after her mother, who translated for the group, and often took her and her girlfriend for walks, thereby allowing them to see more than the rest of their party. He took no steps to continue the acquaintance after their return to Moscow. "Yet it's interesting that he didn't forget that they had known each other and helped her many years later," reminisced Raitman. Her mother sought to return to Paris in the 1970s when it became theoretically possible to accept private invitations; however, her application got turned down time and again. "Then she searched out the telephone number of that very Sergey Ivanovich and called him. They met and he said he knew what the problem was. Shortly afterward he called her and said 'Try again,' and she did and received permission. It was unbelievable that she saw Paris a second time," interjected Raitman. "She traveled several more times before getting another rejection. But this time, Sergey Ivanovich told her 'you went, that's enough. I can't help anymore.' That ended their contact."

Raitman recalled another episode that demonstrates how the shady organization operated. After a group of American children visited School No. 20, she and many of her classmates corresponded with their new foreign friends. One of Raitman's classmates, Tatyana, exchanged letters with her American pen pal for several years, only to have this come back to haunt her. When she later applied for a job that required a security clearance, she had forgotten all about the correspondence; however, the security police had not. Tatyana got the job she wanted, but had some explaining to do.

Mikhail Markovich admitted to several instances of KGB interference: "We got through it all, suspecting that in each organization there was someone who informed on us. You had to be careful." As Vladimir Mikoyan explained, "The spirit of caution was, I think, instilled in just about everyone. People knew where, how, and with whom to express themselves." Moscow's Boris Shtein put it this way: "The KGB was a threatening symbol in my life that resulted in a certain level of self-censorship. I never had any direct contact with the KGB but it indirectly made itself felt. We always thought about what we were saying." At what point did Shtein become conscious of this? "As a child my parents warned me not to tell others what was said at home."

Understandings of freedom are specific to the culture and society in which it is experienced. The Russian sociologist L. G. Ionin suggested that Soviet citizens did not feel lack of political freedom as a lack of freedom per se. "The Soviet people chose from among the available choices and understood freedom as having choices from among what was." In this regard, for a free person, the Soviet Union was a free society. Freedom existed as a real choice, as an individual emotional experience.[20] Freedom, Soviet style, included informing for the KGB. Some did so because they had been compromised, but others chose to do so, or not to, in order to exercise their freedom.

"HOW COULD WE FALL FOR ALL THIS NONSENSE?"

The widening gap between the Baby Boomers' personal experience exercising their freedom and proclaimed government ideals produced deficits in what might be called the Soviet myth economy. The government not only used the school system to indoctrinate but also subjected its people to two systems of propaganda, one based on the mass media, the other on oral communication through lectures and seminars presented by Party activists as part of state "cultural enlightenment" activities. Controlling information and data, the government offered a sanitized version of the past, suppressed information it found damaging, and falsified facts. It used data and cultural artifacts from the West, including feature films, to criticize the capitalist world. The more flexible and dynamic covert propaganda allowed the state to transmit messages it considered inappropriate for the mass media. For instance, it used oral communication to discredit Khrushchev after his ouster, to tarnish the reputation of the dissidents, and to cast a Soviet gloss on the "Jewish question." In turn, people expected to hear things from lectures that found little or no resonance in the press or on radio or television. Oral propaganda became necessary because, in opening up, Soviet society grew more sophisticated. This was especially true of the intelligentsia who, more than any other group, resisted the government's attempts to mythologize reality through propaganda.

What myths did the Soviet government want people to believe in to inspire patriotism? "The main myth was that Soviet power was the best and most just in the world," observed Saratov's Aleksandr Trubnikov. "'Just' was the key word. We didn't have exploitation of man by man as you did under terrible capitalism. Everything we had belonged to the people. We didn't have private property, which is the source of all misfortune. I honestly believed that it was a good thing that everything belonged to the people, because it was mine, too." People internalized these myths at an everyday level, which became stereotypical ways of thinking. Natalya P. believed that "we were the most powerful country in the world, that things were fine here and that everything in the West was terrible." Tatyana Luchnikova knew that the Soviet Union "was the best country in the world, with the greatest possibilities, free education, free healthcare, free everything." As an etiquette book from the time reads, "Unlike the capitalist order, where 'man is wolf to man,' in our society man is comrade and friend to man."[21] "In my opinion," Irina Chemodurova maintained, "the majority firmly believed, and I believed, and believe today, that we were given social guarantees, that the main thing was to work honestly, that we, our country, defended the world."

Saratov and Moscow Baby Boomers alike remembered how, in their youth, they took for granted that the Soviet Union was building communism and that the Soviet system had the advantage over all others. "We didn't go to bed with thoughts of communism on our mind, but we believed in our Motherland," clarified Saratov's Galina Poldyaeva. The myth that everyone who worked responsibly would enjoy material plenty under communism appealed to Aleksandr Trubnikov. "It really had an effect on me. Many really believed that communism was a good thing, when we'll have full equality, when everything will be in abundance, when there will be no poor, no hungry, and when everyone will be employed." Natalya Pronina remarked that "the central myth that we were building communism strongly united people. Everyone was in favor." Sergei Zemskov certainly was: "We really *did* begin to build communism. We lived under communism, for it was a carefree life." Boris Shtein commented on the related Khrushchev-era campaign to overtake America. "Of course, this myth-making affected us, especially the promise 'to each according to his abilities, to each according to his needs' because no one really wanted to work. I think everyone lived the myth. It was an attractive one and our minds weren't yet developed enough for us to understand that it wouldn't work."

Like so many others, Saratov's Aleksandr Virich agreed that the central myth of his youth was "that we were building some sort of ideal future that would be just." But delayed gratification had its drawbacks: "Then, sometime in your twenties, you realize that an ideal future is not for everyone." He asked if I had heard that communism had been built, but only "inside the Kremlin walls." None of the Baby Boomers claimed to have known any true Communists from among people their age. Most people, however, accepted the fundamentals of the Soviet system, still strong enough to punish and discipline, but put their own material interests ahead of those of the state.[22] Sociological research confirms that the values of private life and individualism became more important for the Baby Boomers than they were for the interviewees' parents.[23]

The Baby Boomers may not have anticipated the system's collapse, but they were ready for it when it came, thereby exposing the ultimate failure of the Soviet myth economy. Olga Kamayurova, for instance, did not lose faith in the system until perestroika, but she maintained that, "by the time we had become adults, the slogans found on buildings seemed silly to us: 'Communism is our goal.' 'Communism is a radiant future.'" She continued, "It was part of our everyday prosaic existence. We didn't even notice. The hammer and sickle was everywhere. It even seemed a bit funny, but, then, with the advent of information, it all caved in and I saw the light. Good heavens, where had I been earlier? Where were my eyes, my ears, my brain? How could we fall for all this nonsense?"

Many fell for it because the media provided people with a pantheon of historical and contemporaneous examples of self-fashioned Soviet heroes. Olga Gorelik, for example, cited the example of Pavel Morozov, "the hero of all Pioneers." And not only: "There were war heroes, labor heroes, female heroines, female labor heroines, and mother heroines. We were all inspired by these examples." There was also the example of Soviet leaders. Irina Chemodurova

When Yevgeniya Ruditskaya and her class posed for their annual portrait in the school auditorium in 1986, Lenin still remained at the center of Soviet mythology—but he would not be for long. *Courtesy of Yevgeniya Kreizerova (Ruditskaya)*

related that "the first book I read when I was four years old was called *Russian Heroes*, and my second one *About Lenin and Stalin*, with celebratory verses that I still remember today. I now understand that the idea of a charismatic leader was deeply rooted in mass, and individual, consciousness." She elaborated, "Everything they did was right. That was the voice of the people." She also recalled seeing portraits of three leaders hanging on the Saratov post office when she was a young girl. Stalin was in the center, flanked by Lenin and Molotov. "Then they changed them." But this did not shake her faith in the system. As Lyubov Raitman explained, later people believed "that things are bad, not because the system is bad, but because of bad rulers." Leonid Terlitsky concurred, "I had an idealistic view of the world, that the system itself is not that bad, but it's the bastards who are running it. So, if you have good people in the government, then things may look different. Sort of like Gorbachev's point of view." Were the bad people at the very top, I asked? "They were everywhere," he snapped.

The myth of the good Lenin lay at the center of the Soviet belief system, especially after Khrushchev's stinging denunciation of Stalin. "There was the myth that if Lenin hadn't died that everything would have been okay," explained Leonid Volodarsky. Like others, Saratov's Yevgeny Podolsky believed in Lenin's greatness. "But when I read his works I was horrified," claimed Podolsky. Lenin's readiness to resort to terror and his animosity toward the intelligentsia appalled Podolsky, as did the fact that Lenin never held a job. Decrying Lenin's reliance on the semi-literate, vodka-infused masses, Podolsky queried, "How could he teach people how to work, when he himself didn't know what work was?" Musing over the course of Russian and Soviet history, he concluded, "They began to shoot and kill people. Beginning with terror is the worst way to build a new society."

Apart from the Lenin cult, a mythologized cult of the Great Patriotic War grew up with the Baby Boomers, replacing the Revolution of 1917 as the foundation story for the Soviet state that people could identify with, because they lived through the conflict. The cult of World War II evolved after 1945 to serve changing state needs, reaching its apogee under Brezhnev. He and his cronies orchestrated an extensive agenda of displays of loyalty, undoubtedly hoping that they would increase popular support for the regime and its goals.[24] In 1965 the state declared Victory Day a national holiday, erecting giant shrines and memorials to shape collective memory. These measures worked. "There was a great deal of respect for everyone who took part in the war," remarked Aleksandr Konstantinov. As Moscow's Leonid Terlitsky so aptly put it, people viewed the war "as something honest as opposed to something fake." Aleksandr Babushkin believed the "victory and heroism of the Russian people" unified the country. He, like countless others, underscored the colossal human losses the Soviet Union suffered: "There were deaths in each family." Ironically, Vladimir Prudkin explained that the war days were the best for his parents' generation "because the absolute worst days of their lives had been between the wars [during the Stalin terror]. They felt happy only in the trenches, in these hardships."[25] They won the war, as Vladimir Sidelnikov put it, "because they were fighting for socialism, and therefore could not lose."

Saratov's Tatyana Kuznetsova pointed out that the war also united the Baby Boomers because they modeled themselves on their parents. "We looked up to them. They were an outstanding example. We tried to take what we considered was best from them." As Pyotor Krasilnikov underscored, "We are perhaps the only generation in Russia that never experienced war. Of course, all of those cataclysms united people. What united us was probably rebuilding the economy. We were brought up in this spirit. We developed new lands, developed Siberia, built all of those factories and apartment buildings."

The Baby Boomers contended that the USSR won World War II. "I still believe that Russia won, and that America certainly made a huge contribution, but for me that's secondary, although I know about the large number of Studebakers, food, and other things," said Igor Litvin.* For him and others, Russia's colossal human losses—27 million—gave them the moral right to claim victory. "I know that my Mama at age sixteen was left an orphan, and I know how this affected her. She suffered from neuroses and illnesses all her life." Explained Yelena Zharovova: "My view of the war was formed without a doubt by the government, because all of the media conveyed the government's point of view. I sincerely believe that the Soviet Union's contribution was decisive. I believe that in the West the role of the Soviet Union in the war is vastly underappreciated." Concluded Zharovova: "Our evaluation has to be objective. One [read: Americans] should never over-emphasize the importance of one's condensed milk or tinned meat, and forget how other people lost their lives."

According to Leonid Volodarsky, before the Great Patriotic War the mythologized Red victory during the Russian Civil War united people until the cult of the Great Fatherland War replaced it. Yet Volodarsky noted that the cult of the war became "exaggerated and inflated" under Brezhnev, who abused the myth: "It was funny that the main hero of the Great Fatherland War turned out to be Brezhnev." Added Aleksandr Konstantinov: "The first cracks in this myth took place when someone argued that it hadn't been necessary to involve so many people in senseless assaults, to lead people into battle regardless of obstacles when things could have been done otherwise. Then someone said that perhaps the Germans weren't responsible for the starvation during the blockade of Leningrad, but Stalin, who senselessly held on to the city. Such questions began to surface, and people looked upon the myth of the war somewhat differently." Indeed, Olga Martynkina felt "we exaggerated the role of the war for far too

---

* A reference to the Lend-Lease Act of 1941, which allowed the U.S. government to ship food, weapons, and equipment to its allies.

long. I agree that in the West many don't know history. Yet we have a warped view of the war. They're still making movies about the war. How much of this can you take?"

Aware of the deficits in the Soviet myth economy, the Brezhnev leadership realized it needed to inculcate a spirit of patriotism and inclusion in the country's younger generations that had not participated in the Great Patriotic War. In 1975 it launched the laying of the Baikal-Amur Magistral Railway (BAM) to link the European and Asian sectors of the USSR. The last of the Soviet Union's great construction projects, BAM's ostensible purpose was to bolster trade with the East Asian economies, securing an alternative transportation route in the event the Chinese seized the Trans-Siberian Railway. At one point, more than 500,000 Komsomolites joined in the wasteful and inefficient endeavor, which wreaked havoc on the ecology of the BAM Zone.[26] Revealingly, none of the Baby Boomers took part in building BAM; the campaign surrounding "Brezhnev's folly" did nothing to bolster their backing of the Soviet system. "We knew that BAM was being built," explained Lyubov Kovalyova. "Songs were written about it, but on the scene things weren't so romantic." Like many others, Leonid Volodarsky recalled that "we didn't take part in it. We were absolutely indifferent, but there was lots of clamor over it." Georgy Godzhello concurred: "It passed us all by. We were already working."

The Saratovites felt similarly about BAM. Yevgeny Podolsky cast BAM as "just another myth, that it was the largest construction project in the world, unlike anywhere else. But why build it? No one posed the question." At the time, Podolsky's work took him to a meeting at the State Committee for Planning, Gosplan, where he spoke with those responsible for building BAM. "It turned out that we built the road in a marsh and much of the expensive equipment sunk and was abandoned. If something broke down, no one repaired it, because each year they'd go to the government with requests for more money and they allotted them exorbitant sums." Complained Podolsky: "People were going hungry, there was nothing to eat, but they bought everything for BAM and built this stupid railroad." Aleksandr Konstantinov remembered that "people's attitudes toward it were tongue in cheek. We understood that there were two sides to things, the official one and the personal one. There were people who exhibited real interest, courage, and probably some romanticism." Did he know any? "No. There were no such people among my acquaintances," he laughed. Some of Irina Vizgalova's coworkers at a major Saratov gas firm took part in building BAM; however, according to her, "there were so many disappointments, because they had left for Siberia on such a positive note." A lone dissenting voice reflecting his attitudes toward the post-Soviet present, Viktor D. believed "The country needed BAM. The fact that they don't use it, that they abandoned it incomplete is not the Communists' fault." But he could not explain why.

As a student, Yevgeny Podolsky took part in a construction brigade in Siberia during the summer of 1969, not far from the place where the Baikal-Amur Magistral Railway (BAM) to link the European and Asian sectors of the USSR would be built. He had little positive to say about the experience, and plenty of scorn for the building of BAM. *Courtesy of Roza Bazyleva*

Some Baby Boomers understood my use of "myth" as something that was not true or else was impossible to achieve. Yelena Kolosova believed the hype surrounding the Cuban Revolution "was a myth." Bakhyt Kenzheyev told me his aunt received a pension of 20 rubles a month. "I remember that amount. It's a myth when they say today that pensioners lived well before perestroika." In emigration, Bakhyt Kenzheyev soon discovered that "it was a far-fetched myth that Americans are like Russians." Criminal investigator Gennady Ivanov recalled how much emphasis was placed "on fighting against crime, which was seen as an abnormal phenomenon. Speaking about myths, here's one for you, that we could eliminate crime in our society. They used to demand that we achieve a 100 percent detection rate, which cost them some good investigators."

Vladimir Prudkin perhaps summed things up best: "All of Soviet society was completely mythologized," he maintained. "After all, the starting point of the society created in Russia was the attempt to realize the ideas of Jesus' Sermon on the Mount through force and violence." Taking me on a personal tour of Russian and Soviet history, Prudkin judged things harshly. No, the majority of people did not realize they lived in a mythical world, "But during the Brezhnev era a healthy cynicism began to develop, as more and more people understood that it's a myth. However, people had to live and somehow establish themselves in the system. And this led to its collapse because common sense prevailed. There was no alternative to the Stalinist regime. You weaken it for a second, its policies, and it collapses." What enabled the Soviet state to organize society, posited Prudkin, was "the two wars, the Civil War and the Second World War. As soon as an external enemy appears, all problems are set aside." In other words, the common sense that brought down the system developed "because there was no World War III." If war had broken out again, people would have "defended the Motherland, relinquishing everything. But there was no war for ten, twenty, thirty years. Life without war became more and more significant as people asked 'what kind of pants am I wearing? What kind of shoes are these? What kind of music am I listening to?'"

"I'M CHANGING ALL THE TIME"

I asked the Baby Boomers what forces shaped their identities and how the Brezhnev years affected them. Apart from the role of state propaganda, the Baby Boomers acknowledged the place that family, friends, books, spouses, career choices, gender, and anti-Semitism played in shaping how they saw themselves in the world of late socialism. Saratov's Natalya P., for instance, believed "the opinions of those surrounding us and our parents" most influenced the formation of her identity. Aleksandr Konstantinov detailed how certain childhood experiences determined his relationship with others, both back then and later. "As a child, I got the message in dealing with my nanny that I was selfish and mean. Moreover, my father was rather rigid. I tried to suppress these character traits, but apparently without success." Drawn toward people who were more spontaneous, he thought "they possessed some sort of internal truth" that he lacked. "I was driven by the mind and they were driven by the soul, by the heart," as he put it. In order to understand who you are, he added, "It's essential to know how the world is ordered, and you do this through reading." He mentioned specifically Dostoevsky, Tolstoy, and Sartre. Moscow's Georgy Godzhello believed one's choice of a profession reflected a confluence of influences: "An engineer, someone in the humanities, and an artist, have altogether different casts of mind," Godzhello observed.

Most of the interviewees shared Vladimir Bystrov's observation that identity-making "is an ongoing process that is not yet over," shaped, as Leonid Volodarsky put it, by "my life experience and nothing else." Vladimir Prudkin elaborated, "I fully realize that I'm changing all the time and will continue to do so, and that I'm unbelievably happy about this and afraid that at some point I'll stop changing." Aleksandr Trubnikov also remarked that "the evolution was very strong throughout my life, beginning with my real desire to become a Soviet patriot." He offered an example from during the Vietnam War, when the Soviet Union backed the North Vietnamese in their fight against Americans: "I remember saying to my father in all sincerity, 'Why don't all the people working in the Soviet Union give a portion of their wages to help battle against American imperialism?'" Trubnikov called his transformation into a Russian émigré a gradual one. "I acquired information through experience, and from what I saw, and from what reached us, say, from abroad. When I began conducting research the difference in the level of science became obvious, despite the fact that the Soviet Union had so many scientists." As a result, he spotted a contradiction between what they wrote in the papers and said at Party meetings at the university. Then people were allowed to immigrate to Israel. "This too had a big impact on me, because one assistant professor working with me left," remembered Trubnikov. "First his mother, an old woman, left. They called a Party meeting and insisted that he denounce his mother, to say that she betrayed her homeland." When he refused to do so, he got sacked from work and ended up following her. "I saw people foaming at the mouth denouncing him and saying that he, too, betrayed his country. This also made a big impression on me," concluded Trubnikov. "At that time much depended upon nationality, and my Jewish friends were almost all quite critical."

The experience of Moscow's Igor Litvin resonates with Trubnikov's assessment of his Jewish friends. Litvin linked his identity to the anti-Semitism he encountered getting into college and landing a job. "When they opened the file and saw my surname their eyes turned blank. And this gave rise to an inferiority complex." Not surprisingly, Litvin later made new friends, also Jews, who "understood that it was time to get out of here, that there was nothing to do in this country."

In all societies, one's professional or work life constitutes a crucial element of how one sees oneself in the world. Arkady Darchenko's experience offers a telling example of how features of the post-Soviet period would come to challenge people's sense of self. For Darchenko, this meant "starting life over three times," by launching new careers. Summed up Darchenko: "The first time I was still young, and I could do it without much difficulty. But when I had to for the second time in 1995 it was really hard, because I was well known at the institute, and I became a nobody, a programmer trainee in a commercial firm. It was very tough going, and I didn't know that I had it in me to pull myself up once again." Darchenko, however, delighted in the fact that he could do it: "Thank God the most important thing that I learned at school and then at the university was how to learn," he concluded. "I don't have a low opinion of myself, since I was able to retool myself three times." In some respects his remarks hold true for many other Baby Boomers, if not for Russia as a whole.

"IT'S HARDER FOR WOMEN TO HAVE A CAREER"

The female Baby Boomers had far more to say about how their gender shaped their identity than their male counterparts, but the statements of both sexes reveal deep-rooted attitudes toward innate gender roles that spilled over from the home into the workplace. Natalya P. spoke for others when she volunteered that "in Russia we women spoil our men. At first we shoulder all of the responsibilities and then wonder why our men stop being men." Natalya Yolshina voiced another widely held view that "men are always more interested in politics while women live more in the emotional realm. If a woman's in politics, it's an exception." Yolshina believed that women do not strive to succeed in a man's world, but that "those who want to, achieve something." Yelena Kolosova found it "interesting being a woman." Raised by her parents "to endure thirst, to rise to the occasion, not to ask, not to complain," she made a name for herself in science "for the pleasure of it, not to get ahead."

Many Soviet women had a highly negative understanding of the label "feminist," as Natalya Yanichkina, who "never" felt discriminated against because she is a woman, suggested: "I've always been very much a woman and very much a man at the same time. I've never differentiated between what might be called men's or women's work. If I have the physical strength and ability to do something, I do it." Yanichkina was quick to point out that "I don't have any feminist feelings of any kind. I'm very much a Russian woman, the kind about whom Nekrasov wrote, who can bring a horse to a gallop and charge into a burning hut if I sense that I'm defending my family."*

The Soviet Union had more women in the workplace and more female scientists and engineers than any other country, but state policies did not necessarily undermine men's traditional attitudes. A case in point, Arkady Darchenko believed that the professions he picked all his life were men's professions, particularly nuclear physics. "It's not that women are inferior, but that they're different. They're more emotional, and emotion has no place in science," he explained. "Moreover, emotion keeps you from concentrating on what's most important, especially when you add to this the distraction of taking care of the household." He also considered computer programming a man's profession. "Although there are female programmers, it's simply not their thing. In the same way that being an electrical engineer is not a woman's thing and a nuclear scientist even more so. It's a guy thing even in regard to your health. The radiation we received affects women even more." When I asked about female physicists, he replied, "We didn't take them seriously." Pressed, Darchenko tried to back out of the corner he had talked himself into. "Women are very smart, but they're smart in a different way. They're just different." Viktor Alekseyev now understands that, back then, he unconsciously assimilated the widely held conviction that the possibilities were greater for men. "In this regard, Soviet society was half-Asian, by which I mean openly oriented toward having men dominate."

---

* Poet Nikolai Alekseyevich Nekrasov is especially appreciated for his "Russian Women" (1872), which paid homage to the wives of the so-called Decembrists, who followed their husbands into Siberian exile when they tried to provoke the introduction of political reform in Russia in 1825.

Despite this widespread belief, a study of Soviet émigrés shows that women, constituting the majority of professional occupations, voiced a remarkably high degree of job satisfaction. In fact, they expressed greater satisfaction with the aspects of life measured in the survey than men, except in regard to the availability of goods. And this is crucial, as the Soviet state sought legitimacy along gendered lines, ascribing an inferior ideological role to women, but empowering them in their capacity as consumers.[27] Be that as it may, both men and women "ranked women's life as more difficult" in the USSR,[28] underscoring the widely acknowledged impact of women's double burden.

Women, and the state, took measures to do something about it. Sociologist Vladimir Shlapentokh documented an exacerbation of conflicts between men and women in the marriage market and at home, where most of the burden of running the household fell on women.[29] The dilemma found reflection in a manners book from the era reminding men that women hold jobs and have endless concerns as mothers. "So, all the household chores rightly should be divided in half," with the men taking on the physically more demanding tasks.[30] Moreover, to counter social trends, under Brezhnev the state stepped up media emphasis on the value of women's feminine appearance and behavior, rehabilitating "natural" female roles connected "with love, family, and children." Yet the marriage rate continued to decline.[31]

The female Baby Boomers' remarks complement the survey findings regarding women's high degree of job satisfaction, regardless of the double burden. Many insisted that they had not encountered professional discrimination in their lives. One of them, Larisa Petrova, had been the class elder at school, a member of her Komsomol bureau, a member of the Communist Party bureau at work, and now academic secretary at her research institute and head of a department. "A female activist," she insisted, "always rises to the top, but I never wanted to occupy any really high posts." Lyubov Kovalyova also claimed never to have encountered job discrimination, but this had much to do with her own attitudes and career choices shaped, undoubtedly, by her childhood when she recalled being terribly disappointed that she had been born a girl: "It was terrible, because boys could run in the woods while we had to wear skirts and tie bows in our hair. But later the question didn't concern me all that much." Being a woman did not limit her; in fact, she maintained, "I began to find definite advantages in it." Her mother was the ideal housewife who took excellent care of the family; however, once her children were grown, she returned to work until well into her seventies. As a result, Lyubov informed me that "I never dreamed of sitting home. Right after finishing school I went to college, then to graduate school. Along the way I got married, gave birth to a daughter, and wrote a dissertation, but it never entered my head that I could stay home and be a housewife." Because she worked as a chemist in the textile industry where women predominated, she observed, "When a man appeared like a ray of sunshine, we'd always elevate him into a leadership role." Although Kovalyova acknowledged that "it's harder for women to have a career," she believed she was "equal with everyone else. Later, I traveled a lot across the Soviet Union on business, and I saw that, in many enterprises, women held the very highest management positions." As a result, she concluded, "I would not say that discrimination affected us women all that much."

Several women ran up against discrimination, but they did not see it as confining. Physicist Olga Gorelik acknowledged that "at conferences they perceived women a bit differently," but her advisor "did not distinguish between men and women. Many women worked in our lab and he demanded the same from everyone." Irina Kulikova encountered some discrimination depending upon the boss. Explained Kulikova: "I had two small children, one after the other, and they naturally got sick and I had to stay home with them. Who wants to have such an employee on board? They sometimes didn't give me a bonus." Yet Kulikova enthused over her collective at work. When she had to go away on business trips, "comrades from work would take my kids to school and feed them. If someone got sick and needed to be attended to in the hospital and the person didn't have any relatives, we took turns sitting with him. The same is true today. I lucked out at school with the group I was with, and again at work."

Many women felt straddled by the double burden, regardless of any job discrimination. Speaking for many others, Natalya P. remarked that "although I think women obtain fulfillment from their family, their children, and their husbands, work also means a lot to them. I'm always trying to find some balance between the two. It's really hard." Tatyana Kuznetsova added, "I enjoy being a woman, but have always had it harder than men, be they in Russia or America. There's work, the home, and the need to at least try to look nice." Olga Martynkina also expressed satisfaction at being a woman and pointed out that her gender did not affect her career in music where, as she put it, "Everything is based on talent. But a man is freer of daily concerns. A woman has to spend a lot of time with the children, the household, and with school. Yet what can I do? I like it. I'm a mother." Yelena Zharovova believed her endless chores as wife and mother complicated her professional life and made her far less interested in politics. She recalled a meeting with Americans during the Soviet era who asked her how much time she spent shopping each week. "It was an incredibly stupid question, especially for those years. A Russian woman always has one foot in a store or thinks about doing so."

Because of the double burden, Olga Kamayurova recalled her married years "as a nightmare. Two children, all the household chores, and work. I couldn't afford to work only one shift, and was always moonlighting somewhere." Books, good movies, and a special friendship saved her: "I'm happy that I have had a close girlfriend for thirty-four years. Some people are blessed with meeting the love of their life, but for me it turned out to be a close friendship." Since divorcing her husband she has had boyfriends, "but I am not dependent upon anyone and no one can demand that I clean or put dinner on the table. You can't believe how much that frees you on a spiritual level. I now breathe freely and pity those who haven't experienced this in their lives." Olga underscored that "I'm not all that typical in this regard. A woman, after all, is supposed to appreciate the family and the home. But not me. I like being alone." Concluding that "this independence has perhaps become the defining feature of my life," she enjoys her work as a pathologist because "no one's supervising me."

Others also lamented women's lot in Russia. Natalya Pronina asserted, "I understood all too well already as a child that things are a lot easier for men. If there's a family, then I have to do everything and free my husband of any responsibility." There was also discrimination at work. "If a man and woman compete for the same vacancy at work, the man gets it. That's 99.9 percent certain." Irina Vizgalova added that she "always had to prove myself as a woman. Maybe it's not this way in America, but here when they'd ask, 'can you do this?' I'd always answer, 'of course, I can. I'd think that, even if I didn't know, I could read about it and learn it. At work I had to prove myself." Irina Garzanova "used to think that my gender didn't limit me, but then something happened in 1995 or 1996." Her boss decided to appoint her head of a department based on her seniority and experience, but he was overruled and the only male in the group was appointed instead. Similarly, the only time Irina Chemodurova felt discrimination "was when there were promotions at work, because they always preferred a man when there was a vacancy." She does not believe much has changed in this regard. "I think the idea that men must be in charge remains intact today, regardless of his talents or even his transgressions."

"IT GAVE US NOTHING BUT CRIPPLES AND DRUG ADDICTS"

The 1970s, so decisive in the Soviet Union's evolution, closed with an arresting example of how stagnation had even influenced Soviet foreign policy. In December 1979 the Red Army invaded Afghanistan because the Politburo feared that the Afghan government, which had come to power in the wake of a revolution in 1978, would drift out of the Soviet Union's orbit. Maintaining that Afghan leaders had requested Soviet help to stabilize the country, the Kremlin established bases throughout the country while much of the rest of the world denounced Soviet actions. To register their discontent, the United States and other countries boycotted the 1980 Summer Olympics in Moscow. The United States and some of its allies likewise provided aid to opposition groups known collectively as the Mujahedeen who battled both Soviet troops and those of the newly minted People's Democratic Republic of Afghanistan. The training and support from the outside strengthened the Mujahedeen's hand, locking the Soviet Union in a guerilla war that some Soviet citizens equated with American efforts in Vietnam, not only in terms of military stalemate and defeat but also in regard to how the ill-fated conflict eventually damaged domestic morale. There were also the losses: most estimates put the number of Soviet troops who perished during the ten-year war at 15,000, with more than 460,000 wounded or otherwise incapacitated.

One Muscovite Baby Boomer who served in Afghanistan, KGB operative Andrei Rogatnev, justified the invasion, but slammed hardened Party ideologists for mechanically applying to this alien culture slogans used during the Russian Civil War to win peasants over to the Bolshevik cause. As he put it, "They decided that the slogans were so universal that they'd work in Afghanistan, but there they had the opposite effect." Rogatnev explained that "even our political advisers didn't understand this. They were mostly regional and oblast Party people with fossilized thinking." Rogatnev thus decried Party (civilian) interference, but praised the younger Soviet military officers who "appeased entire regions, not by force, but by reaching agreements with people." Whether he intended to or not, Rogatnev conceded that the USSR's prosecution of the war exposed some deep-rooted problems back home.

All of the other Muscovites denounced their country's invasion of Afghanistan, either from the start or in time. Vladimir Sidelnikov spoke for many in reminding me that "no one needed the Afghan war. Our soldiers died there in vain." Indicting the Brezhnev leadership for attempting to shore up a feeble Communist government in Kabul, he repeated what the Afghans themselves purportedly told invaders, "'You'll never defeat us.' And we didn't." News of the offensive disheartened Anatoly Shapiro, especially because the people with whom he

KGB officer Andrei Rogatnev served his country in Afghanistan in 1985, the year M. S. Gorbachev came to power. In February 1988, Gorbachev announced the withdrawal of Soviet troops from the country. *Courtesy of Vyacheslav Starik*

worked, retired military officers, KGB agents, and Ministry of the Interior officials, "were delighted." Shapiro recalled the reaction of one of them who read
the sour look on his face when he heard the news: "'You're an individualist,' a
former colonel told me. It was terrible. These people were unpleasant, and
I worked with people such as this practically all my life."

Some Muscovites initially did not give the matter much thought, but eventually condemned the invasion. Igor Litvin remembered, "When the first young
men began to return and we saw how psychologically damaged they were and
heard about their experiences, we understood that a carnage was taking place and
that things weren't at all as we had presumed, that we were helping a brotherly
country so that there'd be socialism there." Mikhail Markovich responded similarly. "We began to understand when the first victims appeared among acquaintances, especially when I visited [relatives in] Yasnaya Polyana. Few of our Moscow
acquaintances went to Afghanistan. But the bodies of the dead from Yasnaya
Polyana began to return. Naturally, for years we were under the impression that it
was a localized conflict and not a war, but then Andrei Sakharov spoke out against
it, there was the radio, and information surfaced. We began to understand things
altogether differently." Aleksandr Konstantinov called the invasion "an absurd
stupidity. This was clear to everyone. I can't recall encountering a single individual
who supported it." He clarified, "People weren't indignant as they were in the case
of Czechoslovakia, but simply astonished by such extraordinary stupidity." Leonid
Volodarsky did not react at all to the news of the invasion, "because we had practice. There was Hungary. There was Czechoslovakia. And now Afghanistan. The
only thing that surprised me was that we couldn't win the war."

The more diverse reactions of the Saratovites also suggest that a tectonic shift
in popular attitudes had taken place during the 1970s. True, a handful had other
things on their minds at the time and simply did not give Afghanistan much
thought. Aleksandr Babushkin, for instance, explained that "it was hard to
understand from afar. Moreover, I'd underscore once again that Saratov is a provincial, although very cultured, city. We didn't pay much attention to these
things. Life in the provinces is all about us." Yet the majority of his classmates
had a far different take on the war. As young college students, some of them had
supported the Soviet invasion of Czechoslovakia in 1968, but they slammed the
Politburo's decision to march into Afghanistan in 1979. As Aleksandr Trubnikov
remembered, "I was very much against it. When the Soviet Union had invaded
Czechoslovakia I didn't understand a thing and 'voted' yes, so to speak. But
when they invaded Afghanistan, people even told me that I might get in trouble,
because I so disliked what had happened." Like many others, "I understood that
it was all too similar to the Americans in Vietnam, but in a worst-case scenario,
and that no one needed this. I knew people who perished there. It was terrible.
By the way, I wasn't the only one who felt this way. This was an altogether different time. Society had matured and most people opposed this." Olga Martynkina
opined that "everyone understood that it was terrible and unnecessary." Irina

Vizgalova said she didn't grasp "why we needed to send our boys to Afghanistan to solve their problems. I think that many felt this way."

As in Moscow, some Saratovites came to have a change of heart about the invasion. Vladimir Nemchenko explained that "at first we didn't realize what was going on, and we were influenced by propaganda." He soon concluded, however, that "you should never force another country to live by your rules." Galina Poldyaeva detailed that at first it was as if "well, the Party decided, so it must have been necessary. But then, when it began to affect acquaintances, relatives, people close to us, when people began to perish, we became apprehensive lest it touch us. Of course, those of us whose husbands were in the army were afraid." Natalya P. linked her response to being a woman: "Any woman who has given birth is against anything that might harm her children. I always say that, if we had a female minister of defense, she'd have solved these problems a long time ago," she opined. "But men decide things. Behind any war there's always big money and the political ambitions of leaders, who think little of who might be affected by this. The ordinary people rarely enter into the equation of politicians, ours or yours."

A few Saratovites succumbed to Soviet propaganda. Nikolai Kirsanov "could not say" that he opposed the attack on Afghanistan. "We were blinded by ideology," he explained. "I accepted the official version that they put out," admitted Olga Kamayurova. "I now understand that it was just like the Americans in Vietnam. They sent our eighteen-year-old boys over there and they died by the hundreds. Many were maimed. It was terrible. But back then I simply didn't understand that we had started the war, that we had invaded another country." Tatyana Kuznetsova, whose family belonged to the local Party elite, did not hesitate to say that "I didn't react as if we had invaded Afghanistan. I always believed that our country was helping. I don't believe that we invaded even now."

Saratovite Gennady Ivanov worked in Afghanistan in 1987–88 and, like Moscow's Andrei Rogatnev, justified his time there, making me all too aware that I was an outsider: "I was there as an advisor on criminal investigations. We had to deal with all sorts of contraband," he related. Unlike any of his classmates, he cloned Soviet boiler-plate justifications for the invasion: "I think going in was the right thing to do. If we hadn't done so, someone else would have. From a legal point of view, there was a mutual aid agreement, so our actions were 99 percent correct. They asked us to go in." Then he got to the real point: "It was far more legal than America's going into Iraq. America felt it had to, so it invaded, although there were absolutely no grounds for doing so, ever the more so because Iraq is far away and the weapons of mass destruction there turned out to be mythical." "But in Afghanistan," he lectured, "they overthrew the [legitimate] ruler. We invaded on legal grounds, yet then got drawn in deeper for nothing. We should have given them more opportunity to do what they needed to do, especially because we had the American experience in Vietnam to go on. In today's world nothing gets decided by the use of force." Despite his emphasis on the USSR's right to intervene militarily in Afghanistan, Ivanov let slip the real reason for the Soviet invasion: "We needed to go in so that we'd have a base there. After all, from the mountains all of Central Asia is visible with radar. It's our weak underbelly," he opined. Letting his guard down, Ivanov drew a conclusion about the Soviet invasion of Afghanistan with which many would have agreed: "Besides heroism, it gave us nothing but cripples and drug addicts."

"HE AND THE OTHERS REMAINED IN OFFICE TOO LONG"

The Baby Boomers' value systems evolved in relation to their personal experiences reaching for the Soviet dream and negotiating late socialism, and to the major social and historical developments that provided the broader context for their individual stories and collective biography. The continued opening up of the Soviet Union and spread of information via tape recorders, foreign radio broadcasts, film, television, *samizdat*, foreign travel, and encounters with foreigners visiting the USSR in the midst of a remarkable expansion of the number of people with a college education represent core elements of the late socialism they experienced, as do the further consolidation of the nuclear family, now shaped by a rising divorce rate and declining marriage rate.

Yet another of late socialism's features is the emergence of a genuine human rights movement. It subjected the Soviet Union to critical scrutiny on the world stage, and posed a fundamental challenge to the Soviet myth economy, since it had evolved organically from within the system. Diluted state repression remained an element of late socialism mostly because it constrained people's choices by switching on their self-censorship. Few Baby Boomers had direct run-ins with the KGB, but all felt its presence. Moscow's Yelena Zharovova admitted her "apprehension that someone could inform about a conversation they had with you, but I soon forgot about this, because I couldn't imagine who among those in my group would be capable of this. Judging from the fact that no one ever called me in, there probably weren't any informants among them."

Zharovova's remark hints at the growing importance of private life for the Cold War generation, as self-interest became far more of a motivating force than self-sacrifice for public, societal, goals. This came about both as a result of successful Soviet social policies which, in the long run, ironically weakened the system, and as a result of failures in the economy, which represented the feature of late socialism that the Baby Boomers encountered everywhere they turned. In omnipresent ways, ideology molded the interviewees, but they also were practical: they had to violate rules and principles in order to make the economy work for them and survive. Resorting to all sorts of strategies to make ends meet and to satisfy their self-interest, they compensated for the shortcomings of the

Soviet economic model, which afforded Moscow a privileged place. Enduring a more precarious economic situation than that of people living in Moscow, many Saratovites traveled to the capital to purchase food and consumer goods. Yet, for the most part, the strategies both cohorts perfected bear an uncanny resemblance: semilegal and illegal economic activities facilitated by *blat*. Bringing individuals together on their own initiative in ways that were not controlled by the state and that were usually frowned on, these strategies further strengthened private life as they weakened people's faith in the system.

Aspirations rising faster than Soviet living standards during the Brezhnev era and the expansion of private life and values eroded the hold of ideology in the 1970s and beyond, but no new belief replaced the one losing its grip.[32] History offers many examples of what happens when aspirations grow faster than the likelihood of their fulfillment. Ironically, privileged Muscovites expressed far more critical evaluations of the Soviet economy than their Saratov counterparts. But stagnation had more to it than just economic concerns, for the Soviet system also created a socialism of deficits in the myth economy. Saratov's Irina Barysheva captured this sentiment when she shared that "there was something missing regarding the moral side of things, what's inside. The phrase 'how lucky we are that we were born in the Soviet Union' always grated on me. I'd think, *why* are we so lucky?" She recalled how her classmates got together when someone traveled somewhere special, say to an international youth camp. "We'd exchange impressions, and I'd have the gnawing feeling that there was something missing in life."

What was it? Tracing the Baby Boomers' life trajectories suggests that their parents' generation experienced a different version of the Soviet dream. Growing up under Stalinism and during the war gave them low expectations and plenty of opportunity for self-sacrifice, upward and geographic mobility, and career advancement. The Soviet dream appeared real to them, but perhaps out of reach for most of the Baby Boomers. Moscow's Sergei Zemskov understood this. Remarking that Brezhnev came "from a very poor gene pool" and that "he and the others remained in office too long," Zemskov concluded, "But our parents' generation propped them up. They, of course, saw that the generation steeling up to them was much stronger than they were. And it's altogether clear that, if you look at our generation, no one, extremely few, made their way [to power]. That's why the regime was the way it was." Zemskov believed that perhaps in the provinces "there were still attempts to break in, but they were anemic. In Moscow that was extremely difficult and complicated." The Cold War generation had reached a glass ceiling in regard to achieving the Soviet dream.

The Soviet invasion of Afghanistan can be understood as yet another facet of the Brezhnev-era stagnation. Although Soviet controls prevented public discussion of the inauspicious decision and its consequences until Gorbachev's era of glasnost, the invasion ultimately pounded another nail into the Soviet system's coffin. Yet this was not obvious at the time, for Soviet society was "perplexingly contradictory."[33] As Saratov's Aleksandr Trubnikov reminded me, Soviet power seemed "really very stable, and it got things done." Trying to make sense of the Soviet use of force in Afghanistan against a larger backdrop, Aleksandr Virich mentioned people's "infantile attitude toward all Party slogans." People were fed up with them, but "no one asked what's the Party doing in Afghanistan." Still, Virich emphasized that "everything was clear to those involved in planning things. True, we didn't think that this would lead to the collapse so soon. I thought that my children and I would have a tranquil future, but things changed when everything came together and Soviet power ended."

6

"BUT THEN EVERYTHING FELL APART"

Gorbachev Remakes the Soviet Dream

In the 1980s, Natalya Yanichkina and her husband left Saratov once again to work in the Soviet Far East, not in Magadan oblast, but this time in the town of Pevek on the Chukhotka peninsula in the Arctic Circle. "It was there that we welcomed Gorbachev to power and experienced perestroika and all that was connected to it," she recalled. "We welcomed his program with open minds, like something we had longed for," she stressed. "You know, it's one thing to discuss things in the kitchen, but another thing altogether to be able to say openly that it's impossible to live like this any longer."

Time Magazine's 1987 "Person of the Year" and 1990 winner of the Nobel Peace Prize, Mikhail Sergeyevich Gorbachev was born in 1931 in a village in Stavropol oblast. Elected to the top leadership position in the Soviet Union in 1985, he remained general secretary of the Communist Party until the last days of the USSR at the end of 1991. His peasant family had experienced first-hand Soviet-style repression, war, Nazi occupation, and hard times. An exemplary worker, talented student, and Komsomol activist, the young Mikhail Sergeyevich—against extraordinary odds—got admitted to Moscow University in 1950 to study law, an accomplishment that presaged his brilliant political career. Stalin died in 1953 while Gorbachev studied at Moscow University, where the atmosphere of free discussion that temporarily reigned there deeply affected him. Returning to his native Stavropol upon graduation, Gorbachev climbed rapidly through the ranks of the local Komsomol and Party organizations, becoming local Party boss in 1970, and shortly afterward a Central Committee member. Apart from his enormous talents and ability to win friends, he had another advantage: located in spa territory, Stavropol attracted Politburo members on vacation, providing Gorbachev with an opportunity to impress Moscow leaders, such as long-term Politburo member Mikhail Suslov, who was responsible for ideology, and Yuri Andropov, both of whom supported Gorbachev's appointment in 1978 as Central Committee secretary responsible for agriculture.

The Politburo members' election of robust, articulate Gorbachev in 1985 not only ended the succession crisis that began with Brezhnev's death in 1982 but also marked the coming to power of a new generation of Soviet leaders that had radically different formative experiences from those of their predecessors. Gorbachev's generation knew repression, but usually not firsthand. Their historical baptism into the twentieth century involved not the Russian Revolution and Civil War, but World War II, the Thaw, de-Stalinization, and the country's ascent to superpower status and opening up to the outside world. Better educated than their predecessors, they joined the Party and began rising through its ranks during Khrushchev's campaign to overtake America. Yet few made it into the top echelons of the Party, owing in part to Brezhnev's "trust in cadres." A reaction to Khrushchev's endless reshuffling of Party cadres in an effort to reinvigorate the organization—and country—this policy guaranteed Party officials that they would hold their posts until death. As a result, the Party leadership ossified into a much maligned gerontocracy. The ailing Politburo that selected Mikhail Sergeyevich had no inkling that they had brought a reformer to power. Gorbachev's writings and speeches, however, soon made clear that he believed in economic reform (perestroika), in the benefits of liberalizing the political system (*demokratizatsiya*), in removing ideology from foreign-policy decision making, and in stopping the fighting in Afghanistan (*novoe myshlenie* or new thinking). And, following the nuclear accident at Chernobyl in April 1986, when news of the disaster came to Soviet citizens from the outside world rather than from within the USSR, Gorbachev came to believe that without glasnost—frank public discussion of all issues, including topics formerly taboo—he could not have perestroika.

Far ranging in its consequences, glasnost narrowed the gap between living in Moscow or Saratov. The same information now became accessible to everyone who sought it out, fashioning new forms of collective consciousness that tended to melt away the disparity in the replies to my questions that I received from Muscovites and Saratovites. Thus I no longer segregate their responses.

The astonishing quickness with which the idea of reform built momentum in society, especially after the glasnost revelations involved tens of millions of people in a public debate over the country's turbulent past and uncertain future, convinced Gorbachev that the system needed not only economic reform but sweeping transformation. Soviet society came to life as the atmosphere of openness enabled political liberalization to evolve to such an extent that, by the summer of 1988, Gorbachev convinced the Party to allow contested elections for a new legislature, the Congress of People's Deputies. Serious transformations also came to the economy as Gorbachev and those he had appointed to power experimented with ways to switch to a socialist market system in 1990. Gorbachev implemented, but then backed down from, an ill-advised radical plan to establish a market economy in five hundred days by privatizing the bulk of Soviet enterprises. The resulting economic chaos and opposition from the Soviet military-industrial complex forced Gorbachev to attempt a compromise between market enthusiasts and those who wanted a regulated market economy. Gorbachev's wavering in this climate of openness, which exposed all the ills of the Stalinist past, encouraged moves toward greater autonomy and even independence in the union republics. This provided the context for the exhilarating but explosive atmosphere that resulted in an attempted coup d'état against him in August 1991 undertaken by Party conservatives short on ideas. The bungled coup doomed Gorbachev's leadership, catapulting Russian President Boris Yeltsin to the top of the political hierarchy. It also encouraged the disaffected nationalities to push for independence. On December 8, 1991, leaders of the three Slavic republics—Russia, Ukraine, and Belorussia—signed the Belovezh Accords, which established the Commonwealth of Independent States (CIS), put an end to the USSR, and forced Gorbachev to resign his post of president of the now defunct empire.

Saratov's Gennady Ivanov reminded me of a joke circulating at the time that captures how many felt about the six years that shook the world. "Do you think perestroika was launched by scientists or by politicians? Of course, by politicians. Scientists would have first experimented on dogs." This sentiment expresses the fact that, even today, Gorbachev remains far more popular outside Russia than at home.[1] How does the Cold War generation evaluate the man who presided over the USSR's transformation and decline? How do its members account for the launching of perestroika? How did they respond to the barrage of information unleashed by glasnost? What sentiments did they express about the breakup of the Soviet Union? Finally, how did the greater freedom of choice and movement ushered in by perestroika impact them?

"THE ROAD TO HELL IS PAVED WITH GOOD INTENTIONS"

Gorbachev certainly fed popular expectations of reform, which unfolded in ways that no one could have predicted. As a result, his policies, which many at first welcomed, disappointed some Baby Boomers. "At first it was very interesting, because of the things he said. It seemed so fresh after all the years of stagnation," remarked Yevgeny Podolsky. "But then he began to get carried away by the sound of his own voice. He talked a lot but did little, and things got worse." Gorbachev's verbosity also irked Irina Vizgalova. "He couldn't give a straight answer. He never answered with a simple yes or no. He was a demagogue." Like others, Aleksandr Ivanov felt that "Gorbachev himself didn't know what he wanted." Aleksandr Babushkin claimed he "liked Gorbachev as a person, but his impetuous perestroika was, of course, wrong. Things should have been done *gradually*."

Irina Garzanova remembered when a colleague told her, soon after Gorbachev came to power, that "'nothing good will come from that Don Cossack.' And he was right," she snapped. Garzanova conceded that Gorbachev had good intentions, "but his mission was doomed to failure because you either had to change everything or nothing at all. And he tried to do things only half-way," she clarified. Judged Leonid Volodarsky: "Perhaps his ideas were good, but everything else was quite wretched. I dislike him, and I wouldn't shake his hand." Others in this camp took pity on the Soviet leader. Lyudmila Gorokhova, for instance, volunteered, "I'm critical, of course, but also feel a bit sorry for him as a person, because he didn't expect what happened. He turned out to be a pioneer. Before him no one dared to raise the Iron Curtain, and to do so required courage."

Some of Gorbachev's critics reminded me that his popularity abroad did not translate well back home. Explained Vladimir Kirsanov: "Probably like any other politician, he is viewed from two points of view, that of his domestic policy and that of his foreign policy." Acknowledging Gorbachev's status in the West, it seemed to Kirsanov that "the majority of people inside the country viewed him negatively." Natalya Pronina voiced similar sentiments, emphasizing that how she and others feel about Gorbachev is "not what you think in the West. That's absolutely for certain." Pinning the blame "for all of our misfortunes over the past ten years" on Politburo members Eduard Shevardnadze, Gorbachev's foreign minister, and Yegor Ligachev, Aleksandr Virich claimed that Gorbachev danced to the West's tune. "That which Shevardnadze did—withdrawing the Soviet army from Germany and Europe [without getting anything in exchange]—was pure betrayal." Yelena Zharovova expressed "amazement" by the enthusiastic reception Gorbachev received from Margaret Thatcher, Ronald Reagan, and others. "I was simply astonished that people were so blinded."

But most Baby Boomers recognized Gorbachev's role and the stumbling blocks complicating what he sought to accomplish, and some even shared Margaret Thatcher's enthusiasm. Irina Barysheva saw Gorbachev "as a ray of light that appeared in a land of darkness." According to Arkady Darchenko, "Gorbachev came along just in time, as, I believe, did Yeltsin. I think there were two turning points, during which God gave us the very interesting and flexible Gorbachev and then the original Yeltsin." Olga Gorelik believed "that Gorbachev did a lot that was good and positive and that he was a good man"; however, she acknowledged that some curse his perestroika. "When Gorbachev came to power he was basically a young man. Besides, he was charming. And when he began to speak so clearly, you wanted to listen," recalled Natalya Yanichkina. "I like Gorbachev a great deal. I know for a fact, no matter what they accused him of later, that it's his colossal achievement to have said that we can't go on living like this any longer. Gorbachev started it all." Yanichkina appreciated the magnitude of what he sought to accomplish: "You have to keep in mind that there was no fail-proof program. Although I don't know much about American history, I think that the United States, too, at one time got things done by trial and error." She concluded, "They wanted things to be better, but they turned out like always.* There were a lot of good intentions in his actions. As they say, the road to hell is paved with good intentions."

Lyubov Kovalyova and others also defended Mikhail Sergeyevich. "As a political figure he was progressive, and as a person, charming enough. Later, former Communists accused him of all sorts of transgressions. But back then people pinned their hopes on him and believed in him." Speaking to the cynicism that pervaded Soviet life, including the Party itself, CPSU member Vladimir Bystrov remarked, "He did a beautiful job of destroying the Communist Party of the Soviet Union. It's unlikely that someone else could have done it. I think historians will appreciate this in the future." Vladimir Glebkin felt this way, too: "Many forget he was one man against everyone else in the Politburo, and he was able to reorganize our society in such a way." According to Glebkin, Gorbachev needed to have been a better intriguer to deal with the troglodytes within the leadership. "Be that as it may, I really liked him back then, and I really like him now. He didn't deserve to be brushed aside. It's unfair to forget what he did." Yevgeniya Ruditskaya also "took a strong liking to Gorbachev," adding, "I think that everyone living in the Soviet Union should be thankful for what he did." Tatyana Luchnikova agreed, "We need to say 'many thanks' to Mikhail Sergeyevich Gorbachev, who raised the Iron Curtain, and gave people some oxygen." Luchnikova acknowledged that most people became disappointed when the long-awaited capitalism became robber-baron capitalism, but she saw no way out of this, since "capitalism in the West developed over a thousand years." Marina Bakutina applauded Gorbachev's contributions, too: "I'm hurt and offended that his fellow countrymen don't give a damn about him, blaming him for the breakup of the Soviet Union."

Bakhyt Kenzheyev saw Gorbachev as a hero. "I like him. I believe he's beyond reproach, a courageous man, smart, and talented. He had only one shortcoming—he was a prisoner of his time. He wanted to perfect socialism. But I'm infinitely grateful to this person who did so much to ruin this monstrous regime." Kenzheyev marveled that the Soviet system produced a Gorbachev: "In some incomprehensible way he wormed his way from the Stavropol region into the Central Committee. He was able to do a great job of deceiving the Central Committee members. He was like the Trojan horse in that he pretended to be a normal apparatchik, but turned out to be a normal person." Kenzheyev concluded by reflecting upon a photograph of Gorbachev's office that Kenzheyev had studied. "To my great surprise and delight I discovered a Bible among the books. I don't think it was placed there on purpose."

---

* Here Yanichkina is repeating an aphorism made famous by Viktor Stepanovich Chernomyrdin, who served as Boris Yeltsin's inarticulate prime minister of the Russian Federation from December 1992 until 1998.

A number of others felt positively toward Gorbachev, but understood why many turned against him. Recalled Larisa Petrova: "It was as if we got a breath of fresh air, and all of us welcomed it. We were all for Gorbachev. It was all so interesting as we began to find out things we didn't know before." However, "all of us had to live on food coupons. We literally faced going hungry." Explained Petrova: "People don't like him because the hopes he gave us did not materialize, but in the beginning it seems to me that 90 percent of the population supported him. I judge by my father, a true Communist. Even he said, 'I want Gorbachev.'" But "as soon as people encountered economic difficulties, they turned against him. The mass of ordinary people, the makers of history, don't like Gorbachev precisely because many literally had nothing to eat." Petrova opined that "he was surrounded by the wrong people who were authoritarian and reactionary." If he had had the right kind of support, she maintained, "He wouldn't have had to blindly take examples from the West and experiment in our country, because Russia is not America, is not Germany, is not England. You have to do things differently here. But he threw himself at the West for help, and things got worse."

Viktor Alekseyev looked more favorably upon Gorbachev when I interviewed him than he did at the time of the Soviet Union's demise. Alekseyev recalled that "at first Gorbachev was an altogether fresh figure, and we had great hopes that he'd take things through to the end. But then, at some moment, this was replaced with strong disappointment. I probably don't differ in that regard from many others. Things began to disintegrate, especially in connection with the exacerbation of ethnic relations in Karabakh and in Azerbaijan* and the use of force that still went on under Gorbachev." Alekseyev continued, "There was the shooting in Tbilisi, and in Lithuania.** We were shocked. However, now I'm able to look back at this more soberly."

Several male interviewees defended Gorbachev yet disparaged his anti-alcohol campaign not only because of its effect on the economy but also because it infringed upon their freedom. Urged on by Yegor Ligachev, Gorbachev supported the drive, launched in 1985, which curbed the production, sale, and distribution of alcohol, damaging an economy that generated revenue from selling spirits and giving rise to ubiquitous moonshine production. The loss of alcohol revenues, moreover, coincided with a drop in world oil prices at a time when the state needed additional funds to clean up after the nuclear disaster at Chernobyl in 1986 and a major earthquake rocked Armenia in 1988. According to Pyotor

---

* Karabakh is an Armenian populated enclave in neighboring Azerbaijan. Glasnost and perestroika inflamed Armenian nationalism, especially over Karabakh, when the Karabakh Soviet in February 1988 called for the territory's transfer to Armenia. Demonstrations followed, prompting Azeris to launch pogroms against Armenians living in Azerbaijan.

** In April 1989, security forces brutally broke up strikes and demonstrations in Tbilisi. In January 1991 Soviet troops took over the television station in the Lithuanian capital, Vilnius, resulting in fourteen deaths and the wounding of many others.

Krasilnikov, "the only time he went too far was with his anti-alcohol campaign, and the uprooting of all those grape vines and the enormous lines this caused in the stores. Because this was a state monopoly, you couldn't get around it. There, of course, were people who were able to buy it in the stores and resell it on the street at a higher price." Viktor D. acknowledged Mikhail Sergeyevich's "positive influence" at first, yet peppered his remarks with lots of "if onlys," especially "if only there hadn't been prohibition. It's been proved through the ages—America went through it—that prohibition is accompanied by a growth in the use of drugs and in the mafia and a sharp rise in the criminalization of the country." Aleksandr Virich slammed conservative Politburo member Yegor Ligachev for encouraging Gorbachev to implement this policy. "It ruined Russia's economy when they uprooted acres upon acres of vineyards, hundreds of thousands of grapevines, and shut down the production of vodka."

In sum, most Baby Boomers appreciated Gorbachev's efforts to end the Cold War, to open up society, and to democratize it. As Boris Shtein put it, "He accomplished the most important thing: he turned the country around. Whether things went well or poorly, it was no longer possible to put a stop to the process." But many of the Baby Boomers, like the majority of their countrymen, decried the unintended consequences of his efforts, especially the economic ones, and the breakup of the Soviet Union itself. Few people like belonging to a former superpower.

"YES, SOCIETY WAS READY"

The personal experiences of the Cold War generation, their family genealogies that offered alternatives to sanitized official histories, and the transformations that came to the USSR in the decades following World War II provided fertile ground for perestroika. The loosening of controls after Khrushchev's denunciation of Stalin in 1956, the cultural Thaw, and the closing down of the Gulag gave the Soviet people "freedom of speech in one kitchen"[2] that eventually evolved into a bona fide human rights movement with which broad strata of the intelligentsia sympathized. The strengthening of the nuclear family and mass exodus from communal flats into single-family apartments fortified the private sphere in the Soviet Union. At the same time, publication of anti-Stalinist literature and the growing availability of alternative sources of information, from foreign radio broadcasts to *samizdat*, made people aware of choices and alternatives Soviet leaders might have followed. The withering of Khrushchev's utopian vision, dramatic rise in the number of college graduates, and ever-creeping corruption during the Brezhnev years furthered the subterranean erosion of Communist ideology. So did the system's sputtering economic performance that deepened skepticism and consumer pessimism by the late 1970s, especially as the Baby Boomers returned home from trips to Eastern Europe not only with newly acquired goods but also with impressions and doubts.

Some interviewees also believed that opportunities for upward social mobility were drying up, too, complementing studies showing that, by the 1970s, Soviet young people were more disenchanted than their elders. The international environment likewise contributed to the preconditions necessary for perestroika. The country's signing of the Helsinki Accords of 1975, and the USSR's controversial invasion of Czechoslovakia in 1968 and Afghanistan in 1979 made some people question official policies. Technology, as well, played a role in bringing about the end, from the mass production of cassette recorders and production of audio cassettes, to the rise of direct telephone dialing to the USSR, and the appearance of VCRs, fax machines, and, later, computers. By the time people openly began to mock Brezhnev, their per capita income was declining and many people, even within the upper echelons of the Party, felt that things could not go on like this. The collapse of détente—usually dated from the Soviet invasion of Afghanistan in December 1979—and the rise of the Solidarity movement in Poland triggered ideological debate within the Central Committee. To be sure, no single development proved primary in reforming the system out of existence, but their lethal interaction changed values and magnified social pathologies.[3] In this regard perestroika represented something far more than another revolution from above launched by Russian tsars and commissars to strengthen the imperial or Communist order. This is why the reforms Gorbachev set into motion came to threaten and ultimately undermine the system.

Western academic and popular understandings of the causes of perestroika tend to run along two axes with plenty of overlap. One line of reasoning sees perestroika's origins in Soviet domestic developments, whether from economic causes or cultural-political ones. The other axis weighs the importance of internal (domestic) vs. external factors in bringing about the Soviet reform movement. Not surprisingly, many analysts see the origins of reform in the country's economic crisis characterized by declining growth rates, standards of living, and overall stagnation, because that is what motivated the Kremlin to act. The ruling elite understood that the Stalinist economic system's shortcomings increasingly manifested themselves as the economy became more complex, accepting the need for reform.[4] Some observers link the economic argument to a military one, locating the "real" cause of perestroika in the leadership's "ambitions to preserve the military parity between the USSR and the West."[5] Still others emphasize that the legitimization crisis—the growing demoralization, public discontent, system of privileges, and ubiquitous corruption—proved as important.

Many interviewees articulated explanations for the origins of reform that reflect these Western understandings. Still others advanced spin-off theories, tracing perestroika to elements within the ruling elite that sought to privatize the property they had accumulated; to a CIA plot; to Gorbachev's democratic design, kept well hidden before coming to power; to generational change as liberal reformers from the Soviet 1960s generation who supported Gorbachev came to power with him; to the sustained pressures applied by dissident groups;

or to the depoliticization of the Party brought about by the rise of an administrative class that placed its own privileges above the common good. Ultimately, how the Baby Boomers understood the sources of perestroika reveals their conception of the country's history and their place in it. These attitudes also help to constrain and enable developments in post-Soviet Russia.

Only a handful of Baby Boomers viewed perestroika as a revolution from above, even though this represents an all too familiar scenario in Russian history. One of them, Natalya Yanichkina, mused, "You know, perestroika came from the top. I say that because, if Gorbachev hadn't set things in motion, they would have continued as before." Anatoly Shapiro also backed a great person view of history. "If someone else would have come to power, we wouldn't have had perestroika." Like many others, Shapiro expounded a secondary argument as well. "The economic situation probably indicated that we couldn't go on living this way. There was nothing being done for the people's general welfare." Calling Gorbachev's contribution "fantastic," Vladimir Glebkin reminded me that "he could have supported the status quo, which could have lasted a long time." Glebkin gave agency to Gorbachev but, unlike Shapiro, believed the economy could have continued bumbling along: "We have oil, we have gas, we have timber, and we can sell it despite our poor economy." Pyotor Krasilnikov stressed Gorbachev's part, too. "It began with Gorbachev's desire to stand out at something. He probably also understood that, for the most part, life was hard, because a lot of money was spent on military needs, and nothing was left for the people. I think he wanted to reach some sort of equilibrium with the West, whereby military spending would be cut back and the funds transferred to better supplying the citizen."

Bakhyt Kenzheyev, who today divides his time between Moscow, Montreal, and New York, also presented a Gorbachev-centered argument for why perestroika came about. Kenzheyev lived in Canada when then Soviet Minister of Agriculture and Politburo member M. S. Gorbachev led a delegation to that country in the summer of 1983. Aleksandr Nikolayevich Yakovlev, who later became one of the most pro-reform members of the Gorbachev team, served as Soviet ambassador to Canada at the time. Many analysts see the visit as a formative one for Gorbachev. So does Kenzheyev, who believed "that we need to thank Canada for perestroika in Russia." Kenzheyev pointed out that Gorbachev traveled throughout the country during his visit. "He was in farmers' homes. He was in workers' cafeterias. He was in factories and plants. He met with masses of ordinary people. And something made an impression on him. I think he felt, what the hell, the country's climate is similar to Russia's yet people live like this." The trip ended in Ottawa, where he met Yakovlev. According to Kenzheyev, "he obviously was able to encourage Gorbachev to be open to an alternative model." Later, when Gorbachev became Party general secretary, "Yakovlev returned from Canada and became Gorbachev's closest confidant. In this regard Canada played an indirect, but very gratifying role."

Kenzheyev proffered an idiosyncratic interpretation of why ordinary people supported perestroika. "The Russian people are very patient." Yet something snapped at the end of the 1970s that he interpreted as the beginning of the end: "Vodka began to go up in price." Moreover, "they began to bottle it in green bottles intended for juice. And they sealed it with a cap made out of foil that had lost its pull-off tab." This offended the Russian people, who could not help but feel that the leadership was treating them like cattle. "There was no tab to pull and you had to open it with your teeth or with a knife. I think the average worker could not help but feel offended, for, I repeat, it showed the authorities' huge lack of respect for people."

The majority of Baby Boomers, however, perceived perestroika as inevitable, and a good number believed it would have taken place even without Gorbachev. Olga Martynkina stated, "As they say, 'no matter how much rope you use to hold things up,' when the time's right it had to happen. It was the period of stagnation. People wanted their freedom. It began with the economy, because it was impossible to go on with it any longer. Society was ready." "Perestroika simply became inevitable. People blame Gorbachev for it, but it was not Gorbachev, it simply happened during his years in office," argued Irina Kulikova. "Yes, there is no doubt that something had to be done. It was necessary to change, it was necessary that the old guard who remained in office for ages left the scene so that a new system could emerge." Stunned by how quickly Soviet society, seemingly a united and ideologically unwavering one, began to unravel, Galina Poldyaeva underscored that society was ready for the changes: "Yes, without a doubt, because of all those conversations in the kitchen and elsewhere. There was a great deal of dissatisfaction." "It was simply all interrelated," clarified Irina Vizgalova. "The system had become obsolete. Something had to happen, because everything had become so interconnected that it had to collapse. Yes, society was ready. It would have occurred even without Gorbachev. If it weren't he, it would have been someone else."

Perestroika, responded Aleksandr Trubnikov, "probably was predetermined by fate, because everything simply gave out. The internal spring broke that kept socialism going." He elaborated, "Money came to an end, oil came to an end, as did everything else. I think that even without Gorbachev, all of this would have come to an end. It was clear that people had changed. They no longer could put up with all of that. It was no longer possible to continue deceiving people." Similarly, Olga Kamayurova explained that "it was time. Everyone says Gorby, Gorby, he got things moving. But it wasn't he. He was simply a pawn in the hands of higher forces. When the need came for such a man, he surfaced. If it were not he, someone else would have gotten things moving. Someone always appears at the right time."

Others highlighted the coming to power of a new generation and the circumstances of the transition that turned the tide in favor of the reformers. Irina Chemodurova believed that "the system simply could no longer keep up because of economic and political conditions, and because the power structure fell short. Society had evolved. Some of those in power understood that they needed to reconstruct the existing government model." She added that these young people who came to power "began to search for alternative ways. Whether or not they were successful will become clear much later." Aleksandr Babushkin also credited agency to the new generation of leaders, since the old ones were "both physically and morally worn out. They could not endure all of the stress. Consider the average age of the Politburo members. How could they lead such an enormous country? And their education level was surpassed by the rest of the country. These people could no longer govern. They were forced out by the times. Perestroika took place because society had evolved, but they hadn't." As Tatyana Arzhanova put it, "It was already time when our generation grew up and reached adulthood, because it was the generation that was not too intimidated."

Vladimir Mikoyan complicated this perspective. He, too, felt the time had come for change, "although there were no preconditions, no revolutionary mood, no crisis that had come to a head, and no uprisings in the country." Mikoyan had positive things to say about Gorbachev. "He was smart enough and had the foresight to accept the new ideology if we were to call it that." Mikoyan maintained that "perestroika was so easy because the mass of people supported greater democratization and openness." This held true of the Party elite, too, even of his father's generation: "When my father's friends visited they had similar conversations and similar feelings. All of them worked within the system. They all were democratic-minded people, who accepted perestroika in the political sense, in terms of democratization, but not in the economic sense, because it would be hard for a normal person to accept." He added, "They morally were prepared for this, despite the fact that they worked in the Central Committee, KGB, Ministry of the Interior, or elsewhere. They were democrats at heart."

Although the Baby Boomers sympathized with the dissidents, it is instructive that, in contrast with a widely held view outside Russia, only one of the interviewees, Igor Litvin, credited them with bringing about perestroika. He had some tangential interactions with the latter, which undoubtedly influenced his thinking. "The contribution of the dissidents, in my view, was like that of a virus. They were courageous people. I personally have the greatest respect for their courage, and I believe it played an enormous role," he opined.

Some Baby Boomers affirmed that things had reached a crisis point, labeling the situation a "revolutionary" one, a phrase that Marxist historical writings had pounded into their heads. Yelena Kolosova believed that "perestroika was like a revolutionary situation when 'the leaders no longer could lead and those being lead didn't want to.' The idiotism of our former life, namely the spiritual emptiness, the falsifications, the trampling of all our ideals, had exceeded all bounds. The Brezhnev-era stagnation had produced such a stench that someone suggested perestroika and it took off. Things had gone too far. That's how things happen in life." She explained, "You have to take things to the absurd, to the point when everything was being pilfered, when things weren't going anywhere, when everyone had taken to drinking." According to Arkady Darchenko, "Gorbachev had some sort of special sense and understood that, if he didn't start to change things from above, they would start to change from below.

Everything collapsed and had rotted through. It was a very dangerous moment. Perestroika came just in time." Added Darchenko: "The fact is that economics determines everything, and objective reality determines consciousness."

Similarly, Vladimir Bystrov lectured, "I try to find economic causes for everything, because economics determines politics." When I tied his remark to a Marxist line of reasoning he barked at me: "That's the way it is. If America were a weak country, would there be war in Afghanistan? Would there be war in Iraq? Of course not." Returning to the topic, he explained, "The economy no longer could endure all of the methods that the Bolsheviks dictated."

Anna Lyovina recalled that "we simply did not realize how much everything had rotted through. I believe it rotted mainly from an economic point of view. We didn't realize that we lived only thanks to oil exports, because everything was secret. You know the economic structure had rotted so much that all it took was one puff, and it came tumbling down." Irina Barysheva likewise used this metaphor: "It was simply that the lie had become so pronounced, that everything had rotted through under old man Brezhnev." Barysheva, too, spotlighted the economy, tracing her awareness of the enormity of the country's problems to her college days, when her economist mother praised Kosygin's reforms* and maligned the socialist economic model. Studying the political economy of socialism in college amounted to sheer torture. "We at long last understood everything. How long can you live in the kitchen? Let's put it like this." She claimed that "from the very beginning there was something I didn't like. I didn't know what, but something was not right. Everyone worked their tails off, but there was nothing in the stores." Aleksandr Virich also evoked Soviet boilerplate language about a revolutionary situation, but put a different spin on it. Late in coming to power, Gorbachev "was always late, by a month, by a year. The first thing he should have done was to dismiss the old Politburo and not hold onto those orthodox ones who, excuse me, could no longer hold their pee."

A cynical offshoot of the economic line of reasoning underscores the ruling elite's desire to legalize its and others' ill-gained fortunes. Interestingly, only Saratovites subscribed to this position, which I believe reflects their understanding of life along the Volga in the years following the Soviet Union's collapse, and which does not detract from the argument that glasnost, by making information accessible to everyone, generally erased the differences between the responses of Baby Boomers from Moscow and Saratov. Aleksandr Kutin maintained that perestroika occurred because "people wanted freedom," but also because "Party activists at the top had deposited so much money abroad that they had to legalize their fortunes." Olga Gorelik commented that "perestroika

---

* Also known as the Liberman reforms after the economist who espoused them, the reforms were sponsored by Aleksei Nikolayevich Kosygin, appointed chairman of the USSR Council of Ministers or prime minister in 1964. The reforms sought to give economic managers greater autonomy.

occurred because a large number of people were unhappy with their lives, those people who felt that they could fulfill themselves, but weren't allowed to. Remember, there was underground manufacturing. To a certain extent they had already accumulated their capital, but it was criminal. It was illegal, but those in power also understood that the money wasn't going where it should."

Irina Garzanova concurred that "there were rich people who simply remained in the shadows. The circumstances satisfied them, but then, I think, they felt that it was time to come out into the open. They were tired of hiding." Gennady Ivanov believed that "nothing takes place without preparation. They stole an awful lot during the last years." I pointed out that many Party members were among those who ripped things off. "Yes, there were Party members, too. During the period of stagnation the wrong people ended up in higher and middle-level Party organs and Soviet organizations." As a result, he concluded, "It had to unfold this way. On the one hand, they had to put their capital somewhere so that they could go abroad and finally talk about this." Similarly, Viktor D. indicted the Brezhnev generation for "grabbing what they could. Having pilfered what they could, they had money. But back then if you had a large amount of money you were obliged to live like everyone else." He continued, "You couldn't show off and flaunt your wealth. They had more in the refrigerator than others and more cars, but they began to demand something more for their money. They wanted to use it. This is where perestroika came from."

Others, too, underscored perestroika's inevitability, but not necessarily at the historical juncture during which it unfolded. Maintained Natalya P.: "Well, probably the country had reached a critical state when something had to give. And probably the role of the individual in history is another. If there had been no Gorbachev, then perhaps someone else would not have been able to manage. And if no one had been given that power, things perhaps would have occurred later or else differently." She concluded, "We see here the role of the individual, of the human factor, and also of chance, upon which much in politics depends." Aleksandr Konstantinov also felt that the Soviet Union could not survive, but he never expected the collapse to come when it did: "In regard to the argument that the Soviet Union had to break up, I'd point out that we didn't know when this would take place or how. But I do have one very clear memory. Schiller wrote a wonderful historical essay about Sparta and Athens,* and when I read it I understood that Sparta was very much like the Soviet Union," he sighed, "and Athens was very much like the United States and that for the very same reasons that Sparta lost to Athens [in the sense that its ideas ultimately prevailed], the Soviet Union would lose to America. Everything hinged on brawn instead of brains, and this eventually resulted in the muscles becoming atrophied. An

---

* Konstantinov is referring to Friedrich Schiller's "The Legislation of Lycurgus and Solon," delivered in 1789, which outlines two alternative conceptions of government, a republican (Athenian) and oligarchic (Spartan) form.

empire not founded on a realistic basis cannot survive for long. However, I could not fathom that this would occur so quickly."

A handful of interviewees dissatisfied with aspects of life in Russia when I interviewed them implicated the West in promoting Gorbachev's radical program. Natalya Pronina pronounced that perestroika "took place owing to the enormous influence of America." When I pressed for the details, she demurred, insisting "you have to understand that it's not something clear and concrete." Yelena Zharovova argued that perestroika came about "when Gorbachev used the plans drawn up by an institute dealing with social issues and simply made the program public that they had given him." But there was more to her explanation: "Secondly, there was very strong influence from the West. I can't say which elements exactly, I can't say which countries. But perestroika took place because they pressured him." Gennady Ivanov likewise believed the West played a hand behind the scenes, giving the example of Gorbachev unilaterally withdrawing Soviet troops from Germany without getting anything in return. "They're withdrawn from there and everyone is astonished that he gets no political or economic benefits from this. Then he gets a Nobel Prize and opens some sort of Gorbachev Fund. However, where does the money for this come from? I think it's clear."

Several Baby Boomers did not understand why perestroika occurred, but voiced strong opinions about how it turned out. As Yevgeniya Ruditskaya retorted, "I don't know why it occurred. However, it changed our life for the better. I'm very grateful to Gorbachev." Her classmate Sofiya Vinogradova felt the same way: "I don't dig so deep. That's not my thing. However, it's a very good thing it occurred." A rare dissenting voice, Leonid Volodarsky snapped, "I don't know where it came from, but I know that it turned out terrible. I see this, and any normal person sees that it's bad, because any period of change such as this should have been carried out under the strictest of controls. We see what happened. Here in Moscow no economic or financial laws are at work. Then there's the rest of Russia."

Father Valentin Ulyakhin's remarks remind us of how one's understanding of history depends upon one's own subjective vantage point. He knew exactly where perestroika came from: "God makes his will known. God creates everything. It's all God's will." Yet perhaps Vladimir Nemchenko spoke for most of the interviewees. He cast perestroika as something that was "historically necessary. How shall I put it?" he asked rhetorically. "The whole world does things one way, and we alone, for some reason, thought we could do things differently. That's silly, isn't it? Maybe Lenin and the Revolution simply came too early. After all, many of the ideas behind it are humane." Aware of the many theories explaining perestroika, Marina Bakutina did not know which one to subscribe to, but emphasized "there is no doubt that it fell on well-prepared soil, at least among the intelligentsia. I don't know what behind-the-scenes intrigues took place, but it's absolutely certain that the ground was prepared." And this is the point on which the vast majority of Baby Boomers agree.

GLASNOST "OPENED EVERYONE'S EYES DIFFERENTLY"

Perestroika sought controlled change and reform, but the revelations of mass repressions, corruption, abuses of power, and outright lies found an appreciative, ready audience among the public, and stirred national independence movements in parts of the USSR. Glasnost also aggravated the political struggle within the Party and beyond, which culminated in the attempt to overthrow Gorbachev in August 1991, because the new, increasingly participatory public life that glasnost brought into play propelled Gorbachev to take still more radical measures. For instance, the introduction of popular elections provided alternatives that eventually forced the Party to relinquish its monopoly on power, as popular forces from below challenged power from above.

Whether intentionally or not, glasnost thus turned into the most successful reform because, in seeking the support of the intelligentsia by promoting glasnost, Gorbachev took a path of no return. There could be no such thing as half or partial glasnost; it was an all or nothing deal. Many in the West have called the Soviet Union a country of words rather than deeds. But to understand glasnost's impact, it must be stressed that in Soviet society words were deeds.[6]

The problem with glasnost, however, as Soviet citizens joked at the time, was that you could not eat it. Marina Bakutina recounted a perestroika-era joke that captured this sentiment. "During the early years of perestroika a dog dies and goes to heaven, where he sees a friend from his years on Earth. The friend, who had been in canine heaven for some years, asks, 'Well, tell me how things are down there. I hear that all sorts of news items are being published and that everyone's talking about perestroika. What's perestroika?' 'Well, as for new things,' says the newcomer to heaven, 'what can I say? Imagine that they lengthen your chain by six feet, but move your food bowl away by twelve feet. Yet you're able to bark at whomever you like and as much as you want."

Listening in on this "barking," anthropologist Nancy Ries observed that, in the early years of perestroika, private discussions with ordinary Russians revealed a penchant for litany and lament that soon spread from people's kitchen tables and the emboldened media into politics. Paradoxically, Ries maintained that this public airing of the country's tragic past did not revitalize Soviet society, as Gorbachev had expected, but indicted the ideals of Soviet socialism—even those worth keeping.[7] In a dramatic ritual inversion, the media now portrayed the capitalist West in idealized terms. Works of long maligned Western historians on Soviet history were now presented as "objective." Nostalgia took hold for prerevolutionary images and forms—including family histories, as people searched out their genealogies. Russia proclaimed itself an Orthodox Christian country. Even the old notion that women should stay home and take care of the family was temporarily resurrected.

Yet the wringing of hands and narratives of victimhood had a powerful cleansing effect, providing people with new, temporary identities as survivors of Soviet power—or of perestroika. How the Cold War generation collectively remembered the past constantly underwent change as they sought to make sense of the historical era in which their lives unfolded by drawing on the larger stories available to them.[8] How the Baby Boomers remembered the Soviet experience and perestroika also reflected their social status as members of the country's well-educated urban intelligentsia.[9] In this regard, what they had to say is emblematic of what so many others of their social standing thought, felt, and said.

Lyubov Kovalyova recalled how the euphoria associated with glasnost eventually gave way to more complex feelings: "At first it was very interesting. Everyone simply lapped up this information. People stayed glued to their television sets, avidly read newspapers, and discussed everything. It made us feel better, but then there was a deluge of all sorts of depressing, and perhaps unnecessary, things." Vladimir Kirsanov recounted, "We didn't read books, but devoured them. The first books that began to appear weren't political publications, but belletristic writings." A physician, Kirsanov read about Soviet geneticists who had fallen victim to the Stalinist terror, as well as works of history. "This literature greatly shaped public opinion," he concluded. According to Marina Bakutina, "it was absolutely amazing! There was such euphoria when they began to publish all of those works that had been forbidden before. It was like a clap of thunder on a clear blue day." She told me how, years earlier, she had wondered aloud with university friends where all the talented writers had disappeared to. "Why is there nothing but mediocrities? There was nothing but ponderous prose and then, suddenly, it was as if the dam broke and there was the feeling that we had been taken for fools all those years." Lyubov Raitman also evoked the excitement of the time "when you could read things in the press, when it became possible to watch things on television and hear them over the radio. It was a bombshell! The newspapers from those years, the magazine *Ogonyok* (Little Flame). It was amazing." *Ogonyok* soared in popularity during perestroika under the editorship of Vitaly Korotich, owing to its stunning revelations about the Soviet past. Indeed, Yelena Kolosova likewise attached importance to that publication. "Nowhere else in the contemporary world has anything like this happened. There was freedom of speech, and *Ogonyok* played a huge role. It was all so interesting for the reading public." She explained why: "Because, after all, you could only, as they say, influence a country that read a lot by publishing something."

Many Baby Boomers mentioned specific books, publications, or bits of information that particularly resonated with them. Vladimir Kirsanov, like millions of others, found Viktor Suvorov's *Icebreaker**—a different kind of history—compelling, because it attempts to document vast Soviet preparations to invade and Sovietize Europe in the summer of 1941 on the eve of the Nazi attack.

---

*   Viktor Suvorov (real name, Vladimir Rezun) served in the Soviet military intelligence. After defecting to England he published *Icebreaker* in 1988.

"I remember that a book by a Soviet dissident, who fled to England, a KGB agent, made an impression on me. It was an altogether unusual view of history." But revelations about the Stalinist terror resonated most with the Cold War generation. Solzhenitsyn's *Gulag Archipelago*, for instance, astonished Kirsanov, who had seen the book for sale in Yugoslavia twenty-five years earlier, but did not risk bringing it back home. He began reading it only during glasnost. "However, I wasn't able to finish it. It was too morally distressing and I couldn't go further." Singling out Yevgeniya Ginzburg's *Journey into the Whirlwind* and Shalamov's tales,* Vyacheslav Starik also found the camp literature disturbing. "After all, you lived not knowing anything about it and weren't even interested in such things."

Some interviewees averred that the glasnost revelations destroyed their belief in the system. "When perestroika began we were flooded with information. I was happy that my father didn't live to see this. I don't know how he would have endured having his ideals destroyed," weighed in Olga Kamayurova. She found this a "horrible thing" for her generation too: "We lost our anchor. We're like a balloon that's lost its air. We began to see things differently. It's really awful to live in a period of extraordinary changes. I'm not speaking of material hardships, but of the collapse of one's belief system. It turned out that everything we believed in, everything that we considered sacred and holy, turned out to be not only unholy, but even the handiwork of the devil." Olga Gorelik also recalled how hard the period was: "It was unpleasant to know that you had been deceived for a long time on so many questions. I remember the feeling; it was as if there was deception everywhere, a conspiracy of silence, and the sense that we really could have lived through those years differently."

The availability of new facts forced some Baby Boomers to reconsider their understanding of Soviet history. As Vladimir Kirsanov remarked, "We were altogether in the dark about the annexation of the Western territories, Western Belorussia, Ukraine, and Moldavia" during World War II.** Pyotor Krasilnikov singled out the scandals exposed about the Communist Parties in the union republics. "They found the first secretary of the oblast Party committee, a public figure, with large reserves of gold and valuables." Revelations about corruption in Uzbekistan also troubled Natalya Yolshina, as did reports that "our leaders were far from innocent." Glasnost enabled her to see how much they had embellished things. "The fact that things weren't so good in regard to our production levels as they always said at Party congresses, and that in agriculture we didn't have the

---

* Yevgeniya Ginzburg's enthralling memoir of her falling into Stalin's repressive Gulag, and writer and Gulag camp survivor Varlam Shalamov's poignant and lyrical fictional tales represent two of the most widely read and acclaimed publications on this dark chapter of Soviet history.

** This is a reference to clauses of the Nazi–Soviet (Molotov–Ribbentrop) Pact of 1939 kept secret from Soviet citizens.

harvests that we might have, for instance." She admitted that she and many of her friends took in the new information with resentment. "The dethronement of Pavel Morozov for many was a real tragedy, but for me it wasn't for some reason." Yolshina, however, railed against attempts to challenge sanitized Soviet depictions of World War II: "I don't want to know or to hear that Zoya Kosmodemyanskaya's feats never happened.* The war was always a sacred topic in my family. I continue to believe that the people fought for justice and for independence and that the country and the people were united like never before. For me the war is sacred, and I don't want to subject this to reexamination." Others felt similarly, since World War II remains a defining autobiographical memory of the Cold War generation's parents and other family members. Victory and sacrifice legitimated Soviet power more than Stalinist repression discredited it. The resulting myth of the Great Patriotic War became a vital aspect of the Baby Boomers' own "post-memory," that is, an emotional investment on the part of those born after the war to remember it based in part on the stories told by their family members who lived through it.[10]

Glasnost also elevated the political consciousness of many Baby Boomers. When visiting London right after Gorbachev had been there in 1989, Yelena Kolosova recalled, "I was so proud, because the elections to the Supreme Soviet had just taken place.** It was one of the greatest moments in history. We watched the Supreme Soviet sessions live over television." Owing to glasnost, Tatyana Arzhanova and Vyacheslav Starik got involved in public life in ways that had been impossible before—and in ways that ultimately disappointed them. "One revelation followed another, and it suddenly became clear that there'd be nothing left, for it turns out that there was nothing about us that was good," Arzhanova remembered. Her political awakening occurred when Nobel Prize winning physicist Andrei Sakharov spoke at the Congress of People's Deputies and Gorbachev switched off the microphone on him. "I cried. I stood in front of the television and stomped my feet. It was so intolerable. It shouldn't have happened," she contended. "This was the only period in my life when I got involved in politics." Tatyana gave her political support to a maverick pilot with political pretensions who lived in her apartment complex. "He was a Communist, he was a Party member, and he decided that he, an honest and decent person who wanted Russia to become a real country where people could live a real life as in the West, had to promote this," she explained. He ran—unsuccessfully—

---

* Komsomol activist and partisan Zoya Kosmodemyanskaya became a World War II hero after being tortured to death by the Nazis for blowing up an ammunition dump. A cult arose in her honor during the war, used by the propaganda machine to whip up patriotism and to instill hatred toward the Teutonic invaders. During perestroika, the media revisited the cult of Zoya, raising questions that poked holes in the Zoya myth.

** The Communist Party's decision to introduce contested elections in 1989 for a new legislature represented a decisive break with the past. A new body, the Congress of People's Deputies of the USSR, elected a smaller body, a bicameral Supreme Soviet.

for various offices, during which time Arzhanova typed all sorts of things for him. "Unfortunately," she concluded, "it didn't amount to anything." Starik related how, in 1989, his team at work spent three months on the job to elect a deputy to the Supreme Soviet. Their candidate had numerous positive attributes: He did not belong to the Party, he came from a simple family, he lived modestly, he distinguished himself at work—and he agreed to be nominated. "We printed leaflets for him. Back then the first laser printer appeared at work. We used the laser printer bought for our aerodynamic experiments to print leaflets for him," confessed Starik. "For two or three months I ran around with him throughout the neighborhood, and, as a result, we won. It was a very interesting experience. But then he sided with the Communist faction. We really resented this!" exclaimed Starik.

A good number of interviewees felt that the essence of glasnost lay not in the specific revelations, but in the act of making them public. "In the early days we walked about stunned by glasnost, because we didn't expect such things at all," shared Natalya Pronina. "We knew all of these things, but it was a shock to be able to articulate them. Don't think, though, that they divulged something new for me. They didn't disclose a single thing I didn't know, absolutely nothing." Aleksandr Babushkin agreed. "You have to understand that any cultured person, intellectual, is able to distinguish between true and false information." He fine-tuned his remark: "It was really interesting and wonderful that they began to tell the truth, but it wasn't shocking. I was prepared for this." Tatyana Artyomova likewise held that nothing shocked "intelligent people, who read and talked to each other."

But, as Tatyana Kuznetsova perceptively pointed out, glasnost "opened everyone's eyes differently." "I'd say that 60 percent of the information that came out between 1986 and 1990 was a shock to us," remarked Aleksandr Virich. "We knew a lot, and suspected a lot, but when they began to speak frankly, began to divulge information—the popular magazine *Ogonyok* was a big hit among us back then—began to say things openly, well, they began to destroy Soviet power by bombardment, and each edition of *Ogonyok* was another round." For many, according to Virich, "'Did you read it?' became a sacred question." Saratov Party member Natalya Yolshina found "glasnost was a real shock, and my faith began to waver when it became clear that things weren't as good as we were accustomed to believe." Irina Vizgalova also felt that "many things were a revelation. There was a great deal that was unexpected." "The truth about how things had been under the Bolsheviks" stunned Vladimir Bystrov. "It was practically genocide of one's own people. The most awful thing was that tens of millions passed through the camps for no reason at all. And one who's passed through the camps remains scarred for the rest of his life." Could Bystrov—a Party member—not have known this, or was his selective memory a strategy for rationalizing his belonging to the organization that had institutionalized the repression? Given the responses of the other Baby Boomers, I suspect the latter. Yet Vyacheslav

Starik reminded me that he had had little access to *samizdat* literature, which he associated with people in the "free professions," not engineers such as himself with a practical bent of mind. "It was things connected with the camps, above all, the repression" that shocked him. No one in Starik's family had been repressed, and this fact may have made his family more receptive to the positive aspects of the Soviet regime and its propaganda.

By barraging people with conflicting viewpoints, glasnost taught the Cold War generation a valuable lesson. Recalled Arkady Darchenko: "I was blown away! It was as if the floodgates had been thrown open, and at first we believed everything that we heard. But it gradually became clear," he admitted, "that much of what was being said was a bunch of nonsense. You begin to understand there is such a thing as yellow journalism, a radical press, and a normal press. We began to discriminate more." Lamented Olga Kolishchyuk: "It always shocked me when they'd praise someone to the skies and then suddenly rub his name in dirt. More than anything else it shocked me when there'd be a switch from one point of view to the opposite one. God and tsar and then suddenly the devil, as they say." The dilemma for Irina Kulikova was that "there was conflicting information about the same thing. It was terrible. How was one to know where the truth lay?" The result? "There was so much that, now, for the most part, no one watches anything, or listens to anything. There's a constant twisting of facts, and I stopped listening to any of it." Galina Poldyaeva agreed: "So much came out that we were stunned. And now we, by and large, quit reading papers."

The revelations created a hostile work climate for some members of the old guard. Larisa Petrova recalled that "I was in favor of glasnost, and my father at first was, too. But then glasnost took on some abnormal tendencies." She criticized the "primitive thinking" of those people who turned yesterday's negatives into today's positives. "When glasnost took on these forms my father turned against it." She blasted the "radical" press for writing that "all of those in the oblast and city Party committees were dishonest and corrupt. Of course, there were some like that; you'd find them in any society," she rationalized. Some of the falsely accused lost their pensions. Her own father, she shared, "became a social outcast. And he had many friends like that." Irina Chemodurova recounted that her father, a historian of the CPSU, was eased out of his job at the university where he had taught since 1944. Yet, remarkably, he and his family found glasnost exhilarating: "We sat from morning until night in front of the television set and watched all of the congresses and wanted Sakharov to speak," Irina exalted. "It was the first time in my life I saw such passion at home. I'd even say we became inspired. My father at age seventy was encouraged, and believed something new was happening. Thank God he lived to see what took place in 1991."

Father Valentin Ulyakhin was hard put to say anything positive about Gorbachev, who remained a Communist and gave only lip service to religion.

But even Ulyakhin had to conclude that "his main service is that he illuminated, threw light on the secrets, that is, glasnost."

"THINKING PEOPLE ACCEPTED PERESTROIKA"

Gorbachev's inconsistent, hesitant move toward market socialism set into motion forces that eventually wreaked economic havoc, resulting during the 1990s in a breakdown of the world's third largest economy on a magnitude not seen since the Great Depression. For this reason, many interviewees' assessments of perestroika singled out economic difficulties as the reform program's most nagging problem with which they had to cope. They did not voice regrets over the program itself, revealing their overall acceptance of market forces. According to Olga Kolishchyuk, "it was great. Perestroika and the introduction of market relations were necessary because the planned economy didn't work. But they didn't think things through and all sorts of problems arose. They should have weighed things more carefully at first, and then tried." "Perestroika was too rushed, and perhaps it all should have been done differently," suggested Olga Gorelik. "On the one hand, it gave freedom to several strata of the population, to the intelligentsia, for example. But, on the other hand, it created complicated economic problems. Not everyone can restructure themselves, namely our generation." As Natalya P. summed up, "I didn't expect some sort of unusual leap forward. But we lived through some hard times when perestroika began. Things are more stable now, far more so. Periods of great change are always accompanied by a downside."

The downside impacted many Baby Boomers' jobs. Irina Vizgalova recalled, "First of all, perestroika affected us in that it became practically impossible to work. Ours was a very large design institute. Not only ours, but others, too. Ours, where there were more than 500 people employed, shrank to 20 people, and there was no work." How did people cope? "The entire nation sold things on the street at the bazaars, because they had to live. I didn't end up on the street, but my colleagues did, and began to peddle things. I moved to another organization, although at first things were not so good there either financially. That's how perestroika affected us—very strongly." She also complained about tuition fees introduced in colleges and her family's concerns over funding her children's educations. Yet her own son got in under the old system and her daughter received a scholarship. "We were in time, but now there are fewer and fewer possibilities of this sort." There's a lesson here: Vizgalova did not end up peddling things on the streets, and her children did get into college without paying.

Numerous Baby Boomers focused less on how perestroika affected them economically and more on how it, and glasnost, altered the climate at work. Vladimir Glebkin, who taught physics in Addis Ababa, Ethiopia, during the early years of perestroika, became more and more outspoken owing to the impact of the heady climate he encountered during his summer visits home to Moscow, and this almost got him into trouble. He recalled an episode that took place in 1988, when the concept of "socialist competition" was introduced among Soviet citizens on foreign assignment. Glebkin did not see the logic in introducing the campaign in Ethiopia. "How could you determine who is better? I asked this in a neutral, nonconfrontational way, but it was seen as a mutiny," he remembered. Glebkin reminded me that "problems with Soviet citizens abroad were solved very simply. Within a week, you were sent back to the Soviet Union, and suddenly this prospect loomed large for me. I'm not sure what happened, but I think that, as my case was reviewed higher and higher up, apparently someone high up understood that it was time to put an end to this, and things came to naught." How does Glebkin evaluate perestroika? "Very favorably. Despite all the shortcomings, no one wants to return to what we had before, with the exception, perhaps, of the very oldest people, who received certain privileges under communism. Yet we didn't receive any, therefore there's nothing to remember; perestroika's an indisputable plus."

Mikhail Markovich saw enormous changes in the publishing world where he worked with the onslaught of perestroika. Before, the publishing house was supervised by "an absolutely horrible person, a Stalinist. We had a huge conflict, and I was planning to quit, because for two years it was impossible to work. Literally things changed with the October plenum that elected Gorbachev. They removed my boss the next day. For me, the Gorbachev period began with a bang." For this reason, Markovich considered 1985 "a turning point for me. The centralized system collapsed, and we very quickly began to understand this. I remember the absolute euphoria in connection with Gorbachev's coming to power." Markovich happened to be in the Baltic when Gorbachev's key advisor Yakovlev spoke there. His visit not only emboldened the Baltic states' popular front movements that soon pressed for independence but also Markovich and his colleagues: "We, in one and a half years, ended censorship. The first independent publishing houses opened," he recalled. "I can honestly say that for three years I unselfishly worked for the good of the country. I'd come to work at 7:00 P.M. and leave the next day at 2:00 P.M."

Perestroika posed unfamiliar challenges at work for television journalist Natalya Yolshina. Before then, she said, "I always felt sorry for those people I had to say something negative about over the air." Then they began a new broadcast. She recalled the time they waited for local "democrats" to show up following political meetings so that they could broadcast live. "They came and said that the Communist Party was bad, that we needed a multiparty system, that you had to abolish it. I began to die inside, but kept my composure before the camera. You must understand that I don't see any internal contradictions between that which I was, not only was, but remain. I was a patriot and a Communist, and I consider this normal, authentic, and correct." She continued, "I saw no contradiction between this and when they began speaking about democracy, about glasnost, about freedom of speech, and the like, and that the government and system should be different. This struck a responsive chord in me, because I really did see some things that were wrong, even in our wonderful society. And I was totally in favor of perestroika." Yolshina welcomed the notion of elected organs that would speak for the people, but expressed disappointment over an elected official from Saratov, who, after settling in Moscow, forgot about his constituents and focused on his self-aggrandizement. As a result, Yolshina concluded, "I don't understand a thing about it." But I was not satisfied with why she backed perestroika, so I pressed. "It was all of the publications at the beginning of perestroika," she replied. In other words, glasnost.

Vyacheslav Starik described how he shut down the Communist Party committee at the Aviation Institute where he worked. He reminded me that, owing to the fact that he could not hold his tongue—a personality trait that had gotten him in trouble already back in school—he irritated a member of his Party cell at the institute. "As a result, two or three times I didn't get to travel abroad, because he didn't let me." This was in the 1980s, but before the Gorbachev era. Once perestroika began, Starik was elected to the Party committee during a period of great uncertainty. "The uncertainty," he clarified, "lay in the fact that it wasn't clear what we should do. This was a period of elections and democracy. What should the Party committee do in this climate?" Starik proposed abolishing the committee.

Others felt like Starik, too. Saratov's Yevgeny Podolsky, who resettled in Moscow in the mid-1970s, saw the writing on the wall: "I turned in a written request to quit the Party in 1990. At the time," he said, "I worked at Gazprom [the Soviet gas industry]. Moreover, I had a serious conflict with my boss. When perestroika began I thought, 'Now's my chance.' I saw things were getting worse. I began to speak at Party meetings, and this led to conflict." He added that "naturally everyone voted to expel me from the Party, but in the corridors each of them came up to me, including some from the administration but not the top bosses, and whispered to me, 'Everything you wrote is true. We'd do the same thing too, but we can't right now. If we write a statement they'd boot us out.'" Podolsky had already decided to quit his job and to strike out on his own, taking advantage of the new opportunities for independent business initiatives that perestroika offered.

Despite the problems the Baby Boomers encountered negotiating the rocky transition to a market economy, many of them, appreciative of the fact that hard times often provide unexpected opportunities, placed great value on the freedoms they had won. For Anna Lyovina, "transitional periods are always a two-sided phenomenon. Perestroika greatly benefited some, but completely ruined the lives of others." Her oldest child was born when she lived in East Germany, where her husband was stationed in the Red Army. "Back then it never entered my head that my children at some point would be able to leave the Soviet Union!" She remarked that "freedom of choice is a wonderful thing, especially when you consider how we were brought up, when everything was decided for us." She offered examples to illustrate her point: "When you'd enroll in college no one asked you where you planned to work afterward. They sent you. A living permit tied you to where you lived. You couldn't move from one city to another if they didn't send you there. There were an insane number of regulations. You were tied to one place, to one social structure, to your level, beyond which you couldn't move or advance." Lyovina acknowledged, however, that perestroika "was a tragedy for others. The ground fell out from under their feet. They psychologically could not restructure their lives, and they suffered a great deal materially." She told me about a cousin in Siberia who could not live on his miserly pension. His children, who also had become engineers, lost their jobs and had no prospects.

Bakhyt Kenzheyev, who had emigrated to Canada before perestroika took off, appreciated the newly won freedoms even from afar. "I'm thankful to Gorbachev for everything, but in particular for what I felt personally. For example, I had a hybrid document called a Soviet passport for citizens living permanently abroad. With this passport I needed a visa to travel to Russia. I remember the day they abolished this. It became a full-fledged passport. I could travel to Russia on short notice, without any visa." There was more: "Then they returned my right to vote. I had been deprived of this when I left. Of course, it wasn't much needed, but nonetheless, the hell with it, it's an attribute of citizenship. I can opt not to vote, but I enjoy having the right to do so."

Aleksandr Virich summed things up: "Thinking people accepted perestroika. Of course, 90 percent of us at first thought that this would be a new current." But old ways of thinking did not change overnight. "On the one hand, people wanted freedom; on the other hand, they didn't want to lose what they had."

"COMMON SENSE LED TO THE COLLAPSE"

In August 1991, hard-line Communists plotted to overthrow Gorbachev to prevent signing of a new union treaty that would have created a Union of Soviet Sovereign Republics. What most upset those engineering the putsch was the tacit understanding that the six Soviet republics not involved in the negotiations— Armenia, Estonia, Georgia, Latvia, Lithuania, and Moldova—were free to go their separate ways. Irina Barysheva recalled, "When they began the putsch, it was in the summer. My mother, who was still alive, said that it was like the state she was in when war began." Those in Moscow felt a more immediate threat— and could do something about it. KGB operative Andrei Rogatnev related that "it turned out that, in 1988, I left for Iraq and returned home in 1991 to an altogether different country. And I didn't return the same. The country moved in one direction, and I in a different one. True," he continued, "the putsch began immediately after my return, and I had no choice and I rushed, as they say, to the barricades. I didn't hesitate over whose side I was on." The turning point for

Rogatnev came when open elections began. He told me a joke from the period: "When were the first democratic elections held? Answer: When God brought Eve to Adam and said, 'Well, Adamchik, choose a wife for yourself.' Our elections were the same. Then, finally, for the first time in my life, I could choose from among three or four candidates."

Like many Muscovites, Mikhail Markovich had spent the weekend before the coup at the dacha. When he returned to work on Monday morning from the suburbs, tanks rolled along the Minsk highway. He remembered remarking to a friend, "'Lyosha, I don't think this will last long. At most, it will last for only a year or two,' because we had already gotten used to living differently, and deciding everything for ourselves. We saw how intelligent people came to power with whom you could carry on a conversation. Before this, things were difficult." When he and an acquaintance, like innumerable other Muscovites, responded to Boris Yeltsin's appeal to the Russian people to resist the conspirators by spending the night of Monday, August 21, at the Russian White House where the Congress of People's Deputies convened, they "experienced nothing but the sticky feeling of fear." Anatoly Shapiro recalled that "the putsch was the most terrifying moment for me, and for my family." Like so many others, he quit the Party that week. Justifying his actions, he pointed out that, "as a petty Party functionary, as secretary of a small Party cell, I didn't convene a single Party meeting the entire time. They should thank me for that. People in my collective more or less understood. I didn't betray them, and they didn't betray me."

Like all great historical events, the Gorbachev revolution and breakup of the Soviet empire has provoked extensive debate in the scholarly and popular literature, as well as in public opinion. Some explanations for the collapse of the Soviet system accent the worsening economy, while others locate the collapse in the very (illegitimate) nature of the Soviet regime itself, or in the burdens of empire. Although caution advises against interpretations that smack of inevitability, the confluence of several developments and the consequences of state policies created the necessary preconditions that made the end of the USSR possible, even likely. That Gorbachev himself was a product of the Soviet system and rose to the Party's top leadership position makes this abundantly clear. Indeed, the Baby Boomers' life stories suggest that the Soviet system reformed itself out of existence, as the stagnating political and economic structure attempted to catch up with changes that had come to society and to people's mentalities. These transformations were, in part, the ineluctable but often unplanned consequences of the state's own social policies. They alone doomed the unreformed regime, since they would have continued to evolve organically toward a further opening of society.

Despite the deep-rooted origins of the decline of the Soviet empire, the Gorbachev years, ironically or tragically, contributed to the collapse.[11] As Lyubov Raitman maintained, "It was no longer possible in the circumstances that had arisen in the country by 1991 to preserve central power and govern an enormous country that had exhausted itself." Raitman did not regret the collapse, but "that, for various reasons, including age, I didn't succeed in taking advantage of the fact that, at one time, it had been one accessible country. Now it's a problem, and it's likely I won't see it all." Yet Raitman harbored no illusions about Soviet times. "The petty rulers, governor generals, and general secretaries of these republics always made an awful impression on me. I understood that these autocrats were extremely dependent on the Kremlin, like puppets, with someone pulling the strings, that this subordination existed, and that something happened that destroyed it."

At the start of the new millennium, 70 percent of Russians polled believed that Russia had lost a great deal owing to the breakup of the Soviet Union.[12] Many interviewees felt the same way. Yelena Zharovova, for example, posited that "glasnost made it possible to let out steam and that was it." Still, she believed that, except for the Baltic states, "the other republics did not want independence from the Soviet Union." Critical of the destabilizing role played by the Baltic states, Zharovova opined, "They received more than other republics, they received more attention, more money, more everything at the expense of Russia and Central Asia. Apparently, he who receives more expects more." Lyubov Kovalyova, too, regretted "that a country so big broke apart. Although, probably many welcomed these events." She clarified what she meant: "It all depends upon the person, upon his or her circumstances, upon what they got from perestroika. It seems to me that, at the moment of the breakup, those who turned out to be working at a feeding trough did alright, but those who weren't, well, they were worse off in a purely material sense." Olga Martynkina believed perestroika was inevitable but "regretted the breakup of the union. It was some kind of explosion. Suddenly everyone wanted their freedom, everyone went their separate ways, despite the economic and cultural ties."

Vladimir Kirsanov explained, "You probably can't overcome human nature. No matter how much nationalism was repressed, it very quickly rose to the surface. I was stunned by how suddenly this occurred, since before there wasn't any evidence of this." Kirsanov believed that Islamic fundamentalism played a big role in this. "It began in Kabul and spread from Afghanistan. God forbid that the soothsayers are right who prophesized that a third world war has already begun." Bitter over the dissolution of the USSR, Kirsanov detailed how the discord between nationalities affected his relatives in Baku. "My brother's family fell apart. An engineer with a Ph.D., he lived in Azerbaijan, in Baku, and worked in one of the ministries. Neighbors denounced his wife, who is Armenian, warning him that 'they're coming to get you.' He packed his wife and young son into the car at night and fled Azerbaijan. They now live in Moscow, where he drives a cab," related Kirsanov. Viktor D. likewise expressed deep dissatisfaction: "It offends me that they're now separate states. Moreover, that's the opinion not only of Russians but of Armenians, Azeris, and all the others. The collapse of the union didn't have a beneficial effect on anyone." Viktor, like many others, regretted how expensive and complicated this has become owing to the breakup of the union.

A minority of the Baby Boomers, however, had no regrets about the unraveling of the union. As Tatyana Luchnikova quipped, "I like the fact that the Soviet Union no longer exists, but that doesn't mean I'm right. Many people I know don't like this. Some of them even say that 'we had communism under Brezhnev. Caviar was cheap at 5 rubles and meat at 2 rubles a kilo,' but what kind of communism was it?"

"WHEN WE LIVED IN SARATOV WE ALWAYS WANTED TO LIVE IN MOSCOW"

Late Soviet society had been on the move; the 1979 census, for instance, revealed that less than half of the population lived where they were born.[13] Gorbachev's revolution furthered this trend by providing opportunities to relocate within the Soviet Union, greater freedom to travel abroad, and more possibilities to emigrate. Nationalist animosities magnified by the breakup of the Soviet Union also created a refugee problem of considerable proportions, as hundreds of thousands fled their homes. Moreover, the dissolution of the USSR resulted in tens of millions of Russians now living in the Near Abroad, as the newly independent states once part of the USSR were now called, giving rise to potentially explosive diaspora problems.

The gap in the living standards between Moscow and much of the rest of the country made moving to the Soviet capital a dream of many from the provinces long before perestroika. Seven members of the graduating class of Saratov's School No. 42 now live in Russia's capital, and two others, both women, left Saratov for other cities to accompany their husbands. I located three of the seven. Each of their experiences reveals strategies for relocating to Moscow at different points in Soviet history. Aleksandr Konstantinov left Saratov for Moscow to attend Moscow University in 1967; his brilliant academic career allowed him to remain there. Marrying a Muscovite represented another way to obtain a Moscow living permit. Yevgeny Podolsky resettled in Moscow in the mid-1970s after meeting his second wife-to-be at the Moscow branch of the Saratov research institute that employed him. Podolsky claimed to have had no desire to leave Saratov and that his wife's parents categorically refused to let her move to Saratov, "so I had to abandon everything there and transfer here." Podolsky stressed that at one point he regretted moving to Moscow. Comparing the situations at work for young specialists, Saratov came out on top. His colleagues in Moscow told him, "'Here the leadership tells us that you won't get promoted for at least seven years.'" This made no sense to Podolsky, who waxed nostalgic about the work climate in Saratov, where, as he put it, "everything was different." What irked him about Moscow was that "the directors were very old.

They had their own clan and didn't admit us into it." After four years, he found a new position with the country's gas monopoly, where he worked until perestroika made it possible for him to strike out on his own.

Larisa Petrova is representative of those who relocated to Moscow during perestroika. As director of the research department of a medical clinic in Saratov, Petrova defended her dissertation in Moscow on lung diseases and work conditions and the work environment. She stated: "They transferred my husband to the Ministry of Internal Affairs when they began to set up an independent Russian one in 1990. In this case no one's parents arranged this. It was purely his personal qualities as a professional that played a role." Owing to the ties she had made while traveling back and forth between Saratov and Moscow to work on her dissertation, she secured a job at the recently opened Institute of Criminology. The moved taxed them, as they "arrived in Moscow at an unfortunate time," as she put it. "When we lived in Saratov we always wanted to live in Moscow. We envied Muscovites." Settling in during a time of critical shortages, they experienced disappointment and had to make compromises. She, for instance, had to settle for a position as a junior researcher. Moreover, Muscovites' attitudes toward provincials irked her. "I'd say we faced hard times for two or three years before things gradually began to fall into place and now I'd say that things are more or less okay."

"THE FIRST TRIP MADE A STUNNING IMPRESSION"

For some Baby Boomers glasnost meant fulfilling a life-long dream of traveling abroad to Eastern Europe, to Russia's other neighbors, or to the capitalist West. Traveling to Varna, Bulgaria, in 1986, Igor Litvin reacted the way his classmates had who preceded him by a decade: "It seemed to us back then that we were abroad, because you could buy cold beer at any stand, whereas in Yalta there would be a line for it." Similarly, Yevgeny Podolsky in 1987 spent "an altogether wonderful trip to Prague, where I worked in an exhibit for six weeks." Underscoring the "night and day" difference between Prague and Moscow, he drew comparisons at the latter's expense: "I saw all of the abundance, everything was affordable, people were polite, and things were beautiful and clean. I was stunned." Podolsky expressed amazement that he was allowed to go abroad because he had divorced in 1985 and had no "hostage" back home. Since then he has traveled across all of Europe.

Those traveling at the start of perestroika felt the suffocating effect of Soviet-era suspiciousness toward its own people. Irina Barysheva, whose husband had a top security clearance, first traveled abroad in 1986 to Finland in part with the help of the mother of one of her pupils, who worked in OVIR, the organization that grants permission to travel. Barysheva had to attend two evening discussions with the KGB before leaving the country. On arriving in Helsinki, she saw that nothing was as she had imagined it, especially after she visited her tour guide's home and observed how ordinary people there lived. "It was then that my eyes opened a great deal," she recalled. Barysheva challenged the restrictions imposed by her Soviet group leader, creating something of a row when she refused to leave a night club to adhere to the group leader's curfew. "There were threats that they'd expel me from the Party and inform my workplace of what happened, and that things would get unpleasant for me. I remember crying my eyes out, even though I don't cry easily. But I didn't repent," Barysheva explained, because she had paid for her own trip and did not understand why she had to submit to the unwelcome interference of her Party chaperone. On the trip home, the Party busybody suggested to Barysheva: "Let's leave everything that happened there behind with us." Irina's husband believed that, "more likely than not, she was afraid that they wouldn't send her abroad any more."

Thanks to perestroika, Vyacheslav Starik spent a month with his wife and daughter in Cambridge, England, and afterward visited the United States. The fact that the first trip materialized did not dampen his feeling victimized by the Soviet bureaucracy. Starik received his foreign passport at 9:00 P.M. on Friday and flew out early the next morning. "Up until the last minute I didn't know whether they'd give me a passport or not, so I didn't pack anything, because, as always, it's a bad sign," he explained.

As perestroika opened up the country, foreign travel for some became routine. Viktor Alekseyev visited Finland in 1989 with his classmate Igor Altshuller. Afterward he traveled with Altshuller to West Germany. "Then, pretty soon thereafter, professional trips began. Within a year I went to Seattle to a conference," he observed. Once perestroika began, Anatoly Shapiro traveled to Sweden, West Germany, and Finland. And he joined his wife for a month in Paris, where she spent four months on a study trip. Yelena Zharovova's husband worked in Holland for several years, during which time she visited him often. In his capacity as principal of a sports school, Georgy Godzhello went to Italy, France, Spain, and Finland, and then to the United States for the 1996 Atlanta Olympic Games. Recalled Godzhello: "The first trip made a stunning impression. But you adapt pretty quickly, ever the more so because changes started occurring here at that time. Rich people began to appear, luxurious buildings began to appear, they began to pay more attention to cleanliness and the like, but the first impression, of course, is a powerful one."

They certainly were for Igor Litvin who, in 1988, flew to California to visit a classmate who had emigrated. There he encountered "the bluest of skies, marvelous, almost spotless automobiles, and clean streets." Larisa Petrova traveled to Edinburgh to visit her sister, who had married a Scotsman. She returned the next year, and in 1996 was in the United States. She later visited Spain, Italy, Germany, Sweden, and France as well. The first thing she noticed in the capitalist countries was "how good their stores are and how lousy ours are." The excellent roads also made an impression. Olga Gorelik vacationed in Turkey and visited Israel, where her daughter now lives. The two of them also traveled to Italy. By then the fully stocked stores did not surprise her, but the abundance of household appliances did. "Daily life amazed me, the fact that everything was more developed and it was easier to live. I observed this visiting relatives and friends, and I thought how easier it all is for them. Sure, they had their own problems, but life is for people and not the other way around." Gorelik emphasized that little things astonished her, quipping: "We fly in space, but eat with tin spoons." She also compared her mother's situation with what it might have been had she been a retired surgeon abroad. "She now lives with us, and it is unlikely that she'd live with dignity, as they say, if she lived alone, because her pension wouldn't be enough." Irina Kulikova visited Katowice, Poland, for only a day in 1990 to attend a funeral; however, she called attention to the cleanliness and order noticeable the minute she crossed the Polish border. "When you returned, it was a nightmare."

Having a top security clearance made it impossible for Arkady Darchenko to go abroad until perestroika. Darchenko, who arrived in East Berlin in 1989, just before the wall came down, remembered: "It was my first time abroad and it goes without saying that I found everything interesting. The German sense of cleanliness stunned me." Another thing he noticed was that "people dressed differently. I could spot a Russian in Berlin in a coat and tie three blocks away. Not like in Russia. It simply wasn't acceptable here." Finally, the quantity and quality of German beer impressed him. "Our beer was terrible back then. I love beer. I drank to my heart's content for the first time there in Berlin." Afterward, he traveled to Belgium, Cuba, and China. About Belgium he recalled that "the quantity of technical equipment in the stores, which I'm not indifferent to, simply blew me away. I had stashed away money and in East Germany bought some decent audio equipment at a special store. But in Belgium, I went into a store and it had everything. My God, I thought, I can't believe how much they produce, and it's all so different. You can buy whatever you want. The colossal assortment. That was my first impression."

Some who traveled abroad at this time (especially former Party members) acknowledged what the West had to offer, but also drew comparisons that validated their own professional attributes. Vladimir Bystrov first traveled abroad in 1988, to East Germany, and then to Chicago, Philadelphia, and Washington, D.C., where he took part in an Emerging Leaders Summit, organized by Rotary International and involving more than 300 people from the Soviet Union representing a dozen disciplines. He found Chicago's skyscrapers and the people to his liking, except for one thing: "They allowed us to bring with us whatever we liked in terms of vodka and cigarettes that we wanted to give away as gifts. But no one smokes there, and no one drinks." Traveling by car, he returned to America to visit "practically all of the universities located between Boston and Washington. You'd take something away that was useful and also saw what we do better," he remarked. Larisa Petrova noticed much to admire in the United Kingdom and United States, but not so in her own area of medical research:

"I believe that the depth of research is more detailed, the digging is deeper, and the desire to get at the heart of things scrupulously is greater in Russian minds," she told me. After retiring, Gennady Ivanov became head of security for a joint Russian-Dutch transportation firm in Saratov, and in this capacity visited Holland. "We traveled around and saw what there was to see, but I was bored there, because toward evening life dies down," he observed.

In sum, like those who went before them in the 1970s, the Baby Boomers who traveled abroad for the first time spotlighted Europe and America's material abundance, the cleanliness of public spaces, and the politeness of the people they encountered. Yet in making it routine for the Cold War generation to travel for professional or personal reasons and far less bureaucratically cumbersome, perestroika allowed the generation to replace imagined Europes and Americas with more life-size ones, especially as the post-Soviet Russian economy shed its autarkic tendencies in favor of integration into the world economy and globalization.

"THINGS ARE FINE WHEREVER WE'RE NOT"

Emigration crossed the minds of just about all Soviet Jews at some point, owing to popular and official anti-Semitism, as well as to prevalent images of the glamour of life abroad. Anatoly Shapiro and his wife considered emigrating, "but the idea was frightening," he explained. His father worked abroad at the time and risked losing his coveted position, but understood what potential obstacles his son faced if he remained in the USSR. "He didn't object," recalled Shapiro, "but he knew that this would end his career." Shapiro's wife backed the idea of leaving, but they ultimately decided to stay put. Lyubov Raitman's family seriously considered emigration in the late 1970s at her husband's initiative. Recalled Raitman: "But we didn't leave because of his family, because they were very much against it and explained to him that, if he left, it would ruin their careers." Pyotor Obraztsov came from an eminent family: his grandfather founded the famous Moscow Puppet Theater, and his aunt, an actress, regularly toured abroad. She put pressure on him to stay put, as did Pyotor's mother and stepfather who was deputy director of the Institute of Africa whom Raitman described as "an important Communist and someone involved in ideological work, a fighter on the ideological front." Ironically, Pyotor—who is not Jewish—wanted to emigrate and Lyubov—who is Jewish—lacked enthusiasm for the idea. "Perhaps I regret that now. I can't say for sure," she proffered.

The Baby Boomer I called Nina in chapter 5 described the "tragedy" Soviet Jews faced under late socialism. She befriended a young man at college who filed papers to leave for Israel and got turned down. Afterward she spent time with him and other so-called "refuseniks," as those denied permission to leave were called. At first Nina did not understand why they wanted to leave, but "when I began to hang out with these people, I came to understand why," she related. Nina's friend had asked her to go with him. "In all honesty, I would have left back then with great pleasure, but I understood that I couldn't do that because they'd sack my mother from work, and it wasn't clear what would have happened to me," she admitted. "For me it was a matter of weighing my choices. It was an awful tragedy." Her father banned the topic from family discussions. Years later, after she married, her father expressed some regrets, suggesting they might consider leaving for Israel. "But my husband never wanted to emigrate. I wanted to all my life, but he never did."

Leonid Terlitsky had a refusenik in his own family. When détente opened up the possibility of emigration in the 1970s, some of Terlitsky's relatives took the risk. His cousin went first, in 1970, but not without high drama. When he tried to emigrate, the government attempted to force him to pay for his education. "He and a group of other scientists staged a hunger strike. Western governments got involved, and eventually they were let out. He moved to Israel, and now lives in Holland," related Terlitsky. His own family considered leaving in 1974, but his father died the next year, so they filed to emigrate in 1976. Only Leonid and his mother received permission to leave. Turned down, his brother spent the next eleven years as an unemployed refusenik. "My mother stayed with him," added Terlitsky. "He supported himself mostly by driving a cab, a gypsy cab."

Taken in by his brother's wife's relatives in Philadelphia, Terlitsky "spent the first three weeks in America on their couch." But, after landing a job in an architect's office, Leonid recalled, "I rented myself a studio in downtown Philadelphia and started my own life." He became a licensed architect, took on some good-sized projects, and then moved to New York in 1981. Returning to Moscow in 1987, eleven years after leaving—he married a woman he had met before emigrating. "It was probably the closest I will ever get to travel in time," declared Terlitsky, "because I ended up in the same apartment from which I left with the same woman who saw me off to the airport with the same towels, cups, and bed linen, with the same stores with the same stuff on the shelves for the same prices, with people at the same addresses in the same jobs with the same telephone numbers. I never experienced anything like it before or after." Terlitsky had no regrets "whatsoever" about emigrating. When I interviewed him, he had been living mostly in Moscow for the preceding eight years and had just purchased a spacious apartment in a prestigious neighborhood near former School No. 20.

Many Soviet Jews who decided not to take the risks involved in applying to emigrate saw things the way Sofiya Vinogradova did. Because her parents would not have left Russia, she did not give the possibility serious thought, although she acknowledged that, if she really had wanted to make things work out, she could have. Her family led a "normal" life in Moscow. Improving their material conditions was not high on their wish lists, and the concept of freedom seemed abstract. In relating her experience, she shared a Russian proverb: "Things are fine wherever we're not." Besides, some of her classmates and relatives who emigrated had a "terribly awful time" and faced all sorts of stresses and even illness.

She and others recognized the USSR's shortcomings, but the country was home and its faults were "familiar." In the 1990s she briefly regretted her decision to remain in Russia; however, these feelings passed as circumstances improved. Taking a philosophical bent, she emphasized she had no regrets about how her life had unfolded and reminded me of the adage that, at life's end, most people would not want to trade their life for someone else's.

"NO ONE SAID THAT WE WERE BETRAYING OUR HOMELAND"

Glasnost took the risk out of leaving Russia, but it also gave Soviet Jews hope that real change would come to their own country thereby decreasing the urge to emigrate for political reasons. For instance, Leonid Volodarsky spent four months in America in 1988. "It's a great country, but not for everyone. It's fine to leave for America with your parents when you're five years old. Within three months you'd become an American. But at a later age, when all of your roots are here and everything else, it's difficult. It's not for nothing that the German writer Erich Remarque said that immigration is always a tragedy," said Volodarsky.

In tracing his decision to emigrate, Viktor Alekseyev acknowledged the role his classmate, Igor Altshuller, played in the evolution of his own thinking on the subject. Altshuller emigrated because he had a parting of ways with the Soviet system and because glasnost disappointed him. "Under his influence and the influence of what I read, I, too, became critical," shared Alekseyev; however, he emigrated in the early 1990s, "without any underlying political motives unlike many others, because it became possible to work abroad, in the West, and this possibility appealed to us." He and his wife received invitations to work abroad, but from different countries, she from Switzerland, and he from Holland. Alekseyev eventually joined her in Switzerland. They lived in Europe for eight years before receiving an invitation to teach in Cleveland. The next year his wife accepted an appointment at the City University of New York and he at the College of Staten Island in New York City.

Tatyana Artyomova visited the United States often before she and her husband settled down in Connecticut in 1996, "only because we were offered jobs, and for no other reason." She emphasized, "I never dreamed of living in America. It was not a goal of mine. You live where you work." Quick to add "but I don't regret this for a minute," she fessed up that she and her husband also wanted to give their daughter an American education.

Yelena Kolosova visited the United States in 1991 as a postdoctoral student. At that time emigration did not seem possible, "because it meant leaving my friends and my parents' graves. It had nothing to do with the idiotic notion that I'd be betraying my Motherland. No, it was simply that it seemed to me that it was impossible to sever ties with everything that made me strong." It was her husband Em, who was Jewish, who forced the issue by filing to emigrate. They received permission to do so in 1994, but Kolosova had a hard time making up her mind when her husband placed the burden on her to come to a decision. "It's not an exaggeration to say that for two weeks I couldn't decide. Then, one day, I came home, put the key in the door, and knew that we'd go." Thus inspired, Kolosova realized that "one of the most important reasons" for leaving was to save her son Misha from service in the Russian army in the Chechen war. They left Moscow in 1996.

Tatyana Arzhanova, who had traveled abroad frequently and had lived in Indonesia before settling in Canada in 1991, admitted that they thought about leaving the USSR for good already during their youth, "but since we're not Jews, we didn't have a chance and couldn't. Neither could we become refugees somewhere." She explained: "First of all, we didn't have any basis to do so, and second, it would have been very dangerous for the relatives we would have left behind." Lest I underappreciate her fear of the possibility of a chain reaction that could harm her loved ones, Tatyana confided that, as a schoolgirl, the father of a friend she made at Pioneer camp unduly suffered because he had written a letter of recommendation for Oleg Penkovsky—arrested in 1962 and later shot for espionage—when he sought to join the Communist Party.[14] Tatyana's mother had taught Penkovsky English. When the Gorbachev revolution made it possible for Tatyana and her husband to work abroad, they seized the opportunity, because she "had an enormous desire not to die and be buried in Russia." She elaborated, "I had interesting work, I had friends, my mother was there, but at some point I really wanted to tear myself away from there, even though it was the most encouraging time in regard to freedom." By this point, her daughter had left Moscow to work as an au pair in Ireland and then in Austria.

Marriage to a foreigner represented a ticket out for Tatyana Luchnikova who, in the early 1990s, worked as a secretary in a Russian-Finnish transportation firm. She recounted: "My future husband was here on a business trip and we met at a party and suddenly got married, because I was tired of everything and thought I'd go with him to Norway. It was too hard here. So, I left the country in 1992, got pregnant, and gave birth that same November. My son and mother came to visit that summer." The marriage of convenience barely survived, especially once Tatyana determined to live vicariously through her son, who fulfilled her own dream of becoming a ballet dancer. Rostislav (Stas) studied ballet in St. Petersburg and thus Norway had no attraction for him. After Tatyana filmed him and sent the videocassette abroad, he was invited to London for an audition. "My husband left for Africa on business and I, along with my baby daughter and her carriage, and my son, arrived in London at Heathrow," she detailed. Her second marriage almost ended when her husband later visited them in London. She had just rented a two-bedroom flat. "I sold all of my family heirlooms at Christie's in order to pay for the apartment, because I didn't want to take my husband back." Then, to her surprise, her son told me he wanted to go to New York to study.

Just before Christmas in 1993 she, Stas, and baby Masha in her carriage arrived in New York. At first they rented a flat in Brooklyn, but then she bought an apartment on West 49th Street, near the Russian Samovar restaurant, which was owned by Roman Kaplan, a teacher at School No. 20. Luchnikova found work as a model. After auditioning with the Moscow Classic Ballet when the company visited America, however, Stas accepted an invitation to return to Moscow. During the next several years she moved back and forth between Moscow, New York, and Norway before settling down in New York with her daughter in 1998. Masha was vacationing with her father on Cyprus when the 9/11 tragedy raised everyone's consciousness of the terrorist threat, after which she was afraid to return to New York. Tatyana turned to yoga, "and this helped me a great deal," she recalled. In fact, she soon left for Arizona to study yoga seriously. "We meditated there, in the mountains. It was a fantastic time. The best in my life," she told me. Eventually, her daughter convinced her to return to Norway in 2003. She considered the five years she lived in the United States "the best time of my life. It was a gift of fate." Separated from her husband, she now thanks fate for bringing her to Oslo, which she has come to appreciate.

One-sixth of the Baby Boomers interviewed for this book emigrated, but only one of them, Aleksandr Trubnikov, now resides in Israel. Trubnikov's decision to live there is not without irony. Half-Jewish, his Russian surname masked his identity and, as a result, he did not suffer discrimination. He emigrated for many reasons, but especially because his eldest daughter, who went to Israel to study for three years, liked it, married there, and had a baby. Moreover, he shared, "I began to intensely dislike Russia at that particular moment. It was during the crisis of 1998 [when the ruble defaulted on the world market, resulting in an immediate, but short-lived crisis]. Over a two-month period, the ruble fell six times. People began to receive unimaginably low wages of about thirty dollars a month. And the outlook was grim, especially for those at the university. Things became really awful for us, because in Russia at the time the work of university professors was not appreciated. We were at the bottom of the food chain. All of this had an effect on me." Trubnikov justified his decision in more than personal and economic terms. "For seventy years they oppressed people. Then, when they opened the locks, everything poured out. And who ended up on top? You know what always rises to the surface, it's always the foam. That's what happened in this case." Trubnikov indicted Soviet power: "It's all understandable, but, unfortunately, we have but one life and I thought why wait until things become normal, it's already so hard." Unlike those who emigrated before perestroika, Trubnikov did not encounter any difficulties. "I remain a Russian citizen. I have a Russian passport and I can return whenever I please. In this regard Russia's become a normal country. A democratic one." Trubnikov's mother and his wife's parents remained in Russia, and emigration did not present the threats to those who stayed behind as it did during the Soviet days. "They were fine about our decision to leave. Life in Russia had undergone sweeping changes. No one said that we were betraying our homeland."

"THE WEST TURNED OUT TO BE DIFFERENT"

The Baby Boomers who emigrated acknowledged the help they received in their new home from friends and relatives who had left the USSR before perestroika. Those who emigrated during the Brezhnev era had faced obstacles finding suitable employment and coming to grips with the fact that the West they thought they understood had been an imagined one. For instance, Bakhyt Kenzheyev married a Canadian graduate student in Slavic literatures who worked as a translator for Progress Publishers in Moscow. Kenzheyev and his Canadian bride, eight months pregnant, arrived in Montreal on June 24, 1982, at the peak of an economic downturn. Confident he would fit into Canadian life, he ran up against some real obstacles, for Canadian realities did not at all live up to his expectations. For instance, after reading job ads in a paper, he applied for a position as a lab technician. "And I went there to be hired, absolutely certain that they'd welcome me with open arms, me, a graduate of Moscow University's Chemistry Department."

Aleksandr Trubnikov and his wife decided to emigrate to Israel after the ruble defaulted in 1998 and many university faculty and research scholars stopped receiving paychecks. This picture of Trubnikov and his family in Israel was taken in 2005. "My first boss was from America, and that, of course, was a direct result of the fact that I had studied English and still kept up my skills," recounted Trubnikov, gold medalist in School No. 42's A Class. *Courtesy of Aleksandr Trubnikov*

The West required some getting used to. "It was one of the biggest shocks that there is. Back home we came into contact only with foreigners who had a special interest in Russia. But when you find yourself in America or Canada you see that, there, absolutely no one's interested in Russia, the entire value system is different, and the entire way of life is different, not worse or better, but simply different," explained Kenzheyev. He also felt victimized by the widespread Soviet belief that Americans had a lot in common with Russians. "It's altogether possible that rednecks are like Voronezh truck drivers. But the difference between the American and Russian intelligentsia and middle class back then on the whole was enormous." Regarding attitudes toward everyday life and toward the world, "there was an enormous difference between a Russian of the 1970s and an American from the 1970s," commented Kenzheyev. "Of course, we didn't know this." In short, "it came as a huge shock. The West turned out to be different."

Yet Kenzheyev felt grateful that he found work to his liking in Canada. The country also broadcast Russian-language radio programs to the USSR, and the Canadian station hired him on the spot. He devoted his first radio broadcast to Xerox machines. Recalled Kenzheyev: "Back then in the USSR, Xerox machines were kept under lock and key. In order to make a single copy, you needed to get three signatures." Thus, his first story spotlighted Western copy shops, where customers could duplicate as much as they liked. Staying with the station for seven years, Kenzheyev liked the atmosphere there, which he found far less politicized than at its American counterpart. During this time he returned to Moscow only twice. Once perestroika began in earnest, he realized that "as a writer, I was obliged to go back as often as I could," so he quit his radio job and signed on with what turned out to be a rogue firm that sold frozen bread dough, but which enabled him to travel to Russia a half-dozen times a year.

The Baby Boomers who emigrated during perestroika or after the collapse of the Soviet Union also faced difficulties, but they adapted well because of the help they received from others who had left Russia earlier, because of the survival skills they learned under late socialism—how to work the system—translated well in their new context, and because they knew English. Aleksandr Trubnikov's knowledge of English helped him land decent jobs in Israel in his field, physics, thereby assuring a smooth transition. At first he found a position in a high-tech start-up firm run by an American, but the company went under with the fall of the high-tech business. He now works for another start-up firm, but one that is more stable. "I'm doing what I did in Russia, but at a somewhat different salary," he ribbed.

Trubnikov felt he had an easier time settling into his new life than those who emigrated to the United States: "I wouldn't really call my move to Israel emigration, as I understand the word—torn from your roots, in a foreign country, hard to adjust, hostility from the native people, etc." Why? "It turned out that, at the time of my arrival, almost all of my close friends, with whom I had been connected for decades in Saratov, lived in Israel. Moreover, there's a tolerant attitude toward repatriates who don't know Hebrew." He explained, "This is something specific to the country—its ideology is founded on the return of Jews to their historical homeland. I received citizenship and all rights immediately, along with a passport. In order to move here I only had to prove my Jewish heritage at the Israeli embassy to get a visa." The Israeli government gave him a free ticket to the country, where his daughter and friends welcomed him. "Within two months, with their help, I found work in my field and ever since then have not experienced any special problems," he maintained. "I get together with my friends more often than I did in Russia, even though we live in different cities. Therefore, I didn't lose the luxury of human contact—and as far as I know that's one of the biggest problems, for example, for émigrés in America."

The Soviet dream shaped émigrés' expectations of the America they had imagined, just as it had for Kenzheyev who emigrated a decade earlier. Tatyana Artyomova and her husband, both economists, traveled extensively to Eastern Europe in the 1970s. She visited the United States for the first time for several weeks in 1980 to see her husband, an exchange scholar at Harvard University, complaining about "the absurd cost of higher education and healthcare." Now that she has built a life in America, she has other concerns, too. "To this day, I can't understand how people can retire," she remarked. The precariousness of the labor market in America also made Artyomova anxious. "I was accustomed to being assured that I'd always have work. Here I have the sense that people lose work not only because of their own fault but also because of circumstances. I can't get used to this."

Before emigrating, Yelena Kolosova thought that the cultural difference she had heard so much about was overdrawn, but discovered that the cultural barrier challenged, as she put it, "my belief in friendship, my unwillingness to squeal on others, and some of my moral values." Adjusting to the world of academic scientific research presented an ordeal, for she found "a lot of pettiness and a reluctance to interact within the collective." Her conclusion: "Everyone suffers here. Everyone needs to protect his job security; everyone has to receive more grants; everyone has to make mortgage payments and pay for his children's education." She found relations at work more patriarchal than back home; however, insofar as she worked at Iowa State University, she encountered many cosmopolitan sorts who traveled a great deal. She acknowledged that some barriers had to do with her "uninhibited personality, of course."

Having lived in Europe for eight years, Viktor Alekseyev and his wife had adapted to Western life. They nonetheless found the difference between Europe and the United States to be "considerable," even though Europe had prepared them for the obvious differences in everyday life, and also for "the different approach to research, different understandings of research standards, a different way of writing up your results." Their young daughter, however, had a harder time. After a stressful year not being able to communicate at school in Switzerland, she began to speak Swiss German, only to find herself shortly thereafter in the United States. "She once again had to master a new language from scratch. We went through a rough period with her, because she was always stressed out."

The prehistory of Marina Bakutina's emigration to the United States began with visits her mother made there in the 1950s and the things she brought back at which Marina marveled, especially the View Master. Her own study trip to England in the 1970s and her working with foreigners as an Intourist guide broadened her horizons further. Then, in 1988, she took part in an exchange program that brought her to Reed College in Oregon. After her stint ended, the college offered her a contract to continue teaching there. "Unlike my mother, I was ready to stay, I wanted to stay, but I had to return to Moscow for my children," related Marina. With great difficulty she managed to renew her foreign passport and come back to America. "I arrived with two suitcases crammed with teaching materials to begin a new life. And I've never regretted this, not for a single day," she added. Marina's parents and her in-laws vehemently opposed her decision to give up her prestigious job in Moscow to return to the United States: "I didn't have a permanent job, I didn't have a place to live, I didn't have a thing. No bank account, nothing." Her husband, a physicist, wanted nothing to do with this "shady enterprise" and divorced her. Eventually her children joined her. In the meantime, Marina accepted a better-paying position as assistant professor at the University of Oklahoma. A year later a man she had met in Oregon, a doctor, proposed to her. They married, and she moved to Portland where she eventually took a position at Portland State. As an only child, she brought her aging parents to Portland, too, because of the terrible conditions older Russians without children or other support systems endure.

Boris Shtein left Russia because his son from Shtein's first marriage lived in America since 1987 and asked Boris to come. Moreover, the collapse of the Soviet Union, constitutional crisis of 1993 that led to violence, and growing anti-Semitism clinched the deal. The fear of pogroms in the early 1990s upset his second wife so much that, on occasion, they even spent the night with Russian friends. Although Shtein acknowledged that she overreacted, he concluded: "I now think that, if we were so afraid, then it was clear that the authorities were too weak to prevent something." His family and friends supported Shtein's decision to emigrate in 1994, for it had become "ordinary" back then. Friends at work saw him off without fear. Shtein and his family lived with his first wife in California for a month, arriving shortly before an earthquake rattled Northridge that year. They spent a week without electricity or water. But other than that the transition proved to be a smooth one. Knowing the ropes, his first wife helped him acquire a Social Security number, a driver's permit, and a license. His classmates who had preceded him offered advice and helped him craft a resume. A week after circulating it, he got called in for an interview—the only one—and an offer soon followed. He started off as a low-level engineer, but over the years rose to become a vice president of the company.

America differed from Shtein's expectations as it had for some of his classmates. "I imagined America to be like Europe, but with a higher living

This book put some Baby Boomers back in touch with each other. Boris Shtein (left) flew from California to Portland, Oregon, in March 2007 to see his former classmate Marina Bakutina and to let me interview him. *Courtesy of Donald J. Raleigh*

standard. But it's an altogether different country." He clarified, "It seems to me the people are different, the tempo and rhythm of life is different, there's greater motivation to work and correspondingly a person has far less time for himself." Shtein came to see this as normal and like it, yet he acknowledged that the social security network was greater in some other countries. Yet he, like others, finds the United States more democratic, especially at the workplace. Moreover, "I think that there are many, many very good people and naturally that's important to me."

"FOR SOME REASON IT'S MORE COMFORTABLE HERE"

None of the Baby Boomers regretted the decision to emigrate, undoubtedly because they can return to Russia whenever they like and because the country today is not the one they left. Yet some of them could not imagine going back for good. Tatyana Arzhanova insisted it was "too late" for her to return to Russia to live. She has kept her Russian passport and visits on occasion. "I haven't parted with my homeland for keeps. It's not my enemy," she explained. "But for some reason it's more comfortable here. I'm calmer here. I like it here." Similarly, despite the difficulty she had adjusting to life on Cyprus, Yevgeniya Ruditskaya made clear that "in all honesty, I really don't want to live in Russia, although it's unlikely that I'll stay in Cyprus. I don't know what the future will bring." Bakhyt Kenzheyev travels to Russia as often as possible, but he would not return there for good. "I can cite Heraclites here: 'it's not possible to step into the same river twice.'" He clarified: "The other reason is that, despite how often I traveled to Russia during the past twenty years, I lost the skills to live in Russia, especially since I didn't have any skills living in *contemporary* Russia. I don't know the culture. I know it from the perspective of a writer and of an observer, but to settle in, to earn money there and live there, you have to know it differently." Kenzheyev added, "It's very important to emphasize that the fact I don't want to return to Russia should not be at all understood to mean that I think Russia is worse. It's not." Tellingly, he acknowledged, "I'm made in such a way that I don't want to live in any one place." Today, Kenzheyev, a Canadian citizen, divides his time between Montreal, Moscow, and New York, where his current wife, a Soviet émigré, lives and works.

Marina Bakutina emphasized that she is the only one of her classmates to have married an American. She has lived in the United States for over twenty years and does not mix with the Russian émigré community. "I feel more at home here in America than I ever felt in Russia," she insisted. So do her children. When she asked them how they felt about her bringing them to the States at such a "tender" age, they told her: "There are more opportunities here to realize your potential. There are more possibilities for finding your own path."

Others told me that they would not discount the possibility of returning to Russia, but no one had plans to do so. Tatyana Artyomova said, "I see no obstacles for myself in returning." She tempered her remark: "But for now I'd like to remain here because things are much more interesting." She admitted that many of her Russian friends who visit cannot understand so many things that Artyomova takes for granted. "You have to live [here], you have to see [for yourself], you have to feel. These things are not found in books. You have to pay your taxes, you have to pay for your own X-ray, you have to pay your co-pay." Emigration is not for everyone, and she knows people who have had nervous breakdowns negotiating American realities. "But if circumstances allow, it's enormously interesting here," she concluded. Similarly, Viktor Alekseyev and his wife have not ruled out returning to Russia someday, "but we have no immediate plans to do so. We like it here." Explained Alekseyev: "My colleagues like me, and I feel good about my university, too." He got tenure. Apart from liking the United States, Alekseyev reminded me that pedagogical psychology in Russia is not in the best of straights and that the academic lifestyle is not what it used to be in Russia. Yelena Kolosova did not exclude the possibility of return-

School No. 20 classmates Tatyana Arzhanova (far left) and Bakhyt Kenzheyev (far right), both of whom immigrated to Canada, at Tatyana's "dacha" outside Montreal in March 2003. Kenzheyev's wife Lena is a lawyer in New York; Tatyana's husband Viktor is a freelance translator.
Courtesy of Donald J. Raleigh

ing to Russia for the benefit of the country in which she was born, but she would not remain there to live. She now looks upon many things from an American perspective, "although," as she put it, "I preserve the memory and some of the baggage of the country where I was born." That said, Russia has changed, and she no longer can imagine living in the new Moscow. "I no longer miss Moscow because it's a different city, although there's a connection of course with the roots from which I grew up."

In reply to my query about the possibility of returning to Russia to live, Aleksandr Trubnikov took a philosophical turn: "This is a really difficult question. Even the Lord is unable to predict what will happen in the future in Russia, in Israel, and in my family. I don't think there'll be a peaceful life any-where—take the example of the World Trade Center as confirmation." The com-plex—and its fate—left an indelible impression on him because he saw the twin towers about two weeks before the tragedy on September 11. Importantly, he does not feel cut off from Saratov: "At least the road back to Russia is not closed. I'm a Russian citizen."

"I'M HAPPY THAT THE PERIOD ENDED WITHOUT BLOODSHED"

Saratov's Galina Poldyaeva marveled: "It's interesting how quickly our society, a unified and ideologically unwavering one, went to pieces." The country's official belief system unraveled because the Soviet people had been changing all along and had become ready for perestroika, most unconsciously, but some con-sciously so. In fact, all of the strategies they had perfected over the years to realize the Soviet dream, to work the system, or to beat the system represent personal "acts of perestroika." Many of them recognized the structural issues that had given rise to stagnation and kept the USSR locked in a race to catch up with the West. Boris Shtein summed it up best: "Educated people increasingly saw eye to eye on things, understanding that the country was at a dead end." Indeed, since Stalin's death, the people of the Soviet Union became more and more aware of how the system functioned; their mastering the rules of the game contributed to the system's downfall.[15] During the Baby Boomers' lifetime, the Soviet Union, despite specific successes "remained an awkward industrial mon-ster," while the West prepared the basis for postindustrial society.[16] Large num-bers of Baby Boomers suspected this, and that is why most of them believed that perestroika had to happen, that something had to give. Still, as the oral testi-mony suggests, it might be less a matter of whether people felt perestroika was inevitable than of *when* they began to think that this was the case. By 1991 the population no longer viewed the system as legitimate; however, that does not mean they felt that way earlier. Regardless, they see the second half of Brezhnev's tenure as a turning point in their country's history and in the evolution of their own consciousness.

For instance, by the time perestroika began, Yevgeny Podolsky "had concluded that the very doctrine [of Soviet socialism] itself had turned out to be false. Although the goals were good ones, in reality everything was just the opposite, absolutely everything." Then perestroika, and especially glasnost, turned their worlds upside down. Irina Barysheva likened the Soviet people's condition to that of her neutered cat who is not allowed out on the street. "Everyone says to me, 'don't let him out. He'll like it immediately, and then it's all over.' And that's what probably happened to all of us. We're different. We no longer can live as we had before. Even if it's worse, but not like that!"

The Baby Boomers believed the Soviet economic model had lost its viability, but not the multinational Union of Soviet Socialist Republics. Remarkably few of them linked perestroika and the collapse of the Soviet Union to what Western scholarship has cast as the USSR's volatile nationalities problem. Tellingly, all but a handful regretted the breakup of the union, remembering the Soviet period, in this specific regard, positively. It is possible that such attitudes might have implications in the realm of foreign policy, since this position might make them critical of outside involvement in the CIS and beyond, and inclined to support government measures to restore some features of the former union, and of the country's superpower status.

In opening the USSR to the outside world, the Gorbachev revolution made travel abroad routine for many. Perestroika facilitated emigration, allowing a sizeable number of Baby Boomers to realize the Soviet dream outside the country. Seventeen members of the graduating class of Moscow's School No. 20 live abroad, all but three of them in the United States and Canada. Perhaps more than anything else, these figures demonstrate how late socialism lost the allegiance of its most educated and in many ways, privileged, class. They also reveal the structural and everyday disparities between Moscow and Saratov. Six of the graduates of Saratov's School No. 42 live outside Russia, three in the United States, two in Europe, and one in Israel. Three of them played their Jewish trump card to emigrate; two of them married foreigners; and another left to join her daughter who had married an American.

The Soviet Union and Russia between 1985 and the early 1990s was a society in disarray yet, despite the untold difficulties, the Boomers demonstrated extraordinary resiliency in negotiating the years of perestroika. Seeing the silver lining in the otherwise dark cloud of despair, Arkady Darchenko, for one, expressed gratitude: "I'm happy that the period ended without bloodshed. It could have turned out violent, because things had reached the limit. I have to say that, no matter what you think of Gorbachev, he's a great man because he was able to avoid bloodshed. There could have been a horrible civil war. Thank God things turned out otherwise." The Soviet experience constrained and enabled developments in the new Russia. Explained Darchenko: "The old ideas still linger. They're good ones, even wonderful ones, but they're the ideas of the 1960s generation and they're not for this life. For this reason we have to retool, too, and it's not easy. But what can you do about it? Life has sped past us. Our entire generation, and I speak for all of us, that is, for our graduating class, welcomed perestroika." Darchenko admitted, "It was really hard. For several years most of us barely got by. Yet we survived, and didn't lose anyone. We all found ourselves. But it's been hard for us. And our children grew up under different circumstances. For this reason they're so different."

7

SURVIVING RUSSIA'S
GREAT DEPRESSION

Saratov's Irina Vizgalova remarked, "Our people laugh even when things are bad. They love to tell jokes about themselves." Recalling the tumultuous 1990s, she shared a joke with me from the time: "'Two friends meet and one complains to the other, 'Everything's so awful. My apartment is small, my salary is low, and my mother-in-law and children live with us. I don't know what to do.' His friend says, 'I suggest you buy a goat.' 'Why?' 'Buy it, and then you'll find out how it helps.' Some time later they meet again. 'So, did you buy a goat?' 'I bought one and things got even worse. It's a real nightmare, with the children, the small apartment, and now a goat.' 'Now sell the goat,' his friend advised. A short time later they meet yet again. 'So, did you sell the goat?' 'I sold it, and things are so good now. We have so much room!'"

For many Russians, surviving the 1990s, a decade of painful economic transition, was like acquiring and then getting rid of a goat. Tens of millions of people associated poverty, loss of "confidence in tomorrow," and a deterioration of cradle-to-grave welfare with the introduction of a market economy, privatization of state-owned industries, and establishment of Russian-style democracy. The statistics say it all: already by 1994, 67 percent of the population had no savings or extra cash. That was the worst year, when the number of murders, suicides, and divorces reached extreme levels, and a million migrants from the Near Abroad poured into the country. As the decade progressed, Russian citizens feared impoverishment and unemployment: the Russian gross domestic product plunged by nearly 50 percent between 1990 and 1997. (The World Bank estimated the per capita GDP at the time to be $4,500.) Between 1992 and 1997 life expectancy for men fell from 67 to 57 years and for women from 76 to 70. Heart disease and stroke followed by accidents, suicide, and murder combined surpassed cancer as the leading causes of death among males. By decade's end, there were 3.7 million fewer children than in 1990, and the suicide rate was twice that of the 1980s. Abortion rates remained extremely high. Tuberculosis and diphtheria had returned. Russia's population declined, despite the influx of over 4 million refugees—Russians and others from the Near Abroad fleeing untenable and sometimes dangerous circumstances. Fearing crime, people had little reason to trust law enforcement agencies. Moreover, all political leaders during the decade depicted the opposition in apocalyptic language, warning that their opponents' policies would result in civil war or social disintegration.[1]

Remarkably, between 1994 and 1997 the number of pessimists in the country expecting bad things to happen declined by 2.5 times.[2] In addition, throughout the 1990s, the percentage of Russians looking favorably upon private property and the market economy stayed relatively fixed at 34 percent.[3] The Cold War generation and young people were among them, especially in Moscow, where, in 1999, 23.3 percent of the population lived below the subsistence minimum, the lowest in Russia (in contrast, 43 percent of the population of Saratov did, ranking the region twenty-seventh out of forty-two regions).[4] True, people had plenty of negative things to say about President Boris Yeltsin's impact on Russia when he announced his retirement on December 31, 1999. Even amid the despair, however, a sizeable minority of respondents polled focused on the positive, acknowledging the rise of democracy and political freedoms; the end of shortages, ration cards, and lines; the acceptance of private ownership; freedom to thrive for motivated people; the removal of Communists from power; and the end of the totalitarian regime and improvement of relations with the West.[5]

There were things to be thankful for. After the breakup of the USSR, about three-fourths of the industrial enterprises, organizations, and institutions remained in Russia. The empty shelves and long lines of 1990–91, and the temporary vanishing of items from the Russian market, gave way to shelves aching with goods as consumers learned how and what to buy, and the state learned how to regulate. Freedom of speech and conscience were real. The state no longer persecuted religion and people could travel abroad and earn money without limits. Many people grew accustomed to the overblown language of Russian politics and did not buy into the belief that things were so disastrous and therefore no longer feared the future.[6] Belligerent Russian nationalism did not become the country's political ideology, despite the fact that the country's leaders increasingly blamed the West, and America in particular, for Russia's troubles.[7] Mass burn out and disillusionment with politics, however, had bred political apathy.

Russia in the 1990s was thus a country in disarray but also a country in the making. This transition period fashioned people's fates as they focused on the necessities of economic survival. How did the transition of the 1990s impact the Baby Boomers? How do they remember and assess the period? How do their views as a cohort correspond to those of their countrymen? How do they evaluate the differences between their generation and that of their children?

"GOD DEALS US ONLY THOSE CARDS WE'RE CAPABLE OF HANDLING"

The painful transition of the 1990s gave rise to conflicting trends that complicated and worsened people's lives in some ways, while enhancing them in others. On the one hand, during that decade, the Yeltsin government managed to prevent massive unemployment, but not the erosion of real pay, government subsidies and pensions, or the loss of personal bank accounts. All of this drastically cut buying power. The quality of preschool education declined, arguably of education in general, and there were fewer opportunities for children's leisure. On the other hand, real trade unions functioned and workers had the freedom to strike and take collective action. The market economy ended consumer deficits and led to a growth in consumption of industrial and everyday technology, greater access to cars and telephones, the ready availability of cultural and political information, the freedom to travel abroad, and the appearance of new free time and leisure activities. The gap between (low) legal pay and the realities of life that required money inspired an astonishing system of hidden salaries located in a shadow economy and criminal action, as people took on work outside their main job, or received illegal pay at their place of employment. Employers, including the government, contributed to these survival strategies by holding up payment of wages, pensions, and welfare, in effect creating no-interest loans. This phenomenon became more widespread from 1996 through 2000, with the fewest people receiving their salaries on time in 1998.[8]

Survival skills learned during the Soviet era helped people navigate the 1990s. Indeed, economist Alena Ledeneva argued that, instead of focusing on what does not work in Russia, we might look at what does. Citing the oft-repeated remark heard in Russia that the imperfection of our laws is compensated for by their nonobservance, she concluded that everyday reliance on unwritten rules represented the result not only of the inefficiency of formal rules and lack of mechanisms for enforcing them but also people's lack of respect for formal rules. As long as the battle between the Soviet past and market-oriented future continues, the demand for unwritten rules will remain a defining feature of economic life.[9]

During the decade, the family also helped people cope with the changes bombarding them.[10] Generally speaking, Soviet "marital quality" did not prove to be highly related to the economic status of families as is often the case in the United States. Instead, educational differences between spouses proved more important in causing difficulties.[11] Yet, several Baby Boomers linked the dissolution of their marriages to the terrible economic situation in the early 1990s, although it is possible that they would have ended regardless the special circumstances. For instance, Olga Kamayurova related that "perestroika had begun and I grew estranged from my husband. The situation at home was strained and we were in awful economic straits. I was depressed. I searched for a way to overcome it." They divorced. Marina Bakutina's first marriage ended when she decided to stay in the United States and bring her children there to live. Her husband could not reconcile himself to her "embarking upon adventures."

Some Baby Boomers, particularly those employed in academic and research institutes, spoke of how, in the new environment, professional status declined as the allure of making money replaced it. "A sharp decline in the prestige of our profession took place," remembered Aleksandr Konstantinov. "This was deeply felt, and it, of course, fundamentally affected my life and the lives of many whom I know." Konstantinov realized how his career would have unfolded if Soviet power had survived. "Then everything fell apart, and people were left to their own devices. There was a loss of valuable reference points." He told me how his younger half- brother insulted their father by calling him a "miserable little professor." Concluded Konstantinov: "Such cheap material interests strongly affected our lives and we ended up in an awful situation. At times we swam and swam toward shore only to see it recede still further, or else we had to start out on our own, not knowing how accurate our navigational equipment was. This perhaps was the strongest sensation."

Many Baby Boomers switched jobs to make ends meet, lost jobs, changed professions, or found ways to supplement their income. Natalya P. gave up her position teaching English at the Pedagogical University in Saratov to take a position at the Police Academy, despite the drop in prestige. Her explanation: "Well, the pay was a lot higher there than what I had been receiving." Lyubov Raitman ended her teaching career at Moscow University when she accepted a job as a secretary. "I had to. The salary they offered me was fifty times greater than what I had been earning. Fifty times! What choice did I have? I probably regret that I was forced to do this. But I didn't regret that, all of a sudden, I had money and possibilities. Within several years," she added, "I understood what a watershed this had been. That is, it was as if my entire life before had been severed." Reiterating that she took on this, and then other jobs "only for the money," she underscored that what happened to her was "not the worst possibility."

Arkady Darchenko changed jobs owing to perestroika, recalling "in connection with perestroika, the institute where I worked practically shut down. Well, it's open, but you can't work there, because they don't pay a thing. I changed my profession in 1995 and became a professional computer programmer, and English, well, I don't think any explanation of its importance is necessary." Darchenko admitted how hard it was for him to let go of his previous job at an institute that manufactured measuring equipment. "I worked there for twenty-five years, from an entry-level engineer to positions of authority. Even though I earn money elsewhere, I now sometimes drop in there once a week, purely out of professional interest, and do what I formerly did," he acknowledged. A professor of (Marxist) economics, Natalya Pronina expressed gratitude for the home economics course required at school that taught girls how to sew: "Later, when we lived through some rough times, during so-called perestroika, I even earned some money on the side sewing, and I am not at all ashamed of this," she told me.

Aleksandr Kutin identified a real dilemma: people were now free to work as they pleased, but the economic downturn often made it impossible to strike out on one's

To her surprise, Natalya P. found fulfillment when she gave up her teaching position in the 1990s at the Saratov Pedagogical Institute for a better paying one at the less prestigious Police Academy. "They didn't have a department, and I started one up from scratch. Everything that exists there now was created under my leadership," she explained. *Courtesy of Natalya P.*

own. Moreover, he added, "I'm not used to working like that. Not all of us are able to set up our own business. I, for one, can't, but some members of my age cohort can and do so successfully, but there aren't many." The experience took one of them, Vladimir Nemchenko to new heights—and depths, as a result of which he likened himself to the philosopher Diogenes, one of the founders of Cynic philosophy. Nemchenko told me, "It was only recently that I woke up, because earlier I harbored thoughts about suicide." He had made a fortune during the privatization of state industries that gave the advantage to insider trading, which he claimed earned him tens of million of dollars. Although he managed to lose it just as easily as he had made it, he was now slowly recovering financially. "I sold two apartments and am living off the money. At the moment I'm not working and decided to gather all of the documentation and try to sue to get my money back. Maybe something will come of this," he posited. Proud that he works for himself and not for others, Nemchenko plans to continue in the world of "business" but at a "less grandiose" level.

A good number of respondents explained how deeply ingrained Soviet attitudes and experiences made it difficult for them to adapt to the new circumstances. Describing the Soviet system of wages, bonuses, and other perks to which he had become accustomed, airplane engineer Vyacheslav Starik concluded that "I never formulated a tie between money and work." Finding it hard to learn how to "work for money," he recalled that, in the old days, he "worked as much as I could, because it was interesting to me." English teacher Anna Lyovina maintained that the Soviet system's leveling process had given rise to a consumerist attitude toward the government. "The government has to decide everything for us, has to provide for everyone. Even if it's only a bit, but it has to give everyone something," she opined. Contesting the Soviet propaganda mantra that there was no unemployment in the Soviet Union, she explained, "There was hidden unemployment especially at the numerous research institutes. At work women sat and knitted or went shopping, and the men walked around and smoked or discussed soccer. There was nothing to do." She blamed this on the overproduction of specialists. "For this reason I believe that seventy years of Soviet power had a pernicious effect on people's attitudes. It created a consumerist attitude toward the government that the government owes us something. Now people are lost when they have to make decisions for themselves."

The emergence of fifteen independent states from the ruins of the former Soviet empire also complicated life for the Cold War generation. As Natalya Yanichkina affirmed, "To be honest, a lot of problems appeared. Before, we lived in a single country, and keep in mind that my husband is from Ukraine. During those years before strict customs were set up we could still manage to visit. When his mother died two years ago the telegram served as our so-called visa to let us enter. But a lot of extortion goes on. They stamp your documents in the wrong place and you have to bribe." Yanichkina also complained about the frustrations she and her husband felt when they completed the voluminous paperwork necessary to bring her husband's sister, in dire need of medical care, to Saratov for treatment. "She needed an operation, so we had to bring her here. But all of those customs and passport and visa controls have separated people. Before we could travel anywhere within the USSR. Not now." Lyubov Kovalyova's personal experience illustrates Yanichkina's point. Kovalyova met her second husband, from Minsk, when the two of them were on work assignments in Hungary. "He had his career and work, and I had mine. Besides, I had a young daughter who was about ten at the time. Moreover, my mother was sick and alone. Therefore, I didn't move there, and somehow it wasn't that hard on us," she explained. A train ticket to Minsk at the time cost only 8 rubles, and an airline ticket, 12 rubles, so they took turns visiting each other. "Everything was wonderful until the awful inflation begun, until Belarus became independent, and until they began to use their own currency," Kovalyova related. "As a result, perestroika took itself out on our family, which fell apart. It's a personal tragedy for me. My husband said the same thing. For us, perestroika turned out sadly."

The wrenching changes associated with the 1990s also corresponded with some momentous life passages. Natalya P. remembered, "First, my father died in 1990. It was a great loss for me. He's absolutely irreplaceable. Then I had other things to think about as my son grew up. A child is a big responsibility. We have closer relations [than Americans do], but they breathe down our necks. They live with us for a long time. This causes problems." Natalya appreciated that wisdom often comes with age—and with hard times. Getting sick in the early 1990s transformed her outlook on life: "I no longer get all caught up in little things. I now know what the most important things in life are. Therefore, it actually became easier for me to live after I got sick, because I found out the true value of life and death. My disposition, my attitude toward life, changed altogether and I'm much happier. What a paradox!" She concluded, "They say that God deals us only those cards we're capable of handling. I'm so happy, knock on wood, that I'm still alive, that I can live and enjoy life, and not sweat the small stuff."

Several Saratov Baby Boomers called attention to an ironic consequence of the economic dislocation of the 1990s regarding the local environment. Both under Soviet power and afterward there was a lot of talk about environmental degradation, but no money to do anything about it. Many Saratovites recalled drinking from the Volga as children, but things changed by the time they reached adulthood. Admitting there had been a problem, Olga Gorelik related that "we nevertheless lived at the dacha, swam in the river, and boated." She acknowledged, however, that guests from Yugoslavia "were afraid to swim." Then came perestroika, explained Aleksandr Virich: "The ecological situation has improved ten or fifteen times for one reason—the majority of military production has stopped. Therefore, there's no polluting. Fish have reappeared and the Volga's become cleaner." Arkady Darchenko concurred: "I can't say that everything's fine now, but the Volga is much, much cleaner because they shut

Like many other Saratovites, Pyotor Krasilnikov noticed an improvement in the Volga's cleanliness—and a willingness to eat its bounty—already in 1994 after the closing of many factories that polluted the river. But no one observed that the river is as clean as he or she remembered it as children. *Courtesy of Pyotor Krasilnikov*

down many of the unproductive [military] factories. What was in effect an economic misfortune was not altogether a bad thing. The Volga became cleaner. The air became cleaner. It had been absolutely disgusting before, but we accepted all this as part of our overall, how shall I put it, standard of living."

"MY HEART, MY SOUL, THAT'S MY CHURCH"

To deal with the turmoil in their lives in the 1990s, the Baby Boomers resorted to time-honored coping mechanisms and leisure activities, likewise taking advantage of the circumstances to explore new ones. Market conditions, for instance, changed the country's reading habits, particularly for this generation of readers. Library use had fallen off significantly by 1991, largely because readers could now readily obtain things they wanted to read on their own. If, during perestroika, Russian readers devoured belletristic and literature exposing the falsifications in official Soviet histories, the most popular book of the early 1990s was *Gone with the Wind*. Russian classics remained in demand, but readers by 2001 also consumed in record numbers detective novels, love stories, adventure books, satire, and humor. Readers under twenty-five expressed less interest in every genre except, to the chagrin of their elders, erotica.[12]

Historically a problem in Russian culture and society, alcohol during the strenuous 1990s served as a dangerous balm for many addicted to the substance. The production and sale of often contaminated spirits that began during Gorbachev's campaign to curb excessive drinking complicated the situation. One Saratov Baby Boomer drank himself to death, and another's disease had progressed so far that I was asked to spare him the indignity of an interview. The transition did not necessarily bring this about, since alcoholism is a progressive illness; however, statistics document alcohol's debilitating effect on the population at this time, owing to the decade's unusual stresses, contributing to declining male life expectancy. Afflicted with alcoholism and a nervous disorder, Vladimir Sidelnikov offered a telling example of how perestroika affected his disease and Sidelnikov materially. His mother had left him a considerable inheritance by Soviet standards, "enough to buy three Zhigulis [cars]," he explained. But the value of the amount evaporated with the hopes he had for living better. "They compensated me recently by giving me ten thousand rubles [roughly $400] in today's money. How much is that? See the television over there? It cost nine thousand rubles. So, I turned from a rich man into a poor one. But I'm an optimist. I believe that everything will be okay." Indeed, Sidelnikov saw himself as "a darling of fate," but that outlook came from his experiencing life's downside, first, when he was expelled from Finland as a student and, again, in 1992, when he was locked up in a mental hospital. "In 1992 they gave me a long-lasting injection, after which I felt terrible for years. Very terrible, and I didn't know what world I lived in. But then the shot wore off." He credited his wife, Lyuba, with helping him afterward. "By the way, she thought back then that I wouldn't come out of it after the shot. But God let me live. And now I have to fulfill some kind of mission in this world. I believe that each person comes into this world with a mission. When I fulfill mine, I'll die."

Given the strong school-age bonds they cherished, many members of the Cold War generation continued to rely on each other for help. Especially close, the members of Class B of Saratov's School No. 42 shared memories of coming to each other's assistance during the challenging decade. Irina Barysheva, for example, turned to a classmate to determine the "biography" of a car she considered purchasing. "He clarified everything literally within a few minutes and called me back. He said, 'Don't risk it! It has a checkered past.'" She likewise remembered how her classmate turned to Olga Kamayurova when her son was dying of lung cancer. "She did everything she could in her hospital. She couldn't save him, but she relieved his pain." Not one for nostalgia, Olga Kamayurova had no desire to meet with her classmates until the 1990s. "I'm [now] drawn to them the same way I am to my relatives. You know, I look at them and I think, my heavens, we've known each other for almost fifty years. They're all my brothers and sisters." Olga Martynkina recalled consulting with a classmate regarding her son's language skills in English. She also singled out Viktor D., with whom she shared a desk at school. Two years before I interviewed her, she—a pianist—fell during an ice storm on New Year's Eve and shattered her arm. Panic-stricken, she asked to be taken to his emergency room. "I said to him, 'Vitya, save me.' And my classmate Vitya found room for me and stayed there himself to help," she disclosed. "It was already evening. He fussed with me for four hours, until 10:00 P.M., and left two doctors to look out for me. He saved my arm."

But time and life's challenges weakened these bonds for many of the cohort, especially in Moscow. As Leonid Volodarsky recapped, "We got together for a while and saw our friends from school, but then, life is life. People dispersed, new friends appeared. Yet there are people from school with whom I still associate." Georgy Godzhello regretted that he has not kept in touch with his classmates except for an occasional reunion at school. Many of his closest friends have emigrated. Tatyana Luchnikova, who moved to Moscow in ninth grade, has not maintained ties with her classmates. "We went our separate ways and everyone was busy with their own lives," she stated.

Experiencing a robust revival at this time, religion also helped some people cope with the decade of promise and turmoil. The cessation of state repression of religion and tough economic straits of the 1990s brought about a religious revival as the Russian Orthodox Church reclaimed its role as a state religion with new freedoms, creating mostly favorable conditions for people to practice alternative faiths as well. Valentin Ulyakhin grew up in a home in which religion was respected and practiced. His personal conversion began with the death of his father in 1974. After his mother died in 1982 he became a "conscious believer." "When you see your relatives lying in their coffins you understand that eternity exists," he explained. Ulyakhin believed

Members of the Saratov B Class meet at least yearly. I interviewed all of those gathered here in 2003, except for Natalya Khamidulina (center), who hosted this get-together in her Saratov apartment, and two others who married foreigners and now reside in Germany and the Netherlands. *Courtesy of Arkady Darchenko*

that World War II, which brought about a religious restoration the state had to embrace, postponed the total destruction of religion in Russia until perestroika, by which time communism was exhausted. After celebration of the thousandth anniversary of Christianity in Russia in 1988, churches and seminaries reopened. In 1991 Ulyakhin enrolled in St. Tikhon Seminary and became an Orthodox priest.

Like so many others, Tatyana Luchnikova got baptized in the 1990s. "I made my own choice and got baptized along with my son. No one forced me. I got there only through suffering." So did Vladimir Sidelnikov, for whom religion played no role in his life until he got baptized at age thirty-nine, "after which life has been altogether different. I understood there's a God and that God will help me. When I came to believe in God, I became an altogether different person," he related. This occurred in 1989, following a difficult stint in a hospital—necessary for him to be recognized as an invalid and to receive government welfare. Released on August 3, 1989, he was baptized on August 5, and met his future wife Lyuba the next day. Elaborated Sidelnikov, "The more I believed in God, the more time I spent with Lyuba and her relatives, the less I drank. And then I stopped altogether." He had been sober for four years when I interviewed him in 2008.

For some Baby Boomers getting baptized in the 1990s began a spiritual journey away from Orthodoxy. Tatyana Luchnikova became a Buddhist while living in New York after meeting a young man in a dentist's office. She took him up on an invitation to visit his Buddhist group: "I showed up, found it interesting, and liked it. And I began to read. I really like this religion because it doesn't weigh upon your mind the way Orthodoxy does. It's more of a philosophy of life than a religion, an attitude." When a teacher asked her whether she had renounced Orthodoxy, she replied, "My God, I said, I haven't renounced anything. What's with the big words? What's with the drama? One does not negate the other." Underscoring the violence and hypocrisy she found in organized religion, she concluded, "My heart, my soul, that's my church, it's all within me. What you reap, you sow." Olga Kamayurova explained how perestroika led her to Osho, to Bhagwan Shree Rajneesh, an Indian mystic,* and to a life of spirituality. Because of economic difficulties that strained her marriage to the breaking point, she became depressed. Searching for a way to overcome it, she discovered Osho. "In the first book I read of Osho's, I came across his understanding of Orthodoxy, of Christianity. It's so odd that Christianity doesn't appeal to me. After all, we live in a Christian country and I should be drawn to that religion, but they altered it basically for the needs of the priests," she stated. "It frightens people, it oppresses them. It's such a strict religion—standing in churches for hours during a service, while they threaten you with hell and terrible punishments. Osho interprets Christianity not as something radiantly joyous but as something that's been radically changed by the clergy," Kamayurova concluded.

Another Baby Boomer who asked to remain unnamed grew up an atheist and did not believe in anything; however, "in 1991 or so we got baptized together. I, my son, then my sister and her son. Perestroika had begun and people flocked to religion, even Party leaders," she emphasized. "There was a flood of positive feelings toward religion and the church. But later I became very negative toward this. My son too." She experimented with transcendental meditation, "but it wasn't enough. I abandoned it, perhaps because I wasn't very good at it. Yet I didn't like the tendency toward making it a business," she clarified. Then astrology captivated her. She studied it seriously, obtaining a "bachelor's" degree in it from the St. Petersburg Academy of Astrology. Practicing for fourteen years when I met her, she exclaimed, "Astrology is my love!" Yet a year and a half before I interviewed her, she also embraced Scientology. "I don't want people to know about this," she explained, "because in Russia people are very critical of Scientology. The patriarch sees it as an irreconcilable enemy." She elaborated: "I'm hostile toward religion. You can't study astrology, you can't study meditation, you can't study Scientology. What's left? As far as I understand things it's to go to church with your money." This handful of testimonials gives some credence

---

* Bhagwan Shree Rajneesh—Osho—was born Rajneesh Chandra Mohan in central India. See ch. 5, p 246.

to the argument of a Russian writer who maintains that Russian society today remains unreligious, because contemporary Orthodoxy does not touch people's hearts, leaving them indifferent.[13]

"PEOPLE ARE FULFILLING THEMSELVES"

A psychological dimension to the transition also weighed on people's psyches and shaped their attitudes. Recalling her carefree childhood, Lyubov Kovalyova insisted, "We lived well back then. I felt that I was born in a large, wonderful, highly regarded country. Perhaps they inculcated this in me during my childhood, but that's how I felt. I personally never experienced any oppression or persecution." Similarly, Natalya Pronina underscored, "It seems to me that, at present, we lack an aim and purpose. If before we had a goal, communism, even if it was an unobtainable one, we at least had a purpose. However, there's none now." Many Baby Boomers, and people throughout Russia for that matter, would agree with Leonid Volodarsky: "I believe our generation had it really tough, because we lived through a revolution. We lived peacefully under Soviet power. Lots of negative things have been said about Soviet power, and they're correct. But there also were many things that were good under Soviet power, and there's no denying that." Volodarsky underscored stability, "which is very important for the overwhelming majority of people." The switch from Soviet-style stability to "robber baron capitalism and not real capitalism" took its toll.

Indeed, some Baby Boomers waxed nostalgic about the comparative low crime rate in the Soviet days, seeing this as another benefit of the former system. But back in the Soviet period, people did not know how much crime actually existed in society. I asked criminal investigator Gennady Ivanov why such information was kept secret. His answer speaks volumes about the cultural differences that help sustain a closed society—and constrain it after it opens: "I'm not sure that all of those headlines that we have today are necessary. The papers describe in detail how a crime was committed and who the victim was. Why? Who needs this?" He added, "There's also a difference in the number of murders today and back then. It's about five times higher. Why tell people that there were a 100 and now they're more than 500? Will this affect the crime rate? Why frighten people so that they're afraid of every shadow they see? What's the sense of telling people that there's a murderer on the loose? It doesn't affect you in the least," he insisted. "Therefore, I'd say it wasn't only that we had less crime back then. It played an altogether different role."

Despite the Baby Boomers' real concerns and even disgruntlement, the vast majority of them—like most members of the highly educated urban intelligentsia of their age cohort elsewhere in Russia—felt that the changes of the 1990s and beyond were worth it, thereby passing strong judgment on the Soviet era. They likewise understood the enormity of the task Russia faced transitioning to a market economy. Explained Aleksandr Virich: "The very first economist, Moses, wandered for forty years. What do you want to achieve in ten? Especially with so much opposition from the Communists in the Duma?" Natalya P. also recognized the difficulty Boris Yeltsin had trying to pick up where Gorbachev had left off, maintaining "people remained the same as before, the country remained the same. It's possible to destroy things in a short time, but to change things fundamentally, time is needed." According to Arkady Darchenko, "We'll never have the order that they have, say, in Germany. We're simply different. In many ways, Americans are more like us. In lifestyle, for instance." That said, Darchenko appreciated an important difference, commenting on the fact that, in Russia, some people used the entranceways to buildings to relieve themselves. "It's basically a matter of the level of cultural development. We need several generations for that. The general level is awful. I believe that change will come, but not tomorrow."

Sofiya Vinogradova did not grasp why perestroika took place, but believed "it's a good thing it occurred. A very good thing. Even though you now have to hold down three jobs to make ends meet, whereas before you could get by on one." True, Vinogradova expressed nostalgia about her carefree childhood, but she liked what was better today. "The fact that you can go out and in five minutes lay the table, the fact that you can buy anything you want if you have the money. That you can buy clothes, travel wherever you like, invite whomever you like to visit, and that you and I can now speak with each other. This is all very good. That's my opinion. And that you can work, and that many doors have opened." The result? "People are fulfilling themselves. I know such people. They're realizing themselves; doors opened for them that they never expected. Before they couldn't work where they wanted because of their nationality or else simply didn't imagine that they could do so. Simply put, new horizons have appeared." She especially appreciated the fact "that it's possible to travel, to see other things, other countries, different cultures, indescribable sites. To speak with people in person, not on the telephone. To accept someone's invitation to come and visit. This was impossible before. Even for my parents. No one could. Even people who didn't emigrate, but worked abroad, couldn't invite their parents to visit."[14]

Some devout Communists also had a change of heart. Bakhyt Kenzheyev's father, for instance, has visited him twice in Canada. "He gradually began to acknowledge that things weren't so good after all" in the USSR. Kenzheyev valued the difficulty of such self-reflection, insisting we have no right to judge the views of earlier Soviet generations. Larisa Petrova, too, acknowledged the positive changes that have come to Russia as a result of the country's switch to a market economy. "But the main thing that dissatisfies me today," she injected, "is my salary. I work from morning until night."

People's optimism continued to rise with the economic stabilization setting in after 1998. Speaking in 2003, Irina Vizgalova remarked, "Now things are a bit better. Now many enterprises are reemerging, there's a lot of new construction going on, and natural gas is being exported."

THE PRESIDENCY OF BORIS YELTSIN

In August 1991 the world watched as Boris Nikolayevich Yeltsin, standing atop a tank in front of the Russian parliament, denounced the attempt by Communist hard-liners to remove Gorbachev from power and to prevent the signing of the new union treaty that would have transformed the USSR into a (voluntary) smaller Union of Sovereign States. Calling for a general strike, Yeltsin issued an appeal to the citizens of Russia to stand firm against the conspirators. This was his finest moment. By the time the coup failed at week's end, Yeltsin had eclipsed Gorbachev as the most influential political leader in the country, becoming, when the USSR ceased to exist in December 1991, independent Russia's first president; he served from 1991 until December 31, 1999. Yeltsin's biographer Timothy Colton acknowledges Yeltsin's flaws, but considers him a hero in history, a democratizer, who commands respect and even sympathy.[15] Yet the most popular Russian leader during the early 1990s ended his decade in power in disgrace at home.

Yeltsin was born in 1931 in the village of Butka in Sverdlovsk (now Yekaterinburg) oblast into a modest family that knew repression firsthand: his father Nikolai, convicted of anti-Soviet agitation, spent a three-year stint in the Gulag, after which he labored as a construction worker. His mother Klavdiya worked as a seamstress. Biographical accounts of Yeltsin mention the fact that, as a youth, he lost the thumb and index finger of his left hand while trying to disassemble a hand grenade. The point: already as a teen, Yeltsin took risks. In 1955 he graduated from the Ural State Technical University in Sverdlovsk, where he majored in construction. Rising through the ranks of the local construction industry, he in time assumed a position of power and authority over this sector of Sverdlovsk oblast. He joined the CPSU in 1961—the year Khrushchev promised to achieve communism by 1980—and in 1976 became head of the Sverdlovsk Oblast Communist Party Committee.

Gorbachev invited Yeltsin to Moscow in 1985, and soon thereafter he became first secretary of Moscow's Communist Party Committee, a position akin to mayor, and was elected a candidate member of the Politburo. Exposing the perks enjoyed by the Party *nomenklatura*, Yeltsin quickly won over the support of Muscovites by rubbing shoulders with them on public transportation, making surprise visits to stores and enterprises, and wrestling to preserve the city's architectural treasures. Anxious, Yeltsin soon blasted the pace of perestroika and its architects—including Gorbachev and the senior Party leadership. That October, Yeltsin reiterated his disappointment with the pace of reform, lashed out at conservative Politburo member Ligachev, and decried the emerging cult of Gorbachev. Angered by Yeltsin's remarks, Gorbachev accepted Yeltsin's resignation and removed him from the Politburo.

In March 1989 elections to the USSR Congress of People's Deputies, the first contested elections in Russia since 1917, created advantageous conditions for Yeltsin's political comeback. Winning 90 percent of the vote in Moscow, Yeltsin got appointed to the new Supreme Soviet. Elected to the Russian (as opposed to the Soviet, or national) Congress of People's Deputies in March 1990, Yeltsin became chair of the Russian Supreme Soviet. In July he demonstrably resigned from the Communist Party. The next summer, the citizens of Russia elected him the first president of the Russian republic (the largest and most important of the fifteen Soviet republics) and thus, unlike Gorbachev who had been chosen president of the USSR by the Congress of People's Deputies and not by popular vote, Yeltsin claimed that he had greater legitimacy. The public enmity between the two leaders intensified as Yeltsin demanded Gorbachev's resignation. This was but one of the events leading to the attempt by hard-liners to remove Gorbachev from power and to prevent the signing of the new union treaty on August 20, 1991.

As president, Yeltsin proved more successful at preventing a Communist restoration and at integrating Russia into the global economy than at creating a stable institutional foundation to underpin the freedoms gained at that time. Yet he had also faced the Sisyphean tasks of establishing a new democratic political order, introducing a market economy, and negotiating a new international position for a now defunct superpower. Given the confluence of circumstances, Yeltsin put off forming a political party, writing a new constitution, and electing a new parliament in order to introduce radical economic reform. Prime Minister Yegor Gaidar, a proponent of shock therapy designed to move Russia as quickly as possible to a market economy, freed most prices on January 1, 1992, while democratic reformer Anatoly Chubais drafted a program to privatize state-owned enterprises. Feeding crime and corruption, these policies pushed Russia to the brink of economic collapse and provoked widespread criticism, even from Vice President Aleksander Rutskoi and the speaker of parliament Ruslan Khasbulatov.[16] Most people were simply not prepared for so sharp a change in their economic lives. Less than a quarter of the population—mostly the young and middle aged with decent incomes—maintained their optimism, compared with 60 percent of the population who saw the situation as catastrophic. People feared social conflict and civil war.[17]

The mounting rift between Yeltsin and the Soviet-era Supreme Soviet over economic reform climaxed in the fall of 1993 when Yeltsin sought to dissolve parliament and hold new elections. The opposition's refusal to submit to Yeltsin's demands prompted him to storm the Russian White House, where parliament met, resulting in more than one hundred deaths. At the time, half the population believed the use of force had been necessary, a figure that inched up to 52.8 percent for the Baby Boomer age cohort and shot up to 62.1 percent for young people under thirty.[18] The showdown sped up ratification of a new super-presidential constitution, which governed parliamentary elections in December.

By then, at least thirteen parties had registered in Russia, including the Communist Party of the Russian Federation (CPRF), successor to the CPSU, led by Gennady Zyuganov, and the Liberal Democratic Party of ultranationalist Vladimir Zhirinovsky, which was neither liberal nor democratic. The architect of Yeltsin's economic policies, Yegor Gaidar and his market-oriented Democratic Choice of Russia won only 15.5 percent of the votes, while the Liberal Democratic Party captured 22.9 percent and the CPRF 12.4 percent.

To accommodate the nationalist–Communist coalition in parliament, Yeltsin eased up on the pace of market reform. Privatization, however, entered its second round, giving rise to a class of rich businessmen, as well as to a cohort of entrepreneurs who had accumulated massive fortunes, soon to be known as the oligarchs, who acquired enormous holdings through insider trading and therefore backed Yeltsin. The resulting social inequality and effrontery of the new rich fed disillusionment with market economics and the democratic political system. Retirees looked back upon the Soviet days with nostalgia.[19] By this point roughly two-thirds of the population felt shame for the position in which Russia found itself, saw the situation as intolerable, and feared growing crime and disorder.[20] Roughly 88 percent of the population believed people needed to respect law and order. Seventy percent felt that Russia needed a strong leader.[21]

By the time Yeltsin ran for reelection in June 1996, his popularity ratings had plunged into the single digits. Moreover, his declining health and excessive drinking, about which there had been much gossip and public discussion since the early days of perestroika, took their toll. Poking fun at his slurred speeches and swollen countenance, popular jokes likened him to a second Brezhnev. The oligarchs and Western supporters funded the election campaign, which presented Yeltsin as liberator of the new Russia and his chief opponent, Zyuganov, as a return to Stalinism. Yet Yeltsin had to face Zyuganov in a second, run-off election, before which he suffered a massive heart attack. Only after Yeltsin won the run-off did news of his fragile health reach the public. Afterward, he underwent quintuple bypass surgery with a long recovery during which his daughter and Chubais ran the country. Seen as an emerging epithet for the Yeltsin era, already in 1997, 40 percent of those polled preferred living in Brezhnev's Russia. People believed the country was mired in dire crisis and that even the economic chaos had reached catastrophic dimensions.[22]

Marked by growing crime and corruption, a constant turnover in the office of prime minister, a troubled economy, and the default of the Russian ruble in 1998, which triggered what fortunately proved to be only a short-lived setback, Yeltsin's second term did nothing to restore his popularity. The monthly salary of the humanities intelligentsia plummeted from $354 to $158, and white-collar workers from $317 to $114. Favoring Yeltsin's forced retirement, the population backed returning strategic industries such as oil, gas, and energy to the state, restoring a state monopoly on alcohol and cigarettes, reinstating government control on prices, and even the state's taking control of large industries. People feared for their children's future. They feared being without resources to survive. They feared getting sick and being without medical care. They feared unemployment. They feared crime.[23] Yeltsin's poor health prompted him to secure his legacy by guaranteeing a successor that would grant Yeltsin and his family immunity. That man proved to be a relatively unknown ex-KGB agent, Vladimir Putin, whom Yeltsin appointed prime minister in 1999. Astonishing the world, Yeltsin resigned on New Year's Eve 1999, announcing that he had done the best he could in leading the country. He was succeeded by Prime Minister Putin, about whom we will hear more later.

"PERIODS OF GREAT CHANGE ARE ALWAYS ACCOMPANIED BY A DOWNSIDE"

Irina Garzanova explained that, born on February 1, Yeltsin was an Aquarius: "It was demanded of Yeltsin to destroy; he was unable to build." She voiced gratitude, however, that Yeltsin won his second term in 1996, "because there was a very real threat of a Communist restoration. We were anxious for Yeltsin to stay in power, because the Communists would have been a step back." In 1996 Yeltsin ran against Zyuganov, head of the Communist Party of the Russian Federation. Although Garzanova had sympathized with the Communists earlier, she declared Zyuganov a "terrible man. I saw his horoscope. He's an awful man." Like many, she backed Yeltsin, believing the alternatives were worse.

Valentin Ulyakhin praised Yeltsin because Ulyakhin became a priest while Yeltsin ruled Russia. "I pray for his health," said Father Valentin. "Because under Gorbachev I couldn't have become a priest. The church's rebirth began for real only under Boris Nikolayevich." Yet Natalya Pronina, for one, maintained that Yeltsin promoted the revival of religiosity as an insincere effort to win popular appeal. Claimed Pronina, Yeltsin "exerted a negative influence on the intelligentsia when he, a Party functionary, suddenly appeared in church and crossed himself. It's deceitful! I don't think that he's a true believer. You can call it what you like, but it's insincere. If this is insincere, how can you believe in other things he says or does?" Those applauding the religious revival, however, did not care what drove Yeltsin to back the church.

Natalya Yanichkina concurred that Yeltsin played a positive role: "I have to agree with Yeltsin that we should take only as much freedom as we're capable of handling. They overstrained themselves a bit. Today's politics are a consequence of what happened back then. But man, after all, descended from the apes, right? He can't learn from others' mistakes, and must experience everything himself. That's what all the fuss is about." She continued, "I was thankful to Gorbachev and Yeltsin. I like Gorbachev a great deal. I like Yeltsin too because, for the most part, I think that a lot was gained during this period." Irina Barysheva chortled, "How we rooted for Yeltsin." So did her mother. In fact, during his first presidential election, her mother was house bound and, when it appeared that she would not be allowed to vote from home, she made phone calls until someone brought her a ballot. "She supported his ideas and the fact that he replaced the Soviet regime." Apolitical, Yevgeniya Ruditskaya, when pressed, acknowledged, "I have a great deal of respect for Yeltsin." Similarly, Vladimir Sidelnikov stressed that he was the first to speak out against the Central Committee. "Yeltsin spoke the truth. The problem was that he drank. Yes, he got drunk, but his politics were correct. Russia had to switch to a market economy, like all of the other countries." As a result of Yeltsin's drinking, Yelena Kolosova believed that Yeltsin was more familiar to the Russian people than Gorbachev was. "He was a massive man who drank, and therefore could be trusted."

Yet most Baby Boomers, like most educated Russians of their generation, spoke ill of Yeltsin. Leonid Volodarsky vehemently opposed Yeltsin's economic policies: "I believe that he's probably the person who, in the entire history of Russia, brought his country the most harm. It's hard to imagine anyone doing something worse for his country." Critical of Gorbachev, Larisa Petrova likewise scolded Yeltsin: "For one thing, he's dishonest. Because of him, crime has begun to strangle Russia. I believe that the years he ruled were unlucky ones for Russia. These were years when much that was started and could have been nurtured got squandered." Viktor D. from Saratov maintained, "He's too much of a specu-lator. He was in the wrong place. He didn't do what was necessary or how it should have been done." Yeltsin disappointed Lyudmila Gorokhova, who did not mince words: "We hate Yeltsin and his entire clique." She griped about the "young snots" populating government bureaucracies, "who lacked an ounce of intellect." They belong to the "lost generation" that came of age during Yeltsin's decade in office, and who were raised on post-Soviet television, whose program-ming comprised a dangerous cocktail of "horror, pornography, and shoot outs."

"He's only for himself," opined Aleksandr Ivanov. "He did nothing sensible for Russia." Ivanov regretted that Putin granted Yeltsin and his family immunity. "Just as the leadership was all for itself back then, the leadership is all for itself now." Bakhyt Kenzheyev cast Yeltsin as an "opportunist." Stressing his lack of interest in making big money and his love of scholarship, Vladimir Glebkin lamented that the need to make ends meet left little room for anything else. "Thus, what Yeltsin did in this regard is a total catastrophe. And no one yet has understood this. Moreover, there are many people today who are spoiled by money. Because when you receive low salaries, you'll readily agree to make more." The resulting corruption even penetrated academia, resulting in a low-ering of standards. Tatyana Artyomova argued that "he appeared at that histor-ical moment when he was given a chance to turn Russian into a real democratic country. But I can't say that he used that opportunity." Speaking condescend-ingly, Vladimir Glebkin reminded me of the gorillas and chimpanzees in the film *Planet of the Apes*, likening the chimpanzees to the intelligentsia and the masses to gorillas, "who only recognized force." To keep the gorillas in check, a rigid structure needed to be in place. "One should never do what Yeltsin did. He let go of everything at once, understanding democracy as allowing everything. Our society was clearly not ready for that."

Andrei Rogatnev opposed the putsch of August 1991 and went to the Russian White House to support Yeltsin, "but I didn't do this so that Yeltsin's daughter could build a palace," he barked. Natalya Yanichkina also castigated the oligarchs for negative developments during the Yeltsin era: "Why did the country's wealth end up in the hands of a few? True, many people were duped by various financial scams, but that's nothing in comparison with what these rich people have done. They took advantage of the situation. I don't think this is right. But I also think there's no going back. Perhaps in time a different political climate will arise."

Others condemned Yeltsin's Chechnya policy. As president, Yeltsin has been credited with promoting a nonethnic definition of citizenship in Russia and for rejecting the use of force on behalf of the estimated 20 to 25 million ethnic Russians living in the Near Abroad. But his launching of two wars against Chechen separatists provoked widespread criticism. As background, the Yeltsin government signed a series of bilateral treaties with the twenty-one "republics" within the Russian Federation populated by ethnic minorities. One of them, Chechnya, had become a center of arms smuggling, drug running, and violence after the dissolution of the Soviet Union. When Chechnya refused to recognize Moscow's authority, Moscow invaded in December 1994, and the war ended in stalemate in August 1996. From the start, critics questioned Yeltsin's reason for invading. Did Russia attack to defend the Chechens' challenge to the state's integrity (indeed, President Bill Clinton called him Russia's Lincoln) or because Yeltsin grasped at any means to recover his declining approval ratings?

Russia invaded a second time in September 1999 following a Chechen attack against neighboring Dagestan and mysterious apartment explosions in Moscow and two other cities that killed more than 300 civilians. Led by Yeltsin's new prime minister, Vladimir Putin, the second war "against terrorism" proved enormously popular—initially—and helped to keep Putin in power after Yeltsin's resignation at year's end. Viktor D. believed he understood the wars in Chechnya the same way everyone else does. "Someone was interested in something; someone needed it, both from the Chechen side and from ours." He was puzzled: "Why did we let go of the Baltic states and Belorussia but not Chechnya? Why did we let go of the Georgians, but not the Chechens?" He worried about his son: "Thank God they invited him to enroll in graduate school when he finished college. Otherwise, I wouldn't know what to do to keep him from being sent to Chechnya. No one has any desire to fight for someone else's interests there. No one." Vladimir Prudkin believed he understood the dynamic that led to war, commenting, "The stealing [of state resources] that occurred in appalling, unprecedented levels in the 1990s was, in fact, a continuation of the stealing of the 1970s and 1980s. It's the same people, the same faces, who, back then, took only small bribes up to 100 rubles, but who take up to 100 million dollars today. That's why they need Afghanistan, Chechnya, and all the other conflicts. It's like a covert Third World War, a latent one." On a lighter note, Georgy Godzhello saw a link between Russia's war against terrorism and the piles of trash that littered city streets. "The garbage reflects a lack of culture, there's no way around it. Yet because of all the terrorism there are far fewer garbage cans," he quipped.

Speaking for those who struck out on their own in the new economic climate, Yevgeny Podolsky acknowledged Yeltsin's "colossal" influence on Russia; however, he owned up that "not enough time has passed" to evaluate him. Podolsky did not deny the many negative things associated with the Yeltsin presidency, but he underscored the fact that Yeltsin broke from the Party and created conditions for a new life. "You have to guarantee your own well being and how you do so is your own business. If you can't work, you can live on welfare." Podolsky did well in the new circumstances but admitted that his parents and their generation adamantly opposed them.

Natalya P. disliked the fact that Yeltsin, "in a flash," had abandoned communism for capitalism. "That means that he either was a bad Communist, or else he wasn't telling the truth now." Acknowledging that people placed great hopes on Yeltsin, she remembered how she and her husband argued over this "until we were blue in the face. He believed in Yeltsin 100 percent, and said that now things would be different. I disagreed. Women are more realistic. Yeltsin, after all, came from the Party elite and he was already of an age that it would be difficult to completely change. For one thing, even if he really wanted to, it's very hard for someone to change after holding office for so many years." Natalya understood that it was easier for the iconoclastic Yeltsin to destroy than it was to create something new. Waxing philosophical, she observed, "We lived through some hard times. Things are far more stable now, far more so. Periods of great change are always accompanied by a downside."

"WHAT DOES YOUR ORDINARY AMERICAN REALLY CARE ABOUT . . . RUSSIA?"

In embracing the "American way" and in teaming up with Harvard economists Jeffrey Sachs and Robert Allison, who promoted economic shock therapy, Yeltsin and his economic gurus expected the United States to pour aid and investment money into the country to ward off a Communist restoration and a global economic crisis. Newly independent, the mainstream Russian media in the early 1990s bashed Communism while supporting shock therapy and idealizing the American other. As a result, many people believed that Russia should model itself after the United States or European countries such as Germany or Sweden.[24]

When economic catastrophe turned expectations into resentments, Russian public opinion became critical of the United States. Making no systematic effort to raise Russia from the ashes of economic ruin, the George H. W. Bush administration (1989–93), concerned above all with the fate of Russia's nuclear arsenal, left assisting Russia to NGOs, philanthropists, companies, and individuals. Instead of a new Marshall Plan for Russia, the country was inundated with chicken-leg quarters that America overproduced and few other countries wanted, known derisively by Russians as "Bush's legs." Injured pride stirred Russian nationalism—and anti-American rhetoric. As Russia searched for a post-Soviet identity, many ordinary people came to believe that the United States consciously sought to keep Russia weak, becoming the scapegoat that many needed.[25] Disappointed with their former Cold War enemy, some saw Russia's future as lying in Europe, while others promoted the country's Eurasian traditions. It is possible that Russian neoconservatism and anti-Americanism resulted from the frustration over loss of Russia's superpower status, lack of economic investment in Russia, and the country's exclusion from important decision making. The worst eruption of anti-Americanism came in 1998–99, following the August 1998 devaluation of the ruble, in which millions lost their life savings. In December the United States and Britain bombed Iraq, ostensibly over Saddham Hussein's noncompliance with United Nations Security Council resolutions. Moreover, the issue of NATO expansion into former Soviet-bloc countries loomed larger as the Russian media portrayed the United States as arrogant and expansionist.[26]

Thus, if at the start of the 1990s people expressed optimism over U.S.–Russian relations, by the end of the decade Russia's romance with America had cooled: Ordinary people voiced disillusionment with American-style privatization and liberalization, feared NATO expansion into the independent Baltic states and elsewhere after the United States announced that Poland, the Czech Republic, and Hungary would join, and decried the NATO-backed U.S. bombing of Kosovo in Serbia in 1999. The latter inflamed Russian public opinion against the United States because of the long-term historical and religious ties between Serbia and Russia, both Orthodox countries.[27]

Some Baby Boomers subscribed to these views of America. Angry at the U.S. bombing of Kosovo when I interviewed him, Sergei Zemskov snapped, "I'd say I had a far better attitude toward the West back then than I do now." In the 1960s "we idealized the West and the Western way of life." The disappointment of the 1990s taught Gennady Ivanov that "no one wishes us well and it's up to us to solve our own problems." Ivanov cynically queried, "What does your ordinary American really care about what goes on in Russia? That was the case back then and probably now, too. What's it to him?" Interestingly, a few Baby Boomers voiced greater concern over cultural issues than over U.S. foreign policy objectives. For instance, Vladimir Prudkin observed that his childhood notion that the West produced individuals who were "highly developed" amounted to something of an illusion. Western popular entertainment, its cult of stars, and other "primitive" features especially troubled him, owing to their popularity in Russia. "Now, when Russia has become freer, it's cloning much of this. Under the weight of the totalitarian regime the level of spirituality here was greater."

Yevgeny Podolsky's attitudes toward the West changed, but for the better. "Before they told us that in a capitalist society they oppress the poor, but in fact it's not like that at all. You work, you earn money, and you live normally. And if you don't work, the government helps you." He saw benefit in the fact that people could be fired for not producing. "We didn't have that. Here people got drunk at work. The proletariat was hegemonic. He could drink, knowing that, if they fired him, he could go across the street and they'd hire him and the same thing would happen." Podolsky's vantage point accounts for his views: today he is a successful businessman in Moscow. He worked hard to achieve what he did playing by Western rules adapted to Russian circumstances.

POWER PERSONIFIED: PUTIN IN POWER, 2000–2008

Born in Leningrad in 1952, only a few years after the Baby Boomers, Vladimir Putin became president of Russia in 2000, confirming that the country is one of great opportunity. Interested in the martial arts and in a KGB career already as a young man, Putin studied law at Leningrad University where he was taught by reform-minded Anatoly Sobchak, who later became mayor of St. Petersburg and a Putin promoter. Assigned to the KGB office engaged in foreign spying, Putin served the KGB in East, not West, Germany, compiling a run-of-the-mill dossier. In 1990 Mayor Sobchak appointed Putin an advisor on international relations and then on foreign investments. His ability to get things done and other personal qualities did not go unnoticed by Anatoly Chubais, who linked Putin up with the person who ran the presidential staff in the Kremlin, Pavel Borodin. He offered Putin a position in Moscow.

Putin's effectiveness and apparent lack of any bald-faced political ambition caught the attention of Yeltsin, who invited Putin to head up the Federal Security Service, the successor to the KGB, in 1998. In August 1999 Yeltsin surprised his countrymen, and the world, by appointing Putin his prime minister and possible successor. That month, Chechen terrorists took credit for blowing up apartment houses in Moscow and two other cities, resulting in over 300 casualties. Demanding action, the Russian people applauded Putin's launching of a new war in Chechnya to defend Russia. Yeltsin's resignation on December 31, 1999, stunned people even more, since it made Putin acting president for ninety days. He then presided over what was still a popular war in Chechnya when he stood for reelection in March 2000. Ordinary Russians voted for the stability Putin represented, electing him in the first round. Putin's popularity can be understood only against the backdrop of Yeltsin's intense unpopularity. In 1999, only 2 percent of the population had nothing bad to say about the Yeltsin era;[28] at the start of the millennium, 88 percent of the population viewed Yeltsin's

resignation positively. Sixty-nine percent applauded the Kremlin's new "antiter-
rorist operation" in Chechnya, and a roughly equal percentage Putin's appointment. Russian liberals and others backing a free market system believed political
freedoms remained as important as a strong leader; however, Russian Communists, nationalists, and supporters of Putin's umbrella organization, Unity,
stressed the need for an authoritarian order in the country.[29]

Either Russia will be great, Putin pronounced, or it will not be at all. Based
on public opinion, Putin's mandate became clear: to win the war in Chechnya,
to overcome poverty, to end corruption, to introduce law and order, and to limit
the influence of the oligarchs.[30] His hard-hitting Millennium Speech of 2000
offered a solution to the country's problems through rebuilding a strong Russian
state. Stabilizing the country owing to fortuitous circumstances on the world
market when prices for energy soared, oil exports over the next several years led
to robust growth rates that boosted Putin's popularity and provided an auspi-
cious climate for his leadership style to emerge. It involved centralizing power,
relying on networks of former KGB officers, the military brass, and others from
his base in St. Petersburg; curbing the independent press; restoring some important symbols of the past such as the Soviet national anthem; and stepping out
confidently on the world stage. He also battled with the oligarchs. With the
backing of almost 75 percent of the population, Putin arrested some oligarchs
who manifested political aspirations.

By the middle of Putin's first term in office pollsters documented a depoliticization or de-ideologization of society. In some respects, however, this
phenomenon reflected a large measure of growing public confidence: In
responding to various scenarios of the Russian future, more citizens believed
that Russia would remain a united state, strengthen its position in the world,
restore its economy, and embrace principles of democracy and a state based
on rule of law than feared that the economy would further deteriorate. Half
of the population wished to have the country's superpower status restored or
to see it become one of the five most developed economies in the world. Less
than 5 percent of the population received its news about domestic and
foreign affairs from foreign television, publications, or the Internet, giving
Putin's subsequent crackdown on the press even greater significance, for it
may have contributed to the country's growing optimism. Between 1998 and
June 2002 the percentage of the population that saw the county's situation
as normal rose from a low of 2 percent to 22 percent; concomitantly, the
percentage of those who felt the situation was catastrophic fell from 51 to 13
percent.[31] It has been argued that the Russian people will accept a new pact
with a government only insofar as it taps into popular elements from the
previous moral economy such as equality, justice, solidarity, faith, and
mutual support.[32] Suggesting the beginning of a break with the Soviet past,
however, 65 percent of those polled replied that they rely on themselves in
solving personal problems, followed by help from those close to them (23

percent). Only 6 percent relied on the government.[33] The 1990s had not been in vain.

Putin's move toward "law and order," "stability," "greatness," and "patriotism" also needs to be understood against the backdrop of Russia's war against terrorism. Opponents at home and abroad had condemned Russia's second invasion of Chechnya, but after 9/11 the Kremlin conflated Chechnya with America's fight against terrorism. This made a military solution there more acceptable, especially when terrorists in October 2002 seized over 800 hostages in a Moscow theater, and in August 2004 approximately 1,200, mostly children, in a school in Beslan, resulting in more than 300 deaths. These events also provided favorable ground for the move toward centralizing power and toward curbing the power of parliament, the activities of political parties, the independence of the media, and the influence of foreign NGOs.[34]

The 1993 constitution prevented Putin from running for a third term in 2008. Elections brought Dmitry Anatolyevich Medvedev (b. 1965) to power, the youngest head of state since Tsar Nicholas II and the first Russian leader without any links to the Communist Party or to the KGB. Well educated with a Ph.D. in law from St. Petersburg University, Medvedev met Putin in Mayor Sobchak's office in the early 1990s and appointed Putin his prime minister. Because of his strong link to Putin, who guaranteed Medvedev's victory in the 2008 elections, some observers have depicted him as Putin's puppet, while others have pointed to strains in the relationship. Given Russia's political culture and the retreat from open to "managed" democracy, it seems doubtful that "dual power" will survive in Russia.

"SOCIETY HAS LOST INTEREST IN POLITICS"

The Putin presidency was in its infancy when I began to interview the Baby Boomers and into its second term when I wrapped up this phase of my research (with one exception). Leonid Volodarsky emphasized that "so far he didn't have enough information" to assess Putin. Volodarsky wanted things to get better, but so far they had not. That said, he appreciated the greater stability that had come to Russian society, affirming a phenomenon captured in public opinion surveys: "People have calmed down and are not politicized. Society has lost interest in politics." Larisa Petrova initially saw Putin as an extension of the Yeltsin clan and therefore did not vote for him. But she later changed her mind about him and explained why: "First, I respect what made him tick. I respect many of his ideas and the things he says. Not all, of course." She backed his taking decisive measures against the oligarchs. "It's okay to put an end to the country's criminals. He's trying to do so, but with timid measures. However, we understand how difficult this is." Echoing a popular sentiment, she added, "At least I'm personally not embarrassed for our president. I was ashamed when Yeltsin was president. I like what our president is doing now."

Natalya Yanichkina approved of Putin but for different reasons: "I like the respect he shows to those who preceded him," she opined, clearly having in mind Putin's granting Yeltsin immunity from prosecution. The only Baby Boomer I interviewed after the 2008 elections brought Dmitry Medvedev to power, Vladimir Sidelnikov, extolled Putin's virtues. In so doing Sidelnikov revealed his upbringing in the 1950s: Putin is "a young, forward looking, wonderful president, and his politics are correct. God help that Medvedev continues these policies. In that case Russia will move forward and, in the end, we'll catch up with and overtake America, not with a socialist economy, but with a capitalist one. Just give us time."

A few others liked Putin, but had plenty about which to complain. Lyudmila Gorokhova, for instance, found Putin "very likable. Although he's not handsome, he has a great deal of charm," she pointed out to me. "His range of interests is indisputably wide, and he's intelligent." Aware of his KGB background, she nonetheless preferred his self-control to Yeltsin's extreme behavior. Nevertheless, she faced the future with trepidation. "Man is wolf to man," she reminded me. As our conversation unfolded she and Galina Poldyaeva lambasted the oligarchs. Like others, they suggested that one had to have the right "disposition" to survive in the new Russia, but the personal traits this required were foreign to them. Concluded Poldyaeva: "In sum, that which is transpiring right now is not to our liking." "It's a crying shame," replied Gorokhova. "They deprive us of all of our achievements and create conditions in which we don't know how we'll live." Besides, added Poldyaeva, "No one is held accountable." "There's no one to complain to," confirmed Gorokhova. Her friend corrected her for my benefit: "Now the courts decide everything. Go sue. That's America for you. They sue each other there on any grounds."

Irina Garzanova liked Putin better when he came to power than she did when I met her. "I believe he's a decent, honest man, who is trying to get something done. But I don't know how real this is. It's possible he won't be able to do anything." As she put it, "I voted for Putin because there really was no alterative." It doesn't matter, she added, "because what will happen is meant to happen, no matter who is in power."

But in September 2000, 38 percent of the Russian population polled already feared the advent of an authoritarian regime.[35] Most Baby Boomers are among them. Seeing Gorbachev, Yeltsin, and Putin as "soul mates," Gennady Ivanov sharply criticized Putin: "Under Putin they say one thing and do another. Take, for example, the fact, that practically not a single nongovernment television broadcast exists any longer." Also disapproving of Putin's attack on the oligarchs, Ivanov emphasized, "It's absolutely illegal to victimize the oligarchs. We need to introduce specific legislation and not just can them. Let them spend time, pay up, and release them. I believe that the laws should work. You need to build a government based on laws." Aleksandr Virich also took a long view: "Look at those in power over the past ten years. Do you see these democrats anywhere?" he queried. "The ones who marched with flags and cried 'give us freedom'? You can't find them anywhere. All those in power are former Party members. Wasn't Mr. Putin, a KGB colonel, a member of the Party? Aren't the directors of factories and the largest construction operations who sit in the Duma former members of the Party?" Ivanov chided Putin for granting Yeltsin immunity from prosecution: "Just as the elite was all for themselves then, that's how they remain now." Ivanov rebuked the Kremlin's pouring of resources into rebuilding Chechnya, now controlled by pro-Moscow Chechen forces, as a result of which officials "made money on it. Why do I as a taxpayer have to give money to pay for the war there? It's unnecessary. Buildings are falling apart here and we're spending money on Chechnya. Who needs this?" He also chastised Putin's making oblast authorities responsible for some matters he saw as federal concerns, such as providing benefits for World War II veterans.

Finally, Ivanov saw Putin's reliance on revenues from exporting oil and gas as a myopic, even dangerous, policy that would create greater problems for the Russian economy in the future. Other Baby Boomers felt this way, too. Viktor D., for instance, saw real improvement in the economy; however, like others, he linked this to higher world oil prices. "There's no rise in industrial production, no improvement in what's necessary for the country to grow rich and the people to prosper. Yet, at the same time, I see order is appearing, but only at certain levels. His first term is coming to a close and I can't say I'm as satisfied as I'd like to be with the young president. I'm not the only one who feels this way." Gennady Ivanov, too, lambasted the fact that "no one is looking for new oil-fields to tap. What will be left for our grandchildren?"

A few Baby Boomers supportive of the demise of Communist rule nonetheless saw few prospects for a better life now. Anatoly Shapiro, for example, related with typical pessimism: "I don't believe in Russia's normal development, because several generations need to die off in order for this country to move along a normal, West European path, not an American one, but a Western one." Stating that the same people, or the same type of people, remain in power as under communism, he observed that he was speaking of Moscow and that it was actually "worse in the provinces." Denouncing the vertical hierarchy of power recreated under Putin, Shapiro concluded that "in the end it will be the same as before and nothing good will come of the economy. At some point the oil reserves will be depleted or something else will happen and things will worsen and we'll have another collapse." Shapiro acknowledged that he had not been in the backwaters of Russia. "But I heard what's going on there. Take any kolkhoz chairman, or whatever he's called today. He's tsar and god. It's the same as before. The courts and police are under him. He can give you an apartment or take one away from you. He can put you in jail or decide not to. It's all about loyalty to him. It's the same everywhere."

Some members of the Cold War generation who emigrated shared their views on Putin, which roughly correspond with what their classmates living in Russia had to say about him. Speaking metaphorically, Tatyana Artyomova said, "You can take out an appendix under a general or local anesthetic, or without either. In Russia they opted to remove appendixes without any anesthetic. What can one do? It's very painful, but necessary." Viktor Alekseyev admitted, "I personally don't like him. I don't like what he's doing. I don't like the people who helped him come to power and create the system around him. Beginning with his image and ending with his economic position, I don't think he bodes well for Russia." Bakhyt Kenzheyev attacked the oft-repeated argument that the Russian people "need a tsar." Instead, he argued, "Putin is a genius at PR. He meets with the people, builds schools and hospitals for them. And after the period of pauperization, which is ending if it hasn't already, after this period people like that a strong man appeared who brought pressure on the oligarchs, who pays people on time. But, in fact, the reason for this has to do only with the high price of oil." Apolitical, Tatyana Arzhanova did not understand Putin's popularity in Russia, but recalled that her mother told her that he would be reelected president in 2004 and that the "other candidates were nominated for show." Yelena Kolosova made a decision upon leaving Russia that she no longer had the right to judge what was going on there. Yet she granted that "Putin is far from being the worst possibility."

Most of the Baby Boomers supported Yeltsin during perestroika, but ultimately expressed disappointment in him, owing to the economic dislocation and corruption associated with his ten years in power. They also acknowledged, however, that he prevented a Communist restoration and allowed religion to thrive. Most look upon Putin with some skepticism, regretting the constraints he placed on the media and on political life. While appreciative of the economic stability that began to set in during his presidency, they nonetheless realized that it was mostly due to revenues from the sale of oil abroad. At the same time, however, they did not see many, if any, real alternatives to his coming to power at the end of the 1990s.

"IF YOU WORK A LOT, YOU MIGHT GET PAID A LOT"

How do the Baby Boomers depict their children's generation, the "children of perestroika" coming of age in the new Russia? Most of the interviewees had children early in their marriages during the 1970s. Those born at that time encountered perestroika during their formative teenage years. Those born later were young children when Gorbachev came to power, completing college during Putin's presidency. I consider all of the offspring as belonging to the same generation, but also point to differentiation within it when possible. As Gennady Ivanov observed about his two sons born in 1971 and in

Attending to the needs of aging parents is a problem affecting Baby Boomers worldwide, and one made more complicated when the parents live on different continents. In September 2007, Tatyana Arzhanova (Koukharskaya) and her husband, Viktor, and two of their grandchildren welcomed Tatyana's mother to Canada, where she moved from Moscow to live with her daughter. *Courtesy of Tatyana Koukharskaya (Arzhanova)*

1981, respectively: "The older one is more like us, and the younger one is more contemporary. A lot changed in those ten years." Ivanov works in the suburbs, rarely visiting downtown Saratov "with its new billboards and advertisements. For me, it's a different city, but my youngest is like a fish in water there."

Coming of age during the challenging transition to a market economy resulted in growing rates of smoking among young people in the 1990s, wider use of drugs and other toxic substances, a rise in alcohol consumption, and a lowering of the age when youth committed suicide.[36] The work of anthropologist Fran Markowitz, however, who interviewed Russian teenagers in the mid-1990s corresponding to the Baby Boomers' youngest children, challenges the widely accepted view that cultural stability is necessary in order to assure that adolescents become well-adjusted adults.[37] Her positive gloss on things also takes issue with adult views of adolescent rebelliousness, which she believes adults confuse with what, at heart, young people perceive as conformist behavior. Similarly, she disagrees with observers who maintain that the children of perestroika opted out of the political and economic fray in order to have fun, indulging themselves in an anticulture based on sex, drugs, and rock music. What amounted to a radical transition for the parents seemed far more "ordinary" to teens. Although they rarely mentioned politics to Markowitz, they detailed the economic impact of perestroika on their lives and the disintegration of the Soviet empire, too. Between 1985 and 1995 they believed life had become "more free," both materially and in regard to their ability to express their individualism. For instance, they appreciated not having to wear school uniforms, voicing far fewer regrets over the lack of Pioneer and Komsomol organizations than their parents.[38]

Markowitz found that, despite the radical economic and political transformations during these years, most teens spoke about their lives in terms of continuity.[39] Busy with getting an education and preparing for adulthood, they felt that their fates hinged on the caprice of the government and fortunes of their parents. But they told their life stories within a framework of stabilization. They welcomed the availability of goods, but not the concomitant crime, corruption, and all-too-visible gap between rich and poor. They wanted to live well, yet they also wanted to reap the benefits of their parents' earlier efforts to transform the world.[40] Her conclusions reassure. Social insecurity, she argues, "may not play as central or discordant a role in teenagers' lives as adults would expect." Impressed by the children of perestroika's pragmatism, she suggests that "their combination of cynicism and doubt plus kindness and ingenuousness should give everyone hope."[41]

Markowitz's findings offer a unique perspective on a period generally viewed through the alarming statistics that otherwise define it. Although crises that affect society negatively can leave their marks for a lifetime, the post-Soviet 1990s also afforded enormous opportunities. Russian youth were not in a position to lead the switch to a market economy; however, they embraced new attitudes and in this way corroborate a historical law of sorts linking change to the young.[42]

In a 2003 conversation, Saratov's Galina Poldyaeva and Irina Kulikova chewed over my question regarding how their children's generation differed from their own. "Young people today are far more grown up than we were at that age," began Poldyaeva. "For some reason they're drawn to this new life." Kulikova saw a downside to this: "I believe it's harder for them to live, although they're more satisfied, better provided for, and freer than we were." Poldyaeva agreed. "We had fewer problems, because we knew that we'd study free of charge, we'd go to college. It depended on us, on how well we did on our exams. When we'd get sick, they treated us free of charge. It's another matter altogether *how* they treated us, but we didn't have to worry about these things." Affirmed Kulikova: "Besides, we knew that we'd receive our salary on time. And people somehow managed, on their wages, to build apartments, to buy cars, and to vacation in the south." Poldyaeva unleashed her parental anxiety in post-Soviet language: "There's no confidence in tomorrow, and we're concerned about our children, because we don't own stocks in any big companies. We don't have any investments that we can leave our children so that they could live off the interest or reinvest it."

Illustrating her earlier point about how hard young people have things today, Kulikova offered the example of her son-in-law, a soldier who served several tours of duty in Chechnya. He's been job hunting for months, "and nothing works out." She believed he's most fit for a military career, but he quit the army, announcing, "'I'm ready to sacrifice my life for my country, but not *there.*' He's worked as a guard, a driver, and a construction worker," Kulikova continued. "Now he wants to start his own business, but he doesn't have any start-up capital." Like parents everywhere, Poldyaeva lamented that her own son does not seem to care that he does not know the things she does: "If you'd ask young people today who so and so was, they probably wouldn't even have heard of him. There are lots of things they don't know, and don't want to know. All of their thoughts are focused on the future and how to get set up well in life." Concluded Kulikova: "Young people have become obsessed with money. We didn't think about money."

Given the age-old clash between generations, the Baby Boomers would have criticized their children's generation even if the country had not unraveled and perestroika had not occurred. For this reason, I often found it hard to separate out the consequences of perestroika from laments over time-honored differences between parents and their offspring. Yet perestroika did affect the country and its people in indelible ways. Considering how the Baby Boomers see their children's generation, then, serves as a foil that reflects back the interviewees' own values, priorities, and historical sensibilities.

Take the example of Lyubov Kovalyova, who claimed that her daughter's generation "catastrophically differs from ours." Acknowledging that "of course, each generation differs from the preceding one, otherwise there'd be no progress and development," she explained her negativity. "We, the preceding generation, had a spiritual tie with our parents and there was continuity between generations. My daughter grew up in altogether different circumstances. Perestroika took place as she was growing up, and not in the best way." Her daughter attended a magnet school and "was under my thumb until the fifth grade." Kovalyova recalled what an honor it had been for her to be inducted into the Pioneers, but when her daughter reached that age "they announced that the Pioneers were awful, that the organization enslaved people." The new freedom and move toward a system with different ideals, according to Kovalyova, "has led to confusion." It resulted from the "rejection of all of the achievements and convictions by which their parents lived." They say, "We're going to live differently. We have perestroika." It stung Kovalyova to hear "you didn't live right, you lived wrong."

Sofiya Vinogradova also felt at odds with her children's generation, "but I can't say that I know why," she admitted. "It also depends on the person. It seems to me that certain moral values have probably been lost. But again, I wouldn't treat them all alike, just as with our generation." She mentioned that "they ask us, why is everything so hard for you? Even now things are hard for us. Yet they promise to do something and don't do it. If I had promised, I would have done it. That's how it was for us. We were responsible." Anatoly Shapiro observed that the generational differences "are very large. Judging by my daughter—I have very complicated relations with her—they have no sense of purpose. I'm not saying that I did, but they also don't have a sense of responsibility. That's a terrible thing. It's not only a matter of coming in at all hours, but of saying you'll do something and not doing it. This upsets me. And they don't want to learn anything," he added. "They have no yearning for knowledge, and if there is, it's to learn something in order to make a career. However, that's not all bad." Hundreds of miles away on the Volga, Aleksandr Babushkin voiced similar sentiments: "The younger generation got worse, it's spoiled, because the living standard is better. We had far better relations with and were closer to our parents." Remarried to a younger woman, Babushkin started a second family and had a young son when I interviewed him. Upset over the strain he felt between himself and his older children, he rationalized: "I'm trying to bring up my son differently. We'll see how things turn out."

A surprisingly large number of Baby Boomers criticized the children of perestroika, but not their own offspring, whom most described in positive terms. By noting that their own children are successfully negotiating the challenges of post-Soviet Russia, they mitigate the otherwise negative impression they give of today's young people in Russia. For instance, according to Aleksandr Ivanov, "the most important thing for them is to have fun. For the most part, they live only for today." Describing how he and his wife struggled to make ends meet, he complained that young people "receive their pay and, a week later, they're broke. They go to cafes all the time. They have nothing in their apartments, and no money." He clarified, "Well, not *our* children, but *today's* youth. Perhaps not all of them, but 50 percent, say." Arkady Darchenko found fault with young people's fashion and taste in music and movies. "It's as if they've followed a different path. We have few points of contact. Yet I have to say that my son's not like most." Although she believed her own generation is kinder, Irina Vizgalova claimed, "Personally I really like my children and their friends, and I share many of their views." She did admit that some children today "don't see or know a thing apart from the computer." More troubling are those who succumbed to the allure of drugs and alcohol. "When they speak they can't do so politely. Every other word's the f-word, and they don't even notice. They can't speak any other way. What especially rankles me is that this, for the most part, is also true of young women." Worse yet are the drug addicts. "It's awful when you see the heroin addicts. It's awful when you look into their eyes." Vizgalova, however, stressed that, although some young people smoke, drink, and take drugs, others are totally abstinent.

One interviewee, who asked to remain nameless because of her interest in Scientology, agreed. "My son always told me, 'Don't compare me with others.

Yelena Zharovova's son Alyosha and his wife Lena on their wedding day, April 26, 2003, outside the Kremlin, where many newlyweds still go to place flowers at the Tomb of the Unknown Soldier (lost in World War II). Like so many others, Zharovova boasted about her children but criticized their generation: "It's the generation that accepts Western standards of living. It's a generation that simply basically doesn't think." *Courtesy of Yelena Proskuryakova (Zharovova)*

I'm different.' And I'm really convinced of this. He never smoked and didn't try alcohol until he was twenty-four years old." I pressed for more. "He now has a goal in mind in Scientology, and he brushes aside everything that keeps him from achieving it. He has an iron will. He can't stand any gathering of young people, and absolutely never even stepped foot inside a discotheque." When I asked how she would characterize her son's generation, she responded, "I believe today's youth are awful." She claimed that, statistically speaking, 20 percent of the male population manifested some form of psychopathic tendencies before perestroika and that the figure had shot up to 80 percent. How, as a doctor, did she understand this phenomenon, I inquired. "Well, it's probably lots of things, but I know the wars contribute a lot. We see many Afghan vets, and many more after the wars in Chechnya. Military action has a very negative effect on people. As a rule, they often become apathetic or depressed." She also called my attention to widespread alcoholism. "I don't know anyone today who has a happy childhood. Very few." Unlike before, she claimed, "our government doesn't need children. Apart from their parents, no one needs children, and when their parents don't need them it's a tragedy. Young parents bring up their offspring poorly. That leaves a tell-tale mark on them."

Like some others, Olga Martynkina found her seventeen-year-old son's generation more patriotic. "Although we didn't suffer from lack of this, there's a rise in patriotism among people his age," she recounted, thereby putting a face on the impersonal statistics showing that Russia's youth tend to support Putin's effort to create a strong Russia. "That's simply astonishing," she continued, "because many kids these days are riff-raff and drug addicts." She also finds her son's generation "more materialistic. They're already disposed to earn money somewhere, to work part-time. We weren't like this. They're more rational." Lyubov Kovalyova also called her daughter a patriot: "She's comfortable living here. She says, 'I don't want to go anywhere. I want to live here. I'm happy here.' And somehow things are turning out for them."

The Baby Boomers who teach at the university level, coincidentally all Saratovites, made sweeping generalizations, often critical, about their students. According to Aleksandr Kutin, "there are kids who are dying to study, and the competition to get into college is significantly greater than, say, five years ago. But during this time some undeserving people came of age, who are probably under the influence of drugs." Carped Kutin: "First of all, there is their inappropriate behavior in public. It's their style of clothing, their shaved heads, their obscene language, their lack of restraint." He observed that those students whose parents paid for their tuition often treated their studies inattentively. "My daughter told me that this is not the case in America. If you pay money for your education, you study day and night until you're kicked out of the library," he noted naively. Natalya Pronina believed that "those who came after us don't think about lofty matters at all." She linked this attitude to the new economic climate. "To buy something cheaper somewhere, to deceive the person next door because he's easier to deceive. These are the attitudes being cultivated right now. It's a shame. I work with young people. I see this. I'm concerned."

Natalya P. cast many of her students as irresponsible. "There is no doubt that there are students today with a very developed sense of responsibility, those who sit from morning till night studying. But more often than not these are students who have no one standing over them and who lack their parents' support. For example, it's the student who arrives from the village who has to make his own way." Why? "The majority of kids these days are spoiled by their parents. A sense of responsibility is a trait that's unfortunately all too rare among today's young people, and they lack a real thirst for knowledge because they're pragmatists. It's the times." She lamented that "there's no longer a Komsomol, no longer any organizations for young people. Children are left to fend for themselves. The parents are either unemployed or work from morning until night—and this gives rise to a bunch of problems." Her Soviet education revealed itself: "Whereas before we discussed whether or not someone acted decently, we now think about whether or not something is advantageous to us. This influence came from the West. Our reality had been different." She added that, before, "You could earn a lot of money only in some criminal way. Now there is a legal way to do so. Speculation is now called business." Vladimir Kirsanov taught at the Saratov Medical Institute before moving to the Law Academy. "In the past, we had to get hold of information on our own by reading books, and by researching something, and this always makes the brain work more actively, but now information is absorbed passively. This is the main thing that distinguishes the two generations. Today's students don't like to read."

The subject of work also took central stage in the Baby Boomers' ruminations about their children's generation. Some interviewees underscored that the Soviet system guaranteed them a job after college, unlike today. As a result, Olga Kolishchyuk judged that things are "more complicated for today's young people. I knew that when I graduated from college, I'd go to work." Echoing an oft-heard refrain, she continued, "We had confidence in tomorrow. We knew we'd go to school, attend college, and get a job. Now, there's school, college, but work? What kind? Where? This remains a big question. You no longer feel pro-tected." Tatyana Artyomova agreed. "Everything was clear to us, but for them nothing's clear. That's the main difference" between Artyomova's generation and that of her daughter, born in 1977. Despite her enthusiasm for today's youth, Olga Gorelik concurred that "it's become more complicated for them to live." Anna Lyovina recalled, "I pounded into their heads, Children, we don't have any *blat*. Get an education on your own. Achieve what you can on your own. I can't help you in any way other than loving you and helping you at home. We can't arrange jobs for you. You'll have to do this yourselves."

Despite the Baby Boomers' concerns about their children's professional futures, the children of perestroika appear to be doing just fine. Vladimir Mikoyan pointed out that his children's generation is "completely without complexes, and unflinchingly change jobs." He gave the example of his oldest daughter: "She's almost thirty and is always learning things for one job, then for another. They're quick on their feet. That's the greatest advantage of today's gen-eration. They're not afraid of change." Aleksandr Virich also cast his son's gener-ation as more mobile: "I know that my son, if he were somehow able to accumulate the start-up capital—which is difficult—would launch his own business. He's smart enough. He grasps things well enough. He knows how to work and found a job on his own as a young specialist who is not poorly paid." Reiterating how mobile his son is, Virich generalized, "Based on his example and on the example of many his age, I know that there's no unemployment among youth. It's a lie that there is. Those who don't want to do anything become unemployed, just as in our time. But in our day they received their 120 rubles for sitting there."

After graduating from college, Irina Barysheva's son turned down a job at one of Saratov's closed military enterprises in order to launch his own business. Following a false start opening a joint stock company, he went into adver-tising, a field with potential once the market economy cranked up. "Of course, at first it was difficult, and he put more money into it than he made," recalled Barysheva, who tried to give him unsolicited advice. But he reminded her that he "'makes money out of thin air. I don't manufacture anything.'" Mikhail Markovich emphasized that his children "are different than we are in regard to how they solve their problems." His daughter is the assistant to the director of a large telecommunications firm. "It's a rather important position. She works there until 9:00 P.M. at night." He explained that "now, if you work they pay you real wages and, if you have money, there are no problems. You can solve them today."

Like many, Arkady Darchenko maintained that "we were most likely a repeat of our parents, but after us came a new generation that was completely different. This change can be seen, moreover, not only in Russia, but globally." That said, he appreciated the impact of perestroika on Russia's youth. "Our children grew up at a time when it was clear that you need money for everything. That is, to work 'for the love of it,' well, that's the other extreme, and that's foolish. They now see us as dinosaurs, as fossils, in the sense that well, 'you still go to work for the same lousy wages. They don't do anything at your research institute. They pay nothing. What do you do there all day? Work?'" When confronted like this, Darchenko would respond, "'Well, you know, I like it, it was my job, it was everything.' 'I don't understand,' they reply. 'I work only if they pay me.'" Darchenko concluded: "That's how the new generation's been brought up. Moreover, for this life it's right. It's likely that our working for 'the love of it' is a remnant of socialism. That is, you could work or not and receive your due." But "they understand that if you don't work, you don't get paid. It's that simple," summed up Darchenko. "If you work a lot, you might get paid a lot. That's how it should be and it corresponds to the laws of nature."

Larisa Petrova also felt that her son's generation differs from her own "far more sharply than we did from our parents." According to Petrova, he's different "because life changed so drastically. He subscribes to the new views. He works in a firm. He didn't go into his major, although what he learned is helping him. They now go where they pay. Their worth is how much money they make, not the graduate degrees they've earned as it was for us. Their self-esteem is linked to their ability to succeed in business. They're building resumes." This created tension at home. "He entered graduate school, but then said 'I don't need this. All my life I watched as you defended your dissertations, and from childhood saw nothing but your back at the desk. And what did this get you?' That's how he thinks."

"I SEE IN THEM A FREEDOM THAT WE DIDN'T HAVE"

The children of perestroika not only have embraced Russian-style capitalism but also the personal—not necessarily political—freedoms unleashed by perestroika and glasnost. Again and again, the Baby Boomers cast their children's generation as freer. Olga Gorelik remarked, "Our children are very free. They're really communicative. Computers are their reference books. They never leave the Internet, and over the Internet chat with people throughout the world. They have their own point of view on absolutely everything." Her daughter had been a Young Pioneer, but her eighteen-year-old son never had to participate in

Soviet-era children's organizations. "He's absolutely free in this regard," she injected. Well prepared for university study, he is majoring in computer science and technical translating. "He's going to become a network translator. He's free, really free, and I think that's wonderful. If I had been that free, I think that it probably would have been easier to live. I think it was a shortcoming that we were raised within limits and had all sorts of hang-ups." Yet she had reservations. "On the other hand, I sometimes wish their spiritual development was greater than it is. It seems to me it was deeper with us in regard to how we related to each other, perhaps because we had more problems or because we had less information."

Olga Kamayurova felt similarly. Describing her son as a "smart young man without hang-ups," she stressed, "He's free. He probably would have had a rough time back in the Soviet Union. We were kept harnessed. Things are hard for him right now in a material sense; he's making his way in life. My married daughter," she added, "gave birth and is more materially minded. She's consumed by daily life. But my son's free and it seems to me that our young people today are better off than we were." Bakhyt Kenzheyev echoed, "Children are absolutely free people in contrast to us. We are veterans of the Soviet system. There's such a thing as war veterans, be it of the Second World War or the Vietnam War, and all of these people are wounded psychologically. They cling to their military experience in the same way that people of my generation hang on to their Soviet experience." A writer and poet, Kenzheyev also observed, "I see in them a freedom that we didn't have. I'm not speaking about the Internet or the possibilities to travel, but the feeling of inner freedom. It's very important for poetry. I'm envious. But on the other hand," he continued, "it's not so clear-cut, because it was an experience that we, to a significant degree, overcame, and Soviet power no longer exists. I don't know what kind of obstacles these young people will have to overcome, and what kind of obstacles you need to overcome in order to write good poetry today."

Some Baby Boomers wondered if there might be too much freedom. Viktor Alekseyev told me about his son, born in 1979. "His generation is freer than is necessary." Alekseyev reminded me that his generation earned the same as their parents and that there had been a great leveling in Soviet society. "But my son became an adult at a time when a sharp stratification took place among people in regard to living standards, in income, and in possibilities. And this strongly affects children in terms of which schools kids go to, what's discussed at school, even who the teachers are, and naturally the quality of instruction." Viktor's son, an actor, took part in an exchange program at Harvard the year before I interviewed Viktor and visited his father in New York. "He told me about his acquaintance who invited him for a ride in a private airplane. They rented a private plane in New Jersey, flew across the bay, and landed somewhere on Long Island. Then they rented a car and returned to Manhattan. They could allow themselves such things, which I could never have imagined."

On a similar note, Natalya Yanichkina told me that her children's generation "differs a great deal. If we were raised strictly, then it sometimes seems to me that today's youth are completely unrestrained. Our freedom had limits. Then we were given complete freedom, but a culture of regulating this freedom has not yet been created. For this reason, this freedom sometimes turns vulgar." Offering an example from an unusual angle, Andrei Rogatnev waxed nostalgic about "our first loves dating back to our school years, which we still remember and cherish, and about which our wives are in the know." He described his classmates' first loves as "very touching. But I look upon my son, who will be twenty-five in the fall, and I recall when he was fifteen or sixteen. Their relations were different. We learned about love only from our parents or from literature available to us, the cinema, theater, and other works of art. Everything was very puritanical, and perhaps that was good because it's more romantic." When his son turned sixteen in 1992, "a flood of eroticism and pornography bombarded them. As a parent I told him one thing, but he saw, read, and heard other things." Rogatnev concluded that "they're richer in terms of sexual experiences, but not romantic ones."

A number of the interviewees linked their children's demonstrable freedom to their absence of fear, contrasting the latter with the Baby Boomers' own experiences. "Our children are altogether different. They're freer, more uninhibited," replied Yevgeniya Ruditskaya. "Perhaps I'm speaking only for myself, but we nonetheless have a certain fear. They don't. We were brought up in such a manner that there are many doors I can't open. But my son can open any door." Anatoly Shapiro agreed that "they lack fear, fear of the authorities, of the police. We were afraid of everything." Tatyana Luchnikova quipped, "My son Stas doesn't give a damn about anything." In contrast, Luchnikova reminded me that "from childhood they taught us not to be upstarts. They needed for all of us to be like mice, like a marching army. And they constantly suppressed our desire to fall out of line." Determined to pursue a career in ballet, her son Stas "lacked the fear I had. He goes after his goals, and doesn't take into account that it was hard for me with an infant to fly across the ocean from London. But he needed this. He said, 'If you don't go with me, I'll fly alone.' How could I let him? That's the difference. I would have subordinated myself to my mother's wishes. He has a lot more egoism. Good egoism," she added. "Perhaps that's why he achieved more than I did." Anna Lyovina expressed gratitude "that my children don't have the genetic fear that I'll never outlive. They're children of the world. They think differently. They already rub shoulders with others internationally. I believe that our future, the rebirth of Russia lies in this, in the passing of the generation of bureaucrats and reactionaries, with their old way of thinking, the Party-line." Summed up Lyovina: "The future is with people who have seen the world, analyzed things, compared, and took what they liked that was good and interesting, from wherever."

The freedom enjoyed by the new generation also finds reflection in the fact that a good number of the Baby Boomers' children live abroad, and not only because their parents emigrated. Aleksandr Kutin looks positively upon his daughter's generation born in the 1970s, "although there's the eternal problem of fathers and children." His description of the choices she made demonstrates how enabling perestroika could be for some. After completing the Saratov Medical Institute, his daughter did her residency in Moscow, set up a private practice in the capital, and supported herself until she married an American tourist. Kutin was hard put to find the right words to tell me what his son-in-law does for a living: "You don't encounter such terms here. They own a building that he rents out. That's where their basic income comes from. He also repairs cars. He can turn a jalopy into a real beauty. He's educated and aware of what's going on there and in Russia."

Born in 1980, Lyubov Raitman's daughter, Anna, traveled abroad for the first time already in 1989, when her mother and grandmother took her to France. "During the final years of school many of my [richer] classmates took regular trips to Europe and summer tours to nearby Europe became popular and nothing out of the ordinary," recalled Anna. Her teen years began with the demise of the Soviet system. She remembered that Russian money kept changing, "completely random imports" flooded the market, and both of her parents changed careers. "Flux was normal! No one knew what would come next." By the time she left to spend her senior year as an exchange student in Wausau, Wisconsin, in 1996, "things started to feel good again and normal." After completing high school in Wausau, Anna graduated magna cum laude from Knox College, took a Ph.D. in psychology from the City University of New York, married a New Yorker, and currently is enrolled at Columbia University, working on a degree in architecture.[43]

Aleksandr Konstantinov's son lives in Arizona with Konstantinov's former wife, and his daughter, a musician, resides in Germany. How do they differ from him? "To answer your question, I'd say that perhaps it's their practicality. I can detect this, for instance, in my daughter. In contrast, it seemed to us that our generation was more concerned with ethical questions. They're more practical than we are and rightly so place greater value on important, practical things." Saratov's Aleksandr Trubnikov, who lives in Israel, shared these sentiments, but it is important to note that his daughter moved to Israel first: "They altogether lack the stereotypes we had. Nothing has been pounded into their head since childhood. I think they're simply normal people. We remain abnormal. Unfortunately, some [from my generation] will remain that way until they die. Probably about half or so. But our children are normal. They're simply people, citizens of the world who live altogether differently. They're normal in that they live without an ideology, unlike us." Olga Gorelik's daughter also lives in Israel. Gorelik had little to say about her daughter's reasons for leaving Russia, but described her daughter as "an altogether independent person, in part thanks to the fact that I devoted a large part of my life when my children were born to their education, despite the fact that I worked." She described her daughter as "well read. She also attended School No. 42. She's an independent person, as they say, who has her own opinion about everything."

According to Leonard Terlitsky, "the generation that followed us was even more cynical than we were if anything, because they were the ones who actually took the system apart." "Yes, they're different," repeated Arkady Darchenko. "But what we call cynicism might be common sense, which we lack." Natalya Yolshina does not have children, but sees her generation as being "more narrow minded. When we'd associate with one another, we believed more in what was said, and what was fed to us. The new generation takes in everything critically, not in the negative sense of the term, but simply in an analytical way. It's more capable of evaluating what's said and done. We were probably less capable of this."

In fact, some of the Baby Boomers put a positive gloss on today's generation. Vladimir Prudkin enthused, "My son's generation is marvelous. First of all, I feel comfortable with them. It's easier for me to socialize with them, with the young generation [his son was then twenty-seven] than with people my age, because when I spoke about my own generation in a certain positive tone, I meant those closed circles in which I mingled. For the most part, the hopes of today's generation are significantly closer to mine than those of people my age, with the exception of that narrow circle I mentioned. They're good kids." Vladimir Bystrov described his thirty-one-year-old son's generation as "more dynamic. They don't have the moral constraints we had. I think it's an interesting generation. It's a very strong generation." His son works in a bank as the assistant manager of a large department.

"For the most part I love our young people," volunteered Igor Litvin, whose daughter graduated from Moscow University. "But I am astonished that they relate very negatively to America. They believe that the intellectual and spiritual potential they have doesn't exist outside their own student milieu and is altogether absent in America. That is, if you're going to mingle, do so with young people from the Sorbonne, or from Oxford, but not with Americans. Their orientation is more toward Europe than in our times." Litvin also gave an example of their freedom of movement, so unimaginable before perestroika. His daughter and her husband had left on vacation when I interviewed him. "She called from Sheremetyevo Airport. 'We're flying to Tunis.' 'Why didn't you say anything about this before?' 'I didn't know myself.' Yegor, her husband, 'surprised me and told me where we're going only at the airport.' For my generation that's like a fairy tale." This generation, mused Litvin, naturally faces "other problems." One is their need to chase after money. "On the one hand, perhaps this is an incentive to work, and on the other hand this deprives many of them, because they spend all of their free time trying to fulfill themselves in business, at work. And the main thing that results from this is that, instead of friends, they have necessary acquaintances, and they chose their friends from among them." Litvin asked if I understood the dual meaning of the colloquialism he used to convey the sense of "necessary acquaintances" (*nuzhnik*). The term also is a slang word for "toilet."

As Georgy Godzhello pointed out, all generations differ and each produces accomplished individuals as well as scoundrels. "That's how things have always been, that's how things are, and unfortunately that's how they'll be." Yet, as an educator, he believed that "each generation has it harder, purely in an objective sense if nothing else, because the volume of knowledge changes that's necessary to know." A universal problem, Godzhello noted its impact on Russia. "Regarding our country, I'd put it like this. We came out of a totalitarian regime, and this, too, affected generations, and not always in a positive way. How it did so in a positive way is clear, but what about in a negative sense? How do I see this?" Godzhello explained that "there are more temptations. If before we really were happy, now you have to exert a lot of your own energy to be happy."

Several Finnish scholars developed a typology of generations that challenged widely held views that negative experiences form or shape generations. The characteristics they identified for Finnish Baby Boomers born between 1945 and 1950 have remarkable similarities to their Soviet counterparts, including the rise of a youth culture, the breakthrough of Western popular culture, more leisure time, a carefree attitude, economic growth, rising living standards and a consumerist culture, and the expansion of education. Concluding that only positive events can serve as a basis for generational experience, they point out that negative events, such as the kind of economic dislocation experienced during the 1990s, do not constitute a generational experience because they are experienced by everyone and there is no relationship to age.[44] If this argument is correct, the collapse of the Soviet economy may have had less of an impact on the children of perestroika than the socioeconomic, psychological, and political consequences of the country's recovery whose pace has stepped up since the late 1990s.

Indeed, some speak of the Putin Generation, those born in the decade between 1983 and 1992. They remember the dissolution of the USSR and the madness that followed, but they completed school and entered adulthood during a period of stability. Mobile phones, the Internet, social networks, the mass media, mass culture, and fast food shape their values. The comparative stability and institutionalization of the rules of the market and political game also shape this generation that looks to the future with confidence. This generation is positive and optimistic. This generation demonstrates initiative. This generation is apolitical, conformist, pragmatic, and has a tendency to plan for the future.[45]

In sum, at the start of the new millennium, the majority of those under thirty voiced appreciation for the introduction of radical market reforms in Russia. They also were the strongest supporters of privatization and of the strengthening of presidential powers. Their parents, the Cold War generation, backed these measures less, but more so than older age cohorts. The Baby Boomers' children see equal opportunity as more important than equal income; they believe Russia was on the right path; and, more so than their parents, they believe that Russia must live by Western rules. Moreover, when asked to assess major historical epochs of the twentieth century, those under thirty voiced the most approval of the reforms of the early twentieth century under Nicholas II, perestroika (1985–90), and the transition to a market economy, and least support for the October Revolution of 1917, industrialization of the 1920s and 1930s, collectivization, and the Brezhnev stagnation. The one lesson to which basically all age groups were in agreement, however, was that Russia can prosper only with a strong leader (28.9 percent of all Russians).[46]

"I WANT TO BELIEVE THAT THE FUTURE WILL BE BETTER"

Boris Yeltsin's presidency coincided with the 1990s, a transitional period that transformed society as Russia searched for a new place for itself in the world. The country's efforts at reform and modernization—constrained by circumstances and by the country's long-standing political culture—created a Russian hybrid system that sharply divided, and continues to divide, public opinion.[47] Surviving the 1990s proved a double burden for Russia. Society as a whole suffered from the former superpower's diminished status on the world stage, while its citizens faced declining living standards and loss of confidence. Remarkably, people did not lose their reference points, despite the harsh economic conditions. Channeling their disappointment with social and political institutions and with those in power, they slammed leaders and institutions but evaluated their own personal situations less anxiously, with more than half the population identifying them as more or less satisfactory.[48] Importantly, the majority supported a democratic market system and a readiness to continue the reforms, despite the cost.[49]

Undoubtedly, support for reform and for a democratic market system had emerged already during the Soviet period in the shadows of the second economy and gradual opening up of the country, and became more fashionable once the glasnost revelations poked holes in the grand narrative of Soviet history. It has been said that "you cannot change values like you change your socks,"[50] a point well taken when considering a public opinion in flux during the ordeal of the 1990s. By decade's end, most people placed material, pragmatic concerns over concern for human freedom (which they may have taken for granted since they had more of it). Yet the population's attitudes regarding Russians' distinguishing personal qualities merit attention: they now saw themselves as more hospitable, patient, and energetic than before, and less impractical than they had believed.[51]

Glasnost had leveled the playing field between Moscow and Saratov in terms of access to information; however, regional differences based on economic realities continued to define local mentalities, because the country's wealth remained concentrated in Moscow and Muscovites lived better than those along the Volga.

As a result, throughout the 1990s, Muscovites in general demonstrated greater appreciation for self-reliance, individualism, and Western ways; they opposed a strong leader, valuing freedom and a market economy. Attitudes in the central black earth oblasts were more paternalistic and conformist, with more leveling tendencies. There, a Western mentality was weakly accepted and freedom meant the right to be one's own boss. Most people welcomed a strong leader.[52] For instance, a party list for the State Duma at the end of 1995 reveals that, whereas 69 percent of Moscow voters supported reformist candidates, only 31 percent did in the Volga region, where 64 percent in Saratov supported conservative candidates.[53] Yet the well-educated Saratov Baby Boomers remained more likely to support market reform and political pluralism and, in this regard, their views did not substantively differ from those of their Moscow counterparts.

In 2004, Russia's Public Opinion Fund carried out a survey of all sixty-five regions of the Russian Federation. Remarkably, on average 50 percent of the respondents were satisfied with their life, while 41 percent were not. More people in Moscow expressed satisfaction than in Saratov, but the national range was not that significant, falling between 55 and 48 percent. Despite sober views regarding the future, as in the 1990s respondents showed considerably more optimism when speaking about their own families than about the situation at large. Their main concerns regarding what is keeping them, and their countrymen, from living better are not surprising: poverty and a depressed standard of living, low wages, unemployment, small pensions, inflation, expensive or inferior housing, followed by concern over their health, crime, terrorism, family problems, alcoholism, and drug abuse.[54]

Despite these problems, what the Baby Boomers had to say about their offspring augurs well for Russia's future. Many of the Cold War generation's children, like much of society, experienced a decline in living standards and poor morale. They are not as close to their parents as the Baby Boomers were to theirs. They do not seem as responsible, as serious, or as reliable. They are more materialistic, and more receptive to outside influences. Ironically, the generation raised as atheists see themselves as more spiritual or ethical than their children who enjoy freedom of conscience. Yet the Cold War generation also sees their children as "freer" and more goal-oriented. They accept reality, are more pragmatic, more rational, and have a non-Soviet attitude toward work. They lack the hang-ups their parents had and are not afraid of change. It bears repeating that, although many interviewees cast the children of perestroika in negative light, they saw their own children as exceptions. No friend of the new order in Russia, Viktor D. expressed appreciation that his four children (the product of joining two families) appeared to be on the right track. "Children are the most important thing. Thank God my four children, without help, without connections, without money, without bribes, are all smart and all graduated with highest honors. All have a college education. Two of the four have Ph.D.s."

The Baby Boomers' accounts afford a fascinating glimpse at Western economic and political forms through the words of those experiencing their implementation, in this case, the college-educated urban intelligentsia who now constitute Russia's new middle, consuming, class. As it reconfigures itself, postindustrial Russia faces daunting problems not only in regard to standard of living but also in regard to quality of life issues. However, the vast majority of Baby Boomers remained hopeful. According to Bakhyt Kenzheyev, "it's still true that in Russia all political figures are thieves. Yet, from a philosophical point of view, I think that everything's normal in Russia now." Although Natalya Yanichkina articulated her worries, she concluded, "I hope very much that everything will get better. I want to believe that the future will be better." "Russia is so creative and has endured so much that things *have* to get better," insisted Viktor D. "I believe in Russia, not in the Soviet Union. And I believe that Russia is hope," concurred Tatyana Luchnikova.

Lyubov Kovalyova enjoyed a comfortable life under late socialism. "For me and for many, many others with whom I came into contact, the Soviet period was not bad," she recounted. She described herself, almost dismissively, as a "typical" and "ordinary" inhabitant. "But probably for the majority, or maybe the minority, it was worse." She acknowledged that many felt the Brezhnev-era stagnation. She acknowledged the unsavory mindset and behavior, the passivity, and the indifference toward work and public property of *Homo Sovieticus*. She acknowledged the existence of a dissident movement. "All of that existed, and we all knew about it. Yet this affected some more than others. Probably in the same way that, today, some have a comfortable life and others less so. However," she concluded, "if this life leads to the further development and prosperity of our country, if life becomes better, as we like to say, even if not for us, but for our children, then we can only welcome all of these changes."

CONCLUSION

"It's they who have always held Russia together"

"I don't regret at all from a political point of view that I was born at that time in this country. I was inspired by these changes. It's like a gift of history. My children don't understand that. They're not even interested," observed Vladimir Mikoyan. Living in extraordinary times, he and the rest of the Baby Boomers chose their fates and their lives both as passive objects shaped by the dominant social policies and trends of their era, and as active agents with real choices that were molded by the particular historical situation—late socialism—in which they found themselves. Looking for the connection between larger historical forces and individual biographies, this book explores what it meant to grow up and "live Soviet" in the second half of the twentieth century for an elite and influential component of the country's urban professional class. No single Baby Boomer could have offered this narrative, but each of them should be able to locate his or her own personal story within it.

Because official histories and state propaganda sought to forget the past, patently falsify it, or sanitize it while individuals often remembered things that did not validate official memories, Irina Vizgalova's father admonished her "don't poke your nose in politics, because they're good at rewriting our history." But so are we. This book is not about "how things really were back then" but, more important, about what the past meant to the Baby Boomers in the new millennium. Just as historians rewrite history to accommodate new evidence or interpretive frameworks or approaches, individuals reshape their memories as current events and experiences help them make sense of earlier ones.[1] The Russian historian D. Khubova argued that, when perestroika undermined the framework for historical interpretation in the USSR, people found it hard to interpret their own memories without having a larger public story to relate them to.[2] When I listened in on what the Baby Boomers had to say a decade later, most were two-thirds through their life stories, revising the plots to make room for the astonishing transformations of the past decade. How they understood their life stories within their broader comprehension of the fate of the Soviet Union not only reflected how they saw themselves but also how they behaved.[3]

In determining what shaped the Baby Boomers' stories, it is necessary to return to the original five questions. First, who and what shaped the Baby Boomers' worldviews while they were growing up? Their testimonials demonstrate how attitudes toward authority are shaped mostly by the family, which imparts its own values and shapes how individuals respond to circumstances. A large percentage of the Baby Boomers' parents belonged to the Communist Party. Others consciously did not join it for ideological reasons. Many parents, especially but not exclusively the non-Communists, identified with the liberal wing of public opinion. Although outwardly conformist in their public behavior toward the system that defined and rewarded their success and conferred status, they imbibed the spirit of Khrushchev's Thaw. Apart from their parents, the Baby Boomers affirmed the often profound role grandparents born before the Revolution, older siblings, and sometimes village nannies played in their lives. Because Stalinist repression struck most families, the Baby Boomers' parents, remaining fearful, instilled a sixth sense in their children—caution. As Igor Litvin commented, "Everyone understood everything. All conversations carried out at home took place behind closed doors. It was like the way you look to the left and to the right when you cross the street and there's traffic. It was automatic."

Khrushchev's condemnation of Stalin and shutting down of the Gulag, however, increased confidence in the system and reinvigorated it, especially since the post-Stalin leadership placed a higher priority on improving living standards. One of the most popular and appreciated manifestation of this was that, during their childhood, the Baby Boomers' families moved into private flats, thereby strengthening the Soviet nuclear family—which, in turn, helped to transform the Soviet system by promoting private life. Moreover, the measured opening up of the country created opportunities for a number of parents—almost exclusively from Moscow—to travel outside the country. The Baby Boomers vividly remembered how items from abroad otherwise unavailable in the Soviet Union stirred their curiosity. Even today, Marina Bakutina gushed over the View Master her mother brought her from America in the last 1950s. "It was truly a window on the West. There was nothing else like it."

The deprived war generation provided their children with all the Soviet system had to offer, including sending them to the country's best schools. These elite magnet schools attracted the children of the *nomenklatura*, of Party and state officials, of career military officers, and of the technical and cultural intelligentsia, in short, well-off people in the Soviet context, where knowledge represented a form of wealth. The schools prepared the Baby Boomers for college and taught them English as well as could be expected given the limitations of the times. As state institutions designed not only to educate but also to bring up the builders of communism, the school system imparted in the Cold War generation core values and a sense of duty and responsibility, exposing the Baby Boomers to state propaganda and to Communist Party youth organizations. But many of the younger teachers identified with the Thaw's openness, questioning, optimism, and sense that more was possible, thereby making unforgettable impressions on their young charges who mostly thought highly of those who instructed them. Starting school the year the launching of Sputnik astonished the world, the Baby Boomers' childhood corresponded with the most confident period in Soviet history, defined by the Thaw, the country's opening up, improved standards of living, Khrushchev's promise to build communism in their life-time, and Soviet achievements in space. Casting Yury Gagarin's flight in space as a grandiose achievement, Irina Chemodurova recalled her generation's "faith in the unlimited possibilities of man through science to transform and perfect everything. We were raised on this. That hard work and science are capable of perfecting and transforming not only man, but the world! This was pounded into our heads through children's magazines, through books, through films, through whatever you like, to say nothing of our education."

The clubs, sports, enrichment lessons, and after-school activities in which the Baby Boomers participated, as well as what they read, saw, and heard, and the friends they shared this with, whether at recess, on the street after school, or dur-ing the summer likewise molded them. This is particularly the case because their individual stories unfolded within the context not only of a larger Soviet one but also of a global one. Endorsing internationalism yet leery of its possible effects, the government found no foolproof way of fostering political orthodoxy while accommodating these influences, especially insofar as the Party also had to monitor foreign radio broadcasts, the appearance of *samizdat*, and a focus on individualism.

The near universal college attendance record of the magnet schools' class of 1967 should not obscure the difficulty many Baby Boomers experienced getting into college and the lessons they drew from this. Good grades were sometimes simply not enough to guarantee admission. As a result, their parents resorted to *blat*, whose many forms included hiring tutors to prepare their offspring for entrance exams who also sat on the admissions committee. For the Jewish Baby Boomers, especially in Moscow, this rite of passage sometimes represented their first encounter with official anti-Semitism. As we saw in chapter 4, even some Baby Boomers of Russian ethnicity admitted this. Vladimir Sidelnikov, it will be recalled, said, "I attended school with many Jews, but it was the rare exception among them that got into MGIMO."

In college the Baby Boomers ran up against forms of politicization that made the ideological content of the magnet schools seem innocent in comparison. To curb the spreading contagion caused by the Thaw, de-Stalinization, and growing contact with the outside world, the Communist Party increased the contact hours devoted to political indoctrination at college and monitored Soviet uni-versities. In stepping up such measures, the government acknowledged that the message it wished to convey to the builders of communism had stiff competi-tion. The Party likewise cracked down on dissent both at home and abroad.

These efforts to end the Thaw and contain liberalizing currents resulted in the Warsaw Pact's invasion of Czechoslovakia in 1968, which divided the Soviet intelligentsia, including the Baby Boomers' parents. Although many interviewees supported the crushing of the Prague Spring, others among them took in the events with skepticism or even disapproval, creating cracks in the edifice. Some began "to understand things differently," particularly since the use of force corresponded with the growing availability of *samizdat*. Tellingly, many link the beginning of their serious listening to foreign radio broadcasts to the events of 1968. As Mikhail Markovich recounted, "Because of the invasion we began to understand that we lacked information." They also began to realize that, despite Khrushchev's dismantling of the Gulag, diluted state repression remained a defining element of late socialism, limiting people's choices by switching on their self-censorship and by rewarding external compliance. Few Baby Boomers had direct run-ins with the KGB, but all felt its presence. Television journalist Natalya Yolshina, for one, expressed gratitude that "the Lord" spared her. "No one ever called me in for any conversations, or brought up the subject." She admitted that an "internal censor" was at work. In fact, "although today there's nothing to hide, it's still at work."

Travel represented another hard-to-underestimate influence that shaped the Baby Boomers' worldviews. The West remained an imaginary space for all but a few; however, many of them, through firsthand experience traveling to Eastern Europe as students and young adults, got access to more information. They complained about the suffocating "red tape" and nonsense they went through obtaining permission to go abroad, about the informers who accompanied them, and about the crushing disappointment they experienced when the authorities denied them permission to travel. Yet they clearly felt the effort and risk of rejection were worth it. When Lyubov Raitman and her husband visited Hungary in 1975, she recalled, "It was a very big shock for us. Hungary was a Soviet-bloc country, but it was utterly alive and altogether different. The living standard was closer to that of Europe than to that of the socialist camp." Some of the Baby Boomers learned a valuable political lesson as well. For instance, when Vladimir Kirsanov traveled to Czechoslovakia on the tenth anniversary of the Soviet invasion, he winced when an angry local demanded, "Why do you prevent us from living how we want?" Moreover, the continued opening of the Soviet Union and spread of information via tape recorders, foreign radio broadcasts, film, television, *samizdat*, encounters with foreigners visiting the USSR, and the rise of a genuine human rights movement that evolved organically from within the system magnified the significance of foreign travel by subjecting the Soviet Union to invidious comparison.

The Baby Boomers likewise experienced anxiety waiting to learn where the government assigned them to work upon graduation. The same strategies that helped get them into college proved useful once again. Moreover, establishing themselves professionally proved a turning point in regard to how important

English would be in determining their careers and life choices. Those who majored in English in college worked in the field afterward in some professional capacity. Research scientists and diplomats (all from Moscow) also tended to draw on their knowledge of the language, while those who went into technical fields or into medicine appear to have had much less practical need to use English. Given the substantial number of Baby Boomers who emigrated, it is clear that knowledge of English increased the likelihood of their leaving Russia.

Deciding whether to seek out Party membership proved to be another issue fraught with consequences for the Baby Boomers. Politically mobilized, they had joined all of the correct political organizations (all of them had enrolled in the Komsomol), and none of them belonged to nationalist or dissident movements. But they were also the most likely to listen to foreign radio broadcasts, read *samizdat*, and worm their way out of participating in Soviet public rituals. They saw nothing particularly anti-Soviet about this behavior; on the contrary, it had become Soviet behavior. Whether the Baby Boomers joined the CPSU was a matter of personal choice and family influence, since Party membership often ran in families. Their attitudes toward the Party also illustrate that it was in serious trouble. Some Baby Boomers maintained that their parents became Party members to advance their careers, while others claimed that their parents joined because they believed in its ideology. Only one Baby Boomer, however, stated that he joined the Party for ideological reasons. Because I had never met a true believer among my age cohort during my many trips to the country beginning in 1971, I was not surprised when Vladimir Bystrov, who joined the Party in 1978 to advance his career, asserted, "I personally never met any true believers. By the time I became a Party member, everything was already obvious to normal people." The daughter of Communists, Marina Bakutina joined the Party the year she graduated from the Institute of Foreign Languages and accepted a job there. According to Bakutina, "we probably believed. Yet it was never some sort of frenzied belief of the kind my in-laws had. My parents didn't even have that. It's hard to generalize about my generation, but I'd say we had nothing like that. If we did, it was probably only up to fifth or sixth grade." Working within the system was not the same as believing in it.

Most of the Baby Boomers married during college or shortly afterward and often ascribed considerable, even decisive, influence to their spouses or their spouses' families for challenging their core beliefs. Irina Tsurkan, for example, disclosed that her second husband "brought me down from the clouds by calling Lenin a tyrant." Children came early in Soviet marriages, complicating women's lives, since, although the Soviet Union had more female scientists and engineers than any other country and a greater percentage of women in the workforce, attitudes regarding home life remained traditional. As a result, the female Baby Boomers experienced a double burden. They worked as professionals, yet bore primary responsibility for childrearing and housework. They had fewer children than their parents and had to rely less on babushka to raise their offspring. Reflecting national averages, about half of them divorced. Several female Baby Boomers, divorced and single today, considered their married years as awfully difficult ones. Most of them, however, despite the double burden, voiced a high degree of job satisfaction. They claimed not to have experienced any gender discrimination or to have encountered minor discrimination that did not seriously impact their careers. If it were not for the lax work environment in most Soviet agencies and enterprises, they probably would have found the double burden even more challenging.

In sum, decades of peaceful, evolutionary change in the Soviet Union following World War II had a revolutionary impact on the Cold War generation's attitudes and expectations. This era was shaped by, and reflected, the Soviet leadership's complicated, shifting policies of reform and counterreform, the opening of the country to the outside world, and the ideas and comparisons this opening provoked. Despite the Baby Boomers' stable and comfortable childhood, many of them as adults realized that this formative period in their lives also bred cynicism that would develop more fully in the 1970s. "I think our school years developed a set of values in us that were not necessarily Soviet approved," explained Leonid Terlitsky. "Although we took our own roads in life and sometimes went very different ways, that set of values had an influence. It certainly did on me." This cynicism also had much to do with the beliefs and attitudes nurtured by the Baby Boomers' identification with a larger global youth culture. A case in point, Aleksandr Trubnikov told me, "I remember how they used to rail at the Beatles, yet we were all swept away by them. I even understood what they were singing about. I really liked them and everything else I was able to get my hands on." Olga Martynkina concurred: "The Beatles are sacred. They're wonderful. We grew up on them!" Moreover, this generation experienced no revolution, no terror, no World War II, no major social cataclysms, but an ill-conceived campaign to catch up with and overtake America. In college singing Beatles songs when they confirmed that the USSR would not surpass the United States in per capita production in 1970, the Baby Boomers were thirty-year-old adults in 1980 telling Brezhnev jokes when the government quietly ignored Khrushchev's promise that by then communism would have been achieved.

What do the Baby Boomers' life stories tell us about what constituted the "Soviet dream," and ultimately about the relationship between the growing emphasis on private life after 1945, the undermining of Marxist ideology, and the fate of the Soviet Union? The evolution of the Soviet system after 1953 and promises associated with the blueprint for building communism shaped the Soviet dream for the young Baby Boomers. They wanted a university degree, a satisfying job, foreign travel, decent housing, an improved standard of living, close friends, true love, a family, children with a good outlook on life, and perhaps a car. It took time for them to realize that the Soviet dream had real limits, because they graduated from college, secured jobs, married, and even traveled. Most of them earned acceptable salaries, lived in decent apartments, owned basic household appliances, and sometimes even automobiles. They appreciated state ownership of industry, free education, subsidized day care, after-school programs for children, socialized healthcare, generous paid vacations, subsidized housing, job security (and slack discipline), and an early retirement age (between fifty-five and sixty). In exchange for compliance, the system offered promotions, safety, stability, and privileges, including travel abroad. The most successful who conformed also might have access to foreign goods, special stores, cash bonuses, dachas, cars, and membership in elite professional associations.[4]

But it turned out that what was "Soviet" about this dream was not its content, with which many readers can identify, but how the Baby Boomers went about trying to reach it. A sharp rise in world oil and gold prices allowed the Soviet government to provide its citizens with many material benefits and to spend more money on agriculture, the development of Siberia, and defense, but not on industrial expansion. By the early 1970s, economic reform had become a dead issue and crisis conditions fell into place, resulting in an economic slowdown that, in the course of the decade, eroded people's confidence in the command-administrative system, even among the elite. There was also the problem of Khrushchev's unspoken legacy: the Soviet Union had not built communism. These developments encouraged corruption and the misuse of power throughout the system—and society. Consumers, not producers, the Baby Boomers survived by resorting to *blat* and the black market, and this helped to subvert the system, as people reacted more strongly to the shortages as they got older. Outwardly compliant, they challenged the system by learning how it functioned. By the end of the decade many of them sympathized with the human rights movement, tested the limits of the permissible, and questioned aspects of the Marxist economic model. Some of them emigrated. The vast majority of them denounced, in private to be sure, their country's ill-fated invasion of Afghanistan, suggesting an all-important shift in popular attitudes since the 1968 suppression of the Prague Spring. Even career soldier Aleksandr Ivanov opposed the invasion: "Who has the right to send me there? They didn't threaten us. I didn't take an oath to go to Afghanistan. When they invade us, I'm obliged to defend my country."

A strict social order such as that of Brezhnev's USSR limits people and leads to "general sclerosis,"[5] but not necessarily to individual sclerosis. The Baby Boomers intuitively grasped this, casting the second half of Brezhnev's tenure as a turning point in their country's history and in the evolution of their own consciousness. Life was stable and predictable, but too much so. Many had reached a glass ceiling at work. Most Soviet myths had become meaningless. Some Baby Boomers voiced amazement by how quickly their seemingly unified and ideologically sound society "went to pieces" once Gorbachev unleashed perestroika. Anthropologist Alexei Yurchak argues that if Gorbachev had not opened public space to alternative voices the system could have gone on for much longer.

However, he does not account for how the system produced a Gorbachev, conflating the entire period from 1950 to 1980.[6] Society "went to pieces" because the Baby Boomers had been transforming it all along and had become ready for perestroika: the strategies they had perfected over the years learning to "live Soviet" contributed to the system's demise. Telling jokes about and mocking Brezhnev shook the foundations of the Soviet order. The Baby Boomers' memories reveal a tectonic shift in people's attitudes from blaming individual Soviet leaders—first Stalin, then Khrushchev—the Party line, in effect—to blaming not only Brezhnev while he was still in office but the system itself, as even elements in the Party understood the need for real change. As the glasnost revelations questioned the system's legitimacy, many Baby Boomers temporarily saw themselves as victims of Soviet power. Perestroika also facilitated emigration, allowing some Baby Boomers to realize the "Soviet" dream outside the country, thereby demonstrating how late socialism lost the allegiance of its most educated and in some ways, privileged, class.

How have the Baby Boomers negotiated the challenging transition to a post-Soviet Russia following the collapse of communism in 1991? Some negotiated the transition by emigrating. For the rest, it is essential to consider how they understood the sources of perestroika. Most Baby Boomers saw it as necessary and even inevitable. Expressing the sentiments of many, Boris Shtein explained, "The former system had exhausted itself; Gorbachev could no longer fool people and could no longer pretend that we were going somewhere when we were standing still. Changes were inevitable." The vast majority backed perestroika, applauded glasnost, embraced free elections, and understood the need to replace the command-administrative system with a market-oriented one. According to Vladimir Sidelnikov, the Soviet Union had made three mistakes: "it had banned God, banned the private sector, and put up the Iron Curtain." Yet many of them, appreciating the peculiarities of Russian political culture and the benefits of the planned economy, cautioned against blindly imitating the West and criticized how Gorbachev and later Yeltsin carried out specific reforms.

This is the case because, in the 1990s, they lived through the equivalent of the Great Depression, during which the survival skills they perfected under Soviet power proved invaluable. Family and close friends helped people overcome the challenges, which, for many, necessitated switching jobs and even changing professions. In addition, they had to cope with life passages common to that age cohort such as caring for ill or dying parents, shepherding children through college, and helping them get established. Some found comfort in religion. Ingrained Soviet attitudes complicated how some of them adapted to the new circumstances, to be sure, but their personal stories mostly inspire: crisis comprises both danger and opportunity, and many of them found ways to fulfill themselves in the new circumstances. As one of them, Igor Litvin, put it, "I now feel totally independent. I'm convinced that these are good times for people in Russia. Anyone can realize his full potential."

Yevgeny Podolsky believed that by the start of the millennium the majority of people had already adapted to the new circumstances, "and they know how to live in this world. A large enough number of people sense this. The same holds true for peasants." Indeed, with few exceptions the Baby Boomers looked favorably upon the market economy. To be sure, they echoed majority sentiment in Russia in denigrating Yeltsin when he retired on December 31, 1999; however, most Baby Boomers saw the silver lining, acknowledging that it would take time for a new system to replace the old one and transform mentalities. Most of them held onto their reference points, aiming their anger at institutions, those in power, and the oligarchs, and not at the fledgling Russian democracy or emerging market system. Support for some sort of democratic market order had surfaced already during the Soviet period, becoming entrenched after glasnost stripped away any remaining illusions about the benefits of the Stalinist model.

The Baby Boomers' attitudes merit attention because they promote liberalization and have become part of Russia's new middle, consuming, class. Like Russian society at large, many of them have lost interest in politics at the top under Putin and Medvedev, but not in the politics of everyday life, ironically focusing their energies as they did in the Brezhnev era on the economic side of life, yet admittedly in vastly different circumstances. Olga Kolishchyuk said it succinctly: "If people are living normally politics doesn't interest them. What interests them is what to make for supper tomorrow." Speaking for many, Anna Lyovina understood the negative features of Russian reality as "the costs of the transition period and of the breaking up of old structures." She voiced confidence, however, that things would take a turn for the better. "They have to." Why? Because "ordinary people set the tone for society, not politicians we see every day on TV. Those who help one another, say a kind word, or stop belligerent behavior on public transportation or in stores. This improves the situation, like the way storms clean the air."

This is also a story of three generations in which the middle one, the Baby Boomers who began school the year Sputnik triumphed and graduated the year the USSR celebrated its fiftieth anniversary, are uniquely privileged because they constitute the generation that experienced the best the Soviet system had to offer yet came to reject it. Spared the fears of the Stalin era and the sustained trauma of World War II, the Baby Boomers believed that their parents' suffering imbued them with values to emulate, but they saw themselves as freer and as more optimistic than their parents. Vladimir Prudkin explained: "The Soviet Union was a doomed structure mainly because it could exist only with the strictest adherence to Stalin's principles. The smallest deviation from these policies led to the collapse of the USSR. My generation and I represent those people who began this small deviation." Significantly, the Baby Boomers saw their children as even "freer," and more goal-oriented than they were. Embracing the new order, the children of perestroika are more pragmatic and more rational

Moscow's School No. 20—like the country for that matter—bears a new name and appearance in the new millennium. Anna Lyovina found modern, well-equipped classrooms when she attended a celebration of the school's forty-fifth anniversary in 2003. *Courtesy of Vyacheslav Starik*

and have a different, non-Soviet, attitude toward work. Lacking their parents' complexes, they embrace change. The fact that many interviewees cast the young generation in negative light—what I see as a traditional generational conflict—but depicted their own children as successful exceptions bodes well for Russia's recovery.

How do the memories of those who grew up in Moscow differ from those raised in a provincial city "closed" to foreigners and therefore to many direct foreign influences? There is no denying Moscow's privileged position within the Soviet structure. As Muscovite Viktor Alekseyev emphasized, "Moscow and the rest of Russia are very different things. Moscow was a special world in the Soviet Union." Because Saratov was closed to foreigners, its inhabitants had far less access to outside influences, a fact of life that confined the magnet school's curriculum and affected people at an everyday level. Although it was harder to come across *samizdat* literature in Saratov, what young students might get away with in Moscow threatened local authorities far more in Saratov, who sent a clear message to the student population that behaving too far outside the box would not be tolerated. Owing to the political climate in Saratov, more local Baby Boomers bought into the Party line regarding the invasion of Czechoslovakia and the crackdown on dissent. Yet once glasnost made information available to everyone, these differences in political views between Saratovites and Muscovites largely evaporated.

Muscovites and Saratovites also experienced the economic aspects of late socialism differently. Saratov Baby Boomers remembered the periodic shopping sprees, commonly subsidized by the workplace, which they carried out in the capital, often buying meat and sausage that could have been produced locally. For the most part, however, the strategies both cohorts perfected bear an uncanny resemblance: semilegal and illegal economic activities facilitated by *blat*. Bringing individuals together on their own initiative in ways that were not controlled by the state and that were usually frowned on, these strategies further strengthened private life as they potentially weakened people's faith in the system. Ironically, Muscovites had more of everything, including cynicism: they lived better than those along the Volga, but expressed greater dissatisfaction.

Although glasnost gave Saratovites the same access to information as Muscovites, regional differences based on economic realities continued to define local mentalities in post-Soviet Russia. The market has made everything available in Saratov as in Moscow, but the country's wealth remained concentrated in the capital and therefore Muscovites articulated greater support for democratic freedoms and the market economy. Saratov voters backed more conservative

Friends for roughly fifty years, Saratov Baby Boomers Aleksandr Kutin (left) and Aleksandr Virich share a quiet moment in the kitchen at a reunion of the B Class in 2004. Their lives changed radically during the 1990s: Kutin switched professions; his daughter married an American and moved to the United States. After suffering a stroke, Virich lives on a disability pension. *Courtesy of Aleksandr Virich*

candidates and welcomed a strong leader; however, the well-educated Baby Boomers among them, with some exceptions to be sure, remained more likely to support market reform and political pluralism.

How have the Baby Boomers' experiences both reproduced and transformed Russian society during the Cold War and afterward? How do their personal stories help us comprehend cultural transmission across generations? In answering this question, it is important to stress that the Soviet propaganda state provided its citizens with the "correct" understanding of Soviet history and the country's place in the world. It gave people facts and frameworks with which to think, an ideological language rich in boilerplate metaphors, dogmas, and slogans; however, it ultimately could not dictate what its subjects thought. Understanding freedom as the range of choices from among which to pick, the Baby Boomers had a great deal of space for agency and moral choice, especially in the years after Stalin's death when the country began to open up and the world became smaller. Lacking their parents' fear, these "unconscious agents of change" in Baby Boomer Sergei Zemskov's felicitous formulation became far more demanding of the Soviet system and therefore more open to transforming it.

The Baby Boomers' stories demonstrate that a distinction needs to be drawn between their public and their private lives, although both reproduced and transformed society. After first telling me that Stalin's terror spared his family, Vladimir Sidelnikov confided that his maternal grandmother had spent fifteen years in the Gulag and that his mother had grown up in an orphanage and later fought to get her mother rehabilitated. His mother, a true believer, understood the tragedy as a "terrible mistake," and neither his mother nor his grandmother ever spoke about it. In fact, "they didn't even tell me she was my grandmother. You couldn't back then, because I might have let the secret out. I called her Granny Masha," remembered Sidelnikov. In this case the propaganda state succeeded in shaping their public behavior—and in encroaching upon private life, too. The son of Party members, Sidelnikov, it will be recalled, attended MGIMO and even flirted with the idea of joining the KGB, until he got sent home from Finland while working there on his senior thesis and suffered a breakdown. We can imagine that his family dealt with this publicly by not talking about it or by presenting what happened in sanitized language. Over the years, however, Sidelnikov came to reject the Soviet system. "Before, I believed in all of those ideas," he remembered, "but then I came realize that it's all a bunch of meaningless rubbish."

The borders separating Soviet public and private life might have been porous and ambiguous, as in the case of Sidelnikov's family, but already by the late 1960s, "privacy began to be seen as the only honorable and uncompromising response to the system of public compromise."[7] Many of the Baby Boomers spoke of a certain duality, of what Vladimir Nemchenko called "the world for everyone, and another where we'd gather in small groups and discuss things with others." As a result, there were two truths "one for everyone, and the other that's inside you." Andrei Rogatnev, who worked for the KGB, acknowledged the double standard that characterized Soviet life: "I lived a two-faced life. At work I was one person, and at home another, from a political perspective. We told political jokes. We were indignant over the outrageous things we noticed and saw. But I was incredibly lucky in regard to the people I met and with whom I associated. They, too, understood everything perfectly." Rogatnev's public behavior reproduced structures of Soviet life; however, his private life—which included the telling of political jokes and discussions of the system's shortcomings—made Rogatnev and those with whom he shared his private self open to change.

The Baby Boomers' outward compliance allowed for an inner freedom that, when Gorbachev came to power, made them receptive to reform, even if they had not espoused it earlier. Perestroika may have been launched as a revolution from above, but unlike earlier attempts by the state to effect sweeping transformation, people were ready, even some among the older generations. Aleksandr Virich gave the example of his grandfather who, in his nineties, learned about the dark chapters of the Soviet past through reading *Ogonyok* during perestroika. His reaction: "Go suck my c___! I'm a fool. I didn't know any of that. They didn't tell me." As Virich put it, "Here's a complete change in one's worldview."

Yet changes of this sort also provide evidence in support of the adage that the more things change, the more things remain the same. In other words, the market system and form of democracy that emerged in Russia turned out to be peculiarly, familiarly, Russian. For example, many Baby Boomers stressed that Russia's historical development made it unique and special, not in the way that each country is different but in the way that Russia has been characterized as different as captured in Winston Churchill's dictum that Russia is "a riddle wrapped in a mystery inside an enigma." Natalya P. articulated this sentiment: "I am a patriot of my country. We don't get to pick where we come from. It's a matter of chance who your parents are or which country you were born in. There are no such things as good countries and bad countries, good nations and bad nations." Then Natalya weighed her words for me as an American. "You Americans are greater realists and pragmatists, while we have our heads in the clouds. Besides, we have a different history, different roots."

Indeed, Aleksandr Virich offered an optimistic prognosis of Russia's market economy, but volunteered that he would vote to establish a constitutional monarchy in Russia today: "Russia became accustomed to living under the tsars over many centuries. When Europe was freely moving from feudalism into capitalism, and from capitalism into, excuse me, socialism, we spent three hundred years under the Tatar yoke. We saved Europe! We have a different path of development." And one that many affirmed defied logic. "If you try to explain anything about this country from a logical point of view you're bound for failure," cautioned Leonid Terlitsky. Similarly, Tatyana Luchnikova dredged up the oft-repeated words of nineteenth-century Russian poet Fyodor Tyutchev: "Russia cannot be understood with the mind alone. No ordinary yardstick can span her greatness: She stands alone, unique—in Russia, one can only believe."

And in her people. Whatever their life trajectories, none of the Baby Boomers cast him- or herself as a victim, perhaps, because, in Aleksandr Kutin's words, "we tend to remember the good and to forget the bad." It certainly is human nature to adapt willingly to that which is better. Anatoly Shapiro stressed that "the fear is gone, at least among those with whom I mingle" "What happened is amazing," enthused Yevgeniya Ruditskaya. "If you had told me fifteen years ago that I'd be living on Cyprus and that my friends would come to visit me from Switzerland, Israel, and America, I would have thought you were crazy. But, it turned out that all of this is now possible." Despite the challenges of going, in Arkady Darchenko's words, "from Stalinism to normal, developing capitalism," they, as a cohort, made the journey remarkably intact. Olga Kolishchyuk cast her classmates, with rare exceptions, as "successful people. We're all normal people who live a normal life and who have found our niche in society." Olga Martynkina offered an example: "In terms of everyday life, things have gone all right. I have a happy family life and a good job. I've grown spiritually. Sure there have been temporary difficulties, some material ones, but that's all."

Recognizing these difficulties, past, present, and yet to come, Anna Lyovina observed that "things get done in the world by people who follow their heart. I'm certain of that. And there are many people like that, and they're holding the country together." Underscoring the need to live compassionately, she added, "There are very, very many modest people of this sort. No one writes about them in the papers. They don't make noise. They don't promote themselves. They don't show off. But it's they who have always held Russia together."

Appendix

The Baby Boomers*

Note: Married names follow maiden names in parentheses.

Alekseyev, Viktor Aleksandrovich. Attended Moscow's School No. 20. CPSU member. Born into a military family, Alekseyev studied child psychology, then a new field, at Moscow University. Today he teaches at CUNY's College of Staten Island and resides with his family in the New York area.

Artyomova, Tatyana Mikhailovna. Attended Moscow's School No. 20. CPSU member. A top student, Artyomova became a professor of economics at Moscow's Plekhanov Institute. She and her husband live and work in America, residing in Stamford, Connecticut.

Arzhanova (Koukharskaya), Tatyana Aleksandrovna. Attended Moscow's School No. 20. Raised in a communal flat in Moscow, Arzhanova studied at Moscow's Food Institute, but her career took a different path when she traveled to the United States as translator for a sports delegation in the 1970s. Later she accompanied her husband to Indonesia when he worked there for a Soviet agency. Today she and her family reside in Montreal.

Babushkin, Aleksandr Yevgeniyevich. Attended Saratov's School No. 42. CPSU member. Trained as a physician, Babushkin went to work for the local government at a police-run sobering up center, a job that came with a four-room apartment. During perestroika Babushkin started a second family.

Bakutina (Braun), Marina Olegovna. Attended Moscow's School No. 20. CPSU member. Bakutina remembered the View Master her mother brought back with her from America in the late 1950s. While a student at Moscow's Institute of Foreign Languages, she traveled to England. Bakutina accepted a position at the IFL and taught there until she immigrated to the United States.

Barysheva (Lukonina), Irina Mikhailovna. Attended Saratov's School No. 42. CPSU member. Chapter 1 began with an account of Barysheva's family history. She detailed the drama of the end-of-school writing exam in Saratov, of

---

* Eight of the Baby Boomers requested that I refer to them by pseudonyms or by not using their surnames.

her first trip abroad, and of her resorting to *blat* to join the CPSU. An award-winning teacher, she has spent her career teaching English in Saratov schools.

Bystrov, Vladimir Vladimirovich. Attended Moscow's School No. 20. CPSU member. Bystrov held a high-ranking administrative post in the USSR Ministry of Education. During perestroika, his work took him abroad, including to the United States. In 2003, he served as first vice-president of the World Technological University in Moscow.

Chemodurova, Irina Davidovna. Attended Saratov's School No. 42. Daughter of a Party historian and one of the few Saratov Jews to remember popular anti-Semitism, Chemodurova completed her graduate work in history in Moscow before returning to Saratov to teach at the university level.

D., Viktor. Attended Saratov's School No. 42. The American Relief Administration fed Viktor's starving grandparents during the Russian Civil War and his father served a stint in the Gulag, family experiences that shaped his attitudes. A medical doctor, Viktor worked for many years in an emergency room in Saratov.

Darchenko, Arkady Olegovich. Attended Saratov's School No. 42. Born outside Magadan, Darchenko moved to Saratov as a young boy. His education as a physicist involved a research stint at the closed science city near Moscow, Dubna, where *samizdat* proved easy to come by. Darchenko has had to change careers three times in his life and has found his knowledge of English essential in each transition.

Garzanova, Irina Aleksandrovna. Attended Saratov's School No. 42. Daughter of a decorated war veteran, Garzanova graduated from the Saratov Medical Institute, after which she was sent to Ulyanovsk oblast, where she met her future husband. They lived in his hometown of Lipetsk for twelve years before she returned to Saratov as a single mother. She works in a subspecialty of psychiatry from the Soviet era that treats alcohol and drug addiction.

Glebkin, Vladimir Dmitriyevich. Attended Moscow's School No. 20. Born into a family of academics, Glebkin belonged to the beat-group at School No. 20. He attended and afterward spent his entire career teaching at his alma mater, Patrice Lumumba Friendship University in Moscow.

Godzhello, Georgy Vladimirovich. Attended Moscow's School No. 20. CPSU member. Raised by his mother and grandparents, Godzhello recalled the strong influence his grandfather played in his life. Today he is principal of Moscow's Sport-Educational College.

Gorelik (Belobrovaya), Olga Yakovlevna. Attended Saratov's School No. 42. Daughter of the deputy editor of Saratov's Party newspaper and of a medical doctor, Gorelik earned a Ph.D. in physics and teaches at Saratov University. Her daughter lives in Israel.

Gorokhova, Lyudmila Vladimirovna. Attended Saratov's School No. 42. One of the few Baby Boomers to have appreciated Pioneer camps, Gorokhova briefly worked as a technical translator after graduating from the Saratov Pedagogical Institute. She switched jobs, divorced her jealous first husband, and married her boss. Gorokhova remembers the Soviet period with nostalgia.

Ivanov, Aleksandr Viktorovich. Attended Saratov's School No. 42. CPSU member. One of the few members of the cohort from a working-class family, Ivanov left School No. 42 to complete a military academy. Serving in Saratov oblast, he pursued a professional military career until his retirement.

Ivanov, Gennady Viktorovich. Attended Saratov's School No. 42. CPSU member. After graduating from Saratov's Law Institute, Ivanov went to work for the police to avoid getting drafted. This decision proved life changing: he recently retired as a police investigator. His work involved a stint in Afghanistan.

Kamayurova, Olga Vladimirovna. Attended Saratov's School No. 42. One of the few Baby Boomers who passively believed in the system until glasnost, Kamayurova spent two years in Romania with her husband, there on work assignment, during the Brezhnev era. Perestroika strained her marriage to the breaking point. A pathologist, she enjoys a rich spiritual life today centered on Eastern traditions.

Kenzheyev, Bakhyt Shkurullayevich. Attended Moscow's School No. 20. Half Kazakh, Kenzheyev worked summers as a guide for Intourist while he was a student of chemistry at Moscow University. After graduating, he stayed on to remain the department's "poet in residence" before marrying a Canadian and emigrating. Writer and poet, he mostly lives with his current wife, also from Moscow, in New York.

Kirsanov, Vladimir Nikolayevich. Attended Saratov's School No. 42. CPSU member. Silver medalist and Komsomol activist, Kirsanov attended the Saratov Medical Institute, where he remained to teach. His Volga German ancestry prevented him from applying to MGIMO. Kirsanov links his political maturation to participation in work brigades in the countryside and to his travel to Czechoslovakia.

Kolishchyuk (Skvornyuk), Olga Andreyevna. Attended Saratov's School No. 42. Born in China, Kolishchyuk graduated from the Saratov Pedagogical Institute. She detailed the shadow economy of *blat* and of shopping sprees in Moscow. Kolishchyuk has taught English at Saratov Technical University until her recent retirement.

Kolosova, Yelena Mikhailovna. Attended Moscow's School No. 20. Scion of an academic family, Kolosova studied at Moscow University. She recounted the difficulty she had resolving to immigrate to the United States in 1996, where she has lived and worked mostly in Ames, Iowa, before moving to Houston, Texas.

Konstantinov, Aleksandr Aleksandrovich. Attended Saratov's School No. 42. "Sasha the Muscovite" grew up in Saratov because his father, who had been taken prisoner during the war, was exiled from Moscow. After graduating from the top of the B class at School No. 42 he enrolled at Moscow University, where he completed graduate studies and remained ever since as a research scientist.

Kovalyova, Lyubov Fyodorovna. Attended Moscow's School No. 20. Trained as a chemist, Kovalyova enjoyed a successful career in the textile industry that involved working in Hungary during the late Brezhnev era. The dissolution of the USSR drove a wedge between her and her second husband, a native of Belarus.

Krasilnikov, Pyotor Mikhailovich. Attended Saratov's School No. 42. Krasilnikov's classmates remember that he played the guitar well and had a great voice. But he ran into difficulty getting into college and had to settle for the evening division of the Polytechnic Institute. Krasilnikov is one of the few to have served in the army.

Kulikova (Yevseyeva), Irina Vladimirovna. Attended Saratov's School No. 42. Born into a working-class family, Kulikova studied in the evening division of the Saratov Economics Institute. Although she experienced job discrimination as a young mother, she also extolled the virtues of her work collective. She found the conflicting information bombarding people during perestroika confusing.

Kutin, Aleksandr Sergeyevich. Attended Saratov's School No. 42. Trained as a mathematician and computer scientist, Kutin has enjoyed a career as a university instructor at various Saratov colleges. He taught at the Saratov State Agrarian University when I interviewed him. His daughter married an American and lives in the United States.

Kuznetsova (Dumcheva), Tatyana Anatolyevna. Attended Saratov's School No. 42. The daughter of a high-ranking Saratov Party official, Kuznetsova downplayed her family's privileges that included sojourns for her at elite Pioneer camps. Sympathetic to the Soviet system, she decried the destruction of old idols. She has taught English at the Saratov Technical University since completing college.

Litvin, Igor Markovich. Attended Moscow's School No. 20. Running up against anti-Semitism when he applied to college, Litvin graduated from the Moscow Pedagogical Institute, after which he held various administrative, translating, and teaching jobs. He is in private business today.

Luchnikova, Tatyana Viktorovna. Attended Moscow's School No. 20. Luchnikova moved to Moscow from Kazan when she was in the ninth grade. She experienced difficulty getting into college and landing a job after completing Moscow's Film Institute. Luchnikova lived for a spell in the United States, where she worked as a model and published a volume of poetry. Today she resides in Norway with her second husband.

Lyovina (Maslova), Anna Fyodorovna. Attended Moscow's School No. 20. Chapter 1 opens with a discussion of Lyovina's family's pre-Soviet ties with the United States. A timid child, Lyovina spoke fondly of the atmosphere at School No. 20 and disparagingly of the politicization at Moscow's Institute of Foreign Languages. She has worked most of her adult life as a part-time teacher and tutor.

Markovich, Mikhail Aleksandrovich. Attended Moscow's School No. 20. CPSU member. Born into a large family that knew Stalinist repression firsthand, Markovich graduated from the Moscow Aviation Institute. Placed by the government in a job in publishing upon graduation, Markovich remained in that field ever since.

Martynkina (Zaiko), Olga Dmitryevna. Attended Saratov's School No. 42. Born into a military family, Martynkina was mostly raised by her grandmother. Martynkina left School No. 42 to attend a special music school, after which she graduated from the Saratov Conservatory and has since enjoyed a career as an accomplished pianist.

Mikoyan, Vladimir Sergeyevich (Sergo). Attended Moscow's School No. 20. CPSU member. Grandson of Politburo member Anastas Mikoyan, Vladimir worked as a career diplomat after graduating from MGIMO. He spent much of the 1970s in the United States. During perestroika, he retooled and has since held various administrative jobs in the world of business.

Nemchenko, Vladimir Ivanovich. Attended Saratov's School No. 42. CPSU member. Nemchenko studied physics at Saratov University, but quit graduate school to work as a mechanic. He made a fortune—and lost it, and his health—during the 1990s.

P., Natalya Fyodorovna. Attended Saratov's School No. 42. Natalya P. recalled being exhausted as a child from being involved in too many extracurricular activities. After graduating from the Saratov Pedagogical Institute, she quit the job assigned her as a technical translator and struggled to build a career for herself as a teacher. Perestroika forced her to quit her job at the Pedagogical Institute to accept a better paying one at the Police Academy.

Petrova, Larisa Nikolayevna. Attended Saratov's School No. 42. CPSU member. Born into an elite Party family in Saratov, Petrova remembered the Brezhnev era as one of considerable professional growth for herself for she directed the research department of a medical clinic in Saratov and defended her dissertation in Moscow. She relocated there with her husband during perestroika.

Podolsky, Yevgeny Mikhailovich. Attended Saratov's School No. 42. CPSU member. Podolsky was born in Kaunas, Lithuania, where his father worked for the KGB before moving to Saratov. After marrying a Muscovite, Podolsky remained in the capital. During perestroika he became a successful businessman and applauds Russia's new order.

Poldyaeva, Galina Yevgeniyevna. Attended Saratov's School No. 42. Poldyaeva spent her toddler years on the Kamchatka peninsula. A silver medalist at School No. 42, she quit Saratov Medical Institute when she married a fellow student, who became an army doctor. Afterward, she lived wherever he was stationed, including East Germany. She is the only Baby Boomer not to have pursued a professional career.

Pronina (Altukhova), Natalya Valentinovna. Attended Saratov's School No. 42. Born in Siberia outside Magadan, Pronina enrolled in School No. 42 in fifth grade and always felt like an outsider. She was the only Baby Boomer to have attended the Moscow Youth Festival in 1957. Pronina wanted to join the CPSU, but was not admitted. An economist, she teaches at a commercial college in Saratov.

Prudkin, Vladimir Markovich. Attended Moscow's School No. 20. The son of a famous stage actor, Prudkin himself enjoyed a career in the theatrical world both as director and in other capacities. He argued forcefully that the Soviet system could not survive once it began to reform the Stalinist order.

Raitman (Obraztsova), Lyubov Samsonovna. Attended Moscow's School No. 20. Raitman's parents both traveled abroad while she attended school. A graduate of the Institute of Foreign Languages, Raitman taught at Moscow University when perestroika forced her to give up her teaching career for better paying work. Divorced, she lives and works in Moscow today. Her daughter Anna resides in New York. My thirty-five-year-old friendship with Raitman, who shared stories of her school years and classmates, served as an inspiration for this book.

Rogatnev, Andrei Glebovich. Attended Moscow's School No. 20. CPSU member. Born into a family of KGB operatives, Rogatnev was in Budapest during the 1956 Soviet invasion of Hungary. After graduating from the Aviation Institute, he joined the KGB, serving in Afghanistan and Iraq in the late Soviet period. After the dissolution of the USSR he went into business.

Ruditskaya (Kreizerova), Yevgeniya Semyonovna. Attended Moscow's School No. 20. Ruditskaya experienced anti-Semitism throughout her life. After graduating from Moscow's Pedagogical Institute, she taught in Moscow schools until perestroika. Since the 1990s she and her husband, a businessman, live mostly on Cyprus.

Shapiro, Anatoly Arnoldovich. Attended Moscow's School No. 20. CPSU member. Born in Austria, where his father served as part of the postwar Soviet trade delegation, Shapiro remembered the fear his parents instilled in him and the anti-Semitism he experienced when he applied to MGIMO. He hated army service and later regretted joining the Party. He has spent his career in the field of banking, finance, and commerce.

Shtein, Boris Yakovlevich. Attended Moscow's School No. 20. Living today in California, Shtein was born into a family of construction engineers and to a father who had been raised in Estonia. Shtein's first wife spent many years battling to emigrate before receiving permission to do so. Shtein immigrated to the United States in 1994, acknowledging the help his classmates who had preceded him extended to him.

Sidelnikov, Vladimir A. Attended Moscow's School No. 20. Born into a Party family, Sidelnikov attended MGIMO, but was expelled from Finland by Soviet authorities when he failed to return home at night, after which he suffered a breakdown. An invalid and recovering alcoholic today, he found sobriety, God, and his wife, Lyuba, whose positive effect on him he acknowledged.

Starik, Vyacheslav Davidovich. Attended Moscow's School No. 20. CPSU member. Starik remembered spending summers in his grandmother's village in Orel oblast. Although he claimed anti-Semitism did not affect him, he described how it impacted his career on several occasions. During perestroika he actively campaigned for a local deputy. Since then he has worked in various capacities, but has found it hard to "work for money."

Terlitsky, Leonid Natanovich. Attended Moscow's School No. 20. Terlitsky recounted the impact his parents' travel abroad had on him already as a schoolchild. He encountered anti-Semitism getting into the Moscow Architectural Institute. Turned down when he sought to emigrate, his brother became a refusenik. Terlitsky emigrated, worked as an architect in America, and returned to Russia to direct the Hebrew Immigration Aid Service.

Trubnikov, Aleksandr Vladimirovich. Attended Saratov's School No. 42. The gold medalist of School No. 42's A class, Trubnikov studied physics and remained working at Saratov University in that field until immigrating to Israel in the late 1990s. He is the only Baby Boomer I interviewed who lives in Israel.

Tsurkan (Yegorova), Irina Semyonovna. Attended Saratov's School No. 42. Tsurkan credits her Moldavian father and Volga German grandmother with shaping her personality, and her second husband with raising her political consciousness by slamming Lenin. A graduate of the Saratov Medical Institute, she works as a pediatrician in Saratov.

Ulyakhin, Valentin Nikolayevich. Attended Moscow's School No. 20. Ulyakhin studied at MGIMO, completed graduate school, and held a position at the Institute of Oriental Studies. But perestroika enabled him to fulfill his father's—and his own—dream of becoming a priest. Today Father Valentin is a parish priest in Moscow.

Vinogradova, Sofiya Semyonovna. Attended Moscow's School No. 20. Raised in a military family in Moscow, Vinogradova took a circuitous path to medical school. She lives in Moscow and works as a family practitioner in a neighborhood clinic. Vinogradova applauded perestroika for ending shortages in Russia.

Virich, Aleksandr Grigoryevich. Attended Saratov's School No. 42. CPSU member. Virich described how he and his classmates clandestinely played Western music at a school dance in Saratov. Virich worked as an engineer, joining the Party in 1987 when Gorbachev was in power "because I had to." A smoker since tenth grade, he suffered a stroke after which he retired.

Vizgalova (Vasilyeva), Irina Valentinovna. Attended Saratov's School No. 42. Vizgalova's deaf grandmother moved to Saratov to help raise her. Vizgalova did not believe Khrushchev's promise to build communism, owing to bread shortages in Saratov. The design institute at which she worked all but shut down during the 1990s, forcing her to find employment elsewhere.

Volodarsky, Leonid Venyaminovich. Attended Moscow's School No. 20. Volodarsky graduated from the Institute of Foreign Languages where his father taught. Finding graduate school not to his liking, he became highly skilled at translating English-language films. He is a bitter opponent of how Yeltsin carried out reform. Today Volodarsky has his own radio program in Moscow.

Yanichkina (Belovolova), Natalya Aleksandrovna. Attended Saratov's School No. 42. Accused of cosmopolitanism, Yanichkina's mother and grandmother served stints in the Gulag in the early 1950s. Yanichkina and her husband—whom she met while vacationing—spent many years in Magadan to earn enough money to establish themselves in Saratov.

Yolshina, Natalya Pavlovna. Attended Saratov's School No. 42. CPSU member. Yolshina went to a special music school before enrolling in School No. 42 in seventh grade after hearing so much about it from a friend. A familiar face in Saratov because she has her own television show, Party member Yolshina welcomed perestroika.

Zemskov, Sergei Yuryevich. Attended Moscow's School No. 20. CPSU member. Zemskov was born into a family of revolutionaries who knew repression firsthand: his own grandfather "sat" for five years. Zemskov had vivid memories of Gulag survivors and old Bolsheviks he met at the family dacha as a child, who, he remembered, harbored no animosity toward communism. He is in private business today.

Zharovova (Proskuryakova), Yelena Vadimovna. Attended Moscow's School No. 20. Silver medalist Zharovova graduated from the Physics Department of Moscow University, completed graduate study, and worked at a research institute of the Academy of Sciences. She and her family reside in Moscow today.

Notes

Introduction

1. Khrushchev's outline for the communist utopia stressed that "the set program can be fulfilled with success under conditions of peace," a point lost on frightened Americans. Harrison E. Salisbury, *Khrushchev's "Mein Kampf"* (New York: Belmont Books, 1961), 132. The very title of the Western publication grossly distorts the document's purpose and message.
2. Here I tweak a term coined by historian Stephen Kotkin, "to speak Soviet." See his *Magnetic Mountain: Stalinism as a Civilization* (Berkeley: University of California Press, 1995).
3. Luisa Passerini, "Introduction," *International Yearbook of Oral History and Life Stories,* Vol. I, *Memory and Totalitarianism,* ed. Luisa Passerini (New York: Oxford University Press, 1992), 8.
4. Daria Khubova, Andrei Ivankiev, and Tonia Sharova, "After Glasnost: Oral History in the Soviet Union," *International Yearbook of Oral History and Life Stories,* Vol. I, *Memory and Totalitarianism,* ed. Luisa Passerini (New York: Oxford University Press, 1992), 96.
5. Alen Blium (Alain Blum) and Sergei Zakharov, "Demograficheskaia istoriia SSSR i Rossii v zerkale pokolenii," *Naselenie i Obshchestvo,* no. 17 (February, 1997).http://www.infran.ru/ vovenko/60years_ww2/demogr1.htm.
6. Today the oblast occupies second place in Russia (after Krasnodar) in the volume of grain production, and the city, with a population just over 900,000, ranks fifteenth in population.
7. This information is drawn from <http://www.saratov.ru>; <http://www. russianamericanchamber.org/regions/Saratov>; and G. A. Malinin, *Saratov: Kratkii ocherk-putevoditel'* (Saratov: Privolzhskoe knizhnoe izdatel'stvo, 1974).
8. Cited in Jan-Erik Ruth and Gary Kenyon, "Biography in Adult Development and Aging," in James E. Birren, et al., eds., *Aging and Biography: Explorations in Adult Development* (New York: Springer Publishing Co., 1996), 4.
9. Here I use a scale on complexity that considers the themes, meanings, plots, characters, relationships, and ways of life found in the oral narratives. See Brian de Vries and Allen J. Lehman, "The Complexity of Personal Narratives," in Birren, et al., eds., *Aging and Biography,* 153.
10. Alessandro Portelli, *The Death of Luigi Trastulli and Other Stories: Form and Meaning in Oral History* (Albany: State University of New York Press, 1991), 51.
11. Birren, et al., eds., *Aging and Biography,* 2. Other works that have shaped my thinking on memory include: Harold Rosen, *Speaking from Memory: Guide to Autobiographical Acts and Practices* (Stoke on Trent (UK): Trentham Books, 1998); Micaela Di Leonardo, "Oral History as Ethnographic Encounter," *Oral History Review* 15 (Spring 1987): 1–20; Jaclyn Jeffrey and Glenace Edwall, eds., *Memory and History: Essays on Remembering and Interpreting Human Experience* (Lanham, Md.: University Press of America, 1992); David Dunaway, "The Oral Biography," *Biography* 14, no. 3 (1991): 256–66; and Rhonda Y. Williams, "'I'm a keeper of information': History-telling and Voice," *Oral History Review* 28, no. 1 (2001): 41–63.

12. Initially interrogating the texts for underlying belief systems, elusive patterns, missing meanings, gaps, and emotional overtones, I soon realized that literary forms of analysis presented the danger of my getting lost in language and that this could obstruct the interpretive value of what my interviewees had to say.

13. Kenneth L. Kann, *Comrades and Chicken Ranchers: The Story of a California Jewish Community* (Ithaca: Cornell University Press, 1993), 12–13.

14. In an oral history of East Germans born in 1949, Dorothee Wierling offers no explicit argument, but underscores the importance of family in understanding life in the GDR. See *Geboren im Jahr Eins: Der Jahrgang 1949 in der DDR—Versuch einer Kollektivbiographie* (Berlin: Ch. Links Verlag, 2002).

15. Yurchak focuses on postwar transformations at the level of discourse, ideology, language, and ritual not to illuminate the causes for the Soviet Union's collapse but "the conditions that made the collapse possible without making it anticipated." Rejecting the notion that the single function of language is to reflect or express, Yurchak looks to the *generative* properties of language, to how the effects of language can enable the performance of an ideology that by no means subscribes to its "constative" statements, ones that present facts or describe reality. Alexei Yurchak, *Everything Was Forever, Until It Was No More: The Last Soviet Generation* (Princeton: Princeton University Press, 2006), 1, 4.

16. James V. Wertsch, *Voices of Collective Remembering* (New York: Cambridge University Press, 2002), 172–73.

Chapter 1

1. Luisa Passerini, "Italian Working Class Culture between the Wars: Consensus to Fascism and Work Ideology," *International Journal of Oral History* 1 (February 1980): 10.

2. N. N. Maslov, "Short Course of the History of the All-Russian Communist Party (Bolshevik): An Encyclopedia of Stalin's Personality Cult," *Soviet Studies in History* 28, no. 3 (1989–90): 42.

3. Anne Applebaum, *Gulag: A History* (New York: Doubleday, 2003), xvii. See also Galina Mikhailovna Ivanova, *Labor Camp Socialism: The Gulag in the Soviet Totalitarian System*, ed. Donald J. Raleigh and trans. Carol Flath (Armonk, N.Y.: M. E. Sharpe, 2000), 188.

4. Feiga Blekher, *The Soviet Woman in the Family and Society: A Sociological Study* (New York: John Wiley, 1979), 49–50.

5. Elena Zubkova, *Russia after the War: Hopes, Illusions, and Disappointments, 1945–1957*, trans. and ed. by Hugh Ragsdale (Armonk, N.Y.: M. E. Sharpe, 1998), 102.

6. Ekaterina Foteeva, "Coping with Revolution: The Experiences of Well-to-Do Russian Families," in Daniel Bertaux, Paul Thompson, and Anna Rotkirch, eds., *Living Through the Soviet System* (New York: Routledge, 2004), 68–92.

7. B. A. Grushin, *Chetyre zhizni Rossii v zerkale obshchestvennogo mneniia: Ocherki massovogo soznaniia rossiian vremen Khrushcheva, Brezhneva, Gorbacheva i El'tsina v 4-kh knigakh. Zhizn' 1-ia: Epokha Khrushcheva* (Moscow: Progress-Traditsiia, 2001), 298–300.

8. The percentage of infants in state nurseries rose to over 30 percent before the end of the 1970s, but this expansion affected the Baby Boomers only as parents. Blekher, *The Soviet Woman*, 163, 166.

9. Between 1960 and 1964, the government shut down 5,457 churches, leaving only 7,873 open as of January 1, 1965. See Tatiana A. Chumachenko, *Church and State in Soviet Russia: Russian Orthodoxy from World War II to the Khrushchev Years*, trans. and ed. by Edward E. Roslof (Armonk, N.Y.: M. E. Sharpe, 2002), 187.

10. Petr Vail' and Aleksandr Genis, *60-e: Mir Sovetskogo cheloveka* (Moscow: Novoe literaturnoe obozrenie, 2001), 262–63.

11. Ibid., 262.

12. Victoria Semenova, "Equality in Poverty: The Symbolic Meaning of *kommunalki* in the 1930s–50s," in Daniel Bertaux, Paul Thompson, and Anna Rotkirch, eds., *Living Through the Soviet System* (New York: Routledge, 2004), 64.

13. The cultural consequences of throwing together families from different social backgrounds into such situations may have complicated the transmission of family values

between generations but, based on the Baby Boomers' memories, did not "bleach out" old class identities as has been argued. Some "formers" managed to minimize the obvious downside of living in congested quarters by taking in extended family members. Doing so would only contribute to a strengthening of their identity as being "other." See Semenova, "Equality," 59, also 64.

14. William Taubman, *Khrushchev: The Man and His Era* (New York: Norton, 2003), 382.

15. Irene A. Boutenko and Kirill E. Razlogov, eds., *Recent Social Trends in Russia, 1960–1995* (Montreal and Kingston: McGill-Queen's University Press, 1997), 7.

16. Viktoriia Semenova, Ekaterina Foteeva, and Daniel Bertaux, eds., *Sud'by liudei: Rossiia XX vek. Biografii semei kak ob"ekt sotsiologicheskogo issledovaniia* (Moscow: Institut Sotsiologii RAN, 1996), 352.

17. Kent H. Geiger, *The Family in Soviet Russia* (Cambridge, Mass.: Harvard University Press, 1968), 207.

18. Grushin, *Chetyre zhizni,* 1: 125, 128, 138–54, and Vladimir Shlapentokh, *Public and Private Life of the Soviet People: Changing Values in Post-Stalin Russia* (New York: Oxford University Press, 1989), 68.

19. A. V. Baranov, *Sotsial'no-demograficheskoe razvitie krupnogo goroda* (Moscow: Finansy i statistika, 1981), 158–59, and Shlapentokh, *Public and Private,* 68.

20. Moshe Lewin, *The Soviet Century* (London: Verso, 2005), 386.

21. Nanci Adler, *The Gulag Survivor: Beyond the Soviet System* (New Brunswick, N.J.: Transaction Publishers, 2002), 122, 177, 183, and Idem., "The Returned of the Repressed: Survival after the Gulag," in Daniel Bertaux, Paul Thompson, and Anna Rotkirch, eds., *Living Through the Soviet System* (New York: Routledge, 2004), 214–15.

22. Alex Inkeles and Raymond A. Bauer, *The Soviet Citizen: Daily Life in a Totalitarian Society* (Cambridge, Mass.: Harvard University Press, 1961), 96–98, 185, 251, 337, 377–93.

23. Zubkova, *Russia after the War,* 160.

24. Walter L. Hixson, *Parting the Curtain: Propaganda, Culture, and the Cold War, 1945–1961* (New York: St. Martin's Griffin, 1997), 159.

25. Zubkova, *Russia after the War,* 199.

26. Vladislav Zubok, *Zhivago's Children: The Last Russian Intelligentsia* (Cambridge, Mass.: Harvard University Press, 2009), 111.

27. Eric Shiraev and Vladislav Zubok, *Anti-Americanism in Russia: From Stalin to Putin* (Basingstoke (UK): Palgrave, 2000), 13.

28. Hixson, *Parting the Curtain,* 185–210. Quotation found on 201.

29. Cited in ibid., 210.

30. Susan E. Reid, "Cold War in the Kitchen: Gender and the De-Stalinization of Consumer Taste in the Soviet Union under Khrushchev," *Slavic Review* 61, no. 2 (2002): 211–52.

31. Alex Inkeles, *Public Opinion in Soviet Russia: A Study in Mass Persuasion* (Cambridge, Mass.: Harvard University Press, 1951), vii, 324.

Chapter 2

1. Cited in Matthew J. Von Bencke, *The Politics of Space: A History of U.S.-Soviet/Russian Competition and Cooperation in Space* (Boulder, Colo.: Westview Press, 1997), 18–19.

2. Cited in <http://www.centennialofflight.gov/essay/SPACEFLIGHT/Sputnik/SP16.htm>.

3. Paul Dickson, *Sputnik: The Shock of the Century* (New York: Walker and Co., 2001).

4. This "achievement" did receive mixed reviews. Its detractors nicknamed Sputnik II "Muttnik" because Laika became the first casualty to space exploration when the satellite overheated.

5. A. A. Demezer, compiler, *Domovodstvo,* 4th ed. (Moscow: Kolos, 1965), 85.

6. Mervyn Matthews, *Education in the Soviet Union: Politics and Institutions since Stalin* (London: George Allen & Unwin, 1982), 19–20, 27.

7. National Education Association of the United States. Division of Travel Service, *Soviet Schools: A Firsthand Report Based on a Trip through the Union of Soviet Socialist Republics by a Group of Sixty-Four American Educators* (Washington, D.C.: Division of Travel Service, National Education Association, 1960), 5–16, 32.

8. Susan Jacoby, *Inside Soviet Schools* (New York: Hill and Wang, 1974), 10–11, 15, 19–20.

9. Urie Bronfenbrenner, *Two Worlds of Childhood: U.S. and U.S.S.R.* (New York: Pocket Books, 1970), xii.

10. See Vsesoiuznaia pionerskaia organizatsiia imeni V.I. Lenina. Vsesoiuznyi leninskii kommunisticheskii soiuz molodezhi. Tsentral'nyi komitet, *Tovarishch: Zapisnaia knizhka pionera na 1961/62 uchebnyi god* (Moscow: [s.n.], 1961), 11–12.

11. The career patterns of three-quarters of the graduates involved use of English. John Dunstan, *Paths to Excellence and the Soviet School* (Rochester [UK]: NFER Publishing, 1977), 93–101.

12. Matthews, *Education in the Soviet Union*, 28.

13. Jacoby, *Inside Soviet Schools*, 109.

14. Daniel Bertaux, Paul Thompson, and Anna Rotkirch, eds., "Introduction," in idem., *Living Through the Soviet System* (New York: Routledge, 2004), 4.

15. Jacoby, *Inside Soviet Schools*, 198.

16. Vladimir Shlapentokh, *Soviet Intellectuals and Political Power: The Post-Stalin Era* (Princeton: Princeton University Press, 1990), 25.

17. See Vsesoiuznaia pionerskaia organizatsiia, *Tovarishch*, 170.

18. Ibid., 74–75.

19. Ibid., 240–41.

20. Ibid., 42–47.

21. See, for instance, Ia. A. Ioffe, *My i planeta: Tsifry i fakty* (Moscow: Izdatel'stvo Politicheskoi Literatury, 1967), 7.

22. Vsesoiuznaia pionerskaia organizatsiia, *Tovarishch*, 10.

23. Vladimir A. Kozlov argues that people protested under Khrushchev because they believed in the system and that they might improve it. See his *Mass Uprisings in the USSR: Protest and Rebellion in the Post-Stalin Years*, trans. and ed. by Elaine McClarnand MacKinnon (Armonk, N.Y.: M. E. Sharpe, 2002).

24. Zubok, *Zhivago's Children*, 192.

25. See Legend No. 22 on the website http://www.s2067.narod.ru/ .

26. Vail' and Genis, *60-e*, 13, 16.

27. Iurii Aksiutin has recently argued that many elements in Soviet society were unprepared for the attack on Stalin and thus on their belief system. See his *Khrushchevskaia "ottepel'" i obshchestvennye nastroeniia v SSSR v 1953–1964 gg.* (Moscow: Rosspen, 2004).

28. Catriona Kelly, "'The School Waltz': The Everyday Life of the Post-Stalinist Soviet Classroom," *Forum for Anthropology and Culture*, no. 1 (2004), 152.

Chapter 3

1. Zubok, *Zhivago's Children*, 99–100.

2. See I. S. Kon, *Druzhba: Etiko-psikhologicheskii ocherk* (Moscow: Politizdat, 1980), 9–11, 25, 29, 133–34.

3. Vladimir Shlaptentokh, *Love, Marriage, and Friendship in the Soviet Union: Ideals and Practices* (New York: Praeger, 1984), 213–45.

4. Vail' and Genis, *60-e*, 64.

5. Vsesoiuznaia pionerskaia organizatsiia, *Tovarishch*, 195. This was true elsewhere as well. See N. B. Lebina and A. N. Chistikov, *Obyvatel' i reformy: Kartiny povsednevnoi zhizni gorozhan v gody nepa i Khrushchevskogo desiatiletiia* (St. Petersburg: Dmitrii Bulanin, 2003), 297.

6. Grushin, *Chetyre*, 1: 460, 488.

7. <http://www.kinoexpert.ru/index.asp?comm=4&num=3452>.

8. Grushin, *Chetyre*, 1: 406.

9. Shlapentokh, *Public and Private*, 147.

10. Ibid., 195–217.

11. Reid, "Cold War in the Kitchen," 232–33.

12. Zubkova, *Russia after the War*, 193.

13. Catriona Kelly, *Refining Russia: Advice Literature, Polite Culture, and Gender from Catherine to Yeltsin* (Oxford: Oxford University Press, 2001), 360.

14. *Poleznye sovety* (Moscow: Moskovskii rabochii, 1959), 491.

15. Anna Rotkirch, "'What kind of sex can you talk about?': Acquiring Sexual Knowledge in Three Soviet Generations," in Daniel Bertaux, Paul Thompson, and Anna Rotkirch, eds., *Living Through the Soviet System* (New York: Routledge, 2004), 106.

16. Igor S. Kon, *The Sexual Revolution in Russia: From the Age of the Czars to Today*, trans. by James Riordan (New York: Free Press, 1995), 86, 88.

17. Ibid., 89.

18. Rotkirch, "'What kind,'" 106.

19. Kon, *Sexual Revolution*, 187.

20. Alex Inkeles, *Social Change in Soviet Russia* (Cambridge, Mass.: Harvard University Press, 1968), 344, and Liudmila Alekseeva, *U.S. Broadcasting to the Soviet Union* (New York: U.S. Helsinki Watch Committee, 1986), 9.

21. Hixson, *Parting the Curtain*, 33, 38-40, 42-54, 63-64, 115-16, 153-56. For the Soviet depiction of VOA, see Inkeles, *Social Change*, 344-45.

22. Georgie Anne Geyer, *The Young Russians* (Homewood, Ill.: ETC Publications, 1975), 157; Ludmilla Alexeyeva and Paul Goldberg, *The Thaw Generation: Coming of Age in the Post-Stalin Era* (Pittsburgh: University of Pittsburgh Press, 1990), 181-82; and Alekseeva [Alexeyeva], *U.S. Broadcasting*, 9.

23. Alekseeva, *U.S. Broadcasting*, 1-3.

24. Vail' and Genis, *60-e*, 281.

25. Alan M. Ball, *Imagining America: Influence and Images in Twentieth-Century Russia* (Lanham, Md.: Rowman and Littlefield, 2003), 19, 39, 62, 179, 183.

26. Shiraev and Zubok, *Anti-Americanism*, 13-15.

27. A. Adzhubei et al., *Litsom k litsu s Amerikoi: Rasskaz o poezdke N. S. Khrushcheva v SShA, 15-17 sentiabria 1959 goda* (Moscow: Gos. Izdatel'stvo, 1959), 25, 149, 269, 508-13.

28. Ibid., 5, 7, 19.

29. This demonstrates that "the high measure of people's dependence on texts of an official political nature and on propaganda." Grushin, *Chetyre*, 1: 69-70, 89-99. Quote on 99.

30. At the time, 16,000 foreigners were studying at Soviet universities and another 12,000 were involved in on-the-job training. See Geyer, *Young Russians*, 64.

31. Ibid., 60, 62.

32. Writings on generations tend to emphasize the role they play in presenting alternatives to the status quo. But what determines a generation? Sociologist Karl Mannheim argued that generations become an actuality only when there is a bond created by instability (such as the Great Depression or World War II). See Bryan Turner and June Edmunds, eds., *Generational Consciousness, Narrative and Politics* (London: Rowman and Littlefield, 2002), 4. However, in emphasizing the impact of the Baby Boomers' generation worldwide, two Finnish scholars point out that instability affects people of all ages similarly and argue instead that change experienced as something positive becomes a "generational experience." Tommi Hoikkala, Semi Purhonen and J. P. Roos, "The Baby Boomers: Life's Turning Points and Generational Consciousness," in Turner and Edmunds, eds., *Generational Consciousness*, 145-46, 159-62, quote on 162.

33. James R. Millar, ed., *Politics, Work, and Daily Life in the USSR: A Survey of Former Soviet Citizens* (New York: Cambridge University Press, 1987), 61, 64, 94-95.

34. Ibid., 27.

35. Svetlana Boym, *The Future of Nostalgia* (New York: Basic Books, 2001), xvi, 58.

36. Vail' and Genis, *60-e*, 121.

37. Vladimir Shlapentokh, *Soviet Public Opinion and Ideology: Mythology and Pragmatism in Interaction* (New York: Praeger, 1986), 137-40.

Chapter 4

1. See, e.g., Moshe Lewin, *The Gorbachev Phenomenon: A Historical Interpretation*, expanded edition (Berkeley: University of California Press, 1991).

2. Millar, ed., *Politics*, x-xii.

3. Shlapentokh, *Public and Private*, 13, 63, 153, 170.

4. Inkeles, *Social Change*, 60.

5. Geyer, *Young Russians*, 49.
6. Matthews, *Education*, 101, and V. T. Lisovskii and A. V. Dmitriev, *Lichnost' studenta* (Leningrad: Izdatel'stvo Leningradskogo Universiteta, 1974), 9.
7. Ioffe, *My i planeta*, 168–69.
8. Lisovskii and Dmitriev, *Lichnost' studenta*, 10–11.
9. Ibid., 42.
10. This was the case, not only owing to a growth of interest in the latter but also to an expansion of polytechnic institutes and related technical colleges. See Matthews, *Education*, 130–31, and Lisovskii and Dmitriev, *Lichnost' studenta*, 43–44.
11. Katerina Katz, *Gender, Work and Wages in the Soviet Union: A Legacy of Discrimination* (New York: Palgrave, 2001), 76.
12. Zubkova, *Russia after the War*, 197.
13. Georgie Geyer observed that, although patriotic, loyal, and proud of the USSR's achievements, "the study of Marxism bores them to death…and so does ideology." Geyer, *Young Russians*, 47.
14. Matthews, *Education*, 124–25.
15. Shlapentokh, *Soviet Intellectuals*, 171.
16. Vail' and Genis, *60-e*, 310–11, 314–17.
17. Lisovskii and Dmitriev, *Lichnost' studenta*, 116, 125–29.
18. In 1970, the average monthly wage in Saratov oblast was 115.9 rubles ($150), slightly below that of Moscow. N. I. Ivanov, *Narodnoe khoziaistvo Saratovskoi oblasti (k 50-letiiu so dnia obrazovaniia oblasti): Statisticheskii sbornik* (Saratov: Privolzhskoe knizhnoe izdatel'stvo, 1984), 50.
19. Alastair McAuley, *Women's Work and Wages in the Soviet Union* (London: George Allen & Unwin, 1981), 29.
20. Blekher, *Soviet Woman*, 83, 110–11, 115–20, 217–23; and Geyer, *Young Russians*, 189.
21. See Bakhyt Kenzheev [Kenzheyev], *Zoloto goblinov: Romany* (Moscow: Izd-vo Nezavisimaia gazeta, 2000).
22. Vail' and Genis, *60-e*, 298–302.
23. David L. Ruffley, *Children of Victory: Young Specialists and the Evolution of Soviet Society* (Westport, Conn.: Praeger, 2003), 7–9.
24. Matthews, *Education*, 113.
25. Millar, ed., *Politics*, 207. See Wesley A. Fisher, *The Soviet Marriage Market: Mate Selection in Russia and the USSR* (New York: Praeger, 1980), 149, and Vladimir Shlapentokh, *Love, Marriage, and Friendship in the Soviet Union: Ideals and Practices* (New York: Praeger, 1984), 68–69, 77.
26. Peter H. Juviler, "The Soviet Family in Post-Stalin Perspective," in Stephen F. Cohen, Alexander Rabinowitch, and Robert Sharlet, eds., *The Soviet Union since Stalin* (Bloomington: Indiana University Press, 1980), 231–33, 243.
27. Shlapentokh, *Love*, 41, 46, 65, 129, and Fisher, *Soviet Marriage Market*, 22, 26.
28. Fisher, *Soviet Marriage Market*, 175, 192, 205, 211, 229, 239, 245; Shlapentokh, *Love*, 173, 176.
29. The government had rescinded its ban on marriage to foreigners in 1953 but greatly discouraged this conduct. In 1976, only 8,000 Soviet women married foreigners and left to live abroad in 110 countries. Few foreign women married Soviet men. Fisher, *Soviet Marriage Market*, 255.
30. Ibid., 2–11, 20–26, 33–37, 41–42, 103.
31. Shlapentokh, *Love*, 123.
32. Kelly, *Refining Russia*, 339.
33. Lebina and Chistikov, *Obyvatel' i reformy*, 289.
34. John Bushnell, "The 'New Soviet Man' Turns Pessimist," in Stephen F. Cohen, Alexander Rabinowitch, and Robert Sharlet, eds., *The Soviet Union since Stalin* (Bloomington: Indiana University Press, 1980), 179–80, 190–93.
35. Shiraev and Zubok, *Anti-Americanism*, 21.
36. Bushnell, "'New Soviet Man'," 192–93.
37. See, for instance, V. M. Matveev and A. N. Panov, *V mire vezhlivosti* (Moscow: Molodaia gvardiia, 1983), especially pp. 10, 29–30, 33 (citation), 40–72.
38. Geyer, *Young Russians*, ii.

39. Millar, ed., *Politics*, 28. In contrast, Soviet bureaucrats, state employees, the peasantry, and blue-collar workers remained impervious to Western culture, indifferent to foreign radio broadcasts, and hostile to Soviet dissidents, associating peace and stability with a strapping state. See Shiraev and Zubok, *Anti-Americanism*, 24.
40. Ruffley, *Children of Victory*, 175–76.

Chapter 5

1. George W. Breslauer, *Gorbachev and Yeltsin as Leaders* (New York: Cambridge University Press, 2002), 4–5, 7.
2. See George Breslauer, *Khrushchev and Brezhnev as Leaders: Building Authority in Soviet Politics* (London: George Allen and Unwin, 1982), and Edwin Bacon and Mark Sandle, eds., *Brezhnev Reconsidered* (New York: Palgrave Macmillan, 2002).
3. Although some of capitalism's most vocal critics have acknowledged that it remains adaptive and able to survive systemic crises, they point to signs of the system's social decay worldwide. Still others insist that the capitalist industrial system has already given way to a modern information society. Supporters of the term "late capitalism" have isolated its features such as accelerated technological innovation and globalization of financial capital, but mostly its negative ones such as states' efforts to exert more social controls, intensified competition, a permanent arms economy, the ever-growing gap between rich and poor (both within and among countries), neocolonialism, and the market's breakdown of traditional social institutions. See, among others, Fredric Jameson, *Postmodernism; or, The Cultural Logic of Late Capitalism* (Durham, N.C.: Duke University Press, 1991); David Harvey, *The Limits to Capital* (Chicago: University of Chicago, Press, 1982); and Timothy Bewes, *Reification; or, The Anxiety of Late Capitalism* (London and New York: Verso, 2002).
4. Shlapentokh, *Soviet Intellectuals*, 172–202.
5. L. A. Gordon and E. V. Klopov, *Poteri i obreteniia v Rossii devianostykh: Istoriko-sotsiologicheskie ocherki ekonomicheskogo polozheniia narodnogo bol'shinstva*. Vol. 1, *Meniaiushchaisia strana v meniaiushchemsia mire: Predposylki peremen v usloviiakh truda i urovne zhizni* (Moscow: Editorial URSS, 2000), 125–26.
6. Blekher, *Soviet Woman*, 136.
7. Vladimir Shalpentokh, *A Normal Totalitarian Society: How the Soviet Union Functioned and How It Collapsed* (Armonk, N.Y.: M. E. Sharpe, 2001), 123.
8. Millar, ed., *Politics*, 33–49.
9. Ibid., 95, 111, 113, 132.
10. Shlapentokh, *Public and Private*, 62.
11. Ibid., 142. As Susan Reid argued, "management of consumption was as significant for the Soviet system's long survival as for its ultimate collapse." See "Cold War in the Kitchen," 212.
12. Moshe Lewin, *The Soviet Century* (London: Verso, 2005), 355.
13. James Millar, "The Little Deal: Brezhnev's Contribution to Acquisitive Socialism," in Terry L. Thompson and Robert Sheldon, eds., *Soviet Society and Culture: Essays in Honour of Vera S. Dunham* (Boulder, Colo.: Westview, 1988) 7–8.
14. Alena Ledeneva, *Russia's Economy of Favours: Blat, Networking, and Informal Exchange* (Cambridge: Cambridge University Press, 1998), 2–3.
15. Ibid., 6–7.
16. "The Soviet government, Soviet society, cannot rid itself of corruption as long as it remains Soviet. It is as simple as that," argued Konstantin M. Simis. See his *USSR: The Corrupt Society. The Secret World of Soviet Capitalism*, trans. by Jacqueline Edwards and Mitchell Schneider (New York: Simon and Schuster, 1982), 205–96, quotation on 300.
17. Cited in Shlapentokh, *Public and Private*, 62.
18. Millar, ed., *Politics*, 132–33.
19. Shlapentokh, *Public and Private*, 157, 154, 157,
20. L. G. Ionin, *Svoboda v SSSR: Stat'i i esse* (St. Petersburg: Fond "Universitetskaia kniga," 1997), 35.
21. A. A. Dorokhov, *Eto ne melochi* (Moscow: Politizdat, 1961), 11.
22. Shlapentokh, *Public and Private*, 229.

23. Boutenko and Razlogov, *Recent Social Trends*, 21.
24. Nina Tumarkin, *The Living and the Dead: The Rise and Fall of the Cult of World War II in Russia* (New York: Basic Books, 1994), 132.
25. Catherine Merridale's book on the common Soviet soldier at war confirms this point. See *Ivan's War: Life and Death in the Red Army, 1939–1945* (New York: Metropolitan Books, 2006).
26. See Christopher Ward, *Brezhnev's Folly: The Building of BAM and Late Soviet Socialism* (Pittsburgh: University of Pittsburgh Press, 2009).
27. In this regard they served as the state's agents "in reforming the material culture of everyday life." See Reid, "Cold War in the Kitchen," 220–21.
28. Millar, ed., *Politics*, 51.
29. Shlapentokh, *Love*, 210–11.
30. Dorokhov, *Eto ne melochi*, 17.
31. Anna Temkina and Anna Rotkirch, "Soviet Gender Contracts and their Shifts in Contemporary Russia," *Idantutkimus: Finnish Journal of Russian and East European Studies* 2 (1997): 7, and Boutenko and Razlogov, *Recent Social Trends*, 54, 60.
32. Shlapentokh, *Love*, 4–5.
33. Bertaux, Thompson, and Rotkirch, eds., "Introduction," 4.

Chapter 6

1. M. K. Gorshkov, *Rossiiskoe obshchestvo v usloviiakh transformatsii. Mify i real'nost': Sotsiologicheskii analiz, 1992–2002* (Moscow: Rosspen, 2003), 418–19.
2. Alexander Dallin, "Causes of the Collapse of the USSR," in Alexander Dallin and Gail W. Lapidus, eds., *The Soviet System: From Crisis to Collapse* (Boulder, Colo.: Westview Press, 1995), 549–64.
3. Ibid., 550–60.
4. Ferenc Feher and Andrew Arato, eds., *Gorbachev: The Debate* (Atlantic Highlands, N.J.: Humanities Press International, Inc., 1989), 5–6.
5. Shlapentokh, *Normal Totalitarian Society*, 186.
6. Vail' and Genis, *60-e*, 329.
7. Nancy Ries, *Russian Talk: Culture and Conversation during Perestroika* (Ithaca, N.Y.: Cornell University Press, 1997), 167–68.
8. Wertsch, *Voices*, 172–73.
9. Ibid.
10. See Marianne Hirsch's *Family Frames: Photography, Narrative, and Postmemory* (Cambridge, Mass.: Harvard University Press, 1997).
11. Dallin, "Causes," 561.
12. B. Z. Doktorov, A. A. Oslon, and E. S. Petrenko, *Epokha El'tsina: Mneniia Rossiian. Sotsiologicheskie ocherki* (Moscow: Institut fonda "Obshchestvennoe mnenie," 2002), 54.
13. Shlapentokh, *Soviet Public Opinion*, xii–xiii, 31–36, 45, 100, 106.
14. See ch. 2, p. 97.
15. Bertaux, Thompson, and Rotkirch, "Introduction," 5.
16. As a result, by the 1990s Russia was, according to some Russian scholars, "a hundred times behind the most developed countries of the West in almost all of the main directions of informatization." Gordon and Klopov, *Poteri*, 1: 29.

Chapter 7

1. Yuri Levada et al., "Russia: Anxiously Surviving," in Vladimir Shlapentokh and Eric Shiraev, eds., *Fears in Post-Communist Societies: A Comparative Perspective* (New York: Palgrave, 2002), 18–22, 27–28, and Anne White, *Small-Town Russia: Postcommunist Livelihoods and Identities. A Portrait of the Intelligentsia in Achit, Bednodemyanovsk and Zubtsov, 1999–2000* (London and New York: RoutledgeCurzon, 2004), 18, 41.
2. Doktorov et al., *Epokha*, 276. As a result of an economic crisis in 1998, however, when the devaluated ruble collapsed, resulting in another short but alarming economic downspin, 50 percent of the population now had positive things to say about the Soviet planned

economy and state distribution of goods. Many Russians held that law and order, stability, social security, a strong state, and a dignified life would (re)unite society. See Iu. A. Levada, *Ot mnenii k ponimaniiu: Sotsiologicheskie ocherki, 1993–2000* (Moscow: Shkola politicheskikh issledovanii, 2000), 437; Doktorov et al., *Epokha*, 87–88, 90.

3. Doktorov et al., *Epokha*, 87–88, 90.
4. White, *Small-Town Russia*, 23. See also p. 30.
5. Gorshkov, *Rossiiskoe obshchestvo*, 306.
6. Levada et al., "Russia: Anxiously Surviving," 28.
7. This rise of anti-Americanism notwithstanding, historians Shiraev and Zubok noted that no Weimar Russia emerged, no backlash, because Moscow, Russia's "Klondike," the political hub of the nation with 7 percent of the country's population, lived better than the rest of Russia, paying 20 percent of its taxes, and remained far more pro-Western than elsewhere. Shiraev and Zubok, *Anti-Americanism*, 59–61. As a corollary, Anne White's study of small-town Russia at the end of the decade confirms a resiliency in communities despite the economic collapse. She found that neighbors trusted one another, that family members supported each other, and that reported crime was remarkably low. She also corroborated that, after 1994, socioeconomic indicators improved until the devaluation of the ruble in 1998. By 2000, however, the economy again showed signs of growth as infant mortality and unemployment dropped, even though male life expectancy and the divorce rate further deteriorated. See White, *Small-Town Russia*, 1, 19–20, 41.
8. Gordon and Klopov, *Poteri*, 1: 2, 208–12, 244, 257, 282–92, 479–80.
9. Alena Ledeneva, *Unwritten Rules: How Russia Really Works* (London: Centre for European Reform, 2001), 1, 7, 9, 37.
10. Boutenko and Razlogov, eds., *Recent Social Trends*, 29–32.
11. Dana Vannoy et al., eds., *Marriages in Russia: Couples during the Economic Transition* (Westport, Conn.: Praeger, 1999), 138, 178–79, 184.
12. O. S. Libova, "Otechestvennaia literatura XX veka v fondakh bibliotek i v chtenii rossiian," in *Chtenie v bibliotekakh Rossii: Informatsionnoe izdanie*. No. 3, *Otechestvennaia literatura v chtenii rossiian* (St. Petersburg: Russian National Library, 2002), 9–14.
13. Ionin, *Svoboda v SSSR*, 29.
14. Shiraev and Zubok, *Anti-Americanism*, 59–61.
15. Timothy J. Colton, *Yeltsin: A Life* (New York: Basic Books, 2008), 8–9.
16. Shiraev and Zubok, *Anti-Americanism*, 36–38, 41–43, 45–47.
17. Gorshkov, *Rossiiskoe obshchestvo*, 49–52, 55.
18. Ibid., 75.
19. Shiraev and Zubok, *Anti-Americanism*, 47–51.
20. Gorshkov, *Rossiiskoe obshchestvo*, 110.
21. Ibid., 118.
22. Ibid., 212, 226.
23. Ibid., 249, 255, 271.
24. Doktorov et al., *Epokha*, 224.
25. Shiraev and Zubok, *Anti-Americanism*, 51–55.
26. Ibid., 80–84, 109–23.
27. That year, 44 percent of the population saw the United States as Russia's number one nuclear threat (as opposed to 10 percent who saw China in this regard), although Muscovites remained more pro-Western than others. Levada et al., "Russia: Anxiously Surviving," 23–25.
28. Doktorov et al., *Epokha*, 88; Levada, *Ot mnenii*, 179–80.
29. During the elections in 2000, the young and those in favor of "law and order" tended to support Putin. People voting against him voiced concern over his close ties to Yeltsin, the fact that he was a relatively unknown dark horse, and his lack of a program. Only 4.5 percent of those polled saw his KGB background as something negative. Gorshkov, *Rossiiskoe obshchestvo*, 394.
30. Ibid., 332, and 414.
31. Ibid., 422–24, 431, 443, 455, 458, 474–75.

32. Daniel Bertaux in collaboration with Marina Malysheva, "The Cultural Model of the Russian Popular Classes and the Transition to a Market Economy," in Daniel Bertaux, Paul Thompson, and Anna Rotkirch, eds., *Living Through the Soviet System* (New York: Routledge, 2004), 48–51.

33. Gorshkov, *Rossiiskoe obshchestvo*, 476.

34. These developments draw on Russian neoconservatism—and on the country's political tradition based on what analyst Lilia Shevtsova has called "power personified." See her *Russia Lost in Transition: The Yeltsin and Putin Legacies*, trans. by Arch Tait (Washington, D.C.: Carnegie Endowment for International Peace, 2007).

35. Levada et al., "Russia: Anxiously Surviving," 26.

36. Boutenko and Razlogov, eds., *Recent Social Trends*, 266–67, 270, 318, 322.

37. Fran Markowitz, *Coming of Age in Post-Soviet Russia* (Urbana: University of Illinois Press, 2000), 33, 4.

38. Ibid., 17, 19, 57, 70, 123.

39. Ibid., 126.

40. Ibid., 171, 175, 177, 195, 196, 203, 207.

41. Ibid., 214, 225. Interestingly, she found them more willing to talk about smoking, alcohol, and drugs than about sex. Russian sociologist Igor Kon's sex survey of Moscow teenagers between the ages of sixteen and nineteen found that 54.8 percent of girls and 77.5 percent of boys claimed to be sexually active. Unfortunately, no comparable data are available from the Soviet period. See ibid., 137, 135.

42 Victoria Semenova and Paul Thompson, "Family Models and Transgenerational Influences: Grandparents, Parents, and Children in Moscow and Leningrad from the Soviet to the Market Era," in Daniel Bertaux, Paul Thompson, and Anna Rotkirch, eds., *Living Through the Soviet System* (New York: Routledge, 2004), 121–22.

43. E-mail letter from Anna Obraztsova to Donald J. Raleigh, June 6, 2008.

44. Tommi Hoikkala, Semi Purhonen and J. P. Roos, "The Baby Boomers: Life's Turning Points and Generational Consciousness," in Bryan Turner and June Edmunds, eds., *Generational Consciousness, Narratjve and Politics* (London: Rowman and Littlefield, 2002), 145–46, 162.

45. "Generation Pu," *Russkii Newsweek*, no. 19, May 25, 2008, 38–45.

46. Gorshkov, *Rossiiskoe obshchestvo*, 393, 494.

47. Doktorov et al., *Epokha*, 7–16.

48. Levada, *Ot mnenii*, 493–94.

49. Gorshkov, *Rossiiskoe obshchestvo*, 487–93.

50. Bertaux, "Cultural Model," 51.

51. Levada, *Ot mnenii*, 405, 448.

52. Gorshkov, *Rossiiskoe obshchestvo*, 496.

53. Levada, *Ot mnenii*, 71–72.

54. Johnson List, no. 1, January 8, 2004, Who lives well in Russia?

Conculsion

1. Donald A. Ritchie, "Foreword," in Jaclyn Jeffrey and Glenace Edwall, eds., *Memory and History: Essays on Remembering and Interpreting Human Experience* (Lanham, Md.: University Press of America, 1992), vi.

2. Khubova connected these remarks to two polls taken in the city of Vladimir revealing that people incorporated into their own personal stories things they had heard on television, clutching at stories to make sense of their own. Khubova, et al., "After Glasnost," 96.

3. Psychologists have shown how people draw on these personal stories in making important decisions in life. See Benedict Carey, "This is Your Life (and How You Tell It)," *New York Times*, May 22, 2007.

4. Shlapentokh, *Soviet Intellectuals*, 172–202.

5. Semenova, *Sud'by liudei*, 4.

6. Yurchak, *Everything Was Forever*, 295.

7. Svetlana Boym, *Common Places: Mythologies of Everyday Life in Russia* (Cambridge, Mass.: Harvard University Press, 1994), 94.

Bibliography

Adelman, Deborah. The "Children of Perestroika": Moscow Teenagers Talk about Their Lives and the Future. Armonk, N.Y.: M. E. Sharpe, 1991.

Adler, Nanci. The Gulag Survivor: Beyond the Soviet System. New Brunswick, N.J.: Transaction Publishers, 2002.

Adzhubei, A., et al. Litsom k litsu s Amerikoi: Rasskaz o poezdke N. S. Khrushcheva v SShA 15–17 sentiabria 1959 goda. Moscow: Gos. Izdatel'stvo, 1959.

Aksiutin, Iurii. Khrushchevskaia "ottepel'" i obshchestvennye nastroeniia v SSSR v 1953–1964 gg. Moscow: Rosspen, 2004.

Alekseeva, Liudmila. U.S. Broadcasting to the Soviet Union. New York: U.S. Helsinki Watch Committee, 1986.

Alexeyeva, Ludmilla, and Paul Goldberg. The Thaw Generation: Coming of Age in the Post-Stalin Era. Pittsburgh: University of Pittsburgh Press, 1990.

Alexievich, Svetlana. Voices from Chernobyl: The Oral History of a Nuclear Disaster. Translated by Keith Gessen. New York: Picador, 2005.

Antonov, A. I., and S. A. Sogrin. Sud'ba sem'i v Rossii XXI veka: Razmyshleniia o semeinoi politike, o vozmozhnosti protivodeistviia upadku sem'i i depopuliatsii. Moscow: Izdatel'skii dom "Graal'," 2000.

Applebaum, Anne. Gulag: A History. New York: Doubleday, 2003.

Atkinson, Paul, Amanda Coffee, and Sara Delamont. "A Debate about Our Canon." Qualitative Research 1, no. 1 (2001): 5–21.

Bacon, Edwin, and Mark Sandle, eds. Brezhnev Reconsidered. New York: Palgrave, 2002.

Ball, Alan M. Imagining America: Influence and Images in Twentieth-Century Russia. Lanham, Md.: Rowman and Littlefield, 2003.

Baranov, A. V. Sotsial'no-demograficheskoe razvitie krupnogo goroda. Moscow: Finansy i statistika, 1981.

Barker, Adele Marie, ed. Consuming Russia: Popular Culture, Sex, and Society since Gorbachev. Durham, N.C.: Duke University Press, 1999.

Bertaux, Daniel, ed. Biography and Society: The Life History Approach in the Social Sciences. Beverly Hills, Calif.: Sage Publications, 1981.

Bertaux, Daniel, Paul Thompson, and Anna Rotkirch, eds. On Living Through Soviet Russia. New York: Routledge, 2004.

Bewes, Timothy. Reification; or, The Anxiety of Late Capitalism. London and New York: Verso, 2002.

Birren, James E., et al., eds. Aging and Biography: Explorations in Adult Development. New York: Springer Publishing Co., 1996.

Blekher, Feiga. The Soviet Woman in the Family and Society: A Sociological Study. New York: John Wiley, 1979.

Blium (Blum), Alain, and Sergei Zakharov. "Demgraficheskaia istoriia SSSR i Rossii v zerkale pokolenii." Naselenie i Obshchestvo, no. 17 (February 1997). http://www.infran.ru/vovenko/60years_ww2/demogr.htm .

Boutenko, Irene A., and Kirill E. Razlogov, eds. Recent Social Trends in Russia, 1960–1995. Montreal and Kingston: McGill-Queen's University Press, 1997.

Bovkin, V. V. *Obraz zhizni Sovetskoi molodezhi: Tendentsii, problemy, perspektivy.* Moscow: Vysshaia shkola, 1988.

Boym, Svetlana. *Common Places: Mythologies of Everyday Life in Russia.* Cambridge, Mass.: Harvard University Press, 1994.

——. *The Future of Nostalgia.* New York: Basic Books, 2001.

Brady, Rose. *Kapitalizm: Russia's Struggle to Free Its Economy.* New Haven: Yale University Press, 1999.

Breslauer, George W. *Gorbachev and Yeltsin as Leaders.* New York: Cambridge University Press, 2002.

——. *Khrushchev and Brezhnev as Leaders: Building Authority in Soviet Politics.* London: Allen and Unwin, 1982.

Bronfenbrenner, Urie. *Two Worlds of Childhood: U.S. and U.S.S.R.* New York: Pocket Books, 1970.

Brown, Archie. *The Gorbachev Factor.* New York: Oxford University Press, 1997.

Brumberg, Abraham, ed. *Russia under Khrushchev: An Anthology from* Problems of Communism. New York: Praeger, 1962.

Byrnes, Robert F., ed. *After Brezhnev: Sources of Soviet Conduct in the 1980s.* Bloomington: Indiana University Press, 1983.

Chumachenko, Tatiana A. *Church and State in Soviet Russia: Russian Orthodoxy from World War II to the Khrushchev Years.* Translated and edited by Edward E. Roslof. Armonk, N.Y.: M. E. Sharpe, 2002.

Cohen, Stephen F., Alexander Rabinowitch, and Robert Sharlet, eds., The *Soviet Union since Stalin.* Bloomington: Indiana University Press, 1980.

Colton, Timothy J. *Yeltsin: A Life.* New York: Basic Books, 2008.

Dallin, Alexander. "Causes of the Collapse of the USSR." In Alexander Dallin and Gail W. Lapidus, eds., *The Soviet System: From Crisis to Collapse,* 549–64. Boulder, Colo.: Westview Press, 1995.

Demezer, A. A., compiler. *Domovodstvo.* 4th ed. Moscow: Kolos, 1965.

DeSoto, Hermine G., and Nora Dudwick. *Fieldwork Dilemmas: Anthropologists in Postsocialist States.* Madison: University of Wisconsin Press, 2000.

Dickson, Paul. *Sputnik: The Shock of the Century.* New York: Walker and Co., 2001.

Di Leonardo, Micaela. "Oral History as Ethnographic Encounter." *Oral History Review* 15 (Spring 1987): 1–20.

Dobson, Miriam. *Khrushchev's Cold Summer: Gulag Returnees, Crime, and the Fate of Reform after Stalin.* Ithaca, N.Y.: Cornell University Press, 2009.

Doktorov, B. Z, A. A. Oslon, and E. S. Petrenko. *Epokha El'tsina: Mneniia Rossiian. Sotsiologicheskie ocherki.* Moscow: Institut fonda "Obshchestvennoe mnenie," 2002.

Dornberg, John. *Brezhnev: The Masks of Power.* New York: Basic Books, 1974.

Dorokhov, A. A. *Eto ne melochi!* Moscow: Politizdat, 1961.

Dunaway, David. "The Oral Biography." *Biography* 14, no. 3 (1991): 256–66.

Dunstan, John. *Paths to Excellence and the Soviet School.* Rochester (UK): NFER Publishing Company, 1977.

Eakin, Paul John. *How Our Lives Become Stories: Making Selves.* Ithaca, N.Y.: Cornell University Press, 1999.

Edmunds, June, and Bryan S. Turner, eds. *Generational Consciousness, Narrative and Politics.* Lanham, Md.: Rowman and Littlefield, 2002.

Ely, Margot, et al. *On Writing Qualitative Research: Living by Words.* London: Falmer, 1997.

Esbenshade, Richard S. "Remembering to Forget: Memory, History, National Identity in Postwar East-Central Europe." *Representations* 49 (Winter 1995): 72–96.

Evangelista, Matthew. *Unarmed Forces: The Transnational Movement to End the Cold War.* Ithaca, N.Y.: Cornell University Press, 1999.

Feher, Ferenc, and Andrew Arato, eds. *Gorbachev: The Debate.* Atlantic Highlands, N.J.: Humanities Press International, Inc., 1989.

Fisher, Wesley. *The Soviet Marriage Market: Mate Selection in Russia and the USSR.* New York: Praeger, 1980.

Fitzpatrick, Sheila. *Everyday Stalinism: Ordinary Life in Extraordinary Times: Soviet Russia in the 1930s.* New York: Oxford University Press, 1999.

Furst, Juliane. *Stalin's Last Generation: Soviet Postwar Youth and the Emergence of Mature Socialism.* New York: Oxford University Press, 2010.

Geiger, Kent H. *The Family in Soviet Russia.* Cambridge, Mass.: Harvard University Press, 1968.

Geyer, Georgie Anne. *The Young Russians.* Homewood, Ill.: ETC Publications, 1975.

Goffman, Erving. *The Presentation of the Self in Everyday Life.* New York: Doubleday, 1959.

Golod, S. I. *Stabil'nost' sem'i: Sotsiologicheskie i demograficheskie aspekty.* Leningrad: Nauka, 1984.

Gorbachev, Mikhail. *Perestroika: New Thinking for Our Country and the World.* New York: Harper and Row, 1987.

Gorbachev, Mikhail, and Zdeněk Mlynář. *Conversations with Gorbachev on Perestroika, the Prague Spring, and the Crossroads of Socialism.* Translated by Georges Shriver with a foreword by Archie Brown. New York: Columbia University Press, 2002.

Gordon, L. A., and E. V. Klopov. *Poteri i obreteniia v Rossii devianostykh: Istoriko-sotsiologicheskie ocherki ekonomicheskogo polozheniia narodnogo bol'shinstva.* Vol. 1, *Meniaiushchaisia strana v meniaiushchemsia mire: Predposylki peremen v usloviiakh truda i urovne zhizni.* Moscow: Editorial URSS, 2000.

Gorshkov, M. K. *Rossiiskoe obshchestvo v usloviiakh transformatsii. Mify i real'nost': Sotsiologicheskii analiz, 1992–2002.* Moscow: Rosspen, 2003.

Gosudarstvennyi komitet RSFSR po statistike. *Narodnoe khoziaistvo RSFSR v 1987 g.* Moscow: Finansy i statistika, 1988.

Grant, Nigel. *Soviet Education.* 4th ed. New York: Penguin, 1978.

Grushin, B. A. *Chetyre zhizni Rossii v zerkale obshchestvennogo mneniia: Ocherki massovogo soznaniia rossiian vremen Khrushcheva, Brezhneva, Gorbacheva i El'tsina v 4-kh knigakh. Zhizn' 1-aia: Epokha Khrushcheva.* Moscow: Progress-Traditsiia, 2001.

———. *Mneniia o mire i mir mnenii: Problemy metodologii issledovaniia obshchestvennogo mneniia.* Moscow: Izd-vo Polit. Literatury, 1967.

Hanson, Philip. *The Rise and Fall of the Soviet Economy.* London: Longman, 2003.

Harvey, David. *The Limits to Capital.* Chicago: University of Chicago Press, 1982.

Hendel, Samuel, and Randolph L. Braham, eds. *The U.S.S.R. after 50 Years: Promise and Reality.* New York: Alfred A. Knopf, 1967.

Hirsch, Marianne. *Family Frames: Photography, Narrative, and Postmemory.* Cambridge, Mass.: Harvard University Press, 1997.

Hixson, Walter L. *Parting the Curtain: Propaganda, Culture, and the Cold War, 1945–1961.* New York: St. Martin's Griffin, 1997.

Hoikkala, Tommi, Semi Purhonen, and J. P. Roos. "The Baby Boomers: Life's Turning Points and Generational Consciousness." In Bryan Turner and June Edmunds, eds., *Generational Consciousness, Narrative and Politics,* 145–64. London: Rowman and Littlefield, 2002.

Humphrey, Caroline. *The Unmaking of Soviet Life.* Ithaca, N.Y.: Cornell University Press, 2002.

Inkeles, Alex. *Public Opinion in Soviet Russia: A Study in Mass Persuasion.* Cambridge, Mass.: Harvard University Press, 1951.

———. *Social Change in Soviet Russia.* Cambridge, Mass.: Harvard University Press, 1968.

Inkeles, Alex, and Raymond A. Bauer with the assistance of David Gleischer and Irving Rosou. *The Soviet Citizen: Daily Life in a Totalitarian Society.* Cambridge, Mass.: Harvard University Press, 1961.

Ioffe, Ia. A. *My i planeta: Tsifry i fakty.* Moscow: Izdatel'stvo Politicheskoi literatury, 1967.

Ionin, L. G. *Svoboda v SSSR: Stat'i i esse.* St. Petersburg: Fond "Universitetskaia kniga," 1997.

Ivanov, N. I. *Narodnoe khoziaistvo Saratovskoi oblasti (k 50-letiiu so dnia obrazovaniia oblasti): Statisticheskii sbornik.* Saratov: Privolzhskoe knizhnoe izdatel'stvo, 1984.

Ivanova, G. M. *Labor Camp Socialism : The Gulag in the Soviet Totalitarian System.* Edited by Donald J. Raleigh. Translated by Carol Flath. Armonk, N.Y.: M. E. Sharpe, 2000.

Jacoby, Susan. *Inside Soviet Schools.* New York: Hill and Wang, 1974.

Jameson, Fredric. *Postmodernism; or, The Cultural Logic of Late Capitalism.* Durham, N.C.: Duke University Press, 1991.

Jeffrey, Jaclyn, and Glenace Edwall, eds. *Memory and History: Essays on Remembering and Interpreting Human Experience.* Lanham, Md: University Press of America, 1992.

Jones, Polly, ed. *The Dilemmas of De-Stalinization: Negotiating Cultural and Social Change in the Khrushchev Era*. London and New York: Routledge, 2006.

Kabakov, Il'ia Iosifovich. *60-e, 70-e, Zapiski o neofitsial'noi zhizni v Moskve*. Vienna: Weiner Slawistischer Almanach, 1999.

Kann, Kenneth L. *Comrades and Chicken Ranchers: The Story of a California Jewish Community*. Ithaca, N.Y.: Cornell University Press, 1993.

Katz, Katarina. *Gender, Work and Wages in the Soviet Union: A Legacy of Discrimination*. New York: Palgrave, 2001.

Keep, John. *Last of the Empires: A History of the Soviet Union, 1945–1991*. New York: Oxford University Press, 1995.

Kelly, Catriona. *Children's World: Growing Up in Russia, 1890–1991*. New Haven and London: Yale University Press, 2007.

———. *Refining Russia: Advice Literature, Polite Culture, and Gender from Catherine to Yeltsin*. Oxford: Oxford University Press, 2001.

———. "'The School Waltz': The Everyday Life of the Post-Stalinist Soviet Classroom." *Forum for Anthropology and Culture*, no. 1 (2004): 104–55.

Kerblay, Basile. *Modern Soviet Society*. Translated by Rupert Sawyer. New York: Pantheon Books, 1983.

Khodakov, M. S. *Kak ne nado sebia vesti*. Moscow: Molodaia gvardiia, 1975.

Khubova, Daria, Andrei Ivankiev, and Tonia Sharova. "After Glasnost: Oral History in the Soviet Union." In *International Yearbook of Oral History and Life Stories*. Vol. 1, *Memory and Totalitarianism*, ed. Luisa Passerini, 89–102. New York: Oxford University Press, 1992.

Klein, Kerwin Lee. "On the Emergence of Memory in Historical Discourse." *Representations* 69 (Winter 2000): 127–50.

Kon, Igor S. *Druzhba: Etiko-psikhologicheskii ocherk*. Moscow: Politzdat, 1980.

———. *The Sexual Revolution in Russia: From the Age of the Czars to Today*. Translated by James Riordan. New York: Free Press, 1995.

Kotkin, Stephen. *Armageddon Averted: The Soviet Collapse, 1970–2000*. New York: Oxford University Press, 2001.

———. *Magnetic Mountain: Stalinism as a Civilization*. Berkeley: University of California Press, 1995.

Kozlov, Vladimir A. *Mass Uprisings in the USSR: Protest and Rebellion in the Post-Stalin Years*. Translated and edited by Elaine McClarnand MacKinnon. Armonk, N.Y.: M. E. Sharpe, 2002.

Lapidus, Gail. *Women in Soviet Society*. Berkeley: University of California Press, 1978.

Lebina, N. B., and A. N. Chistikov. *Obyvatel' i reformy: Kartiny povsednevnoi zhizni gorozhan v gody nepa i Khrushchevskogo desiatiletiia*. St. Petersburg: Dmitrii Bulanin, 2003.

Ledeneva, Alena V. *Russia's Economy of Favours: Blat, Networking, and Informal Exchange*. Cambridge: Cambridge University Press, 1998.

———. *Unwritten Rules: How Russia Really Works*. London: Centre for European Reform, 2001.

Levada, Iu. A. *Ot mnenii k ponimaniiu: Sotsiologicheskie ocherki, 1993–2000*. Moscow: Shkola politicheskikh issledovanii, 2000.

Levada, Yuri, et al. "Russia: Anxiously Surviving." In Vladimir Shlapentokh and Eric Shiraev, eds., *Fears in Post-Communist Societies: A Comparative Perspective*, 11–28. New York: Palgrave, 2002.

Lewin, Moshe. *The Gorbachev Phenomenon: A Historical Interpretation*. Expanded edition. Berkeley: University of California Press, 1991.

———. *The Soviet Century*. London: Verso, 2005.

Libova, O. S. "Otechestvennaia literatura XX veka v fondakh bibliotek i v chtenii rossiian," *Chtenie v bibliotekakh Rossii: Informatsionnoe izdanie*. No. 3, *Otechestvennaia literatura v chtenii rossian*, 8–31. St. Petersburg: Russian National Library, 2002.

Lisovskii, V. T., and A. V. Dmitriev. *Lichnost' studenta*. Leningrad: Izdatel'stvo Leningradskogo Universiteta, 1974.

Lourie, Richard. *Russia Speaks: An Oral History from the Revolution to the Present*. New York: Edward Burlingame Books, 1991.

McAuley, Alastair. *Women's Work and Wages in the Soviet Union.* London: George Allen and Unwin, 1981.

Mace, David, and Vera Mace. *The Soviet Family.* Garden City, N.Y.: Doubleday and Co. Inc., 1963.

Madison, Bernice. *Social Welfare in the Soviet Union.* Stanford, Calif.: Stanford University Press, 1968.

Malinin, G. A. *Saratov: Kratkii ocherk-putevoditel'.* Saratov: Privolzhskoe knizhnoe izdatel'stvo, 1974.

Markowitz, Fran. *Coming of Age in Post-Soviet Russia.* Urbana: University of Illinois Press, 2000.

——— . "*Russkaia Druzhba*: Russian Friendship in American and Israeli Contexts." *Slavic Review* 50, no. 3 (1991): 637–45.

Maslov, N. N. "Short Course of the History of the All-Russian Communist Party (Bolshevik): An Encyclopedia of Stalin's Personality Cult." *Soviet Studies in History* 28, no. 3 (1989–90): 41–68.

Matthews, Mervyn. *Education in the Soviet Union: Politics and Institutions since Stalin.* London: Allen and Unwin, 1982.

——— . *Privilege in the Soviet Union: A Study of Elite Life-Styles under Communism.* London: Allen and Unwin, 1978.

Matveev, V. M., and A. N. Panov. *V mire vezhlivosti.* Moscow: Molodaia gvardiia, 1983.

Medvedev, Roy A. *Post-Soviet Russia: A Journey through the Yeltsin Era.* Translated and edited by George Shriver. New York: Columbia University Press, 2000.

Medvedev, Roy A., and Zhores A. Medvedev. *Khrushchev: The Years in Power.* New York: W. W. Norton and Co., 1978.

Merridale, Catherine. *Ivan's War: Life and Death in the Red Army, 1939–1945.* New York: Metropolitan Books, 2006.

Millar, James R. "The Little Deal: Brezhnev's Contributions to Acquisitive Socialism." In Terry L. Thompson and Robert Sheldon, eds., *Soviet Society and Culture: Essays in Honour of Vera S. Dunham,* 3–19. Boulder, Colo.: Westview, 1988.

Millar, James R., ed. *Politics, Work, and Daily Life in the USSR: A Survey of Former Soviet Citizens.* New York: Cambridge University Press, 1987.

Moos, Elizabeth. *Soviet Education: Achievements and Goals.* New York: National Council of American-Soviet Friendship, 1967.

Morrison, John. *Boris Yeltsin: From Bolshevik to Democrat.* New York: Penguin, 1991.

National Education Association of the United States. Division of Travel Service. *Soviet Schools: A Firsthand Report Based on a Trip through the Union of Soviet Socialist Republics by a Group of Sixty-Four American Educators.* Washington, D.C.: Division of Travel Service, National Education Association, 1960.

Neuenschwander, John A. "Remembrance of Things Past: Oral Historians and Long-Term Memory." *Oral History Review* 6 (1978): 45–53.

Nove, Alec. *Glasnost in Action: Cultural Renaissance in Russia.* Boston: Unwin Hyman, 1989.

Ortner, Sherry B. *New Jersey Dreaming: Capital, Culture, and the Class of '58.* Durham, N.C.: Duke University Press, 2003.

Osterman, Lev. *Intelligentsiia i vlast' v Rossii (1985–1996 gg).* Moscow: Gumanitarnyi tsentr "Monolit," 2000.

Oushakine, Serguei Alex. *The Patriotism of Despair: Nation, War, and Loss in Russia.* Ithaca, N.Y.: Cornell University Press, 2009.

Pahl, Ray, and Paul Thompson. "Meanings, Myths, and Mystifications: The Social Construction of Life Stories in Russia." In C. M. Hann, ed., *When History Accelerates: Essays on Rapid Social Change, Complexity, and Creativity,* 130–60. London: Athlone Press, 1994.

Paperno, Irina. "Personal Accounts of the Soviet Experience." *Kritika* 3, no. 4 (2002): 577–610.

——— . *Stories of the Soviet Experience: Memoirs, Diaries, Dreams.* Ithaca, N.Y.: Cornell University Press, 2009.

Passerini, Luisa. "Introduction." *International Yearbook of Oral History and Life Stories.* Vol. 1, *Memory and Totalitarianism,* 1–20. New York: Oxford University Press, 1992.

Petro, Nicolai N. *The Rebirth of Russian Democracy: An Interpretation of Political Culture.* Cambridge, Mass.: Harvard University Press, 1995.

Pilkington, Hilary, ed. *Gender, Generation and Identity in Contemporary Russia.* London and New York: Routledge, 1996.

Poleznye sovety. Moscow: Moskovskii rabochii, 1959 and 1960.

Portelli, Alessandro. *The Battle of Valle Giulia: Oral History and the Art of Dialogue.* Madison: University of Wisconsin Press, 1997.

———. *The Death of Luigi Trastulli and Other Stories: Form and Meaning in Oral History.* Albany: State University of New York Press, 1991.

Putin, Vladimir. *First Person: An Astonishingly Frank Self-Portrait by Russia's President.* With Nataliya Gevorkyan, Natalya Timakova, and Andrei Kolesnikov. Translated by Catherine A. Fitzpatrick. New York: Public Affairs, 2000.

Raleigh, Donald J. *Russia's Sputnik Generation: Soviet Baby Boomers Talk about Their Lives.* Bloomington: Indiana University Press, 2006.

Reid, Susan E. "Cold War in the Kitchen: Gender and the De-Stalinization of Consumer Taste in the Soviet Union under Khrushchev." *Slavic Review* 61, no. 2 (2002): 211–52.

Remnick, David. *Lenin's Tomb: The Last Days of the Soviet Empire.* New York: Random House, 1993.

———. *Resurrection: The Struggle for a New Russia.* New York: Random House, 1997.

Ries, Nancy. *Russian Talk: Culture and Conversation during Perestroika.* Ithaca, N.Y.: Cornell University Press, 1997.

Ritchie, Donald A. *Doing Oral History.* New York: Twayne Publishers, 1995.

Rosen, Harold. *Speaking from Memory: Guide to Autobiographical Acts and Practices.* Stoke on Trent (UK): Trentham Books, 1998.

Ruffley, David L. *Children of Victory: Young Specialists and the Evolution of Soviet Society.* Westport, Conn.: Praeger, 2003.

Samuel, Raphael. *Theatres of Memory.* Vol. 1, *Past and Present in Contemporary Culture.* London: Verso, 1994.

Semenova, Viktoriia, Ekaterina Foteeva, and Daniel Bertaux, eds. *Sud'by liudei: Rossiia XX vek. Biografii semei kak ob"ekt sotsiologicheskogo issledovaniia.* Moscow: Institut Sotsiologii RAN, 1996.

Seniavskii, Andrei S. *Rossiiskii gorod v 1960-e—80-e gody.* Moscow: Institut rossiiskoi istorii RAN, 1995.

Severiukhin, Dmitrii. *Vecher v letnem sadu.* St. Petersburg: Izdatel'stvo im. N. I. Novikova, 2000.

Sherbakova, Irina. "The Gulag in Memory." *International Yearbook of Oral History and Life Stories.* Vol. 1, *Memory and Totalitarianism,* ed. Luisa Passerini, 103–16. New York: Oxford University Press, 1992.

———. "Voices from the Choir: Reflections on the Development of Oral History in Russia." *International Yearbook of Oral History and Life Stories.* Vol. 1, *Memory and Totalitarianism,* ed. Luisa Passerini, 188–91. New York: Oxford University Press, 1992.

Shevtsova, Lilia. *Russia Lost in Transition: The Yeltsin and Putin Legacies.* Translated by Arch Tait. Washington, D.C.: Carnegie Endowment for International Peace, 2007.

Shiraev, Eric, and Vladislav Zubok. *Anti-Americanism in Russia: From Stalin to Putin.* Basingstoke (UK): Palgrave, 2000.

Shlapentokh, Vladimir. *Love, Marriage, and Friendship in the Soviet Union: Ideals and Practices.* New York: Praeger, 1984.

———. *A Normal Totalitarian Society: How the Soviet Union Functioned and How It Collapsed.* Armonk, N.Y.: M. E. Sharpe, 2001.

———. *The Politics of Sociology in the Soviet Union.* Boulder, Colo.: Westview Press, 1987.

———. *Public and Private Life of the Soviet People: Changing Values in Post-Stalin Russia.* New York: Oxford University Press, 1989.

———. *Soviet Intellectuals and Political Power: The Post-Stalin Era.* Princeton: Princeton University Press, 1990.

———. *Soviet Public Opinion and Ideology: Mythology and Pragmatism in Interaction.* New York: Praeger, 1986.

Siddiqi, Asif A. *Sputnik and the Soviet Space Challenge*. Gainesville: University of Florida Press, 2003.

Sidorova, Liubov'. *Ottepel' v istoricheskoi nauke: Sovetskaia istoriografiia pervogo poslestalinskogo desiatiletiia*. Moscow: Pamiatniki istoricheskoi mysli, 1997.

Siegelbaum, Lewis H., ed. *Borders of Socialism: Private Spheres of Soviet Russia*. New York: Palgrave MacMillan, 2006.

Simis, Konstantin M. *USSR: The Corrupt Society. The Secret World of Soviet Capitalism*. Translated by Jacqueline Edwards and Mitchell Schneider. New York: Simon and Schuster, 1982.

Smith, Kathleen E. *Mythmaking in the New Russia: Politics and Memory during the Yeltsin Era*. Ithaca, N.Y.: Cornell University Press, 2002.

Stahl, Sandra. "The Oral Personal Narrative in Its Generic Context." *Fabula: Journal of Folklore Studies* 18 (1977): 18–39.

Statisticheskoe upravlenie Saratovskoi oblasti. *Narodnoe khoziaistvo Saratovskoi oblasti v 1959 godu*. Saratov: Gos. Stat. izd-vo, 1959.

Taubman, William. *Khrushchev: The Man and His Era*. New York: Norton, 2003.

Temkina, Anna, and Anna Rotkirch. "Soviet Gender Contracts and their Shifts in Contemporary Russia." *Idantutkimus: Finnish Journal of Russian and East European Studies* 2 (1997): 6–24.

Thompson, Paul. *The Voice of the Past: Oral History*. New York: Oxford University Press, 1978.

Titma, M. Kh., and E. A. Saar. *Molodoe pokolenie*. Moscow: Mysl', 1986.

Titon, Jeff Todd. "The Life Story." *Journal of American Folklore* 93, no. 369 (1980): 276–92.

Tonkin, Elizabeth. *Narrating Our Pasts: The Social Construction of Oral History*. New York: Cambridge University Press, 1994.

Trace, Arthur S., Jr. *What Ivan Knows that Johnny Doesn't*. New York: Random House, 1961.

Tsentral'noe statisticheskoe upravlenie. *Narodnoe khoziaistvo SSSR v 1985*. Moscow: Finansy i statistika, 1986.

Tsentral'noe statisticheskoe upravlenie RSFSR. *Narodnoe khoziaistvo RSFSR v 1977 godu: Statisticheskii ezhegodnik*. Moscow: Statistika, 1978.

Tumarkin, Nina. *The Living and the Dead: The Rise and Fall of the Cult of World War II in Russia*. New York: Basic Books, 1994.

Turner, Bryan, and June Edmunds, eds. *Generational Consciousness, Narrative and Politics*. London: Rowman and Littlefield, 2002.

Vail', Petr, and Aleksandr Genis. *60-e: Mir Sovetskogo cheloveka*. Moscow: Novoe literaturnoe obozrenie, 2001.

Vannoy, Dana, et al., eds. *Marriages in Russia: Couples during the Economic Transition*. Westport, Conn.: Praeger, 1999.

Vladimirov, Leonid. *The Russian Space Bluff: The Inside Story of the Soviet Drive to the Moon*. Translated by David Floyd. New York: Dial Press, 1973.

Von Bencke, Matthew J. *The Politics of Space: A History of U.S.–Soviet/Russian Competition and Cooperation in Space*. Boulder, Colo.: Westview Press, 1997.

Vsesoiuznaia pionerskaia organizatsiia imeni V.I. Lenina. Vsesoiuznyi leninskii kommunisticheskii soiuz molodezhi. Tsentral'nyi komitet. *Tovarishch: Zapisnaia knizhka pionera na 1961/62 uchebnyi god*. Moscow [s.n.], 1961.

Ward, Christopher. *Brezhnev's Folly: The Building of BAM and Late Soviet Socialism*. Pittsburgh: University of Pittsburgh Press, 2009.

Wertsch, James V. *Voices of Collective Remembering*. New York: Cambridge University Press, 2002.

White, Anne. *De-Stalinization and the House of Culture: Declining State Control over Leisure in the USSR, Poland and Hungary, 1953–1989*. London: Routledge, 1990.

——— . *Small-Town Russia: Postcommunist Livelihoods and Identities. A Portrait of the Intelligentsia in Achit, Bednodemyanovsk and Zubtsov, 1999–2000*. London and New York: RoutledgeCurzon, 2004.

White, Stephen. *After Gorbachev*. New York: Cambridge University Press, 1993.

——— . *Russia's New Politics: The Management of a Postcommunist Society*. New York: Cambridge University Press, 2000.

Wierling, Dorothee. *Geboren im Jahr Eins: Der Jahrgang 1949 in der DDR—Versuch einer Kollektivbiographie*. Berlin: Ch. Links Verlag, 2002.

Williams, Rhonda Y. "'I'm a keeper of information': History-telling and Voice." *Oral History Review* 28, no. 1 (2001): 41–63.

Woll, Josephine. *Real Images: Soviet Cinema and the Thaw.* New York: I. B. Tauris, 2000.

Yanowitch, Murray. *Controversies in Soviet Social Thought: Democratization, Social Justice, and the Erosion of Official Ideology.* Armonk, N.Y.: M. E. Sharpe, 1991.

Yeltsin, Boris. *Against the Grain.* New York: Summit, 1990.

———. *The Struggle for Russia.* New York: Random House, 1994.

Yurchak, Alexei. *Everything Was Forever, Until It Was No More: The Last Soviet Generation.* Princeton: Princeton University Press, 2006.

Zajda, Joseph I. *Education in the USSR.* New York: Pergamon Press, 1980.

Zdravomyslova, O. M., and M. Iu. Arutiunian, eds. *Lichnost' i sem'ia v epokhu peremen.* Moscow: RAN, Institut Sotsial'no-ekonomicheskikh problem narodnonaseleniia, 1994.

Zubkova, Elena. *Russia after the War: Hopes, Illusions, and Disappointments, 1945–1957.* Translated and edited by Hugh Ragsdale. Armonk, N.Y.: M. E. Sharpe, 1998.

Zubok, Vladislav. *Zhivago's Children: The Last Russian Intelligentsia.* Cambridge, Mass.: Harvard University Press, 2009.

Index

THE OXFORD ORAL HISTORY SERIES

J. TODD MOYE (University of North Texas), KATHRYN NASSTROM (University of San Francisco), and ROBERT PERKS (The British Library Sound Archive), *Series Editors*
DONALD A. RITCHIE, *Senior Advisor*